# Tonality: An Owner's Manual

# OXFORD STUDIES IN MUSIC THEORY

*Series Editor* Steven Rings

*Studies in Music with Text*, David Lewin

*Metric Manipulations in Haydn and Mozart: Chamber Music for Strings, 1787–1791*, Danuta Mirka

*Songs in Motion: Rhythm and Meter in the German Lied*, Yonatan Malin

*A Geometry of Music: Harmony and Counterpoint in the Extended Common Practice*, Dmitri Tymoczko

*In the Process of Becoming: Analytic and Philosophical Perspectives on Form in Early Nineteenth-Century Music*, Janet Schmalfeldt

*Tonality and Transformation*, Steven Rings

*Audacious Euphony: Chromatic Harmony and the Triad's Second Nature*, Richard Cohn

*Music as Discourse: Semiotic Adventures in Romantic Music*, Kofi Agawu

*Beating Time and Measuring Music in the Early Modern Era*, Roger Mathew Grant

*Mahler's Symphonic Sonatas*, Seth Monahan

*Pieces of Tradition: An Analysis of Contemporary Tonal Music*, Daniel Harrison

*Music at Hand: Instruments, Bodies, and Cognition*, Jonathan De Souza

*Foundations of Musical Grammar*, Lawrence M. Zbikowski

*Organized Time: Rhythm, Tonality, and Form*, Jason Yust

*Flow: The Rhythmic Voice in Rap Music*, Mitchell Ohriner

*Performing Knowledge: Twentieth-Century Music in Analysis and Performance*, Daphne Leong

*Enacting Musical Time: The Bodily Experience of New Music*, Mariusz Kozak

*Hearing Homophony: Tonal Expectation at the Turn of the Seventeenth Century*, Megan Kaes Long

*Form as Harmony in Rock Music*, Drew Nobile

*Desire in Chromatic Harmony: A Psychodynamic Exploration of* Fin de Siècle *Tonality*, Kenneth M. Smith

*A Blaze of Light in Every Word: Analyzing the Popular Singing Voice*, Victoria Malewy

*Sweet Thing: The History and Musical Structure of a Shared American Vernacular Form*, Nicholas Stoia

*Hypermetric Manipulations in Haydn and Mozart: Chamber Music for Strings, 1787–1791*, Danuta Mirka

*How Sonata Forms: A Bottom-Up Approach to Musical Form*, Yoel Greenberg

*Exploring Musical Spaces: A Synthesis of Mathematical Approaches*, Julian Hook

*The Musical Language of Italian Opera, 1813–1859*, William Rothstein

*Tonality: An Owner's Manual*, Dmitri Tymoczko

# Tonality

*An Owner's Manual*

DMITRI TYMOCZKO

# OXFORD
UNIVERSITY PRESS

Oxford University Press is a department of the University of Oxford. It furthers the University's objective of excellence in research, scholarship, and education by publishing worldwide. Oxford is a registered trade mark of Oxford University Press in the UK and certain other countries.

Published in the United States of America by Oxford University Press
198 Madison Avenue, New York, NY 10016, United States of America.

© Oxford University Press 2023

All rights reserved. No part of this publication may be reproduced, stored in a retrieval system, or transmitted, in any form or by any means, without the prior permission in writing of Oxford University Press, or as expressly permitted by law, by license, or under terms agreed with the appropriate reproduction rights organization. Inquiries concerning reproduction outside the scope of the above should be sent to the Rights Department, Oxford University Press, at the address above.

You must not circulate this work in any other form
and you must impose this same condition on any acquirer.

Library of Congress Control Number: 2022042508

ISBN 978–0–19–757710–3

DOI: 10.1093/oso/9780197577103.001.0001

Printed by Sheridan Books, Inc., United States of America

*to anyone who cares enough*
*to make it all the way through*

# Contents

| | |
|---|---|
| *Preface and Acknowledgments* | xi |
| 1.  Implicit Musical Knowledge | 1 |
|     1.  Gesualdo's trick | 4 |
|     2.  The quadruple hierarchy | 10 |
|     3.  Philosophy | 15 |
|     4.  Statistics | 22 |
|     5.  Schema | 26 |
|     6.  Outline | 33 |
| Prelude:  Transposition Along a Collection | 37 |
| 2.  Rock Logic | 47 |
|     1.  A melodic principle | 48 |
|     2.  A harmonic principle | 54 |
|     3.  A first loop family | 57 |
|     4.  Two more families | 61 |
|     5.  Shepard-tone passacaglias | 64 |
|     6.  Minor triads and other trichords | 68 |
|     7.  A fourth family | 71 |
|     8.  Other modalities | 74 |
|     9.  Function and retrofunction | 78 |
|     10.  Continuity or reinvention? | 82 |
| Prelude:  The Tinctoris Transform | 87 |
| 3.  Line and Configuration | 96 |
|     1.  The imperfect system | 97 |
|     2.  Voice exchanges | 103 |
|     3.  Other intervals | 107 |
|     4.  The circle of diatonic triads | 113 |
|     5.  Voice exchanges and multiple chord types | 119 |
|     6.  Four-voice triadic counterpoint | 125 |
|     7.  Thinking within the chord | 132 |
|     8.  Seventh chords | 138 |
|     9.  Harmony and counterpoint | 146 |
| Prelude:  Sequence and Function | 151 |
| 4.  Repetition | 155 |
|     1.  Repetition reimagined | 155 |
|     2.  Repeating contrapuntal patterns | 159 |
|     3.  The geometry of two-voice sequences | 165 |

viii CONTENTS

|  |  |
|---|---|
| 4. Three voices and the circle of triads | 171 |
| 5. Three voices arranged 2 + 1 | 175 |
| 6. Four voices | 179 |
| 7. Contrary-motion sequences | 184 |
| 8. Melodic sequences and near sequences | 188 |
| 9. Near sequences | 193 |
| 10. Sequences as reductional targets | 198 |

Prelude: Three Varieties of Analytical Reduction 203

5. Nonharmonic Tones 210
   1. The first practice and the SNAP system 211
   2. Schoenberg's critique 221
   3. Monteverdi's "Ohimè" 227
   4. The standardized second practice 235
   5. A loophole 240
   6. After nonharmonicity 246

Prelude: Functional and Scale-Degree Analysis 253

6. The Origins of Functional Harmony 257
   1. The logical structure of protofunctionality 258
   2. Similarities and differences 264
   3. Origin and meaning 269
   4. Harmony and polyphony 275
   5. The *Pope Marcellus* Kyrie 282
   6. A broader perspective 290
   7. "I cannot follow" 296

Prelude: Could the Martians Understand Our Music? 303

7. Functional Progressions 311
   1. A theory of harmonic cycles 311
   2. A more principled view 316
   3. Rameau and Bach 321
   4. Functional melody, functional harmony 326
   5. Fauxbourdon and linear idioms 330
   6. Sequences 336
   7. Bach the dualist 343

Prelude: Chromatic or Diatonic? 357

8. Modulation 361
   1. Two models of key distance 361
   2. Enharmonicism and loops in scale space 366
   3. Minor keys 371
   4. Modulatory schemas 376
   5. Up and down the ladder 379
   6. Modal homogenization and scalar voice leading 384
   7. Generalized set theory 393

Prelude:  Hearing and Hearing-As · 402

9. Heterogeneous Hierarchy · 407
   1. Strategy and reduction · 407
   2. Two models of the phrase · 412
   3. Chopin and the Prime Directive · 419
   4. An expanded vocabulary of reductional targets · 426
   5. Simple harmonic hierarchy · 433
   6. The four-part phrase · 437
   7. Grouping, melody, harmony · 443
   8. Beyond the phrase: hierarchy at the level of the piece · 446

Prelude:  Why Beethoven? · 451

10. Beethoven Theorist · 457
   1. Meet the Ludwig · 458
   2. From schema to flow · 465
   3. The *Tempest* · 472
   4. The Fifth Symphony · 482
   5. The "Pastorale" sonata, Op. 28 · 495
   6. Schubert's *Quartettsatz* · 504
   7. The prelude to *Lohengrin* · 518

Conclusion · 527

*Appendix 1: Fundamentals* · 533
*Appendix 2: Deriving the Spiral Diagrams* · 545
*Appendix 3: Sequence and Transformation* · 555
*Appendix 4: Corpus Analysis, Statistics, and Grammar* · 569
*Terms, Symbols, and Abbreviations* · 575
*Bibliography* · 583
*Index* · 599

# Preface and Acknowledgments

This book grew like a city, each gleaming draft built over the ruins of a previous version. The earliest stratum is pedagogical. After many years of teaching tonal harmony, I had accumulated an unstructured miscellany of ideas, techniques, and analyses. Some were the product of computational corpus study—a practice I adopted around 2000, first using MIDI files and Max/MSP, and then using Python, music21, and actual scores. My plan was to use this material to put pressure on what I took to be theoretical oversimplification. I wanted to demonstrate, against Schenkerian orthodoxy, that harmonies in baroque and classical music followed a largely nonhierarchical chord-to-chord grammar. I wanted to show that upper-voice configurations in four-voice counterpoint obeyed a simple grammar of hand positions. I wanted to argue that nonharmonic tones were not "merely decorative," and to trace the "irreducible seventh" back to the Renaissance. I wanted to identify protofunctional tendencies in sixteenth-century music. The goal was to provide more detailed information than could be found in standard textbooks, augmented by conceptual heuristics I used in the classroom.

This led to the aesthetic or critical layer. For the more I dove into the grammatical minutiae, the more I began to question the value of disinterested description: by avoiding issues of musical *relevance*, I was tacitly accepting assumptions that should instead be put into question. This felt increasingly problematic, pedagogically, aesthetically, and even morally. Why should twenty-first-century musicians care about the detailed grammar of sixteenth- or eighteenth-century practice? Who needs a truly accurate account of largely extinct functional-harmonic conventions? What is the aesthetic value of recapitulation? Though I love music, and consider it intrinsically worthy of study, I felt increasingly strongly that aesthetic *significance* should be a component of grammatical inquiry. Music theory without philosophy is empty.

The final, theoretical layer introduced the spiral diagrams that were to play a central role in the completed book. Originally designed as pedagogical simplifications, I gradually came to realize that they were something more. For by freeing the mind from the burden of imagining higher-dimensional voice-leading geometry, they left more energy for understanding genuinely musical relationships, often in a way that connected past and present. A major development here was my discovery that Princeton graduate composers were interested in ideas I had taken to be purely theoretical and historical. Their influence pushed me to connect sequences to repetition and transformation more generally, to think about how one might use complex motivic networks in contemporary contexts, and to consider how pieces like the *Waldstein* might serve as models for contemporary composition. More

## xii PREFACE AND ACKNOWLEDGMENTS

significantly, these connections led to the idea of the *quadruple hierarchy*, one of the central themes in the manuscript as it now stands. The result is that the oldest and newest sections of the book are found side-by-side: for while I had long used the heuristics of OUCH theory in the classroom (§3.6), I happened upon the general picture of chords-as-scales only after I thought the book was essentially finished (§3.7).

This last revision, so drastic and so late, raised the disturbing possibility that I had ceased writing a book in any conventional sense: what had begun as a journey had turned into a way of life, my manuscript evolving into a repository for my latest thinking on all things music. Every time I learned something new, or changed my mind, I updated the relevant file on my computer. Having faced the prospect of spending the rest of my life endlessly writing and rewriting the same words—along with the attendant familial disapproval—I resolved to stop. The result is this snapshot of my thinking as of the time of publication. Already I worry that readers will be reluctant to climb so far out on my own little conceptual limb. And though I have tried to be clear, I am aware that the material is extremely challenging.

Many people helped me along the way. Thirty-five years ago, John Stewart sat next to me at the piano and showed me his version of OUCH theory, planting seeds that were to bear fruit decades later. In a graduate seminar at UC Berkeley, David Huron taught me about corpus study and computational musical analysis. Richard Cohn introduced me to musical geometry and provided valuable support when my thinking was in its early stages. Clifton Callender, Noam Elkies, Rachel Hall, and Ian Quinn joined me in working out the geometrical approach to voice leading.

More recently, Nick DiBerardino, Robert Andrew Scott, Jacob Shulman, and Steve Taylor provided invaluable comments on drafts of the manuscript. Robert's incredibly detailed copyediting, of both music and examples, went well beyond the call of duty. Jason Yust not only read the manuscript, and shared portions of it with his class, but also served as a useful sounding board for many half-baked thoughts. Mark Liberman was a gracious consultant about linguistic and statistical matters. Michael Bruschi and Christopher Peacocke read early drafts through chapter 5, the former leading me to add preludes to each chapter. I have already mentioned the graduate students in Music 527: Jenny Beck, Yihan Chen, Wei Dai, Nick DiBerardino, Molly Herron, Natalie Miller, James Moore, Mauro Windholz, and Zhoushu Ziporyn. The next semester, undergraduates in Music 306 user-tested portions of the book—leading to yet more rewriting. Others who have helped me, by some combination of reading excerpts, answering emails, and providing materials, include Giovanni Albini, Matthew Arndt, Fernando Benadon, Ed Berlin, Eli Berman, William Caplin, David Cohen, Michael Cuthbert, Harrison Davis, Donnacha Dennehy, Chris Douthitt, Noam Elkies, David Feurzeig, Kenneth Forkert-Smith, Andrew Gelman, Robert Gjerdingen, Aaron Grant, Dan Harrison, James Hepokoski, Julian Hook, Nori Jacoby, Corey Kendrick, Megan Long, Rudresh Mahanthappa, Nathan John Martin, Nathaniel Mitchell, Marco Buongiorno Nardelli, Drew Nobile, Ali Rahmjoo, Peter Schubert, Ian Sewell, David Temperley,

Yo Tomita, and Dan Trueman. I am sure that this list is incomplete, and I apologize to anyone I have missed.

My children, Lukas and Katya, allowed me to share their journey into music, gently teaching me that I wasn't as smart as I thought. Several of their pieces turned into musical examples.

Last but not least comes my partner, emotional lodestone, and intellectual hero Elisabeth Camp, who makes a cameo in a few footnotes. I am embarrassed that neither of my books is good enough to be dedicated to her.

# 1

# Implicit Musical Knowledge

Twenty-first-century musicians inherit a canon of notated, largely triadic music originating before Palestrina and stretching past Joplin. This triadic tradition has long been central to classical concert life, the focus of orchestral performances and chamber-music recitals. It is the music of the movies, which in their most dramatic moments reach for the tropes of the nineteenth-century orchestra. It occupies a central place in undergraduate curricula, which often emphasize the imitation of earlier styles even though analogous acts of mimicry are unknown in other areas. Its rich syntax attracts significant scientific attention. And for all its distance from contemporary music, it is the yardstick against which recent work is judged—one that tells us our efforts are alternately too simple or too complex, too intuitive or too cerebral. For many listeners, the baroque, classical, and Romantic eras represent a pinnacle of musical achievement, the perfect balancing of emotion and intellect. The intervening centuries may have seen their share of intellectual progress, but the notated triadic tradition remains, rightly or wrongly, the epitome of learned composition.

And yet this music remains oddly foreign. The central problem is that *musical knowledge is largely implicit*—which is to say, embedded in compositional, improvisational, and perceptual habits that may not be available to conscious reflection. This is why composers can write without being able to explain what they are doing and why listeners can understand without being able to describe what they hear. And it is why music-making has often been taught through ungrounded injunctions of the form "do *this* when you find yourself in *this* situation." Modernism brought with it a distrust of inherited convention and a sense that substantial portions of musical practice were outdated or dogmatic. One consequence was the withering of a vast tradition of implicit knowledge, with composers proposing artificial systems to replace the natural grammars of earlier times. Another was the rejection of a whole host of very general concepts, including scale, sequence, consonance, and nonharmonic tone, all on the grounds that they were associated with the specific idioms of an outdated past. A third was a shift in the economic value of implicit and explicit, as musical culture came to value the ability to describe functional-harmonic grammar more than the ability to speak the language. Finally, lacking an embodied compositional counterweight, pedagogy and scholarship gravitated toward strict laws and speculative generalizations. Where "composer theory" leans

---

*Tonality.* Dmitri Tymoczko, Oxford University Press. © Oxford University Press 2023. DOI: 10.1093/oso/9780197577103.003.0001

2   TONALITY: AN OWNER'S MANUAL

toward the piecemeal and empirical, "theorist theory" inclines to the systematic *a priori.*

Compounding these difficulties is the fact that our musical ancestors inhabited a vastly different intellectual world, bounded by conventions that we now consider unjustified: near-universal avoidance of parallel perfect intervals, drawing a sharp boundary between consonance and dissonance, using only some of the available triadic progressions, limiting scalar vocabulary to a small number of modes, satisfying the formal demands of fugue and sonata, returning to the opening key at the end of the piece, and so on. These conventions were born of a Platonic conception of music as objective and extra-human—once basic science, part of the quadrivium alongside mathematics and astronomy, music has been demoted to a kind of fancy fun, its "rules" reconceived as conventions rather than laws of nature. The result is a past that is simultaneously paradigmatic and problematic. Our pedagogy tells a story of self-alienation: introductory harmony textbooks devoted to functional-harmonic conventions that have largely lost their force, counterpoint manuals shockingly similar to those of the sixteenth century, and advanced analytical methodologies explicitly designed to establish the aesthetic superiority of the White Germanic Genius.

All of which leads to a dilemma. On one side is the imperative of diversification: recognizing the many varieties of musical pleasure, acknowledging the systematic prejudice that led to a White male canon, and grappling with pedagogical traditions that no longer seem appropriate to contemporary musicians. On the other is the imperative of conservation, expressed by the belief that for all its problems, the notated tradition is vital and important in a way that contemporary markets may not always recognize—and that it can still be worthwhile to engage in the relatively unprofitable act of performing and studying this music, or composing new pieces that show its influence. We need a new way of connecting our past to our future, reconceptualizing music not from the standpoint of the native speaker, but from the standpoint of the sympathetic foreigner who is interested in something new. We need to scrub away the irrelevant dogma and reveal the core practices of continued interest.

I have written this book because I believe recent music theory allows us to understand music in a way that is more responsive to contemporary intellectual and aesthetic values, explicitly describing a vast field of formerly implicit knowledge. Indeed, I think we can now generalize the core techniques of earlier music, including voice leading, counterpoint, sequence, motivic development, nonharmonic tones, and modulation, so that they apply to any chords and scales whatsoever—recognizing and using those techniques in a vast array of contexts, from Renaissance polyphony to jazz, rock, and contemporary notated composition. To call this a "generalized tonal theory" would be a misnomer, for its techniques are broad enough to embrace extremes of consonance and dissonance, encompassing both tonality and atonality. My goal in this book is to explain this generalized theory in a way that is both comprehensible and comprehensive, starting with the analysis of existing pieces and considering how these ideas might also be used to make new music.

The properties I am interested in have clear and audible effects, producing distinctive sonic signatures that are easily identified: the characteristic sound of rock harmony or J. S. Bach's counterpoint, Chopin's distinctive approach to chromaticism, Beethoven's fondness for contrary-motion sequences. But I am primarily interested in musical *knowledge* as it is revealed by compositional and improvisational behavior, and my starting point will typically be the composer's perspective rather than the listener's. The following chapters will explore four distinct characterizations of musical knowledge. First, it is *mathematical,* a matter of knowing how to move through abstract spaces of musical possibility. This aspect is highly susceptible to generalization and modeling, revealing surprising structure across a very wide range of practices. Second, and somewhat opposed to this, it is *particular,* a matter of internalizing idioms and tendencies conforming to no general laws. Like knowledge of fashion or slang, knowing a musical style is often a matter of knowing to do things *this* way and not another, for no particularly good reason. Third, musical knowledge is often *implicit*—which is to say, embedded in compositional and improvisational practice in a way that is not available to conscious reflection. In this respect, it is comparable to a natural language whose grammar displays complex structure going beyond the explicit understanding of its speakers. Fourth and finally, musical knowledge has often been *dogmatic,* shaped by avoidances we now consider unmotivated or superstitious.

Each of these aspects of musical knowledge calls for different theoretical tools. The theory of voice leading, pioneered by Richard Cohn, uses geometry and mathematics to elucidate the connection between harmony and melody, revealing fascinating structure in specific pieces, in the work of individual composers, and across genres. Statistical corpus studies, cultivated by David Huron and brought to the masses by Michael Cuthbert, reveal tendencies invisible to conventional analytical methods. The *particularity* of musical knowledge is the purview of schema theory, deriving from Leonard Meyer by way of Robert Gjerdingen. Finally, there is analytic philosophy, introduced into music theory by Milton Babbitt and helping us separate dogmatic assertion from valid logical argument.[1] Together these different strands of inquiry allow us to pursue music theory as continuous with cognitive science, modeling the internal mental representations that underlie compositional competence—or *what we know when we know how to compose.*[2]

This knowledge is technical, detailed, and difficult to acquire. It is the knowledge of exactly which shades of paint combine to produce a vivid sunset, of which

---

[1] Babbitt was a partisan of logical positivism, whose narrowminded and aggressive skepticism drove many theorists away from analytic philosophy as such; however, I believe that music theory has much to learn from its emphasis on clear reasoning.

[2] This is not the only project that music theorists can undertake: we can study perception, either using experiments or introspection; we can study the historical concepts that have actually guided music creation; we can engage in various forms of criticism and evaluation. I will be concerned with these issues only secondarily, focusing instead on the intuitive knowledge of basic pitch structure.

## 4 TONALITY: AN OWNER'S MANUAL

signs mark an animal's track through a forest, of how to write a compelling legal brief. It is being able to navigate your house in the dark. This book exists because I love peering over other composers' shoulders to see intelligible patterns emerging from the tens of thousands of decisions that jointly produce a musical composition. (And, of course, trying to hear those patterns as I listen or play at the piano.) Those who are bored by detailed analysis should close this book immediately. Those who stay, hopefully, will find it exhilarating to go beyond pedagogical platitudes, understanding musical practice in real and specific detail—not least because it reveals a music that is less systematic, and sometimes differently systematic, than textbooks make it out to be.

Done well, analysis gives a sense of ownership, allowing us to understand how flesh-and-blood humans might find their way to composing beloved works. I am aware that this metaphor can suggest rapaciousness, capitalism, or untrammeled power.[3] Yet we speak of taking ownership of our own words, and in our society people sometimes come to own objects of significant public concern—a historic home, a well-known work of art, an ecologically significant wetland, or a beloved sports team. In these cases, to be an owner is to be a custodian, temporarily inhabiting an office with responsibilities and duties that we might not have chosen. My suggestion is that contemporary musicians are in an analogous position. My hope is that a vigorous reexamination of the past may ease the sense of conflict between conservation and diversification, allowing us to see the commonalities between such figures as Carlo Gesualdo and Rudresh Mahanthappa, Heinrich Schütz and Carole King, Fanny Mendelssohn Hensel and Meredith Monk, Dmitri Shostakovich and McCoy Tyner. This is in keeping with my belief that jazz is a natural continuation of an extended common practice beginning before Palestrina and including musicians like Debussy and Stravinsky—a repository for the sort of implicit knowledge that was once pervasive.

## 1. Gesualdo's trick

Gesualdo's "Moro Lasso" opens by sliding from C♯ major to A minor to B major to G major (Figure 1.1.1). Where earlier theorists might have seen arcane contrapuntal wizardry, or perhaps a specific chromatic idiom, twenty-first-century musicians will recognize a general technique: outer-voice tenths moving downward by semitone, forming triads by alternately adding a minor third above and below this dyadic core.[4] One could perhaps label the first of these a "progression between hexatonic poles" and the second a "standard iv⁶–V," but this would bifurcate a unified sequence into two unrelated harmonic moves.[5] The pattern appears

---

[3] McCreless 2011 considers the metaphor of musical ownership from many different points of view.

[4] Note that Gesualdo substitutes G major for the G minor implied by the sequence (§4.9).

[5] Cohn 1996 and 2012, pp. 106–9.

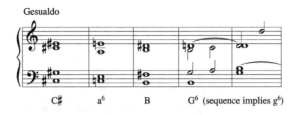

Figure 1.1.1. The opening of Gesualdo's "Moro Lasso" (1611). Underneath, I analyze the underlying three-voice schema: two voices moving down by semitone, harmonized by a minor third either above or below this interval. This pattern is then reregistered so that the parallel thirds are always in the lowest voices.

Figure 1.1.2. Gesualdo's trick in Beethoven's Seventh Symphony (1812), IV, mm. 136–146; Schubert's "Morgengruß" (1823), mm. 12–15; and Debussy's *Prelude to the Afternoon of a Faun* (1895), m. 107. Beethoven and Debussy use three voices; Schubert uses Gesualdo's four-voice version.

in both three and four voices, and can be found throughout the Western tradition (Figure 1.1.2).

When confronted with a passage like this, I try to follow what I call the Prime Directive:

*whenever you find an interesting musical technique, try to generalize it to every possible chordal and scalar environment.*

6 TONALITY: AN OWNER'S MANUAL

**Figure 1.1.3.** In mm. 73–76 of K.309, I, Mozart uses Gesualdo's trick but with parallel minor thirds rather than major.

In this case we have two voices moving in parallel with the third alternating between prime and inverted forms of a sonority, arrayed in close position and without voice crossings. Thus generalized, Gesualdo's trick can be found in many other places: Figure 1.1.3 shows Mozart using it in the first-movement development of his C major piano sonata K.309, now with descending minor rather than major thirds; Figure 1.1.4 shows one of its several appearances in *The Rite of Spring*, with the parallel voices forming major sevenths; Figure 1.1.5 shows Rudresh Mahanthappa using it in the twenty-first century. Figure 1.1.6, meanwhile, applies the technique in *diatonic* space whose unit of distance is the scale step. Here two voices are separated by diatonic third, moving downward in parallel, with the last voice alternately a fifth and sixth above the bass. What results is the descending-third "Pachelbel" sequence (rechristened the "Romanesca" by Robert Gjerdingen), a central idiom of both modal and functionally tonal composition.[6] From the standpoint of the Prime Directive, Gesualdo, Stravinsky, Mahanthappa, and Pachelbel are all doing the same thing.

We can go further. Any chord can be inverted so as to preserve any two of its notes; by moving these in parallel we can construct analogues to the three-voice

---

[6] Hook 2002 reports that John Clough (2000) offered a similar analysis.

IMPLICIT MUSICAL KNOWLEDGE 7

**Figure 1.1.4.** The second measure of R114 in *The Rite of Spring*. Here the parallel voices form major sevenths and articulate a melody; the third voice is alternately a tritone above the bottom voice and a tritone below the top.

**Figure 1.1.5.** Rudresh Mahanthappa's 2006 composition "The Decider" linearizes Gesualdo's trick, moving the perfect fourth in parallel, the middle voice alternately a major second below the top voice and a major second above the bottom.

**Figure 1.1.6.** The Pachelbel sequence moves two voices in parallel diatonically, alternately adding the third above and below.

8  TONALITY: AN OWNER'S MANUAL

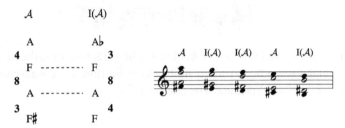

**Figure 1.1.7.** At R57 of *The Rite of Spring*, Stravinsky uses Gesualdo's trick, inverting a four-voice sonority so as to preserve its eight-semitone middle interval.

passages we have just considered. Figure 1.1.7 shows a prominent theme from *The Rite of Spring*, in which superimposed major and minor thirds create a delicious polytonal clash. Inversion around the middle interval exchanges upper and lower thirds.[7] Rather than mechanically alternating between these two chord-forms, Stravinsky moves the upper voices *diatonically* along the white-note collection, superimposing three distinct scales. (Here he exploits the fact that the diatonic scale's two-step intervals, its "thirds," are either three or four semitones large, the top and bottom intervals of his chord.) The end product is an unusual blend of horizontal and vertical coherence: the harmonies all form 014 trichords while the melodies move along three diatonic scales. For all its near-parallelism, it is a remarkable feat of counterpoint.

Collectively, these analyses exhibit several features of my approach to music theory. First, a composer-centered perspective that uses modern tools to generalize and extend implicit cognition: theory as "rational reconstruction" of the compositional process. Typically, my goal will be to produce sketches that are simple enough that readers could imagine inventing them, while also being rich enough that readers could imagine expanding them into the finished piece. Though this activity is not science, I imagine it to be within shouting distance of that enterprise, broadly

---

[7] Stravinsky's four-voice passage involves the same abstract registral configurations as Gesualdo's, with alto doubling bass in one chord form and tenor doubling soprano in the other. In both passages, the four-voice sonorities are related by pitch-space inversion.

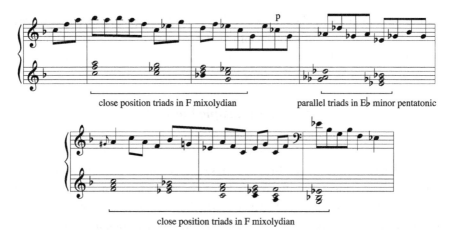

**Figure 1.1.8.** In mm. 18–23 (1'27") of his solo on "Passion Dance" (from *The Real McCoy*), McCoy Tyner plays a descending line that moves from close-position diatonic triads to close-position pentatonic triads and back, deploying the same technique in different scales. Black noteheads on the bottom staff are not played.

conceived. Second, a fluid understanding of stylistic boundaries such that modal, functionally tonal, and nontonal music participate in a shared dialogue. Third, the identification of specific techniques used throughout the history of Western music, a fundamental *language of counterpoint* grounded in the abstract structure of musical space, and encompassing both schematic routine and idiosyncratic innovation. Fourth, analyzing triadic music using *dyadic* logic, embodied by the parallel voices in the preceding analyses. Fifth and finally, an implied aesthetic attitude: I find beauty in such connections, and write for those who take joy in the thought that similar techniques can be found from Gesualdo to the present.

The Prime Directive functions as an analytical maxim encouraging us to ask whether superficially different idioms arise from a unified musical logic. It is not necessary that *composers themselves* understood that logic; indeed, it is more likely that their practice developed intuitively and without any abstract theoretical framework. Yet the Prime Directive can still serve an *explanatory* function, allowing us to understand why certain idioms might have survived. (For example, the preceding examples all combine harmonic consistency with parallel stepwise motion in two voices, features valued by composers in many different styles.) It can also serve a *generalizing* function, allowing us to adapt earlier techniques to new harmonic domains. But we can sometimes find moments where musicians seem to exhibit a more general understanding: in Figure 1.1.8, for example, McCoy Tyner builds a stepwise descending line using close-position triads in two different scales, F mixolydian and E♭ minor pentatonic; because of the scale change, the pentatonic "triad" looks superficially like a fourth chord.[8] In §9.3 we will find Chopin doing

---

[8] Later in the same solo, Tyner uses the technique with four-note pentatonic subsets (Figure A3.11).

something similar, using the same voice-leading techniques in a variety of different contexts. Here we see a more abstract understanding of contrapuntal possibility, one that detaches musical techniques from specific chordal and scalar environments.

## 2. The quadruple hierarchy

The Prime Directive leads to my guiding idea, that Western music displays a hierarchical structure in which the same basic procedures occur on multiple levels simultaneously. This is the *quadruple hierarchy* of surface voices moving inside chords that move inside more familiar scales that are themselves moving through chromatic space—or as I will sometimes call it, the *collectional* hierarchy, as the number of levels can vary. Figure 1.2.1 presents a clear example, the pianist's right hand moving sequentially along three voices that articulate the familiar "omnibus" schema.[9] It is not unreasonable to think that these triadic voices form a three-note scale, a series of melodic positions available throughout the piano's range, with right-hand melody moving systematically along this scale very much like "doe a deer" moves along the diatonic collection. Yet these three voices form triads that would normally be considered chordal.

The quadruple hierarchy opens a new analytical project of determining the precise combination of background and foreground motion that reproduces a given passage. In some cases, this can lead to unexpected insights. Figure 1.2.2 analyzes

Figure 1.2.1. In mm. 38–41 of Beethoven's Op. 54, II, voices move systematically along the top three notes of the omnibus pattern, as if they formed a three-note scale.

---

[9] Yellin 1998, Telesco 1998, and §4.6.

IMPLICIT MUSICAL KNOWLEDGE 11

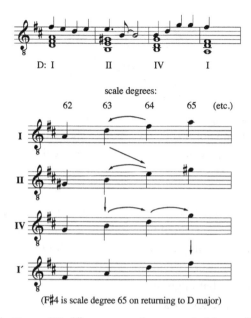

**Figure 1.2.2.** "Eight Days a Week" returns to the same pitch but a different scale degree.

the verse of the Beatles' "Eight Days a Week"; if we are willing to treat the harmonies as small scales, then we can say that the melody alternates between two different scale degrees, 64–63, 64–63, and 63–64, moving up to degree 65 to finish the phrase.[10] What is interesting is that the melody returns to its starting *pitch* but not its starting *scale degree*: the F♯ that starts the verse is, on this analysis, scale degree 64, while the F♯ that finishes it is scale degree 65. Melody and harmony thus cancel out, the chords continually sinking while the melody ascends in order to stay fixed in register—countervailing motion on two hierarchical levels. Here, modeling chords as scales allows us to assert two seemingly contradictory observations: that the music repeats more or less exactly, and that it articulates a continuous descent at a deeper, scalar level. The result is a psychologically complex *repetition* that also *continues* an ongoing process of scalar descent.[11]

One obstacle to recognizing the quadruple hierarchy is our difficulty imagining how transposition can be applied to notes *outside* the relevant collection. For example, it may seem impossible to transpose a figure like C–D–E along the C major triad, since the note D is foreign to that harmony. Here it helps to realize that musical objects can contain intervals at multiple hierarchical levels. Figure 1.2.3 shows two interpretations of the C–D–E figure, one on which the D is an incomplete neighbor a scale step above the initial C, and another on which it is a scale step *below* the final E; either interpretation allows us to move the figure along the C major triad.[12] This

---

[10] Throughout this book I notate scale degrees so that middle C is as close to 60 as possible.
[11] Lewin (1986, p. 355, note 19) makes a similar point about Schubert's "Morgengruss." Whether the Beatles were explicitly thinking in these terms is a complex and likely unanswerable question.
[12] If we interpret D as a passing tone connected by step to both C and E, then it is unclear how to start the figure on G.

**Figure 1.2.3.** Transposing the motive C–D–E along the C major triad. The top line interprets the second note as being a scale step above the first; the bottom line interprets it as a scale step below the second. These lead to different forms on G.

same strategy works when we need to transpose chromatic figures such as C–C♯–D along the diatonic scale, or virtually any collection of notes along any other. Indeed, we will see that this idea is implicit in a wide range of practices from motivic development to the "tonal answer" of baroque counterpoint.

Another obstacle is what might seem like an ontological gulf between chord and scale. The paradigmatic chord is a concrete object localized in both pitch and time, its notes situated in specific octaves and sounding together. The paradigmatic scale is instead a collection of *melodic slots* that are localized neither in time nor in register. Imagine hearing C4, E4, G4 in a C major context. While we can typically answer questions like "what voice is sounding the chord's fifth, and what octave is it in?" we cannot answer the analogous questions about notes not currently sounding. In what octave is the leading tone? The question makes no sense: the leading tone is a potentiality, a melodic location existing a step below every tonic and two steps above every dominant. It is in every octave and none, a *pitch class* rather than a pitch.

However, this distinction is determined by function rather than inherent musical structure. In twentieth-century languages such as impressionism or jazz, seven-note collections can act as concrete chords. Conversely, smaller collections can act like scalar fields of play. Figure 1.2.4 shows the first half of the remarkable mid-sixteenth-century motet *Heu me Domine*, likely written by Vicente Lusitano. This triadic background is as abstract and rigorous as anything in Ligeti or Reich, ascending semitonally from E3 to A6 before falling back to the cadence. Virtually all the melodic lines can be generated from this structure, which does not explicitly appear in the music; instead, the concrete musical voices switch between "background" scale degrees so as to remain within their registral bounds, generating musical variety while avoiding contrapuntal malfeasance (e.g., second-inversion triads and forbidden parallels). This is the inverse of the pattern we found in "Eight Days a Week," the concrete lines moving downward along the ever-ascending background—like walking on a treadmill, expending energy just to stay in the same place. The result is a paradoxical combination of registral stability and endless ascent, reminiscent of the barber-pole illusion, known to musicians as "Shepard tones."[13]

---

[13] Shepard tones can be used to produce a sequence that appears both to fall continuously and also to remain fixed in register; the illusion is accomplished by gradually fading in higher-register harmonics while fading out the lower-register harmonics (Shepard 1964).

IMPLICIT MUSICAL KNOWLEDGE 13

**Figure 1.2.4.** A reduction of the first half of Lusitano's 1553 motet *Heu me domine*. Rhythmic durations have been halved. The background accounts for virtually all the notes in the piece.

This leaves analysts with a choice between two different kinds of reduction. In a piece like *The Well-Tempered Clavier*'s first C major prelude, we can understand figuration as a purely rhythmic phenomenon, outlining a series of concrete voices whose notes belong to particular registers. In *Heu me domine*, the reduction produces something more abstract, a scale-like structure whose voices can appear in any octave. Schenkerian theory does not recognize this distinction, its reductions typically delivering concrete pitches, with octave shifts understood as a matter of "register transfer"—displacing a chorale's voices from their "true" or "obligatory" home. When we reduce to a scalar background, there is no "obligatory register" since the background object is a scale existing in every octave and none. As we will see, this perspective opens a host of new analytical possibilities, allowing us to reconceive some portion of Schenkerian practice in a more scientifically reputable way.[14]

Implicit in these examples is the idea that scales can be linked by particular voice leadings. Typically, it is the *regularity of the surface* that leads us to postulate voice leadings at the scalar level. It is natural to read Figure 1.2.5 as presenting a surface voice moving regularly along a scalar field *whose notes are themselves shifting*. That is: the abstract melodic slot F moves up by semitone to F♯ while the surface voice continues to articulate the same series of melodic intervals ("up by two, down by one"). In *A Geometry of Music*, I used the metaphor of a frog hopping along a

---

[14] Peter Westergaard (1975) asserted that leaps of a third or more *inherently* marked a change of voice below the surface, a claim that initially sounds counterintuitive. But when background voices are triadic and connected by stepwise voice leading, the statement is almost tautologous: since the background of *Heu me Domine* contains almost no leaps, leaps on the surface are necessarily due to motion from one background strand to another, precisely as Westergaard suggests.

14   TONALITY: AN OWNER'S MANUAL

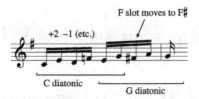

**Figure 1.2.5.** Here the voice moves according to a regular pattern ("up by third, down by step") along a series of melodic slots that are themselves moving. The example is drawn from the first movement of Mozart's G major piano sonata, K.283.

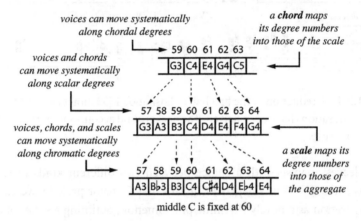

**Figure 1.2.6.** The quadruple hierarchy.

circular arrangement of lily pads, making regular patterns—for example, "clockwise by two pads, counterclockwise by one"—while the pads themselves drift. The result is a deep analogy between *scale degrees* and *musical voices*: at some level, scale degrees *are* voices, articulated not by concrete musical instruments but by abstract structures of melodic possibility. Terminologically this means we need to be careful to distinguish concrete or *surface* voices, which articulate perceptible melodies, from *abstract* voices, which are scale degrees or melodic slots. The right-hand melody in Figure 1.2.1 presents a single surface voice moving along three abstract voices.

   Central to the idea of the quadruple hierarchy is the claim that transposition and inversion are available not just at the chromatic level, as in atonal set theory, or at the scalar level, as in diatonic set theory, but also at the *chordal* level—where they form a new, "chordal set theory" governing the motion of voices. Figure 1.2.6 attempts to visualize this situation, numbering chromatic, scalar, and chordal degrees so that middle C is 60. These numbers allow us to represent intervals using addition and subtraction at all levels. Motion along the chord occurs on this top layer: the chordal interval +1 in Figure 1.2.1 moves one step to the right, −2 moves two steps to the left, and so on. The chord in turn provides a translation or mapping from its own degrees to those of the scale. Intervallic patterns like the (+2, −1) of

Figure 1.2.5 occur on this level. The scale in turn maps *its* degrees to the chromatic degrees at the bottom of the graph, offering yet a third opportunity for collectional motion. (The chromatic neighbors of Figure 1.2.1 move along this level.) Together the collections form a recursive architecture that will be more familiar to computer scientists than to music theorists, yet it is one that every musician intuitively grasps.

Motion at different levels of the hierarchy gives rise to a diverse range of phenomena: motion of scale within aggregate produces modulation, motion of chord within scale produces voice leading, motion of voice within chord produces motivic development, chordal inversion, and what I call "structured arpeggiation" (§4.8). Particularly important is the technique of counteracting, or nearly counteracting, an operation at one level with its analogue at another: combining transposition along chord and scale to produce efficient voice leading, or combining *inversion* along both chord and scale to produce Gesualdo's trick (appendix 3).[15] Musicians have learned to manipulate the hierarchy in special cases, typically mediated by idioms and schemas. The general picture, however, is likely to exceed our intuitive comfort. Here then is an opportunity for theory to add value—starting with the analysis of earlier music, abstracting its techniques in accordance with the Prime Directive, and showing how hierarchical set theory can be applied in a range of musical environments.

## 3. Philosophy

Another motivation for this book is my sense that music theory presents philosophical challenges whose complexity is not always appreciated. As a discipline that crosses the boundary between science and art, it requires both musical intuition and methodological sophistication, yet it is extremely difficult for a single human being to acquire expertise in both domains. The result is a tendency to neglect some of the most perplexing issues in what is an inherently challenging intellectual enterprise.

The most obvious issue is the divergence between eye and ear, between structure apparent in musical scores and what can be heard by even well-trained listeners. This is a familiar problem in twentieth-century contexts, exemplified by worries about the audibility of twelve-tone and other modernist modes of musical organization.[16] But analogous problems surround earlier music as well: for instance, both introspection and experimental research suggest that long-term tonal closure (the return to the tonic at the end of a long piece) is *not* particularly salient for most listeners, yet the architecture of sonata form seems to presume its importance—the

---

[15] The investigation of hierarchically embedded musical "alphabets" begins with Simon and Kotovsky 1963, continuing with Simon and Sumner 1968, Deutsch and Feroe 1981, and Lerdahl 2001. The idea of extending set-theoretical techniques to arbitrary collections is implicit in Clough 1979a and 1979b. This book fuses these ideas with the theory of voice leading, considering arbitrary hierarchies of arbitrarily moving collections, with analogous transformations occurring at each hierarchical level, and motion at one level often counteracting motion at another.

[16] Lerdahl 1988.

purported function of the recapitulation being to resolve the "large-scale dissonance" created by the appearance of the second theme in a "foreign" key.[17] Were
earlier composers fixated on structures that even well-trained listeners cannot hear?
Did they wrongly expect their audience to experience recapitulation as resolving a
dissonance? Was classical music written for a small elite with absolute pitch? These
are uncomfortable questions, and contemporary theorists are understandably reluctant to confront them head-on, yet they are essential for understanding the aesthetic significance of classical music.

The divergence between eye and ear undermines the common music-theoretical
inference from patterns-in-scores to listeners' awareness of those patterns. This
*what-you-see-is-what-you-hear* principle is central to projects as different as Fred
Lerdahl's a prioristic psychology, which assumes that "experienced listeners"
recreate in their minds a completely accurate copy of the musical score, and
Gjerdingen's historicist "schema theory," which proposes score analysis as a tool for
reconstructing the "situated psychology" of earlier listeners.[18] Thus Leonard Meyer
writes, "the structure of the affective response to a piece of music can be studied
by examining the music itself," a statement echoed by Gjerdingen and Byros.[19] We
know this statement is false in the case of long-term tonal closure, and we have
reason to worry that it fails in other cases as well: for instance, earlier composers
avoided parallel perfect intervals even in cases where they are very difficult to hear
(e.g., when tucked away in inner voices). Consequently, any identification of *what is
seen* with *what is heard* will underestimate the complex mixture of aural and conceptual, of heard and imagined, at play in the Western notated tradition.[20]

To be clear, I accept that musical styles are characterized, in part, by recurring
regularities and patterns, and that our ability to perceive such patterns underwrites
our ability to appreciate and understand music. Furthermore, I agree that theory
can enrich our perceptual experience by sensitizing our ears to structure: having
written this book, I regularly find myself hearing the idioms and patterns I discuss, even when listening to unfamiliar pieces without a score. But I reject the claim
that structure-in-scores is *ipso facto* available to listeners' conscious reflection,
or even that an ideal listener *should* consciously try to track compositional technique. Gjerdingen compares the listener to a figure-skating judge observing a series
of standard moves like the Lutz or triple axel. I will argue that music perception
is more complex than that: composers can navigate spaces of musical possibility

[17] Charles Rosen writes, "material presented outside the tonic *must* have created, in the eighteenth century,
a feeling of instability which demanded to be resolved" (1971, p. 74, my italics). The experiments of Cook 1987
and Marvin and Brinkman 1999 suggest that this may not be true.

[18] The diagram in Lerdahl 2020, p. 23, formalizes the inference from the musical surface to the "heard
structure." See Tymoczko 2020a for more.

[19] See Meyer (1956, p. 32), Gjerdingen (1996, pp. 380–81, and 2007, pp. 16–19), and Byros (2012, pp. 282–
84, which is admirably clear about these issues, and from which several of the preceding references are
drawn).

[20] Aural comprehension is sometimes used as a criterion of musical content—which we might call the
*what's-there-is-what-you-hear* principle. For example, Hadjeres, Pachet, and Nielsen 2017 use listener data
to judge whether a computer can be said to "compose like Bach." I doubt those listeners were sensitive to the
structural details that interest theorists, composers, and analysts.

without being able to say exactly what they are doing just as listeners can understand what they are hearing without being able to describe their understanding in words. Music is written for *audiences*, not judges.

One way of putting this point is that there is no fixed relationship between compositional technique and communicative meaning, or *how something is made* and *what it says*. In some circumstances, artists efface their methods, deliberately aiming to create illusions. (Outside of music we have magic tricks and special effects; inside it, we have Chopin's arpeggiation patterns or Ligeti's "touches bloquées," simple physical gestures creating outsized impressions of complexity.) In other cases, technique is meant to be apprehended only holistically and tacitly: for example, sound engineers and record producers make countless decisions about reverb, panning, filtering, microphone placement, and amplification, all in service of creating a coherent and aesthetically pleasing sonic field, but with no expectation that audiences will consciously track these decisions ("wow, nice use of a high-pass filter"). In still other circumstances there is a closer connection between technique and content, as when composers intend listeners to recognize the return of a theme. But many practices are difficult to categorize: when it comes to sonata form there is a genuine question about whether we should expect an idealized listener to consciously track specific technical events such as the "medial caesura" or whether we should think of those events as *tools* for creating compelling energetic trajectories. Much the same might be said for galant schemata, which some theorists might compare to words in a language and others might consider technical tools for generating a certain sort of musical flow.

If theory's fundamental challenge is the gap between eye and ear, then the runner-up is inferring *aesthetic norms* from musical evidence. This is an issue that can arise even with perfect perception of every musical detail. For suppose we notice that rock and classical music use different harmonic progressions: should we conclude that rock musicians are *deliberately rejecting* classical norms, or simply speaking a novel musical language?[21] Or we observe Beethoven effacing standard sonata-form signposts such as the medial caesura: should we read this as a deliberate rejection of the past or as a new set of formal conventions that can be understood on its own?[22] Do popular music's pervasive accents on beats 2 and 4 represent a deviation from a genuine psychological expectation that beat 1 should carry the strongest accent, or an alternate metrical norm? Here it is all too easy to project inappropriate expectations onto earlier styles, powering up the hermeneutic engines when our oversimplifications fail.

Consider the nineteenth-century theorist Ebeneezer Prout's approach to one of the more vexed problems in historical theory, the prohibition on parallel perfect

---

[21] Stephenson 2002, chapter 5. The issue here is comparable to questions about whether a speaker uses "bad grammar" or speaks a slightly different dialect; chapter 2 interprets rock music with reference to specifically modal norms.

[22] Hepokoski's notion of "dialogic form" (2010) places a very heavy weight on inferred cultural norms; chapter 10 interprets Beethoven as less beholden to existing convention.

509. VI. As a suspension is only a temporary substitute for the harmony note which follows it, a progression which would be incorrect without a suspension is not justified thereby.

For example,

the suspension (*a*) involves the same consecutive octaves as are seen at (*c*); and (*b*) the same consecutive fifths as at (*d*). This rule, however, is not always strictly observed by the old masters in the case of fifths, where the progression is less unpleasing than with the octaves.

If the suspensions are omitted here, we have clearly consecutive fifths between the two upper parts; but the effect of the passage is quite unobjectionable.

Figure 1.3.1. Prout's 1889 discussion of suspension-masked parallel perfect intervals.

intervals in the presence of nonharmonic tones. Prout endorses the common view that suspensions represent (or "substitute" for) their tones of resolution, and thus cannot be used to mask parallels. He then immediately concedes that this norm was not obeyed by the "Old Masters" in the case of perfect fifths, proposing a sonic explanation—that this violation is "less unpleasing" and "quite unobjectionable" (Figure 1.3.1). This notion of *a musical rule not followed in practice* should make us suspicious, for how are we to know that a norm exists, if not through practice? Textbooks are unreliable, as authors might just be wrong about the music they intend to describe. (Consider the prohibition of split infinitives, a more-or-less illusory rule with no grounding in actual linguistic behavior.[23]) Perhaps instead of describing composers as *habitually violating their own rules* we should look for *rules that accurately describe compositional behavior*. Or perhaps our so-called rules are generalizations *theorists* have made about complex musical traditions—with apparent departures better described as limitations of the generalizations themselves. Here it is important that earlier composers were trained from an early age and in a hands-on manner, a pedagogical approach that can preserve idioms resisting systematic generalization.[24] In replacing this hands-on tradition with textbooks and college classes, we tend to reify the regularities, endowing them with a metaphysical weight they do not deserve.

---

[23] Pullum and Huddleston 2002. Weber (1817–1821) 1846 is impressively nondogmatic about musical practice.
[24] Gjerdingen 2020.

Prout's struggles point to an ambiguity in the notion of a grammatical "rule." In both music and language, it is easy to come up with generalizations that are true yet incomplete: music theorists rightly say that nonharmonic tones do not generally license parallel fifths, just as linguists correctly say that English does not allow one word to be inserted into another. Yet there are rare but systematic exceptions to these generalizations (e.g., "unbebloodylievable"). Grammatical norms, in other words, are *multilayered*, with one and the same utterance simultaneously violating a true generalization while also conforming to a more nuanced set of rules. Misunderstanding this point sometimes leads theorists to insist on universality against the evidence of our senses—as when Prout postulates persistent violations of an imagined rule forbidding suspension-masked parallels. Conversely, it can lead us to dismiss rules just because of the occasional exception—as when contemporary theorists reject Roman numerals because of their various limitations.[25]

A third philosophical issue involves norms of linguistic meaning, and in particular a set of antiquated assumptions inherited from figures like Schenker and Schoenberg. These can lead to dogmatic stipulations about how words *must* be used: that the label "I⁶" necessarily presupposes inversional equivalence, that "V–I" implies the primacy of the bass voice, or that "modality" must mean something more than a largely diatonic language with a range of possible tonal centers.[26] By contrast, for the better part of a century, philosophers, psychologists, and cognitive scientists have been suspicious of strict definitions, emphasizing that words often acquire their meanings by virtue of complex and ever-changing networks of practice. A single term can thus support a range of uses varying with context, speaker, and time.[27]

Wittgenstein famously wrote about the difficulties of defining "game."[28] Many of his arguments could also be applied to terms like "seventh chord." It is a truism of music history that seventh chords came to be accepted as genuine sonorities somewhere around the time of Monteverdi; before that, it is said, they are mere byproducts of nonharmonic tones. But the history of seventh chords is like a river with many tributaries, and chapter 5 will describe the "Renaissance seventh," a common idiom in which sounding seventh chords *cannot be analyzed as nonharmonic decorations of a consonant background*; this idiom evolves seamlessly into the ii§–V cadence of baroque music, where the seventh was explicitly recognized. In other words, the history of music presents us with a continuous evolution in which one and the same vertical structure, the irreducible seventh, gradually acquires more and more independence, occurring initially only in one context and slowly acquiring new uses.

---

[25] This point is further obscured by the music-theoretical conflation of the grammatical and the pedagogical: introductory textbooks simultaneously function as our most complete descriptions of musical syntax, leaving us with an extensive literature articulating true but simplistic generalizations, and comparatively little scholarship which tries to describe musical norms at a more granular level.

[26] See the prelude to chapter 6 for specific references.

[27] Margolis and Laurence 2003. Hilary Putnam notes that "momentum equals mass times velocity" was once true by definition; yet in special relativity this statement is false, true only in the limit of very small velocity (Putnam 1988, p. 8).

[28] Wittgenstein 1953.

## 20 TONALITY: AN OWNER'S MANUAL

Are the earlier instances "truly" seventh chords? The question, like the quest for a simple definition of "game," is not particularly productive. We can if we like try to demarcate the "true" seventh chords from the false, but this is to impose discreteness where history gives us continuity. It seems more fruitful to say that the vagueness of the term "seventh chord" reflects the continuity of compositional practice; instead of a bright line separating seventh from non-seventh, we have a central core of paradigmatic cases surrounded by a penumbra of increasingly problematic examples.[29] Much the same could be said for terms like cadence, dominant, second theme, sonata, tonic, meter, and indeed the entire practice of Roman numeral analysis.

If we respond to this fuzziness by insisting on strict definitions, we will invariably fall into dogmatism. When William Caplin says that a classical-style authentic cadence *must* involve a root-position dominant chord *that lasts right up until the arrival of the tonic*, he is committing himself to withholding the term "cadence" from a host of moments that may sound or feel cadential.[30] When James Hepokoski and Warren Darcy assert that a sonata's second theme *must* as a matter of definition be preceded by a "medial caesura," they commit themselves to denying what may for all the world sound like second themes—or alternatively, to defining "medial caesura" as *whatever comes before a second theme*.[31] The issue here is not so much moral as intellectual, for the risk is that we will transform important generalizations ("the passages we feel to be second themes are very often preceded by a pause") into trivial assertions of linguistic convention ("I will refuse to use the term *second theme* unless I can identify a preceding pause").[32] This is very close to what philosophers call the "no true Scotsman fallacy."[33]

In this book I will try to honor the fuzziness of conceptual boundaries in two ways. First, by avoiding, inasmuch as possible, fruitless disputation about whether a musical object "really" deserves a particular name or not—whether a certain passage "really" is a second theme, or whether a certain progression "really" is a cadence, whether two figures "really" are versions of the same motive, and so on. Many of these questions simply have no objective or interesting answers, much

---

[29] See Rosch 1978, which develops Wittgenstein's observations in a scientific context. Caplin (2013, p. 127) associates this attitude with "postmodernism," but I think it is close to the consensus among analytic philosophers and cognitive scientists, two groups not known for their postmodern attitude. Lawrence 2020 observes that Caplin operates with a "classical" theory of concepts.

[30] For instance, Caplin 2004, example 6, Mozart K.310, III, mm. 173–174, and the opening themes of Beethoven's Op. 127, I and IV. Richards's term "closural function" (2010) is virtually synonymous with the pre-Caplin "cadence," underscoring the potentially terminological nature of the debate. Burstein 2015 also critiques Caplin's approach.

[31] Effacing the medial caesura is, as Mark Richards (2013a, 2013b) has noted, a common tactic in Beethoven's music (Figure P10.4, §10.3).

[32] I think Caplin is right to point out that $\hat{5}$–$\hat{1}$ bass motion typically plays an important role in signaling strong cadences in the classical style, just as I think Hepokoski and Darcy are right to note that second themes are very often preceded by pauses. But in making these true observations into definitions, they reject the very possibility of counterexamples. I see Brown 2005 as declaring that he will only use the word "tonal" to describe pieces that are susceptible to Schenkerian analysis.

[33] The fallacy begins with a claim that "no Scotsman would do *x*" (Flew 1975). When presented with a counterexample, a Scotsman who does in fact do *x*, the claimant responds by arguing that the doer is "no *true* Scotsman." In this way it becomes definitionally true that no Scotsman would do *x*, since anyone who does *x* is not a (true) Scotsman. This renders a potentially true generalization into a trivial fact about linguistic usage.

like the question of whether a hot dog really is or is not a kind of sandwich.[34] We encounter no intellectual or methodological difficulties if we acknowledge that there are grey areas where concepts, from "bald" and "sandwich" to "cadence" and "closing theme," simply fail to grip.

Second, I will try to favor "thin" uses of music-theoretical terms involving only minimal presuppositions, as opposed to "thicker" or methodologically freighted definitions. For me, the term "modality" will refer to largely diatonic music with a wide range of possible centers, making no assumptions about the presence of reciting tones or the utility of the plagal/authentic distinction. Thus "D phrygian" means "music that generally uses the two-flat diatonic collection while articulating D as its tonal center."[35] Similarly, Roman-numeral labels like "I⁶" will mean "scale degrees 1, 3, and 5 with 3 in the bass" carrying no presumptions about roots or inversional equivalence. This is, in the first instance, because I think simpler terms are better suited to a slowly evolving musical practice in which stylistic boundaries are inherently fuzzy. But it is also because the insistence on "thick" terminology has the effect of balkanizing us into distinct linguistic communities, baking our beliefs into words themselves, so that disputes about music are complicated by bickering about language. The risk is that the already-small field of music theory will be even further divided, with historicists, *Formenlehre* theorists, Schenkerians, and empirical musicologists each cultivating their own little gardens of terminological presupposition.

A final philosophical issue involves humility and openness to criticism. Some intellectual communities are relatively hospitable to robust debate, placing a premium on empirical confirmation and an open-minded consideration of alternatives. Others, such as politics and the law, are more likely to view argument as a tool for establishing predetermined goals—the point being for your side to win rather than to discover unexpected truths. I believe there is too much of this second attitude in music scholarship. The field labors under the shadow of figures who made claims far outstripping the evidence available to them, holding to their views even in the face of reasonable counterargument.[36] This has led to a culture in which pointed criticism is sometimes taken to be impolite or even insolent. Both inclination and upbringing lead me to believe that vigorous give-and-take is our best mechanism for improving understanding, and for the most part I have tried to engage with theorists who I feel have genuinely contributed to our understanding; in disagreeing, at various points, with Fétis, Schenker, Schoenberg, Gjerdingen, Cohn, Caplin, or Hepokoski and Darcy, I do not mean to belittle their ideas, but

---

[34] For sandwiches see Lund 2014 and Scherer 2015; Burstein (2015, p. 105) notes that traditional theorists often emphasized the importance of judgment in concept application.

[35] Powers 1992b, p. 212: "Nowadays professional folksingers and composer of folksongs talk glibly about their Dorian and Mixolydian tunes, and so too sophisticated jazz practitioners and textbooks alike, just as composers and theorists of art music used to compose using 'dominants' with 'flatted leading-tones' and call it 'modal harmony.'"

[36] Both Schoenberg and Schenker, for example, placed a heavy emphasis on musical relationships of dubious perceptibility, justifying their methods by appeals to a nebulous and problematic notion of "genius" (Arndt 2013).

22 TONALITY: AN OWNER'S MANUAL

rather to honor their contributions by trying to refine them. Nor, for the most part, do my criticisms undercut their fundamental achievements, instead identifying points where they may have drawn overly broad conclusions or gone too far. Understanding is a process, and criticism is the engine that makes it go: future theorists will no doubt find lacunae and errors in this book, refuting some claims and improving others.

## 4. Statistics

Where earlier scholars worked intuitively, twenty-first-century theorists can be more systematic: with computers it is possible, for example, to list every instance of parallel perfect intervals found on the surface of Palestrina's mass movements. With a little work we can go further, identifying all the parallels that appear in the "harmonic skeleton" that has been shorn of nonharmonic tones. This gives us hope that, for the first time in history, we can produce an empirically adequate account of the prohibition on parallel perfect intervals. Corpus analysis thus provides a "ground truth" against which we can evaluate traditional theoretical claims, much as historians of science can evaluate previous theories against what is now known.[37] Computational corpus studies thus stand alongside geometry as an important twenty-first-century addition to the music theorist's toolbox.

The new data allow us to extend our conception of "music theory" beyond the explicit statements contained in written treatises, to the theories implicitly encoded in musical works themselves. Language users can be said to have implicit theories of grammar, revealed for example by whether they allow themselves to split infinitives—theories absorbed through imitation and implicit learning. The history of English grammar is constructed by the interaction between these implicit theories and the explicit theories of grammarians, which both affect and are affected by the implicit theories. (Sometimes we may even find cases where a single person's implicit theory diverges from their explicit beliefs.[38]) In much the same way, composers have implicit views about theoretical issues both small and large, which we can recover (if imperfectly) through a careful study of their music—thus revealing an intuitive "composer theory" that stands alongside the explicit statements of "theorist theory."[39] Corpus data allow us to reconstruct the dialogue between explicit and implicit, a history of musical ideas written jointly by theorists and composers.

---

[37] There are interesting analogies between the history of science and the history of music theory, which both struggle to chart a path between the twin dangers of triumphalism (or "whiggishness") and relativism. I suspect that the history of music theory, having survived whiggishness in the form of a Hegelian-Schenkerian progressivism, is currently in the late stages of its relativist or historicist phase, with a more realist, computational era on the horizon. See Wootton 2015.

[38] Labov 1975 describes a case in which a speaker used constructions he declared to be ungrammatical.

[39] Compare Weber (1817–1821) 1846, pp. 453–54: "Theorists really possess incomparably less of theory than practitioners themselves. For the former teach false rules while the latter act according to those which are true. The rules which the former lay down, infinitely more often prove erroneous than correct; while the latter produce elevated works of art, from which we might and should long since have deduced better rules."

Unfortunately, musical scores are for many computational purposes opaque: D–F–A can be a tonic in D minor, a supertonic in C major, a mere agglomeration of nonharmonic tones deserving no chordal label, and many other things as well. Linguists dealt with analogous issues by constructing substantial corpora of hand-analyzed data that served both as primary objects of study and as training sets for automatic language-parsing algorithms.[40] For this book, I have followed their lead, creating machine-readable Roman-numeral analyses of more than one thousand pieces stretching from Dufay to Brahms; as I explain in appendix 4, all this material is freely available on the internet—music, data, code, and instructions for reproducing all the graphs, tables, statistics, and analyses in the book. Over the last decade I have carefully checked this corpus, improving it as I use it.[41] Handmade annotations greatly increase the power of computational analysis, but at the cost of introducing subjectivity—an issue that will be explored in later chapters.

The recent explosion of musical data has the potential to transform our understanding of a wide range of questions. Consider Paul von Hippel and David Huron's investigation of the traditional claim that melodic leaps tend to lead to a change in direction—a principle found in Western counterpoint texts both ancient and modern.[42] Given the resources available when they wrote, von Hippel and Huron had to explore this question using a limited sample of just over 200 heterogeneous works: 35 Schubert lieder and 176 folk songs from diverse cultures. Finding no compelling evidence for reversal in this small dataset, they proposed that "post-skip reversals" might instead be explained by tessitura: large leaps, they observe, are more likely to take vocalists to their registral extremes, and registrally extreme notes are likely to move toward the center of their range. This led them to a *memory-free* mechanism whereby all notes seek the center of a vocalist's register, in contrast with the traditional view that melodic direction depends on the size of the preceding interval.

Figure 1.4.1 combines the vocal parts in virtually all of Palestrina's mass movements, a sample large enough that we can inspect melodic behavior at every point in the tessitura. We see a substantially greater tendency for leaps to change direction throughout the range, a tendency that is also present in the fugues of *The Well-Tempered Clavier*, while being severely reduced in artificial "memory-free" music that uses the same distribution of melodic intervals at every point in the range.[43] It is now easy to perform this sort of analysis on a wide range of corpora from the thirteenth century to the present, a vastly greater sample than von Hippel and Huron were able to access. Such analyses suggest that melodic leaps often do

---

[40] McEnery and Wilson 1996.

[41] Mistakes no doubt remain, however, and readers are invited to send corrections by email.

[42] Von Hippel and Huron 2000.

[43] The artificial datasets are amnesiac or "Markov twin" versions of the musical data that have the same (first-order) melodic statistics: note $x$ in the Markov twin uses the same intervals, with the same probabilities, as note $x$ in the original music, but has no memory of the previous interval. For more, see von Hippel and Huron 2000. Note that the artificial datasets *do* exhibit a tendency toward "post-skip reversal" at their registral extremes; Huron and von Hippel are not wrong about the existence of this effect, just about its magnitude.

24    TONALITY: AN OWNER'S MANUAL

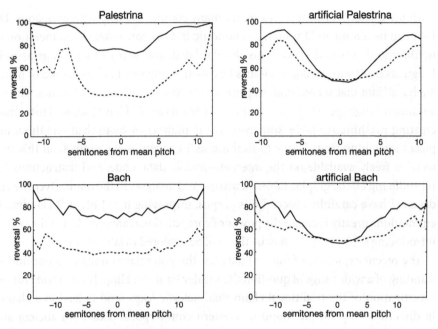

**Figure 1.4.1.** The tendency for leaps (solid lines) and steps (dotted lines) to reverse direction in Palestrina's masses, the fugues from *The Well-Tempered Clavier*, and artificial music based on these. In the real music, there is a substantial tendency for leaps to reverse direction, even in the middle of the tessitura; this tendency is much smaller in the artificial music.

preferentially change melodic direction over and above what can be explained by register alone—in Josquin, Palestrina, Monteverdi, J. S. Bach, Beethoven, Sacred Harp vocal polyphony, rock music, and other genres as well (Figure 1.4.2). This tendency is greater in some styles than in others, and particularly pronounced in Western notated music, both vocal and instrumental; but it does not seem to be entirely an artifact of tessitura.

Such evidence needs to be viewed with caution, not just out of general principle but also because musical concepts, including "voice" and "step," can be difficult to pin down. In sophisticated tonal music we find melodies alternating between two logical voices, arpeggiating chords (i.e. moving by step along a nonscalar collection), and inserting embellishing tones between leap and reversal (Figure 1.4.3). These examples remind us that the principle of post-skip reversal is native to the context of *counterpoint instruction*, a simplified environment in which many musical techniques are off the table.[44] Simple counting will not necessarily answer the musical question.

---

[44] Von Hippel and Huron were concerned both with the universal claims of Leonard Meyer and Eugene Narmour, and also with the situated pronouncements of Western pedagogues. Their data more directly bears on the former.

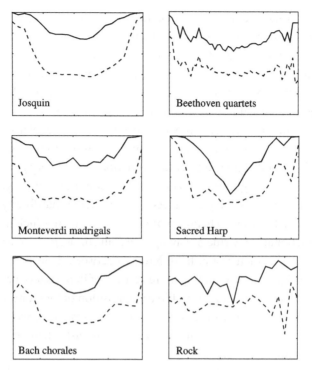

**Figure 1.4.2.** The tendency of melodic leaps to reverse direction in a variety of repertoires. Due to the frequent use of the pentatonic scale, a three-semitone interval has been classified as a step in Sacred Harp and rock.

**Figure 1.4.3.** Skips that do not immediately reverse direction due to multiple abstract voices, stepwise motion along a triadic alphabet, and melodic embellishment.

What we can say is that computational analysis often provides limited and defeasible evidence in favor of music-theoretical common sense. Leaps lead disproportionately to changes of melodic direction in many repertoires. Vast tracts of Renaissance polyphony decorate triads with the nonharmonic tones of traditional contrapuntal theory. And, of course, countless functionally tonal passages exhibit the tonic-subdominant-dominant-tonic organization described in harmony texts. Here and elsewhere empirical investigation undercuts the more extreme forms of music-theoretical skepticism—a complete rejection of "post-skip reversal," or of Roman-numeral analysis, or of the very notion of nonharmonicity.[45] In the past,

---

[45] Schenker rejected (local) Roman-numeral analysis while Schoenberg rejected the very notion of nonharmonicity. These views are echoed by contemporary figures such as Robert Gjerdingen (1996) and Ian Quinn (2018).

26 TONALITY: AN OWNER'S MANUAL

such skepticism has often served theoretical ambition, the rejection of received wisdom paving the road for more radical alternatives. It is difficult to see how this approach can survive the era of abundant musical data.

At the same time, however, the following chapters will uncover numerous challenges to textbook verities: nonharmonic tones that cannot be "reduced" to consonances, or classical idioms that do not conform to any simple model of harmonic progression. Conversely, we will find untheorized regularities in a variety of genres. Perhaps the most consequential are the continuities between sixteenth-century modality and eighteenth-century functionality—a very gradual harmonic simplification beginning in the Renaissance and continuing through the classical era, often invisible to the analytic eye. As a result, there is hardly any music that is purely "modal" in the sense of being untainted by functional principles, nor any that is purely "functional" by virtue of having shorn all connections to earlier practice. Consistent with this picture are the differences between dialects of functional tonality, with baroque music retaining more vestiges of Renaissance practice. Corpus analysis thus suggests we replace the binary opposition of modality and functional tonality (and perforce the assumption that these represent separate and coherent "systems" of musical thinking) with a more continuously changing set of contrapuntal and harmonic conventions.[46]

We are, in other words, led in equal and opposite directions: on the one hand to the conclusion that traditional theory is generally correct, and on the other to the realization that its basic assumptions sometimes fail. One might draw an analogy to Newtonian physics, which provides accurate descriptions of the macroscopic world despite being fundamentally wrong about its microscopic structure. To the engineer, these failures are minor and can often be ignored. To the philosopher, they are cataclysmic, for the failure of Newtonian physics points to a fundamentally counterintuitive picture of the universe. For all the success of classical mechanics, the world simply is not made of tiny billiard balls proceeding along deterministic paths. Something altogether different is going on.

## 5. Schema

A good candidate for this *something* is the idiom or schema—contemporary music theory's answer to its earlier Newtonianism. Here the pioneering figure is Robert Gjerdingen, who proposes to scrap much of the apparatus of traditional theory in favor of a "construction grammar" in which composers recombine atomic patterns.[47] Musical behavior, on this view, is not lawlike at its deepest level—instead it is an unruly and messy enterprise whose basic objects are specific gestures, often tied to particular formal contexts. In many ways, Gjerdingen favors a return to a

---

[46] For the "two systems" see Dahlhaus 1990, pp. 59–65.
[47] Gjerdingen and Bourne 2015. Gjerdingen's project is influenced by Meyer 1996.

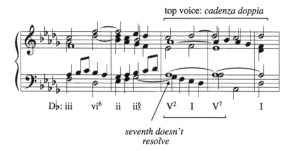

**Figure 1.5.1.** An idiom from the first B♭ minor fugue in *The Well-Tempered Clavier*, mm. 21–24. The bass of the V² steps down to the tonic without resolving.

pre-Rameauian conception of musical structure, rooted in the inherently particular injunctions of seventeenth- and eighteenth-century pedagogy.[48]

Figure 1.5.1 shows an unusual cadential formula that can be found throughout J. S. Bach's work. The main point of interest is the bass, which unsettles two fundamental presuppositions about eighteenth- and nineteenth-century music:

(1) That dissonant chordal sevenths invariably resolve downward by step to a chord tone; here $\hat{4}$ moves through passing $\hat{3}$ and $\hat{2}$, with the next chordal note a fourth below.[49]
(2) That nonharmonic tones are essentially decorative and irrelevant to syntacticality; for this figure almost never involves the bass $\hat{4}$ leaping to the tonic. Apparently, Bach felt that the stepwise motion was important to the sense of resolution.

Gjerdingen's work offers an antidote to two powerful music-theoretical temptations. The first is to declare unusual moments nonsyntactical or ungrammatical simply because they violate oversimplistic generalizations; instead, he suggests that idioms are as important to Bach's idiolect as the procedures of textbook harmony. The second temptation is the construction of *ad hoc* analyses seizing on particular features of the local context to justify the "violations of the rules"—hermeneutic narratives that purport to explain why Bach might have turned outlaw at just this particular moment. For what initially seems like a violation may simply be a second-order default, a rare but legitimate syntactic option. Schema theory encourages us to consider that "exceptions to the rules" might simply be features of a practice, explained by no more general principle or law. Here one could draw an analogy to English phrases such as "a whole nother kettle of fish" or "unbebloodylievable," exceptions to the general truth that English words cannot be inserted inside one another.

---

[48] The connection is explicit in Holtmeier 2007.
[49] If we assert that the bass F ($\hat{3}$) is a chord tone, then the upper-voice E♭4 on the second quarter is the seventh of iii⁷ (F–A♭–C–E♭), which moves up by step.

28  TONALITY: AN OWNER'S MANUAL

Figure 1.5.2. Unusual resolutions of the seventh in Bach's chorales. In "Christus, der uns selig macht" (Riemenschneider 198, BWV 283), mm. 7–8, and "Ich dank dir, Gott, für all Wohltat" (Riemenschneider 223, BWV 346), m. 11, the tenor steps down to the tonic. In "O Welt, sieh hier dein Leben" (Riemenschneider 117, BWV 244.10), mm. 9–10, the bass steps down by fourth but on unusual scale degrees; the seventh is resolved in register by another voice.

The task is then to characterize Bach's idiom accurately: is it just a fact that his sevenths sometimes move down by fourth? Or does this happen only with dominant seventh chords or only in cadential contexts? How can we improve upon the largely correct generalization that sevenths usually resolve down by step to chord tones? We cannot dismiss these questions out of a distaste for abstract theorizing, for the question is precisely how to characterize "this" idiom—as a specific cadential gesture, a technique for resolving the seventh, or in some other way. It is just here that statistical generality can help schema-theoretic particularity: given a set of scores along with a labeling of their chords, it is possible to identify *all* the moments in which sevenths resolve anomalously; these can then be examined individually to determine the scope of a composer's actual practice. In Bach's chorales we find that this idiom *usually* occurs in the context of this particular schema ($V^2$–I–V–I, often with the *cadenza doppia* in one of the voices), largely at cadences, but occasionally at other points in the phrase, and very occasionally in inner voices (Figure 1.5.2).[50] The cadential schema thus stands at the center of a network surrounded by progressively more uncommon variants.[51] Without detailed empirical investigation it is simply impossible to describe the scope of the idiom.

---

[50] The "cadenza doppia" is the formula in the top voice of Figure 1.5.1, where the leading tone moves up to the tonic, often forming a suspension, before ultimately moving back to the leading tone and resolving once again to the tonic.

[51] In discussion, theorists have sometimes suggested that Bach's cadential idiom "works" because the bass and upper voices become temporarily out of sync, with the seventh resolving to 3̂ prematurely, before the upper voices reach the tonic. But consider this explanation from the point of view of a student attempting to imitate Bach: here it is crucial that the "falling out of sync" (if that is what it is) almost always occurs in a

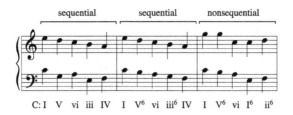

**Figure 1.5.3.** Sequential and nonsequential variants of Robert Gjerdingen's "Romanesca" schema.

Gjerdingen has provided an important corrective to speculative overreach, and I fully endorse his claim that musical style is idiomatic at its core, employing schemas and patterns that sometimes violate broader grammatical generalizations. But I reject the thought that generalization is inherently suspect, for it seems entirely likely that composers learn *both* specific idioms *and also* more general and systematic principles: the "rules" of functional harmony—traditionally expressed by precepts such as "V does not go to ii"—are generalizations of this sort, learned implicitly in something like the way that children learn the grammar of their native language.[52] Something similar can be said for the precepts of traditional counterpoint theory, which accurately describe techniques for augmenting consonant harmonies with passing tones, suspensions, and the like. These "rules," or rather *approximately true generalizations*, are broader than Gjerdingen's idioms, more conducive to genuine creativity, and roughly comparable to the implicitly learned principle that English has a subject-verb-object norm. Schema theory is best understood as *augmenting* rather than *replacing* the generalizations of familiar theory.

Consider, as a point of contrast, galant composers' preference for $I^6$ over iii in the nonsequential "Romanesca" (Figure 1.5.3). Gjerdingen explicitly disavows any attempt to explain this preference by "chord grammar," the "rise of tonality," or "other grand abstractions," instead proposing that eighteenth-century musicians play by "eighteenth-century rules" grounded in the solfege and unfigured-bass traditions.[53] By contrast, I think that we can often explain why schemas are the way they are. Indeed, the ionian-mode preference for $I^6$ long predates the eighteenth century (Figure 1.5.4); this general favoring of $I^6$, I will claim, is both a rudimentary manifestation of "chord grammar" and an early stage in the development

particular context and on a particular set of scale degrees. This limitation is apparent only when we switch perspectives from that of the passive listener, confronting a fixed body of earlier music, to that of the composer, who needs to know when the idiom is permissible.

[52] Temperley 2006 also argues for abstract schemas, while Byros 2017 distinguishes "microtheory" from "macrotheory." Rabinovitch (2018, 2019, and 2020) also tries to systematize schematic thinking, though from a different point of view. Holtmeier 2011 notes that eighteenth-century musicians had easy access to an elaborate theoretical discourse containing generalizations about topics such as sequences, the rule of the octave, and the fundamental bass.

[53] Gjerdingen 2007, p. 34.

30  TONALITY: AN OWNER'S MANUAL

| | |
|---|---|
| Bach | 92 |
| Corelli | 90 |
| Monteverdi | 80 |
| Morley | 90 |
| Palestrina (ionian) | 61 |

**Figure 1.5.4.** The percentage of triads above $\hat{3}$ that are in first inversion.

**Figure 1.5.5.** Three ways to harmonize stepwise descending thirds with alternating $\frac{5}{3}$ and $\frac{6}{3}$ sonorities. The first is common in virtually all triadic music; the second can be found in the baroque but is rare thereafter; the third is common only in modal music. Here "D4A2" means "descending fourth, ascending second."

of functional harmony. From this point of view, the puzzle is not the use of I$^6$ in the nonsequential "Romanesca" but rather the persistence of iii in sequential contexts: indeed, the Pachelbel sequence was originally just one of many related idioms in which descending thirds alternately support $\frac{5}{3}$ and $\frac{6}{3}$ sonorities (Figure 1.5.5); the gradual pruning of these options, to the point where only the Pachelbel progression remains, was part of the lexical narrowing that produced functional tonality. These might be grand abstractions, but they are grounded in concrete data.

One of my goals, therefore, will be to combine the schematic approach with an openness to regularity and generalization. To that end I will argue that many schemas originate in constraints inherent to our materials: rather than the figure skater's codified moves, they are responses to the contours of musical space—a rock climber taking advantage of a particularly prominent outcropping. The musical analogue of the rock face is a contrapuntal geometry that funnels intuitive exploration toward certain solutions. These can take on different rhetorical roles in different styles: Gjerdingen's "Prinner," for example, may function as a precadential "riposte" in the galant period, and a cadence in the Renaissance. This difference is built atop a deeper level of constraint arising from the fundamental logic of musical possibility.[54] Thus we should distinguish the "deep Prinner," a very general voice-leading schema used from the Renaissance to the present, from the "shallow Prinner" that is a specific galant mannerism.

---

[54] Holtmeier 2011 makes a similar point.

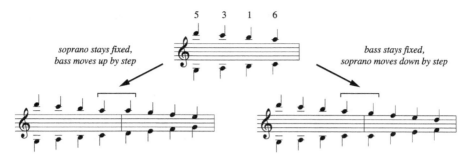

Figure 1.5.6. Two contrary-motion sequences featuring diatonic consonances. They can be reversed to create registral expansion.

Another general principle, tacitly understood by composers in many genres, is that contrary-motion sequences are most balanced when they move by about half an octave. The idiom in Figure 1.5.6 appears in virtually all modal and functionally tonal styles, the two voices moving stepwise to enumerate the diatonic consonances—fifth, third, octave, sixth. The pattern can be continued in two obvious ways, either lowering the top voice to move the pattern down by fifth (or, in the other voice, up by fourth), or raising the bass to move up by fifth (down by fourth in the other voice).[55] Repeating one of these options produces a sequence, while using them in alternation produces a quasi-sequence that returns to its starting point after two iterations (Figure 1.5.7). Thus what might initially seem like an arbitrary figure of speech, drawn from an infinite reservoir of equally good alternatives, can be plausibly described as an optimal path through a preexisting geometrical space of musical possibilities. The advantage of the general approach is that it allows us to connect traditional practices with those of our time. In Figure 1.5.8, for example, we find Meredith Monk using diatonic contrary motion to generate the same sort of fifth relationship found in Western classical music, only now featuring seconds and fourths. I think it is useful to recognize the continuity between this excerpt and the more schematic contrary motion patterns of the classical style. This is possible only if we ground schematic particulars in broader potentialities.

Without general principles, the schematic approach can devolve into a picture of composition as the mindless stitching-together of precomposed chunks, reminiscent of jazz textbooks that teach only licks or "artificial intelligence" programs that recombine preexisting music to produce the illusion of something new. Genuine musical thinking requires novel solutions to high-level compositional problems: Fanny Mendelssohn Hensel harmonizing a traditional diatonic schema in an unusual way, Meredith Monk adapting a familiar technique to dissonant dyads. The goal of this book is to describe some of the general techniques that can be found throughout Western practice: "thinking within the chord," hierarchically nested transposition, repeating contrapuntal patterns, and many others as well. These

---

[55] These two intervals, the fourth and fifth, are the diatonic scale's closest approximation to a half-octave.

32 TONALITY: AN OWNER'S MANUAL

Figure 1.5.7. Two examples of a contrary-motion schema alternating thirds and sixths: Fanny Mendelssohn Hensel's "Januar," mm. 15–18 (from *Das Jahr*, H. 385); and a passage from Klaus Badelt's film score *Pirates of the Caribbean: Curse of the Black Pearl* (2002, heard at 2:07:32). The first forms a brief fifth sequence, while the second combines an ascending and descending fifth to return to its starting point.

Figure 1.5.8. A motive from Meredith Monk's *Anthem* (2020), analyzed in relation to the traditional contrary-motion schema. Both feature "antiparallel" motion where the upper voice ascends by fifth ($T_4$ or four diatonic steps), while the bottom voice descends by fourth ($T_{-3}$).

general principles are the source of the particular schemas that help to define specific styles.

Schema theory shares with Schenkerian theory a focus on outer-voice contrapuntal patterns, privileging line and dyad over triad and seventh chord; it differs from Schenkerian or Roman-numeral theory in favoring *particular idioms* over general principles. I will try to triangulate between these approaches, describing *general principles governing the interdependence of harmony and counterpoint*. To that end I will introduce a family of geometrical models that allow us to view any given passage under a dyadic, triadic, seventh-chord, or scalar lens. What results is a generalized analogue of schema theory, combining linear ideas from Schenker with harmonic ideas from Rameau, and revealing connections between a wide range of practices from the Renaissance to the present day.

## 6. Outline

This book is framed by two largely analytical chapters. Chapter 2 argues that a variety of rock progressions, all unusual from the standpoint of classical theory, reflect straightforward features of musical geometry—and hence that the intuitive competence of the rock musician is in part a matter of knowing one's way around the space of chromatic triads. This chapter is meant to provide an accessible introduction to my general approach. Chapter 10 makes a broadly similar point about Beethoven, focusing on what I call the "Ludwig" schema, and considering some of the philosophical challenges his music poses. This is more of a culmination, linking technical issues in voice-leading geometry with philosophical questions about analysis. Together, the two chapters suggest that a range of different musical styles can be linked by a subterranean geometrical logic.

Sandwiched in between are seven more theoretical chapters examining various features of modal and functionally tonal syntax. Chapter 3 considers the *voice-leading system*, arguing that counterpoint is not fundamentally a matter of avoiding parallels, or even balancing of independent melodic lines, but of understanding the interdependence between harmonic and melodic forces. As we will see, general linear impulses such as the preference for descending stepwise melodies will tend to generate different kinds of harmonic progressions in different contexts—so that one and the same melodic tendency produces modal results in one situation and functional results in another. My approach here recalls the Schenkerian idea that melodic phenomena generate harmonic patterns "at the musical surface." But unlike Schenker, I argue that the voice-leading system often generates a distinctively *modal* logic which reverses classical harmonic norms.

Chapter 4 then zeroes in on the particular subject of repetition, proposing a new theoretical device, the *repeating contrapuntal pattern*, that can be found from the Renaissance to the present day. This is perhaps the newest chapter of the book, using abstract notions of symmetry to identify an aspect of musical competence

34 TONALITY: AN OWNER'S MANUAL

crossing stylistic boundaries; its argument continues in appendix 3, which connects classical sequences to twentieth-century transformations. Chapter 5 considers the *nonharmonic system* coordinating the behavior of dissonant and nonharmonic tones. I argue that nonharmonic tones are not simply "decorative," particularly in the case of suspensions. This leads to a more general consideration of the ways in which nonharmonic tones can serve harmonic ends—and hence the impossibility of drawing a clean distinction between harmonic and nonharmonic realms. The discussion again serves as a case study for my broader approach: traditional theories of nonharmonicity work well in general, while also breaking down in alarming ways.

The latter part of the book turns to the *harmonic system*, a set of initially implicit norms that were eventually codified by figures such as Rameau and Riemann. Chapter 6 interprets the rise of harmonic functionality as a gradual process spanning more than two centuries, using analysis and corpus study to tease out a simpler form of *protofunctionality* appearing early in the sixteenth century. Chapter 7 analyzes the local procedures of mature functionality as the product of three independent subsystems—harmonic cycles, fauxbourdon, and sequences. Here the main innovations are (1) tracing functional practice to basic affordances of geometrical space; (2) using the circle of diatonic thirds to highlight the quasi-sequential nature of functional harmony; (3) including fauxbourdon as a core functional subsystem; and (4) expanding our conception of sequential practice. Chapter 8 discusses scales and keys, which I present as chordlike objects operating at a higher hierarchical level; I also use voice leading to propose a new theory of enharmonicism. Chapter 9 turns to higher-level organization, considering melodic strategies, harmonic recursion, and eight-bar phrase structure.

Each chapter is prefaced by a short prelude setting the stage for the more detailed investigation to follow; for some readers, these may provide the most concentrated source of interesting material. Where appropriate, I end each chapter by considering twentieth- and twenty-first-century applications of its techniques. Some readers will want to chart a path reflecting their particular interests: the examination of earlier music is mostly confined to chapters 2–6, while functional tonality is the focus of chapters 7–10. Those who are interested in analysis can find detailed discussions of Monteverdi's "Ohimè, se tanto amate" in §5.3, the opening of the Rondo-Burlesque from Mahler's Ninth Symphony in §5.5, the Kyrie of Palestrina's *Pope Marcellus Mass* in §6.5, Marenzio's "Ahi Dispetata Morte" in §6.7, four "dualist" pieces by J. S. Bach (invention, prelude, chorale, and fugue) in §7.7, several Chopin pieces in §9.3, and, in chapter 10, five nineteenth-century movements by Beethoven, Schubert, and Wagner. Once the basic framework of chapters 2–4 is taken on board, chapters can be read out of order, as loosely connected essays on different aspects of musical structure.

Any theory that is concerned with voice leading needs to grapple with Heinrich Schenker, whose musical ideas are in equal parts insightful and infuriating—and whose moral and aesthetic views are often downright repulsive. One of the major surprises for me, over the course of my writing, is how often I have found myself close to Schenkerian insights.[56] Like Schenker, I believe music is often governed by a deep contrapuntal logic that is obscured when we focus too closely on roots and Roman numerals. I endorse the Schenkerian idea that chords can exist "below the musical surface," though for me this means treating them as small scales along which voices move. I likewise share Schenker's perception that sequences are fundamentally connected to certain sorts of linear intervallic structures, or "repeating contrapuntal patterns" as I call them. I frequently adopt a broadly Schenkerian strategy of analyzing music by "reducing" it to familiar templates or schemas, eliminating surface detail to reveal a simplified backbone. On a more detailed level, I often follow Schenker by assigning voice exchanges to the musical surface.[57] Finally, I use voice leading as a lens for understanding higher-level phenomena such as modulation. In all these ways, I will try to infuse the relatively flat models of voice-leading geometry with a richer hierarchical structure.

But beyond these broad similarities are a host of important differences. The biggest is that I am fundamentally skeptical about the long-range connections that characterize so much Schenkerian practice—the idea that there are aesthetically and perceptually meaningful connections between notes separated by dozens or hundreds of measures. In my view this represents a fantastical disregard for human perceptual limitations.[58] Almost as important are two different conceptions of musical reduction: for me it is a process of *modeling*, speculative hypotheses about the cognitive structures that might produce a musical passage, whereas for Schenker it reveals something like a musical essence.[59] Furthermore, I view *scales* (both familiar and generalized) as important bearers of harmonic structure, while Schenkerian theory affords them no privileged status. I also think *sequences* can provide alternatives to the chorale-like backgrounds of Schenkerian analysis, allowing us to understand an irregular musical surface as distorting a more-regular background. Finally, I am largely unconcerned with unity as an aesthetic value and with reductional stages beyond the first. All of which is to say that I try to incorporate Schenkerian insights in ways that are both empirically informed and epistemologically modest, tempered by geometry, corpus study, and schema theory.

The notated tradition has often been a source of undue anxiety. We are bad listeners if we do not have a sense of resolution when a sonata recapitulates its second theme in the tonic key. We are bad historians if we hear tonic-dominant resolution in sixteenth-century music. We are bad composers if we need the piano, or

---

[56] Burstein (forthcoming) describes the difficulties of assigning a univocal view to Schenker himself or Schenkerians more generally. In this book, I will typically be concerned with views shared by many different scholars—what Burstein describes as a "Schenkerian practice" originating with an "idealized" Schenker.

[57] Cf. Brown 2005, p. 78.

[58] Forte 1959 aptly compares Schenker to Freud, whose work was considered much more scientific in 1959 than it is now.

[59] Cf. Schenker (1935) 1979, p. xxiii: "The musical examples which accompany this volume are not merely practical aids; they have the same power and conviction as the visual aspect of the printed composition itself (the foreground). That is, the graphic representation is part of the actual composition, not merely an educational means."

fail to imagine an entire piece in a single blazing instant. We are aesthetically unsophisticated if we happen to prefer rock to Wagner. Over and over again, we are told that we are Ordinary while the dead composers are Geniuses—and that we should subordinate our preferences to those of our aesthetic betters. One possible response is to reject the learned tradition in favor of simpler and more accessible styles. My hope is that this book could point toward another: that by generalizing and demystifying basic compositional techniques, it will allow us to appreciate the notated tradition's virtues while also defusing some of its elitism—giving us a middle path between uncritical acceptance and outright rejection. This is the final and most unlikely meaning of my title.

# Prelude
## Transposition Along a Collection

If I had to identify the single most important concept in music theory, I would pick *transposition along a collection*, the operation that shifts musical material along a chord, a scale, or any other set of notes. Here the collection acts like a musical ruler, providing a unit of musical distance that allows us to move objects by one or more steps. Alternatively, we can think of a collection as a slightly uneven ladder: the conceptual trick is to measure distance with ladder rungs (steps) rather than some fixed unit like inches (semitones). Figure P2.1 turns "doe a deer" into "ray a drop" by shifting each note upward one rung along the diatonic ladder; this operation preserves scalar distance, or distance as measured in scale steps. In "West End Blues," Louis Armstrong uses the same operation to move his motive successively downward along an E♭ major triad; this preserves distances as measured in triadic steps, or steps along the three note "scale" E♭–G–B♭ (Figure P2.2). Actually, that oversimplifies: it is only the last two notes of the motive that move along the triad, with the first a neighbor note one scale step above the second note; to analyze the passage we therefore need to juggle scalar and chordal distances simultaneously.

In Figure P2.3, Domenico Scarlatti transposes along *both* chord and scale, the right hand moving up by one triadic step while the left hand ascends by two scalar steps. (For the sake of illustration, I am ignoring the slight difference between the hands' patterns and considering some notes to be nonharmonic.) We see that for A–C–E, transposition by triadic step (C–E–A) is almost equivalent to transposition by two diatonic steps (C–E–G). Readers can explore this idea by shifting arbitrary motives along the *intrinsic scale* defined by their own notes; this produces a range of interesting results, particularly when combined with transposition along the scale, or when one declares some notes to be nonharmonic. The passages in Figure P2.4 lie somewhere between traditional motivic development and modern set theory; as a group, they suggest that musical identity is *up to us*, determined by an object's transformational properties rather than fixed for all time by its intrinsic constitution.

While motion-along-a-collection is most familiar in melodic contexts, it plays an important role in the harmonic domain as well. Consider the notion of "registral inversion." Students are taught to construct inversions by moving a chord's bass to its soprano, a procedure that works well in the conventionalized language of classical music, where harmonies are always familiar, bass and melody are paramount, and the precise configuration of inner voices is secondary. In other contexts, the

*Tonality*. Dmitri Tymoczko, Oxford University Press. © Oxford University Press 2023. DOI: 10.1093/oso/9780197577103.003.0002

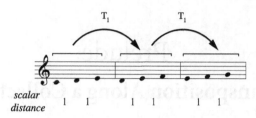

**Figure P2.1.** Moving a three-note motive up by step along the diatonic scale ($T_1$).

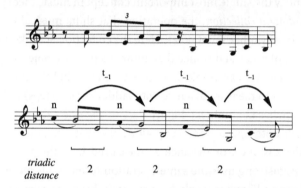

**Figure P2.2.** In m. 7 of "West End Blues," Louis Armstrong transposes the second two notes of his motive downward by chordal step along the E♭ major triad ($t_{-1}$), with the first note a neighbor one scale step above the second.

procedure becomes problematic. The chord in Figure P2.5 has one high note and two low notes close together. As we move bottom note to top, we destroy its characteristic spacing: the first inversion has one low and two high notes, while the second inversion has all three notes high and close. Worse yet, another inversion does not bring us back to our starting point but to a configuration in which all notes are close together.

An alternate strategy moves each voice upward by step *along the chord itself*. First we compress the chord's notes into a single octave, forming a scale from its notes; then we move each voice by the same number of steps along that scale. This yields a series of voicings sharing the same abstract registral arrangement and returning to their initial configuration in a higher octave (Figure P2.6).[1] Once again, transposition *along* a collection preserves intervals *as measured by* that collection: here, the middle note is always one chordal step above the lowest, while the top is four chordal steps above the middle. This approach is familiar in guitar pedagogy, where it is used to construct inversions that keep the left hand in roughly the same position; in chapter 3 we will find that it plays a role in traditional figured-bass theory as well.

---

[1] If we start with a chord whose notes are compressed within a single octave, the new algorithm returns the same results as the traditional process of moving bottom note to top.

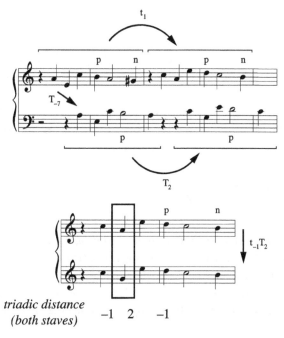

**Figure P2.3.** Domenico Scarlatti's Sonata in A minor, K.3, mm. 3–6. The right-hand motive moves up by chordal step ($t_1$), while the left-hand variant moves up by two scale steps ($T_2$), with the two transpositions producing very similar results. (Here and elsewhere, I use p and n for passing and neighboring notes.) Since $t_1$ and $T_2$ are almost the same, $t_{-1}$ almost cancels $T_2$ so that the combination $t_{-1}T_2$ does very little. The bottom system analyzes the efficient voice leading between the top system's (A, C, E) and the bottom system's (G, C, E) as a combination of transpositions along both chord ($t_{-1}$) and scale ($T_2$).

Transposition along the chord is significant here because it preserves a tangible aspect of musical structure: *voicing*, or the pattern of registral spacing measured in steps along the chord itself. It is also important because the most efficient voice leading between two chords—the mapping that collectively moves the voices by the smallest overall amount—will always connect chords that are voiced in the same way. Thus if we want to find efficient voice leading between two chords, we should arrange them using the same spacing-in-chordal steps. Figure P2.7 maps the preceding example's C3–D3–A4 to a minor triad spaced in exactly the same way. There are three fundamental possibilities depending on whether the C in the initial chord is mapped to the root, third, or fifth of the minor triad.[2] We conclude that chordal-step distance will be relevant whenever composers are concerned with efficient voice leading, which is much of the time. Indeed, composers might find themselves using transposition-along-the-chord unknowingly, as a byproduct of

---

[2] The next chapter's prelude will explain how to derive the remaining spacing-preserving voice leadings from these three options.

40   TONALITY: AN OWNER'S MANUAL

**Figure P2.4.** Transposing two motives along the *intrinsic scale* defined by their pitches. Two different stepwise transpositions are shown, one treating all notes as harmonic, the other treating some as nonharmonic. Boldface **n** labels potential chromatic neighbors, regular n labels potential diatonic neighbors. The last measure of the third line transposes a triad along its fifth, interpreting the second note as a third above the first.

**Figure P2.5.** Forming registral inversions by moving a chord's bottom note to the top.

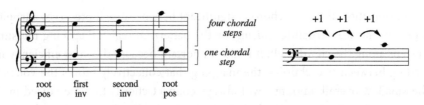

**Figure P2.6.** Forming registral inversions by moving each voice along the intrinsic scale formed by the chord's notes.

**Figure P2.7.** Three spacing-preserving voice leadings from C3–D3–A4 to a minor triad; the first maps the C to the triad's root, the second to the triad's third, and the last to the triad's fifth. All chords are voiced with the middle note one chordal step above the bass and four chordal steps below the soprano.

trying to minimize contrapuntal motion. In motivic contexts, composers intentionally move musical objects along the chord; in contrapuntal contexts, these same transformations can arise implicitly and without conscious knowledge. The phenomenon of transposition-along-a-collection spans the border between implicit and explicit.

The deep point is that any collection of notes, from chord to motive to set, can be associated with two different scales: an external or *enclosing scale*—chromatic, diatonic, or some other contextually relevant collection—and the *intrinsic scale* formed from its own notes. To transpose along the first scale is to transpose in the ordinary sense, preserving intervals as measured along the scale; to transpose along the second is to generalize the notion of chordal inversion as just described, preserving intervals as measured along the chord. Recent music theory has largely concerned itself with the first of these transformations, whereas traditional theory often concerned itself with the second, either implicitly (e.g., as a means of obtaining efficient voice leading) or explicitly (e.g., close and open position). The intrinsic scale is a missing link between traditional tonal theory and modern set theory, obscured by the habit of conceiving sets in exclusively chromatic terms. Once we train ourselves to think within a variety of different scales, starting with "diatonic set theory" and generalizing from there, we will eventually find our way to the intrinsic scale and the concepts implicit in traditional theory.

There are many other uses for the concept of the intrinsic scale. One, to be discussed in the next two chapters, harmonizes melodies using transposition along both chord and scale. Another connects chords related by *pitch-class inversion* and voiced in the same way; such spacing-preserving progressions will invariably preserve the distance between at least one pair of voices.[3] What results are exactly the passages we explored in §1.1, where two voices move in parallel while the remaining notes alternate to create similarly spaced, inversionally related chords. In other words, the seeming contrapuntal wizardry of Gesualdo et al. is a straightforward consequence of a concern for efficient voice leading, or attention to chord voicing as measured in chordal steps (Figure P2.8). The recent discipline of "neo-Riemannian theory" is largely concerned with these progressions, and particularly those where the parallel voices are stationary; the concept of the intrinsic scale gives us an intuitive handle on this complex literature, and on the musical practices motivating it.[4]

Transposition along the chord and transposition along the scale combine to form a kind of *doubly parallel motion* along a pair of hierarchically nested collections. I will notate $x$-step transposition along the chord as $t_x$, with a lowercase "t," and $y$-step transposition along the scale as $T_y$, using a boldface T for chromatic

---

[3] NB: "inversion" here means "pitch-class inversion," the turning-upside-down of a chord's intervals, rather than "registral inversion," the rearranging of its notes in register. In this case, the identity of the parallel voices is determined by the registral inversions of the chords in the progression.

[4] Spacing-preserving voice leadings between inversionally related chords can be obtained by inverting a chord twice, along both the intrinsic and extrinsic scale; see appendix 1, appendix 3, and Tymoczko 2020b for more.

**Figure P2.8.** Spacing-preserving progressions from a chord to its pitch-class inversion. Intrinsic spacing is listed to the right of each staff. Open noteheads show the parallel voices. The progressions on the left move to different registral inversions of the same target chord in a voicing-preserving way. The progressions on the right also transpose the destination chord chromatically.

transposition and regular T for transposition along scales such as the diatonic.[5] Together, the two operations generate a wide range of harmonies from a single starting point, all broadly similar in arranging the same intervals in the same abstract registral configuration; indeed these two transpositions are the *only* operations that preserve both chord type and distance in chordal steps.[6] For an $n$-note chord in an $o$-note scale, transposition by $n$ chordal steps is equivalent to transposition by $o$ scale steps, so we can always replace $t_n$ with $T_o$ and vice versa. The two operations commute, so $t_x T_y$ ($t_x$ and then $T_y$) is the same as $T_y t_x$ ($T_y$ and then $t_x$). Subscripts add as we would expect, with $t_x T_y$ and $t_a T_b$ combining to form $t_{x+a} T_{y+b}$. We will see that there are even circumstances in which we might want to consider *inversion* along both chord and scale, notated $i_x I_y$.

Remarkably, there is a simple and intuitive geometry of hierarchically nested transposition, equally applicable to voice in chord, chord in scale, and scale in chromatic aggregate. We can use the following recipe to represent transposition along both an $n$-note collection ("chord") and an $o$-note collection ("scale") containing it.

A. Draw a spiral with $n$ loops, attaching its end to its beginning. In this book I will always a draw clockwise spiral beginning at 12 o'clock and moving inward until it reaches 9 o'clock for the $n$th time, then connecting the end of the spiral clockwise to its starting point (Figure P2.9).
B. Mark off $o$ equally spaced points along this spiral, labeling them with consecutive scale tones. To do this, divide the circle into $o$ equal pie slices; move along the spiral placing a point at the border of every $n$th slice, with $n$ the

---

[5] This notation was first used by Julian Hook (2003, 2008).
[6] Here I am using "chord type" to mean "transpositional set class." If we consider pitch-class inversions (like the major and minor triad) to be the same, then we need to include the "generalized neo-Riemannian voice leadings" that send a chord to its similarly spaced inversional partner as shown in Figure P2.8 (e.g., the "parallel" voice leading that lowers a major triad's third by semitone or raises the minor triad's third by semitone). These act as half a transposition-along-the-chord (Tymoczko 2020b).

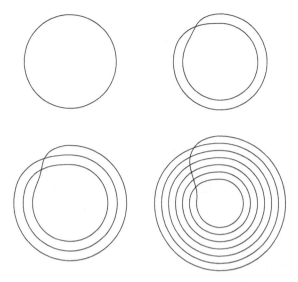

**Figure P2.9.** Spirals representing chords with one, two, three, and seven notes.

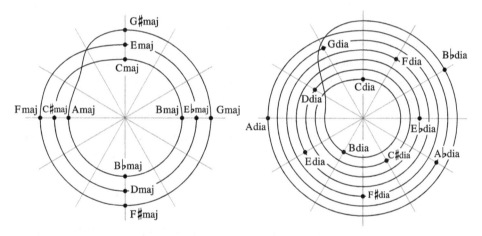

**Figure P2.10.** Spiral diagrams for major triads in the chromatic scale and seven-note diatonic collections in the chromatic scale. Each point represents a complete chord: "Cmaj" in the first example represents the C major triad, while "Cdia" in the second represents the C diatonic scale.

size of the chord: every border for one-note chords, every other border for two-note chords, every third for three-note chords, and so on. In this book I will usually place the C chord at the innermost point at 12 o'clock and move clockwise along the spiral in a descending fashion, labeling B, B♭, A ... for the chromatic scale, B, A, G ... for the diatonic, and so on.

Figure P2.10 shows the resulting diagrams for major chords and diatonic scales in chromatic space. Each point represents an *entire collection of notes*, a complete major chord or complete diatonic scale. (In my experience, readers can be confused

44  TONALITY: AN OWNER'S MANUAL

by this point, so I will repeat it: in this book, points on the spiral diagrams will always represent *entire chords* rather than single notes.) The major-chord spiral winds around the circle three times, with chords positioned at 12, 3, 6, and 9 o'clock (every third clock position); the scalar spiral winds around the circle seven times, with chords placed at every seventh slice. Readers can verify that a chord's angular position corresponds to *the sum of its pitch classes*, with each one-slice clockwise motion decreasing the chord's sum by one.[7] Given a diagram, we can determine the size of the chord from the number of loops and the size of the scale from the number of points. Do not be concerned by the line's self-intersection, as this is an artifact of depicting an intrinsically higher-dimensional geometry on a flat piece of paper; as appendix 2 explains, the actual line does not intersect itself.

There are three rules for moving around the space.

1. *Sliding* along the spiral corresponds to transposition along the larger scale-like collection, shifting the chord's notes upward or downward by the same number of scale steps. In this book clockwise motion descends and counterclockwise motion ascends. (This is because descending musical motion and clockwise circular motion are both defaults.) One needs to move $n$ slices clockwise to transpose an $n$-note chord down by scale step.

2. A full *loop* around the center of the space corresponds to a transposition along the smaller chord-like collection, moving each note upward or downward by one chordal step as if the chord were a scale. A clockwise loop moves notes downward by one chordal step while a counterclockwise loop moves notes upward by one chordal step. (This requires "jumping rings," or leaving the spiral at some point, as discussed in appendix 2.) A double loop moves each voice by two steps, a triple loop by three steps, and so on. An $n$-fold loop transposes each voice by octave and is equivalent to sliding along the complete spiral. Unless otherwise noted, I will always use "loop" to mean *loops enclosing the center of the spiral*; paths that return to their starting point without enclosing the center leave each voice exactly where it began.

3. Two paths on the spiral represent the same voice leading when they begin and end at the same points and involve the same total quantity of angular motion. This total quantity of angular motion will always be equal to the sum of the intervals moved by the voices.[8]

---

[7] Here we need to use "clock arithmetic," where we take the remainder when divided by the size of the scale. So, for instance, the C major triad contains C, E, and G or 0, 4, 7 in pitch class notation, which together sum to 11 (0 + 4 + 7). A♭ major contains A♭, C, and E♭, or 8, 0, 3, which also sum to 11. E major is E, G♯, and B, or 4, 8, and 11, which sum to 23, which is 11 when we divide by 12 and take the remainder. B major, G major, and E♭ major are three pie-slices clockwise, since their notes sum to 8 modulo 12.

[8] Rule 3 is equivalent to the statement that two paths correspond to the same voice leading if one can be smoothly transformed into the other without breaking the path or moving its endpoints; such deformations are studied by topologists (Tymoczko 2020b). In summing the intervals in each voice, we do not use clock arithmetic but rather real numbers representing *paths in pitch-class space* (appendix 1, Tymoczko 2011a).

Figure P2.11 illustrates. The third rule is in many ways the most important, as it allows us to understand *every* path as a combination of loops and slides, or chordal and scalar transpositions. Before using a particular model, we will typically calculate the voice leading linking nearby chords; this is the combination of loops and slides that counteract each other as much as possible, and it changes from diagram to diagram. Chapter 2 will explain how to do this.

The rest of this book will use the spiral diagrams to model intuitive musical knowledge—and particularly the efficient voice leadings that result when an operation-along-a-chord nearly counteracts the corresponding operation-along-a-scale. We will focus on a small collection of spaces, analyzing rock music with the

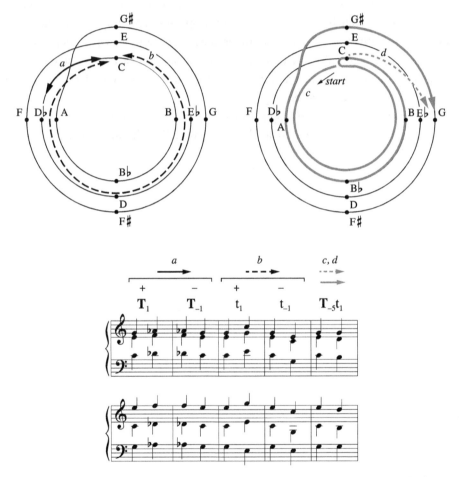

Figure P2.11. In the spiral diagrams, clockwise motion descends and counterclockwise motion ascends (− and + respectively). Path *a* slides along the spiral and transposes along the scale. Path *b* loops around the space and transposes along the chord; this requires leaving the spiral at some point. Paths *c* and *d* represent the same voice leading as they start and end at the same point and involve the same total quantity of angular motion (90° clockwise). Path *c* shows that this voice leading is $T_{-5}t_1$, combining a clockwise loop ($t_1$) with a five-step counterclockwise slide $T_{-5}$.

3-in-12 graph of chromatic triads, early music with the 2-in-7 and 3-in-7 graphs of diatonic dyads and triads, and functionally tonal modulation using the graph of 7-in-12 diatonic scales. In modeling melody, we will sometimes consider very small scales such as the 2-in-3 graph of two-note triadic subsets. We will also use multiple spiral diagrams to describe nested musical motion, the same basic structure representing the motion of voice in chord, chord in scale, and scale in aggregate. With a little practice, the reader can learn to translate geometrical path to musical notation and vice versa; with a little more practice, the reader can construct and manipulate the spiral diagrams for any chord in any scale. The spiral diagrams can also be extended to include multiple chord types and a wider range of voice leadings, including those with voice exchanges, and those in which chord tones are doubled.[9] No mathematics is required, and no particular music-theoretical skill beyond an ability to manipulate hierarchically nested transposition. My hope is that the spiral diagrams can function as the music-theoretical equivalent of a consumer product, allowing readers to enjoy the benefits of sophisticated musical geometry without mastering its details—much as we can use GPS without fully understanding the general-relativistic calculations it performs.

Readers who want to dive straight into the technical details can turn to appendices 1 and 2; those who prefer a more analytical introduction should instead proceed to chapter 2.

---

[9] Readers may find it useful to visit the website https://www.madmusicalscience.com, where they can find movies and software.

# 2
# Rock Logic

In many musical styles, melodic steps tend to descend while leaps tend to ascend.[1] In Figure 2.0.1, for example, the singer steps downward from $\hat{3}$ to $\hat{1}$, descending by step within the chord before leaping back to $\hat{3}$ to start the next verse. It is reasonable to think that the melody motivates the song's inversion of traditional harmonic norms: if we decide to associate each melodic note with a major triad in the D major scale, the I–V–IV–I progression is one of a small number of possibilities. The subversion of the tonic-subdominant-dominant paradigm, in other words, may not be a rebellion against classical harmonic practice, but rather a straightforward solution to a basic musical problem.

This chapter will use this idea to motivate a model of rock harmony, one that emphasizes the melodic origin of its harmonic idioms. Though the underlying techniques apply equally well to ascending or leaping melodies, my main focus will be on stepwise descent. The goal is to understand the implicit knowledge of talented but possibly untrained musicians—principles that they might plausibly absorb from thousands of hours of listening and playing. This project is broadly comparable to that of constructing a grammar for natural language, another formal system that humans learn without explicit instruction. This embodied and intuitive grammar contrasts with the explicit doctrines of the notated tradition, from species counterpoint to twelve-tone composition.

Figure 2.0.1. "Helpless" by Neil Young.

---

[1] This asymmetry can also be found in birdsong and human speech, suggesting a potential origin in respiration, the sharp intake and gradual release of breath required for both speaking and singing. See Tierney, Russo, and Patel 2008 (music and speech), Tierney, Russo, and Patel 2011 (the "motor constraint hypothesis"), and Savage, Tierney, and Patel 2017 (birdsong and music).

## 1. A melodic principle

Suppose a melody embellishes a stepwise descent from one tonic-triad note to another. For simplicity, imagine that we decide to harmonize each note with a root-position major triad—ignoring minor chords for the moment. What sorts of progressions should we expect to find? Figure 2.1.1 identifies all the two-chord progressions beginning with C major and supporting a stepwise melodic descent, with points representing major triads and lines the different steps: thus, C and G are connected by a thick solid black line indicating that the root of C major can descend by semitone to the third of G major, and a thin dotted black line indicating that the third of C major can descend by major second to the fifth of G major. The figure can be understood as a musical "gameboard" describing the local moves available to musicians interested in descending steps. Simple tabulation shows that descending steps preferentially give rise to what are sometimes called "weak" root-progressions: ascending fifths rather than descending fifths, ascending minor thirds rather than descending minor thirds, and descending rather than ascending steps (Figure 2.1.2).[2]

The model has Schenkerian overtones in suggesting that *harmonic* patterns can arise out of fundamentally *melodic* aims—in this case, phrase-level descending motion from one tonic-triad note to another. But rather than trying to show that stepwise descending melody necessarily reproduces the conventions of functional harmony, I will suggest that it leads to different kinds of progressions in different harmonic contexts. In *A Geometry of Music*, I used complicated geometrical models to try to capture this interdependence of harmony and melody, describing twisted,

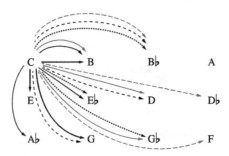

Figure 2.1.1. A musical gameboard depicting the possibilities for stepwise melodic descent between triads. Each letter represents a complete major triad. Solid lines represent the possibility for a note to descend by semitone while dotted lines represent a major-second descent. A thick dark line descends from the root, a thin dark line descends from the third, and a lighter line descends from the fifth.

---

[2] For the terms "strong" and "weak," see Meeùs 2000. Stephenson 2002 makes a similar observation about the prevalence of weak progressions in rock, though he explains the phenomenon differently.

|  | strong progressions || weak progressions ||
| harmonic interval | root prog. | descending melodic possibilities | descending melodic possibilities | root prog. |
| --- | --- | --- | --- | --- |
| perfect fourth | +5 semitones | 1 | 2 | −5 s.t. |
| minor third | −3 | 0 | 2 | +3 |
| major second | +2 | 2 | 3 | −2 |
| minor second | +1 | 1 | 3 | −1 |
| *major third* | *−4* | *1* | *1* | *+4* |

**Figure 2.1.2.** "Weak" root progressions (ascending fifths and thirds, descending steps) generally permit more opportunities for stepwise descent, with the major third being the only interval equally balanced between strong and weak.

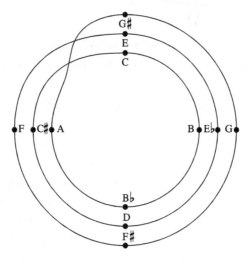

**Figure 2.1.3.** The spiral diagram for chromatic triads. Each point represents a complete major triad.

singular, and higher-dimensional spaces in which each musical voice is represented by its own dimension. Here I will use the simpler spiral diagrams for the same purpose. Figure 2.1.3 reproduces the voice-leading space for major triads in the chromatic scale. For reasons to be explained in §2.6, I label points using the triad's root; readers should keep in mind, however, that each point represents an entire chord.

We know that slides along the spiral correspond to transposition along the scale while loops represent transposition along the chord. Unfortunately, it is not obvious from these principles how to understand *radial* motion between nearby chords, say from C major vertically outward to E major. This is a general problem: for each new spiral diagram, we will need to calculate the voice leadings between nearby points. Here, transposition-along-the-chord largely counteracts transposition-along-the-scale, leaving efficient voice leading as the result.

50    TONALITY: AN OWNER'S MANUAL

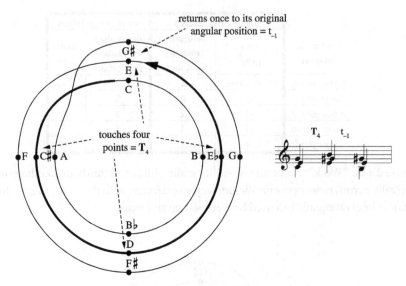

**Figure 2.1.4.** Calculating the radial path from C to E. We move counterclockwise along the spiral by four steps to reach E, for $T_4$; we pass our original angular position once, for $t_{-1}$.

There is a general recipe that works for any spiral diagram: to find a direct path between two chords, slide your finger in the desired direction (clockwise or counterclockwise) from one to the other along the spiral; if you are looking for a purely radial path, then both directions are equivalent.[3] The number of chords you touch, not counting the first, is the transposition along the scale ($T_x$), with positive and negative values of *x* corresponding to counterclockwise and clockwise motion respectively. Meanwhile, the number of times you revisit your initial angular position, *y*, becomes the transposition along the chord $t_{\pm y}$, with its sign *opposite* that of the scalar transposition. The two combine to form $T_x t_{-y}$ or $T_{-x} t_y$, a composite representing the most direct voice leading between the two chords.

*Example 1. Radial motion from C to E.* Imagine sliding counterclockwise along the spiral from C major to E major. Not counting our starting point, we touch four chords for $T_4$. (Remember that I use boldface **T** for chromatic transposition, and regular T for transposition along a scale such as the diatonic.) We return once to our initial angular location of 12 o'clock, for $t_{-1}$, with a negative sign because our scalar transposition is positive. The combination of these two motions, shown in Figure 2.1.4, moves C down to B, keeps E fixed, and moves G up to G♯; this is the LP voice leading of neo-Riemannian theory.[4] The same reasoning shows that radial

---

[3] In general, the initial direction is important. If you want a short clockwise path from C to F, you need to start by sliding clockwise; the algorithm in this paragraph will produce the path $T_5 t_{-1}$. If you were to instead slide counterclockwise, the algorithm will calculate the shortest *counterclockwise* path from C to F, $T_{-7} t_1$; this is a different but equally important voice leading. For a purely radial path the two directions produce the same result.

[4] The "LP" voice leading moves a major triad's root down by semitone and fifth up by semitone; "PL" moves a major triad's third down by semitone and fifth up by semitone. I call this "the major-third system" (Tymoczko 2011a). For a comparison between voice-leading geometry and neo-Riemannian theory see appendix C of Tymoczko 2011a and Tymoczko 2020b.

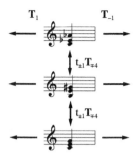

**Figure 2.1.5.** The voice leadings on circular chord space represented in notation: vertical motion corresponds to $t_{-1}T_4$ or $t_{-1}T_{-4}$ (LP or PL) while horizontal motion corresponds to chromatic transposition ($T_x$).

motion from E major out to A♭ major, and from A♭ major inward to C major, also produces $T_4t_{-1}$ or LP.

*Example 2. Radial motion from E to C.* Now we slide clockwise from E down to C, returning once to our starting point for $T_{-4}t_1$. This is the opposite of the voice leading in the previous example: G♯ moves down to G, E stays fixed, and B moves up to C. This is the PL voice leading of neo-Riemannian theory. Similar reasoning shows that radial motion from A♭ to E, and from C to A♭, also produces $T_{-4}t_1$, or the PL voice leading. This allows us to express all motions on the diagram in musical notation (Figure 2.1.5).

*Example 3. 90° counterclockwise motion from C to F.* We could simply reapply the algorithm, sliding counterclockwise five steps for $T_5$ and passing our original radial position once for $t_{-1}$. Alternatively, we can add a chromatic transposition to one of the radial voice leadings just calculated. For instance, to calculate the counterclockwise path from C to F, we start with the outward radial motion from C to E, representing the voice leading (C, E, G) → (B, E, G♯).[5] To this we add a quarter turn along the spiral from E to F, transposing each note up by semitone and giving us the composite (C, E, G) → (C, F, A). Symbolically, $T_4t_{-1} + T_1 = T_5t_{-1}$. This voice leading holds root fixed, moves third up by semitone, and fifth up by two semitones. A quarter-turn clockwise from F to C has the opposite effect, moving F down to E, A down to G, and holding C fixed ($t_1T_{-5}$). Similarly, clockwise motion from C to G moves C down to B, E down to D, and holds G fixed. Clockwise motion from C to B♭ ($T_{-2}$) lowers each voice by two semitones, while counterclockwise motion between the same two points generates the voice leading (C, E, G) → (D, F, B♭), or ($t_1T_{-2}$).

Proceeding in this way, we see that the descending stepwise melodies recorded on our earlier "graph of melodic possibilities" (Figure 2.1.1) are exactly those that are produced by radial or short clockwise motion on the new spiral graph. It

---

[5] As appendix 1 explains, this notation means "C moves to B," "E moves to E," and "G moves to G♯."

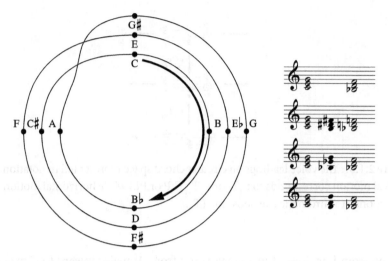

**Figure 2.1.6.** Geometrical representations encode relations of "betweenness." Here we see that B major, E♭ major, and G major are all between C major and B♭ major; this means we can insert them between C and B♭ without disrupting the stepwise descending voice leading.

follows that a *musical* preference for descending stepwise melodies will be modeled by a *geometrical* tendency to move radially or clockwise. The spiral diagram also encodes a musically useful notion of *distance*, since larger motions represent larger voice leading. Finally, the graph gives us a notion of *betweenness*, showing how larger voice leadings can be factored into smaller moves: for example, Figure 2.1.6 shows that the two-step clockwise progression from C major to B♭ lowers each voice by major second; there are exactly three chords lying between C and B♭ on the spiral, each preserving the stepwise descending voice leading. The model's geometrical structure thus encodes the musical intuition that the G major chord lies "on the way" from C major to B♭ major, as do B and E♭ major. Here, a picture is worth a thousand words in the sense that these intuitions of "betweenness" are packed into a single percept, rather than many disconnected verbal descriptions.[6]

In exploring voice leading, it is often useful to consider what I call the "Principle of Musical Approximation," which encourages us to think of nearly even chords as perturbations of completely symmetrical chords. Figure 2.1.7 shows a sequence of semitonally descending augmented triads, which can be labeled in a number of ways: $C^+$–$B^+$–$B♭^+$, $C^+$–$E♭^+$–$G♭^+$, $C^+$–$G^+$–$D^+$, and so on. Since the augmented triad is completely symmetrical this is a conceptual rather than sonic difference. The major triad is *nearly* symmetrical—just a single semitone away from the augmented triad—and divides the octave into three almost-even parts. We can obtain a variety of descending major-chord progressions by lowering any

---

[6] Camp 2018.

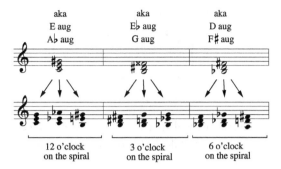

**Figure 2.1.7.** (*top*) A descending sequence of augmented triads that can be labeled in a variety of ways. (*bottom line*) By lowering a note of each augmented triad, we can obtain a variety of root progressions exhibiting descending stepwise voice leadings. These progressions all move one step clockwise on the spiral diagram.

note of each augmented triad: C–B–B♭, C–E♭–G♭, C–G–D, and so on. These are the same root progressions we obtain in the augmented case, only now they are sonically distinctive; any members of this collection can be related by applying *major-third substitution* ($t_1T_{-4}$ or $t_{-1}T_4$) to their constituent chords; because of the triad's near symmetry, this major-third substitution has only a small effect on the voices. Musically, we can think of the resulting progressions as slight distortions of a continuous parallel descent, an asymmetrical major-chord analogue to the perfectly parallel augmented-chord model.[7] We can repeat this derivation to obtain descending sequences of minor triads (raising an augmented-triad note), diminished triads, and so on.

A sophisticated treatment of melody is necessarily hierarchical, allowing voices to move inside a chordal field that is itself moving. This can be modeled by combining two separate spiral diagrams: a 1-in-3 diagram representing the motion of voice inside chord, and a 3-in-12 diagram representing the motion of chord inside chromatic collection. For the sake of simplicity, this chapter will generally adopt an alternate approach in which the melodic voice is stationary relative to the triadic field, being "carried along" by the triadic motion. (We can think of the inner voices as moving in doubly parallel motion with the melody, using the same combination $t_xT_y$.) This allows us to avoid the more complex hierarchical picture, treating 3-in-12 motions on the circle as metonymic for the melodic motions they produce. From this point of view, it is the bass that provides contrary motion, moving *relative* to the shifting triadic field. Figure 2.1.8 shows that we can think of the bass as following its own double transposition, sharing the same chromatic transposition $T_x$ but a different scalar transposition $t_y$. We will return to this thought in §3.7.

---

[7] Yust 2015a explores distorted and quantized sequences.

**Figure 2.1.8.** In this chapter, we will generally imagine inner voices moving in doubly parallel motion with the melody while the bass moves independently.

## 2. A harmonic principle

Progressions like C→B and C→G♭ are contrapuntally plausible but musically rare, at least in major-mode songs. This is presumably because they are felt to move between distant chords, implying very different diatonic scales.

Figure 2.2.1 formalizes the notion of "diatonic distance" using the circle of fifths: any diatonic scale is distance 0 from itself, and distance 1 from those collections a fifth away: thus C and G diatonic are one unit apart, since just one semitonal shift (F→F♯) relates them, while C and D diatonic are two units apart, since it takes *two* semitonal shifts (e.g., C→C♯ and F→F♯) to transform one into the other. This conception of "diatonic distance" is a *voice-leading distance* that reflects how far the scale's notes have to move to get to their destination; this is similar to, but not quite the same as, a model based on common tones. Scalar voice-leading distance can be represented by the circular graph of diatonic scales in chromatic space, where motion between adjacent points represents the single-semitone voice leading between fifth-related diatonic collections, and angular distance is equivalent to scalar distance (Figure P2.10). We will return to this idea in chapter 8.

I will define the harmonic distance between two major triads as *the smallest distance from a scale containing one chord to a scale containing the other* (Figure 2.2.2). Thus the C major triad is distance 0 not just from F major and G major (since the C, F, and G triads all belong to the C diatonic scale), but also from D major (since the G diatonic scale contains both C major and D major triads) and B♭ major (since F diatonic contains B♭ major and C major). Meanwhile, the C major triad is one unit away from the E♭ major triad (since C major belongs to F diatonic, and E♭ major belongs to B♭ diatonic, and the B♭ diatonic scale is one step away from F diatonic). By similar reasoning the C and A major triads are one unit away from each other. Major-third-related triads, like C and E, or C and A♭, are two units away from each other, whereas semitonally related triads are three steps away. Maximally separated are tritone-related triads, which are four steps apart. This notion of triadic distance is very closely related to the circle-of-fifths distance between triads, here justified by the fact that fifth-related triads create coherent diatonic

ROCK LOGIC   55

| Interval | Distance | Common Tones | Example |
|---|---|---|---|
| 0 | 0 | 7 | C↔C |
| 5 | 1 | 6 | C↔F |
| 2 | 2 | 5 | C↔B♭ |
| 3 | 3 | 4 | C↔E♭ |
| 4 | 4 | 3 | C↔E |
| 1 | 5 | 2 | C↔D♭ |
| 6 | 6 | 2 | C↔G♭ |

**Figure 2.2.1.** Voice-leading distance between diatonic collections.

| Interval | Distance | Example |
|---|---|---|
| 0 | 0 | C↔C |
| 5 | 0 | C↔F |
| 2 | 0 | C↔B♭ |
| 3 | 1 | C↔E♭ |
| 4 | 2 | C↔E |
| 1 | 3 | C↔D♭ |
| 6 | 4 | C↔G♭ |

**Figure 2.2.2.** Diatonic distance between major triads, defined as the minimum distance between a diatonic scale containing the first chord and a diatonic scale containing the second.

D diatonic → A diatonic: 1 step on the circle of fifths
A diatonic → D diatonic: 1 step on the circle of fifths

**Figure 2.2.3.** Measuring the total diatonic distance of a progression; the progression D–A–E–G has diatonic distance 2, since it requires modulating from D diatonic to A diatonic and back.

backgrounds or *macroharmonies*.[8] It is, in other words, a voice-leading distance at another hierarchical level.

The distance traversed by a repeating chord progression can then be defined as the total number of modulatory steps involved in the entire progression, with the proviso that we return to the initial chord and scale (Figure 2.2.3). My proposal is that rock musicians favor chord progressions that are *diatonically close*—that is, lying in a single diatonic scale or a small collection of closely related scales. If this is so, then we should expect more fifth-related triads like C and F, and major-second related triads, like C and B♭, than semitonally or tritone-related triads (like C and B

---

[8] See Tymoczko 2011a.

## 56 TONALITY: AN OWNER'S MANUAL

| root prog | all pieces | major | minor | average (maj/min) |
|---|---|---|---|---|
| P5 | 77.5 | 82.7 | 50.7 | 54.6 |
| M2 | 18.9 | 15.7 | 26.5 | 33.2 |
| m3 | 2.0 | 0.8 | 13.2 | 7.0 |
| m2 | 1.0 | 0.3 | 8.0 | 4.15 |
| M3 | 0.6 | 0.5 | 0.7 | 1.0 |
| TT | 0 | 0 | 0 | 0 |

**Figure 2.2.4.** Progressions connecting two major triads in *Rolling Stone*'s "500 Greatest Songs of All Time." Ascending and descending motions are grouped together, P5 is "perfect fifth," M2 is "major second," and so on. The columns show the percentages in all the pieces, the major-mode pieces, the minor-mode pieces, and an average of the two modes.

or C and F♯).[9] The suggestion is that rock musicians have implicitly absorbed a weak diatonic norm through extensive exposure to Western music.[10]

Because this norm is often learned implicitly, it is not absolute; we can therefore expect to find progressions between triads not belonging to the same diatonic scale—with progressions by minor third more prevalent than major third, major third more prevalent than semitone, and semitone more prevalent than tritone. This is what we see in Figure 2.2.4, which records the root progressions between major chords in the top 200 of *Rolling Stone*'s "500 greatest songs of all time."[11] (Note that this figure does not distinguish ascending intervals from descending intervals; we will ignore that issue for the moment.) The ordering of intervals is precisely what the model suggests, with fifths being the most frequent root motion, followed by major seconds, minor thirds, major thirds, and minor seconds.[12]

Figure 2.2.5 rewrites the spiral diagram using Roman numerals, with darkness representing harmonic proximity to the tonic chord. Once again, the figure leads us to expect an abundance of progressions by ascending fifths, ascending and descending major seconds, and, to a lesser extent, ascending minor thirds. It does not give us reason to expect many descending fifths or descending thirds, progressions traditionally associated with functional tonality. For this reason, I will say that the

---

[9] To be sure, there are some styles, like heavy metal, that emphasize these diatonically distant progressions precisely for their ominous and unusual quality; we will ignore this "contratonal" music for the time being. For "contratonality" see Huron 2007a, p. 339.

[10] Of course, many rock musicians have absorbed this norm through musical training as well.

[11] De Clerq et al. 2011. See also Figure 3.4 in Temperley 2018. Pinter 2019 surveys the early history of ♭VII in popular music.

[12] Note that there is not a single tritone progression on the list—and that there is a huge gap between the diatonic intervals of a fifth and major second, and the rest. The relatively greater popularity of fifths over major seconds, which both have diatonic distance 0, is likely explained by the longstanding norm of fifth motion. A secondary factor may be the fact that fifth-related triads are diatonically "superclose" since each pair belongs to two different diatonic collections, whereas major-second-related pairs belong to just a single collection.

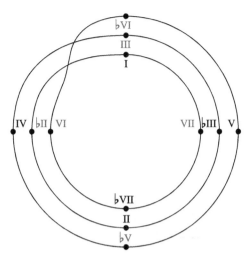

**Figure 2.2.5.** The spiral diagram for major triads, rewritten with Roman numerals and with dark chords being harmonically closer to I.

gameboard embodies a *retrofunctional* norm.[13] Starting with two very basic musical preferences—descending melodic steps and a preference for diatonically close progressions—we have derived substantive expectations about rock harmony, expectations that are both different from those appropriate to classical music, and (as we will shortly see) consistent with what we find in the repertoire.

Conversely, the rules of functional harmony are precisely *not* the rules you would come up with if you were to construct a musical syntax on your own (if, say, you were a talented but not formally trained musician sitting in your bedroom with a guitar). Instead, you would be more likely to come up with the inverse—a *retro*functional norm, favoring ascending rather than descending fifths and ascending rather than descending minor thirds. This retrofunctional norm, I will argue, is an intuitive counterknowledge arising from the deep structure of musical space, a subterranean musical practice distinct from, and to some extent opposed to, the culturally sanctioned routines of the notated tradition.

## 3. A first loop family

Neil Young's "Helpless" features simple but powerful musical forces operating in concert, its melody descending from third to root, while its harmonies articulate

---

[13] Stephenson 2002 notes that the chord progressions in rock music are the opposite of those in classical music, and suggests that this is the explanation for their popularity: rock harmony, in his view, is fundamentally oppositional, a matter of doing what was not done in earlier styles. My explanation instead proposes that rock musicians are making affirmative use of the possibilities afforded by deep musical relationships; if anything, rock harmony is more intuitive than classical harmony. Their oppositional quality is more byproduct than motivation—though unfamiliarity is likely part of their attraction.

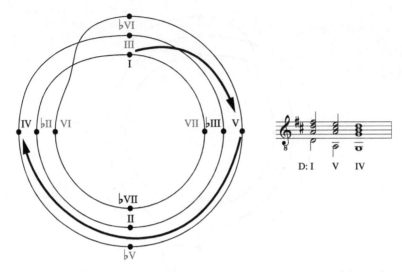

**Figure 2.3.1.** "Helpless" graphed on the spiral diagram.

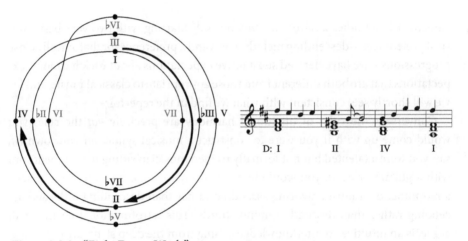

**Figure 2.3.2.** "Eight Days a Week."

one- and two-step clockwise motions on the 3-in-12 spiral (Figure 2.3.1). The result is an endlessly repeating, endlessly falling root-position I–V–IV–I, a diatonic progression that is exquisitely logical yet alien to more than two centuries of functionally tonal music-making. It is, one might say, both natural and forbidden—natural in being an obvious musical solution to a deep musical problem, and forbidden because it violates strong cultural norms.

The Beatles' "Eight Days a Week" traces an equally forbidden path through the space, replacing the D–A–G with D–E–G (Figure 2.3.2). Once again, the melody outlines a $\hat{3}$–$\hat{2}$–$\hat{1}$ descent, though now embellished with additional notes that imply multiple voices. Classically oriented music theorists have puzzled over this progression, wondering whether the E major chord should be understood as "predominant" or "thwarted secondary dominant." I reject this dichotomy: rather than feinting

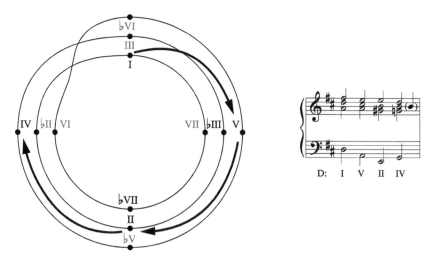

**Figure 2.3.3.** "Rose Parade."

toward a dominant that never appears, the II chord is a thing-in-itself, largely unknown in classical harmony and not reducible to its categories. Like "Helpless," "Eight Days a Week" embodies a nonclassical norm, harmonizing descending stepwise melodies with closely related major triads.[14]

Elliott Smith's "Rose Parade" features a I–V–II–IV progression that takes one chord from each radial position (Figure 2.3.3). This progression fuses the chords of "Helpless" and "Eight Days a Week" precisely as they appear on the circle—almost as if they had been combined in the popular-music equivalent of a particle accelerator, smashed together to produce an undiscovered byproduct. Once again we have an unadorned $\hat{3}$–$\hat{2}$–$\hat{1}$ melody in the voice, with Smith's self-destructive lyrics annihilating the cheerful harmony, bubblegum pop concealing an almost unprecedented expression of rock-star self-hatred.[15] Like Kurt Cobain, Smith dares us to take pleasure in his expressions of self-torment—bringing to mind Dorothy Rowe's description of depression as "a prison where you are both the suffering prisoner and the cruel jailer."[16] The power of this song lies precisely in the use of iconic musical material to express extreme emotion.

It is interesting to think of "Rose Parade" as a maximal progression, an archetype which generates the others by elision: eliminating II gives us "Helpless" while eliminating V gives us "Eight Days a Week." From this point of view, the four positions on the chromatic chord circle can be thought of as "slots" that can be either filled or left open—a purely contrapuntal analogue to the familiar

---

[14] See §3.9 for more on the origins of this progression. It represents a popular-music instance of what Samarotto 2004 describes as the "sublimating" of ♯$\hat{4}$.
[15] "When they clean the street, I'll be the only shit that's left behind."
[16] Rowe 1983.

```
I    V    II   IV
I    V         IV
I         II   IV
I    V    II
```

**Figure 2.3.4.** A family containing all the progressions that can be generated by eliminating a nontonic chord from the "Rose Parade" progression.

**Figure 2.3.5.** "Knockin' on Heaven's Door."

harmonic categories we call "tonal functions."[17] A third possibility is to eliminate IV, producing I–V–II–I (Figure 2.3.4). This is rare, though a variant does appear in Bob Dylan's "Knockin' on Heaven's Door." (The use of the minor ii, shown in Figure 2.3.5, does not unsettle the descending stepwise voice leading, as we will discuss.) That song again harmonizes $\hat{3}$–$\hat{2}$–$\hat{1}$, alternating the I–V–II of "Rose Parade" with the I–V–IV of "Helpless"—as if hinting at the full "Rose Parade" progression without ever stating it. Here the ii–I has the character of an interruption, a musical "comma" demanding the more definitive IV–I close.

Dylan's song uses an important technique that can be found throughout the triadic tradition, harmonizing its melody by transposing along the prevailing chord. My example shows that the background voices shadow the main melody at a distance of two steps along a changing sequence of harmonies—producing a scalar interval of a sixth or fifth depending on the chord. This is essentially just parallel motion within a (modulating) scale, but using three-note scales rather than seven-note scales. Once again we see the importance of a flexible approach to musical distance: measured in chordal steps, the two melodies move exactly in parallel, maintaining their two-step distance; measured in diatonic or chromatic steps, they diverge. Similar parallelism can be found whenever voices maintain the same spacing along the sounding harmonies. Chapter 3 will use this idea to develop a general theory of four-part counterpoint.

---

[17] My argument is not that ♭III, V, and VII are *harmonically* similar, the way dominant chords like V and vii° are; instead, they are *contrapuntally* similar in the sense that any of them can be inserted between I and ♭VII without disrupting the stepwise descending voice leading. For the claim that major-third relations can play similar harmonic functions, see Cohn 1999; this view, as Cohn notes, is cousin to Lendvai's minor-third-based "axis system" (§3.8).

Collectively, these examples show how the spiral diagrams can help us perceive relationships that would not otherwise be apparent: on first hearing, one would not think to associate the progressions of "Helpless" and "Eight Days a Week"; but in the context of "Rose Parade" and "Knockin' on Heaven's Door" the similarities become much clearer. This is characteristic of what philosophers call a "family resemblance"—like a genetic family, our "chord-loop family" (or "loop family") is united by features that are more obvious when we consider the group as a whole than when we attend to pairs of individuals. By revealing the different paths through chord space, the spiral model gives us a collection of loop families that can be used to categorize and conceptualize rock norms. It also hints at a picture of rock music as *nearly sequential*, repeatedly taking short clockwise motions through an abstract harmonic space. These are not *exact* sequences as there are a variety of options at each angular position; instead they represent a disguised or distorted regularity that we will encounter elsewhere.

## 4. Two more families

"Sympathy for the Devil" uses the same progression as "Helpless," reinterpreted as a mixolydian I–♭VII–IV rather than ionian V–IV–I.[18] This is one of the most characteristic progressions in hard rock, featured in the Who's "I Can't Explain," AC/DC's "Back in Black," and many other songs. Mick Jagger's melody vacillates between $\hat{5}$ and $\hat{4}$ until the chorus, where it descends to $\hat{3}$ over a $V^7$–I progression (Figure 2.4.1). The music thus combines rock retrofunction in its verses with functional tonality in the chorus, using harmonic syntax to reinforce its form. ("I Can't Explain" does something similar, moving to V just before the old-fashioned I–vi–IV–V chorus.) The mixolydian I–♭VII–IV can be embedded inside a I–♭III–♭VII–IV which, like the progression of "Rose Parade," is geometrically maximal—selecting one harmony from each of the four angular positions in the spiral diagram. This progression appears in Status Quo's "Pictures of Matchstick Men," Seals and Crofts's "Summer Breeze," the White Stripes' "The Air Near My Fingers" (shown in Figure 2.4.2), and countless other songs. As before, we can generate three-chord progressions by eliminating one of the nontonic chords (Figure 2.4.3). All three possibilities are reasonably common: I–♭VII–IV–I is ubiquitous (e.g., "Tangled Up in Blue"), I–♭III–♭VII–I is pervasive in hard rock, often with a minor tonic ("Stairway to Heaven," "Locomotive Breath," "Paranoid," see §2.6 for discussion of minor triads), and I–♭III–IV–I, though not quite as popular as the others, is also found ("I Can See for Miles"). Again, we might not think to associate these songs without the spiral model.

At the level of the phrase, rock songs tend to adopt one of two strategies. "Helpless" and "Back in Black" return to the tonic at the start of each two-bar unit,

---

[18] Temperley (2018, p. 35) surveys the many writers who have commented on the dual meanings of this progression.

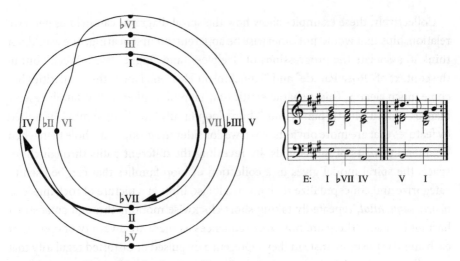

Figure 2.4.1. "Sympathy for the Devil."

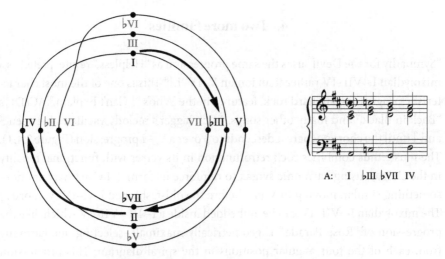

Figure 2.4.2. "The Air Near My Fingers."

|   |     |      |    |
|---|-----|------|----|
| I | ♭III | ♭VII | IV |
| I | ♭III |      | IV |
| I |     | ♭VII | IV |
| I | ♭III | ♭VII |    |

Figure 2.4.3. Progressions that can be generated by eliminating a nontonic chord from the "Air Near My Fingers" progression.

overlapping their phrases to generate a feeling of constant forward progress. Here, harmonic arrival coincides with melodic departure, and the music is largely devoid of cadences in the sense of phrase-terminating pauses. "Eight Days a Week," "Sympathy for the Devil," and "I Can't Explain" instead return to the tonic at the

C:  I        V      ♭VII     IV

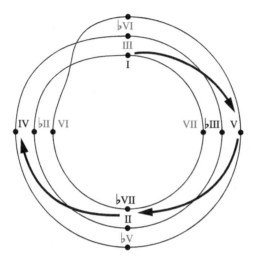

**Figure 2.4.4.** "Natural Woman."

end of each two-bar unit; this creates a much stronger sense of arrival, allowing for a feeling of rest between each repeating unit. Here it is reasonable to speak of cadences in a relatively traditional sense.[19]

The third loop family is built on the I–V–♭VII–IV progression featured in songs like "Natural Woman" (written for Aretha Franklin by Goffin and King) and Duran Duran's "Rio." The former is shown in Figure 2.4.4, the descending voice leading clear on the musical surface. This 6–5 progression is the retrograde of the classical tradition's ascending 5–6 sequence (Figure 2.4.5), giving rise to a descending chromatic line. Unlike the other progressions we have considered, it plays a significant role in the classical tradition—appearing in the music of Beethoven (Op. 31, no. 1, the *Waldstein* sonata), Schubert (the late G major quartet, etc.), and many other composers. In classical contexts it usually articulates a descent from tonic down to dominant, whereas in popular music it often returns plagally to the tonic after just four chords.[20] Thus classical composers *embed* the progression within a broadly

---

[19] See Moore 2012, p. 85, on "open" and "closed" phrases.
[20] In the Eagles' "Hotel California," the descending 6–5 moves from tonic to dominant in tonally functional fashion. Temperley 2018, p. 57, notes the descending chromatic line. One can interpret this as a variant of

**Figure 2.4.5.** Ascending and descending 6–5 sequences.

functional movement from tonic to dominant whereas popular music is more likely to use it as an *alternative* to tonic-dominant functionality. The four-chord pattern generates two three-chord progressions we have already encountered, I–♭VII–IV–I and I–V–IV–I, and one new progression, I–V–♭VII–I, used in the Beatles' "I'm a Loser" and Guns-N-Roses' "Sweet Child O' Mine."

## 5. Shepard-tone passacaglias

Figure 2.5.1 offers two interpretations of the repeat in Neil Young's "Helpless": according to the first, we take two steps clockwise around the circle before rewinding, moving back to the start via ascending voice leading that resets all voices to their initial position; according to the second, we return from subdominant to tonic by way of another clockwise motion, completing a full circle in chord space. This circle, we know, has the effect of transposing *down one step along the chord*, sending F♯ down to D, D down to A, and A down to F♯. Musically, it represents a hearing in which D of the IV continues as an inner voice of the following tonic—a hearing that is supported by a subtle feature of Neil Young's Massey Hall performance, the guitar's high G4 ($\hat{4}$) entering just as the vocal melody arrives at its D4. This suggests that the G major IV chord continues *downward* to the D major tonic, the entire piece an endless descent. As in "Eight Days a Week," the melodic voice has to ascend relative to this descending background in order to remain in place, returning to the same pitch but a different scale degree.

Figure 2.5.2 traces this endless *Urlinie* throughout the progression: the note D4, which ends the vocal line, continues downward by step in the guitar to C♯ (over V) and then B (over IV) before arriving at A3 at the next repeat—whereupon it continues downward to G3 before shifting upward by octave to the guitar's high G4. The music thus embeds a hidden *canon* or *round* endlessly descending by step (Figure 2.5.3). Unlike a traditional round, however, where the melodic lines are articulated by actual instruments, this canon is constructed by listeners—supported by rich, strummed guitar chords that suggest but do not completely determine specific voices. It is *we* who connect the D4 in the vocal melody to the subsequent D4 in the guitar, *we* who hear the common tones and stepwise motions linking each chord to the next. Nevertheless these are reasonable connections to make: the stepwise

---

Gesualdo's trick where a single voice moves chromatically while the other two alternate between root position and first inversion.

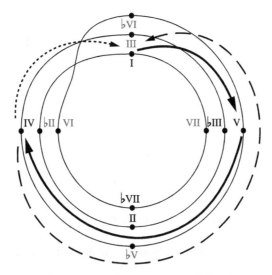

**Figure 2.5.1.** Two ways of conceiving the repeat in "Helpless."

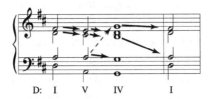

**Figure 2.5.2.** Each voice in "Helpless" connects to the next-lowest voice across the repeat.

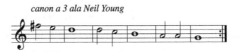

**Figure 2.5.3.** "Helpless" embeds a three-voice continuously descending canon. Voices enter every two measures.

motions in Figure 2.5.2 are really there in the music, and can be identified even by the casual listener. (Sing the canonic line along with the recording and you will realize how obvious it is.) To me this is one of the most fascinating differences between voice leading in classical music and rock—in the former, it is embodied in notation while in the latter it is partially constructed by the audience.[21]

"Helpless" thus presents an endless stepwise descent, sinking ever downward while somehow remaining stationary. This description once again evokes the

---

[21] The composer Paul Lansky has spoken about composing so as to allow the listener to chart their own way through a piece (Perry and Lansky 1996).

66   TONALITY: AN OWNER'S MANUAL

Figure 2.5.4. The canon in "Eight Days a Week." Voices enter every two measures.

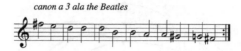

Figure 2.5.5. "You Won't See Me" explicitly articulates a continuous stepwise descent.

Shepard tone, an endless glissando that somehow remains in place. David Feurzeig coined the term *Shepard-tone passacaglia* to refer to progressions in which voices connect nontrivially across the repeat, as when soprano becomes alto, alto tenor, and so on: here, what initially seems like *repetition* can also function as a *continuation*, in this case because the lines continue their trajectories.[22] Expressively, this endless, tumbling descent—moving always forward yet also staying the same—functions as an apt representation of helplessness, capturing the persistence of memory alongside inexorable progression of time, the chords staying fixed as the years tick by. It is, perhaps, one of the reasons we are inclined to listen to these three harmonies over and over, always progressing yet never reaching a conclusion.

These Shepard-tone passacaglias are easy to find once you start to listen for them: indeed our three loop families all give rise to analogous canons (Figure 2.5.4). The canon will sometimes be obscure and hard to follow, but sometimes very close to the musical surface—as in the Beatles' "You Won't See Me," where the main melody encircles the background vocals to create a continuous scale (Figure 2.5.5). That descent was apparently a focus of compositional attention: the verse ends with a turn to V/IV, allowing the composite melody to descend by almost a complete octave, reaching the low tonic just as the chorus arrives.

It is natural to wonder how many of these repeating, pseudocanonic rock progressions there are—that is, how many progressions (a) begin and end at the tonic; (b) move clockwise through a single turn in chord space, selecting one of the three chords at every angular position; and (c) contain no harmonically "distant" chords whose roots are related by semitone or tritone.[23] It turns out there are just

---

[22] Feurzeig 2010 cites examples from Miles Davis ("Blue in Green") to Philip Glass (the "Spaceship" harmonies from *Einstein on the Beach*) and Ligeti (the fourth movements of the Horn Trio and Violin Concerto), including the Shostakovich passage analyzed in §2.6.

[23] There are various other ways to characterize this class of progressions, for instance as those involving a diatonic distance less than 6, or those whose roots lie in a pentatonic scale (Biamonte 2010).

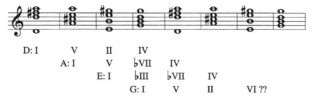

**Figure 2.5.6.** A single progression heard in four different ways.

**Figure 2.5.7.** Three songs in three keys played at the same time without dissonance.

four: the three families we already considered and I–V–II–VI, a sequence of ascending fifths. This last progression is almost entirely unknown in popular music, at least as a repeating four-chord loop; this is likely because VI–I makes for an unsatisfying return to the tonic, particularly in comparison with the IV–I that ends the other three progressions.[24]

Remarkably, these four progressions are all identical under rotation. That is, they all can be expressed as a repeating sequence of major triads D–A–E–G, but with a different choice of tonic: if D is tonic, we have the "Rose Parade" progression (I–V–II–IV); if A is tonic it is "Natural Woman" (I–V–♭VII–IV); if E is tonic it is "The Air Near My Fingers" (I–♭III–♭VII–IV); and if G is tonic, it is the unused I–V–II–VI (Figure 2.5.6). What this means is that our three song families are all in some deep sense *the same*, and in fact they can be superimposed to good effect. Figure 2.5.7 tries, lamely, to illustrate. (It is much better to sing it with friends.) Here we have a strange sort of *polytonality without dissonance*, the different keys largely a function of where one feels the four-bar hypermetric accent. If you know the original songs, it is possible to flip back and forth between interpretations, creating an unstable situation where scale degree is a function of attention—a musical analogue of the famous duck/rabbit illusion.[25] Figure 2.5.8 represents the canon implied by this

---

[24] See Temperley 2011b. In rock, IV chords are almost as likely to go to I as V chords are. The Alt-J song "(Interlude 3)" from *An Awesome Wave* presents a four-chord ascending-fifth sequence F–C–G–D, but I hear G and not F as the tonic despite the hypermetric accent on F.

[25] This is a picture that can be perceived either as a duck or a rabbit, but not both at the same time.

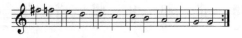

**Figure 2.5.8.** The fundamental canon of rock. Voices enter every two measures.

ubiquitous four-chord sequence, a line that can be described, only half-jokingly, as the "fundamental canon of rock." It is what we might call a *deep schema*, rarely grasped explicitly but existing in the musical unconscious—and manifesting in many seemingly unrelated ways.

One moral is that rock centricity is often a matter of phrasing and musical emphasis rather than abstract pitch relationships. O-Zone's "Dragostea Din Tei" provides a marvelous example, modulating from C major in the chorus to A minor in the verse without ever departing from its repeating C–G–a–F loop (to be discussed shortly). This is initially accomplished hypermetrically, prolonging the G chord for two measures so that the verse begins on A minor rather than F major (16 bars into the music, at about 0'30"). The remaining modulations operate entirely by orchestration, the bass synthesizers dropping out a bar before each section change; their return creates a musical accent which, along with the melody, helps shift the sense of tonal center back and forth between A minor and C major, even while preserving the four-bar harmonic rhythm. These modulations suggest that centricity can be a matter of delicate hints rather than unmistakable signposts.[26]

Our progression C–G–D–A–(C), with its three ascending fifths and one ascending minor third, is cousin to the most famous minor third in all of music theory, Rameau's *double emploi*. Rameau interpreted functional harmony using a sequence of four descending diatonic fifths d–G–C–F whose phrase structure was offset relative to its harmonic structure: C–F–d–G–(C) rather than d–G–C–F–(d). His "double emploi" is the minor-third juncture between the ends of the fifth sequence, sometimes elided into a ii$^6_5$ composite. These two chord loops are retrogrades: three fifths and a minor third, ascending in rock and descending in functional harmony. This resemblance underscores the sense in which rock music is genuinely *retrofunctional*, its chords inverting classical expectations—not out of cussedness but for reasons of contrapuntal logic.

## 6. Minor triads and other trichords

By now, readers will be wondering how to fit minor triads into the spiral model. A first answer is that Figure 2.1.3 can be used to represent *any* type of three-note chord in chromatic space: major chords, minor chords, diminished triads, 026

---

[26] One can make a similar point about Boston's "Peace of Mind," which may seem to shift into C♯ minor at the start of the chorus despite its generally E major tonality. See Harrison 2016, pp. 70–72 (on "Cherry Cherry"), Doll 2017, and Nobile 2020.

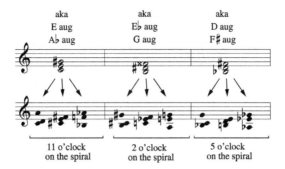

**Figure 2.6.1.** The position of 025 chords on the spiral diagram.

trichords like C–D–F♯, three-note chromatic clusters, and so on. (This is why I labeled the figure by root, without specifying the complete chord type.) That is, its basic principles are completely independent of a chord's specific intervallic content, depending only on the size of the chord and the size of the scale: sliding along the spiral transposes along the scale, while looping around the space transposes along the chord, so that moving radially outward, in any twelve-tone scale, combines transposition down one chordal step with transposition up four chromatic semitones ($t_{-1}T_4$). For the C minor triad, radial motion corresponds to the voice leading (C, E♭, G) → (B, E, G); for an 026 trichord it is (C, D, F♯) → (A♯, E, F♯); and for a chromatic cluster it is (C4, D♭4, D4) → (F♯3, E4, F4).[27] (Inward radial motion is the inverse, transposing one step upward along the chord and four semitones chromatically downward.) In each case, radial motion involves the same total amount of upward and downward semitonal motion, so that the sum of the paths in all voices is zero semitones. This universality is one of the most remarkable features of the geometry, a single *n*-in-*o* graph describing any *n*-note chord in any *o*-note scale.

There is, however, one important difference between these various spiral diagrams: the closer the chord is to the augmented triad, the tighter the connection between clockwise motion and descending stepwise voice leading. Figure 2.6.1 distorts augmented triads to obtain the 025 trichords on the spiral diagram. With a nearly even chord, like the major or minor triad, we do not need to distort the augmented triad very much, and the result is smooth descending voice leading (e.g., Figure 2.1.7). The 025 triad requires a larger amount of distortion, and this makes for a larger amount of contrary motion as we move clockwise along the spiral diagram. In the aggregate, adding the motion in all voices, descent still dominates: each clockwise turn produces a voice leading whose melodic intervals sum to −3. But as chords become more and more uneven, the connection to stepwise melodic motion is less and less clear (appendix 1).

Of course, we would really like to represent both major and minor chords at the same time. One way to do this is to superimpose two versions of our graph on top

---

[27] In this last example, I use pitches to show how voices move, as discussed in appendix 1.

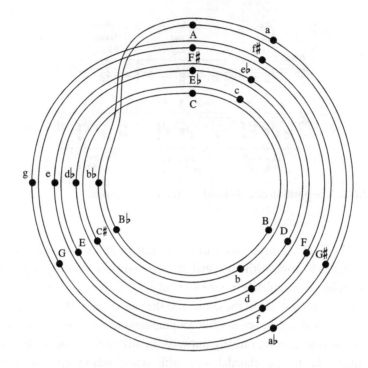

**Figure 2.6.2.** Superimposing major and minor spiral diagrams.

of each other, as in Figure 2.6.2.[28] To use this new figure we need to know that the direct clockwise path between parallel major and minor triads is the "parallel" voice leading that alters the chord's third by semitone: thus moving clockwise from C major to C minor lowers E to E♭, moving from A major to A minor lowers C♯ to C, and so on.[29] (Naturally enough, the reverse paths raise the minor triad's third.) This allows us to calculate the voice leading corresponding to any other path on the graph: for example, to figure out the voice leading from C major to E minor, we combine the radial voice leading from C major to E major, (C, E, G) → (B, E, G♯), with the "parallel" voice leading (B, E, G♯) → (B, E, G); the result, (C, E, G) → (B, E, G), is the "leading-tone exchange" that lowers the root by semitone.[30] We can use this graph to represent chromatic triadic sequences such as those in Gesualdo and Mozart (§1.1).

Another option is to use Figure 2.1.3 to represent major *or* minor triads, with the single point "C" standing for both C major and C minor. This allows us to use a simple graph to represent a family of closely related progressions, each equivalent up to the exchange of parallel major and minor. Figure 2.6.3 uses this approach to model the upper voices in the passacaglia from Shostakovich's E minor trio. The

---

[28] This graph is similar to familiar music-theoretical constructions such as the Tonnetz and Douthett and Steinbach's "Cube Dance" (1998). Here we reconstruct these graphs by *superimposing* spiral diagrams (appendix 1).

[29] To determine this, we can ask what spacing-preserving voice leading from C major to C minor moves its voices by intervals collectively summing to –1; see Tymoczko 2020b.

[30] As before, different paths between the same points represent different voice leadings: the counterclockwise path from C major to E minor, for example, corresponds to the voice leading (C, E, G) → (E, G, B).

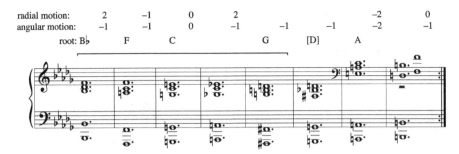

**Figure 2.6.3.** The passacaglia from Shostakovich's E minor piano trio. The numbers above the figure show how to interpret these motions on Figure 2.1.3, using a single point to represent major, minor, or diminished triads with that root. For augmented triads, the three radial points collapse into a single chord.

phrase begins with ascending fifths and stepwise descending melodies: B♭, F, C, G, with an upper voice C diminished chord between C and G; the next chord should be D major, but we instead get the augmented chord F♯–B♭–D, a single semitone away from each of the triads at the bottom of the circle (here forming the top of a G minor-major seventh chord); we then proceed to the expected A, with its voices exactly where they would be had the sequence continued. The top voice of the final chord, B diminished, leads naturally to the tenor B♭ across the repeat; its doubled F serves the same musical function as the G4 in Neil Young's "Helpless," melodic overlap creating the illusion of endless descent. This resonance is neither coincidence nor a matter of influence, but rather the independent rediscovery of similar solutions to similar problems.

In the rest of the chapter, I will mostly follow the strategy of grouping major and minor together, sacrificing detail in the name of graphical simplicity; readers who prefer more precision can use Figure 2.6.2 instead. Chapter 3 will introduce the diatonic analogues of these structures, in which major and minor triads appear as transpositionally related species of the same genus, the diatonic triad. This provides yet a third strategy for simultaneously modeling major and minor triads.

## 7. A fourth family

My last loop family involves five chords again arranged in an ascending-fifth pattern so as to be maximally close diatonically. Its best-known representative is "Hey Joe," made famous by Jimi Hendrix.[31] When I first learned the song, I was puzzled by its combination of dark lyrics and "bright" ascending-fifth major chords. (Why I thought of them as ascending fifths rather than descending fourths is a bit mysterious, but I did.) It was not until decades later, when I focused on its voice leading, that I understood the musical logic: closely related triads and stepwise descending

---

[31] The song is credited to Billy Roberts but likely derives from Niela Miller's 1955 "Baby, Please Don't Go to Town."

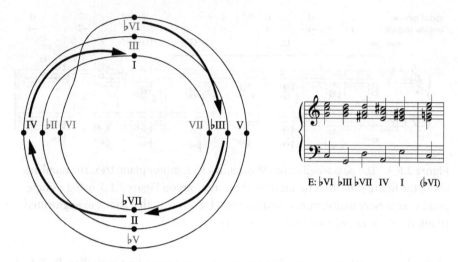

**Figure 2.7.1.** "Hey Joe." Despite the ascending semitone B–C, we can hear a canonic descent E–D–C♯–B–(C), with the melodic E descending to the inner-voice C across the repeat.

|  C  |  G  |  D   |  A  |  E  |                   |
|-----|-----|------|-----|-----|-------------------|
| ♭VI | ♭III| ♭VII | IV  | I   | Hey Joe           |
| VI  | III | VII  |     | I   | Dragostea din tei |
| IV  | I   | V    |     | vi  | Let It Be         |
| VI  | III |      | IV  | i   | 867-5309          |
| VI  |     | VII  | IV  | i   | Let It Go         |
| VI  |     |      |     | i   | Ask The Angels    |
| VI  |     |      | IV  | I   | Heart-Shaped Box* |

**Figure 2.7.2.** Progressions in the "Hey Joe" family. "Heart-Shaped Box" is starred because its progression usually features ascending voice leading.

melody, an endlessly sinking lament (Figure 2.7.1). Here, however, C major and E major occupy the same registral position, producing an ascending semitone B→C across the repeat. The loop can be found in any number of classic-rock songs including the Beatles' "A Day in the Life" and "Here Comes the Sun," Al Green's "Take Me to the River," and "Time Warp" from *The Rocky Horror Picture Show*. It is notable that the progression can be played with the five major triads that do not require barring in standard guitar tuning (C, G, D, A, E).

Figure 2.7.2 shows some of the many songs that can be derived from this pattern by eliminating chords and replacing major with minor. These are some of the most important progressions in all of rock, including i–VI–VII–i and a–F–C–G, which can appear either as i–VI–III–VII in A minor or I–V–vi–IV in C major.[32] Since the outer chords in the five-chord sequence occupy the same angular position, they

---

[32] These and many other progressions are discussed in Doll 2017, an extensive survey of rock harmony. Richards 2017 focuses on the "axis progression" a–F–C–G.

**Figure 2.7.3.** Neil Young's "Keep on Rockin' in the Free World" uses subsequences of the progression e–G–D–A–C.

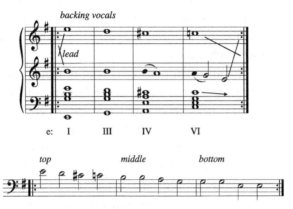

**Figure 2.7.4.** The vocal parts in "Steppin' Stone" articulate a continuous stepwise descent, while the harmonies present a four-chord subsequence of e–G–D–A–C. The vocal pitches are implied by the triads' descending voice leading.

are linked by symmetrical voice leading in which one note ascends and one note descends; from the standpoint of the spiral diagram, neither belongs "before" or "after" the other. We can therefore exchange them to obtain E–G–D–A–C. Neil Young's "Keep on Rockin' in the Free World" uses the progression's three-chord subset e–D–C in its verse and the four-chord e–G–D–C in the chorus, the minor tonic creating a completely diatonic progression while allowing for stepwise descent from VI to i (Figure 2.7.3). Another four-chord subset, E–G–A–C, appears in Dave van Ronk's version of "House of the Rising Sun," to be discussed in §2.10. Boyce and Hart's "Steppin' Stone," recorded by Paul Revere and the Raiders, uses van Ronk's progression in the context of an explicit and continuous melodic descent: the backing melody $\hat{8}$–$\flat\hat{7}$–$\hat{6}$–$\flat\hat{6}$ connects smoothly to the main vocal $\hat{5}$–$\hat{4}$–$\flat\hat{3}$–$\hat{1}$, forming a descending octave (Figure 2.7.4).[33] Interestingly, the melodic composite articulates the canon implicit in the version of the progression that has a minor tonic; it is not inconceivable that the writers heard this line in the progression, writing the melody in the way a listener might track the Shepard-tone passacaglia in the final product.

---

[33] Minor Threat's version expresses the continuity between these two vocal lines, the single vocalist alternating between them.

74  TONALITY: AN OWNER'S MANUAL

From this perspective, the melody's G–e descent, rather than a departure from a stepwise norm, is faithful to the progression's inner logic.

It is extraordinary how many iconic rock progressions can be derived from ascending fifths—perhaps with some chords eliminated, and perhaps with the phrase structure misaligned with the fifths-sequence. That this is so attests not just to the inner consistency of rock harmony, but also to the way ascending fifths mediate between the demands of harmony and counterpoint, generating descending melodies while keeping triads diatonically close. My own musical education deemphasized ascending fifths in favor of the descending fifths of functional music, with the latter treated as "normal" and the former exceptional. One of my goals in this book is to correct this misapprehension, restoring the ascending fifth to its central place in both modal and functionally tonal theory.

At this point it is useful to pause for a moment of metatheoretical reflection. Grant for the sake of argument that rock music exhibits a retrofunctional regularity, with descending melodic steps generating harmonic patterns in the way I have described. According to schema theorists like Meyer, Gjerdingen, and Byros we should be able to use these objective musical patterns to draw conclusions about the listening public's subjective experience. But I think this is misguided; after all, *we* are the historical audience for this music, and we can simply ask whether we have always been explicitly aware of these structures. In my case, the answer is a resounding "no!" While I may have had some vague and intuitive sense of "what rock harmony sounds like," I have been genuinely *surprised* by the degree of structure to be found in music I have spent my life playing, writing, and listening to. Here we have clear regularities in a genre, explained in part by the structure of musical space, but not explicitly present in the mind of at least one historically situated listener. If objective musical structure were a reliable guide to listener psychology, then this sort of surprise should be impossible. This suggests we need a more nuanced account of the relation between observable musical patterns and the psychology of composers and listeners.

## 8. Other modalities

Figure 2.8.1 shows the spooky prayer near the end of Heinrich Schütz's setting of Psalm 84 ("Wie lieblich sind deine Wohnungen"), the eighth of his *Psalmen Davids* (1619, SWV 29). It is an intensely powerful rendering of the Psalm's most direct address to God, eleven consecutive root-position triads of uncertain tonal provenance—the unmetered homophonic chant a sharp contrast with the preceding polyphony. When I first encountered this music, I heard resonances with rock that led me to gently question my sanity. Why should Schütz's early seventeenth-century composition remind me of Jimi Hendrix or Aretha Franklin? It took some time before I was ready to accept these resonances as something more than accidental; and it took longer still before I was confident enough to imagine

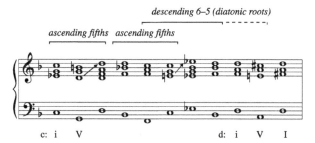

**Figure 2.8.1.** "Wie lieblich sind deine Wohnungen," mm. 136–146.

that they might reflect deep musical values—a shared interest in closely related harmonies and stepwise descending melody. I now think it is not so surprising that we should find resemblances here: rock musicians and early seventeenth-century composers both operated in a context where functional-harmonic constraints were comparatively weak, available options rather than inviolable laws. In such environments, musicians are free to explore the fundamental geometry of triadic voice leading, and in particular the connection between descending voice leading and retrofunctional harmony.

In other words, this music represents a largely unrecognized species of *quasi-chromaticism*. We are accustomed to using "chromaticism" in connection with the nineteenth century, where efficient voice leading provides shortcuts between remote harmonic locations; Schubert moving directly from C major to A♭ major, exploiting efficient voice leading to modulate between distant keys.[34] I am arguing, in effect, that similar strategies can be found in repertoire that is more resolutely diatonic. My claim has two components. First, this diatonic music, like nineteenth-century chromaticism, allows *contrapuntal* forces to operate relatively free of harmonic constraints: in the nineteenth century this led to surprising chromatic shifts; while in modal music it leads to "nonfunctional" progressions that may or may not lie within a single diatonic scale. Second, insofar as this music involves a diatonic norm, it is weak, controlling the departures from the prevailing key and limiting chromatic excursions. The progressions we have been exploring constitute a species of *heavily diatonic chromaticism* in which the diatonic scale exerts a greater gravitational force than it does in the nineteenth century. Yet the underlying principles are similar.

What is true of this early music is equally true of later modality. Figure 2.8.2 shows the Intermezzo of Grieg's "Watchman's Song" (Op. 12, no. 3, written in about 1866).[35] The spooky i–VII–♭II–IV–V progression represents the Spirit of the Night, nearly parallel four-bar phrases outlining an $\hat{8}$–$\hat{7}$–$\hat{6}$–$\hat{5}$ melodic descent. In classical

---

[34] See Cohn 1996, 1999, 2012, Tymoczko 2011a. Agmon's "within-key chromaticism" (2020) is very close to my own.
[35] For an insightful treatment of Grieg's late style, see Taylor 2019.

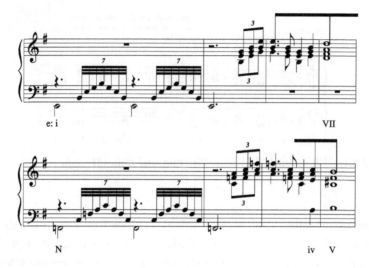

**Figure 2.8.2.** The Intermezzo of Grieg's Op. 12, no. 3.

music this line would likely be accompanied by a familiar functional progression; in Grieg it breaks free, the unusual D–F–a–B harmonies more obviously related to Schütz and rock than to Corelli or Haydn.

The counterintuitive association between early and late modality is one of the main motivations for this book. My idea is that there is a triadic "state of nature" that is most directly accessible when harmonic function is weak, and which is correspondingly harder to see in more harmonically regimented styles. This protogrammar arises not from any human convention but from the underlying geometry of three-note chords—a geometry which is intrinsically neutral with respect to harmonic progression, acquiring directionality from external factors such as the preference for descending melody. Because this geometry is deep, rooted in constraints both mathematical and psychological, it produces resonances across very different musical styles—Shostakovich and Neil Young, the Beatles and Grieg. My goal is to take these resonances seriously, allowing them to guide us toward a better understanding of music outside the classical tradition.

As a general rule, these sorts of retrofunctional progressions are uncommon in baroque and classical styles. Nevertheless, we can find traces of this nonfunctional default woven throughout that music—in the ascending-fifth sequences that so often feature in developments (§8.5), in the retrofunctional progressions that make up the "fauxbourdon rule of the octave" (§7.5), in familiar yet harmonically anomalous idioms such as the *Waldstein* sequence (§3.7), and in many other undertheorized corners of the tradition. Retrofunctional techniques thread like a hidden cantus firmus throughout functionality, an unruly strip of wilderness surrounded by the well-charted territory of rule-governed harmony.

Occasionally, this musical Other rears its head. Figure 2.8.3 shows Mozart using stepwise descending voice leading to answer IV–I in the tonic with IV–I in the

**Figure 2.8.3.** Retrofunctional motion in Mozart's piano sonata K.333, III (mm. 40ff).

**Figure 2.8.4.** A retrofunctional sequence of ascending fifths at the end of Bach's "Es woll uns Gott genädig sein" (BWV 311, Riemenschneider 16).

subdominant, a striking departure from harmonic decorum.[36] Figure 2.8.4 shows the retrofunctional ending of one of J. S. Bach's phrygian-melody chorales, the music modulating from D to b along an ascending-fifth sequence; once again, we have the impression of a temporary suspension of functional harmony, the music briefly reverting to earlier norms.[37] These moments underscore the importance of viewing functional harmony against the background of modal practice, a more general default that can help explain and contextualize these exceptional moments. Such "retrofunctional" progressions are utterly clear in their contrapuntal logic, and not intrinsically strange. What is unusual is just to find them *here*—tiny moments where harmonic convention fails to grip, allowing us to glimpse the world beyond the borders of textbook harmony.

---

[36] The chord sequence C–G–F–C, with descending voice leading, evokes the "fauxbourdon rule-of-the-octave" idiom, I–V$^6$–IV$^6$–I$^6_4$, though here it occurs over a different bass and in the wrong key (§7.5).

[37] Bach frequently modulates from major to relative minor by a sequence of ascending fifths (§7.7). The bass here instantiates something very close to Byros's "*le-sol-fi-sol*" schema (2012) but on the wrong scale degrees.

## 9. Function and retrofunction

One of the most interesting features of rock is the coexistence of modal and functional harmony. Songs like "Sympathy for the Devil" and "I Can't Explain" juxtapose mixolydian I–♭VII–IV–I verses with functional dominants in their choruses. The Beatles' "With a Little Help from My Friends" does something similar, beginning with ascending fifths supporting a two-voice compound melody (Figure 2.9.1).[38] The retrofunctional fifths then reverse direction to produce a functional ii–V$^7$–I progression, now supporting $\hat{2}$–$\hat{3}$ in the melody. In the figure, I interpret this $\hat{2}$–$\hat{3}$ as moving between voices, with the arrival on $\hat{1}$ implied but not explicitly stated. (The tonic scale degree arrives in measure 3 but without harmonic support, while the accompaniment clearly states the $\hat{4}$–$\hat{3}$ descent.) The chorus harmonizes a strong $\hat{2}$–$\hat{1}$ with an archetypal rock-mixolydian progression, ♭VII–IV–I. This ascending-fifth pattern then shifts up by fifth, from ♭VII–IV–I to IV–I–V, arriving on a functional half-cadence with the guitar part recapitulating the phrase's $\hat{5}$–$\hat{4}$–$\hat{3}$–$\hat{2}$ descent. The verse's three-chord units thus alternate ABAB between function and retrofunction. In the second verse, this ABAB alternation is highlighted by the vocals, with Ringo Starr taking the modal unit (I–V–ii) and the background vocals singing the functional unit (ii–V$^7$–I). This association continues through the bridge, where the background singers ask a functional question (vi–V/V) which the lead vocal answers retrofunctionally (I–♭VII–IV). The contrast between harmonic styles is thus reinforced by the orchestration.

"In rock music the harmonies tend to go backwards, except when they don't." This sounds like a parody of untestable theorizing . . . yet it is entirely possible that rock music *does* in fact juxtapose distinct harmonic subsystems, one functional and one modal, each with its own characteristic repertoire of harmonic moves.[39] Insofar as

**Figure 2.9.1.** The Beatles' "With a Little Help from My Friends" alternates functional and retrofunctional motion.

---

[38] Steve Forbert's "Goin' Down to Laurel," from *Alive on Arrival*, uses the same progression.

[39] Many other theorists have commented on rock harmony's polystylistic qualities, including Everett 2004, Osborn 2017, and Temperley 2018 (pp. 54ff).

ROCK LOGIC    79

the systems are kept separate, occurring for instance in different sections of a song, then it is not unreasonable to declare the music to be harmonically polyvalent. Such juxtapositions have been dubbed "code switching" by Richard Cohn, borrowing a term from linguistics to describe nineteenth-century chromaticism.[40] Just as bilingual speakers can move smoothly between two different languages, so too do popular musicians shift between the default voice leading of the modal system and more conventionalized functional routines. To be sure, the line between languages can vary from individual to individual: to my ears, tunes like "With a Little Help from My Friends" really do move back and forth between distinct harmonic styles, but for others the song may be unified creole, a coherent fusion of elements that are no longer distinct.

I hear a similar sort of code switching in a piece such as Thomas Morley's "April Is in My Mistress' Face" (1596), whose 38 measures are divided into four short sections, each setting a single line of text. The opening is strongly functional, with paired voices articulating T–(S)–D–T progressions that would be unobjectionable in the high baroque (Figure 2.9.2).[41] The second phrase shifts to B♭, its ascending-fourth progressions including a series of ascending leading tones. The third phrase is homophonic and declamatory, starting with primary triads in B♭ major and shifting to G minor as the thought of fall is introduced. Here it is possible to perceive the major/minor opposition as carrying some of the "happy/sad" valence it acquires later.[42]

After so much functionality, the last 16 measures make a striking shift away from functionality. The music uses a common Renaissance idiom, the diatonic version of the descending 6–5 sequence, here decorated with a voice exchange that creates an outer-voice canon—one that veils but does not obliterate the descending voice leading (Figure 2.9.3). I hear a sharp musical contrast, the ending dark and modal where the opening was bright and functional. The root-position chords throw the nonfunctional progressions into relief: ascending thirds and descending fourths that counter functional expectations.

Compare this music to Grieg's "In My Homeland," the nineteenth of the *Lyric Pieces* (Op. 43, no. 3, written in about 1886 and shown in Figures 2.9.4–5). Once again, the functional outlines are generally clear even when the local progressions avoid strong dominants. The twelve-measure phrase begins with a version of Morley's descending 6–5, outer voices hinting at the very same canonic structure (though substituting $I^6$ for the expected mediant); this proceeds to a strongly functional I–vi–V/V–V cadence. The dominant then moves nonfunctionally across the phrase boundary to IV, beginning an "up by step, down by third" sequence in sevenths.[43] That phrase ends with another stereotypical cadence, leading to a proto-Debussyian

---

[40] Cohn 2012.

[41] The F♮ in m. 9 provides a hint of modality.

[42] See Meier 1988, Part II, chapter 7.

[43] The voice leading recalls that of mm. 10–11 in Wagner's *Tristan*, which is (C, F, A♭, D) → (B, F♯, A, D♯) when we remove crossings. Here, the A♭→A voice becomes G♯→B.

80  TONALITY: AN OWNER'S MANUAL

**Figure 2.9.2.** Thomas Morley's "April Is in My Mistress' Face" begins functionally, but ends retrofunctionally.

**Figure 2.9.3.** The end of Morley's piece is based on a diatonic version of the descending 6–5 decoration, embellished with a voice exchange. The voice exchange highlights the canon in the outer voices.

**Figure 2.9.4.** The twelve-bar core of Grieg's Op. 43, no. 3.

alternation of ii and V. Grieg thus uses two of the three Renaissance sequences that typically harmonize stepwise descending thirds (cf. Figure 1.5.5), reviving progressions that had been neglected for decades.[44] His melodic logic is so clear that one may not notice the absence of dominant-tonic progressions.[45]

---

[44] The parallel thirds appear in the first sequence's alto and tenor (disrupted by the substitution of I⁶ for the iii) and as sixths in the second sequence's soprano and tenor.

[45] Note the ubiquitous parallel tenths between outer voices.

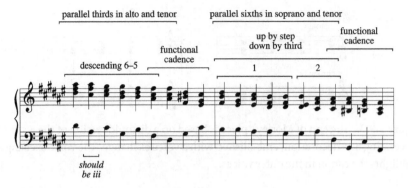

**Figure 2.9.5.** A reduction of Grieg's Op. 43, no. 3.

These cross-stylistic resonances suggest a new starting point for twenty-first-century pedagogy. Harmony textbooks often begin and end with functionality, as if the TSDT archetype were the norm and anything else a departure. But the eighteenth century's rigid harmonic laws are more exception than rule: in seventeenth-century music, as in contemporary rock, we find alternative models in which functionality is just one option among many—music in which the deep logic of voice leading sometimes takes the lead. It would make sense to begin our curricula with these harmonically flexible styles, which often feel more relevant than the more rule-governed language of chorale and sonata. One suspects that our reluctance to do so is not a matter of considered deliberation, but of the lack of appropriate conceptual tools: we know how to teach the principles of functional harmony but not the deep contrapuntal logic that animates other music.[46] The theory of voice leading can help fill this gap, giving us a more rigorous understanding of contrapuntal possibility—and in the process dampening the pedagogical echoes of classical-music chauvinism.

## 10. Continuity or reinvention?

The connection between early music and rock is in one sense obvious: bands had names like "Renaissance," wrote lyrics about knights and royalty, and played folksongs like "Scarborough Fair." Amidst political turmoil, an idealized past provided an alternative to an unsatisfactory present, with modal harmony its sonic emblem. This was clear to conservative musicians, who largely rejected modality in favor of functional harmony—to the point where one can have a pretty good sense, even before listening, of the harmonic vocabulary of a song like "The Ballad of the Green Berets" or "Stand by Your Man." What results is a strange historical inversion

---

[46] Ewell (2020) has emphasized that this focus on functional harmony is also a reflection of elitist, ethnocentric, and racist forces.

**Figure 2.10.1.** Ashley and Foster's 1933 recording of "The House of the Rising Sun."

whereby an older modal practice was associated with progressive politics while newer functionality symbolized traditional values.

When I was young, I assumed the triadic modality of rock was linked by a continuous tradition to the modality of the Renaissance. Surely, I imagined, people never stopped strumming dorian and mixolydian tunes in informal venues such as pubs and homes, uncorrupted by the learned tradition. What happened in the 1960s, I imagined, was simply that this marginalized and ubiquitous musical tradition was raised to public consciousness. But having looked for evidence of this continuity, I find myself much less convinced than I used to be. American and English folk recordings made before 1950 tend to be harmonically sparse, featuring either unaccompanied melodies, drones, or perhaps oscillating between two chords. It is surprisingly difficult to find recordings that are (a) clearly modal, (b) made before 1950, and (c) feature three or more distinct triads.[47] Insofar as these recordings are representative, folk modality tends toward monody.

Furthermore, the picture of folksongs as rigid vessels for modal practice is at odds with the extraordinary flexibility of the vernacular tradition: surveying early twentieth-century recordings, one finds the same tunes appearing in different forms—changing modes and time signatures, and acquiring a variety of harmonizations. Consider the earliest recording of "The House of the Rising Sun," made for Vocalion in 1933 by the Appalachian musicians Clarence ("Tom") Ashley and Gwen Foster, under the name "Rising Sun Blues." The piece, transcribed in Figure 2.10.1, is a sixteen-bar major-mode blues with an ABBC structure, a

---

[47] There are a number of continuous modal traditions that are unlikely to have served as a historical bridge between Renaissance and rock. Gregorian chant is one. Irish folk music is another, with modal elements present from the transcriptions of Edward Bunting (1773–1843) to the recordings of the early twentieth century.

84   TONALITY: AN OWNER'S MANUAL

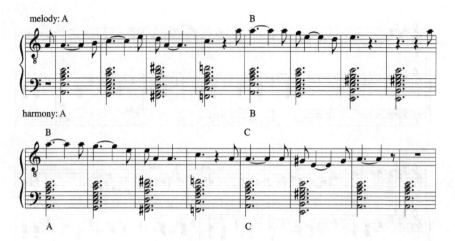

**Figure 2.10.2.** Bob Dylan's 1962 harmonization of "The House of the Rising Sun." The melody is an idealization that does not try to capture the nuances of Dylan's performance.

standard twelve-bar blues that repeats its middle four bars. As such it is largely functional, oscillating between I and IV before reaching the V–I cadence. Its most unusual chord—a iv$^2$ that occurs under a melodic $\flat\hat{7}$ not present in the harmony—can perhaps be seen as a minor subdominant (an instance of "modal mixture") though it also has an affinity with the VI that appears in later versions of the tune. (In some verses of the Ashley/Foster recording, this iv$^2$ moves to V$^4_3$ on beat three.) A 1935 variant by Homer Callahan (under the name "Rounder's Luck") has simple i–V–i harmony, while other versions are monophonic (Georgia Turner, 1937), or blues-based (Roy Acuff and His Smoky Mountain Boys, 1938). These performances are considerably more functional than most of the songs in this chapter, and indeed a later recording by Ashley and Doc Watson sands down the rough edges of the first version, softening the iv$^2$ and hewing more closely to blues convention.

The route to the rock harmonization of "Rising Sun" is instructively circuitous. Bob Dylan's 1962 acoustic recording borrows its chords from Dave van Ronk; it features an a–C–D–F progression over an $\hat{8}$–$\hat{7}$–$\sharp\hat{6}$–$\hat{6}$ descending bass that sounds for all the world like a tonally functional lament, albeit interrupted by a root-position tonic where a classical composer would use i$^6_4$ (Figure 2.10.2).[48] Here there is no dramatic rejection of functional norms: the subdominant, so central to the blues, is subsumed within the descending bass, the reharmonization producing an ABAC harmonic structure at odds with the vocal line's ABBC. If anything, Dylan's version feels more conventional than Ashley's, the blue notes of the original melody now supported triadically.[49] By contrast, the Animals' 1964 recording speaks the

---

[48] Rings (2013) notes a similar progression in the work of Len Chandler, an oboist in the Akron Orchestra, who would likely have been familiar with the learned modality of the early twentieth century. See Grieg's *Elegie* (§8.7) for the sort of descending bass line that might be the ancestor of Dylan's lament.
[49] Wagner 2003.

ROCK LOGIC    85

Figure 2.10.3. Gordon Heath and Lee Payant's 1955 version of "Scarborough Fair."

language of rock: Dylan's stepwise descending lament is moved to an upper voice and its harmonies placed in root position—an aggressive progression that feels much less functional than its predecessor. Far from being the relic of an ancient tradition, these retrofunctional triads are a recreation, a reimagined past as artificial as Debussy's.[50]

A similar story can be told about "Scarborough Fair," initially recorded in 1955 by Gordon Heath and Lee Payant (Figure 2.10.3). Their major-mode version features simple I–V–I harmonies, the jaunty vocal declamation evoking a comedic Renaissance figure. Like much vernacular music, it is in a "loose duple" that permits the occasional extra beat; my transcription locates this beat in the third measure of each phrase, resetting the downbeat to the final syllable and allowing for a comfortable pause between lines.[51] This version is followed in 1957 by Ewan MacColl and Peggy Seeger's harmonized dorian version, its melody collected ten years earlier.[52] Audrey Coppard made a monophonic dorian-mode recording in 1958, and Shirley Collins released a very similar take in 1959. Meanwhile Peggy Seeger released a functional major-mode recording in 1960, while Marianne Faithfull provided a functional minor-mode harmonization in 1965. The tune appears with its now-canonical dorian chords on Martin Carthy's 1965 debut album; Carthy taught it to Simon and Garfunkel, who used it in their 1966 medley—a top-ten hit that eventually became standard.

Such examples suggest that, in the absence of recordings, folk songs are an unlikely vehicle for the faithful transmission of modal harmony. Instead of fixed and unchanging songs we find endless interpretations, united chiefly by lyrics and secondarily by melody. As far as I can tell, early twentieth-century American and English folk music is if anything *more* functional than its descendants: triadic modality, with its blatantly nonfunctional progressions, is largely a phenomenon of

---

[50] Later uses of the progression, such as "Stairway to Heaven," further detach it from its origins in the lament: here, the i–III$^6_4$–IV$^6$–VI$^{maj7}$ returns to i, decorating the idiomatic modal-rock VI–VII–i rather than the functional-harmonic i–V–i.

[51] Compare measure 3 of Figure 7.2.6.

[52] Kloss 2012 presents a thorough archaeology of the song, showing that both major and minor variants have an extensive history. The earliest published transcriptions resembling the standard modern version appear in the very late 1870s, though in aeolian rather than dorian.

the late 1950s and 1960s, not obviously continuing any widespread folk practice.[53] In this sense, the modality of the 1960s is best understood as the delayed echo of modernism, popular musicians rejecting functionality a half-century after classical composers did.

Thus if there are resonances between Renaissance and rock, this is likely due to intrinsic triadic logic rather than actual historical connection. What sustains the modal "state of nature," what leads to its reappearance in disconnected eras, is that it offers straightforward solutions to basic musical problems—stepwise descending melodies and closely related triads. In other words, it is a "syntax" supported not by convention but by constraints inherent in our musical materials. Musicians need not be aware of these constraints to be bound by them; they simply need to be interested in writing music that *feels right* (with their intuitions prioritizing stepwise melody, diatonically close harmonies, and so forth). By analyzing this feeling of rightness we can transform the implicit into the explicit, revealing hidden roads connecting different musical languages. If we are lucky, this new understanding will suggest new compositional possibilities as well.

---

[53] We see a similar progression when we consider other folk traditions, such as shape-note polyphony: the clear modality of its eighteenth-century tunes is gradually regularized and made more functional in the nineteenth century, returning only as twentieth-century practitioners become more interested in historical authenticity. Thanks here to Rachel Hall.

# Prelude
## The Tinctoris Transform

Students are taught to understand counterpoint as the braiding of independent lines, with melodies the primary objects of attention and harmonies the byproducts of their interaction. This chapter will introduce a complementary perspective that is central to a good deal of musical thinking both practical and speculative, one that emphasizes vertical shapes or *configurations* having different locations or *centers of gravity*—so that harmonies are salient and melodies more like byproducts. Where the first perspective deals in descriptions like "one voice is at A4 and the other at D4," the second instead uses phrases like "one voice is a fifth above the other, forming a vertical interval centered on F4." This has the result of highlighting the contrast between parallel motion, which preserves the vertical configuration, and contrary motion, which changes it. The two perspectives are mathematically equivalent, and one can switch between them without loss of information; indeed, I suspect many musicians regularly do so without realizing it.

We can think of these as different musical coordinate systems. In both cases, we begin by numbering pitches in some enclosing scale, using chromatic or diatonic or other pitch-labels as appropriate. We then choose some arbitrary order for our musical voices. In the familiar system, pitch numbers are used to label each voice's position, yielding a list containing the notes in the first voice, second voice, and so on. In the second system, we instead label voices by their distance from one "reference" voice (usually the first), whose coordinate is necessarily 0; this gives us a *configuration*, or collection of relative distances that can be instantiated anywhere in pitch space. To specify the configuration's location, we need another number recording the average of the pitches; I will call this its *center of gravity*.[1] The difference between the two systems is illustrated by Figure P3.1. The second system is closely related to what physicists call the *center-of-mass* coordinate system.[2]

Though it may seem newfangled and mathematical, the configuration-based approach is in fact very old. Johannes Tinctoris used it to analyze two-voice counterpoint in his 1477 *Liber de arte contrapuncti*, arranging part of the book so that chapters correspond to starting intervals and subsections destination intervals,

---

[1] Since the reference voice has position 0, the two systems both use $n$ changing numbers to label the notes of an $n$-note chord. We could also measure the configuration's location using the sum of the chord's pitches instead of their average.

[2] Transposition is a structure-preserving perceptual symmetry, much as "translation" (physical movement) is a symmetry of 3D space. By factoring out transposition and translation, we can simplify musical or physical problems.

---

*Tonality.* Dmitri Tymoczko, Oxford University Press. © Oxford University Press 2023. DOI: 10.1093/oso/9780197577103.003.0004

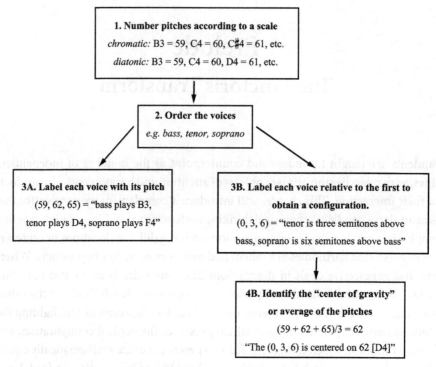

**Figure P3.1.** Two musical coordinate systems.

with each section describing how the combination can appear.[3] The result is a tedious verbal description of what is essentially a matrix or spreadsheet (Figure P3.2). Contemporary musicians will be tempted to dismiss Tinctoris's approach as unbearably pedantic, a residuum of the scholastic obsession with enumeration and lists. (C. S. Lewis once wrote that, of all the inventions of modernity, the medieval mind would be most impressed by the card catalogue.[4]) But there is purpose to Tinctoris's pedantry, and something to be learned from his approach.

One advantage of the configurational perspective is that it clarifies the phenomenon of efficient voice leading. This is because the most efficient voice leading between two vertical configurations will necessarily minimize the change in center of gravity. This simple observation helps elucidate some important patterns found throughout Western music: among the center-of-gravity-preserving progressions in Figure P3.3 we see the major-third triadic progressions beloved by Schubert, the minor-third tetrachordal progressions of Wagner, Debussy, and Stravinsky, and a host of familiar fifth-progressions; each combines a changing vertical shape with a relatively stable center of gravity. The example shows that transpositionally related dyads can be connected by efficient voice leading when their roots move by tritone

---

[3] Tinctoris measures an interval's location relative to the tenor (his "reference" voice), rather than the interval's center of gravity; this difference is not fundamental, as the location of the tenor can be computed from the center of gravity and vice versa.

[4] Lewis 1964, p. 10.

|          | −4  | −2              | 0     | 2              | 4   |
|----------|-----|-----------------|-------|----------------|-----|
| −4 (ch. 6) | ... | ...             | ...   | ...            | ... |
| −2 (ch. 4) | ... | 0, ±1, ±2, ±3, ±4 | 0, −1 | 0, −1, −2, −3, −4 | ... |
| 0 (ch. 3)  | ... | 0, ±1, ±2, 3, 4  | 0     | 0, ±1, ±2, −3, −4 | ... |
| 2 (ch. 4)  | ... | 0, 1, 2, 3, 4    | 0, 1  | 0, ±1, ±2, ±3, ±4 | ... |
| 4 (ch. 6)  | ... | ...             | ...   | ...            | ... |

**Figure P3.2.** Some of Tinctoris's recommendations in matrix form. The row labels record the starting configuration, measured in diatonic steps from tenor to counterpoint voice; the column labels record the destination configuration measured in the same way. Numbers in the cells refer to the motion of the tenor in diatonic scale steps. Thus, if the harmonizing voice is a third above the tenor in the first chord (row label 2), moving to a third below the tenor in the second chord (column label −2), then the tenor can ascend by 0–4 scale steps (i.e., up to a fifth). Similarly, if the harmonizing voice starts a third below (row label −2) and is moving to the unison (column label 0), the tenor can either stay fixed (0) or descend by step (−1).

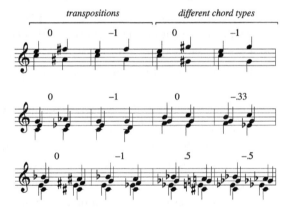

**Figure P3.3.** Efficient voice leading minimizes the change in a chord's center of gravity. The example presents dyadic, triadic, and seventh-chord progressions in chromatic space; above each I identify the change in center of gravity, equivalent to the average of the melodic motions in all voices.

or near tritone (i.e., fourth or fifth), three-note chords when their roots move by major third or near major third (i.e., minor third or perfect fourth), four-note chords when their roots move by minor third, tritone, or intervals nearly equal to these, and so on.[5] These relationships underwrite many important idioms from the Renaissance to the present day.

---

[5] These root motions correspond to $12/n$, where 12 is the size of the octave and $n$ is the size of the chord. As we move away from these optimal intervals, we increase the size of the resulting voice leading.

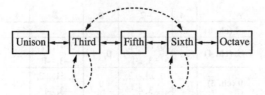

**Figure P3.4.** The diatonic consonances spanning an octave or less, arranged from small to large. Composers often move along the arrows.

They are also manifest in the structure of our geometrical models, where the amount of angular motion corresponds to the change in center of gravity. For example, on the 3-in-12 diagram (Figure 2.1.3), radial motion from C major to E major lowers the root by semitone while raising the fifth by semitone; since the ascending and descending semitones cancel, center of gravity is preserved. In general, two chords will have the same angular position when they can be linked by voice leading in which the change in center of gravity due to looping (transposition along the chord) exactly counteracts the change in center of gravity due to sliding (transposition along the scale): in this case $T_4$ raises the center of gravity by one third of an octave, while $t_{-1}$ lowers it by that same amount. Readers who look ahead to Figures 4.2.7 and 3.8.4 will see that tritone-related perfect fifths occupy the same radial position in 2-in-12 space, while minor-third-related seventh chords occupy the same radial position in 4-in-12 space; this is the geometrical origin of the idioms in the previous paragraph.

Efficient voice leading also requires that vertical configurations themselves change by only a small amount. Figure P3.4 arranges the diatonic consonances by size. Two-voice consonant counterpoint tends to move by short distances on this graph: in the two-voice passages of Palestrina's masses, for example, about 90% of the fifths move to sixths or thirds, while about 80% of the unisons move to thirds.[6] (Note that this claim implicitly uses the new coordinate system: to say "fifths often move to sixths" is to say that voices configured as a fifth often move so that they end up configured as a sixth.) By contrast, imperfect consonances often move to other imperfect consonances by parallel or contrary motion. Putting these points together, we can formulate a useful rule of thumb: if you are on a perfect consonance, move along Figure P3.4 to a nearby imperfect consonance (or, less likely, jump over an imperfect consonance to reach the nearest perfect consonance); if you are on an imperfect consonance, move about half the time along the dotted lines to another imperfect consonance, and otherwise to a nearby perfect consonance. This *positive counterpoint* gives musicians an affirmative goal, a set of plausible options going beyond a negative approach built on prohibitions. It aims to capture the intuitive knowledge of a composer who knows *what to do next*: "if I am located at *this*

---

[6] Motion from unison to unison, fifth to fifth, or octave to octave will produce parallel perfect intervals so long as the center of gravity changes.

**Figure P3.5.** Two of Thomas Campion's contrapuntal categories, along with his notation of the shared vertical configurations. The arrows and T labels are my own, showing that progressions within each category are related by the independent transposition of each chord.

point in musical space, then my most obvious destinations are . . ." Such knowledge becomes increasingly important as additional voices bring more contrapuntal options, or when composers are constrained by harmonic rules.

A second advantage of the configurational perspective is that it helps us focus on structural relationships that are independent of transposition; in this respect it is the earliest forerunner of what we have come to call *musical set theory*.[7] Two progressions can be said to belong to the same category if they exemplify the same series of vertical configurations, differing only in transpositional level: "an octave followed by a major sixth," "a major triad in ⅝ position followed by a minor triad in ⁶₄ position," "a root-position half-diminished seventh in close position followed by a root-position dominant seventh in close position," and so on. In 1614, Thomas Campion used this idea to categorize four-voice voice leadings between root-position triads, extending the Tinctorian perspective from two voices to four (Figure P3.5).[8] In *A Geometry of Music* I said that such progressions are *individually transpositionally related*; here I will say they are *related by the Tinctoris Transform*.

---

[7] See Nolan 2003 and Schuijer 2008 for histories of set theory that begin more recently.

[8] This example comes from Schubert 2018, who hypothesizes that Thomas Tallis may have used it in composing his 1570 *Spem in Alium*. I think we can find evidence for the strategy throughout the sixteenth century, most obviously in those repertoires that make extensive use of close-position root-position triads (§6.1).

Paths on our spiral diagrams are related by the Tinctoris Transform if they differ only in the amount of sliding involved; this is true whether we are considering a simple diagram representing only the transpositions of a single chord type or a more complex diagram superimposing multiple chord types. By ignoring slides, we can group together a large number of superficially different possibilities, revealing similarities that may not be intuitively obvious. The 3-in-12 diagram of chromatic major triads, for example, contains only three fundamental kinds of motion, the clockwise loops of 0, 1, or 2 turns ($t_0$, $t_{-1}$, $t_{-2}$); all other motions can be obtained by adding slides to these (Figure P3.6). This sort of simplification can be analytically useful: for example, the three canonic sequences in Figure P3.7 repeatedly apply a transformation of the form $T_x t_1$, differing only in the amount of sliding involved. While they might initially seem unrelated, they are similar from the configurational point of view.

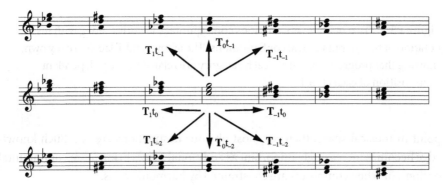

**Figure P3.6.** Voice leadings from the central C major triad to triads on each line differ only in their transpositional component.

**Figure P3.7.** Three canonic sequences that repeatedly apply the same voice-leading pattern, differing only in their diatonic transposition.

Finally, configurations can help us understand the logic behind some seemingly arbitrary prohibitions of traditional pedagogy. For example, many textbooks prohibit similar motion into perfect consonances ("direct fifths and octaves"), but Figure P3.8 shows that similar motion is rare *regardless of destination interval*: the general scarcity of similar motion is at least as striking as the difference between the perfect and imperfect consonances. Our new perspective helps explain why this is so: the change in center of gravity will be zero when two voices move in exact contrary motion; as the change in center of gravity increases, the voice leading becomes more and more unbalanced and the largest leap gets larger and larger (Figure P3.9). This situation persists until we reach the boundary of oblique motion, where one voice remains fixed and all the motion is in the other voice. As we move into similar

|          | Ockeghem |      | Josquin |      | Palestrina |      |
|----------|----------|------|---------|------|------------|------|
|          | Perf.    | Imp. | Perf.   | Imp. | Perf.      | Imp. |
| Contrary | 36       | 24   | 34      | 27   | 30         | 33   |
| Oblique  | 60       | 38   | 63      | 32   | 69         | 28   |
| Parallel | 0        | 33   | 0       | 36   | 0          | 37   |
| Similar  | 4        | 5    | 4       | 4    | 1          | 3    |

**Figure P3.8.** Approaching perfect and imperfect consonances in Ockeghem, Josquin, and Palestrina. Values are percentages, with each column adding up to 100 (within rounding).

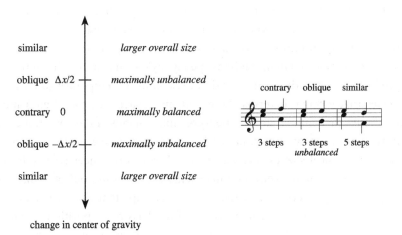

**Figure P3.9.** (*left*) An abstract diagram relating a dyad's change in center of gravity to its overall size. When the change is zero, the voice leading involves perfectly contrary motion and the overall voice-leading size is minimized; voices move in a balanced way by approximately the same distance. As we increase the change, the melodic intervals become more unbalanced, until we reach oblique motion, where all the movement is in one voice; beyond this, we have similar motion where the overall size of the voice leading increases. (The line of obliqueness is half the change in interval size.) (*right*) A concrete example using imperfect consonances. Underneath each progression, I count the total number of melodic steps in all voices.

motion, the total motion in both voices starts to increase. It follows that there is a basic incompatibility between similar motion and the principle that voices should move by small distances: given any instance of similar motion, we can reduce the melodic intervals in each voice by reducing the change in center of gravity. Much the same point could be made about "voice overlap," a form of similar motion where one voice crosses another's starting point.[9] Our new coordinate system allows us to understand the *don't*s of negative counterpoint in terms of affirmative *dos*—in this case, minimizing melodic motion by keeping the center of gravity approximately fixed.

Hierarchical set theory supplements the Tinctorian perspective by providing a new way to measure the intervals in a vertical configuration. We can formalize the intuitive notion of a *voicing* as a pattern of spacing in chordal steps: a "close position" voicing is a voicing in which each note is one chordal step above its lower neighbor (e.g., C4–E4–G4) while an "open position" voicing places each note *two* steps above its lower neighbor, as in C4–G4–E5. We can think of voicings as *set classes*, collections of pitch intervals measured along the intrinsic scale: for triads, close position is the (pitch-set) set class 012, measuring along the intrinsic scale from bass to soprano, open position is the (pitch-set) set class 024, and so on. Thus any chord presents multiple set classes simultaneously: a chromatic set class determined by its pitch classes, a diatonic set class determined by the extrinsic scale, and an intrinsic pitch-set set class determined by its voicing (Figure P3.10). In different musical situations different sets can be more or less salient, with pitch-class content often more perceptible for small chords in close position, and intrinsic spacing more important as chords grow larger or are voiced in unusual ways.

The Tinctorian tradition of configurational thinking continues into the eighteenth century, reflected in figured-bass pedagogy's terms for describing the shapes played by the keyboardist's right hand. It lives on in contemporary guitar manuals that categorize voicings in terms of their intrinsic spacing ("drop 2," etc.) and jazz-theory books that enumerate the open-position voicings of the pentatonic scale.[10] Its most comprehensive manifestation is set theory, whose even-more-general vocabulary of musical shapes is sufficient to describe *any* conceivable collection of notes. Set theory shares with its antecedents the factoring out of transposition, leaving behind a description of relative relationships that can be instantiated at any transpositional level: an interval, a figured-bass hand position, a voicing, a "set class." The connection between these traditions has been obscured by three factors. First, traditional set theory is unusually indifferent to registral position, disregarding vertical spacing entirely to focus on pitch-class content alone.[11]

---

[9] Here the reasoning is more complicated. The prohibition on voice overlap dictates that large melodic intervals be harmonized not with near-parallel motion but significant changes of spacing. These changes of spacing increase voice independence and are often, but not always, more efficient than the near-parallel alternatives.

[10] For example, Laukens 2019 or Levine 1989.

[11] This amounts to discarding some of the information contained in the relative configuration, for instance by treating its numbers as unordered and conceiving them modulo the octave. Morris 1995 incorporates both pitch and pitch-class information.

|     | CHR | DIA | CHORD |
|-----|-----|-----|-------|
| F–A | 4   | 2   | 2     |
| C–F | 5   | 3   | 2     |
| G–C | 5   | 3   | 2     |
| D–G | 5   | 3   | 2     |

|      | CHR | DIA | CHORD |
|------|-----|-----|-------|
| E–A  | 5   | 3   | 2     |
| B–E  | 5   | 3   | 2     |
| G♯–B | 3   | 2   | 2     |
| C–G♯ | 8   | 4   | 2     |

**Figure P3.10.** Both Bill Evans's "So What" chord and Schoenberg's "Farben" chord are voiced as open-position pentachords, spaced as two-step intervals along the intrinsic scale. The tables show how the two five-note chords each present three set classes; "CHR" measures the size of their chromatic intervals, "DIA" is the scalar size along the white-note or A melodic-minor scale, and "CHORD" is the spacing along the chord's intrinsic scale. Since the chordal spacing is identical, the chords are voiced in the same way.

Second and related to this, the early set theorists were not concerned with voice leading, a core topic of traditional theory. Third and finally, set theory originally assumed chromatic space whereas traditional theorists delt with the diatonic world. In recent years, however, theorists have started to extend set-theoretical concepts to include both diatonicism and voice leading, uncovering surprising connections between different intellectual traditions. Chapter 3 will continue this line of inquiry.

# 3

# Line and Configuration

Musicians learn their way around abstract spaces of musical possibility, developing an intuitive understanding of the contrapuntal paths between sonorities of various kinds. This knowledge is typically schematic and style-specific, the relevant pathways changing from one circumstance to another. This chapter will use spiral diagrams to provide a more general perspective. The central claim is that a wide range of musical practices subsist on an underlying geometrical structure: across many styles, the desire for certain kinds of melodies, such as those that move by step, combines with a desire for consistent harmony to constrain compositional possibilities. These constraints, which are as much mathematical as aesthetic, shape the syntax, idioms, and schemas that characterize many different genres. Something similar can be said for the idiosyncratic progressions found in composers like Gesualdo or Mahler. Both rule and exception can be understood geometrically.

On a technical level, I will analyze polyphony not just as the superimposition of independent melodies but also as successions of vertical configurations obeying their own higher-level laws. This perspective has long been used to provide practical heuristics for creating idiomatic counterpoint—as in §3.6, where it underwrites a simple system for teaching four-part chorale harmonization. But it is also intimately connected to set theory and geometry, leading to a convergence between modern theories of voice leading, which arose in response to nineteenth-century chromaticism, and traditional diatonic pedagogy, which in turn inspired contemporary schema theory. Attending to vertical configurations can contribute to our embodied musicianship while also deepening our appreciation for subtle musical mathematics.

The plan is to gradually increase complexity, starting with two and three voices before considering four-voice composition with both triads and seventh chords. At a certain point, this purely quantitative increase of voices leads to a qualitative change in perspective: for while it is possible to understand two- and three-voice counterpoint using nonhierarchical models, four-voice triadic counterpoint is more consistently hierarchical, with voices often moving *inside* an abstract and scale-like harmony (§3.7). As we progress, we will encounter several intertwining themes, including the persistence of two-voice logic in three- and four-voice contexts, the geometrical foundations of common idioms (e.g., the "Quiescenza" or the common-tone diminished seventh), a collection of "wrong-way" resolutions

*Tonality.* Dmitri Tymoczko, Oxford University Press. © Oxford University Press 2023. DOI: 10.1093/oso/9780197577103.003.0005

in which familiar objects move contrary to our expectations (the ascending-fifth resolutions of the diatonic third, the subdominant triad, and the dominant seventh), and a set of practical tools for understanding traditional counterpoint ("OUCH theory"). Inspired by the Prime Directive, we identify similar phenomena reappearing in different environments, the same abstract relationships manifested in increasingly sophisticated ways.

A word of warning: this is one of the most dense and difficult chapters in the book, discussing almost all the geometrical spaces needed later. Readers who want a break can read the opening of chapter 4 after they finish part 1, returning to part two before reading §4.4. Similarly, the opening of chapter 5 can be read without absorbing this material, though part 3 is needed in §5.5.

## PART 1. TWO VOICES

### 1. The imperfect system

Some of the deepest mysteries of counterpoint arise from the geometry of imperfect consonances. Figure 3.1.1 presents the spiral diagram for thirds and sixths in diatonic space.[1] Here, the unit is one scale step and "diatonic seconds" such as C–D and E–F have size 1 (appendix 1).[2] Since our chords have two notes, the line of transposition winds twice around the circle before returning to its starting point; since the diatonic scale has seven notes, there are seven equally spaced points along the

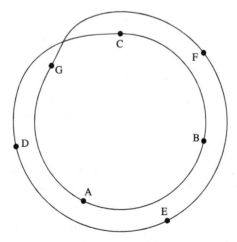

**Figure 3.1.1.** The spiral diagram for diatonic dyads.

---

[1] Visit https://www.madmusicalscience.com/cs.html for interactive versions of this space, and https://www.madmusicalscience.com/graphs/2in7.pdf for a printable version of the graph. Other graphs can be found by replacing "2" and "7" with the appropriate numbers.
[2] For more on this perspective, see chapter 4 of Tymoczko 2011a.

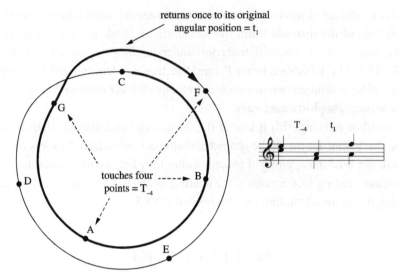

**Figure 3.1.2.** Moving one clockwise step from C to F combines $T_{-4}$ and $t_1$. The third moves up by step and the root moves down by third.

spiral. Sliding along the spiral transposes along the scale, looping around the spiral transposes along the chord, turning thirds into sixths and vice versa.

We can calculate the effect of single-step clockwise motion from C to F using the recipe in §2.1. Sliding clockwise from C to F touches four points for $T_{-4}$, passing our initial radial position once for $t_1$. Figure 3.1.2 shows that these two motions combine to form the voice leading (C, E) → (A, F), moving the third's root down by two scale steps and its third up by one step. I call this the *descending basic voice leading* for diatonic thirds, since it connects every point on the graph to its nearest clockwise neighbor.[3] Single-step counterclockwise motion generates the inverse voice leading, sending the third up by two steps and the root down by one step. I call this the *ascending basic voice leading*. (When context is clear, I will not specify the direction.) Repeatedly applying the basic voice leading moves through the two inversions or "modes" of the interval (third and sixth), touching on each inversion of every imperfect consonance before returning to the initial chord, now with the notes transposed by octave (Figure 3.1.3).

There are two nonobvious ways to analyze motion along the diagram. The first is to assign every path a number corresponding to the angular distance traveled, or, equivalently, the number of basic voice leadings required to generate that path. Since there is only one chord at every angular coordinate, radial motion is completely determined by angular motion; as we will see, this allows us to collapse the spiral into a circle. Alternatively, we can adopt the Tinctorian strategy of decomposing

---

[3] This voice leading reduces the dyad's center of gravity by one: if we number notes so that C = 0, D = 1, E = 2, and so on, then the chord (E, G) is (2, 4), with a sum of 6 and center of gravity (or average) of 3; the basic voice leading sends (E, G) to (C, A), or (0, 5), with a sum of 5 and an average of 2.5.

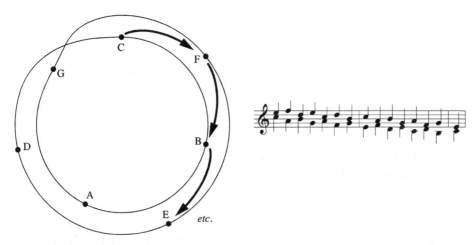

**Figure 3.1.3.** A series of clockwise moves in the space produces a descending-fifth progression in which thirds and sixths alternate.

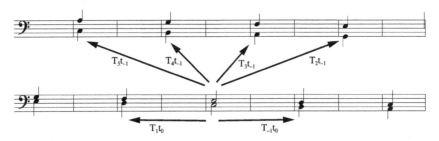

**Figure 3.1.4.** The voice leadings along the dyadic circle expressed in musical notation; the top staff applies an odd number of basic voice leadings, combining transposition along the scale with one-step transposition along the dyad ($t_1$); the bottom staff applies an even number of basic voice leadings and involves no transposition along the dyad.

voice leadings into combinations of transposition along both chord and scale, or loops and slides. From this perspective, there are just two basic possibilities, corresponding to those that transpose along the chord and those that do not; these use an odd or even number of basic voice leadings, respectively. Within each category, voice leadings differ only by a change in center of gravity, controlled by the scalar transposition $T_x$ (Figure 3.1.4).

It follows that purely contrapuntal relationships will tend to privilege fifth motion: if we are in two-note diatonic space, then fifth-related dyads are literally adjacent to one another. This dyadic "circle of fifths" is independent of both the *acoustic* circle of fifths and the circle of fifths connecting diatonic scales (chapter 8). We should therefore expect that linearly oriented music will contain a plethora of fifth-related imperfect consonances, even when roots are not the explicit objects of compositional attention. Figure 3.1.5 shows that the opening of Palestrina's mass *Ave regina coelorum* contains four instances of the diatonic third's basic voice leading. The fifth-motion here arises from two distinct sources, the contrapuntal logic of

100    TONALITY: AN OWNER'S MANUAL

**Figure 3.1.5.** The opening of the Palestrina's mass *Ave regina coelorum*. The numbers below the example indicate angular motion on Figure 3.1.1, with negative numbers corresponding to clockwise (descending) motion.

**Figure 3.1.6.** The start of the last movement of Beethoven's E♭ major piano sonata, Op. 27, no. 1.

diatonic thirds and the converging voices of the cadence. The rise of functional tonality involves the integration of these two, assigning harmonic significance to the fifth-progressions that are inevitably produced by the system of diatonic dyads. This is more or less explicit in a passage like Figure 3.1.6, where the dyads of the main theme articulate the basic voice leading while the root progressions conform to tonally functional expectations, the descending fifths of the cadence of a piece with those within the phrase.

The dyadic logic of the 2-in-7 spiral interacts with the triadic system in complex ways. In the descending voice leading the initial dyad is almost always the root and third of a triad, while the second dyad can either be root/third or third/fifth, producing authentic and deceptive resolutions respectively (Figure 3.1.7). A passing tone is often inserted into the melodic third to create a resolving tritone. The ascending-fifth voice leading embeds into a wider range of progressions; here again a passing tone yields $\hat{6}$–$\hat{7}$–$\hat{1}$ against $\hat{4}$–$\hat{3}$, combining plagal root motion with an authentic resolution of the tritone ($\hat{7}$–$\hat{1}$/$\hat{4}$–$\hat{3}$). In baroque music this figure is often harmonized as shown in the middle column of Figure 3.1.7, producing a pair of eighth-note harmonies over a stable bass (ii–vii°6 or IV–vii°$^6_4$).[4] The rightmost

---

[4] As Nicolas 2019 points out, Étienne-Denis Delair's 1690 *Traité d'accompagnement pour le théorbe, et le clavessin* recommends the ascending basic voice leading for ascending-fifth bass lines, often producing a quasi-functional result.

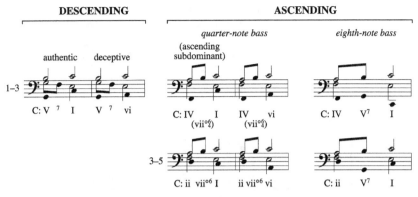

**Figure 3.1.7.** Triadic harmonizations of the diatonic third's basic voice leading. The descending form typically appears as root and third of the initial triad (top line, "1–3"), moving either to root-third or third-fifth of a second triad. The ascending form can also appear as third-fifth of the initial triad (bottom line, "3–5"). In both cases, a passing tone can create a resolving tritone. The rightmost column harmonizes the dyadic progression with a change of bass.

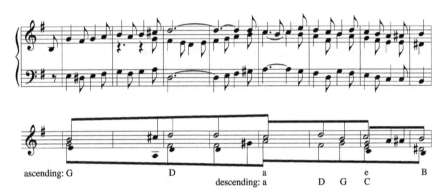

**Figure 3.1.8.** The second theme of the first movement of Beethoven's Op. 23 violin sonata. While the root progressions are mysterious, the sequence of basic voice leadings is systematic, ascending by fifth, descending, and then ascending again.

column instead supports the voice leading with a changing bass, an option that is increasingly preferred as functional harmony develops. The contrast between these two approaches reflects a shift from a dyadic-contrapuntal conception of functionality, where linear patterns are predominant, to a later and more triadic orientation.

Attending to these dyadic patterns can reveal subterranean levels of musical structure obscured by Roman numerals. In the second theme of the first movement of Beethoven's Op. 23 violin sonata, for example, the root progressions are mysterious while the sequence of basic voice leadings is completely clear, moving up and down the ladder of fifths (Figure 3.1.8).[5] This dyadic organization is concealed

---

[5] The end of the phrase ends with an e–b ascent that continues the G–d–a pattern of the opening phrase, though I would not put much emphasis on this connection.

**Figure 3.1.9.** The opening of the middle section of the second mazurka in Clara Wieck Schumann's *Soirées Musicales*, Op. 6. The top staff shows various appearances of the ascending and descending basic voice leadings, designated by open and closed noteheads respectively. The annotations indicate whether the basic voice leading appears as the bottom (b) or top (t) third of the triad.

by the third's changing position, appearing initially as the triad's third-fifth rather than root-third. In the recapitulation, Beethoven normalizes the music so that roots follow upper voices, replacing a–G–d with C–G–d and clarifying the theme's sequential structure.[6] Similarly, Figure 3.1.9 shows Clara Wieck Schumann presenting a period whose two endings exploit the two different basic voice leadings of the dyad (C♯, E); the surrounding music embeds the ascending basic voice leading into three of its four possible triadic positions, appearing as the bottom thirds of successive triads, the top thirds, and the top and bottom. Here the logic is one of *chordal subsets* rather than complete triads. Roman numerals are not so much wrong as incomplete, taking a back seat to other relationships.

The dyadic circle is also the source of a number of schemas central to functional tonality. Figure 3.1.10 analyzes four patterns discussed in Gjerdingen's *Music in the Galant Style*: the converging cadence takes a single clockwise step from $\hat{2}$–$\hat{4}$ to $\hat{5}$–$\hat{7}$, augmented by passing tones in each voice. The "Fonte," or descending-fifth sequence, makes a series of clockwise moves. The "Monte," or ascending-step sequence, alternates clockwise steps with three-step counterclockwise moves, transposing up by

---

[6] See m. 182; this is one of countless instances of Beethoven transforming a theme so as to reveal a disguised sequence.

**Figure 3.1.10.** Common schemas and patterns analyzed as paths on the imperfect consonance's spiral diagram.

step at every other chord. The "Quiescenza" alternates rightward and leftward steps, tonicizing a pair of fifth-related harmonies with ascending and descending basic voice leadings. To these I have added a common I–IV–V–I pattern not identified as schematic by Gjerdingen; like the Quiescenza, it juxtaposes rightward and leftward motions. Such examples suggest that the basic idioms of functional composition are not so much arbitrary conventions as responses to the basic affordances of musical space: beneath the conventional and schematic surface lies a deeper geometrical logic featuring short-distance motions in the space of imperfect consonances.[7]

## 2. Voice exchanges

Any voice leading can be decomposed into two parts: a crossing-free component that preserves spacing as measured along the intrinsic scale and a *voice exchange* rearranging the notes of a single chord, with paths collectively summing to 0.[8] (As we will see, this factoring of voice leadings into voice exchanges and a crossing-free residue is a point of contact between Schenkerian theory and voice-leading geometry.) The diatonic third has two elementary voice exchanges, a small one moving each voice by two steps (third down to root and root up to third), and a large one moving each voice by five steps (third up to root and root down to third). More complicated voice leadings—for instance, keeping the third fixed while moving the root up by octave—can be generated from these two, perhaps in combination with one or more transpositions along the chord.[9] Figure 3.2.1 uses curved arrows to represent the

---

[7] Rabinovitch (2018, 2019, 2020) likewise grounds schemata in deeper contrapuntal principles; though he starts from very different theoretical principles, I believe his approach is largely consistent with mine. The link between galant schemas and dyadic geometry is also supported by Holtmeier's observation that galant composers favored outer-voice imperfect consonances (2011).

[8] The voice leading (E4, G4, C5) → (D4, A4, E5) can be decomposed into the voice exchange (E4, G4, C5) → (C4, G4, E5) and the spacing-preserving (C4, G4, E5) → (D4, A4, E5); the latter has both chords in "open position," with each voice two steps above its predecessor. When chords are related by transposition, the spacing-preserving component is a transposition along the chord.

[9] To move the root up by octave while keeping the third fixed, we can transpose both notes up along the chord, sending C up to E and E up to C. We then apply the five-step voice exchange to move E up to C and C down to E. The result leaves E fixed and in the same voice while raising C by octave in the other. In other words, we have (C4, E4) → (E4, C5) → (C5, E4), for a composite of (C4, E4) → (C5, E4).

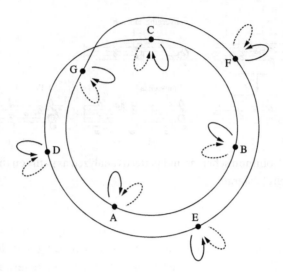

**Figure 3.2.1.** Curved arrows represent voice exchanges: dotted and solid lines are the two- and five-step exchanges, $c_0$ and $c_1$.

elementary voice exchanges. This new geometry can represent every two-voice voice leading connecting any imperfect consonances in the same diatonic collection.

The voice leadings on this augmented graph are again fundamental to functionally tonal composition, schematic but more general and flexible than idioms as we tend to think of them. A single voice exchange combines with a single basic voice leading to produce "antiparallel" motion in which the voices move in contrary motion by *almost* the same amount. For instance, the basic voice leading (C4, E5) → (A3, F5) combines with the two-step voice exchange (A3, F5) → (F3, A5) to produce (C4, E5) → (F3, A5), with the root falling by fifth and the third ascending by fourth; that same basic voice leading combines with the five-step voice exchange (A3, F5) → (F4, A4) to produce (C4, E5) → (F4, A4), now with the root ascending by fourth and the third descending by fifth. These voice leadings are *contrapuntally balanced* in the sense that they move their voices by approximately the same distance—a fourth and a fifth. If we move further along the circle, say by combining a three-step clockwise motion with one of the voice exchanges, we get more and more unbalanced motion (Figure 3.2.2). Here again diatonic fourths are contrapuntally privileged: fourth-related thirds, as geometrical neighbors, allow for antiparallel motion in which the voices are almost exactly balanced, and hence minimize the largest distance moved by either voice; other root motions produce less-balanced counterpoint, with larger leaps in one of the voices. This is why we find fifth-relations in diatonic contrary-motion passages from Monteverdi to Meredith Monk (e.g., Figure 1.5.8).[10]

---

[10] The fifth is the closest diatonic approximation to the half-octave. In a scale with an even number of notes, such as the chromatic or octatonic, then tritone transposition allows for perfectly balanced contrapuntal motion, connecting maximally close thirds.

**Figure 3.2.2.** (*top*) Antiparallel motion decomposed into a basic voice leading and a voice exchange. (*bottom*) Antiparallel motion between fifth-related thirds involves the most balanced intervals in the two voices; as we move away from the fifth, the motion moves to one voice.

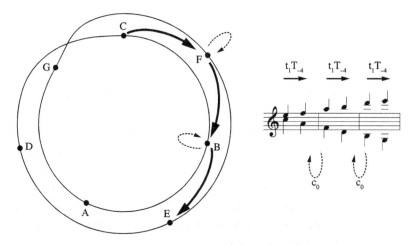

**Figure 3.2.3.** Alternating the basic voice leading and the two-step voice exchange leads to a wedge sequence in which harmonies move by fifth.

We can also apply the two-step voice exchange separately from the basic voice leading to produce the sequence in Figure 3.2.3. Here the voices move apart in near contrary motion, the bass descending by thirds while the top voice alternates steps and thirds. Figure 3.2.4 shows the opening of the last movement of Beethoven's A♭ major piano sonata, Op. 26. The music begins with the basic voice leading in a descending-fifth sequence that continues across the textural change. (Here the schema appears in the context of shifting scales tonicizing ii and vi, adding chromatic variety without disrupting the contrapuntal logic.) Beethoven follows this with the two-step voice exchange, moving the hands apart so that the tenor plays A♭ while the top voice plays C;

106   TONALITY: AN OWNER'S MANUAL

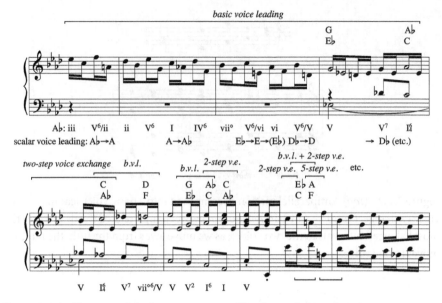

Figure 3.2.4. The start of the last movement of Beethoven's A♭ major piano sonata, Op. 26.

the basic voice leading then produces F–D, or vii°6/V, at which point the pattern restarts between alto and bass under an upper-voice pedal. The opening music now returns but with the two hands in contrary motion—vertical dyads cycling through the two-step voice exchange, the "antiparallel" voice leading, the five-step voice exchange, and a second antiparallel voice leading. Here we have all the imperfect system's atomic moves: the basic voice leading, the two voice exchanges, and their combination. This fusion of contrapuntal and harmonic is typical of Beethoven, its joyous simplicity laying bare the fundamental mechanisms of functional coherence.

One way to internalize these relationships is to focus on the voices' third-or-sixth arrangement, which can either oscillate back-and-forth to preserve the dyad's spacing-in-chordal-steps or form a contrary-motion wedge. Figure 3.2.5 shows a few common idioms that can be obtained by moving one hand along some familiar pattern—such as a scale or arpeggio—while the other moves from third to sixth and back, augmented with occasional parallel motion. (Parallel motion and shifts between third and sixth generate all the moves on the expanded diagram of Figure 3.2.1.) My practical, improvisational understanding of functional tonality improved significantly when I developed an intuitive feel for these patterns. Both Schenkerian theory and schema theory have emphasized outer-voice idioms of this sort; here we take the additional step of tracing them to the spiral geometry of musical possibility, an abstract logic constraining musicians' linear impulses and leading them toward a small collection of musical possibilities.

LINE AND CONFIGURATION 107

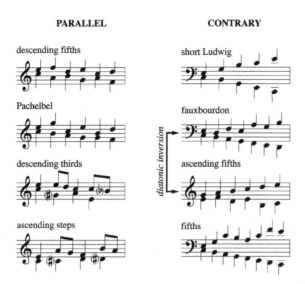

**Figure 3.2.5** Third-and-sixth patterns that can be generated with the expanded circle of Figure 3.2.1. On the left, parallel patterns that preserve spacing in chordal steps; on the right, contrary-motion patterns.

## 3. Other intervals

Chapter 2 showed that a single graph can be used to represent voice-leading relationships among the chromatic transpositions of any three-note chord. The same is true of the other spiral diagrams: to generate Figure 3.1.1 we need only the size of the chord, which tells us how many times our "line of transposition" wraps around the circle, and the size of the scale, which tells us how many equally spaced points to place on the line. This means that the graph represents any two-note interval in any seven-note scale: no matter what scale we choose, we can label its notes with the letters A–G, redefining the familiar names to refer to the notes of our new scale, and no matter what interval we choose, we can form a descending "basic voice leading" combining four-step descending transposition along the scale with one-step ascending transposition along the chord, or $T_{-4}t_1$ (Figure 3.3.1). Though superficially different, these "basic voice leadings" move their voices in structurally similar ways.

The development of the first movement of the first Beethoven piano sonata superimposes two basic voice leadings, the outer voices in thirds and the inner voices in fifths; because of their structural similarity, the two dyads stay in sync with each other, moving down by step every other chord and combining to produce triads with doubled root (Figure 3.3.2). The resulting four-voice pattern is ubiquitous throughout functional harmony, one of the main voice-leading schemas used for descending-fifth sequences. Figure 3.3.3 shows some other formulae containing the diatonic fifth's basic voice leading: a standard 7–6 fauxbourdon

108  TONALITY: AN OWNER'S MANUAL

**Figure 3.3.1.** The basic voice leadings for diatonic fifths, seconds, and unisons. The figure shows how they all combine four-step transposition downward along the scale with one-step transposition upward along the chord, or $T_{-4}t_1$.

**Figure 3.3.2.** A sequence from the development of Beethoven's Op. 2, no. 1 (mm. 73–80), combining basic voice leadings for thirds and fifths.

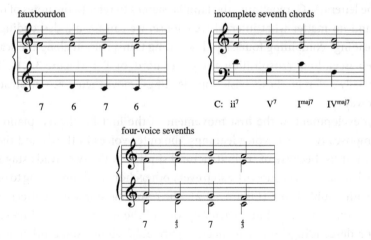

**Figure 3.3.3.** The diatonic fifth's basic voice leading can be embedded into a fauxbourdon 7–6 sequence, a sequence of incomplete descending-fifth seventh chords, or a four-voice descending-fifth sequence of root-position and second-inversion seventh chords. The last sequence contains two separate copies of the pattern.

pattern, a descending-fifth sequence of incomplete seventh chords, common in virtually all functional music from the baroque to jazz, and a descending-fifth sequence of seventh chords fusing these two. Baroque sequences often trade on the similarity of these patterns, blurring the boundary between "merely linear" fauxbourdon and robustly harmonic descending fifths (§7.5). Here again, functional schemas exploit the structure of a preexisting space of musical possibilities.

Of course, thirds and sixths predominate in the Western tradition, partly because composers favor imperfect consonances and partly because *all* the derived voice leadings are permissible—parallel motion, antiparallel motion, and the basic voice leading itself. Perfect consonances require more cautious treatment due to both forbidden parallels and the ambiguous status of fourths and tritones. However, there are genres that are less squeamish about these matters: Figure 3.3.4 uses the spiral to analyze a phrase from the Sacred Harp tune "Heavenly Spark," exulting in its perfect-consonance harmony. More complex are the opening eight bars of Thelonious Monk's "Pannonica," where the upper voices outline a diatonic fifth that sinks slowly downward, much like the previous chapter's rock songs (Figure 3.3.5); the left hand

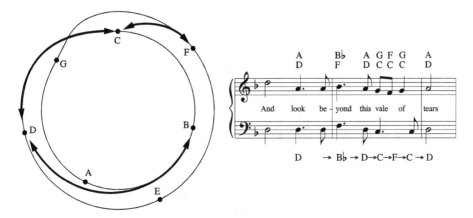

**Figure 3.3.4.** A phrase from "Heavenly Spark" represented on the circular space for diatonic fourths.

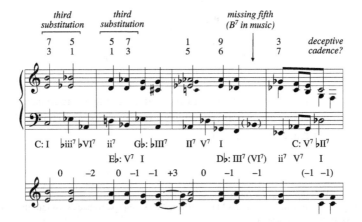

**Figure 3.3.5.** The opening of Thelonious Monk's "Pannonica" decorates a pair of upper voices forming fourths and fifths (bottom staff).

110  TONALITY: AN OWNER'S MANUAL

subposes various bass notes under this right-hand core so that the upper voices move from third-seventh to root-fifth and back, and then up to sixth/ninth.[11] These basic diatonic patterns are further elaborated by a variety of scale shifts, the music implying a variety of black-note keys before returning to C major. Jazz often involves similarly sophisticated manipulation of diatonic geometry, exploiting the link between descending-fifth harmonic progressions and efficient voice leading.

Beethoven superimposed two basic voice leadings in a musical context, and we can do the same in the theoretical domain. Figure 3.3.6 combines the circular spaces for all three diatonic consonances, with unisons and octaves on the outside, fourths and fifths in the center, and thirds and sixths between those two. Angular position on this graph represents the sum of the chords' pitch classes, while radial position mirrors the prelude's abstract graph of diatonic consonances; small radial motions thus change the vertical configurations by small amounts (Figure 3.3.7). This is essentially the Möbius strip representing all two-note diatonic consonances, reconstructed as the sum of three separate spiral diagrams.[12] Expressed in musical notation, its basic motions appear as shown in Figure 3.3.8, horizontal lines embedding the contrary-motion pattern

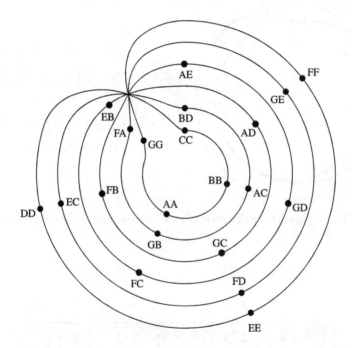

**Figure 3.3.6.** Superimposed spiral diagrams for the three diatonic consonances. Changes in interval size correspond to radial motion in this space; changes in center of gravity correspond to angular motion.

---

[11] Thanks here to Gunnlaugur Björnsson.
[12] In this space, the line of unisons acts like a mirror, "reflecting" paths backward into the interior of the graph. See Tymoczko 2011a, chapter 3.

LINE AND CONFIGURATION 111

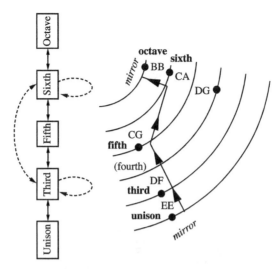

**Figure 3.3.7.** The cross section of dyadic chord space embeds the graph of dyadic consonances from Figure P3.4.

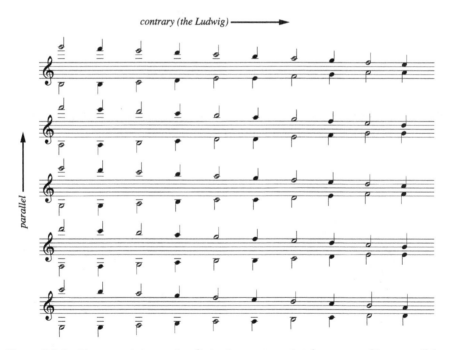

**Figure 3.3.8.** Consonant, two-voice diatonic counterpoint decomposed into parallel and contrary motion. Open noteheads show imperfect consonances.

of Figure 1.5.6 (a version of the "Ludwig" schema [§10.1]) and the vertical direction representing parallel motion. This is a Tinctorian approach to two-voice counterpoint, emphasizing parallel and contrary motion rather than the locations of the individual voices.

112   TONALITY: AN OWNER'S MANUAL

Figure 3.3.9 presents an even more abstract version of the space, taking advantage of the fact that diatonic spirals contain exactly one chord at every angular position: the new space compresses the spiral's two strands into a single circle, each angular segment representing a basic voice leading and switching between the interval's two inversions (fourth and fifth, third and sixth, unison and octave). Despite its abstraction, it represents the very same voice leadings as the earlier spiral diagrams, providing a simple model of many different intervals (Figure 3.3.10).

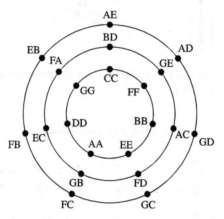

**Figure 3.3.9.** An abstract graph of two-note diatonic consonances. Set class corresponds to radial position while center of gravity corresponds to angular position.

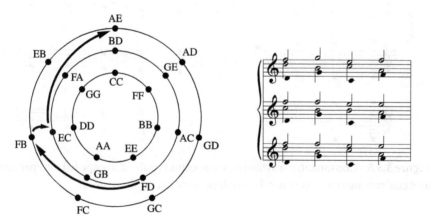

**Figure 3.3.10.** Three sequences with descending-fifth root progressions. In the first, the upper voices move clockwise along the middle ring from FD to GB to EC; in the second they move along the outer ring from FC to FB to EB. The third mixes these two as shown by the dotted lines.

## PART 2. THREE VOICES

### 4. The circle of diatonic triads

We start our study of three-voice counterpoint with the spiral diagram representing diatonic triads (Figure 3.4.1). Since a triad has three notes, the line of transposition winds three times around the circle; since the diatonic scale has seven notes, this line contains seven equally spaced points. To find the basic voice leading we slide clockwise along the spiral from C down to E, touching five chords for $T_{-5}$ and passing by our initial radial position twice for $t_2$; the two operations combine to produce $T_{-5}t_2$ (or equivalently $T_2t_{-1}$), a voice leading in which the triad's root descends by one diatonic step, lowering the chord's center of gravity by ⅓.[13] This links diatonic triads in a chain of thirds connected by single-step voice leading, reaching the descending-step transposition at every third iteration:

$$(C, E, G) \to (B, E, G) \to (B, D, G) \to (B, D, F) \to \text{and so on.}$$

As before, iterating the basic voice leading produces all possible combinations of transposition along the chord and transposition along the scale—or in other words every three-voice triadic voice leading that preserves spacing in chordal steps.[14] Once again, the same graph represents any three-note chord in any seven-note scale.

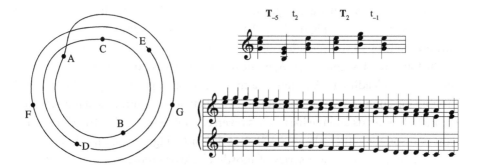

**Figure 3.4.1.** The circle of diatonic triads, along with its basic voice leading. Repeated applications of the basic voice leading pass through each inversion of each triad before returning to the initial configuration transposed by octave.

---

[13] $T_{-5}t_2$ is equivalent to $T_2t_{-1}$ since $T_7t_{-3}$ does nothing and $T_{-5}t_2 + T_7t_{-3} = T_2t_{-1}$. Three applications of $T_{-5}t_2$ produces $T_{-15}t_6$ or $T_{-1}$ since $T_{-14}t_6$ also does nothing. The descending basic voice leading turns (E, G, B), or (2, 4, 6) in diatonic note-numbers, into (D, G, B), or (1, 4, 6), decreasing the sum from 12 to 11 and center of gravity from 4 to 3.66.

[14] These voice-leading patterns were the subject of explicit discussion in early figured-bass treatises; see, for example, the examples on p. 77 of Buelow 1992 or the discussion on pp. 202–3 of Bach (1762) 1949.

**Figure 3.4.2.** Chromatic "major third" substitution compared to diatonic "third substitution"; the former changes chord-quality dramatically while the latter preserves its harmonic character. As a result, the progressions on the right sound reasonably similar while those on the left sound very dissimilar.

The previous chapter used a chromatic version of this space to explore how stepwise descending melodies can be combined with triadic harmonies. There, contrapuntally close chords such as C and E major could be harmonically quite distant. The circle of diatonic triads is special insofar as it encodes a kind of harmonic similarity as well: adjacent chords on the circle are close both contrapuntally (linked by single-step voice leading) and harmonically (sharing two of three notes). It follows that the diatonic analogue of chromatic third substitution will preserve a good degree of a chord's harmonic quality (Figure 3.4.2). This linking of harmonic and contrapuntal similarity is crucial for the development of functional harmony (§7.2).

The triadic circle allows us to deploy the theoretical strategy of chapter 2 in a fully diatonic context, revealing how melody and harmony constrain one another. Consider the "Et incarnatus est" passage from the Credo of Palestrina's mass *Spem in alium*, shown here as Figure 3.4.3. The music is largely homophonic and almost entirely made up of root-position chords whose upper voices are in close position. As the top voice descends C–B–A, we hear a series of ascending fifths F–C–G, with the last chord leading to A minor as a modal subtonic, producing a VI–III–VII–i progression common in popular music.[15] We then hear a symmetrical i–iv–i before the melody ascends and the harmonies reverse, leading to a i–VII–III–VI progression that sounds rather like vi–(IV⁶)–V–I–IV in C. Figure 3.4.4 models the palindromic upper voices as a series of mostly clockwise moves (F–C–G–a–d) that unwind themselves exactly (d–a–G–F–C). The resulting music is extremely clear in its association of melody and harmony, the descending melodic steps leading to ascending fifths while ascending melodic steps generate a much greater sense of functionality.

Renaissance music is suffused with "generalized fauxbourdon," or three-voice passages in which triads descend through a variety of triadic inversions. In Figure 3.4.5 Ockeghem alternates ⁶₃ and ⁵₃ chords to produce a descending 6–5 sequence; on the triadic circle, the passage moves by one and two clockwise steps. Figure 3.4.6 presents a series of ascending-fifth progressions from C to G to D to A, moving two

---

[15] Chapter 6 will discuss the application of Roman numerals in an early-music context. These near-palindromic phrases are fairly common in the Renaissance (e.g., Figure 8.6.11 or the start of Palestrina's "Stabat Mater").

LINE AND CONFIGURATION 115

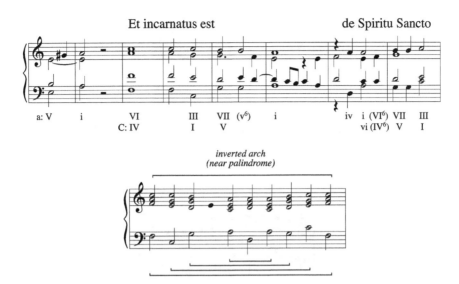

Figure 3.4.3. The "Et incarnatus est" from the Credo of Palestrina's mass *Spem in alium*. Its harmonies form an embellished inverted palindromic arch.

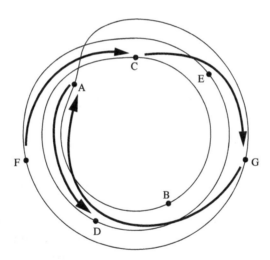

Figure 3.4.4. The path traced by the first five chords in the "Et incarnatus est"; the music then retraces its steps.

steps clockwise on the triadic circle. (Here I consider the d$^6_4$ chord to be harmonic, a reading that will be discussed in chapter 5.) These are diatonic analogues to the passages in chapter 2, and indeed there is plenty of rock music that can be modeled on the diatonic spiral—for example, Israel Kamakawiwo'ole's version of "Over the Rainbow," where the melody descends almost by octave while the harmony loops around the spiral three times (Figure 3.4.7).[16] Something similar could be said

---

[16] Note that the top line of the ukulele jumps above the vocal at the dominant, producing the familiar effect of overlap.

116  TONALITY: AN OWNER'S MANUAL

Figure 3.4.5. Ockeghem, Gloria from the mass *De plus en plus*, mm. 127ff. Numbers represent steps on the triadic spiral diagram (positive counterclockwise, negative clockwise).

Figure 3.4.6. Palestrina, Kyrie from the mass *Descendit angelus Domini*, mm. 39–40.

Figure 3.4.7. Israel Kamakawiwoʻole's "Over the Rainbow."

about the McCoy Tyner passage in Figure 1.1.8, though that music passes through the pentatonic scale as it descends.

Of the many possibilities for generalized fauxbourdon, a few survive to become functional schemas. Figure 3.4.8 shows three idioms featuring a pair of stepwise voices: the Pachelbel and Prinner progressions, joined here to descend through a melodic octave; the standard "rule of the octave" ascent; and what I call the "fauxbourdon rule of the octave," a mostly parallel-sixth pattern that often harmonizes descending bass lines (§7.5).[17] Things are complicated by the fact that descending melodic motion tends to correlate with *retrofunctional* progressions (Figure 3.4.9). Thus where modal composers could freely use short clockwise steps on the triadic circle, functional composers need to restrict themselves to a small number of harmonically acceptable options.[18]

---

[17] The Pachelbel/Prinner combination is an exact A2D4 sequence that has been truncated and repeated: b°–C–G–a–e–F–C–[b°]. Caplin (2015, p. 51) mentions this progression.

[18] Free use of small clockwise steps can sometimes be found in functional music, for example the opening of Mozart's G minor quintet K.516 (g–f♯°6–f6–C♯46–E♭6–D6), the opening of the *Waldstein* (§3.7), or the Chopin excerpts in §9.3.

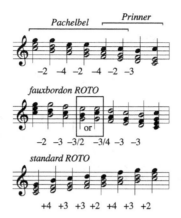

**Figure 3.4.8.** Three common functional patterns involving consistent clockwise or counterclockwise motion on the triadic circle.

| Progression | C→E | C→G | C→B | C→D | C→F | C→A |
|---|---|---|---|---|---|---|
| Clockwise steps | 1 | 2 | 3 | 4 | 5 | 6 |
| Stepwise descents | 1 | 2 | 3 | 2 | 1 | 0 |
| Interval from start | +third | +fifth | −step | +step | −fifth | −third |

**Figure 3.4.9.** The possibilities for stepwise descent, starting from a C diatonic triad. The first line shows clockwise steps on the circle of diatonic thirds; the next line shows the number of voices that descend by step; the third shows the interval connecting the roots. For each interval, "weak" progressions permit more descents than "strong" progressions: ascending-third progressions allow for one descending voice whereas descending thirds permit none; ascending fifths allow for two descents, while descending fifths allow for one; and descending steps allow three descents, whereas ascending steps allow only two.

Two further points about functional harmony: first, the primary triads I, IV, and V divide the triadic circle nearly evenly, into arcs of length 2, 3, and 2; this means that as a group they collectively minimize common tones, articulating three maximally distinct harmonic poles. There are two other nearly even divisions of the circle that contain the tonic triad, I–ii–V–I and I–IV–vii°–I, both paradigmatic T–S–D–T progressions; this suggests a geometrical interpretation of harmonic functions as maximally disjoint regions of triadic space, involving triads with the fewest possible common tones.[19] Second, there is an interesting symmetry between the two fifth-progressions IV–I and V–I: each has a direct voice leading in which two voices move stepwise, ascending for the dominant and descending for the subdominant, and an indirect voice leading in which two voices move by third and one moves by step (Figure 3.4.10). Both of these indirect voice leadings can be embellished with passing tones to create a diminished triad, producing a

---

[19] Agmon 1995 and Quinn 2005.

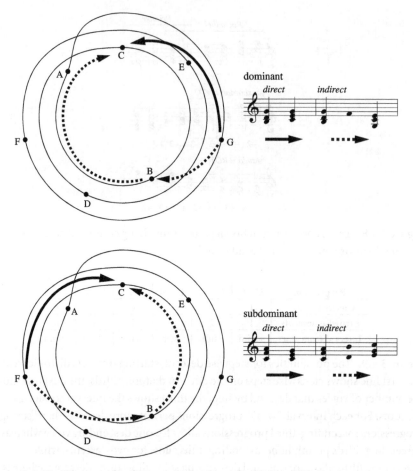

**Figure 3.4.10.** Direct and indirect voice leadings for V–I and IV–I progressions.

standard descending-fifth progression and an "ascending subdominant" respectively. The dualistic symmetry between these two kinds of fifth motion, and the tension between functional tonality and descending stepwise voice leading, will be topics for chapter 7.

To see how these relationships can play out, consider "Liebst du um Schönheit," the fourth song in *Liebesfrühling*, Robert Schumann's Op. 37 and Clara Weick Schumann's Op. 12. Clara's music, shown in Figure 3.4.11, presents a sixteen-bar ABAC period whose A sections are arranged as four-bar sentences. Both consequents harmonize outer-voice tenths, the first using the diatonic fifth's descending basic voice leading to suggest the seventh-chord idiom at the bottom of Figure 3.3.3; the second embellishing the Pachelbel/Prinner hybrid with the diatonic third's *ascending* basic voice leading, here tonicizing the second chord in each ascending-fifth pair.[20] Meanwhile, the join between the period's two halves exploits

---

[20] Compare Figure 3.4.8 and Figure 3.1.7; see also the first measure of J. S. Bach's chorale "O Haupt voll Blut und Wunden" (BWV 244.54, Riemenschneider 74), which uses the same Pachelbel/Prinner hybrid, starting on $\hat{4}$ rather than $\hat{6}$.

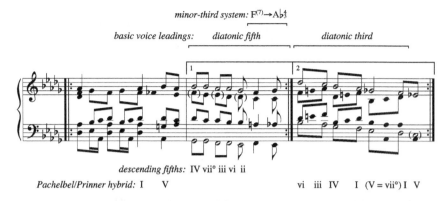

**Figure 3.4.11.** An outline of Clara Wieck Schumann's "Liebst du um Schönheit," Op. 12.

the chromatic proximity of minor-third-related seventh chords, moving directly from $F^7$ to $A\flat^7$ (§3.8 below). The resulting music is both effortless and dense, a spontaneous yet conceptually intricate combination of linear, harmonic, dyadic, triadic, and seventh-chord patterns. How did earlier composers manage to become fluent in such an extraordinarily difficult musical language?

The answer, I think, is that its basic conceptual structures are neither the homogenized harmonic patterns of Roman-numeral analysis, nor the equally homogenized linear patterns of Schenkerian analysis, nor the highly particular idioms of existing schema theory. Instead, they are somewhere in between, linear/harmonic hybrids arising from the fundamental geometry of diatonic objects: a small set of moves on various spiral diagrams. These hybrid structures are more general than schemas and more specific than "dominant-tonic progressions" or "parallel motion in tenths"; instead, they are that subset of contrapuntal possibilities that is compatible with Roman-numeral harmonic grammar, pruned from the larger vocabulary of earlier music. A major lesson of voice-leading geometry is that this subset is both small and surveyable: that the linear drive to write parallel tenths, if it is to be compatible with functionally harmonic grammar, will manifest itself in a limited number of ways. These are not idioms so much as possibilities. It is not that harmony or counterpoint is primary; instead, only a few moves have both harmonic and contrapuntal virtues.

## 5. Voice exchanges and multiple chord types

The Tinctoris Transform gives us an alternate perspective on two-voice counterpoint: instead of independent musical lines entwined like affectionate snakes, it depicts a series of verticalities waxing and waning as their shared center of gravity rises and falls. To model three-voice counterpoint we could replace vertical intervals with registral configurations such as $\frac{5}{3}$, $\frac{6}{3}$, and $\frac{6}{4}$, using two numbers to record the relative positions of three voices. However, it is traditional to adopt broader categories representing more general classes of vertical configurations

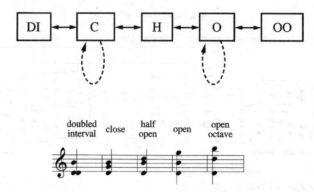

**Figure 3.5.1.** Five upper-voice configurations and a diagram of their most common connections.

or hand shapes. Eighteenth-century figured-bass pedagogues recognized three positions for a keyboard's right hand: the default "close position," with three voices articulating a complete triad and spanning less than an octave (encompassing $\frac{5}{3}$, $\frac{6}{3}$, and $\frac{6}{4}$), the "doubled interval" position in which two adjacent voices sound the same pitch with the third note less than an octave away, and a "half open" position in which two voices are an octave apart with the third voice between them.[21]

If we require that voices sound at least two distinct pitch classes, and that adjacent voices be separated by an octave or less, then there are two other possibilities, the "open" configuration where the voices sound a complete triad, with each voice two triadic steps above the next-lowest voice, and the "open octave" position where two voices are an octave apart with the third note outside this interval, less than an octave from the nearest voice. This yields the five possibilities of Figure 3.5.1. These can be divided into the complete triadic voicings (close and open) and incomplete voicings in which one note is doubled (doubled interval, half open, open octave). Within categories, configurations are related by octave displacements: we can turn DI into H, C into O, and H into OO, by transposing the middle voice by octave. As mentioned in the prelude to this chapter, these generalized hand positions are vertical configurations measured along the intrinsic scale defined by the voicing's notes.[22]

Though these categories were originally designed to describe the upper voices of four-voice figured-bass accompaniments, we can repurpose them for counterpoint in three voices. Once again we describe three-voice music using a center

---

[21] See Buelow 1992 and Bach (1762) 1949. Robert Gauldin (1997) calls my "half open" configuration the "open/octave" position.

[22] For example, imagine we form a scale containing two notes in all possible octaves (i.e., ... C3, G3, C4, G4 ...). Measured in steps along that scale, DI is 001 or 011 and corresponds to collections like C3, C3, G3 or G3, G3, C4. In this same scale H is 012 (i.e., C3, G3, C4 or C3, G3, G4) while OO is 013 (C3, G3, G4) and 023 (C3, C4 G4). For C and O, we form a scale containing three distinct notes in every octave (i.e., ... C3, E3, G3, C4, E4, G4 ...). Three consecutive notes in that scale form a close-position triad (C, or 012 in steps along that scale), while three notes such as C3, G3, E4 form an open-position triad (O or 024).

**Figure 3.5.2.** The Kyrie of William Byrd's Mass in Three Voices (~1591).

of gravity and an upper-voice configuration. In Figure 3.5.2 the center of gravity undulates gently, rising from 60.33 to 62.33 in m. 5, descending to 58.33 in m. 7, and ending near its starting point on 60. Meanwhile upper voices are largely in O and OO positions, with just three shifts to C in mm. 3–4 and 8.[23] The four O→O voice leadings move their roots by fifth, taking two steps on the triadic circle. The open-octave chords always move to complete triads, usually open but occasionally close. Most of the open-octave chords are doubled thirds, with the exception of the two doubled fifths in the final phrase.

This pedagogical theory of "hand positions" maps more-or-less directly onto the concepts of set theory and musical geometry. Figure 3.5.3 shows all possible diatonic three-voice consonances: as in Figure 3.3.9, one-step angular motion represents the basic voice leading, increasing or decreasing the center of gravity by one third of a diatonic step; radial motion, meanwhile, corresponds to changes of vertical configuration.[24] Though the figure looks similar to the earlier dyadic graph, it is in fact somewhat more abstract, its radial dimension modeling a space that is intrinsically two-dimensional. Figure 3.5.4 presents a more faithful representation of the two-dimensional cross section of the three-dimensional space of ordered diatonic trichords. Here our five consonant configurations are disjoint regions arranged left-to-right, while changes in center of gravity move in the third

---

[23] The chord at the end of m. 4 is either half-open or open, depending on how we read the melodic A4–G4–A4 figure (§5.1).

[24] For instance, the descending basic voice leading moves (D, D, A) or (1, 1, 5) to (C, F, F) or (0, 3, 3), changing the chord's sum from 7 to 6 and the center of gravity from 2.33 to 2.

122 TONALITY: AN OWNER'S MANUAL

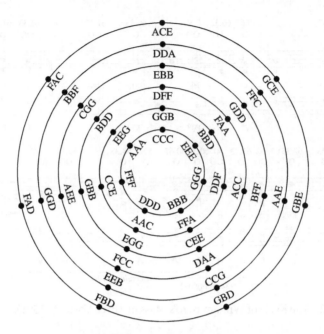

**Figure 3.5.3.** An abstract model of three-voice diatonic counterpoint.

dimension, out of the page.[25] Once again, there is a direct line from figured-bass terminology to set theory and geometry: thinking in vertical configurations *is* geometrical thinking, with terms like "close position" corresponding to compact regions in the space of musical possibility.

We can sharpen our understanding of these configurations by considering the issue of parallel perfect intervals. One close-position triad can move to another without creating parallels except when both are in root position. Similarly, open-position triads can be linked without parallels except when both are in root position or both are in first inversion. Half-open chords can progress to half-open chords only when the outer-voice octave stays fixed. Doubled-interval and open-octave positions are slightly more flexible, since the doubling can shift voices; however, such motions are rare.[26] As a general rule, then, we can expect that three-voice progressions will conform to the map on Figure 3.5.1—either moving from close to close, open to open, or horizontally by one step. Thus DI typically moves to C, OO moves to O, and H moves to C or O. About 75% of the three-voice transitions in Palestrina and Victoria follow these rules; for Josquin the number is closer to 70% as crossings are more common.[27]

---

[25] Again, efficient voice leading requires small changes in configuration: when every voice moves efficiently, the total configuration moves by short distances on the graph.

[26] For example, (D4, D4, F4) → (C4, E4, E4).

[27] Readers might notice that this figure is remarkably similar to the graph of two-note consonances (Figure P3.4), with close position playing the role of thirds and open position playing the role of sixths—a curious and largely coincidental resonance between two rather different music-theoretical constructions.

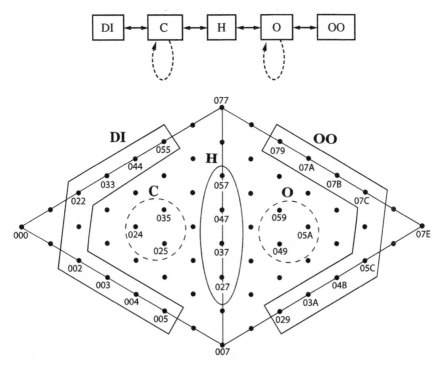

Figure 3.5.4. The five three-voice hand positions correspond to regions in trichordal ordered pitch space. These contain all configurations of three diatonic voices ordered in pitch with no two adjacent voices more than an octave apart.

Theorists since Zarlino have enjoined composers to write complete triads whenever possible.[28] However, three-voice composition involves an unusually strong tension between harmony and melody: the desire for harmonic richness pushes toward complete triads, while the desire for melodic elegance pulls toward incomplete sonorities. As a result, *doubled thirds* are more common than first-inversion triads (Figure 3.5.5). One might say that the fundamental three-voice triadic harmony is the third, which is accompanied either by a fifth, a doubling, or a sixth (in that order). Furthermore, it is a mathematical fact that any three-voice voice leading between consonant diatonic sonorities will have two voices connecting imperfect consonances unless one of the sonorities contains no imperfect consonances at all.[29] This means that three-voice voice leadings will often have two voices behaving according to the "imperfect system" of §3.1, moving between imperfect consonances by some combination of parallel motion, voice crossings, and a basic voice leading.

---

[28] Zarlino (1558) 1968, Schubert 2008.
[29] A three-voice diatonic consonance contains either zero or two imperfect consonances. If both chords in the voice leading contain two consonances, then at most one of the three pairs of voices in each chord contains an interval that is not an imperfect consonance. So the third pair must contain an imperfect consonance in both chords.

| | Ockeghem | Josquin | Palestrina |
|---|---|---|---|
| **3, 5** | 26 | 29 | 35 |
| **3** | 29 | 29 | 27 |
| **3, 6** | 20 | 19 | 19 |
| **5** | 11 | 11 | 7 |
| **6** | 8 | 7 | 7 |
| **4, 6** | 3 | 3 | 4 |
| **1** | 3 | 3 | 1 |

**Figure 3.5.5.** Configurations of three-voice consonances in a range of Renaissance music; numbers are percentages with each column adding to 100 (within rounding).

It can sometimes be useful to attend to these voices. In Byrd's "Kyrie," for example, we find that the first two phrases share the dyadic sequence (F, A) → (E, G) → (F, A) → (D, B♭)→ (F, A), with the lower voice moving from bass to tenor in the repeat: we begin with I–V$^6$–I–IV$^6$–(vii°)–I, with the parenthesized chord the basic voice leading's resolving tritone; in the repeat, the new bass line instead gives us I–V–I–ii–vii$^{o6}$–I. It is easy to imagine that Byrd heard the V chord in the second phrase as being similar to the V$^6$ in the first, and the IV–(vii°) pair as analogous to ii–vii$^{o6}$, a modal precursor to inversional equivalence arising from dyadic voice leading. The third phrase, meanwhile, is less dyadic and functional, featuring a descending 6–5 progression overlapping with a series of ascending fifths.[30] The sequence should lead back to (D, F) → (C♯, E) in the outer voices, but the middle voice instead leaps to take the bass's role, allowing for a root-position cadence. As a whole, the piece is a nice example of triadic music's ability to juggle different logics, moving from dyadic organization in the first two phrases to triadic organization in the third.

Our five upper-voice configurations are sufficient to represent any consonant three-voice diatonic voice leading in which adjacent voices do not cross and are no more than an octave apart. We can model voice crossings by considering the three fundamental voice exchanges that swap a chord's adjacent pitch classes along equal and opposite paths: for the triad, these are the two-step voice exchanges that swap root and third or swap third and fifth, and the three-step voice exchange that swaps root and fifth (Figure 3.5.6). Voice crossings are fairly rare in the Renaissance and even rarer in later music.[31] Furthermore, there is a tendency for the ear to filter out crossings, associating voices registrally rather than by instrument.[32] Nevertheless, these are important possibilities that we sometimes need to consider. Readers who care about contemporary music might find it interesting that the five positions

---

[30] As discussed in §5.2, I consider the $^6_4$ chord to be harmonic. The phrase also features a conspicuous point of imitation, with the middle voice picking up the top voice's "Kyrie" a bar later.

[31] A simple computer survey suggests they occur in less than 3% of Renaissance voice leadings. See also Huron 1991.

[32] Huron 2016.

**Figure 3.5.6.** (*top*) The three basic pairwise voice crossings, exchanging root and third, third and fifth, and root and fifth. (*bottom*) We can factor any triadic voice leading into a combination of a crossing-free voice leading (here connecting close-position E minor and B diminished triads) plus a series of pairwise voice exchanges.

discussed here, when conceived as patterns of spacing-along-a-chord, can be applied to any trichord in any scale.

## PART 3. FOUR VOICES

### 6. Four-voice triadic counterpoint

While two- and three-voice counterpoint can be usefully analyzed using spiral diagrams, four voices require a different approach. This is because the spiral diagrams model doubly parallel motion along both chord and scale. Any appearance of contrary motion is thus a byproduct of the unevenness in the chord's internal structure, and in some sense not counterpoint at all.[33] Genuine contrary motion instead arises from motion between chord types (represented by the different rings on Figures 3.3.6 or 3.5.3) or voice exchanges (represented by the curved arrows on Figure 3.2.1). Thus triadic counterpoint has to change as we add voices: with two or three voices, composers have access to multiple types of consonance, but with four or more voices, they are largely restricted to a single sonority and hence more reliant on voice exchanges.[34] Historically, two and three voices often feature in counterpoint classes, with four voices relegated to the domain of harmony; at a

---

[33] When a chord divides the scalar octave exactly evenly, "spacing in chordal steps" is equivalent to "spacing in scale steps." As the chord divides the octave less and less evenly, the two notions diverge.

[34] It is interesting to ask whether (C, G) and (C, C, E) should be considered sonorities in their own right or subsets of a triad; Renaissance and functional composers would likely give different answers.

126   TONALITY: AN OWNER'S MANUAL

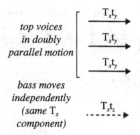

**Figure 3.6.1.** A schematic diagram of C→C and O→O counterpoint.

more fundamental level, however, this is a difference within counterpoint itself, a boundary we inevitably cross when the number of voices increases beyond the size of our harmonies.

The philosophical implications of this change will be discussed in the next section. Here I want to introduce a simple and broadly useful strategy for writing in four voices: modeling the upper three voices as in the previous section, and treating the bass as an independent actor. Thus the top voices can be conceived as moving along Figure 3.5.1, typically from C to C, O to O, or between adjacent positions such as DI and C. The most common situation has the upper voices moving from close position to close position, or open position to open position; this produces the situation in Figure 3.6.1, where two groups of voices articulate different dual transpositions—three upper voices moving in doubly parallel motion along both chord and scale, and a bass moving independently.[35] This reduces the four voices to two fundamental lines, alto and tenor shadowing soprano in a nonobvious fashion.

Figure 3.6.2 shows the distribution of upper-voice configurations in the four-voice passages from Palestrina's masses and J. S. Bach's chorales. Palestrina's upper voices are generally close, concentrated toward the left side of the graph, while Bach focuses on the C↔H↔O subsystem. (This reflects the greater importance of voice crossings in Palestrina.) Figure 3.6.3 shows the most popular triadic upper-voice transitions in the chorales: more than 30% connect close-position triads, with another 12% connecting open to open; the next seven transitions connect adjacent positions on the model. The only surprise is the frequency of motion between C and O, which is slightly more popular than motion to and from the open-octave position.

Figure 3.6.4 updates our upper-voice model by incorporating C↔O transitions and relabeling DI and OO as "U" for Unusual. When I teach Bach-style harmony, I use the mnemonic "OUCH theory" to refer to these possibilities, providing students with a simple and symmetrical set of guidelines: $U_{DI}$ goes to C, C goes anywhere except $U_{OO}$, H goes to C or O, O goes anywhere except $U_{DI}$, and $U_{DI}$ goes to O. (In these contexts, the "U" label is useful in producing a snappy mnemonic while reinforcing the configurations' rarity.) I introduce the configurations gradually, asking that students first use only close-position triads, then only open position,

---

[35] This is comparable to Figure 2.1.8, only now with a wider range of inversions in the bass.

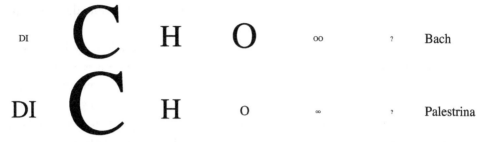

Figure 3.6.2. Upper-voice configurations in the four-voice passages of Bach's chorales and Palestrina's mass movements; size is proportional to frequency.

| voice leading | % of total |
|---|---|
| C→C | 31.8 |
| O→O | 11.8 |
| C→H | 9.1 |
| H→C | 8.5 |
| H→O | 4.6 |
| O→H | 4.3 |
| C→DI | 3.6 |
| DI→C | 3.5 |
| H→H | 3.3 |
| O→C | 3.1 |
| C→O | 2.8 |
| OO→O | 1.7 |
| O→OO | 1.6 |

Figure 3.6.3. The most popular triadic upper-voice transitions in Bach's chorales.

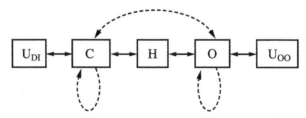

Figure 3.6.4. A grammar of triadic upper-voice configurations, extended to allow for C↔O transitions. DI and OO have been relabeled as Unusual (U) to reflect their rarity in Bach.

128 TONALITY: AN OWNER'S MANUAL

then open and close, and finally open, close, and half open. Only after they are comfortable with these possibilities do I introduce the rest.

These rules account for about 85% of the four-voice triadic voice leadings in the Bach chorales and about 75% of those in the four-voice passages of Palestrina's masses. The approach simplifies the long lists of voice leadings sometimes found in textbooks, allowing students to produce idiomatic part-writing with a minimum of pain: the focus on upper-voice configurations helps them avoid parallels, encourages them to think about spacing, and gives them a *positive* set of options to pursue.[36] They know, for example, that if they are in H position they will be moving to either C or O on the next chord; furthermore, they know that it is impossible for upper voices to form parallel octaves when following these rules, and unlikely for them to form parallel fifths.[37] The rules generalize traditional figured-bass pedagogy, extending its upper-voice configurations to *all possible arrangements* (consistent with the principles of good spacing), and not just those that lie comfortably under the hand. More importantly, they clarify that changes in one line have implications for the others, arising from norms of vertical spacing.

It can be instructive to label vertical configurations in preexisting pieces. Let us imagine that Bach began composing Figure 3.6.5 with the bass and harmony—perhaps improvising at the keyboard while paying particular attention to the outer voices. Now observe that the upper voices use a default, close-position harmonization right up to the point at which this would produce parallels (C♯–D in the tenor and bass). Here he shifts to the half-open position by moving the tenor down one triadic step, to A rather than D. At this point one might expect him to return to close position, but given his harmonic choices, this would double the leading tone and produce an augmented fourth in the tenor. A second half-open voicing would create parallel octaves while O and $U_{DI}$ are equally problematic; Bach's best option is to move the tenor down another triadic step to F♯ and an open-octave voicing. At this point, he is free to return to close position, which he does for the rest of the phrase. So far there is nothing particularly marvelous about the individual melodies; it is only when Bach seizes the opportunity to add tenor-voice passing tones that the counterpoint comes alive, transforming an awkward harmonic skeleton into something attractive. "OUCH theory" provides a plausible if speculative genealogy of the passage—one that suggests how an attention to vertical configurations can help create a genuine counterpoint of melodic lines. My suspicion is that composers rarely if ever conceive of counterpoint in purely linear terms, always keeping one eye on the subtle play of vertical configurations.

The "Hosanna" from Palestrina's *Spem in alium* mass evinces similar thinking in a different style. On Figure 3.6.6 I have labeled the upper-voice configuration

---

[36] For examples of long lists of options, see Kostka and Payne 2003, who borrow from McHose 1947.

[37] For example a DI↔C transition can produce parallel fifths only if moving between a close, root position triad and a fifth with one note doubled; H↔O transitions can produce parallel fifths only between adjacent voices, as in (**D4, A4, D5**) → (**C4, G4, E5**).

**Figure 3.6.5.** A hypothetical derivation of the opening of J. S. Bach's "Ich dank' dich, lieber Herr" (BWV 347, Riemenschneider 2).

of every four-voice chord, marking crossings with a ×. The passage is divided into five phrases, each supporting a repetition of the text ("Hosanna in excelsis") and featuring a motive that moves from an ascending interval (usually a step, occasionally a third) to a stepwise descent. Overall, about 65% of the chords are in close position, 14% open, and 11% half open, with the doubled interval and open-octave positions together accounting for 5% of the sonorities; the only move not on Figure 3.6.4 is the m. 18 leap from C to OO. The first, third, and fourth phrases exhibit a similar structure, starting with widely separated voices and moving to a close-position cadence: we have O→H→C in the first and fourth phrase, and OO→O→H→C→DI in the third, systematically enumerating the five positions. In each case, the compression of the voices is driven by an inner-voice entry of the "Hosanna" motive. Harmonically, the music is suffused with retrofunctional progressions: ascending fifths (especially the six connecting B♭ major to E major in mm. 20–23), ascending thirds (F–a–C in mm. 14–15), and ascending and descending steps. This is a beautiful example of counterpoint leading harmony, an idiomatic Renaissance analogue to the patterns we found in rock.

130  TONALITY: AN OWNER'S MANUAL

Figure 3.6.6. The "Hosanna" from Palestrina's mass *Spem in alium*.

OUCH theory works because upper voices often form complete triads while the bass moves independently. This naturally raises the vexed question of doublings. Bret Aarden and Paul T. von Hippel have produced an astonishing survey of pedagogical advice on the subject, considering forty different texts, all of which seem to disagree.[38] A particular focus of controversy is the permissibility of doubling the bass in first-inversion major triads such as I⁶; the question is whether these chords can support upper voices in C or O position, or whether they should instead use one of the other configurations. For all the theoretical disagreement, compositional practice is surprisingly clear: Figure 3.6.7 shows that in Bach's chorales, the bass is the most frequently doubled note except when it is a leading tone.[39] And in Palestrina's masses we find something even more remarkable. If we conceive vertical configurations as combining bass, middle element (a third or fourth above the bass), and top (fifth or sixth), then Palestrina's practice is to double the bass most

---

[38] Aarden and von Hippel 2004.
[39] Note that the bass is doubled if and only if the upper voices are in C or O position.

| | Bach | | | Palestrina | | |
|---|---|---|---|---|---|---|
| | bass | 3 or 4 | 5 or 6 | bass | 3 or 4 | 5 or 6 |
| I | 92 | 7 | 2 | 84 | 10 | 6 |
| I⁶ | 50 | 27 | 23 | 55 | 30 | 15 |
| I⁶₄ | 75 | 7 | 18 | 96 | 4 | 0 |
| ii | 72 | 21 | 6 | 81 | 14 | 5 |
| ii⁶ | 55 | 26 | 19 | 51 | 43 | 6 |
| iii | 64 | 32 | 3 | 78 | 21 | 1 |
| iii⁶ | 85 | 2 | 12 | 83 | 11 | 6 |
| IV | 73 | 19 | 7 | 76 | 15 | 9 |
| IV⁶ | 64 | 18 | 18 | 49 | 49 | 2 |
| V | 91 | 2 | 7 | 94 | 3 | 3 |
| V⁶ | 7 | 48 | 45 | 12 | 64 | 24 |
| vi | 64 | 31 | 5 | 54 | 39 | 6 |
| vi⁶ | 64 | 26 | 10 | 83 | 14 | 2 |
| vii° | 3 | 94 | 3 | 80 | 20 | 0 |
| vii°⁶ | 71 | 28 | 1 | 60 | 40 | 0 |

**Figure 3.6.7.** Doublings in four-voice passages in J. S. Bach's chorales and selected Palestrina masses. Each number is a percentage representing the proportion of chords of that type with the given doubling.

often, the middle element next, and the top last.[40] The major exception is $V^6$, where the leading tone is less likely to be doubled. Palestrina's reluctance to double the top voice may reflect its status as an active or variable note, free to move between fifth and sixth while still forming a consonance; doubling this note would eliminate that freedom by turning one of these options into a dissonance.

I know of no substantial body of music that avoids doubling the bass of first-inversion chords. Certainly, the practice of Palestrina and Bach quashes any attempt to ground this supposed prohibition in acoustics or aesthetics: Palestrina and Bach knew a good deal about sonority, and it is reasonable to follow their practice rather than the opinions of pedagogues.[41] My own suspicion, shared by Gottfried Weber, is that the avoidance of the doubled third arose not out of aesthetics but rather out of the exigencies of figured-bass realization: here doubling the bass of a first-inversion chord can lead the unwary improviser into parallels, and the half-open position generally allows for more melodic options (Figure 3.6.8).[42] It is possible that this purely pragmatic consideration gradually acquired an illusory aesthetic weight, mutating into an analytically unsupportable prohibition on doubled thirds.

---

[40] Huron 2016 tries to derive doubling practices from principles of upper-voice spacing, but he exaggerates the rarity of the DI position; in Palestrina, DI is very common, and in Bach, it is reasonably common. I describe it as "unusual" only in a pedagogical context.

[41] Aarden and von Hippel 2004 contains a good summary of the justifications given for various doubling rules. Schoenberg ([1911] 1983, p. 59) argues that the doubled third is acoustically defective.

[42] Weber (1817–1821) 1846, pp. 190–92.

**Figure 3.6.8.** Using half-open chords to avoid parallels. In the first measure, upper-voice close-position triads create parallels between bass and alto; replacing the second close-position triad with a half-open voicing removes the problem.

## 7. Thinking within the chord

The heuristics in the previous section divide bass from upper voices in a way that may be untrue to a piece's intrinsic organization. This is not necessarily a problem for the practitioner, as they generate a very wide range of musical possibilities—again, all those voice leadings without voice crossings in pitch space and in which upper voices are no more than an octave from their neighbors. But they are theoretically unsatisfactory, allowing us to produce four-voice counterpoint without necessarily understanding it very deeply.

We can obtain a richer perspective by allowing for more flexible groupings of voices, so that any pair or triple can move in doubly parallel motion. The first passage in Figure 3.7.1 uses the standard OUCH strategy, the three upper voices moving against an independent bass; the second instead groups voices into pairs; while the third groups the bottom three voices together. The soprano and bass are the same in each passage; the only difference is which voice the inner voices follow. Underneath I identify the motion of voices inside the triad ($t_x$) and the motion of the triad inside the scale ($T_x$). We can assign these to different musical levels, imagining the chord to move along the scale in the background while the voices move along the chord in the foreground.

In other cases, we might want to postulate background voice leadings that themselves combine transposition along chord and scale: abstract voices that function as scale degrees along which the surface voices move. Back in Figure 1.2.1, we saw upper voices ascending along a three-note scale that participated in the "omnibus" schema—a pattern so familiar and commonplace that it is recognizable despite the right-hand figuration. In that example, an upper-voice melody moved along a triadic background that itself moved by $t_1 T_{-3}$ from the start of one sequential unit to the next. Figure 3.7.2 uses this strategy to analyze the opening of Beethoven's *Waldstein*. On the bottom staff we have a triadic background that generates three scale degrees which I number from bottom to top: abstract voice 1 descends semitonally, sounding C–B–B♭–A, while abstract voices 2 and 3 descend in whole steps, sounding E–D–D–C and G–G–F–F respectively. The pianist's left hand is stationary relative to this structure, its motion entirely produced by the background. The surface voices of the right hand,

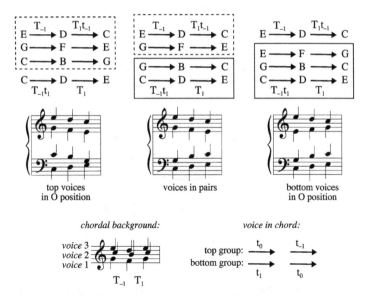

Figure 3.7.1. Three progressions grouping voices in different ways. In each case, the top group moves by $T_{-1}$ and $T_1 t_{-1}$ while the bottom group moves by $T_{-1} t_1$ and $T_1$. Underneath, I analyze these motions as combining motion of chordal background inside scale, and motion of voices inside chordal background.

Figure 3.7.2. The opening of the *Waldstein*. The background voice leading is shown in the lowest staff, creating three abstract scale degrees. The left hand always sounds degrees 1 and 3 while the right hand ascends along this three-note scale.

meanwhile, ascend along the background to form a chain of ascending thirds E–G–B–D–F–A–C, with the alto one or two chordal steps below the soprano.[43] (For simplicity, my analysis omits the tonicizations of G and F, which exploit the

---

[43] A fact that first came to my attention a few years back, when I awoke from a deep sleep, sat bolt upright in the middle of the night, and said to myself, "Holy cow, how did I never notice the ascending thirds in the *Waldstein*?" Whereupon my waking self had to reconstruct this analysis to figure out what I meant.

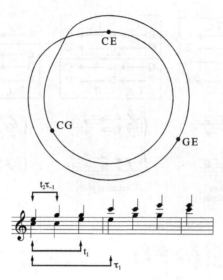

**Figure 3.7.3.** The spiral diagram for two voices inside a three-note triad. Here t represents transposition along the triad while τ represents transposition along the dyad.

diatonic third's ascending basic voice leading; I also rectify octave displacements to show the continuing pattern of ascending thirds.) Familiar chromaticism is here embellished hierarchically, the stepwise voice leading sublimated into the background.

We can model this geometrically with the smallest nontrivial spiral diagram, that of two voices moving within a triad. Its basic voice leading moves the voices by alternating triadic step, producing a series of one- and two-step verticalities (Figure 3.7.3). Beethoven's right hand outlines a series of short counterclockwise motions in this space, moving between thirds, fourths, and fifths while the left hand remains motionless (Figure 3.7.4). This, however, only represents the voices' motion *within* the triadic background. To represent the background's motion, we need a second spiral diagram representing triads in chromatic space. This background is very similar to the models in chapter 2, now augmented by an additional hierarchical layer that creates an expanding wedge. For the first time we need *two* diagrams rather than a single spiral on its own. This hierarchical depth is characteristic of four-voice music.

I call this *thinking within the chord*: an abstract chorale provides scale-like collections within which surface voices move. One can imagine a metaphorical harp (or autoharp) sounding a chord's notes in every octave, providing a field of contrapuntal play.[44] Those

---

[44] Autoharps play triads, which are the collections relevant to this discussion, but provide no voice leading from one chord to the next; harps supply voice leadings via their pedals, but sound seven-note collections.

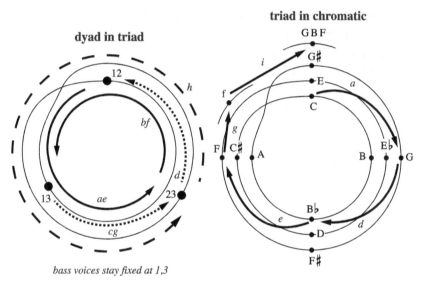

**Figure 3.7.4.** The *Waldstein* opening plotted on a pair of spiral diagrams. Letters above the music correspond to labeled paths on the diagrams. Here there are three levels of transposition: τ refers to transposition along the right-hand dyad, t to transposition along the triad, and T to chromatic transposition.

slots shift as the chord changes, typically by efficient voice leading; the surface voices' motion-within-the-chord is unperturbed by the shifts, like a melodic sequence inside a modulating scale (e.g., Figure 1.2.5). This description resonates with the Schenkerian insight that voice leading often takes place in a musical "background" simultaneously real and yet not always obvious in the score. More specifically, it allows us to implement the Schenkerian strategy of relegating doublings and voice exchanges to the surface, as artifacts of voices moving within a simpler background.[45] My approach gives

---

[45] Previous theorists have tried to translate Schenker's metaphors of "surface" and "depth" into perceptual terms, postulating that humans naturally experience harmony in hierarchical fashion (Lerdahl and Jackendoff 1983, Lerdahl 2001, and Rohrmeier 2020).

## 136   TONALITY: AN OWNER'S MANUAL

**Figure 3.7.5.** The opening of *Tristan*. The lower staff shows a background voice leading with voices or scale degrees numbered from bottom to top. The melodic "Desire" motif ascends along these scale degrees, sounding voice 1, voice 2, voice 3, voice 4, and then voice 1 in a higher octave.

nonmetaphysical meaning to the claim that the right-hand B3 and D4 in mm. 3–4 of the *Waldstein* are "the same" as the left-hand B2 and D3—that is, the same abstract scale degrees articulated by different concrete voices.

The *Waldstein*'s ascending thirds are produced by voices ascending within a tertian background that slowly descends. The *Tristan* prelude opens with a similar chain of ascending thirds arising in a similar way (Figure 3.7.5); the technique reappears at the prelude's climax when the outer voices expand in an uncontrolled frenzy (Figure 3.7.6).[46] In later chapters we will encounter analogous passages in Chopin's "Revolutionary" Etude (§9.3), Schubert's *Quartettsatz* (§10.6), the prelude to Wagner's *Lohengrin* (§10.7), and, in the conclusion, a composition exercise of my own devising. These are all structurally analogous to the *Waldstein*, ascending melodic thirds refracting the tertian structure of standard harmony through the distorting lens of a nontrivial background.

OUCH theory thus treats as universal what is really just one particular way of organizing musical lines, setting bass against upper voices; this is why it struggles when voices are divided into pairs or when the soprano is opposed to the lower voices. With more parts come even more possibilities: the first forty-voice voice leading in Thomas Tallis's *Spem in alium* traces a very large number of paths from G major to C major (Figure 3.7.7). It would boggle the mind to try to analyze this progression in forty-note chord space where every triad appears more than fifty thousand times, each corresponding to a different doubling. Much more intuitive is the idea that the forty voices move *within* a shifting three-note scalar field, pursuing their own independent combinations of scalar and chordal transposition. As in Figure 3.7.1, we can

---

[46] Milton Babbitt (1987, p. 148) emphasized that the opening of *Tristan* spells out a "Tristan" chord in its upper voice (G#–B–D–F# on Figure 3.7.5). I see this as the byproduct of the same general relationships that produce the ascending thirds in the *Waldstein*.

LINE AND CONFIGURATION  137

**Figure 3.7.6.** The climax of the *Tristan* prelude, mm. 77–83. The lowest staff shows the background against which the outer voices move.

imagine harmonies moving in parallel along the scale ($T_y$) while voices move inside them ($t_x$).[47]

There are three basic points here. The first is that as a very general matter, triadic counterpoint in four or more voices often sets groups of voices against one another: bass in contrary motion to the upper voices, soprano and alto against tenor and bass, and so forth. The second point is that over the course of Western music history composers seem to have become increasingly aware of the hierarchical possibilities inherent in this arrangement, writing music in which surface voices move along abstract backgrounds whose scale degrees themselves articulate nontrivial voice leadings, a significant musical development occurring within the functional era. The third point, which will be the focus of chapter 8, is that functional tonality adds yet another hierarchical level, with voices moving inside scale-like chords that move within seven-note scales that are themselves modulating through chromatic space: wheels within wheels, spiral diagrams nested like the epicycles of Ptolemaic astronomy.

---

[47] Schubert 2018 proposes a similar analysis.

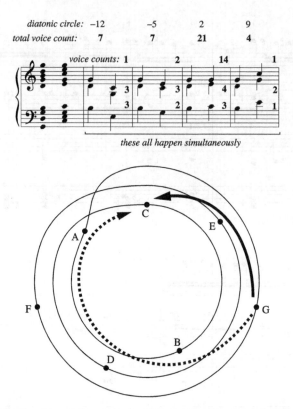

**Figure 3.7.7.** The first forty-voice voice leading in *Spem in alium*. Boldface numbers show how many voices sound each interval. The voices together articulate four voice leadings on the triadic circle, two of which are shown: the clockwise five-step path and the counterclockwise two-step path (labeled –5 and 2 on the figure). The remaining paths, labeled –12 and 9, can be obtained by sliding counterclockwise and clockwise along the spiral respectively. Together, the four voice leadings contain all the intervals in which voices move by fifth or less.

## 8. Seventh chords

A diatonic seventh chord contains a fifth between root and fifth, and another fifth between third and seventh. Figure 3.8.1 shows that as we move clockwise along the spiral, we apply a basic voice leading to each of the fifth-pairs in turn. It is as if the seventh-chord diagram divides the dyadic fifth-diagram in half: two steps on the seventh-chord diagram takes one step on each fifth-pair's dyadic diagram; where the fifth's basic voice leading links fifth-related harmonies, the seventh's basic voice leading links third-related harmonies, with the diatonic third being half the diatonic fifth.

Because of this, seventh chords again allow for a seamless integration of melodic and functional-harmonic logic: where clockwise steps in triadic space feature ascending-third roots, clockwise steps in seventh-chord space produce

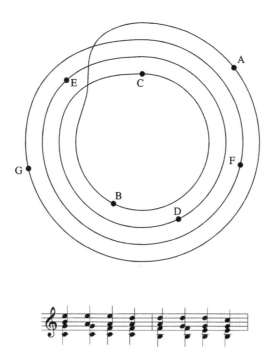

**Figure 3.8.1.** Clockwise one-step motion on the circle of diatonic sevenths produces a sequence of descending-third progressions in which the seventh descends ($T_{-2}t_1$). Two-step motion produces descending-fifth progressions ($T_{-4}t_2$, e.g., from $C^{maj7}$ to $F^{maj4}_3$), while three-step motion produces ascending steps ($T_{-6}t_3$, $C^{maj7}$ to $D^{maj2}$). The stems show that the four-voice voice leadings can be factored into two pairs of voices each articulating the diatonic fifth's basic voice leading.

**Figure 3.8.2.** "All the Things You Are" outlines the descending-fifth sequence of seventh chords. Open noteheads show melodic tones.

*descending-third* root progressions; two clockwise steps make a descending fifth. This geometry is the basis of many familiar songs: "All the Things You Are" oscillates between the notes of one fifth-pair in the descending-fifth sequence, descending by almost a complete octave (Figure 3.8.2); songs like "Autumn Leaves" have a very similar structure. Rock and pop occasionally use the same strategy, as in "I Will Survive" (Figure 3.8.3), where the melody descends stepwise from tonic to subdominant before ascending. This is exactly the sort of pattern we found in chapter 2, only now with seventh chords rather

**Figure 3.8.3.** "I Will Survive," written by Freddie Perren and Dino Fekaris and sung by Gloria Gaynor, also follows the descending-fifth logic. During the C major chord, the melody descends to a lower voice.

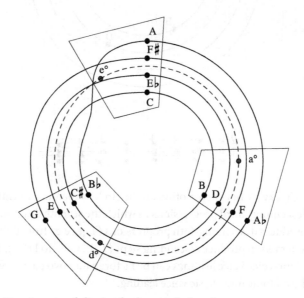

**Figure 3.8.4.** Dominant and diminished seventh chords.

than triads. The addition of a fourth voice magically converts retrofunctionality into functionality.

Meanwhile, the space of *chromatic* sevenths is vital to understanding a range of nineteenth- and twentieth-century idioms. Figure 3.8.4 superimposes the circular voice-leading spaces for dominant and diminished seventh chords. The trapezoidal boxes enclose dominant sevenths sharing three notes with the same diminished seventh, a relation that lends them a degree of harmonic similarity. The situation here is intermediate between the space of chromatic triads (where nearby chords, like C major and E major, can be harmonically quite different) and diatonic triads (where nearby chords are harmonically similar): minor-third- and tritone-related dominant sevenths, while not quite equivalent, have a definite harmonic resemblance.[48]

---

[48] Erno Lendvai (1971) argues that major or minor chords have the same function when their roots belong to the same diminished seventh, at least in Bartók's music. I find this somewhat plausible in the case of dominant-functioning chords, less so in the case of tonic and subdominant.

E: ct°⁷   V⁷   E♭: vii°²   V⁷   D: vii°⁷/V   V⁷

**Figure 3.8.5.** Motion from diminished to dominant seventh: one counterclockwise step corresponds to the "common-tone" resolution (+3); in-box clockwise motion preserves three common tones and can function as vii°⁷–V⁷ (−1); one out-of-box clockwise step corresponds to an authentic resolution (−5).

F: V⁷   V⁴₃/V   e: Ger⁶₅   V⁷   F: V⁷   V²/ii   F: V⁷   D♭: V⁴₃

**Figure 3.8.6.** One-step clockwise motion from one dominant seventh to another. This produces either an authentic resolution, its tritone substitution, a deceptive motion from V⁷ to V²/ii, or a descending major-third progression.

Progressions from a diminished seventh to its in-box dominant-seventh neighbors can function as vii°⁷–V⁷, with a single voice descending by semitone. Clockwise motion from diminished seventh to the nearest out-of-box dominants produce authentic resolutions, usually acting as vii°⁷/V–V⁷. Counterclockwise steps, meanwhile, are the "common-tone resolutions" of second-semester theory, with three voices ascending by semitone; the counterclockwise direction reflects the progressions' predominantly ascending voice leading. Figure 3.8.5 shows that these familiar voice leadings are all equivalent under the Tinctoris Transform, differing only in the transposition of the destination chord.

One-step clockwise motion between dominant sevenths produces the four quasi-authentic voice leadings in Figure 3.8.6. Three of them are reasonably common: the first is a standard descending-fifth progression between dominant sevenths, while the second is its tritone substitution, initially associated with the resolution of the German augmented sixth. The third, (C, E, G, B♭)→ (C, D, F♯, A), occasionally functions as a deceptive resolution, particularly in J. S. Bach (V⁷→V²/ii in the old key, IV⁷→V² in the new).[49] The final progression (C, E, G, B♭)→ (C, E♭, G♭, A♭) is quite unusual, and I do not know of many examples from the literature. All four feature predominantly descending voice leading and a seventh resolving down by step.

One-step counterclockwise motion produces a package of unusual resolutions that evoke the common-tone diminished seventh: each of the progressions in Figure 3.8.7 simply replaces the standard common-tone diminished chord with

---

[49] See, for example, m. 12 of the second E major fugue from *The Well-Tempered Clavier* or mm. 19, 31, and 71 of the second F major fugue.

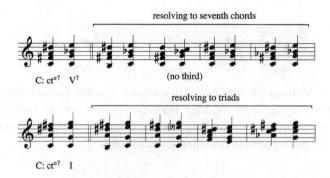

**Figure 3.8.7.** The "common-tone dominant sevenths." Each replaces a common-tone diminished seventh with a dominant seventh sharing three of its notes.

**Figure 3.8.8.** Ascending-fifth progressions in Mahler's Ninth Symphony, I, mm. 408–409, and Beethoven Op. 59, no. 3, I, mm. 42–44.

a dominant seventh sharing three of its notes. For that reason, I call these chords "common-tone dominant sevenths," even though some of the progressions feature no common tones![50] One is the reverse of the dominant-seventh resolution, with seventh rising upward to the leading tone—a dramatic deceptive motion that becomes increasingly important over the course of the nineteenth century (Figures 3.8.8–9). A second has the dominant seventh acting as a neighbor to the dominant seventh a major second below; it appears in Haydn and Mozart and has a clear resemblance to the common-tone diminished seventh (Figure 3.8.10; Figure 3.8.11 shows a variant resolving to a triad).[51] The third option, a semitonal

---

[50] The name is meant to emphasize their relation to the common-tone diminished seventh, not the presence of common tones in the actual progression. Clendinning and Marvin 2016 use the term "common-tone German sixth" to describe one of these progressions.

[51] Other examples can be found in Haydn's Symphony no. 100 ("Military"), I, mm. 195–197 (VI$^6_5$ →V$^7$), Beethoven's Symphony no. 2, I, mm. 40–43 (V$^6_5$/V→vii$^{o7}$/V→V$^4_3$/IV), and Kabalevsky's "Sonatina" (Op. 27, no. 18, mm. 33–36, II$^2$→I).

**Figure 3.8.9.** A dominant seventh on IV in Grieg (Op. 68, no. 3, mm. 26–34).

**Figure 3.8.10.** V/ii acting as a neighboring chord to $V^7$ in Mozart's C major piano sonata K.309, I, mm. 3–4.

**Figure 3.8.11.** Supertonic dominant sevenths moving directly to the tonic in Grieg (Op. 68, no. 4, mm. 52–53) and John Williams ("Hedwig's Theme" from the *Harry Potter* movies). In the last example, the common-tone dominant seventh replaces the cadential dominant.

lower neighbor, (B, D♯, F♯, A) → (C, E, G, B♭), is relatively rare, though with a triadic arrival it becomes a deceptive resolution of the dominant seventh. One of my favorite nineteenth-century idioms—perhaps the most colorful of its many altered and substitute dominants—combines this pseudo-common-tone resolution with

144   TONALITY: AN OWNER'S MANUAL

**Figure 3.8.12.** Common-tone voice leading over an authentic V–I bass: Beethoven uses this pattern in Op. 59, no. 1, I, mm. 361–362; in Chopin's Op. 50, no. 2, mm. 77–79, the common-tone diminished seventh arrives while the bass is still on $\hat{5}$, and is sustained through the tonic arrival.

a dominant-tonic bass, fusing dominant and common-tone functions (Figure 3.8.12).[52] The fourth possibility is often found with a triadic chord of resolution, usually as Ger$^6_5$ →I$^6_4$ and but occasionally as a more generic neighboring progression. Late nineteenth- and early twentieth-century American music often used these ascending resolutions to harmonize blue notes, explicitly linking them to the common-tone diminished sevenths of the classical tradition (Figure 3.8.13).

Finally, one diminished seventh can ascend semitonally to another—a move particularly characteristic of Beethoven (Figure 3.8.14).[53] In the context of the previous examples we can understand this as yet another variant of the

---

[52] This chord originates in the baroque minor-mode use of III$^{+maj7}$ as a dominant, which sometimes progresses deceptively to VI rather than i (e.g., the second C minor prelude in *The Well-Tempered Clavier*, mm. 3–4 and 24). This deceptive III–VI then becomes an authentic major-mode V–I in the nineteenth century (e.g., "Estrella" from Schumann's *Carnaval*, mm. 5–6 and again in m. 7). The major triad on VII appears in early rock-and-roll as a semitonal lower neighbor ("Jailhouse Rock"); it is interesting to try to hear a connection to these earlier idioms.

[53] Other examples include the endings of the first D major and second G major preludes in *The Well-Tempered Clavier*, m. 80 of the WTC's first A minor fugue, chorales such as BWV 40.3 (Riemenschneider 43, m. 14), 309 (R166, m. 5), 60.5 (R216, m. 5), 272 (R340, m. 3), and 248.42 (R360, m. 10), Mozart's Clarinet Concerto K.622, I, mm. 141ff, Beethoven's Op. 10, no. 3, II, mm. 5–8 (which interposes a dominant seventh between diminished sevenths), and Figures 10.3.4 and 10.4.11.

**Figure 3.8.13.** Three passages that link common-tone dominant and diminished sevenths, in contexts that evoke the blues IV$^7$: Scott Joplin's *Pine Apple Rag* (1908, mm. 2–4 of the trio); Charles Trevathan's racist "Bully Song" (1896, mm. 1–10, harmonizing ♭3 with VI$^7$ rather than IV$^7$); and Antonio Maggio's "I Got the Blues" (1908, mm. 8–11).

**Figure 3.8.14.** A semitonally ascending diminished seventh in Beethoven's Op. 2, no. 1, IV, mm. 28–29.

common-tone diminished seventh—indeed, we would hardly question the association in cases where a dominant seventh briefly intervenes between the two diminished sevenths.[54] The four-note spiral diagram thus allows us to generalize the "common-tone diminished seventh" to contexts where common tones are no longer

---

[54] I hear these diminished sevenths on $\hat{4}$ as having a dominant function which is then thwarted by the ascending-semitone resolution.

146 TONALITY: AN OWNER'S MANUAL

present, moving beyond a specific idiom to a more general form of tetrachordal retrofunctionality in which seventh chords resolve contrary to our expectations.

Our model sorts seventh-chord progressions into categories: the pseudo-authentic resolutions moving one step clockwise, the neutral voice leadings moving radially, and the retrofunctional or quasi-common-tone resolutions moving one step counterclockwise. As the nineteenth century progresses, seventh chords are gradually liberated from their contrapuntal obligations, the "dissonant" seventh increasingly permitted to ascend. This in turn allows for a more thorough exploration of tetrachordal geometry. There is, I think, a strand of nineteenth- and twentieth-century music in which the diagram's categories are analytically relevant, with minor-third-related dominants having a kind of equivalence, and clockwise and counterclockwise motion corresponding to more and less expected progressions.[55] The evolution culminates in the twentieth century, when musicians begin speaking of the intersubstitutability of minor-third and tritone-related dominants.[56]

## 9. Harmony and counterpoint

Analysts are accustomed to finding elaborate contrapuntal machinations in nineteenth-century music, where chromatic voice leading provides an alternative to functional-harmonic organization. Chapter 2 identified similar processes in the unlikely setting of popular music, describing a quasi-chromaticism in which the diatonic scale exerts greater gravitational force. This chapter has extended the argument to purely diatonic counterpoint from the sixteenth century onward, using spiral diagrams to model the interdependence of harmony and counterpoint in a range of modal and functionally tonal styles. The ubiquity of these relationships reflects the power and generality of voice-leading geometry: we can construct spiral diagrams for any chord in any scale, allowing us to observe how similar linear forces lead to different harmonic outcomes in different musical environments.

With diatonic thirds, a preference for descending melodic motion produces descending-fifth progressions and a distinct sense of functionality; indeed, a random series of short clockwise motions in the spiral diagram will tend to produce the impression of harmonic function (Figure 3.9.1). By contrast, triadic geometry associates descending melodies with retrofunctional progressions, leading to sharper conflicts between melodic and functional norms: random clockwise steps in the space of chromatic triads sound more rock than classical, while clockwise steps in the space of diatonic triads evoke the weightless progressions of the Renaissance. Four-note diatonic music once again lends itself to functionality—and indeed, this is one reason for the seventeenth-century embrace of seventh chords

---

[55] See, for example, Grieg's "Salon" (Op. 65, no. 4).
[56] See Okazaki 2015, p. 98.

**Figure 3.9.1.** Simple dyadic counterpoint randomly generated by a series of mostly clockwise steps on the dyadic circle.

**Figure 3.9.2.** A descending-fifth seventh-chord progression embedding the nonfunctional triads from "Moro Lasso." Randy Newman uses the descending-fifth progression in "When She Loved Me" from *Toy Story 2* (at "still I waited for the day").

(§7.4). Thus there is no simple relationship between linear procedure and harmonic outcome, but rather a shifting and context-dependent set of implications.

This is beautifully illustrated by the reappearance of nonfunctional triadic patterns in four-voice functional contexts: for example Randy Newman's "When She Loved Me" uses a descending-fifth sequence of seventh chords that embeds the eerie descents of Gesualdo's "Moro Lasso" (Figure 3.9.2, compare Figure 1.1.1).[57] What might initially seem like a mere curiosity instead reflects the fact that

---

[57] Thanks to Zhoushu Ziporyn for this example. Cohn 2012, p. 148, discusses Wagner's use of this progression in *Parsifal*.

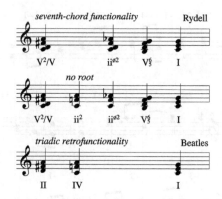

**Figure 3.9.3.** The Beatles' I–II–IV–I derived from a functional seventh-chord idiom.

descending voice leading tends to be retrofunctional with triads, but functional with seventh chords. A similar relationship connects the II–IV–I progression of "Eight Days a Week" to its functional ancestor, the $V^7/V$–$ii^{ø7}$–$V^7$–I of Bobby Rydell's "Forget Him."[58] Rydell's progression is a Romantic trope, combining a secondary dominant with so-called modal mixture and exploiting descending semitonal voice leading.[59] In translating this idiom into retrofunctional triads, the Beatles turned it into something genuinely new (Figure 3.9.3).[60] Our two examples thus move in opposite directions, Randy Newman incorporating a nonfunctional idiom within a functional progression, the Beatles drawing nonfunctional triads out of functional sevenths.

This approach contrasts with more fixed conceptions of the relation between linear and horizontal. Schenkerians tend to favor a "compatibilist" view according to which contrapuntal forces, acting on their own, inevitably generate the progressions of functional tonality.[61] Richard Cohn, meanwhile, leans toward a more *incompatibilist* outlook, proposing chromaticism and functional harmony as separate and opposed musical forces.[62] I think these perspectives each capture only part of a larger story: the relationship between horizontal and vertical is fundamentally context-dependent, with different geometrical environments providing different harmonic affordances. This in turn reflects a more general continuum of musical practice: on one side we have idioms in which counterpoint

---

[58] The first Beatles song to use II–IV is "She Loves You," presenting it as both a dominant approach and as a plagal progression in its own right; it was almost certainly influenced by Rydell's song. See Everett and Riley 2019, pp. 64–65.

[59] On modal mixture, see Tymoczko 2011a, §6.6; Rydell's idiom appears in Figure 9.3.1.

[60] The IV→VI–I progression in Otis Redding's 1965 "I've Been Loving You Too Long" is perhaps comparable, a triadic analogue of IV–iv⁷–I. The I–II–IV progression also appears at the end of Mendelssohn's Op. 120, no. 1, first as part of a "fauxbourdon ROTO" idiom (§7.5) and then in root position. The bass voice converts more-or-less idiomatic music to something more unusual.

[61] Headlam 2012 and Yust 2018, chapter 10. For the term "compatibilism" see Tymoczko 2011a, chapter 7.

[62] See Cohn 2012, pp. 199–203. Cohn's book is largely concerned with chromatic triads, focusing on an unusually retrofunctional environment. This leads him to describe the progression in Figure 3.9.2 as "feign[ing] a red-herring tonality" (2012, p. 148) rather than exemplifying the compatibility of tetrachords, descending semitonal voice leading, and functional progressions.

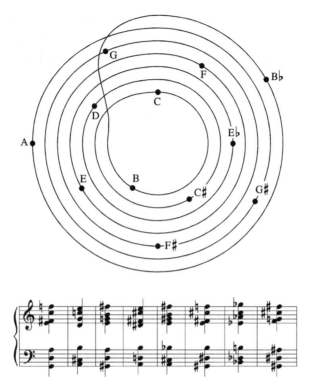

**Figure 3.9.4.** A chorale built from the basic voice leading for a seven-note chord in twelve-note space; each chord is $T_7 t_{-4}$ of its predecessor and is voiced 3, 5, 3, 2, 3, 3 in intrinsic steps.

and functional tonality work together smoothly; toward the middle, linear forces generate occasional harmonic hiccups that do not dislodge our sense of tonal functionality; and at the other extreme, we find passages that totally efface the sense of functionality and sometimes even centricity.[63] The spiral diagrams allow us to visualize this spectrum of musical practice, showing exactly how harmony and counterpoint relate.

Composers can use these ideas to explore unfamiliar combinations of chord and scale. Figure 3.9.4 uses a spiral diagram to generate a chorale from my piece *The Thousand Faces of Form*. The basic chord is a gapped stack of fifths, F–C–G–D–A–E–[B]–F♯, initially appearing with G–D–A–E in the bass and F♯–C–F at the top: a dominant-seventh sharp nine over a tonic pedal and with an additional major ninth. The chorale takes a series of clockwise steps that pass through seven inversions, repeatedly applying the basic voice leading before returning to the one-semitone transposition of the opening chord. This is abstractly parallel motion, with each chord belonging to the same set class and spaced in the same pattern of

---

[63] See §9.3. As Cohn notes, a range of figures from Dahlhaus (1967) to Lerdahl (2001) to Charles Smith (1986) advocate for a more unified perspective.

150   TONALITY: AN OWNER'S MANUAL

chordal steps—and though the progression is complex and clangorous, I hear its chords as audibly similar, reflecting their similar spacing and intervallic constitution. One could use this chorale to generate even-more-complex passages in which different groups of voices combine different transpositions along the chord $t_x$ with the same transposition along the scale $T_y$, as in §3.7. Here we start to glimpse how we might generalize traditional compositional procedures to arbitrary chord-and-scale environments, precisely as suggested by the Prime Directive.

# Prelude
## Sequence and Function

The last movement of Beethoven's *Pathétique* contains a brief tutorial in the many varieties of repetition. Its A♭-major episode opens with a *canonic sequence* whose melodic intervals move from voice to voice, the counterpoint almost entirely generated by "antiparallel" voice leading in which one voice ascends by fourth and the other descends by fifth, with the motions switching hands after every dyad. Despite this alternation of intervals, the left hand always sounds the root and the right hand the third.[1] Figure P4.1 graphs the passage on the 2-in-7 diagram, where it moves clockwise at each turn, combining the descending basic voice leading with alternating two- and five-step voice exchanges. Zooming out to the level of the bar we find a *transpositional sequence* that moves each voice down by step.

Since the diatonic scale has an odd number of notes, the voices exchange intervals when they return to the tonic: where the right hand initially ascended from C by fourth, it now descends from C by fifth, and where the left descended from A♭ by fifth, it now ascends from A♭ by fourth (Figure P4.2). The humor lies in the impression of invertible counterpoint: in the consequent, each hand plays the *intervals* of the antecedent's other hand, but on the same *notes* as before. To my ear, contour and rhythm trump pitch-class content, and the theme seems to switch hands. (The quarter-note delay contributes to this impression by directing our ears to the left hand.) The passage manages to sound trivial and brilliant at once, a paradoxical effect of "counterpoint" that is hardly worth the name.

On the brilliant side of the ledger, the final left-hand fourth is decorated by stepwise contrary motion, producing Gjerdingen's "converging cadence." In the opening, this forms a half cadence, tonicizing E♭ while reinforcing its status as dominant; it also serves the rhythmic function of filling four measures with seven chords. In the consequent the voices start converging one chord earlier, on F rather than B♭—a result of the hands having exchanged melodic intervals. (Rhythmic displacement conceals this, the consequent's left hand only one quarter-note ahead of the antecedent.) This creates a stronger sense of B♭-as-dominant, and hence a stronger tonicization of the final E♭, reinforced by the melodic E♭. This is a nice example of the power of schematic vocabulary: the two phrases are nearly identical, descending by fifth from A♭ to E♭, yet because of the different positions of the converging cadence

---

[1] See Caplin 1998, chapter 16, for more on these rounded-binary interior episodes. Steve Taylor observed that this passage echoes the consequent of the slow-movement opening theme; it is also very similar to the third variation of Op. 1, no. 3, III (discussed in §4.10), and the second theme of Op. 18, no. 5, IV (mm. 36ff).

*Tonality.* Dmitri Tymoczko, Oxford University Press. © Oxford University Press 2023. DOI: 10.1093/oso/9780197577103.003.0006

**Figure P4.1.** Beethoven's *Pathétique* sonata, III, mm. 79–86, in notation and on the dyadic circle. Dotted and solid curved arrows represent the five- and two-step voice exchanges respectively, each occurring before the radial motion.

**Figure P4.2.** The opening phrase as a single sequence.

they manage to form a period, moving from a half cadence to a full cadence on the dominant. At which point the sequence has returned to its original state so that the repeat follows organically—meaning that the restatement is also a *continuation* of the underlying process. The result is almost deconstructive in its simplicity, the nearly pure unfolding of an algorithm that generates invertible counterpoint, a canon, a tonally functional period, a half cadence, a modulation to the dominant, and the conventionally mandated repeat. It is simultaneously funny and profound.

The four-bar middle section, meanwhile, presents a *near sequence* that states a brief melody on E♭, D♭, and A♭.[2] Figure P4.3 shows that the motive outlines an octave-displaced version of the diatonic third's ascending basic voice leading. The circular pattern of roots E♭–B♭–D♭–A♭–E♭ outlines a reordered fifth sequence

---

[2] It is also a microscopic version of what we will call, in chapter 8, the up-and-down-the-ladder schema.

**Figure P4.3.** The contrasting middle section, with the diatonic third's ascending basic voice leading stated successively on E♭, D♭ (the upper third of B♭ minor), and A♭.

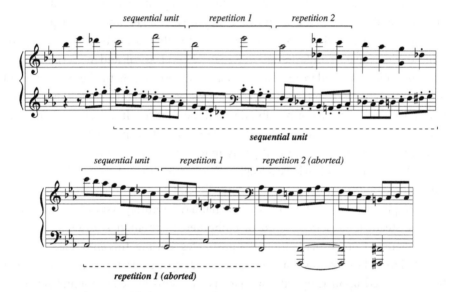

**Figure P4.4.** The episode's final section features a one-measure contrary-motion sequential unit embedded inside a four-measure canonic sequential unit.

D♭–A♭–E♭–B♭–(D♭) perturbed by the insertion of a minor third (§2.5). Here the thirds on B♭ and D♭ are superimposed to form a B♭ minor triad, producing the three-chord sequence E♭–b♭–A♭–E♭. (We can also imagine the basic voice leading displaced by triadic step, appearing as third-fifth of B♭ minor rather than root-third.) This is a nice example of triadic music's ability to juggle two- and three-note logics, embedding a dyadic sequence in nonsequential triads: E♭–b♭–A♭–E♭, the unusual root progressions normalized by tonicization. This music reverses the descending fifths of the opening measures, moving upward along the ladder of fifths, though the perturbation ensures that we end just where we began.

The final measures present a one-bar *contrary-motion* sequence that moves the hands an octave farther apart with each iteration; this is accomplished by altering

154 TONALITY: AN OWNER'S MANUAL

the opening music so that one hand consistently falls by fifth rather than alternating fifths and fourths (Figure P4.4). This one-bar sequence is embedded inside a four-bar canonic sequence, with the descending scalar eighths switching hands from left to right. The larger sequence is not a contrary-motion sequence since one hand stays fixed (C6 to C6) while the other descends by three octaves (A♭5 to A♭2); a complete second statement would therefore move the right hand down by three octaves while keeping the left hand fixed, returning the hands to their original configuration. But the four-measure pattern breaks off in favor of a standing-on-the-dominant in C minor, preparing the main theme's return.

Beethoven's rounded-binary episode is thus composed of three sequences in close succession, a canonic sequence, a near sequence, and a contrary-motion sequence, all presented with insistent simplicity, the music wearing its structure on its sleeve. Its omnipresent repetition illustrates Beethoven's love of patterns while hinting at a conception of functional harmony as inherently repetitive, its patterns disguised, distorted, and blurred to the point where they are no longer obvious. Chapter 4 will provide a comprehensive framework for analyzing this sort of transformed repetition, considering its manifestations in Renaissance, classical, and modern music.

If we sometimes underestimate this sort of repetition, that is because we tend to conceive counterpoint negatively, in terms of rules and prohibitions, rather than positively, in terms of possibilities and affordances. It is just this habit that led Charles Rosen to claim that writing counterpoint is "not after all a very difficult craft."[3] Rosen was right that pretty much anyone can follow rules, avoiding forbidden parallels and awkward leaps and so forth. But at the same time genuine *contrapuntal understanding* can be quite difficult to obtain.[4] Beethoven's deliberate simplicity is compelling for reasons that have nothing to do with schoolbook rules; instead, it presents a kind of embodied mathematics, drawing musical consequences from a small number of postulates. For me, this embodied aspect is essential to its beauty: this is a mathematics that grows out of practice rather than being imposed upon it by external fiat. Its theorems are contrapuntal schemas, embedded in works of art and untheorized even to this day. Understanding this music is difficult and creating it doubly so, just as living a meaningful life requires more than avoiding arrest.

[3] Rosen 1998, p. 545.
[4] C. P. E. Bach advertised his father's "original thought" in the contrapuntal domain (Wolff 2001, p. 8). One component of this originality is Bach's distinctive approach to the diatonic third's ascending basic voice leading (§3.1, 4.6, 7.7).

# 4

# Repetition

Voice leadings are atomic musical moves that can be combined arbitrarily. One of the central discoveries of the Renaissance was that they could be *repeated*, chained together algorithmically to convert an isolated event into an ongoing process. Repeating contrapuntal patterns are an important feature of sixteenth-century music, where they are often subtle and disguised (e.g., the ascending fifths in Figure 3.6.6, whose sequential structure is not immediately obvious).[1] This disguised repetition evolves into the overtly repetitive sequences of the baroque, which embed repeating contrapuntal patterns into larger musical blocks. Nineteenth-century composers make increasing use of contrary-motion "wedge" sequences, sometimes nontonal, paving the way for the very flexible transformations of modern music—a style that permits almost any conceivable transformation at any level of the quadruple hierarchy. Appendix 3 considers this practice as an extension and generalization of the traditional sequences that are the focus of this chapter.

## 1. Repetition reimagined

If we want to repeat a passage, the most obvious thing to do is play it unchanged. Less obviously we can transform it so as to preserve some essential features of its structure. The most familiar structure-preserving transformations are *transpositions* moving the music through pitch and *permutations* moving it through the instrumental ensemble; these are the basis of sequences and rounds respectively (Figure 4.1.1). Combining transposition and permutation produces a *transposing round* where the lines move through both pitch and ensemble, as in the third passage of Figure 4.1.1. While transposition and permutation are not the only possible transformations, they are central to a great deal of music and will occupy us for the rest of this chapter.[2]

A general model of repetition should therefore combine three elements, a "cell" or "unit" consisting in a set of melodic lines to be repeated, a collection of *transpositions* applied at each repeat, and a *permutation* or "twist" moving the lines among the available voices. Figure 4.1.2 adapts a notation originating with the

---

[1] See Schubert 2008, chapter 8, on the Renaissance aesthetic of disguised repetition.
[2] The octave, permutation, and transposition symmetries (OPT) are discussed in Callender, Quinn, and Tymoczko (2008) and Tymoczko 2011a; appendix 3 will incorporate inversion (I) as well.

*Tonality.* Dmitri Tymoczko, Oxford University Press. © Oxford University Press 2023. DOI: 10.1093/oso/9780197577103.003.0007

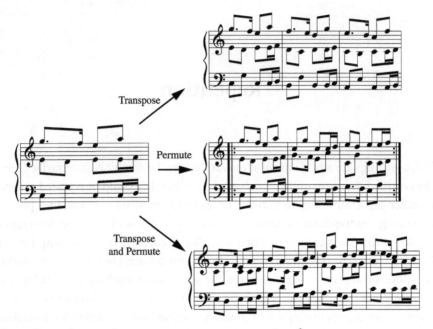

**Figure 4.1.1.** In repeating a passage, we can transpose it to form a sequence, permute its voices to form a round, or do both to form a transposing round.

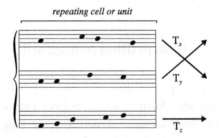

**Figure 4.1.2.** An abstract model of repetition in which a cell's melodic lines are transposed and permuted as they repeat.

Russian theorist Sergei Taneyev, using arrows to generate new sequential units from their predecessors.[3] Each arrow points from source to destination and is labeled with a transposition: thus, whatever music is in the top voice is transposed by $x$ and placed in the second voice, and whatever music is in the second voice is transposed by $y$ and is sent to the top; the music in the third voice is transposed by $z$ and remains in that voice. In most sequences, the arrows form a stable structure that stays fixed as the music repeats. In a *transpositional* sequence, all the transpositions have

---

[3] Taneyev [1909] 1962, Segall 2014, and Collins 2015 and 2018; the notation is also similar to Henry Klumpenhouwer's model of voice permutation (Klumpenhouwer 1991, see also Harrison 1988). Thanks here to Julian Hook.

the same subscript, and arrows do not cross: each voice retains its own melodic material and is transposed in exactly the same way. Crossed arrows create *canonic* sequences, partitioning the voices into groups sharing the same melodic content. A three-voice sequence can either have no crossings and hence no canon, a pair of crossed arrows forming a two-voice canon, or all three arrows crossing to form a three-voice canon (Figure 4.1.3).

This model resolves some longstanding difficulties surrounding the identification of repeating sequential units. We can distinguish the *simple period*, which is the length of the minimal block of music sufficient to generate the sequence, or the cells as I have defined them, from the *grand period*, which is the time it takes for all voices to cycle back to their initial melodic positions, all transposed by the same amount (not counting octave displacements that may differ from voice to voice). Previous

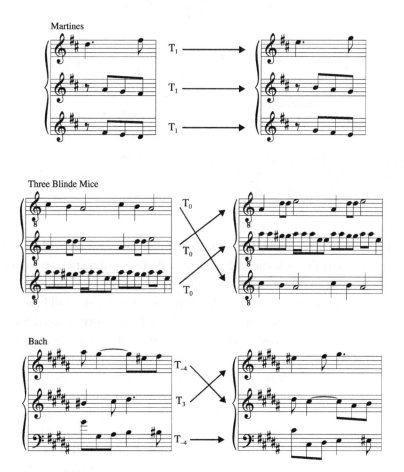

**Figure 4.1.3.** Three examples of the schema. (*top*) An ascending-step sequence from Marianna Martines's "Vo solcando un mar crudele" (from *Scelta d'Arie Composte per suo diletto*, 1767), mm. 122ff. (*middle*) "Three Blinde Mice" (1609) uses permutation but not transposition. (*bottom*) A sequence with both transposition and permutation from the first G♯ minor fugue in *The Well-Tempered Clavier*, mm. 86ff.

158  TONALITY: AN OWNER'S MANUAL

**Figure 4.1.4.** Schoenberg's "Angst und Hoffen" (*The Book of the Hanging Gardens*, Op. 15, no. 7) contains a wedge sequence that transposes the voices by different amounts.

**Figure 4.1.5.** An invertible-counterpoint sequence in mm. 57–60 of the second E minor prelude in *The Well-Tempered Clavier*. The sequence uses invertible counterpoint at the twelfth (mm. 1–2).

theorists have often focused on the grand period to the exclusion of the simple period; in large part this is because they have neglected permutation as a sequence-generating operation.[4] In the presence of permutation, however, the grand period will contain multiple simple periods: the sequences in Figure 4.1.3 all have a simple period of one bar, but it takes three bars for "Three Blinde Mice" to cycle back to its original melodic configuration and two bars for the G♯ minor fugue to do so. In some cases, different groups of voices will have different simple periods (e.g., Figure 4.5.7).

Sequences can be stable or unstable in two different ways. A collection of transposing arrows is *harmonically* stable when its transpositions differ only by octave. These sequences are structure-preserving in a very general way, producing transpositionally related blocks regardless of their cells' content. Harmonically *unstable* sequences create contrary-motion "wedge" patterns that move through unrelated vertical states (Figure 4.1.4). Here again the grand period will typically

---

[4] See Bass 1996, Moreno 1996, Harrison 2003, Ricci 2004, Sprick 2018, and Waltham-Smith 2018. Both Bass and Schoenberg ([1911] 1983, p. 283) require that sequential periods contain multiple chords, which is false of many descending-fifth sequences (e.g., Figure 4.3.2). It was the work of David Feurzeig, many years ago, that provoked me to think about the sequential role of permutation.

contain multiple simple periods, the voices cycling through different transpositions until they return to their initial alignment. In earlier music, unstable sequences often exploit unique features of the sequential unit to create a consonant result. This typically involves the sort of invertible counterpoint found in Figure 4.1.5.[5]

*Registrally stable* sequences preserve distance between voices from one grand period to the next, while *contrary-motion* sequences alter those distances by one or more octaves. A collection of canonic voices, whose parts are interlinked by arrows, is always registrally stable, as each line passes through the same sequence of transpositions with each grand period. In the bottom passage of Figure 4.1.3, for example, the music in the top voice moves down four steps and then up three steps while the music in the middle voice moves up three steps and down four; in both cases the total is –1 and the lines transpose down by diatonic step. The bass voice, meanwhile, moves down by eight diatonic steps with each grand period, forming a contrary-motion sequence. Note that my term "contrary motion" encompasses both oblique and similar motion from one grand period to the next—as in this last example, where the top voices descend by step while the bass descends by a ninth.

Readers are encouraged to be patient, as it can be genuinely difficult to wrap one's mind around the full range of effects that can be obtained from this simple model: while working on this book I have been repeatedly surprised to discover that yet another familiar passage could be described with transposing arrows. I take some comfort in the thought that the difficulty is not so much theoretical as it is musical—it is not that I am overcomplicating something simple, but rather that composers have made extremely sophisticated use of transformed repetition.[6] To be sure, I am trying to understand this practice abstractly, replacing particular schemas with a general framework. (And to be fair I sometimes exercise the analyst's privilege of asserting permutations not found on the musical surface—as in §2.5, where I identify canons created by the listener's ear rather than the composer's pencil.) But the real issue here is the wide range of effects that can be obtained by simply doing the same thing over and over.

## 2. Repeating contrapuntal patterns

Look at the left side of Figure 4.2.1 while covering the right side with your hand. If you wanted to repeat this voice leading, how would you do it?

Rather than a single correct answer there are two possibilities: continuing the melodic motions within each voice to form a contrary-motion wedge, or permuting the melodic intervals so that they move from voice to voice. Either yields a sequence

---

[5] Taneyev (1909) 1962. Any sequence with differing transpositional subscripts technically involves some sort of invertible counterpoint.

[6] There is a repetition calculator at https://www.madmusicalscience.com/ allowing users to explore repeating contrapuntal patterns in a hands-on way.

160  TONALITY: AN OWNER'S MANUAL

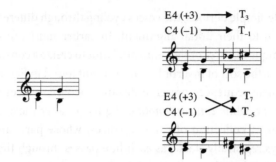

**Figure 4.2.1.** Two ways to repeat the voice leading on the left.

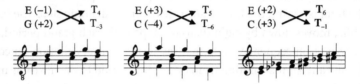

**Figure 4.2.2.** Three sequences whose units have just a single chord. (*left*) Josquin, from the Sanctus of the mass *L'Ami Baudichon*, mm. 14ff; (*middle*) the Beethoven passage in Figure P4.1; (*right*) one of the main motives of Stravinsky's *Firebird*.

with a repeating cell that is just one note long.[7] I will call these one-note sequences *repeating contrapuntal patterns*. Repeating contrapuntal patterns can be associated with phrases like "voice X moves up by 3 semitones and then this melodic interval moves to voice Y; voice Y moves down by one semitone and then this motion shifts to voice X." We can think of them, loosely, as combining two separate voice leadings, one that determines the melodic intervals ("move voice X up by three semitones") and another that permutes these melodic intervals among the voices ("its motion moves to voice Y").[8] Figure 4.2.2 contains repeating contrapuntal patterns from Josquin, Beethoven, and Stravinsky.

There is something potentially confusing about the notion of a single-note sequential unit. With larger units, the lines' internal structure allows us to draw transpositional arrows on the basis of just two iterations: looking back at Figure 4.1.3, it would be easy to reconstruct the arrows were they to disappear. With a repeating contrapuntal pattern, however, we need at least *three* chords to identify the sequence. After all, the left side of Figure 4.2.1 contains two chords, yet permits two equally good continuations. This is because repeating contrapuntal patterns are characterized by the melodic intervals that occur *between* units—in Figure 4.2.1,

---

[7] Readers may notice that the two solutions recall the first two phrases of the *Waldstein*, which opens with a contrary-motion wedge and continues with the diatonic third's ascending basic voice leading (§3.7).

[8] Geometrically, this resembles the operation known as "parallel transport," the moving of a vector along another vector. Here we move a path (the voice leading) along another path that determines the permutation; in wedge sequences the second path is the same as the first, while in harmonically stable sequences it is the line of transposition.

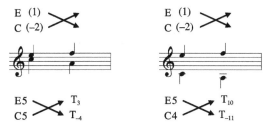

**Figure 4.2.3.** When voices shift octaves, the melodic-interval notation stays the same while the transpositional notation changes.

the ascending minor third and the descending semitone. It takes two notes to identify those intervals, and three for us to observe them moving around the texture. When analyzing repeating contrapuntal patterns, I will therefore include each voice's initial melodic interval in parentheses, measured in diatonic or chromatic steps as appropriate; these intervals move around the texture following the arrows. This interval-and-arrow notation is slightly more general than the transposition-and-arrow notation, as it is insensitive to the notes' initial registral positions (Figure 4.2.3). For any initial registral position, however, melodic intervals and transpositional labels carry the same information, and we can compute one from the other.

I have said that a sequence is harmonically stable if its transposition arrows differ only by some number of octaves. For a repeating contrapuntal pattern, this means, first, that it connects transpositionally related chords; and second that the melodic intervals are linked to specific chordal elements (e.g., root, third, and fifth). Thus we can associate harmonically stable repeating contrapuntal patterns with phrases like "shift the root and third down by step while keeping the fifth constant." *Any such sequence will necessarily correspond to a type of motion in one of our spiral diagrams.* For we have seen that motion on the spiral diagrams can be described by abstract instructions for moving chordal elements: for instance, in the 2-in-7 graph of imperfect consonance (Figure 3.1.1), every clockwise step moves the root down by third and the third up by step ($T_{-4}t_1$, the descending basic voice leading). It follows that a harmonically stable repeating contrapuntal pattern is just a repeated pattern of motion through a spiral diagram. We can highlight this connection with a change in notation: rather than using scalar transpositional arrows to link notes *across* voices, we can instead use hierarchically nested transpositions to link notes *within* voices, as in Figure 4.2.4. This clarifies that little-t transposition is inherently canonic, cycling voices through different chordal elements. Indeed, even a trivial passage like Figure P2.6 has an imitative structure, its three voices ascending C–D–A in a one-beat canon.

The upshot is that there are deep connections between the seemingly distinct domains of repetition, canon, and voice leading. These are reflected by two different ways we can conceive of repeated moves on a spiral diagram: as harmonic sequences and as generators of canons. This connection is in the first instance theoretically surprising, as one might not expect that repetition had anything to do

**Figure 4.2.4.** Two interpretations of the same repeating contrapuntal pattern. The first uses diatonic transpositions to connect notes in different voices; the second uses double transposition along chord and scale to relate notes within voices.

**Figure 4.2.5.** The ascending basic voice leading in the top two voices of the Sanctus of Palestrina's mass *Ave regina coelorum*, mm. 18–20.

with canon. It is also interesting historically, as it is likely that the canonic aspect was initially paramount: in a passage like Figure 4.2.5, Palestrina was presumably more concerned with imitation than the ascending-fifth pattern of harmonies.[9] As time passed, however, these moments of close imitation perhaps came to be valued for their harmonic patterning as well; thus when J. S. Bach or Mozart make sequential use of the diatonic third's basic voice leading, its harmonic aspect is ascendant (Figure 4.3.2). In this way, a concern with counterpoint and imitation could gradually yield to a focus on harmonic repetition without any clear line dividing the two. Chapter 6 will argue that repeating contrapuntal patterns could also spark awareness of abstract structural concepts such as "root" and "fifth," thus setting the stage for inversional equivalence.

In large-unit sequences, repeating contrapuntal patterns connect analogous chords in adjacent units. For example, the expositional sequence of *The Well-Tempered Clavier*'s first E minor fugue articulates the diatonic third's ascending basic voice leading across units (Figure 4.2.6). The repeating core of Ligeti's *Passacaglia Ungherese* is structurally if not expressively similar, a series of major thirds and

---

[9] Repeating contrapuntal patterns are an important part of the Renaissance practice of *stretto fuga* (Milsom 2005).

**Figure 4.2.6.** The exposition of the first E minor fugue in *The Well-Tempered Clavier* (mm. 11–12) is a sequence with two-measure units, whose initial notes articulate the basic voice leading from one unit to the next.

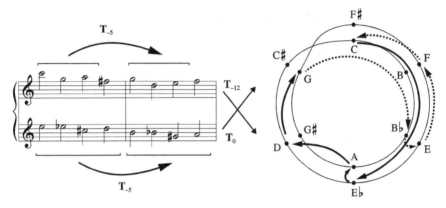

**Figure 4.2.7.** The round in Ligeti's *Passacaglia ungherese* makes a complete circle in the space of chromatic major thirds.

minor sixths that compose to form a one-step transposition along the chord (Figure 4.2.7). (Note that one will not necessarily find *the same* voice-leading relationship between all analogous pairs of chords in a large-unit sequence: changes of spacing within the unit can change the $T_x t_y$ relationship between analogous chords, as in Figure 4.2.8.) This explains why we can describe sequences either using the crossed $T_x$ arrows of §4.1, or by identifying the voice leading connecting analogous chords in successive units, as with the uncrossed arrows of Figure 4.2.4; when considering large sequential units we typically want to use transposing arrows, but when concerned with repeating contrapuntal patterns, we may prefer the latter.[10] In either case, there is a two-way mapping between sequences and voice leadings: every sequence determines a repeating contrapuntal pattern between analogous chords of successive units; and every voice leading can be expanded into a larger-unit sequence. The theory of voice leading and the theory of sequence are one and the same.

Indeed, there is a general recipe for constructing a sequence from a voice leading between transpositionally related chords: starting with any such voice leading, draw transpositional arrows between the notes, and then use those arrows to form either

---

[10] Each notation has distinct advantages: crossed T arrows apply to larger sequential units, but are sensitive to chords' position in register; dual transpositions $T_x t_y$ are not sensitive to register and generalize more readily, but may apply only to some chords in the sequence.

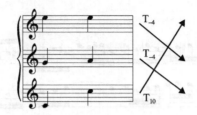

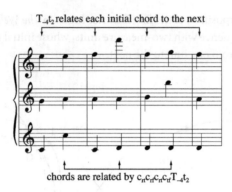

**Figure 4.2.8.** In a large-unit sequence, not all chords need be related by the same voice leading. Here, the first chords in each unit relate by $T_{-4}t_2$, while the second add the complicated voice exchange $c_{rt}c_{rf}c_{rt}c_{tf}$, with $c_{rt}$ the pairwise voice exchange of root and third, $c_{rf}$ root and fifth, and $c_{tf}$ third and fifth.

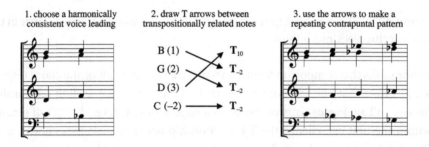

**Figure 4.2.9.** A recipe for converting a voice leading into a sequence. We start with a voice leading connecting chromatic 0457 chords, or major triads with added fourth. The grand period is three chords long.

a repeating contrapuntal pattern or a larger-unit sequence containing it. Figure 4.2.9 goes through the process for a voice leading using nontertian tetrachords. It is somewhat surprising that contemporary musicians do not learn this recipe, for it is a useful technique that could easily be incorporated into the university theory curriculum—one that allows us to explore the full spectrum of transposed and permuted repetition. Its absence reflects our tendency to think about sequences schematically, as a set of idioms characteristic of functional tonality, rather than as manifestations of a general transformational technique.

## 3. The geometry of two-voice sequences

The isomorphism between sequence and voice leading allows us to use the spiral diagrams to explore the geometry of sequential possibility. For suppose we have a two-voice, harmonically consistent repeating contrapuntal pattern: if it has no voice exchanges then it is either *canonic* or *transpositional*, depending on whether it takes an odd or even number of steps on the dyadic spiral; if it has voice exchanges, then it is either *canonic* or *contrary-motion*, again depending on how many steps it takes (Figure 4.3.1).[11] Readers will recall that these sequence-types—transpositional, contrary-motion, and canonic—were all discussed in this chapter's prelude. The spiral diagrams show that they are the *only* harmonically consistent two-voice possibilities. Geometry also justifies our decision to include permutation alongside transposition as a sequence-generating operation: after all, any harmonically stable voice leading generates a sequence, and some of these permute their voices.

With no voice exchanges, canonic sequences take an odd number of steps on the dyadic circle and transpositional sequences take an even number of steps. (Refer back to Figure 3.1.4, where the top-line voice leadings generate canonic sequences,

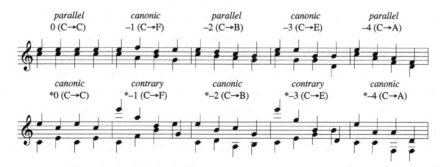

Figure 4.3.1. Sequences generated by repeated clockwise motion on the dyadic circle. The top line does not involve any voice exchanges while the bottom line incorporates the two-step voice exchange (symbolized by the asterisk; see the dotted curves on Figure 3.2.1). This turns parallel sequences into canonic sequences and canonic sequences into contrary sequences.

---

[11] Thus contrary-motion sequences require voice exchanges. This follows from the fact that crossing-free voice leadings preserve spacing in chordal steps; contrary-motion sequences change spacing and thus require voice exchanges.

166   TONALITY: AN OWNER'S MANUAL

**Figure 4.3.2.** The development sequence of Mozart's K.545, I, mm. 37–38, and a sequence from the first C minor fugue in *The Well-Tempered Clavier*, mm. 9–10.

with each voice alternating root and third, while the bottom-line voice leadings generate parallel sequences.) The most common pattern is just single-step motion on the spiral, producing the diatonic third's basic voice leading; this schema appears in a substantial proportion of baroque and classical sequences, embellished lightly if at all. Classical sequences usually feature descending fifths, whereas earlier styles more frequently use ascending fifths, often embellished with passing tritones as described in §3.1 (Figures 4.3.2–3).[12] We can find three-step motion on the circle as well (e.g., Figure 4.5.4).[13] Larger motions, such as five or seven steps, make for awkward melodic leaps and are correspondingly rare. Meanwhile, sequences that take an even number of steps on the circle are transpositional; these typically occur in explicitly parallel passages (e.g., fauxbourdon) or else at the beginning of longer sequential units.

For sequences with an odd number of voice exchanges, canons result from an *even* number of steps on the dyadic circle, while antiparallel motion results from an odd number of steps (bottom staff of Figure 4.3.1). The most common sequences use the two-step voice exchange: on its own it produces a simple round; combined with one-step clockwise motion it produces antiparallel motion in which one voice

---

[12] For example, Figures 4.2.2, 4.2.5, or 5.3.4.
[13] For other examples see Mozart's F major piano sonata K.533, I, mm. 24–25, or Beethoven's C minor piano sonata, Op. 10, no. 1, mm. 151ff.

**Figure 4.3.3.** The diatonic third's ascending basic voice leading in the second E minor prelude of *The Well-Tempered Clavier*, mm. 23–28.

moves by fourth and the other moves by fifth in the opposite direction. The combination of stepwise motion with the two-step voice exchange is also reasonably common, particularly in its ascending form (e.g., Figure 7.6.10). For a sequence with an even number of voice exchanges, the situation is reversed: an odd number of steps produces a canonic sequence, and an even number produces antiparallel motion. Sequences with larger motions on the dyadic circle tend to be rare as they involve more unbalanced motion between the two voices.[14]

We now turn to harmonically *unstable* sequences. Any two-voice canonic repeating contrapuntal pattern, whether harmonically stable or not, will preserve its canonic structure when either of its dyads is moved by exact contrary motion.[15] This means that any such pattern can be generated by applying contrary-motion distortion to either parallel motion or *Pathétique*-style alternating antiparallel intervals, depending on the interval of transposition as measured from one grand period to the next (Figure 4.3.4).[16] For a particular interval, the various possibilities will be represented by a matrix such as that in Figure 4.3.5. The most common harmonically unstable canon is the dyadic 5–6; it can be embedded into a triadic sequence as root-fifth, fifth-third, or both simultaneously—in which case we have three canonic voices, one sounding third and fifth, another fifth and root, and another root and third (Figures 4.3.6–7).[17] This structure can be transformed via dyadic expansion into a 5–10 sequence (e.g., the outer voices on the right side of Figure 2.9.3).

---

[14] One sometimes finds patterns like (E5, G5) → (D4, F5) → (C3, E5), as at the end of the *Pathétique* episode discussed in the prelude.

[15] Suppose we have a two-voice canonic repeating contrapuntal pattern with the top voice moving by interval $x$ from first chord to second, and bottom voice moving by $y$. Since the sequence is canonic, the top voice moves by $y$ from second chord to third while the bottom voice moves by $x$; both voices move by $x + y$ from first chord to third. If we keep the first and third chords the same, while expanding the second so that the top voice moves by $x + 1$ and bottom voice by $y - 1$, we preserve the canonic relationship. If we are willing to use fractional scale-steps (e.g., quarter-tones), then *any* sequence can be turned into a purely parallel sequence in this way.

[16] Voice exchanges are a particular kind of contrary-motion expansion and contraction; the "threads" in Gosman 2012 unwind voice exchanges to reveal the parallel motion, much as we are discussing here.

[17] Harmonically unstable sequences involve invertible counterpoint: in the case of the 5–6, the ascending step is initially a fifth above the constant lower voice, and then a sixth below the constant upper voice; this is invertible counterpoint at the tenth.

168 TONALITY: AN OWNER'S MANUAL

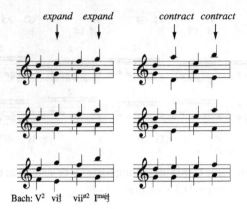

Figure 4.3.4. Two-voice canonic sequences derived from either parallel or antiparallel motion by expanding or contracting every other chord. This produces sequences with even or odd intervals of transposition respectively. On the bottom left, a pattern from m. 56 of the second B♭ minor fugue in *The Well-Tempered Clavier*.

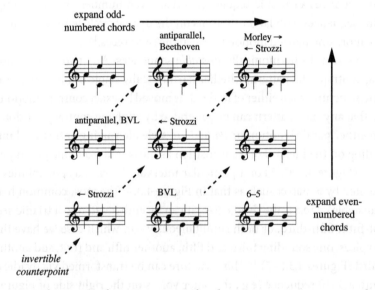

Figure 4.3.5. The matrix of two-voice, two-chord canonic patterns repeating down by step. The examples can be read right-to-left to produce ascending-step patterns.

The music in Figure 4.3.8 makes sophisticated use of these possibilities: my reconstruction begins in the top line with an antiparallel ascending-fifth sequence; every other chord is then subjected to contrary-motion contraction, the top three voices lowered by step while the bass rises by the same amount; finally we apply "third substitution" to the last three chords, lowering the bass by third and raising the fifth of the upper-voice triad. This produces a familiar harmonic loop, four descending fifths and one third, b–e–A–D (§2.5).

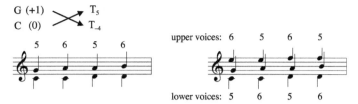

**Figure 4.3.6.** The 5–6 voice-leading pattern is an example of invertible counterpoint at the tenth, with the G–A voice moving down by fifth to C–D while the C–C voice moves up by sixth to A–A. This is equivalent to transposing G–A down by tenth and transposing the whole pattern up by sixth. This figure can be embedded in a triadic 5–6 sequence in two separate ways.

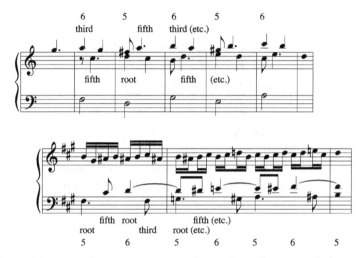

**Figure 4.3.7.** Two ascending-step sequences from *The Well-Tempered Clavier*, each involving a canonic relation among two voices. The top system is a reduction of mm. 13–19 of the second C major fugue, and has the canon between the third-fifth and fifth-root voices; the bottom is from the second F♯ minor fugue, mm. 47–48, and has its canon between the root-third and fifth-root voices.

The interesting conceptual point is that canon and contrary motion arise as byproducts of the basic mechanics of sequential voice leading, rather than requiring deliberate compositional artifice: they are outcroppings that the rock-climber may choose to grasp or not. The presence or absence of canonic patterning is thus a matter of whether composers decide to *draw out* the canonic potential latent in their material, with noncanonic sequences often *obscuring* preexisting canonic relationships (Figure 4.3.9).[18] In the case of contrary motion, the handhold is less commonly grasped, though there are circumstances where it is analytically useful to be aware of it: a nice example comes from the opening of Beethoven's *Tempest*

---

[18] In 1719, Moritz Johann Vogt explicitly noted the imitative qualities of the diatonic third's basic voice leading (Morgan 1978, p. 84).

170   TONALITY: AN OWNER'S MANUAL

Figure 4.3.8. Barbara Strozzi's "Il Contrasto dei Cinque Sensi," mm. 3–4. The top staff presents an antiparallel fifth sequence; on the second staff, the voices of every other chord are moved together by step; the third staff applies third substitution to the final three chords, lowering the bass by third and raising the alto by step.

Figure 4.3.9. Measures 9–12 of the trio of Maria Szymanowska's Polonaise no. 1, from *18 Dances of Different Genres*. The figuration disguises rather than highlights the canon inherent in the voice leading.

sonata, a sequence that could form a contrary-motion wedge, though Beethoven chooses not to (Figure 10.3.2).[19] These facts allow us to unpack metaphors like "the will of the tones," connecting low-level musical affordances to high-level compositional devices like canon and contrary-motion.[20] An intuitive sense for this connection lies behind a good deal of compositional expertise.

---

[19] In other places, such as the development of Op. 59, no. 1, IV, mm. 123ff, Beethoven realizes the same motive's contrary-motion potential.
[20] Arndt 2011.

All of this has an obvious resonance with Schenkerian theory. Schenker famously denied that sequences exist, preferring instead to speak of linear motion.[21] But what are these linear motions if not repeating contrapuntal patterns? Schenker was certainly right that it can be useful to focus on the voice leading connecting chords at the start of successive sequential units, for if we do, we will almost always find common patterns that, when iterated enough times, transpose each voice by the same amount— which is to say, linear motion. (Indeed, it is definitionally true that the chords at the start of each grand period are always related by transposition.) This reveals an important mathematical link between the local voice leadings connecting adjacent chords, and nonlocal relationships occurring across larger timespans. It is all too easy to pass from this mathematical truth to the musical conclusion that sequences are *essentially* linear devices with no harmonic significance, or that a sequential unit *represents* its initial chord, or perhaps even that "sequences" (as distinct from linear motion more generally) do not exist. While I do not subscribe to these views, I suspect they are based on genuine insight. Perhaps Schenker looked at countless sequences and noticed that their initial chords frequently spelled out familiar contrapuntal moves that often occur on the musical surface. If he drew questionable conclusions from this observation, then that may be because he lacked the mathematical tools needed to unravel this extremely intricate knotting of harmonic and contrapuntal forces.

## 4. Three voices and the circle of triads

With larger chords, the subject of voice exchanges becomes much more complex. Setting them aside for the moment, we can repeat the preceding analysis: for an $n$-note chord, an $n$-step motion on the spiral diagram, or motion by any integer multiple of $n$, will produce a transpositional sequence in which all voices move in parallel; any other motion will produce canonic sequences. Figure 4.4.1 generates three-voice sequences by taking one, two, four, five, and seven clockwise steps on the triadic circle. The resulting schemas are all very common. Because the triad divides the octave very evenly, short motions on the triadic circle produce little melodic activity and the canonic imitation is very subtle.

The five- and seven-step sequences, by contrast, create the clear impression of canon. Five-step motion produces a fifth-sequence whose lines sound an ascending triadic arpeggio, typically filled out with passing tones. Figure 4.4.2 shows the pattern over an independent bass, its third entry divided between alto and tenor. Figure 4.4.3 shows a sequence from *The Well-Tempered Clavier*'s second C♯ minor fugue; this is the same idiom in its descending form, disguised by a suspension and incorporated into a longer sequential unit. Seven-step motion embeds the triadic arpeggio within a round that moves by chordal step at each repeat. In "L'amante modesto," Barbara Strozzi uses this sequence to create a bravura expansion whose

---

[21] Slottow 2018.

**Figure 4.4.1.** Repeating contrapuntal patterns generated by short clockwise motion along the triadic circle. Each column is related by the Tinctoris Transform. The −2 and −4 patterns contain descending three-note scale fragments, while the −5 and −7 patterns contain descending triadic arpeggios. The examples can be read backwards to produce ascending sequences (+1, +2, etc.).

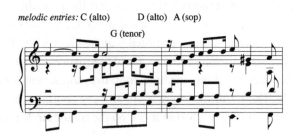

**Figure 4.4.2.** An ascending-fifth canonic sequence from Barbara Strozzi's "Gli amanti falliti," mm. 32–33. This uses the +5 sequence, the retrograde of the −5 pattern in the previous example.

aural complexity belies its straightforward structure (Figure 4.4.4). The technique is reminiscent of the "Shepard-tone passacaglias" in §2.5, only ascending rather than descending, and directly embodied in the score rather than constructed by the listener.

Remarkably, these two patterns can be combined—each new triadic arpeggio either a fifth above or at the same pitch level as the previous entry (Figure 4.4.5). This combined pattern appears from Josquin to Beethoven, often at moments of expressive urgency; for reasons that will become clear at the end of chapter 6,

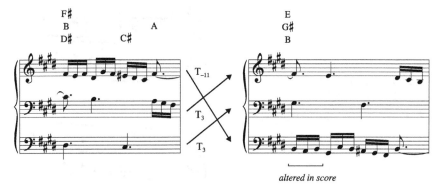

**Figure 4.4.3.** A sequence from the second C♯ minor fugue in *The Well-Tempered Clavier*, mm. 10ff. The sequence uses the descending-fifth canonic voice leading labeled −5 on Figure 4.4.1.

**Figure 4.4.4.** The opening of Barbara Strozzi's "L'amante modesto" uses the +7 sequence, the retrograde of −7 on Figure 4.4.1.

I call it the *Chase schema*. Figure 4.4.6 shows Orlando Gibbons using it to generate a quasi-sequential pattern of ascending fifths F–C–g–d. The unison entries function to slow the harmonic rhythm, to avoid second-inversion triads, and to extend the melodic lines into longer scales. Figures 4.4.7–8 show two of the countless examples found throughout the literature.[22] The Chase schema is both sequence and canon, appearing in virtually every Renaissance composer's music and surviving well into the nineteenth century. From the standpoint of the Prime Directive, it is essentially similar to the two-voice canon generated by the diatonic third's basic voice leading.

We end this section with a six-voice sequence that superimposes two separate triadic patterns. The left hand in Figure 4.4.9 plays a standard 5–6 sequence, here analyzed as a two-voice canon whose lower voice is doubled a third below; the right

---

[22] For more, see the end of the Agnus of Palestrina's eight-voice mass *Fratres ego enim accepi*, the final phrase of Bach's "Meine Seele erhebet den Herren" (BWV 10.7, Riemenschneider 358), mm. 17–21, the second F major fugue in *The Well-Tempered Clavier*, mm. 29–33, and the first movement of Beethoven's Second Symphony, mm. 88–95. Traces can also be found in mm. 11–12 of Morley's "April Is in My Mistress' Face" (Figure 2.9.2). The parallel thirds in Gosman 2009 are closely related.

**Figure 4.4.5.** (*left*) Each new entry can appear either a fifth above the previous entry, or at the same pitch level. (*right*) Using repeated entries to avoid second-inversion triads.

**Figure 4.4.6.** The Chase schema in Orlando Gibbons's *In Nomine a 4*, mm. 17–19.

**Figure 4.4.7.** In mm. 190ff of Josquin's "Benedicite, omnia opera," we have a descending-fifth sequence featuring two superimposed instances of the diatonic third's descending basic voice leading, with all four voices in canon. After a brief ascending-step sequence, where the upper voices continue to inhabit the circle of imperfect consonances, we have seven entries of a canonic sequence based on the Chase schema.

hand adds a three-voice canon that takes four clockwise steps along the triadic circle (pattern −4 on Figure 4.4.1, with a grand period of three bars). The two sequences come together to sound a pure triad on the weak beat of every measure, but the right hand's descending voice leading allows the strong-beat ninth chord to be rationalized as a suspension. This is an example of how to build complex multivoice

**Figure 4.4.8.** A Chase-schema variant in mm. 96–111 of the scherzo of Beethoven's Third Symphony Op. 55. The upper staff is a reduction of Beethoven's actual music, while the lower shows the three-voice Chase schema.

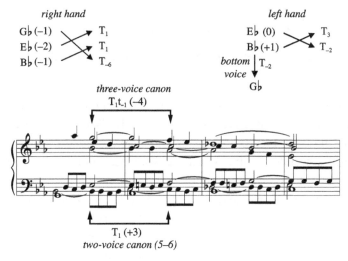

**Figure 4.4.9.** Measures 158–161 of the six-part Ricercare from *The Musical Offering*, BWV 1079. The sequence superimposes a triadic canon in the right hand with a dyadic canon in the left.

textures by superimposing smaller schemas. Once it might have struck me as an example of inexplicable genius; now I see it as a clever but comprehensible manipulation of familiar relationships, exactly what I expect in baroque music. Bach's talent lies not so much in his understanding of triadic geometry but in his expressive use of that understanding.

## 5. Three voices arranged 2 + 1

Contrary-motion sequences require that the transpositional arrows separate the voices into at least two independent groups. This means a two-voice sequence cannot be simultaneously contrary and canonic. Three or more voices, however, can combine canons within groups with contrary motion between them. The structure of the crossed arrows typically determines the best geometrical analysis: when

176  TONALITY: AN OWNER'S MANUAL

**Figure 4.5.1.** Two passages that take advantage of the tritone's symmetry, moving the bass down by fifth and the upper-voice tritone down by semitone.

**Figure 4.5.2.** Descending seventh chords in chromatic and diatonic space.

all three arrows cross, we will usually want to model the sequence on the triadic circle; but if only two cross it is often better to use dyadic geometry instead.

On the left side of Figure 4.5.1 the upper voices descend by semitone while the lower voice descends by fifth. While we would generally expect superimposed interval cycles to produce clashing harmonies, here they remain vertically aligned: because of the tritone's symmetry, semitone and fifth transposition reproduce the same pitch classes, and the vertical interval is always a tritone. We do not often find these bare tritones prior to the twentieth century, but we *do* find a variant in which the bass has been transposed relative to the upper voices; the result is a sequence of incomplete dominant sevenths in which the upper voices descend by semitone while the bass falls by fifth. (Or, in deference to registral limitations, alternates descending fifths and ascending fourths.) This is an important sequence in virtually all functionally tonal music from the baroque onward.[23]

The Principle of Musical Approximation tells us that nearly even chords can approximate the behavior of perfectly even chords (§2.1). This means we can replace tritones with chromatic or diatonic fifths, once again transposing the bass relative to the upper voices (Figure 4.5.2). Here the upper voices move *almost* by semitone, alternating steps and unisons. The canonic structure in Figure 4.5.1 was latent, evident only if we calculated that third and seventh change voices at every chord; here it is overt, the voices descending by step in alternation. Since the diatonic third is less even than the diatonic fifth, it produces a canon with even more melodic activity, upper voices alternating descending thirds and ascending steps (Figure 4.5.3). Readers will recognize both patterns as basic idioms of functional tonality.

---

[23] Examples include the second D minor fugue in *The Well-Tempered Clavier* (mm. 11–12), the second theme of Mozart's Symphony no. 40, I (mm. 56–58), and Brahms's Op. 116, no. 2 (m. 63).

**Figure 4.5.3.** The same pattern using diatonic thirds. The upper voices can either be root-third or third-fifth pairs.

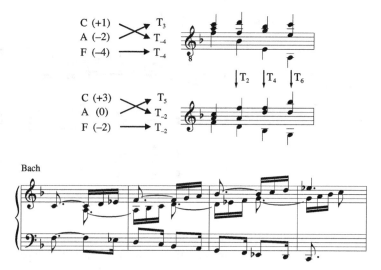

**Figure 4.5.4.** (*top*) We can transpose the chords of the sequence to shift the motion to the upper voices, turning a descending-fifth sequence into a more balanced descending-third sequence. (*bottom*) The second F major fugue in *The Well-Tempered Clavier*, mm. 57–60.

The preceding examples have the bass leaping and upper voices moving stepwise. A package of related progressions shifts the melodic motion toward the upper voices: Figure 4.5.4 appears in *The Well-Tempered Clavier*, the bass descending by third while upper voices take turns ascending by fourth. In Beethoven's first D major piano sonata, the asymmetry is even more extreme, with the bass descending by step while the upper voices ascend by fourth and fifth (Figure 4.5.5).[24] These passages are quite different from one another, and one might not think to associate them; yet they exhibit a fundamentally similar organization. The differences are (a) the interval in the upper voices (fifth, third, etc.); (b) how the bass is transposed relative to the upper voices; and (c) the degree of transpositional motion applied

---

[24] Note that the (G, B) → (F♯, D) progression in the second measure belongs *both* to the opening contrary-motion fifth pattern *and* the subsequent fauxbourdon pattern. That fauxbourdon pattern links the top voice to the middle voice, suggesting a series of voice overlaps; this could be modeled using voice crossings in the two-note scale containing the chord's root and fifth.

178   TONALITY: AN OWNER'S MANUAL

**Figure 4.5.5.** Beethoven's Op. 10, no. 3, IV, begins with contrary-motion thirds, leading to contrary-motion fauxbourdon in the second full measure. That passage relates via the Tinctoris Transform to the sequences we have been exploring.

to the underlying pattern. Together, these parameters generate a range of options whose sonic diversity disguises their shared structure.

Triadic composers also make extensive use of rounds dividing the voices 2 + 1, typically as a device to enliven static harmony. The most common pattern dates back to the early sixteenth century, adding passing tones to the two-voice round marked *0 in Figure 4.3.1 (Figure 4.5.6; see Figure 6.1.7 and §6.7 for Renaissance examples). It can appear either as IV–I or as V–I to form "Prinner," "Fenaroli," and "standing on the dominant" schemas.[25] Figure 4.5.7 contains one of my favorite classical rounds, the nonschematic build to the final cadence of the first movement of Beethoven's Op. 10, no. 3. One would hardly think to look for contrapuntal trickery here, yet the upper voices embed a two-voice canon in contrary motion with the bass.[26] Such rounds differ from standard sequences only in that their harmonies do

---

[25] Examples include Mozart's C minor piano fantasy, K.475, mm. 102–105 (standing on the dominant), Haydn's C major quartet Op. 50, no. 2, IV, mm. 211ff (ambiguous between dominant and predominant), and Mozart's C major piano concerto K.467, II, mm. 45–50. Bass 1996, note 3, describes the last example as a "purely melodic" sequence.

[26] The right-hand dyads ascend systematically through 2-in-3 space (Figure 3.7.3), moving clockwise and skipping the D–A perfect consonance: (A, F♯) → (D, F♯) → (F♯, A) → and so on, alternating $\tau_{-1}t_2$ and $t_1$, with $\tau$ being transposition along the dyad and t transposition along the triad. The example also shows that the left hand hints at its own canonic structure.

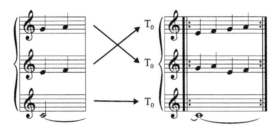

**Figure 4.5.6.** A common three-voice round.

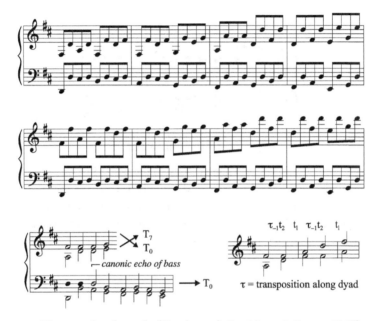

**Figure 4.5.7.** The round at the end of Beethoven's Op. 10, no. 3, I, mm. 333ff.

not transpose; by grouping them with familiar sequences we can deepen our appreciation for the many functions of transformed repetition.

## 6. Four voices

Four voices can be divided as two pairs, a triad plus an independent voice, or a single four-voice unit. The simplest four-voice sequences superimpose two basic voice leadings moving along their own spiral diagrams, as in Figures 3.3.2 and 4.4.7. Figure 4.6.1 instead moves its voices in contrary motion: here each pair forms a two-step interval containing every other note of a four-note scale, with consistent contrary motion reproducing the complete collection at every step. (This "thinking within the chord" is analogous to a familiar whole-tone technique discussed in appendix 3.) Figure 4.6.2 shows a related passage from the beginning of Louis Andriessen's *De Staat*, with fifths moving by contrary stepwise motion along the

180 TONALITY: AN OWNER'S MANUAL

Figure 4.6.1. Measures 43–44 of Wagner's *Tristan* prelude, with pairs of voices moving in contrary motion within a four-note chord, initially A–C–D♯–F♯, then G♯–B♯–D♯–F♯; this produces the complete four-note collection at every step. Geometrically, the voices move in opposite directions along the 2-in-4 spiral diagram, which has only one loop since the two-step interval is transpositionally symmetrical.

Figure 4.6.2. The opening of Louis Andriessen's *De Staat*, with pairs of voices moving in contrary motion along the scale B–C–E–F. Each hand alternates between the fifths F–C and E–B, always forming the full tetrachord.

scale B–C–E–F. In such cases, the evenness of the four-note scale will determine the regularity of melodic intervals: for the diminished seventh, voices always move by three semitones; for other chords they move by *approximately* three semitones, with the value of "approximate" depending on the chord's unevenness (distance from

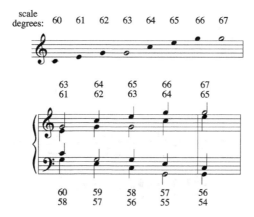

**Figure 4.6.3.** A contrary-motion sequence that moves along a four-note collection with two copies of the note G; each verticality states the complete four-note collection (C major with doubled G). The technique appears in mm. 19–24 of Burgmüller's "Ballade" (Op. 100, no. 15); it can be generalized to any trichord.

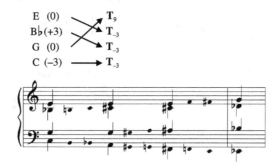

**Figure 4.6.4.** The "omnibus" sequence features three voices sounding the third, fifth, and seventh of the dominant seventh chord (a diminished triad), with the fourth voice sounding the root.

the completely even diminished seventh). This contrary-motion pattern can be extended to triadic contexts by doubling a note (Figure 4.6.3).

Other sequences divide the voices in a 3 + 1 fashion, typically with upper voices forming a canonic group while the bass sounds chord roots and moves in contrary motion. The "omnibus," for example, has upper voices ascending canonically against a bass that descends by minor third (Figure 4.6.4). The diatonic sequence from Haydn's E minor sonata has the same basic structure, though here the bass doubles an upper voice and the canon is almost completely inaudible (Figure 4.6.5). More prosaic, but still essentially similar, are the Renaissance idioms in Figure 4.6.6; in each case upper voices form a canonic group, moving regularly along the 3-in-7 circle of diatonic triads, while the bass moves sequentially in contrary motion.

When all four voices form a single cycle, the analytical situation can become bewilderingly complex. The repeating contrapuntal pattern of Figure 4.6.7 is a four-voice Chase schema taking a two-step counterclockwise path on the space of triads

182    TONALITY: AN OWNER'S MANUAL

**Figure 4.6.5.** Measures 72–78 of Haydn's E minor sonata, Hob. XVI:34.

**Figure 4.6.6.** Four-voice contrary-motion sequences in which the upper three voices move as a unit in contrary motion to the bass. The sequences on the right both appear in Figure 3.6.6.

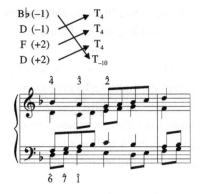

**Figure 4.6.7.** A repeating voice-leading pattern that generates a four-voice ascending-fifth canon. The pattern moves the root and one third down by step, and the fifth and a second third up by third (by way of passing tones). J. S. Bach often uses this pattern with scale degrees $\hat{4}$–$\hat{3}$–$\hat{2}$ in the top voice against $\hat{6}$–$\hat{7}$–$\hat{1}$ in the bass.

**Figure 4.6.8.** The hidden canon at the end of "Was mein Gott will, das g'scheh allzeit."

with doubled third, equivalent to Figure 3.8.1. This schema was a favorite of J. S. Bach's, permeating his four-voice music and likely internalized as part of his improvisational practice.[27] Figure 4.6.8 shows a marvelously disguised appearance at the end of the chorale "Was mein Gott will, das g'scheh allzeit" (BWV 244.25, Riemenschneider 115). We hear two literal instantiations of the schema before the harmonic rhythm halved. This is accomplished in two different ways: first by staggering the ascending-third melodies so that they occur separately, and second by expanding the harmonies so that they last for two beats instead of one (in the second line of the example). Despite its complexity, the ascending-fifth canon remains audible through the penultimate chord.

Together these passages exemplify what might be called the subterranean mathematics of Western music, a mathematics that becomes increasingly complex as we add voices. I imagine that earlier composers were proud of their sequential discoveries, rightly considering them novel solutions to ubiquitous compositional challenges—and a way to stamp their individuality on the shared language

---

[27] Other examples include the end of "Es ist das Heil uns kommen her" (BWV 155.5, Riemenschneider 335), and Figure 7.7.9.

of functional harmony. In earlier times, such solutions would need to be learned or discovered piecemeal, without the benefit of an overarching theoretical framework. For a composer working in a consensus style, this schematic approach might be entirely sufficient. In our own more fragmented time, the more abstract approach can be useful, allowing us to apply sequential techniques to any chord in any scale.

## 7. Contrary-motion sequences

Contrary-motion sequences help guide the transition from nineteenth-century functionality to twentieth-century modernism, with regular melodic motion providing access to new and unusual harmonic states (e.g., Figures 4.1.4, 10.2.7, and 10.7.10). But with some notable exceptions, they are not central to earlier practice. This is in large part because there are so few options; indeed, every contrary-motion sequence can be derived from the list of diatonic consonances in Figure 4.7.1. This list is in the first instance a contrary-motion sequence with a grand period of four notes; less obviously, it is *almost* a repeating contrapuntal pattern—that is, it is *almost* the case that each step involves a common tone in the upper voice and an ascending third in the lower, the only exception being the lower-voice ascent from C to D. In other words, the enumeration of consonances is a minimal deformation of a repeating contrapuntal pattern, as close to a sequence as it is possible for a nonsequence to be.

We can apply the Tinctoris Transform to produce sequences that move by fifth, third, and step (Figure 4.7.2). The numbers show how the voices transpose from one grand period to the next: −4/+3 means one voice descends by fifth (−4 diatonic steps) while the other ascends by fourth (+3). As in the enumeration of consonances, harmonies progress third-octave-sixth-fifth-third, though these vertical intervals are transposed differently in each case. Brackets identify chords belonging to the same enumeration of consonances, with one voice staying fixed. This is easiest to see at the bottom of the example: the −1/+6 and +1/−6 sequences each use four consecutive intervals from an enumeration of consequences, with the top voice sounding the same note four times in a row before being transposed by step; the −2/+5 and −5/+2 sequences meanwhile use *two* consecutive intervals

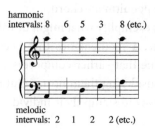

**Figure 4.7.1.** An enumeration of the diatonic consonances under a fixed A. The pattern repeats every four chords.

**Figure 4.7.2.** Contrary-motion fifth sequences derived by transposing the enumeration of consonances. Brackets show chords belonging to the same enumeration of consonances.

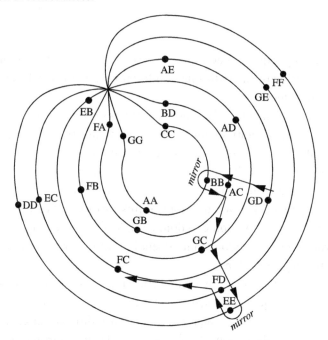

**Figure 4.7.3.** The –4/+3 sequence moves largely radially through the space of diatonic dyads. The other sequences add more radial motion to this basic pattern.

from the same enumeration; and the –4/+3 and –3/+4 sequences include two singletons and one pair. (Note that in some cases brackets identify chords belonging to an enumeration of consonances *above* a fixed note, with the lower voice fixed.) On the spiral diagram, the top line is special insofar as it systematically enumerates the consonances available at every radial position before moving angularly between fifth and sixth (Figure 4.7.3). These sequences are, in other words, as efficient and contrary as it is possible for a consonant sequence to

186  TONALITY: AN OWNER'S MANUAL

Figure 4.7.4. The "Morte" schema uses the ascending-fifth wedge, often with an augmented sixth tonicizing the dominant.

Figure 4.7.5. With an added voice, the four-beat step sequence becomes a two-beat fifth sequence.

be. The remaining sequences add some degree of angular motion to this contrary template, increasing the melodic intervals but not changing the Tinctorian structure of the harmonies.

Parenthesized accidentals show how dominants are most often inserted into the patterns. These alterations turn perfect fifths into tritones, with the added benefit of making the sequence fully invertible at the octave. The −4/+3 and −3/+4 patterns are what I call the "Ludwig schema"—center-of-gravity-preserving enumerations of diatonic consonances, by far the most common of all these sequences. Figure 4.7.4 shows that John Rink's "Morte" schema uses the −3/+4 combination to move from tonic to dominant; its first three notes are often used to move from tonic to subdominant, ascending-fifth counterpoint articulating a descending-fifth progression.

The −1/+6 and −6/+1 patterns require special comment, for their outer voices form genuine step-sequences that, despite the bass, do not factor into a pair of fifths. It is possible to create a fifth-sequence by adding an additional voice: in Figure 4.7.5 the upper voices use the diatonic fifth's basic voice leading, forming a half-note sequential unit that exploits the bass's preexisting periodicity. Many contrary motion step-sequences factor into a pair of fifths in exactly this way: the climactic sequence in *The Well-Tempered Clavier*'s first F major fugue is a good example, featuring descending steps in the canonic upper voices against ascending sevenths in the bass (Figure 4.7.6).[28] Figure 4.7.7 shows the *Hammerklavier*'s opening theme, where ascending steps B♭–C–D appear against descending sevenths, again factored into a pair of descending fourths. Once again the middle voice completes the diatonic

---

[28] Thanks to Daniel Harrison for bringing this example to my attention.

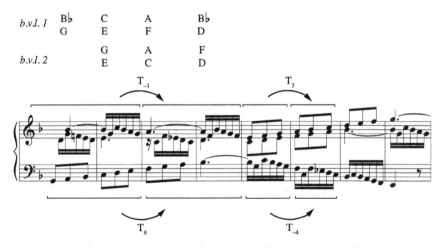

**Figure 4.7.6.** Contrary motion in the first F major fugue from *The Well-Tempered Clavier*, mm. 56ff. The first sequence has a two-measure melodic period and moves by step/seventh; the second has a one-measure period and moves by fourth/fifth. (In the first, the upper voices articulate two instances of the diatonic third's basic voice leading, as shown above the music.) Across the juncture between them, the sixteenth-note figure moves down by third and the ascending eighth notes are doubled a third below. We can imagine B♭–C–D in the left hand of the fourth measure continuing smoothly with E–F–G in the next.

**Figure 4.7.7.** Beethoven's *Hammerklavier*, Op. 106, mm. 5–6, is a contrary-motion sequence. The outer voices, on their own, are a step-sequence with a one-measure period; the middle voice creates an ascending-fifth sequence with a half-measure period.

third's ascending basic voice leading, though you would never notice unless you were looking for it.

The interesting point is that all these contrary-motion sequences are similar from the Tinctorian perspective, sharing the same pattern of relative motion between the hands; we can derive all of them by transposing the list of consonances and (perhaps) eliminating some dyads. All these patterns exemplify the same basic constraint on antiparallel motion: when the harmonic interval is the fifth, the motion is balanced, with the voices moving by almost the same interval; as we move away from this interval, to the third, second, and finally unison, the voices become less and less balanced until the melodic motion is confined to one voice and we recover our original list of consonances. Conversely, since there are only a few ways

188 TONALITY: AN OWNER'S MANUAL

to harmonize contrary-motion patterns with traditional contrapuntal and harmonic principles, contrary motion becomes an important tool for nineteenth- and twentieth-century harmonic expansion—as in passages like Figure 4.1.4, where voice leading is the engine that generates the atonal harmonies.

Transpositional sequences are public knowledge, found in virtually every composer's work and discussed in virtually every harmony textbook. Contrary-motion sequences are more esoteric, a secret compositional art not often subjected to theoretical or pedagogical scrutiny. One gets the sense of magic tricks jealously guarded from the public—and perhaps not equally fascinating to every composer. (These sequences are ubiquitous in Beethoven, common in J. S. Bach and Domenico Scarlatti, and rare in Mozart.) Insofar as theorists have managed to penetrate this veil of secrecy, they have typically glimpsed only a fraction of the whole, identifying isolated sequences without realizing they are species of a single larger genus.[29] In part this reflects a gap in our theoretical knowledge: without the Tinctoris Transform, it is difficult to see the unity among these patterns, or why there would be anything interesting to say about contrary motion in general. Readers are hereby enjoined to keep faith with this esoteric tradition, revealing only what is absolutely necessary to those who have not yet purchased a copy of this book.[30]

## 8. Melodic sequences and near sequences

Textbooks explain that sequences can be purely harmonic, with no melodic repetition, or purely melodic, with only some of the texture's voices repeating. These are special cases of a broader category of *near sequences* in which repetition is disguised or inexact. Analysts have not always been sensitive to the full range of near sequences in the literature, a lacuna that can suggest that regularity is a rigid norm. In fact, however, some of the most sophisticated examples of musical patternmaking are irregular to some degree: like most musical laws, the law of sequence is flexible, with the *impression* of repetition persisting despite small alterations here and there.

The most basic form of melodic sequence is *structured arpeggiation*, in which a surface voice systematically articulates a series of background lines that need not themselves be sequential. The opening of J. S. Bach's first G major cello suite, shown in Figure 4.8.1, is a well-known example, arpeggiating three voices in what is initially a very systematic way; at first, these voices appear in fixed octaves, suggesting a chorale-like background containing specific pitches; as the piece progresses, however, the voices begin to switch octaves, suggesting a more abstract scalar background. The use of nonharmonic tones is also interesting, with the top voice always decorated by a diatonic lower neighbor; consequently, the G in m. 6 is *both* an octave displacement of voice 1 and a lower neighbor to voice 3. (Chopin's A minor

---

[29] Yellin 1998, Rice 2015.
[30] Just kidding.

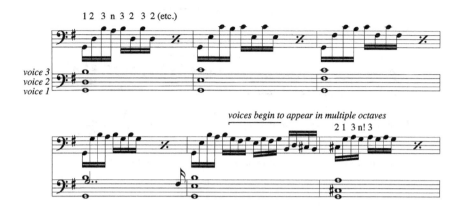

Figure 4.8.1. Structured arpeggiation in the opening of J. S. Bach's first cello suite, BWV 1007.

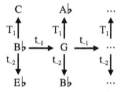

Figure 4.8.2. The sequence in Louis Armstrong's "West End Blues" (Figure P2.2) modeled with both horizontal and vertical arrows. The horizontal or between-motive arrows transpose the harmonic tones along the E♭ major triad; the vertical or within-motive arrows generate nonharmonic tones by transposing along the E♭ diatonic scale.

prelude, to be considered in §9.3, is very similar.) Here the sequence is a foreground phenomenon, the product of surface voices moving regularly along a nonsequential background.

More closely analogous are melodic patterns that transpose as they repeat. These are theoretically interesting because they often imply hierarchical networks in which the distinction between harmonic and nonharmonic plays a structural role. In the prelude to chapter 2, we saw Louis Armstrong moving a motive downward along the E♭ major chord, with the first note a diatonic upper neighbor to the second (Figure P2.2). We can model this with two different kinds of transformational arrow, little-t arrows representing intervals within the triad and big-T arrows representing intervals within the scale (Figure 4.8.2). Here the distinction between harmonic and nonharmonic has a *transformational* significance, with different kinds of tones moving differently from one motive-form to another.

Things get more complicated when composers transpose along both chord and scale. Amy Beach's "Fire-Flies" (Op. 15, no. 4, Figure 4.8.3) begins by moving a quarter-note motive upward along both the D and A melodic-minor scales. Beach then moves a variant motive upward by one step along the A minor triad (acting as the top of F♯ half-diminished in the last measure). The two motives

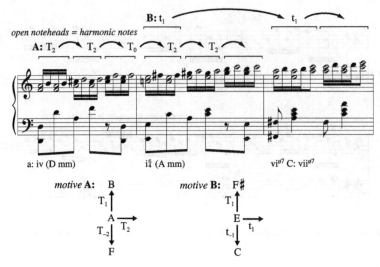

Figure 4.8.3. Transposition along both chord and scale in mm. 9–11 of Amy Beach's "Fire-Flies," Op. 15, no. 4.

interpret similar pitch structures with different transformational arrows: in the first, the vertical dyad is two scale steps, while in the second it is a one-step triadic interval and hence either a third or a fourth. Distinguishing these two kinds of transposition can be difficult: a good rule of thumb is that, over a fixed harmony, transposition along the chord preserves the distinction between harmonic and nonharmonic, while transposition along the scale does not. This is shown by the open noteheads, which change positions in the first motive but stay fixed in the second.

Once again, these examples show that intervallic content is not something fixed, but rather a variable whose value is revealed by musical development: one and the same motive can be subjected to multiple interpretations, treated first as a collection of scalar intervals and then as a collection of triadic intervals. This is particularly important in the analysis of fugue subjects, whose notes can be associated either with the tonic or dominant scale degree; the former are answered down by fourth while the latter are answered down by fifth (Figure 4.8.4). Thus, rather than thinking of tonal answers as *distorting* or *altering* the original subject, we can think of them as *exact* transpositions of complex hierarchical structures.[31] In other words, a fugue's alternating tonic-dominant entries are an *exact* melodic sequence that moves along the tonic-dominant perfect fifth. Creating a fugue subject involves not just writing a melody but also deciding on its pattern of hierarchical dependencies.[32]

---

[31] The tonic note moves down by fourth, the dominant down by fifth; consequently, composers can choose between a real answer in the dominant, a nearly subdominant answer, or some mixture of the two. In many of *The Well-Tempered Clavier*'s fugue subjects, only the first dominant note is echoed at the fifth below; but some have more thoroughly subdominant answers (e.g., the first E♭ major and G♯ minor fugues).

[32] Similarly, Shostakovich's more chromatic fugue subjects combine diatonic and chromatic intervals.

**Figure 4.8.4.** The subject and answer to the first B♭ minor fugue in *The Well-Tempered Clavier*; here, "t" refers to transposition along the root-fifth dyad. The subject's G♭5 sounds like a displaced neighbor to the preceding F5; however, it transforms as a sixth above the initial B♭.

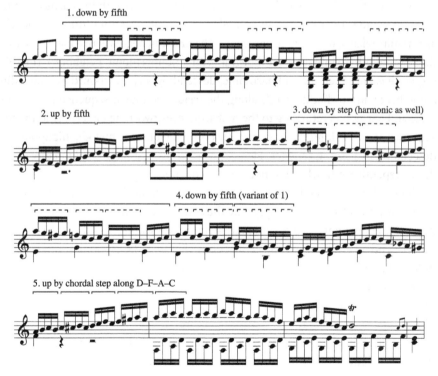

**Figure 4.8.5.** Five melodic sequences in the second theme of Mozart's K.310, I.

Once we sensitize ourselves to these phenomena, a new world of structure comes into focus. Figure 4.8.5 shows the second theme of the first movement of Mozart's A minor piano sonata, whose twelve measures contain no fewer than five melodic sequences. This music would not ordinarily be considered sequential—in the language

**Figure 4.8.6.** Measures 136–138 of "October," from Fanny Mendelssohn Hensel's *Das Jahr*, H. 385. The music presents two short sequences that move along the four-note scale A♭–B♭–C–E♭ (the "horn fifth scale"). The passage uses two-step intervals within the four-note scale, always forming either A♭–C or B♭–E♭.

of chapter 7, it belongs to the subsystem of harmonic cycles rather than the sequential system. Yet there is a sense in which the melody is pervasively and insistently repetitive. The opening measure is an exact melodic sequence that shifts position relative to the nonsequential harmony, starting on the root of the I chord and descending by fifth to the third of the ii chord; it then descends in conjunction with the harmony to the thirds of V and I. The next measure contains a two-unit ascending-fifth sequence that again shifts relative to the static harmony. (The first unit begins with a harmonic tone, the chordal fifth, while its second begins with a nonharmonic neighbor.) The third sequence is both melodic and harmonic, descending-step fauxbourdon embedding a one-beat pattern that descends along the triad. The fourth sequence is both melodic and harmonic, returning to the first sequence's two-note pattern. And the fifth sequence ascends along the ii$^7$ chord, regaining the phrase's melodic highpoint and descending to a strong cadence. Here we start to see that functional tonality can be deeply repetitive even when it is not strictly sequential.

Though I have studied classical music for more than three and a half decades, I have only recently come to appreciate the complexity of its melodic procedures—its motives moving in regular and quasi-regular ways along chords, scales, chordal subsets, and a variety of bespoke collections (Figure 4.8.6).[33] Sometimes it can be difficult to unpack the relative contributions of transposition along chord, transposition along the scale, and structured arpeggiation. And sometimes we find operations not easily captured by familiar music-theoretical terminology: in Figure 4.8.7, Mozart moves an intervallic pattern from a three-note triad to a four-note seventh chord, collections that are not themselves related by transposition. Debussy used this sort of "interscalar transposition" to shift melodies from the seven-note diatonic collection to the six-note whole-tone scale and back. Mozart's chordal use of this technique is more likely to pass unnoticed, in large part because we think we understand his music better than we do.

---

[33] This "horn fifths" pattern exploits the same structure that gives rise to Figures 4.6.1–3, alternating between the vertical dyads A♭–C and E♭–B♭.

**Figure 4.8.7.** The second movement of Mozart's K.533, mm. 96–98, presents the same melodic intervals in four-note and three-note collections.

## 9. Near sequences

Another important type of near sequence is the *variable* sequence in which some feature changes slightly: either the unit, the transposition, or the permutation. Figure 4.9.1, from the penultimate phrase of Louise Farrenc's Op. 19 *Souvenir des Huguenots*, combines two of the most common sequential alterations, changing the interval of transposition and compressing the sequential unit from two bars to one. The first change ensures that the sequence returns to the tonic after just four iterations; the second creates variation and increases excitement. (Changes in transpositional level also function to avoid undesired tonicizations, in this case the major-mode mediant.) We can notate the alteration in transpositional level with a *list* of transpositions through which each voice cycles in a circular fashion. A substantial number of sequential passages have small changes of this sort—including many fifths-sequences in which the bass alternates ascending fourths with descending fifths (e.g., the lower passage in Figure 4.3.2, where the music is exactly sequential at the level of the bar and nearly sequential at the level of the half bar).

Another class of near sequence arises from the elimination of sequential units, creating a moment of surprise that allows the sequence to be extended without taxing the listener's patience. The development of the first movement of the first Mozart piano sonata, K.279, contains a memorable example: after switching to the dominant minor and ascending by fifths, the music begins a harmonic sequence of 11 descending fifths (A–d–G–C–[F]–B♭–E–a–D–g–C–F, shown in Figure 4.9.2); the bracketed F major does not appear, leading to a glitch in the harmonic structure—a descending jolt that sets up the turn to A minor and the change of texture. Note that the first three and a half beats of the B♭ major measure are in the exact registral arrangement mandated by the sequence, reinforcing the suspicion that a measure has simply been deleted. The resulting music conveys a sense of a process imprecisely carried out, the background engine of fifths continuing despite a momentary hiccup—reminiscent of the "broken systems" in twentieth-century music.[34]

---

[34] Russell 2018.

**Figure 4.9.1.** The variable sequence just before the end of Louise Farrenc's *Souvenir des Huguenots*, Op. 19.

Still a third form of near sequence repeats one of the progressions in a two-chord sequence such as the Pachelbel or ascending 5–6: that is, rather than alternating D3, A4, D3, A4, a composer repeats a progression to obtain A4, A4, D3 or D3, D3, A4. This can lead to a sense of consistency despite the deviation from sequential exactness. In many cases, composers will repeat a chord to keep the repeating root-progression in its expected rhythmic location. Figure 4.9.3 shows how this works in the case of the ascending 5–6, with a chord repetition generating consecutive ascending-fourth or descending-third progressions—and preserving the sequence's repeating V–I structure while varying the underlying harmony. In Duke Ellington's "Satin Doll" the repeated A chord allows for two consecutive fifths without disrupting the ii–V organization of each bar (Figure 4.9.4). Figure 4.9.5 shows a classical example that substitutes diminished triads for dominant chords, leading to free ascent in the three triadic voices. We will encounter similar near sequences in Beethoven's Fifth Symphony and his second Razumovsky quartet (Figures 10.4.14 and 8.4.3 respectively).[35]

---

[35] See also Figure 4.3.8, Monteverdi's "Cosi sol d'un chiara fonte" (Madrigals, Book 8, no. 4, part 2 of "Hor ch'el Ciel e la Terra," mm. 14ff), and Beethoven's First Symphony, Op. 21, I, mm. 81–86. When triads are in

**Figure 4.9.2.** The development of Mozart's piano sonata K.279, I, begins with a long sequence of descending fifths from which one chord has been eliminated.

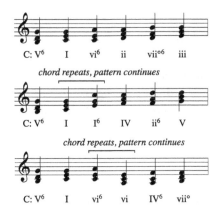

**Figure 4.9.3.** This passage alters the standard ascending-step sequence in two ways—first repeating the C major chord that functions as a quasi-tonic, and second repeating the A minor chord that functions as a quasi-dominant; this leads to consecutive descending fifths (V–I–IV) or consecutive descending thirds (I–vi–IV).

Stepping back a little further, we can locate sequences within the broader class of *transformationally restricted* passages. Where a standard sequence repeatedly applies a *single* transformation, these latter passages draw from a small collection of transformations, often closely related. The five excerpts in Figure 4.9.6

---

close position, this can produce free alternations of descending thirds and fifths, with either the fifth or the third and fifth moving up by step.

196  TONALITY: AN OWNER'S MANUAL

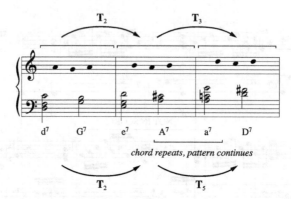

Figure 4.9.4. Duke Ellington's "Satin Doll" starts as a standard ascending-step sequence, but with the units expressing ii–V rather than V–I functionality. At the third iteration, the root stays fixed while the melody ascends by three semitones, continuing the pattern in an unpredictable way.

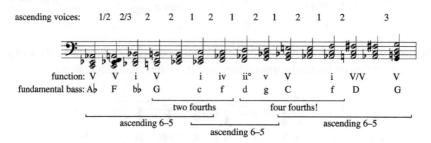

Figure 4.9.5. The ascending 5–6 in the *Waldstein* sonata's first-movement coda, mm. 251ff, with first-inversion chords functioning as both tonics and dominants. The fundamental bass contains the roots of the triads that would normally have those harmonic functions.

exhibit broadly similar structure, lines divided into groups that move in doubly parallel motion along both chord and scale. The first is exactly sequential; the second is almost sequential, alternating between three- and four-step descending diatonic transposition, while the last three combine the two transpositions more freely; taken together they suggest a continuum from sequence to free composition, determined by which features of contrapuntal structure are held fixed. Figure 4.9.7 models one region of that continuum, exemplifying the various combinations of repeating contrapuntal pattern (R), harmonic consistency (H, or the use of a single chord-type), and preservation of spacing-in-chordal-steps (S). The passages featuring R are all paradigmatically sequential; the combination SH is not, as it permits arbitrary combinations of transposition along both chord and scale. Yet the result is regular enough so as to bear comparison with sequences in the strict sense.

**Figure 4.9.6.** Palestrina's passage is an exact sequence whose upper voices have a one-chord unit and whose bass has a two-chord unit; Beethoven's is a near sequence in which the scalar transposition varies irregularly between descending fourth and fifth. The last three passages freely combine transposition along chord and scale.

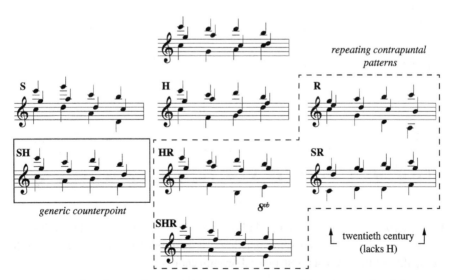

**Figure 4.9.7.** Combining three properties: preservation of spacing-in-chordal-steps (S), harmonic consistency (H), and repeating contrapuntal pattern (R). The top measure uses different chord types, different voice leadings, and different spacings; the bottom uses the repeating contrapuntal pattern $t_1 T_{-4}$. The boxed SH measure uses a variety of patterns of the form $t_x T_y$.

## 10. Sequences as reductional targets

In *A Geometry of Music*, I analyzed Chopin's E minor prelude as a descending-fifth sequence disguised by a series of semitonal descents, with each dominant seventh's third, fifth, and seventh descending freely *en route* to the next dominant seventh (Figure 4.10.1).[36] I think this sort of analysis can provide a sense of ownership, helping us imagine how we might arrive at such unusual melting harmonies—that is, that we might embellish a sequential middleground with chromatic descent. That the descents traverse the edges of a four-dimensional hypercube provides an additional and more cerebral analytical payoff.

Now let us consider the theme of the variations movement in Beethoven's piano trio, Op. 1, no. 3. The basic structure here is the circle-of-fifths sequence generated by the diatonic third's basic voice leading. In Figure 4.10.2, Beethoven subposes a new bass underneath the dyadic sequence, creating primary-triad harmonies that avoid the functionally awkward vii°–iii–vi; this transforms a regular dyadic sequence into a quasi-regular triadic sequence, seven descending fifths becoming a pair of TSDT cycles. My suggestion is that this quasi-regular structure is further distorted to produce the final version of the theme, the C moving from the inner voice of chord 5 to the upper voice of chord 6. The music reveals this quasi-sequential structure only gradually, first presenting eight notes of the pattern (Figure 4.10.3, iteration 1), then ten, then sixteen. This is the technique of the *disguised model*, moving from obscurity toward clarity as the music progresses.

It is not until the third variation that Beethoven becomes fully explicit about the harmonic logic, lifting the curtain on his compositional process to reveal a

Figure 4.10.1. Chopin's E minor prelude embellishes a middleground descending-fifth sequence with a series of semitonal descents on the surface. These freely lower the third, fifth, and seventh of the structural seventh chords.

---

[36] See chapter 8 of Tymoczko 2011a.

**Figure 4.10.2.** (*top*) The circle of fifth-related diatonic thirds augmented by a bass line that creates a pair of TSDT harmonic cycles; (*middle*) a distortion of this schema using I⁶ and ii⁶ and shifting the fifth chord's C to the sixth chord; (*bottom*) the end of the theme from Beethoven's Op. 1, no. 3, II (mm. 21–24).

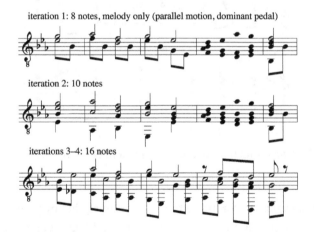

**Figure 4.10.3.** Three iterations of the theme of Beethoven's Piano Trio, Op. 1, no. 3, II. The basic voice leading becomes increasingly clear each time.

completely sequential structure (Figure 4.10.4).[37] Or perhaps what is revealed is the nature of functional music more generally, since Beethoven's theme is about as typical as one could imagine. In either case, the result is a profound reimagining of the variation form, proceeding not by progressive *embellishment* (embodied in

---

[37] In the last variation the falling fifths of the third variation are factored into falling thirds (§7.2).

200 TONALITY: AN OWNER'S MANUAL

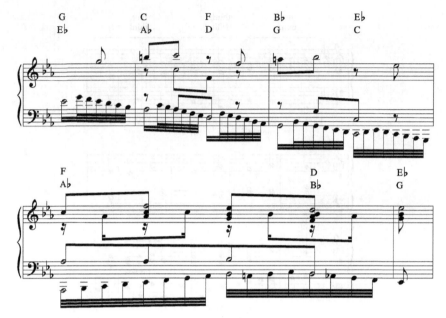

Figure 4.10.4. Overtly sequential structure at the end of the third variation of Beethoven's Op. 1, no. 3, II.

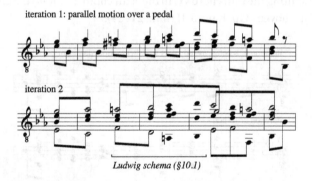

Figure 4.10.5. Transformations of the consequent in Op. 1, no. 3, II.

ever-faster note values decorating a thematic original), but by progressive *analysis*, stripping away decoration to reveal a latent musical logic (Figures 4.10.5–6). The entire third variation is a series of perturbed fifths, reminiscent of the *Pathétique*'s A♭ major episode. One can hardly appreciate the profundity of this moment unless one is sensitive to the near sequences buried within the ostensibly freely composed theme.

Here again we can see the sequential structure as a template or middleground. Like Chopin, Beethoven presumably started with a ubiquitous schema, altering it to produce something less obviously regular. This suggests a form of analytical "reduction" that traces irregular surfaces back to their simpler origins. Notice, however, that where the Chopin analysis removed *notes*, stripping away the semitonal

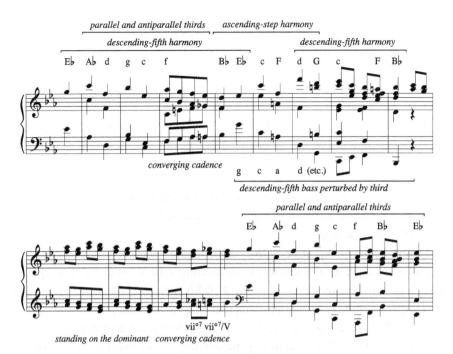

**Figure 4.10.6.** A reduction of the third variation in Beethoven's Op. 1, no. 3, II. Aside from the two descending thirds E♭–c and F–d, the harmony is entirely composed of descending-fifth progressions.

descents to reveal a shorter background, the Beethoven analysis instead postulates a template of more or less the same length; instead of removing notes it removes *compositional decision points*, transforming the irregular into the regular—a machine that, once started, runs without the need for composerly input. My suggestion is that Beethoven's surface is derived by a process of tinkering with the machine's output, producing a result that is more complicated but no longer than the original.

Sequence-based reduction reflects the belief that a great deal of music is covertly repetitive even where it might not initially appear to be. To the extent that listeners perceive this regularity, it shapes their expectations. To the extent that it is disguised, it can create the magical experience of inexplicable inevitability, of an aural logic that cannot be easily described. From this perspective, disguised repetition—as opposed to the more overt repetition in rock or minimalism—is a defining characteristic of functional tonality. In its simpler forms we have the *Pathétique*'s A♭ major episode, which uses octave displacements and converging cadences to disguise its falling fifths, or the Chase schema, where composers can change the harmonic rhythm by bringing in voices at either the unison or the fifth. At a more sophisticated level we have Chopin's E minor prelude, where longer sections of music are governed by submerged musical patterns. In other cases, we have entire movements constructed from a handful of sequences (§10.3). Chapter 7 will connect this approach to Rameau's claim that *harmonic functionality* is itself a quasi-sequential phenomenon, disguising descending-fifth architecture with

**Figure 4.10.7.** A Schenkerian analysis of mm. 21–24 of Beethoven's Op. 1, no. 3, II. The original music is shown at the bottom of Figure 4.10.2.

surface-level transformations.[38] In other words, rather than imagining sequences as deviant, we can reconceive nonsequential functionality with reference to a fundamentally repetitive norm.

Contrast this perspective with a Schenkerian approach that consigns sequential structure to the surface, as decorating a fundamentally nonsequential middleground. The reduction in Figure 4.10.7 is typical, its nonsequential analysis running roughshod over the almost-regular pattern pervading Beethoven's musical surface.[39] I would argue that this represents a problematic devaluing of repetition *and also* that the $\hat{3}$–$\hat{2}$–$\hat{1}$ descent is genuinely important. In other words, we seem to be in the presence of two complementary truths: that functional tonality often features near-sequential organization, repeating harmonic and melodic patterns in a slightly disguised fashion, and also that it features stepwise melodic connections between nonadjacent notes, a "slower melody" taking place behind the musical surface. This tension between the mechanistic and organic devolves through an extended chain of reasoning into the conflict between traditional harmonic theory and Schenkerian analysis. Our challenge is to balance these vital but seemingly incompatible perspectives.

Chapters 7 and 9 will explore these issues further. Readers who are particularly interested in modern music—or who would like to see "Gesualdo's trick" analyzed as a hierarchical sequence-by-inversion—might want to read appendix 3 while these topics are still fresh.

---

[38] Meyer 1982, Gosman 2009, and Yust 2015a all explore ideas related to sequential reduction. Christensen 1993a refers to Rameau's "mechanization" of harmonic motion.

[39] This analysis is my own simplification of one by David Damschroder (2018, p. 30), who should not be held responsible for it. The melodic F is viewed as a decoration of the A♭, while the other melodic thirds are treated differently.

# Prelude
## Three Varieties of Analytical Reduction

Central to contemporary analysis is the practice of *reduction*: eliminating "surface" musical activity to reveal a "background" clarifying a piece's logic. Theorists generally pursue three kinds of reductive analysis. The simplest is *nonharmonic reduction*, the removal of nonharmonic notes to leave behind a "harmonic skeleton" containing only chord tones. A second is *textural reduction*, transforming complex instrumental textures into chorales typically exemplifying the laws of good counterpoint. The third and most far-reaching is *summarizing reduction*, removing notes to show long-range connections between nonadjacent events. Though fundamental to virtually all analytic endeavor, these different forms of reduction are poorly understood, in part because music-theoretical scholarship has not always distinguished them, in part because there is reason to suspect that earlier composers did not share our reductive instincts, and in part because the topic raises difficult philosophical questions.

Broadly speaking, nonharmonic reduction is a kind of *syntactic* analysis analogous to the parsing of a sentence into its component clauses. By dividing music into "structural" harmonies decorated by nonharmonic tones, we clarify its organizational logic, reducing a complex surface to a small number of stereotypical harmonies decorated in a small number of stereotypical ways. This is, in the first instance, a pedagogical tool for helping students come to grips with earlier music in all its intimidating complexity. But it can also be said to reveal the rules of the game that is musical composition: rules for constructing consonances, rules for decorating them with dissonances, and rules governing the progression of consonances themselves. This form of reduction is most appropriate when genres have strict policies regarding harmonic content and melodic embellishment; it makes more sense for Palestrina and Bach than for Debussy or Sonic Youth.

Even in strict styles, however, we sometimes find that nonharmonic reduction fails, either because there is no way to eliminate the purportedly nonharmonic notes, or because those notes seem to have genuinely harmonic functions. In Figure P5.1, for example, nonharmonic analysis forces us to choose between two equally plausible readings: an intervallic view in which we have parallel tenths between the two hands and a chordal view in which we have parallel triadic arpeggiations. (These two interpretations in turn evoke the traditions of modal counterpoint and functional harmony.) If we think a piece's harmonies are straightforwardly real and nonharmonic analysis a matter of uncovering an objectively existing "harmonic skeleton," then one analysis must be right and the other wrong. But I prefer

*Tonality.* Dmitri Tymoczko, Oxford University Press. © Oxford University Press 2023. DOI: 10.1093/oso/9780197577103.003.0008

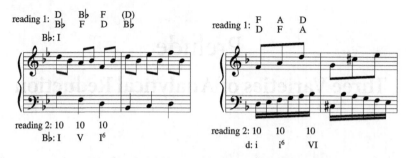

**Figure P5.1.** (*left*) The opening of the first Minuet from Bach's Partita in B♭, BWV 825. (*right*) Measures 3–4 of Bach's D minor two-part invention BWV 775.

**Figure P5.2.** Beethoven's Op. 54, II, mm. 14–15. De-arpeggiation turns the D♯ into a chromatic neighbor.

to imagine the music as suspended between these two poles; if so, then even this simple form of reduction is fundamentally interpretive, producing partially true models of complex and ambiguous musical surfaces.[1]

*Textural reduction* can also serve a syntactic purpose, rationalizing anomalous notes by postulating multiple voices: on a literal reading, the melodic D♯3 in Figure P5.2 is what I call a "rogue note," an unusual dissonance that is leapt-to and leapt-away-from; if we postulate multiple voices, however, it becomes a chromatic neighbor.[2] This simple form of textural analysis might be called "de-arpeggiation," as it converts an arpeggiated texture into a chorale containing the very same pitches; it is the inverse of what §4.8 called "structured arpeggiation." A more sophisticated form of textural reduction, introduced in §1.2, postulates surface voices moving along backgrounds that are more abstract and scale-like. Figure P5.3 contrasts these two approaches: in the first analysis, the figuration stands for a three-voice chorale whose relation to the surface is somewhat oblique; in the second, we have a melodic pattern that moves along a three-note scale that is itself moving. This second analysis in turn appears in two variants, one postulating efficient scalar voice leading but starting each iteration of the melodic pattern on a different scale

---

[1] Ian Quinn first alerted me to the complexities of nonharmonic reduction.
[2] Christoph Bernhard ([~1640] 1973) was one of the first theorists to distinguish surface and abstract voices.

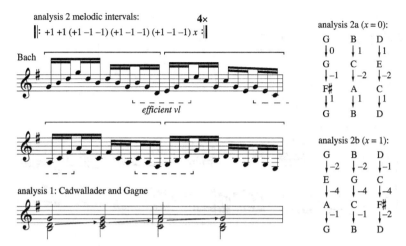

Figure P5.3. Three analyses of the right hand at the start of the first G major prelude in *The Well-Tempered Clavier*. The first postulates a three-voice chorale, while the others postulate a melodic sequence moving along a small scale. The choice of the pattern's final melodic interval determines the scalar voice leading.

degree, the other postulating less-efficient voice leading but starting each pattern on the same scale degree—and hence more closely tracking the surface.[3]

The scalar strategy can help ameliorate some awkward analytical problems. While most Alberti-style patterns can be verticalized to form law-abiding concrete voices, some cannot (Figure P5.4). Similarly, many classical-style IV–I progressions suggest parallel octaves with the melody, often softened by suspensions or incomplete neighbors; indeed, such parallels are closer to rule than exception, even in large-ensemble contexts (Figure P5.5). And of course there are numerous chordal skips that would produce parallels were they straightforwardly de-arpeggiated (Figure P5.6). It is not so much the frequency of these moments as their character that is problematic: a composer who genuinely imagined Alberti-style patterns to represent concrete voices simply would not write the music in Figure P5.4, as it is clearly and obviously defective from that point of view. This is a place where pedagogical oversimplification can cause real damage, for students will often avoid these idioms even if their teacher allows them—wanting to "play the game right," they will no more violate the musical "rules" than they would follow a coach's suggestion to cheat during a sporting event.[4] But earlier composers *did* write such passages, frequently and, one presumes, without guilt. The issue, then, is their *obvious wrongness*, a wrongness suggesting composers did not always think of arpeggiated textures as representing chorale-like backgrounds.

Schema theorists would argue that this gap between theory and practice can be explained by the way earlier composers learned their trade—as a practice, a set of

---

[3] Thanks here to Ian Sewell. The scalar approach is both highly constrained and yet capable of recreating some characteristic features of Schenkerian analysis.
[4] Burstein 2020 tries to justify traditional pedagogical strictness, but I worry that his arguments resort to unjustified ideology (e.g., that upward resolutions of the cadential six-four chord necessarily represent the standard descending resolution, or that occasional inner-voice parallel fifths create a perceptible weakening of voice independence).

206  TONALITY: AN OWNER'S MANUAL

**Figure P5.4.** Passages where Mozart's accompaniment suggests parallel fifths.

musical routines, a spoken language whose grammar was not explicitly theorized. (And of course at an early age, rather than as young adults in college classrooms.) English speakers naturally and unconsciously accept the dummy subject in a sentence like "it's raining": by the time we are old enough to wonder what "it" is, we are so accustomed to the phrase that we do not feel its strangeness. In much the same way, a young musician might play hundreds of passages such as those in Figures P5.4–6 before noticing that they could be said to contain forbidden parallels. Such passages would simply be part of the language, the way "it's raining" is part of ours. As a result, we should not be surprised to find arpeggiated accompaniments suspended somewhere between genuine polyphony and undifferentiated harmony.

This response is fine as far as it goes, but I suspect that there is also a deeper issue here: eighteenth-century musicians recognized a class of musical objects that were qualitatively different from, and analytically irreducible to, chorale-like arrangements of pitches—nonspecific "accompanimental stuff" that augments the concrete soprano and bass voices of figured-bass notation. The picture of chords-as-scales allows us to model this richer ontology without abandoning analytical rigor: in Figure P5.7, for example, we can postulate a concrete bass and soprano, the latter articulated by the top of an arpeggio that moves along a shifting triadic alphabet.[5] This arpeggio activates a background not localized to any specific register and substantially immune to standard contrapuntal strictures. (There is no possibility of

---

[5] The extreme notes of an arpeggiation pattern tend to be treated as belonging to a concrete voice when they form the outer voice of a musical texture; thus Mozart would typically avoid parallels between a concrete melody and the lowest note of the Alberti patterns in Figure P5.4, which represent a concrete bass line; similarly, Beethoven would typically avoid parallels between a concrete bass line and the highest notes of a pattern such as that in Figure P5.7. Once again, this recalls figured-bass thinking, which often combines concrete soprano and bass with abstract harmonies.

**Figure P5.5.** IV($^6_4$)–I progressions suggesting parallel octaves: Haydn, Symphony no. 100, I, mm. 97–98; Mozart Piano Concerto no. 23, K.488, III, mm. 213–215; Beethoven, Symphony no. 7, Op. 92, I, mm. 74–75; Chopin, Mazurka, Op. 30, no. 2, mm. 33–34.

forbidden parallels *within* the abstract background, nor *between* background and surface; parallels occur between concrete voices only.[6]) From a hierarchical perspective there is nothing suspect about this passage; but if we try to reduce it to specific pitches, then we can avoid parallels only at the cost of radically inconsistent analysis.[7]

*Summarizing reduction*, is, paradoxically, both the most speculative and least problematic form of reduction: here we boil a complex passage down into something

---

[6] In pitch-class space there is no distinction between parallel fifths and parallel fourths, and parallel octaves occur only in the (extremely rare) situation where we want to postulate scale-like backgrounds with scale steps of size 0. Surface voices move *inside* the pitch-class background, and cannot form parallels with it.

[7] Weber (1817–1821) 1846, p. 827, explicitly argues that arpeggiated lines are not actual parts but only "imagined" parts, and hence are less strictly bound by the rule against parallel fifths (p. 836).

208　TONALITY: AN OWNER'S MANUAL

**Figure P5.6.** Idiomatic passages where verticalization of chordal skips produces parallels: Marianna Martines, A major Sonata IMM 14, II, m. 15–16 (1765); Mozart, K.333, III, m. 17; and Bach's chorale "Gelobet seist du, Jesu Christ" (BWV 91/6, Riemenschneider 51), mm. 1–2.

**Figure P5.7.** The start of the trio of Beethoven's Op. 2, no. 3. Carl Schachter's reduction postulates a doubled A3 that is not motivated by the music; my alternative features a regular melodic sequence in a shifting scalar background.

simpler, finding familiar musical patterns guiding longer stretches of musical time. If nonharmonic reduction reveals the rules of the musical game, then summarizing reduction provides conjectures about a composer's *strategic* ends, analogous to the suggestion that an expert chess player intends to put pressure on a specific square. In this way it can provide a hypothetical blueprint, an outline or plan that helps us understand how a composition might have been made.[8] Such analysis is inherently speculative, requiring a careful alignment between composer and analyst—a good sense of a composer's tendencies and characteristic moves. One major achievement of recent schema theory is to reveal a much wider range of strategies, directing our attention to a host of common patterns such as the "Prinner," "Indugio," and "Morte."

Crucially, schemas are often occluded by *diminution*, with important schematic notes hidden among a wealth of decorative figuration. Schenkerian theory typically understands diminution as a matter of less important notes *representing* more important notes "at a deeper structural level," a "standing for" that derives from our experience with the nonharmonic system. This habit of thinking is so ingrained that it is surprising to realize that it is superfluous. For consider a summary of a movie: when we omit episodes extraneous to the main plot, we do not imply that this material *represents* or *prolongs* the core narrative. Or imagine a group of improvising actors beginning with the skeletal outline of a plot to be embellished spontaneously.[9] Or a skilled chess player pausing their offense as they fight off an opponent's threat. In all these cases, there is a higher-level plan that contains within it a variety of subsidiary lower-level events, which we can eliminate from our summaries without invoking the notion of representation.[10]

From this point of view, summarizing reduction gives us something like a *paraphrase* of a composer's musical ends, akin to those we apply to sports or games or movies. Though these reductions can be important analytical tools, they are by their nature tentative: we should no more aspire to come up with a singular correct summary of a piece than we should strive to produce the perfect paraphrase of a movie. (For this reason I am skeptical of attempts to automate or quantify the process of summarizing reduction, which inherently requires high-level understanding.[11]) Nor is there any reason to expect that our paraphrases will take some specific form—that they will conform to the principles of species counterpoint, that bass lines will always move from tonic to dominant, or that the melodic structure of an entire piece will necessarily descend from a tonic-triad note to the root. Here I think the music-theoretical community could benefit from more informality: rather than conceiving of summarizing reduction as a syntactic project analogous to nonharmonic reduction, it would be better to imagine it as producing hypotheses about composers' intentions. We will return to this point in chapter 9.

---

[8] For similar approaches to reduction see Temperley 2011a, Cook 1989, Sewell 2021. The Schenkerian analyses in Figures P5.3 and P5.7 are discussed by Sewell; the scale-based alternatives are my own.

[9] Gjerdingen (2007, chapter 1) cites the *commedia dell'arte* as a model for musical schemas. Reef 2020 provides a nice example of a Bachian template that sits somewhere between schema theory and Schenkerian theory.

[10] Yust (2015, 2018) questions the connection between representation and prolongation, though he ends up much closer to standard Schenkerian practice than I do.

[11] See, for example, Lerdahl 2001 and Kirlin 2014.

# 5

# Nonharmonic Tones

Western music has traditionally been a music of rules: rules about how chords are constituted, rules constraining the relation between harmonic and nonharmonic, rules governing the avoidance of parallels or antiparallels, rules about which notes can be doubled, rules about how chords progress, and countless others besides. The rules regulating nonharmonic tones are perhaps the most important, in large part because they ensure a certain sort of *teachability*—allowing us to mark our students right and wrong without consulting our aesthetic preferences. They are also intimately connected to the practice of reductive analysis, the replacing of nonharmonic tones with their harmonic partners. In many styles this produces a *harmonic skeleton* that can be said to carry the weight of the musical argument. The nonharmonic system thus allows theorists to play the role of structural engineers, distinguishing the load-bearing and ornamental walls of the musical house.

All of which works much better in theory than in practice. For as we will see, received views of nonharmonicity are empirically inadequate, assimilating suspensions to decorations even though they resist our best attempts at reduction. They are plagued by inconsistency, as when they treat the permissibility of parallel fifths on different musical levels. And they are aesthetically problematic, encouraging us to ignore the myriad ways in which nonharmonic tones can contribute to fundamentally harmonic narratives. We do not have to stray far from the Austro-Germanic canon to find composers like Domenico Scarlatti blatantly disregarding traditional rules—or styles in which the distinction between "chordal" and "nonchordal" is inherently blurry.[1] These problems have provoked some theorists to protest against the very notion of nonharmonicity, searching for alternatives in which harmonic and nonharmonic are on a more equal footing.[2] Indeed, this is one motivation for the recent turn to figured-bass nomenclature, where there is a less-sharp distinction between the harmonic and linear realms.[3]

One issue here is the theoretical tendency to overvalue rules at the expense of concrete idioms, a Platonic streak running throughout the history of Western musical thought. Beyond that, however, is a deeper and more uncomfortable fact about

---

[1] Sutcliffe 2003, chapter 5.
[2] See, for example, Schoenberg (1911) 1983, Narmour 1988, or Quinn 2018.
[3] See Gjerdingen 2007 and Holtmeier 2007, who essentially invert Riemann's argument that figured-bass notation makes too *little* distinction between harmonic and nonharmonic (Riemann 1896, p. 107).

*Tonality.* Dmitri Tymoczko, Oxford University Press. © Oxford University Press 2023. DOI: 10.1093/oso/9780197577103.003.0009

the language itself, namely that composers sometimes viewed the nonharmonic system with a degree of irony, writing music in which purportedly nonharmonic notes had important harmonic effects. The nonharmonic system was less like a system of moral commandments than it was like the speed limit, often seen as a nuisance and sometimes obeyed only grudgingly.[4] (This is obviously true of Monteverdi, Domenico Scarlatti, and Mahler, but I believe it holds for Palestrina and J. S. Bach as well.) Like the speed limit, the rules were real enough, explaining behavior that would otherwise remain inexplicable. But a deep understanding of earlier music requires acknowledging the gap between the theoretical precepts of the nonharmonic system and the meaning of the music produced under its aegis. This leads to an awkward terminological problem, for we should neither claim that "nonharmonic tones are harmonic" nor assert its negation. Nonharmonicity, or perhaps ~~nonharmonicity~~, is an inherently unstable notion, both useful and misleading, explanatory and yet false to the music it purports to describe.[5]

Misunderstanding this point sometimes leads pedagogues to discourage the very techniques that enabled composers to express themselves freely. Thus we forbid practices that were merely somewhat uncommon: consecutive strong-beat parallels, parallels masked by suspension, and antiparallel fifths in four or fewer voices.[6] Haydn's reported comments about Kirnberger aptly express this point: "too cautious, too confining, too everlastingly many infinitely tiny restrictions for a free spirit."[7] This persnickitude is often associated with the abdication of aesthetic responsibility, for by forbidding antiparallels we allow ourselves to avoid questions about whether a particular passage is pleasing or stylistic: the whole subject is simply off the table. An alternative would be to deemphasize rules in favor of more directly musical questions, emphasizing fluid creativity over legalistic niceties. Sometimes what looks like rigor is really just a desire to make it through the day with our red pencils intact.

## 1. The first practice and the SNAP system

The first great era of nonharmonic control was based on what I call "the SNAP system": suspensions, neighbors, anticipations, and passing tones. Though often said to originate with Josquin, this *prima prattica* stabilized somewhat later, in

---

[4] In the course of a sensitive discussion, Weber (1817–1821) 1846, p. 830, protests against "the furious persecution against every thing that has the name of fifths."

[5] For clarity, I will continue to use the standard term "nonharmonic" even though it occasionally leads to paradoxical language.

[6] Sometimes pedagogues forbid practices that are actually common, such as cadences in which inner-voice leading tones do not resolve, or doubling the third of a first-inversion tonic. Some of these superstrict prohibitions can be traced back to dogmas contemporaneous with the music in question, suggesting a longstanding conflict between theoretical regularization and compositional heterogeneity. See, for example, Vicentino's prohibitions on simultaneous leaps in ensembles of various sizes (Vicentino [1555] 1996, book 2, chapter 30, Arthur 2021).

[7] Quoted in Mirka 2015, p. 165.

**Figure 5.1.1.** Unusual nonharmonic tones. In mm. 106–107 of Josquin's motet "Liber generationis," we have both an incomplete neighbor and an upward-resolving suspension (A–B on beat 4). In mm. 18–19 of Clemens's "Concussum est Mare," we have a nonharmonic tone that is both leapt-to and leapt-away-from.

the music of Palestrina and contemporaries such as Lassus and Byrd.[8] Earlier polyphony features an array of incomplete neighbors, upward-resolving suspensions, and the occasional inexplicable moment (Figure 5.1.1). The Palestrina style largely eliminates these, retaining the cambiata as the sole surviving incomplete neighbor. The resulting music is astonishing in its systematicity, almost completely free of the occasional glitches that mark most human productions. Among his other achievements, Palestrina was one of the great proofreaders in human history.

This music is highly susceptible to computational analysis—partly because musical voices are directly embodied in the notation, partly because it contains relatively few changes of tonal center, and partly because there is little need for concepts such as the "nonharmonic consonance."[9] Consequently, it takes just a few hours of programming to produce a reasonably accurate survey of nonharmonic usage in Palestrina's work.[10] The success of such simple algorithms testifies to the tight constraints governing the vocabulary: virtually all the nonharmonic tones can be labeled and removed algorithmically, leaving behind a triadic skeleton exactly as described in textbooks. This is perhaps the closest that Western music has ever come to the theorist's dream of purely consonant harmony decorated by clearly nonharmonic embellishment.

Palestrina's nonharmonic tones can be said to be decorative in the specific sense that they rarely obscure the entire duration of a consonance. This means, first,

---

[8] See, for example, Taruskin 2005, volume 2, chapters 14–16, which identifies Josquin as the source of the "ars perfecta." Monteverdi's brother Giulio Cesare instead identifies Ockeghem (Strunk 1950, p. 408). Counterpoint textbooks tend to take Palestrina's practice as representative of this broader and more varied tradition.

[9] See the prelude to chapter 7. John Miller performed the extraordinary service of digitizing all of Palestrina's well-attested masses. See Sailor and Sigler 2017 for a quantitative study focusing on dyadic pairs.

[10] Unfortunately, further improvements take much more work; as with most programming projects, a small amount of effort produces the lion's share of the results.

**Figure 5.1.2.** In m. 51 of Élisabeth Jacquet de La Guerre's Sonata no. 1, I, an upper-voice échappée occurs as the suspension resolves, so that the chord never sounds. Chopin's Mazurka Op. 6, no. 3, m. 89, presents the same échappée, only now lasting the entire duration of the dominant chord.

**Figure 5.1.3.** Suspensions in Palestrina lasting the entire length of a consonance: the Agnus from the mass *De Beata Marie Virginis* (III), m. 23, and the Gloria from the mass *Veni Sancte Spiritus*, m. 3.

that each individual nonharmonic tone takes up only a part of a consonance; and second, that nonharmonic tones rarely conspire so as to obscure a consonance entirely. Consonances are thus *real sonic objects* usually sounding at some point during their lifespan. In later music, harmonies are often obscured in a way that suggests they are abstract entities or conceptual templates (Figure 5.1.2).[11] The main exception here is the suspension, which even in Palestrina can occupy an entire sounding consonance (Figure 5.1.3). This is a first hint that suspensions have a unique role in the nonharmonic system.

---

[11] This is one way of understanding Schoenberg's statement that dissonances are "comprehended" with reference to consonances (Schoenberg 1984, p. 259, and Tymoczko 2011a, p. 185): that the nontriadic surface is understood in terms of a triadic object that never appears.

214 TONALITY: AN OWNER'S MANUAL

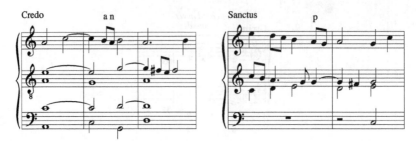

**Figure 5.1.4.** Different meanings for similar figures. In mm. 163–165 of the Credo of Palestrina's mass *In duplicibus minoribus* (II), neither the B nor the A is harmonic; it is sensible to identify a lower neighbor A decorating a quarter-note anticipation B. In mm. 19–20 of the Sanctus of the mass *De Beata Marie Virginis (I)*, however, we need to read the A as a passing tone to avoid the parallel B–A/E–D fifths.

One advantage of computers is that they allow us to look at repertoires *cross-sectionally*—for example showing us every instance of a certain progression, or every nonharmonic tone that resists standard reduction. This cross-sectional view can reveal regularities that would otherwise escape the analytic eye. For instance, it turns out that Palestrina almost always uses anticipations in the context of suspensions—to the point where it might make more sense to speak of a "suspension/anticipation system" rather than of anticipations as a freestanding class of nonharmonic tone.[12] At the same time, and in uncomfortable conflict with this point, decorated anticipations form one of the style's most ambiguous idioms: the top voice on the left passage in Figure 5.1.4 is most naturally read as an anticipation decorated recursively by a neighbor tone. Yet the same reading of the passage on the right would imply parallel fifths between outer voices.[13] Thus a single melodic formula can play different structural roles. When both readings are possible, they can lead to very different interpretations: the suspension in the last measure of the left passage in Figure 5.1.4 can be understood to resolve either on the second or the third beat of the measure, depending on whether the first F♯ is treated as a chord tone or an anticipation. (For what it's worth, I prefer the latter interpretation.) And one occasionally finds passages suspended between these two possibilities, submitting to no fully satisfactory analysis (Figure 5.1.5).[14]

Computational analysis also forces us to confront practices that we might prefer to ignore, including ♮ chords that act as fully fledged harmonies or passing and

---

[12] By my count, freestanding anticipations, not decorating suspensions and not themselves decorated by other notes, comprise less than 1% of Palestrina's dissonances—making them less frequent than ascending neighbors. Freestanding anticipations are much more common in Josquin.

[13] This figure sometimes appears in eighth notes (sixteenths in our notation), as in m. 10 of the Benedictus of the mass *Ave Regina coelorum*.

[14] Knud Jeppesen ([1946] 1970, p. 124) notes that accented third-species dissonances are acceptable for Palestrina *only* when they form this slippery figure, and not in the context of unidirectional melodic lines.

NONHARMONIC TONES 215

Figure 5.1.5. An idiomatic passage in m. 9 of the Kyrie of Palestrina's mass *Dilexi quoniam*. Underneath I provide two analyses. In the first, there is a C$^6_4$ chord and the bass B and A are passing; in the second, there is no C$^6_4$ and the A–G–A is a half-note anticipation decorated by a neighbor.

Figure 5.1.6. In mm. 9–11 of the Benedictus of Palestrina's mass *Io mi son giovinetta* (1570), the fourth above the bass resolves a suspension. In mm. 5–6 of the Kyrie of the mass *Ave regina coelarum*, the leapt-to A is harmonic, which suggests that the alto F is similarly harmonic; otherwise, it has to stand for the following E.

neighboring tones that cut across the binary division of the beat (Figures 5.1.6–7).[15] By far the most significant of these is the *Renaissance seventh*, a sounding seventh chord, formed by suspension, that cannot be reduced to a consonance—an idiom appearing as early as Dufay and used throughout the Renaissance.[16] Figure 5.1.8

---

[15] I call these "121 passing and neighboring tones": three melodic notes with durations 1, 2, and 1, with the nonharmonic tone having duration 2 and the harmonies progressing in a 2, 2 rhythm. Bach uses the 121 neighboring and passing tones in BWV 393 (Riemenschneider 275) m. 3 and BWV 103.6 (Riemenschneider 120) m. 4.

[16] See m. 47 of the Gloria of Dufay's mass *Ave Regina coelarum* (three voices) and m. 25 of the Credo of the mass *Se la face ay pale* (four voices). Dufay's music contains many other moments that resist nonharmonic

**Figure 5.1.7.** "121" neighbor and passing tones that cut across the binary division of the beat, sometimes called "fake suspensions," from Palestrina's *Pope Marcellus Mass* (Gloria, m. 9) and Adrian Willaert's motet *O salutaris hostia* (m. 36). This idiom often gives rise to a $\smash{\substack{6\\4}}$ chord, occupying the first half of the nonharmonic tone's duration.

**Figure 5.1.8.** Three irreducible seventh chords in mm. 72–75 of the Gloria of Palestrina's mass *Veni Sancte Spiritus*. The starred notes cannot be dissonances according to standard contrapuntal theory.

shows a short passage containing three examples in close succession. One would like to say that the tenor B♭ on beat 3 of the second measure is "just a suspension," but replacing the nonharmonic tone with its tone of resolution forms a *second* seventh chord, now in first inversion rather than root position (i.e., C–E♭–G–A rather than C–E♭–G–B♭). The problem is the starred G, a step away from the suspension's resolution; it is approached and left by leap and hence cannot be assimilated to any known species of Renaissance dissonance. We are forced either to invent an entirely new nonharmonic tone solely to account for this figure, or else admit that there are suspensions that cannot be reduced to a consonant background.

For all its strangeness, this idiom admits a fairly straightforward explanation. Let us suppose, first, that the voices not sounding the dissonant suspension tend to form a consonance, and second, that this consonance tends not to contain the tone of resolution except in the case of the 9–8 suspension over a root-position triad.

---

reduction—for example, m. 7 of the Kyrie of the mass *Ave Regina coelorum*, where an irreducible seventh is formed by passing motion. In Palestrina's music, the idiom occurs at least once per movement on average. Gauldin 1995a discusses this figure.

**Figure 5.1.9.** The Renaissance seventh's standard resolutions. From a modern perspective, all involve root progressions of a descending third or descending fifth.

**Figure 5.1.10.** Suspensions masking parallel fifths in the harmonic skeleton, in the Kyrie of Palestrina's mass *Assumpta est Maria* (m. 54), and Bach's chorale *Ich hab mein Sach Gott heimgestellt* (BWV 351, Riemenschneider 19, m. 7).

If the suspended note is a dissonant C, this means that the remaining voices can sound either G or G–D (a 4–3 suspension), a root-position B♭ triad (the 9–8), or some subset of D–F–A, the maximal consonance not containing C or B. It is this last option that produces the Renaissance seventh: since the collection D–F–A is dissonant with the suspension resolution B, the voices have to move as the suspension resolves (Figure 5.1.9).[17] Everything makes sense *so long as we abandon the idea that there is a definite consonance governing the entire texture at the moment of suspension*. It would be easy to abandon this assumption were we talking about late-medieval pieces whose lines were composed successively. The difficulty is that the assumption of a governing consonance works well in virtually every other late-Renaissance context.

Suspensions are also unique in being the only nonharmonic tones that regularly license parallels at the level of the harmonic skeleton—both in the Renaissance and later (Figure 5.1.10). This poses another obstacle to the view that suspensions are merely decorative, as it seems incoherent to say that the first passage in Figure 5.1.11 is grammatical, the second is nongrammatical, and the first stands for, embellishes, or represents the second. The challenge is exacerbated by the cadential idiom in Figure 5.1.12; here parallels are often said to be permissible because they occur "only on the surface," disappearing when we consider the harmonic skeleton. But how can it be that some parallels are allowed because they

---

[17] Guillotel-Nothmann 2018 connects suspension resolutions to the origins of root functionality.

**Figure 5.1.11.** The progression on the left is common, while the progression on the right almost never appears. Should we say that the former stands for the latter?

**Figure 5.1.12.** An idiom in which parallel fifths appear "on the surface." Here the anticipated tonic appears alongside $\hat{5}$–$\hat{4}$–$\hat{3}$ to create fifths. For an example, see Bach's Chorale "Freuet euch, ihr Christen" (BWV 40.8, Riemenschneider 8, m. 4).

occur only on the surface while others are allowed because they occur only in the harmonic skeleton?

The suspension's ambiguous status, I suspect, is connected to its cadential role as a signal for *musica ficta* and the leading tone. Equally important, though less easily quantified, is its role in generating the tension released by the cadence itself: suspensions are *dissonant harmonic events* and not mere decorations. Thus, rather than being sprinkled throughout the phrase, as we might expect from the example of fourth-species counterpoint, suspensions tend to cluster near cadences (Figures 5.1.13–14). A passage like Figure 5.1.15 might look ionian to the modern eye; to a Renaissance musician, the suspension chain would signal an impending cadence even before the leading tone appears. Indeed, Renaissance sevenths tend to have cadential function: the most common form resembles and evolves into the baroque predominant seventh, while other forms occasionally produce sounding dominant sevenths (Figure 5.1.16).

Fétis wrongly claimed that these dominant seventh chords originated at the end of the sixteenth century, mistaking standard Renaissance practice for a harbinger of the future.[18] The paradox is that the Renaissance seventh is simultaneously new and old—an idiom that antedates the notion of a "governing triad" while also evolving into the seventh chords of the classical era. Seventh chords are the inevitable

---

[18] Fétis (1840) 1994, pp. 32–33, and Christensen 2019. Christensen emphasizes the unpreparedness of some of Monteverdi's sevenths (p. 33 of Fétis [1840] 1994), whereas I am more focused on Fétis's apparent misunderstanding of the suspension idiom (p. 32 of same).

NONHARMONIC TONES 219

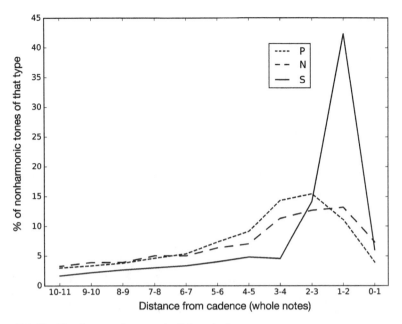

Figure 5.1.13. Nonharmonic tones in Palestrina's masses.

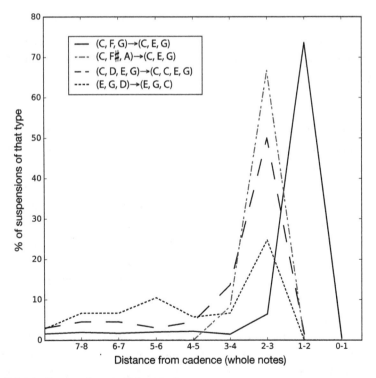

Figure 5.1.14. Suspensions in Palestrina's masses.

**Figure 5.1.15.** The second Agnus from Palestrina's mass *Assumpta est Maria*, mm. 44–47. The suspension chain in the last measure should lead us to expect a D major chord, which in fact does appear.

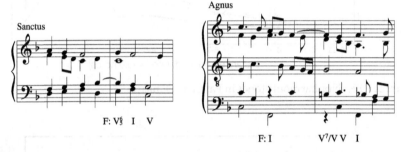

**Figure 5.1.16.** Sounding dominant seventh chords in mm. 11–12 of the Sanctus of Palestrina's mass *Aeterna Christi munera* and m. 38 of the Agnus of the mass *In semiduplicibus majoribus* (II).

result of attempting to reconcile the earlier practice with the philosophical view that nonharmonic tones must necessarily be decorative.[19] If the suspension *always* stands for its tone of resolution, then the B♭3 in m. 2 of Figure 5.1.8 cannot be a suspension, and therefore must be harmonic: this syllogism is appropriate in J. S. Bach, inappropriate in Josquin, and of indeterminate validity during much of the intervening time. Which means that the idealized consonant style of the counterpoint textbooks never actually existed: while Palestrina's music can *almost always* be understood as using nonharmonic tones to decorate exclusively consonant harmonies, it retains idioms that stubbornly resist nonharmonic reduction—inherited from the past and pointing toward the future. It is as if Palestrina wrote *just before* and *just after* an imaginary consonant era.

It is natural to contrast the embodied and intuitive grammar of rock harmony with the more explicit precepts of the nonharmonic system, codified in books from Tinctoris to the present. But we have just seen that nonharmonic usage, even in Palestrina's style, resists simple formalization: the true grammar of the

---

[19] Compare Lerdahl (2020, p. 18): "once passing and neighboring tones and suspensions are stripped away in Classical music, every chord is a triad."

nonharmonic system, the regularity that can be inferred from compositional practice, is inherently schematic, more complex and interesting than the simplifications found in textbooks. The theoretical tradition's reluctance to acknowledge this complexity testifies to a Platonistic conviction that "surface" dissonances *have to* decorate a consonant harmonic skeleton. In reality, however, this belief is just an approximately true generalization, a model *we* apply to music that was composed by people who thought differently. It is a fairly good approximation to be sure: like Newtonian mechanics, it should neither be rejected out of hand nor accepted as the complete truth.[20]

## 2. Schoenberg's critique

The most famous critique of nonharmonicity occurs in chapter 17 of Schoenberg's *Harmonielehre*:

> I come now to one of the weakest points of the old harmonic system, to the point where it suddenly abandons its usual procedure and, as I said in Chapter I, is patched up with another system, which is not a system, in order somehow to include the most familiar harmonic events. It is remarkable that this point has not yet occurred to anyone: *Harmony, its theory, its pedagogy, is concerned with non-harmonic tones!* But non-harmonic matters have just as little place in a textbook of harmony as do non-medical matters in a textbook of medicine. (Significantly, the word *medizinfremd* is not used.) Whatever belongs in such a textbook is there precisely because it is not non-medical: if it were, it would not be there. The expression, "non-harmonic" tones, I can interpret only to mean that a number of tones are declared unsuitable, or under certain conditions unsuitable, for forming harmonies; that such tones, because they intrinsically lack the ability to form harmonies, i.e. chords (*Zusammenklänge*), are designated as having nothing to do with music and consequently are thrown out of the art and out of its theory. [ . . . ] Either there is no such thing as non-harmonic tones, or they are not non-harmonic.[21]

As written, Schoenberg's complaint seems to be a purely verbal one that could be resolved with a simple change of terminology: instead of "nonharmonic tone"

---

[20] Numerous theorists have considered suspensions "essential" or "primary" dissonances, as opposed to the less-essential, more decorative nonharmonic tones: Vincenzo Galilei (Palisca 1956, p. 88), Christoph Bernhard ([~1640] 1973, p. 79), Fux ([1725] 1971, p. 55), Fenaroli and other partimento theorists (Sanguinetti 2012, pp. 103 and 125ff), and Jeppesen (1946) 1970. Even Rameau often assigns a different fundamental bass to a suspension and its resolution (Christensen 1993a, pp. 123ff; this view is echoed in Schoenberg [1911] 1983, pp. 316–17). Others instead treat suspensions as purely decorative, including Riemann (1896, p. 107), Prout (Figure 1.3.1), and Schenker ([1910] 1987, I, pp. 261 and 266). Beach 1974 identifies Kirnberger as the progenitor of this second perspective. Thanks here to David Cohen.

[21] Schoenberg (1911) 1983, p. 309. The claim about medicine is outdated: health-care providers have learned that they often need to consider non-medical matters such as economics, environment, and sociology.

**Figure 5.2.1.** Two interpretations of the $^6_4$ chord in the Kyrie from Palestrina's *Descendit angelus Domini*, mm. 39–40.

we could agree to use a more neutral term like "linearly constrained tone" or "tone of the second classification." In this respect Schoenberg betrays a naïve conception of language, as if meaning was determined by words themselves rather than our behavior—the same rigidity that might lead someone to insist that a sea cucumber *must* be a vegetable, as a simple matter of lexicography. Yet behind the verbal complaint we can discern the deeper observation that nonharmonic tones range from what might be called "merely connective," serving primarily melodic aims, to those whose purpose seems to be to create a specific *sound*. In these latter cases, uncritical allegiance to "nonharmonicity" can keep us from understanding a genuinely harmonic logic.

Figure 5.2.1 returns to the $^6_4$ chord in Palestrina's mass *Descendit angelus Domini* (Figure 3.4.6). The example provides two interpretations of the chord, one recording the standard claim that suspensions represent their tones of resolution; from this point of view, the second inversion triad is "really" an A–F–C sonority whose third is decorated by an inessential suspension. The issue with this reading is that the second-inversion triad appears in the context of a common sequential pattern, two-step clockwise motion on the circle of diatonic triads, producing ascending-fifth harmonies in which root and third repeatedly descend; it is difficult to do justice to this sequence without treating the $^6_4$ as a harmony. Another problem is that the $^6_4$–$^5_3$ pattern is ubiquitous in Palestrina, accounting for almost 10% of his suspensions (Figure 5.2.2). Meanwhile, $^6_4$ suspensions almost never resolve to $^6_3$ chords, with $^6_4$–$^5_3$ resolutions outnumbering $^6_4$–$^6_3$ by a factor of about 30 to 1. Thus, rather than being accidental or inessential, the 6–5 motion is virtually *mandated* by the presence of the 4–3. Once again, it seems perverse to argue that something ubiquitous "stands for" something that almost never occurs. Like the Renaissance seventh, the $^6_4$ is a suspension with harmonic significance.

There is an old-fashioned view that Renaissance music is fundamentally linear: a matter of lines and intervals, with harmonies simply the byproducts of melodic logic.[22] This picture is consistent with the formalist vision, promulgated

---

[22] Jeppesen (1931) 1939, p. xi.

| Suspension | Resolution | % |
|:---:|:---:|:---:|
| C, F, G | C, E, G | 34.7 |
| C, F, G | C, E♭, G | 7.6 |
| C, E♭, B♭ | C, E♭, A | 6.2 |
| C, F, A♭ | C, E♭, G | 3.5 |
| C, F, A | C, E, G | 3.3 |
| C, E, B | C, E, A | 2.4 |
| C, D, E♭, G | C, C, E♭, G | 1.9 |
| C, G, A | D, F♯, A | 1.9 |
| C, F, A♭ | C, E, G | 1.9 |
| C, E♭, B♭ | C, E♭, A♭ | 1.4 |
| C, E, G, B | C, E, A | 1.2 |
| C, E♭, G, B♭ | C, E♭, A | 1.1 |
| C, F, G | C, E, C | 1.1 |
| C, E, G, A | D, F♯, A | 1.0 |

Figure 5.2.2. The most common suspension figures in Palestrina's masses, transposed so that the bass of the first sonority is C.

by Babbitt and others, that musical styles are logical systems with different axioms or postulates.[23] Historically, Renaissance counterpoint functioned as the first of a triad of disconnected styles, with functional harmony and twelve-tone music its canonical successors. (We see traces of this view in curricula that contrast the vertical approach of "tonal harmony" with the supposedly horizontal approach of "modal counterpoint.") Yet Palestrina's music is filled with idioms like the $\frac{6}{4}$–$\frac{5}{3}$, which are harmonic in the sense that they cannot be explained as the byproducts of independent melodic lines obeying the prohibitions of standard counterpoint.[24] Chapter 6 will argue that functional harmony began with precisely these sorts of idioms, understood intuitively and not explicitly theorized; over decades they gradually strengthened and grew more complex, metamorphosing into the lawlike regularities of the eighteenth century.

One can make a similar point about the "ascending subdominant"—an ascending-fifth progression from IV to I, where one of the voices moves from $\hat{6}$ to $\hat{1}$ through a "merely passing" $\hat{7}$; this ascending passing tone can create a sense of dominant functionality, particularly when reinforced by $\hat{4}$–$\hat{3}$ to create a resolving tritone.[25] Ascending subdominants are found throughout the Renaissance and

---

[23] For an interpretation of functional tonality and twelve-tone music as formal systems, see Boretz 1970 and 1972, Westergaard 1975, and Dahlhaus 1990, pp. 61–62 (particularly the thought that there may not exist additional "systems").

[24] Note that in making this claim, I am using the term "harmonic" in a minimalist sense, essentially as a label for residual preferences that cannot easily be explained by linear or melodic factors; I do not presuppose inversional equivalence, root functionality, or any other sophisticated theoretical ideas. Quinn (2018) offers an alternative definition of "harmonic" in terms of *tonic-independent principles*; on this definition, the tendency for $\frac{6}{4}$ to resolve to $\frac{5}{3}$ would be a purely contrapuntal law—as would a preference for descending-fifth progressions, if I read Quinn correctly.

[25] Harrison 1994 considers harmonic function as arising from particular scale-degree motions; while this is not how I always think of function (§7.1), I find it analytically useful here.

224  TONALITY: AN OWNER'S MANUAL

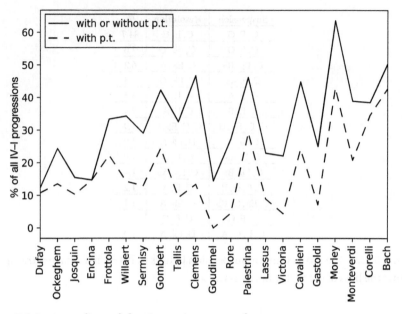

Figure 5.2.3. Ascending subdominants in a range of composers.

baroque and are particularly important in J. S. Bach (Figure 5.2.3, §7.7).[26] The analytical challenge is that they span the gamut from harmonic to nonharmonic: some of the ascending leading tones in Figure 5.2.4 require a Roman numeral, others support one only shakily, and others do not call for one at all. To do justice to this continuum of musical practice, we need to recognize that nonharmonic tones can participate in harmonic narratives.

The previous section showed that some contrapuntal configurations resist reduction, in the sense that there is simply no way to reduce them to a consonant background. Here we are dealing with the more delicate fact that even when we *can* "reduce out" the nonharmonic tones, we may have good analytical reason not to do so. Sometimes a nonharmonic tone has harmonic effects. And some progressions only appear when accompanied by nonharmonic tones—such as the $V^2$–I in Figure 1.5.1, which Bach used only when passing tones disguise the unusual treatment of the bass seventh. In still other cases, a variety of nonharmonic tones conspire to produce a single sounding sonority, such as Chopin's beloved dominant thirteenth: that so many *different* contrapuntal configurations generate the *same* harmonic object suggests that harmony is goal rather than byproduct (Figure 5.2.5).[27] A similar point could be made about the Tristan chord: while it often can be explained as the byproduct of nonharmonic tones, it is so ubiquitous that it is reasonably considered harmonic (Figure 5.2.6). And I am sure that readers can

---

[26] The ascending $\hat{7}$ passing tone is virtually mandatory when the $\hat{6}$–$\hat{1}$ is in the bass, the $IV^6$ chord leaping to I only in the context of $IV$–$IV^6$–I arpeggiations.

[27] Narmour 1988 makes a similar argument.

NONHARMONIC TONES 225

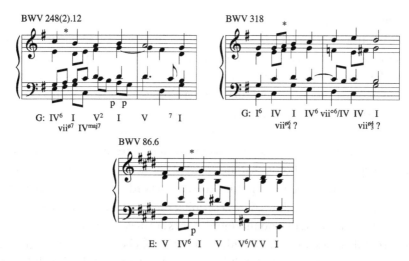

Figure 5.2.4. Ascending subdominants in Bach's chorales. In "Ermuntre dich, mein schwacher Geist" (BWV 248(2).12, Riemenschneider 9, m. 3), the leading tone supports a clear harmony. In "Menschenkind, merk eben" (BWV 318, Riemenschneider 18, m. 10), the harmony is more unusual. In "Es ist das Heil uns kommen her" (BWV 86.6, Riemenschneider 18, m. 9), the leading tone is passing.

Figure 5.2.5. Many different nonharmonic tones conspiring to produce the same "dominant thirteenth" sonority in Chopin's mazurkas: Op. 6, no. 3, mm. 89–90; Op. 41, no. 1, mm. 41–44; Op. 41, no. 2, mm. 1–2; and Op. 41, no. 2, mm. 18–20.

Figure 5.2.6. Three appearances of the "Tristan chord" that could be analyzed as the byproduct of nonharmonic tones.

226 TONALITY: AN OWNER'S MANUAL

cite other moments where the nonharmonic system seems to be a *means* for producing nontriadic ends: the F♯ in Monteverdi's "Tu se' morta," Domenico Scarlatti's countless dominant-sevenths-with-an-added-tonic, the gently overlapping horn calls at the end of the first movement of Beethoven's "Lebewohl" sonata, and so on.

All of which, I propose, shows that Schoenberg was fundamentally right: a musically sensitive theory cannot treat nonharmonic tones as having "nothing to do with music" or even as having nothing to do *with harmony itself*. Sometimes tones which are properly classified as "nonharmonic," at least from the standpoint of textbook theory, produce chords that are clearly "harmonic" in the broader compositional sense. (As Schoenberg put it, "these are chords: not of the system, but of music."[28]) What then is achieved by describing these notes as "nonharmonic"? The safest answer, I think, is that nonharmonic tones are *melodically constrained* in ways that harmonic tones are not. Consider Palestrina's ⁶₄ chords: even if we grant that they are harmonically significant, it is nevertheless true that the fourth is almost never doubled and almost always resolves downward—indeed the downward resolution of the suspension is as close to an inviolable law of the style as one can find. By contrast, the sixth of the ⁶₄, though usually moving downward, is more flexible, available for doubling and sometimes moving differently.[29] (A similar point can be made about the Renaissance seventh, which invariably resolves down by step.) The real significance of the nonharmonic system lies in these linear constraints, which forbid certain vertical configurations *except* in the context of specific melodic obligations.

Schoenberg, of course, went farther than this, denying the existence of "nonharmonicity" altogether. As a historical claim this is flatly unconvincing, asking us to ignore unmistakable regularities in nonharmonic usage. (The Monteverdi-Artusi controversy was about *something*, after all![30]) As an aesthetic proposal, however, it becomes more plausible: our experience with the whole panoply of twentieth-century music—from Debussy and Schoenberg to jazz and rock—has taught us a more flexible attitude toward the harmonic domain, making those long centuries of compositional obedience seem somewhat baffling in retrospect. How, we might wonder, could a composer as inventive as Mozart have been so utterly conventional when it came to dissonance treatment? Was the nonharmonic system merely a convenient tool for writing music quickly? Did composers invest its conventions with metaphysical force? In asking these questions, we can find ourselves in an uncomfortable relation to the past, valuing its music while questioning the conceptual framework intrinsic to its creation. Certainly the nonharmonic system was key to an incredible tradition of well-ordered composition. Our challenge, as inheritors of this tradition, is to balance our love for this style with our sense that its underlying syntactical principles have lost their force. Once, the

---

[28] Schoenberg (1911) 1983, p. 322.

[29] Compare the Sanctus of Palestrina's mass *Assumpta est Maria*, m. 31, or the Sanctus of the *Pope Marcellus Mass*, m. 53.

[30] Recall also that the harmonic/nonharmonic distinction has a transformational significance (§4.8).

grammar of nonharmonicity helped justify the music itself; now the music is the only thing sustaining the grammar.

## 3. Monteverdi's "Ohimè"

Schoenberg argued that composers sometimes used the nonharmonic system to introduce harmonically significant notes, expanding their expressive range while paying lip service to traditional counterpoint rules. This is more or less uncontroversial in the case of Monteverdi, a composer born less than fifty years after Palestrina. Glancing through his scores, we recognize all manner of unusual moments, including unprepared and unresolved sevenths, voices leaping away from suspensions, pedal tones, leaping anticipations, incomplete neighbors, upward-resolving suspensions, Brahmsian rhythmic syncopations, parallel perfect intervals, and notes that seem to defy reduction altogether (Figure 5.3.1). Nonharmonic tones occasionally conspire to produce nontertian sonorities or even challenge the very notion of "underlying harmony" (Figure 5.3.2).[31] And yet for all this strangeness Monteverdi was a man of his time, a composer working in the broad tradition of the late Renaissance. Critics love to wax offended at his "shrieking" dissonances and unprecedented text-painting; but to ears raised on Metallica and Penderecki, these dissonances can pass unnoticed, being less salient than the bold triadic language he shares with Marenzio and Morley.[32] Paradoxically, hyperbolic rhetoric functions to legitimize the nonharmonic system, suggesting that even minor contrapuntal unorthodoxies are shocking to the ear: this is Victorian primness gussied up in postmodern garb.[33]

Let us therefore look at Monteverdi's setting of Giovanni Battista Guarini's "Ohimè, se tanto amate," published in 1602 in his fourth book of madrigals. The piece presents a range of characteristically Monteverdian devices, including unprepared sevenths, suspensions resolving by leap, incomplete neighbors, extraordinary chromaticism, and a few notes that seem to defy nonharmonic analysis altogether. Along the way, we will revisit some contrapuntal techniques from the previous chapters—including a wealth of sequences and near sequences exploiting the geometry of diatonic dyads and triads.

---

[31] Christoph Bernhard ([~1640] 1973, p. 90) associates many of these effects with improvisation, an association echoed by Palisca (1994, pp. 54ff). The tradition of using nonharmonic tones to produce quartal harmonies, often evoking folk music, continues in works such as Schubert's C major string quintet, D. 956, III, and Chopin's Mazurka Op. 6, no. 2.

[32] See, for example, Fétis (1840) 1994, p. 31, or the heightened language in McClary 2004, pp. 183ff ("shriek," "grinding dissonances," "shouting," "BITCH!," "transgression," "bitter," "unpleasant," "brutal assault").

[33] McClary's extreme language is no doubt intended to get us to hear Monteverdi's dissonances as striking and outrageous, as his contemporaries might have. However, it is not obvious that ordinary Renaissance listeners (as opposed to theorists) would have had such extreme reactions—perhaps the fleeting dissonances would have eluded earlier ears precisely as they elude so many contemporary listeners. Or perhaps Renaissance audiences were accustomed to more extreme levels of dissonance in improvisational contexts, as suggested in Palisca 1994, chapter 3.

228 TONALITY: AN OWNER'S MANUAL

4.1, 95 = "madrigal book 4, piece 10, measure 95"

Figure 5.3.1. Some contrapuntal oddities in Monteverdi's madrigals. In A the upper voices are easiest to understand as rhythmically displaced passing tones rather than suspensions: the F5 in m. 1 is dissonant and hence not a preparation. In B the lowest voice arrives at F♯ a quarter note before the rest of the voices; this could be either a leapt-to anticipation or a weak-beat suspension of the E. In C the top voice resolves the suspension D upward to E. Example D is a standard cadential figure occurring under an upper-voice pedal D5. In E the C5 seventh is unprepared. In F the top voice leaps away from the seventh (G5 down to C).

Figure 5.3.2. The nonharmonic tones in A conspire to produce fourth chords. In B the harmonies are difficult to identify.

I hear the piece in four sections: the first stretches to m. 19 and makes use of the diatonic third's basic voice leading; the second stretches to m. 38 and is constructed from two 9.5 bar phrases; the third, mm. 39–43, lasts just five measures but contains the central poetic and dramatic conceit; while the final section, mm. 44–67, features two parallel twelve-bar phrases. The first contrapuntal anomaly occurs in m. 2, where the falling-third "alas" motif seems to articulate a

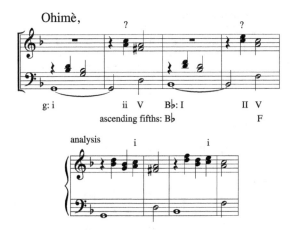

**Figure 5.3.3.** The beginning of "Ohimè," along with a reading in which the incomplete neighbors embellish their predecessors.

V⁷ chord with an unprepared seventh (Figure 5.3.3). If we imagine the V⁷ to start on beat 3 then the upper voices' A–C are "rogue notes": nonharmonic tones not connected by step to any chord tone. (The variant in mm. 3–4 compounds the strangeness by using E♮ where one might expect E♭.) One interpretive option is to take them at face value, as leaping-third anticipations not entirely foreign to the tradition (e.g., the first passage in Figure 5.4.6). Another is to imagine a hocket with rhythmic and registral displacement, analyzing the high-register A and C in m. 2 as incomplete neighbors attached to the *preceding* low-register G and B♭ (Figure 5.3.3). This is how the figure later appears (e.g., top two voices of mm. 6–8, and alto and tenor in mm. 9–11). This reading also reflects the text, sundering the sighs into male and female (low and high), rather than allowing them to sound together as a unified syntactical structure.[34] In either case, the crucial point is that nonharmonic reduction has become an interpretative rather than mechanical process: as in late nineteenth-century music, it is genuinely unclear how to reduce the surface to a well-behaved harmonic skeleton—with none of the answers being completely convincing.

The next six measures ("se tanto amate di sentir dir "Ohimè" / "if you so love to hear me say alas") present a familiar ascending-fifth sequence that develops the preceding bars both melodically and harmonically (Figure 5.3.4).[35] Cantus, tenor, and alto sing a six-beat melodic canon that incorporates the "alas" motif, with Quinto and alto doubling at the third below; this canon is essentially the ascending version of the diatonic third's basic voice leading, split into different octaves and with the bass sounding chord roots. The sequential unit's third half-note is harmonically variable, supporting a first-inversion triad with a bass that either sustains the

---

[34] Octave-displaced melodies also appear in the bass voice at mm. 16, 25, and 35.
[35] That is, the ascending B♭–F fifth of the previous phrase continues to the C–G–D–A of the next; this is noted in Chafe 1992 (p. 92). Salzer 1983 reads the opening chords as a prolongation of G minor.

230  TONALITY: AN OWNER'S MANUAL

**Figure 5.3.4.** "Ohimè," mm. 5–19, with brackets marking the six-beat sequence. Underneath, an analysis of the opening canon.

preceding bass note or descends by third.[36] As in rock modality, these ascending-fifth root progressions produce descending-step voice leading.[37] One can admire the compositional technique in designing the incipit of the canon to fit with the "Ohimè" continuation, so that what initially sounds like development transmutes into something more like resolution or explanation.

---

[36] Chafe 1992 proposes that Monteverdi's language is hexachordal and based on major and minor triads (pp. 24–31). The sequence in mm. 6–12, however, suggests that it is fruitful to include the diminished triad alongside major and minor: the b°6 in m. 6 plays a similar role to the g6 in m. 10; these are both instances of a ubiquitous Renaissance voice-leading pattern, which can appear either in authentic (vii°6–I) or plagal (♭vii6–I) forms. To capture this similarity, it is useful to treat the diminished triad as a genuine sonority, and hence to postulate a diatonic rather than hexachordal background.

[37] Salzer 1983 interprets the chords in the fifth-sequence as dominants of their predecessors rather than "ascending subdominants" of their successors. I think this is an anachronistic flattening-out of a three-dimensional Renaissance harmonic landscape.

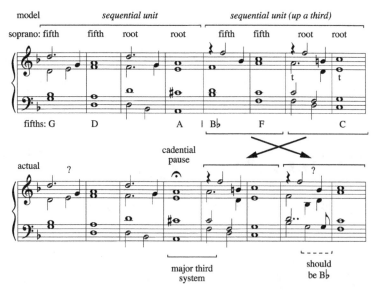

**Figure 5.3.5.** A hypothetical derivation of mm. 8–15. Question marks are suspensions resolved by leap. The result is an ABBA palindrome.

The next text fragment ("deh perché fate" / "then why do you") features a new motive that overlaps with the end of the canon; here the suspensions resolve by leap.[38] Figure 5.3.5 analyzes the passage as a distorted ascending-third sequence. The outer-voice counterpoint here is essentially parallel, with the top voice initially singing chordal fifths and then roots ("thinking within the chord," §3.7). Monteverdi obscures this structure in two ways: first by reversing the order of the phrases in the sequential repeat, and second by reaching a cadence at the end of the first unit. This makes the second unit feel like both a continuation and a phrase beginning; our ears hear *some* of the organization in Figure 5.3.5 but only obscurely. (The A cadence also ends the ascending-fifth harmonic motion that began in m. 3, B♭–F–c–g–d–A crossing motivic and phrasal boundaries.) The reordering transforms the relatively standard deceptive progression A–B♭ into the more dramatic A–F ("the major-third system"). The passage continues with "chi dice 'Ohimè' morire?" ("kill the one who says 'Alas?'"), returning to the A major triad via another major-third progression, with the cadential dominant extensively decorated by incomplete neighbors, an unprepared seventh, and octave-displaced passing motions—a free counterpoint of lines decorating a stable but hazy harmony.

The piece's second large section starts with the upper two voices moving in parallel thirds (Figure 5.3.6), freely harmonized by descending steps and descending fifths, and shifting position from root-third to third-fifth. (The underlying logic here is shared with the Pachelbel progression, which features descending melodic voices and is codified as a specific piece of functional vocabulary; in the

---

[38] To my ear, these figures have less the character of a true seventh, or even a suspension, than of a syncopation or perhaps a resonance that has been sustained just slightly longer than the harmony it belongs to—like a fleeting pedal tone.

232 TONALITY: AN OWNER'S MANUAL

Figure 5.3.6. "Ohimè," mm. 20–38, along with a reduction of each phrase's opening.

Figure 5.3.7. "Ohimè," mm. 39–43.

Renaissance, the same basic relationships are exploited more freely.) This quasi-sequence dissolves in a wonderful reduction of the harmonic rhythm, the voices singing a slow, sad "doloroso" on ascending scale fragments. The voices take turn ascending by fourth and fifth, harmony secondary to linear motion until the final cadence on D. The phrase repeats up a fourth and with a fuller texture; the last melodic ascent is displaced upward by third, producing a ♭9 incomplete neighbor and an unapologetic seventh chord in m. 37. It is interesting that the two phrases both start on a root-position D triad: the first begins with the descending second (d–d–C–F– . . .), the parallel thirds sounding root-third, while the second begins with the descending fifth (D–g–F–B♭– . . .), the parallel voices sounding third-fifth.[39]

Figure 5.3.7 presents the poem's "turn" ("but if, my love, you wish to let me live and live for me . . ."), set in a lydian-inflected B♭ and one of just two phrases in the

---

[39] This is the "chord repeats, pattern continues" technique discussed in §4.9.

Figure 5.3.8. "Ohimè," final section.

piece that are not immediately repeated.[40] The shift to a faster tempo and brighter tonality effectively conveys the poem's move toward amatory hope. Harmonically it is the piece's most straightforward music, replete with functional progressions and organized around an ascending bass line from B♭2 to B♭3, with the upper voice outlining a stepwise descent from F5 to B♭4.[41] Contrapuntally, it is noteworthy for the dissonances in mm. 41–42, particularly the cluster G–A–B♭ and the semitone A–B♭.

The final section delivers the punchline, the promise of endless satisfying sighs shared between lovers (Figure 5.3.8). We begin with emphatic V–I–V progressions in G and C minor, the second containing undisguised parallel fifths. The music then returns to the opening "Ohimè," now harmonized with parallel first-inversion triads; these create deceptive-resolution pairs (e.g., D–E♭, C–d, B♭–c), leading to a b$^6$–g cadence closer to Poulenc than standard Renaissance harmony. (Here the opening bars' octave-displaced hocketing has been regularized to a single line.) The lower voices then echo this music, alternating tonic and dominant dyads in G dorian and recalling some of the analytical challenges of the opening (Figure 5.3.9).

We then get a varied repeat of this twelve-bar phrase: the homophonic declamation returns, replacing the V–I–V with I–V–I, and transforming the fauxbourdon "down a third/up a step" progression into descending fifths (mm. 60–61). The lower two voices articulate the basic voice leading and the top voice doubles at the third. (The interchangeability of descending fifths and "down a third up a step"

---

[40] See Theune 2007 on poetic turns.
[41] Salzer 1983 reads the phrase as an interruption form.

**Figure 5.3.9.** In mm. 53–55, we can read harmonies changing in quarter notes, as in the surrounding phrases, or syncopated half-note motion.

**Figure 5.3.10.** An interpretation of "Ohimè," mm. 63–67.

fauxbourdon is characteristic of baroque tonality, as we will see in chapter 7.) As before, the ambiguity of the opening "Ohimè" seems to be resolved, with each note assigned its own chord. Ambiguity returns, however, with the utterly baffling measure that follows. My best guess at an analysis is shown in Figure 5.3.10, where I try to capture the sense of half-note harmonic motion.[42] Crucially, this requires turning around the ubiquitous "Ohimè" figure, so that it has appoggiaturas rather than escape tones: in almost every previous appearance, the unaccented "Ohi" has been nonharmonic, with the accented "mè" the genuine harmony; here it is difficult to make that reading work with the two inner voices. (This reinterpretation has a nice poetic significance, mirroring the transformation from sighs of sorrow to sighs of passion.) We are left with music that makes sense to the ear—a descending scalar rush of notes congealing on the cadential $\substack{6\\4}$—while resisting technical analysis. The nonharmonic system has momentarily lost its authority.

This is the sort of passage that provoked the most famous police action in Western music history, Giovanni Artusi's attempt to enforce the authority of the learned tradition. Much of the commentary around this incident centers on Giulio Cesare Monteverdi's suggestion that text-setting justifies a *seconda prattica* that departs from strict counterpoint. To my mind, however, that is something of a red herring. More fundamental is the attempt to shift the debate from *inviolable musical rules* toward *acts of aesthetic judgment*. The crucial point, in other words, is the suggestion that we need to consider whether a given passage is *aesthetically fitting*, rather than whether it obeys the time-independent rules of the *prima prattica*.[43]

---

[42] One might try a quarter-note reading where the first two beats are B♭$^{maj7}$ followed by a°, but this involves an unusual harmonic progression and a nonstandard resolution of the seventh.

[43] On "fittingness" in aesthetics, see Danto 1981, p. 207, and Camp 2017. McClary is similarly suspicious of what she calls the "'the words made me do it' defense" (2004, p. 182).

To be sure, the particular judgment Monteverdi asks us to make is one that compares musical effects to poetic texts, but put that aside for the moment; focus instead on the general *form* of the question. "Do I find this particular musical passage to be compelling?" *That* question can be asked without reference to a text, precisely as we do when modern music takes a more flexible attitude toward the nonharmonic realm. Here the Monteverdis can start to seem uncannily contemporary, as if they had anticipated modernity three centuries too early: for the fundamental freedom they desired—to have counterpoint judged by its aesthetic effects rather than by an unquestionable set of musical laws—was one that composers did not obtain until the early twentieth century. By contrast, Artusi seems to think that aesthetic judgment should come into play only *after* we have verified that the music conforms to the timeless norms of the strict style. What makes Monteverdi radical is the subjecting of *the rules themselves* to aesthetic evaluation: for each of his unusual contrapuntal effects, we are supposed to ask, "do I appreciate this passage?" regardless of whether it violates traditional norms.[44]

Construed like this, the debate starts to look like a draw at best.[45] Historians have sometimes dismissed Artusi as an ineffectual conservative, pointlessly resisting the inexorable force of musical progress. This may be justified so long as we focus narrowly on the question of *prima prattica* rules. But if we turn to the more general question "should nonharmonic tones conform to *some* rigorous contrapuntal grammar, whatever it may be?" then we have to admit that history gave an answer more Artusian than Monteverdian. Yes, the classical tradition incorporated some of Monteverdi's specific innovations, but it subjected them to rules as inviolable as those of the *prima prattica*: in this sense, Monteverdi was an evolutionary dead end, an unheard avatar of compositional freedom. While it may be true that Artusi had a fundamentally scholastic mind, it is also true that the notated tradition retained a scholastic streak right up to the twentieth century. That scholasticism still survives, for though we live in a Monteverdian world, we tend to become Artusi the moment we step into our classrooms.

## 4. The standardized second practice

Eighteenth-century composers embraced a number of new contrapuntal devices: seventh chords, the cadential $\frac{6}{4}$, incomplete neighbors, and pedals.[46] We

---

[44] These two perspectives—one humanist and evolutionary, the other scholastic and timeless—map onto broader worldviews whose conflict was playing out during these same decades. See Tomlinson 1990 and Wootton 2015.

[45] Palisca 1994 makes a similar point, as does Chafe (1992, p. 5): "what distinguishes Monteverdi's music from both late Baroque rationality and the sixteenth-century style is the relative unpredictability of his dissonances and rationalizations."

[46] Christoph Bernhard's unpublished 1640 treatise contains one of the most interesting seventeenth-century discussions of nonharmonicity; interestingly, it does not discuss pedal tones.

|        | accented      | unaccented          |
|--------|---------------|---------------------|
| before | appoggiatura  | incomplete neighbor |
| after  | ?             | échappée            |

**Figure 5.4.1.** The four species of incomplete neighbor.

**Figure 5.4.2.** Two examples of the missing incomplete neighbor (accented and connected by step to the preceding tone): Chopin's Mazurka Op. 33, no. 1, mm. 23–24; and "The Streets of Laredo," sometimes considered traditional and sometimes attributed to Frank H. Maynard. In both cases the note can be interpreted as an added sixth.

**Figure 5.4.3.** An incomplete neighbor in m. 5 of "Wie schön leuchtet der Morgenstern" (BWV 172.6, Riemenschneider 323).

will discuss the first two of these in chapter 7. Figure 5.4.1 classifies the incomplete neighbors according to metrical weight (accented or unaccented) and direction of stepwise connection. Three of the four combinations are common, and two have their own names; the fourth possibility, an accented incomplete neighbor connected by step to its predecessor, is extremely rare (Figure 5.4.2). These neighbors are interesting insofar as the notes they represent, for the purposes of reduction, are not necessarily the notes to which they are connected by step: in Figure 5.4.3, for example, the bass B♭ is a melodic decoration of the following C, but would be replaced upon reduction by the preceding F.[47] Like the other nonharmonic tones, incomplete neighbors can also decorate each other recursively, as in Figure 5.4.4, where an incomplete neighbor decorates an appoggiatura.[48]

---

[47] Christoph Bernhard describes this explicitly: "part of a note is cut off, so that this may be placed in front of the following note in the degree immediately below" ([~1640] 1973, p. 108).

[48] A modest degree of recursion is characteristic of the nonharmonic system: in Figure 5.1.4, for example, we have an anticipation being decorated by a neighbor. One can also find neighbor tones decorating passing tones and suspensions, and so on.

**Figure 5.4.4.** An incomplete neighbor to an incomplete neighbor in m. 6 of the second B♭ major fugue in *The Well-Tempered Clavier*.

Pedal tones are more complicated, in part because they are both a rhetorical effect and species of nonharmonic tone: one can create the *sense* of a pedal by changing chords over a static bass note, even if that bass is always part of the prevailing harmony. Formally, a pedal tone is any note that is initially harmonic and sustained through one or more chord changes.[49] In practice, however, this definition is overbroad, encompassing such phenomena as Monteverdi's "suspensions that resolve by leap," which may not feel much like pedals. Actual pedal tones are more schematic, almost always occurring on the tonic or dominant scale degree, and typically returning to harmonic status before they move: to my knowledge, Mozart's piano sonatas contain no exceptions to these principles among their hundred or so pedals, though J. S. Bach's chorales do contain a few (Figure 5.4.5).[50] Pedals are unique in the nonharmonic bestiary insofar as they are *irreducible*: where the other nonharmonic tones can be said to embellish some specific note, pedals do not; removing them requires recomposition rather than reduction. Many textbooks dodge this issue by stipulating that the rest of the music *embellishes the pedal tone itself*, but I think this conflates the syntactic process of nonharmonic reduction with the very different enterprise of summarizing reduction.

By the late baroque, many composers had once again become formulaic in their treatment of nonharmonic tones. J. S. Bach in particular can be astoundingly systematic: of more than ten thousand nonharmonic tones in his chorales, all but about ten are well behaved. Most of the anomalies, illustrated in Figure 5.4.6, involve what might be called "arpeggiated anticipations," where an arpeggiating voice (always moving down by third, usually from tonic to subdominant) reaches the next harmony an eighth note early; this is reminiscent of the start of "Ohimè." There are a few other unusual moments, including a trio of weak-beat suspensions, the nonstandard pedals in Figure 5.4.5, a couple dozen "121" passing and neighboring tones, a few upward-resolving suspensions, and so forth. Here Monteverdian

---

[49] This minimal definition is found in Gauldin 1997. Other textbook authors such as Aldwell and Schachter (2002) and Kostka and Payne (2003) place more restrictions on pedal tones. The bass G in Figure 9.3.1 is unusual: if we want to consider the ii$^{ø7}$ to be harmonic then the chordal G is attacked a measure too early; it is perhaps comparable to the bass A in m. 13 of Figure 5.5.2.

[50] Pedal tones are the only species of nonharmonic tone largely limited to specific scale degrees. Some genres, such as string quartets, are more lenient with pedal tones.

238 TONALITY: AN OWNER'S MANUAL

Figure 5.4.5. Three unusual pedal tones in the Bach chorales: "Jesu Leiden, Pein und Tod" (BWV 245.14 Riemenschneider 83, mm. 11–12), "Nun danket alle Gott" (BWV 252, Riemenschneider 330, mm. 3–4), and "O Gott, du frommer Gott" (BWV 399, Riemenschneider 315, mm. 1–2).

Figure 5.4.6. Anomalous nonharmonic tones in the chorales: "Herzlich lieb hab ich dich, o Herr" (BWV 245.40, Riemenschneider 107, mm. 14–15), "Meinen Jesum laß ich nicht, weil..." (BWV 154.8, Riemenschneider 152, mm. 10–11), "Christus, der uns selig macht" (BWV 245.15, Riemenschneider 81, mm. 11–12).

anarchy has been domesticated, standardized into a "second practice" whose rules are almost as inviolable as Palestrina's. This system remains in force throughout much of the eighteenth and nineteenth centuries, with few composers coming anywhere close to Monteverdi's radical freedom.

This is a subtle point, so it is important to be clear. My claim is that the vast majority of the nonharmonic tones in the Bach chorales can be labeled according to traditional counterpoint rules: we find suspensions, neighboring tones, passing tones, anticipations, and the occasional pedal, more or less in line with textbook theory. There are, in other words, very few outright obstacles to nonharmonic reduction. But this does *not* mean that nonharmonic reduction is analytically unproblematic: one often finds irreducible pedals (Figure 5.4.5), suspensions masking parallel fifths (Figure 5.1.10), and nonharmonic tones that play a vital role in the harmonic argument (Figure 5.2.4).[51] Nonharmonic reduction is *theoretically feasible* in the sense that it is possible to program a computer to do it reasonably well. But it does not follow that reduction is analytically or aesthetically advisable. One might say that the *syntax* of the music allows for a reduction that sometimes leads us to misunderstand the music's semantics.[52]

This standardization imposes a powerful constraint on musical analysis: given a passage of baroque or classical-style music, the theorist needs to find an analysis that rationalizes *both* the melodic and harmonic behavior. That is, the task is to identify harmonies such that (a) dissonances belong to some recognized species of nonharmonic tone; and (b) harmonic successions obey functional norms (§7.1). These requirements are highly restrictive, implying for example that notes both leapt-to and leapt-away-from must necessarily be harmonic.[53] Thus it is rather remarkable that we can analyze Bach's chorales such that more than 95% of the chord progressions conform to a standard "grammar" of functional harmony, while all but a handful of nonharmonic tones behave recognizably.

We can put these constraints to computational work by using the nonharmonic system to "score" harmonic interpretations of particular musical passages based on how well-behaved its voices are; this is accomplished by assigning penalties to nonharmonic tones, with higher penalties for the less-common varieties.[54] (One can apply this procedure recursively, first by scoring all the single-harmony interpretations of a measure, then all the interpretations with two half-measure harmonies, then those with four quarter-measure harmonies, and so on.) Figure 5.4.7 shows that this produces a reasonably good automatic analysis of the opening measures of the first Mozart sonata; for the sonatas as a whole, it correctly identifies the chord about 75% of the time, which is an excellent result for a simple algorithm not specifically tuned to the style.[55] Here we see one practical use for the nonharmonic system—despite legitimate grounds for skepticism about its metaphysical status.

---

[51] Bach's keyboard music occasionally presents additional anomalies, including suspensions resolving by leap.

[52] Or, more neutrally, its significance; I use "semantics" in a general and metaphorical sense.

[53] Or that they represent multiple voices as discussed in the prelude to this chapter.

[54] That is, one might have a small penalty for the standard notes of the SNAP system (ensuring that the computer prefers an analysis with *no* nonharmonic tones to one with some), a slightly higher penalty for incomplete neighbors and pedal tones, and the highest penalty for "rogue notes" with no standard explanation. The strategy was devised by my student Jeffrey Hodes in his undergraduate thesis (Hodes 2012).

[55] Assuming the key is correct.

**Figure 5.4.7.** A computer analysis of the opening of the first Mozart piano sonata. The analysis is mostly accurate, with the main issue being the unnecessary chord changes in mm. 6–8.

## 5. A loophole

The nonharmonic system does not directly deal with sonic resultants, but only with the linear behavior of dissonant voices—a technical loophole licensing almost any imaginable dissonance.[56] Beethoven's Ninth Symphony uses incomplete neighbors to sound a complete harmonic minor scale, the same scandalous set that stomps away at the opening of Stravinsky's "Dance of the Adolescents" (Figure 5.5.1).[57] This *Schreckensfanfare* is one of several famous moments where Beethoven uses nonharmonic tones to create unusual harmonies, joined by the *Eroica*'s "false horn entry," and the end of the first movement of the *Lebewohl* sonata. If such anomalies are rare in earlier music, it is largely for reasons of taste: as a general rule, earlier composers *intended* to create consonant surfaces in which nonharmonic tones avoided extreme dissonances.[58] These intentions start to change over the course of the nineteenth century even while the musical syntax remains the same. The risk is that we focus too much on the stable syntax at the expense of the evolving aesthetics.[59]

---

[56] This is something like the converse of the twelve-tone technique of creating consonant music by hiding unwanted notes in an unobtrusive instrument.

[57] Steve Taylor notes that the same chord appears at m. 327 of the first movement of Mahler's Second Symphony.

[58] One sign of this intention is that nonharmonic tones generally form consonances with each other.

[59] Meyer 1996 also emphasizes Romantic composers' repurposing of earlier techniques.

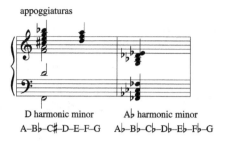

**Figure 5.5.1.** The same seven-note sonority appears in the last movement of Beethoven's Ninth Symphony (m. 208, just before the first vocal entrance) and Stravinsky's *Rite of Spring*.

Beethoven used this loophole sparingly, as a special effect; in the "Rondo-Burlesque" from Mahler's Ninth Symphony, it is pervasive. Viewed from a distance, the music articulates clear harmonic zones that act in recognizable ways—though to be sure, its harmonies are sometimes extended or altered. But like a pointillistic painting, the notes get harder and harder to rationalize the closer you look. Figure 5.5.2 reduces the opening forty-five measures to a harmonic skeleton, trying to synthesize the musical chaos into an easily playable piano reduction; it is my attempt to imagine the kind of sketch that Mahler might have used as a basis for his orchestration. That this reduction is a riot of late-Romantic harmonic invention is one of the main obstacles to convincing analysis; in making my reduction, I felt a constant worry that there might be a more logical alternative.

The piece begins off tonic, an unharmonized melody outlining a C♯ half-diminished seventh chord. We then hear the same melody transposed down a major third and extended into a nearly complete scale, the melodic A–B–C in m. 3 the sequential counterpart to the earlier C♯–D♯–E. After this six-bar introduction, the music settles into a series of eight-bar phrases. In the first, the unremarkable Roman numerals paper over several anomalies: the V–(VI–i) in m. 9, for example, would normally occur with the VI on a strong beat, as a variant of the iv$^6_4$–i cadential decoration (§9.5); similarly, the tonic bass arrives in m. 14, a bar before the cadence. Less unnerving but still problematic is the pickup C–E in m. 9, with the C belonging neither to the V/V in m. 9 or the V in m. 10.

The next eight-bar phrase presents two counterbalanced sequences. The first ascends by fifth from D minor (with added sixth) to A minor (with subposed F♯) to E minor to the dominant of B minor and then to B minor itself. This is reminiscent of mm. 5–11 of Monteverdi's "Ohimè," particularly since the ascending fifths sometimes move through the dominant of the next chord to articulate the "ascending subdominant" schema. (Note that Mahler expands the final unit's harmonic rhythm so that e–vii°/b occupies two measures rather than one.) The arrival on B minor, v of the dominant, overlaps with a root-position fauxbourdon descent to a bare fifth on the dominant E. Once again, the descending-step logic is clearer

242    TONALITY: AN OWNER'S MANUAL

**Figure 5.5.2a.** A reduction of the opening 23 measures of the Rondo-Burlesque from Mahler's Ninth Symphony.

when we postulate added-sixth chords, treating the second chord in m. 22 as F major rather than D minor in first inversion. Note also the melody's flexible relation to the harmony, with B–C–D–C–B over D minor echoed as F♯–G–A–G–F♯ over E minor, the melody ascending by fifth while the harmony moves by step. The impression is less of harmony as container for the melody than of melody as an independent actor that creates tension by shifting its relation to the harmonic structure.

The music now turns to the relative major, oscillating between I, V, and various decorations of V (mm. 24ff). The general technique—extensive chromatic activity above a dominant pedal—is familiar, here taken to Mahlerian extremes. Measure 26 gives us a flurry of eighth notes, $A^7$ leading to $G^7$, the most conventional of the common-tone dominant sevenths (§3.8). The chromaticism increases as the melody rises: in m. 28 we have a second flurry on another common-tone

**Figure 5.5.2b.** A reduction of measures 24–46 of the Rondo-Burlesque.

244   TONALITY: AN OWNER'S MANUAL

dominant, B[7] over G.[60] This leads to the remarkable explosion of mm. 29–30, with the upper voices descending at different speeds along the minor seventh G♯–B–D♯–F♯, each note acquiring a semitonal upper neighbor.[61] The result is gleaming and uncategorizable, as deliciously painful as nitrous oxide in a dentist's chair.

The second phrase echoes its predecessor, now with a chipper violin melody and still circling around the "B[7] over G" dominant (mm. 32ff). This leads to a long sequence of descending triads that I hear pointing to E[7], or V/V in D minor. The expected cadence is elided with the start of the next phrase, the only interruption of the four-bar phrasing since m. 7. This is a fine example of Mahler's ability to use purely instrumental forces to convey complex emotional states like intrusion, digression, and hesitation. The subsequent music once again invokes the ascending voice leading of the common-tone diminished seventh: here we have a surprising E–G–B–D moving to the expected E–G♯–B–D, with the G ascending to G♯ over the course of two measures, the E minor seventh the distant cousin of the standard common-tone diminished seventh E–G–A♯–C♯.[62] This ascending semitonal voice leading continues through the phrase, moving through F–A–B(♭)–D, to F♯–A–B–D♯, seventh chords ratcheting upward underneath a truncated opening motif.[63] I found this passage completely unintelligible until I became aware of the retrofunctional idioms in §3.8.[64]

So goes my account of the opening section's harmony. On the page it may seem straightforward, but it was formulated over countless hours spread over many years, with many wrong turns and rethinkings along the way. I have no expectation that readers will agree with it, and indeed Mahler's surface presents numerous details that argue against my reading.

1. The V/V in m. 8 occurs over an E–A fifth that does not belong to the underlying harmony, creating a D–D♯–E cluster on the downbeat; I treat the E as a reattacked pedal tone surviving from the preceding harmony, though it appears in a new octave as part of an active bass line (Figure 5.5.3). As in an improvisation, the bass player simply arrives at the harmony a bit late.

2. My analysis treats the wind parts in mm. 15–18 as largely independent of the underlying harmony, the neighbor notes moving from weak to strong eighth notes with every repetition of the four-note motive (Figure 5.5.4, top staff). Here they act as a kind of orchestrational thickening hinting at pandiatonicism.

[60] Note that the "A[7] over G" common-tone dominant resolves to G[7] and is associated with the diminished seventh C♯–E–G–B♭; the "B[7] over G" resolves to C and is associated with C–D♯–F♯–A.

[61] See Lewis 1983, pp. 148–50, for a polytonal interpretation involving the dominant of E minor. My analysis evokes what jazz musicians call "upper structures," chromatic, stacked-third extensions of what is fundamentally V[7] in C (cf. Levine 1989).

[62] It is also possible to identify the chord on m. 38 as a G[7], with bass E an accented neighbor, though that makes the underlying voice leading less clear.

[63] The B/B♭ oscillation once again evokes the common-tone diminished seventh.

[64] Note the three-note trumpet figure landing successively on G, D, and A.

**Figure 5.5.3.** Measures 7–9 of the Rondo-Burlesque.

**Figure 5.5.4.** Measures 15–18 of the Rondo-Burlesque.

**Figure 5.5.5.** Measures 23–26 of the Rondo-Burlesque.

3. The suggestion of a stable V in mm. 23–26 is undercut by bass motion that could be taken to represent chord changes (Figure 5.5.5).
4. The "e minor seventh" in m. 38 is actually a minor ninth, occurring over a towering clash: C–C♯–D–E–F–A on beat 4 of m. 37 and D–E–F–G on beat 1 of m. 38 (Figure 5.5.6). The D–E–F bass could suggest that E is passing.

These are genuine issues, but I know of no better analysis. The problem is that Mahler's language is so contrapuntally and harmonically inventive as to make objective analysis almost impossible; there are simply too many ways to parse the extended chords, pervasive linear dissonances, and unusual progressions.[65] (As we will see in the prelude to chapter 7, nonharmonic reduction typically requires some

---

[65] Lewis 1983 contains a careful reading of the opening measures that disagrees with mine in almost every detail.

246  TONALITY: AN OWNER'S MANUAL

Figure 5.5.6. Measures 38–41 of the Rondo-Burlesque.

prior understanding of the music's harmonic vocabulary.) While I strongly suspect that Mahler imagined *some* reductive template along the lines of Figure 5.5.2, that template is all but unrecoverable. The upshot is that nonharmonic reduction is no longer something broadly intersubjective or syntactical, but rather autobiographical and interpretive, a record of one's personal coming-to-terms with a refractory and ambiguous musical surface. Here we have the familiar modernist slippage between compositional process and musical result, albeit in the context of functional tonality.

Once again, I find myself pulled in two directions. In some sense, the basic theoretical picture of "skeleton with decoration" seems reasonably apt: if one function of analysis is to tell us how we might make a piece, then I find my reduction to be successful, for I can just about imagine turning Figure 5.5.2 into Mahler's actual score. (And when I listen to the piece, I have a sense of tonal coherence that seems consistent with the reduction.) At the same time, the very act of reduction slights Mahler's frenzied counterpoint, its lines careening as close to chaos as those of Nancarrow or Schoenberg. If Western norms of dissonance treatment were produced by a conversation between composer and theorist, one gets the sense that the dialogue has broken down. This is virtually explicit in the movement's sardonic dedication "to my brothers in Apollo": superficially, the music proves that Mahler could write counterpoint; but the pervasive delirium is the sign of something deeper—an ironic attitude toward syntax itself. If the meaning of this music lies in its clashes, extended sonorities and vectors of dissonance, then it represents a deliberate challenge to the very idea of nonharmonic reduction.

## 6. After nonharmonicity

The opening of Shostakovich's Ninth String Quartet is in a flexible E♭ major, the violins snaking in and out of the key to create a marvelous sequence of tensions (Figure 5.6.1). These lines have their own individual logic and character, the first violin articulating a series of 015 and 016 trichords (the two three-note sets containing both semitone and fifth) against the second violin's octatonic fragments, G–A♭–B♭–B–C♯–D and C–D–E♭–F–G♭, intersecting to saturate chromatic space

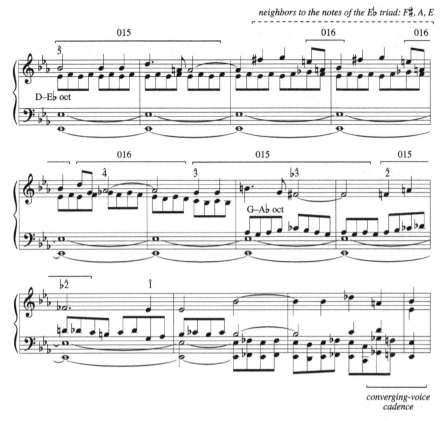

**Figure 5.6.1.** The opening of Shostakovich's Ninth String Quartet.

from B♭3 to E♭4. The beauty of this music, to my mind, lies in the skillful blending of multiple logics—one nontonal and set-theoretical, another tonal and harmonic, a third emphasizing a descending fifth from B♭4 to E♭4. The same combination can be found in jazz, originating with the blues and theorized under the rubric "playing outside" (Figure 5.6.2). Unlike their weightless atonal cousins, these sets acquire differential significance as they move in and out of the key, flashes of color like fish in a coral reef.

Here we can speak about the "emancipation of the dissonance" in a very precise sense, for notes outside the harmony are no longer required to resolve to harmonic notes according to rigid formulas. Indeed, the very distinction between "inside the harmony" and "outside the harmony" becomes problematic. This emancipation is a feature of virtually all twentieth-century music whether notated or not. (In popular-music scholarship, it is known as "the melodic-harmonic divorce."[66]) This loosening of restrictions should be distinguished from a very different and more radical view that denies or abrogates the distinction between consonance

---

[66] Temperley 2007 and Nobile 2015. Christopher Doll modifies this to "melodic/harmonic stratification" (2017).

**Figure 5.6.2.** The fourth chorus of McCoy Tyner's solo on "Pursuance," from *A Love Supreme*. Brackets show moments where the melodic 035 sets align with the harmony.

and dissonance altogether.[67] In Shostakovich's music there is a fundamental sense of "inside" and "outside," of tension and release created by shifts relative to the prevailing harmony.[68] This more limited emancipation of the dissonance begins with composers like Chopin, Mahler, and Debussy, who realized that harmonies could acquire sixths and ninths without losing their meaning. It was radicalized by Stravinsky, who allowed the nonharmonic tones to become chromatic, sometimes acquiring their own secondary centricity.[69]

This is the freedom for which Monteverdi advocated, realized only centuries after his death. To evaluate this music, it is neither necessary nor sufficient to consult a list of timeless rules; instead, we have to listen and make an aesthetic judgment. The freedom was fueled by the near-contemporaneous development of sound recording—a technology allowing musicians to bypass notation and formal education (itself a significant force in sustaining the nonharmonic system), communicating directly through sound. Once again, the blues played a central role: in "Rising Sun Blues" (Figure 2.10.1), the most striking nonharmonic tone is the sustained D♮ against the A minor seventh, a note that neither belongs to the chord nor obviously embellishes any chord tone, contributing to a five-note sonority that is aurally hard to parse. Then there is the G♮ deliciously clashing against the E major chord, essential to the blues but utterly foreign to the nonharmonic system. Connected to this, and not apparent in the notation, is all the delicate microdetail of Tom Ashley's singing, the scoops and glides that I have quantized into the semitonal grid. It is

---

[67] Whether Schoenberg himself distinguished these two senses of "emancipation" is an interesting question. As Hinton 2010 and Arndt 2011 point out, his description of emancipation changed over time, from something anticipated to something that had occurred.

[68] Exactly what determines this sense of "belonging" is a very complex matter; in popular music, instrumentation plays a vital role, with guitars often playing pure triads while the vocalist provides additional notes.

[69] See Figure 1.1.4, which suggests a distorted B♭ minor. When the embellishing tones acquire their own centricity, we have "polytonality." Thus there is a hidden connection between the emancipation of dissonance and polytonality.

genuinely unclear whether this music has a "harmonic skeleton" in the traditional sense, and whether it admits of anything like nonharmonic reduction.

The most vigorous protest against this new style of musical thinking came from Schenker, who like Artusi felt that the rules of the nonharmonic system were the foundation of musical coherence itself. Schenker frequently insisted on the connection between traditional counterpoint and his own analytical techniques, and he certainly seemed to treat the abandonment of the former as a threat to the latter.[70] Supercharging Artusi's scholasticism with an infusion of Hegelian metaphysics, Schenker insisted that great music necessarily permits an analysis rooted in traditional contrapuntal laws. Here one can hardly avoid the thought that the nonharmonic system functioned as a form of cultural power: power that distinguished learned from unlearned, legitimate from illegitimate, and whose exercise ensured the viability of a certain kind of analytical reduction. Its collapse, as Schenker sensed, represented not just a change of musical fashion but a threat to an entire species of intellectual authority.

Central to Schenker's theory is the assertion that nonharmonic notes serve no harmonic function whatsoever:

> Between the dissonant passing note and the sustained note, therefore, no composite sound exists. Anyone who, in disregard of this fact, posits a composite sound at the upbeat—between the dissonance and the cantus firmus note—has not grasped the nature of dissonance, of the passing note as strict counterpoint teaches it.[71]

This commitment could lead him into analytical contortions, as when he asserted that the ear spontaneously decomposes the parallel thirds of Figure 5.6.3 into a series of staggered semitonal motions. One can sympathize with Schenker's predicament: a straightforward reading would have the sliding at once nonharmonic, embellishments of the V–I motion, and harmonic, forming major thirds whose sonic character is musically significant. One wonders how Schenker would've dealt with the passage in Figure 5.6.4, where Chopin slides an entire triad from dominant to tonic, chromatic passing tones creating beautiful and harmonically significant flashes of color. Or for that matter Figure 5.6.5, where chromatic thirds have become the music's primary harmonic engine. Committed to the absolute nonharmonicity of the passing note, Schenker was poorly situated to theorize such moments, and by extension the changing role of nonharmonicity over the course of the nineteenth century.

---

[70] This comes out most clearly in his various complaints over modernism, most notably "Further consideration of the Urlinie: II." The precise role of traditional contrapuntal principles, and their specific applicability or inapplicability to various levels of reductive analysis, is a major point of disagreement among Schenkerians.

[71] Schenker (1926) 1996, p. 10. This point is echoed by Rothgeb ("the passing tone is . . . totally without harmonic significance," 1975, p. 268) and Lerdahl (2020, p. 18).

250   TONALITY: AN OWNER'S MANUAL

**Figure 5.6.3.** Mozart's Symphony no. 36, K.425, mm. 158ff, with Schenker's hypothesized perception of the chromatic ascent.

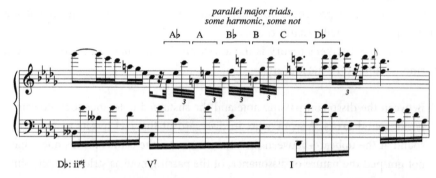

**Figure 5.6.4.** Chopin's Nocturne, Op. 27, no. 2, mm. 32–33, in which complete triads slide chromatically from dominant to tonic.

In effect, Schenker took passing tones as the model for all dissonances, and nonharmonic reduction as the model for reduction more generally.[72] Here I have reversed his argument, suggesting that suspensions are fundamentally less reducible than passing tones, and using that irreducibility to propose that reduction is generally problematic. My claim is that the nonharmonic system, rather than a means of *prolongation*, is a mechanism for *generating dissonances whose meaning and metaphysics is up for grabs*—with musicians and theorists sometimes disagreeing about their status. In the bottom passage of Figure 5.2.4, it is vital to hear the "composite sound" formed by the passing D♯ and the harmonic A; just as in Figure 5.2.1 it is vital to hear the composite sound of the ♯ formed by the suspension and the consonant sixth. If this is right, then there is an inconsistency at the heart of traditional musical syntax, a mismatch between the grammatical rules composers followed and the harmonic meaning of the music they made.

One underappreciated feature of that grammar is its combining of intervals from distinct alphabets (§4.8). In earlier music, nontriadic alphabets usually produce

[72] Schenker (1910) 1987, I, pp. 261ff, and Rothgeb 1975, pp. 273–74.

**Figure 5.6.5.** The end of Kabalevsky's "Ditty" (Op. 30, no. 2), where parallel chromatic major thirds create the harmonies.

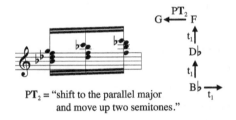

**Figure 5.6.6.** *The Rite of Spring*, upper voices at R196.

decorative notes subordinate to those of the prevailing harmony.[73] Twentieth-century musicians sometimes combined alphabets without this sort of subordination: Figure 5.6.6, from the end of Stravinsky's *Rite of Spring*, is similar to Louis Armstrong's line in "West End Blues" (Figure P2.2, §4.8), lower notes moving along the B♭ minor triad, with the top voice moving along the C major triad, two or three semitones above its lower neighbor; here, a complex transformational network creates a variety of set classes sharing the same abstract structure. While the network is reminiscent of the one we used to describe Armstrong's phrase, it has a very different meaning: the first note of Armstrong's motive is an out-of-harmony neighbor that resolves to a chord tone, whereas the top note of Stravinsky's chord is part of the harmony itself.

The combination of different intervals produces a harmonic variety not easily captured with any available analytical language, a hidden musical logic that tickles the ear. Figure 5.6.7 shows how we might use this technique in tonal and atonal contexts, deploying hierarchical networks whose structure is revealed by their

---

[73] Fugue subjects are an exception, using different interval types to relate harmonic notes (§4.8).

**Figure 5.6.7.** Two passages that transpose complex musical objects along both chord and scale. The fourth note of the first motive is a diatonic step below the fifth note; the third note of the second motive is a minor third above the fourth note.

transformations. Generalized in this way, the techniques of the nonharmonic system provide an extraordinarily flexible resource for twenty-first-century musicians. We can still take pleasure in the way motives and melodies move in and out of the prevailing chord or scale, and we can still enjoy the similar-yet-different configurations that result from complex intervallic relationships. If we broaden our thinking as suggested by the Prime Directive, the past starts to feel present again.

# Prelude
## Functional and Scale-Degree Analysis

Since there is a one-to-one correspondence between standard Roman numerals and tertian structures over a bass, we can interpret Roman numerals as *referring* to those structures. Thus a symbol like "I⁶" can be taken to mean "the $\frac{6}{3}$ sonority over scale degree 3" or "scale degrees 1, 3, and 5 with $\hat{3}$ in the bass." This is *scale-degree analysis*, a "thin" and relatively theory-neutral record of the tertian sonorities in a piece. Pure scale-degree analysis is a relatively modern phenomenon; the traditional or *functional* approach uses harmonic symbols that are "thick" and theory-laden—encoding the analyst's phenomenological impression of a chord, beliefs about its behavior, theory of its historical origins, or claims about its "essence."[1] Thus a scale-degree theorist would label the starred chords in Figure P6.1 as mediants while the function theorist might use V to record the claim that they behave or sound like dominants. To a scale-degree analyst, it's just a fact that mediants sometimes appear where we would ordinarily expect dominants; to a function theorist the label "III" betrays a misunderstanding.

The tradeoff here is between simplifying the process of chord-identification and simplifying the grammar of harmonic progressions. Rameau analyzed the deceptive cadence as a descending-fifth progression in which the tonic chord is represented by the root, third, and *sixth* above the fundamental bass; this yields a simple harmonic rule ("dominants descend by fifth to the tonic") at the expense of complicating the identification of the fundamental bass (since either tonic or sub-mediant can now serve as fundamental bass for scale degrees 6, 1, and 3).[2] In much the same way, traditional theorists have often treated vii° as a dominant seventh missing its root; once again this simplifies the grammar of progressions ("V goes to I") while complicating the process of chord identification ("V⁷ sometimes lacks its root"). This same philosophical difference underwrites the longstanding dispute about the proper labeling of the cadential six-four: to the scale-degree theorist, I$\frac{6}{4}$ means "scale degrees 1, 3, and 5 with $\hat{5}$ in the bass," and it is just a fact that this chord sometimes occurs between predominant and dominant. The function theorist prefers to say that ii⁶ progresses to a *dominant* that is sometimes embellished by a $\frac{6}{5}$–$\frac{5}{3}$ progression above the bass. This gives an efficient grammar at the expense of an ambiguous notation in which "V$\frac{6}{4}$" can refer to two different chords: scale degrees 1, 3, and 5 with $\hat{5}$ in the bass and scale degrees 5, 7, and 2 with $\hat{2}$ in the bass.[3]

---

[1] See Rothgeb 1996.

[2] Rameau (1722) 1971, pp. 71–73 (book 2, chapter 6).

[3] This debate can be traced back at least to Weber (1817–1821) 1846, pp. 463–64; for more recent discussions see Beach 1967 and Ninov 2016.

*Tonality.* Dmitri Tymoczko, Oxford University Press. © Oxford University Press 2023. DOI: 10.1093/oso/9780197577103.003.0010

**Figure P6.1.** (*top*) The fifth phrase of Bach's chorale "Jesu, meine Freude" (BWV 64.8, Riemenschneider 138), where III$^{+6}$ acts like a dominant; (*bottom*) the last measures of Robert Schumann's "Am Kamin" from *Kinderszenen*, along with John Rothgeb's analysis. Above the music, I show how the passage can be viewed as a "down by third, up by step" sequence (with mixed chromatic and diatonic elements). On this reading the bracketed g$^6$–a$^6$ cadence repeats the bracketed final g°–[a] sequential unit.

Discussions of this issue, when they do not immediately degenerate into outright invective, often terminate in naïve philosophy. Many theorists have claimed that labels like "I" and "I$^6$" *necessarily* imply similarity, indicating that both chords have the fundamental quality of *tonicity* or *tonic-triadness*.[4] But this is not how language works: the sea cucumber is biologically an animal despite its name. Philosophically, the scale-degree theorist is fully justified in using Roman numerals to refer to collections of scale degrees: from that perspective the relation between "I" and "I$^6$" is a matter for investigation rather than a presupposition of the notation. Roman numerals, as used by the scale-degree theorist, are largely equivalent to figured-bass symbols.

To be sure, the difference between these approaches is one of degree rather than kind: in reality there is a continuum between almost completely mechanistic analyses that label every sounding consonance, and highly interpretive enterprises that provide almost no information about scale-degree content at all (cf. the prelude to chapter 7). Nor can harmonic analysis entirely avoid questions about whether sonorities are harmonic or nonharmonic—questions that are extremely complex in the functional era but arise in other styles as well (Figure P6.2). But we can

---

[4] As Carl Schachter puts it, "there is no such 'thing' as a I chord in C major, but only an *idea* that can find expression" in manifold ways; that single "idea" is presumably what is labeled by the Roman numeral "I" (Schachter 1990, p. 166, quoted in Rothgeb 1996; my italics). Damschroder 2016, p. 5, expresses a similar sentiment.

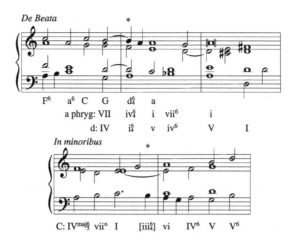

**Figure P6.2.** (*top*) The second-inversion triad in m. 19 of the Agnus from Palestrina's mass *De Beata Marie Virginis* (II) (starred) is plausibly harmonic, occurring in a sequence of four ascending fifths (or five, if we ignore the a⁶). (*bottom*) The second-inversion triad in m. 21 of the Agnus of the mass *In minoribus duplicibus* (starred) has a much weaker claim to harmonicity, being produced by a passing tone.

acknowledge these theoretical points while still hoping to separate, inasmuch as it is feasible, the project of *labeling* harmonies from that of *theorizing about their meaning and role*, using harmonic labels as a relatively neutral ground for evaluating claims about syntactic behavior. From this point of view, the behavior or origin or essence of a chord should have little influence on its label.

In this book, I generally default to a fairly strict form of scale-degree analysis. First, because it gives us a vocabulary for exploring how collections like iii⁶ can gradually change their function (e.g., moving to IV in the Renaissance, largely disappearing in the classical period, and acquiring dominant function in the nineteenth century). Second, because it gives us a common language in which to express disagreement or uncertainty about a chord's perceived function: for example, one listener may hear the cadential $^6_4$ as a dominant, while another may be more sensitive to its tonic qualities, with neither being right or wrong.[5] Scale-degree analysis provides a shared vocabulary for discussing these disagreements, rather than encoding the purportedly "correct" interpretation directly in its notation.[6] And third, because the scale-degree approach leads to greater methodological clarity. For the scale-degree theorist, a term like "dominant" is roughly synonymous with "V or vii°" and "dominants proceed to tonics" is a testable claim: we simply check whether scale degrees 5, 7, and 2 typically proceed to scale degrees 1, 3, and 5. This is something even a computer can do.

By contrast, functional analysis can sometimes come dangerously close to circularity: at the extreme, labels like "dominant" are utterly divorced from their

---

[5] Rothgeb 1996 describes functional analysis as recording what a "perceptive listener" hears; such perceptions are much more variable than scale-degree content.

[6] In this respect my proposed reconceptualization of Roman numerals is consonant with the trend toward the more theory-neutral labels of figured bass (Gjerdingen 2007 and Holtmeier 2007).

256   TONALITY: AN OWNER'S MANUAL

scale-degree content, applied to *any* chord that is perceived (*by the analyst*) as engendering a certain kind of expectation.[7] Here the claim "dominants progress to tonics" becomes *definitional*, free of any empirical content whatsoever—an introspective report that some sonority arouses an expectation of a tonic arrival.[8] Here, harmonic analysis becomes a language for talking about one's experience—sometimes described as a matter of "chord meaning."

None of which is to imply that it is misguided: describing subjective experience is a reasonable pursuit, and there is certainly something to be gained from the thought that tonic function can be expressed by scale degrees 1, 3, and either 5 or 6. Problems arise when one particular approach is tacitly assumed to be the only option. Eminent scholars have claimed that Roman numerals *necessarily* presuppose inversional equivalence, or that terms like "dominant" assume the primacy of the bass voice.[9] Similarly, theorists sometimes complain about the "trivial transliteration of note-content"—as if it were a mistake to aspire to somewhat objective descriptions against which we can test our assertions.[10] (Very often these same theorists underestimate the degree of regularity to be found in local harmonic progressions, regularity that becomes unmistakable when we stoop to the level of "trivial transliteration.") In rejecting scale-degree analysis, theorists deprive themselves of a useful tool for charting the development of harmonic functionality—indeed, virtually the *only* tool that can trace the subtle ways in which configurations of scale degrees change their behavior over the course of the sixteenth and seventeenth centuries.

My argument can be reformulated as a question. Suppose a musician is interested in scale-degree content, desiring a relatively theory-neutral account of the tertian harmonies in a piece. How should they go about this? The two options are to create an entirely new language that is virtually equivalent to, and intertranslatable with, familiar Roman numerals (for instance, using "scale degrees 7 and 3 over $\hat{5}$" in place of "iii$^6$"), or, alternatively, to use familiar Roman numerals with a slightly different set of implications. The first has massive costs in time and effort: when confronted with these new terms, readers need to stop and think about what is meant, whereas traditional Roman numerals can be immediately associated with collections of scale degrees. The second runs the risk of unwanted implications, but this can be forestalled by being clear about how one is using words. One approach requires that readers internalize an entirely new nomenclature, all in the fruitless attempt to stave off misunderstanding; the other requires only that we trust our readers to be attentive, flexible, and charitable enough to take us at our word.

---

[7] Some theorists divorce terms like "dominant" from scale-degree content altogether (Lerdahl 2001, Nobile 2016).

[8] Some theorists use "subdominant" to refer to IV chords that progress plagally to the tonic rather than authentically to V, so that "subdominant chords progress to tonics" becomes a matter of definition; for the scale-degree theorist these same words constitute a falsifiable claim (Swinden 2005, p. 253).

[9] Dahlhaus 1990, p. 73. Speaking about the Renaissance cadence, Taruskin writes: "the progression in the bass, from the fifth scale degree [ ... ] to the final, is congruent with what we are accustomed to calling a V–I or dominant–tonic progression. *To call it that is to think of the motion of the lowest part as the essential cadential approach*, and to associate the gesture toward closure with the 'dominant' harmony" (Taruskin 2005, vol. 2, p. 496, my italics).

[10] Rothgeb 1996, paragraph 11.

# 6

# The Origins of Functional Harmony

Scholars have situated the origin of functional tonality in the early 1400s, the popular music of the early 1500s, Monteverdi's works of the early 1600s, Corelli and the 1670s, and even after J. S. Bach.[1] To my mind this is like trying to identify the precise moment in which dinosaurs evolved into birds: functional harmony developed gradually over centuries, and there is no single point at which the process began or ended.[2] This is because the transition was largely *implicit*, a matter of composers learning patterns and idioms without necessarily recognizing them explicitly—embodied routines that only later became the subject of explicit theoretical attention. To trace its development, we need to look toward the musical knowledge implied by music itself. Statistics are essential here, if only to point us in the right direction.

Once we understand the development of tonal functionality as gradual and implicit, we can incorporate a number of earlier insights. In what follows, I will agree with Lowinsky that a simple form of *protofunctionality* appeared in the early 1500s as an optional set of ionian-mode idioms emphasizing root-position I, IV, and V.[3] Over the next two centuries, these routines colonized an increasing swath of music, ultimately coming to resemble universal laws rather than genre-specific tendencies. During this time, they also increased in complexity, moving beyond simple oscillations to longer progressions featuring a wider variety of sonorities. Thus I also agree with Fétis and Dahlhaus, who have drawn attention to the early 1600s as a time when additional functional vocabulary was being standardized. The mid-seventeenth-century enthusiasm for sequences represents another inflection point, and a reason for highlighting Corelli.

Where I depart from earlier theorists is in rejecting a unified or essentialist conception of functionality. The evolution of functional harmony, like the evolution of birds, involved numerous separate processes occurring at different times. One is the restriction of harmonic vocabulary to a small number of chords and progressions. Another is modal homogenization, the reduction of the available modes to just major and minor. The development of inversional equivalence is a third. Broad

---

[1] Korte 1929, Georgiades 1937, and Besseler 1950 (early 1400s, all cited in Dahlhaus 1990, p. 83); Lowinsky 1961 (early 1500s); Dahlhaus 1990 and Fétis (1840) 1994 (Monteverdi); Bukofzer 1947 (Corelli); Gauldin 1995b (after Bach).

[2] This view is consonant with Christensen 1993b and Taruskin 2005, vol. 2, pp. 471–72. On avian evolution, see Varricchio and Jackson 2016.

[3] Lowinsky 1961.

*Tonality.* Dmitri Tymoczko, Oxford University Press. © Oxford University Press 2023. DOI: 10.1093/oso/9780197577103.003.0011

258 TONALITY: AN OWNER'S MANUAL

acceptance of seventh chords and second-inversion triads is a fourth. A fifth is the standardization of modulatory pathways. Interest in sequential patterning is another. Yet others concern melodic routines, from the leading tone's increasing tendency to resolve, to the development of the $\hat{3}$–$\hat{2}$–$\hat{1}$ and $\hat{5}$–$\hat{4}$–$\hat{3}$–$\hat{2}$–$\hat{1}$ templates that underlie so many baroque and classical phrases. My guiding principle is that these processes are largely independent, separable, and linked by no single logic.[4] As a result, we find some varieties of functional tonality that are focused on primary triads, and others that make heavy use of seventh chords, secondary diatonic triads, or sequences. No one key unlocks all the doors.

Again, many of these changes occurred in musical practice long before they were noticed by theorists. To say this is not to imply that history is guided by a hidden hand, or that it evolves toward greater artistic perfection, but merely that it sometimes develops in a way that is akin to natural language: from 800 to 1400, for example, English gradually lost its case markers in a bottom-up process driven by the changing behavior of ordinary speakers. To study this process by looking at medieval grammars, rather than the records of linguistic behavior, is to get things backward—for the grammarians neither noticed nor cared about these changes as they were occurring.[5] The development of harmonic functionality is analogous, a very gradual regimentation of musical behavior that focuses musical attention on a core set of harmonic and melodic routines. To explore it, we need to consider the utterances of musical speakers, rather than the theories surrounding those utterances. Paradoxical as it may sound, it is possible that contemporary theorists, using contemporary tools, may end up understanding some aspects of this grammar better than its native speakers.[6]

## 1. The logical structure of protofunctionality

A precondition for understanding the origin of functional harmony, and a topic to which I as a nonhistorian can contribute, is a clear and principled understanding of the phenomenon itself. We can start with simple counting. In a typical major-key passage by J. S. Bach or Beethoven, more than half of all sonorities will be either I, $I^6$, or $V^{(7)}$. The flip side of this popularity is the remarkable scarcity of sonorities like iii, $iii^6$, and $vi^6$, which in classical music typically comprise less than 1% of all chords. Such frequencies are sometimes known as *zeroth-order* properties, as they are context-independent. They contrast with *first-order* properties that describe

---

[4] Compare Taruskin's suggestion that there is a unified logic based on fifths: "we [modern readers] are therefore much more fully aware than anyone could have been at the time of *the range of implications* the new cadential structure [i.e., the root-position V–I cadence] *carried within it*" (2005, vol. 2, pp. 471–72, my italics).

[5] In fact, there were relatively few such grammars; medieval grammarians were largely concerned with Latin rather than "vulgar" language. In contrast to the standard practice of historical linguistics, Bent explicitly recommends founding musical grammar on contemporaneous grammatical theorizing (1998). This view is so foreign to historical linguistics that I am unable to find any linguists who have considered it.

[6] For a linguistic analogue see Labov 1975, p. 107: "this puts us in the somewhat embarrassing position of knowing more about a speaker's grammar than he does himself."

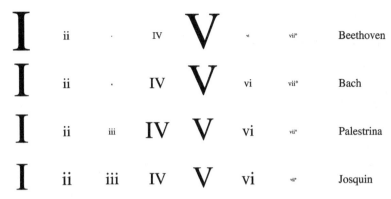

Figure 6.1.1. Chord roots in a range of composers, with size proportional to frequency.

the likelihood that one chord will progress to another: for example, the probability that V will go to I. Theories of functionality often highlight first-order properties—associating the experience of "dominantness" with that chord's tendency to move to the tonic.[7] But to my mind functionality is first and foremost a matter of chordal vocabulary.

Figure 6.1.1 presents the distribution of diatonic sonorities in the ionian and major-mode music of a range of composers.[8] Here we see harmonic vocabulary gradually coming to focus on the tonic, dominant, and the two main predominants, ii and IV, while the mediant grows so infrequent as to become invisible. Particularly interesting is the gradual reduction of the submediant, a narrowing that continues from J. S. Bach to Beethoven, as if the process that *led to* functionality also persists *during* the functional era. It is also interesting that IV appears to increase from Josquin to Palestrina, only to decrease thereafter—suggesting a protofunctional practice emphasizing I, IV, and V. These kinds of changes show that a harmonic theory cannot be phrased solely in terms of rules like "chord X can go to chord Y": we also need to consider the basic preference for some chords over others.

We see these same tendencies when we look at specific pieces. Figure 6.1.2 shows the opening of the pavane of Dalza's first *Pavana alla Venetiana*, published in 1508 in the fourth volume of Petrucci's lute intabulations. The music is grouped into sixteen-bar periods whose antecedents end with two bars of V and whose consequents end with a bar of V and two bars of I. More than 95% of the piece is spent on the root-position primary triads I, IV, and V; all but three chords are in

---

[7] The opposition between zeroth-order and first-order is broadly related to Dahlhaus's opposition between Riemannian and Rameauian conceptions: Riemann tends to emphasize zeroth-order chord categories ("functions"); while Rameau tends to emphasize first-order progressions (Dahlhaus 1990, Christensen 1993). Bobbitt (1955) and Meeùs (2000, 2018) emphasize first-order probabilities. There are also second-order probabilities concerning the likelihood that a two-chord sequence such as ii⁶–V will continue in a particular way, third-order probabilities governing the successors to three-chord sequences, and so on.

[8] This figure categorizes chords by root; one gets a very similar graph if one looks only at root-position triads.

Figure 6.1.2. The opening of Dalza's first *Pavana alla Venetiana*.

root position. The only substantial departures from functionality are the ♭VII⁶ in m. 9, the ♭VII in m. 27, and the occasional use of F♮ over the C major chord.⁹ One gets the sense that each period embellishes a single harmonic template, rather like a variations form—for instance, antecedent phrases always start with four bars of I and end with two bars of V, but mm. 5–6 can contain either IV or I; similarly, consequents always end with a bar of V and two bars of I, but the preceding five measures are more flexible. There is also an eight-bar "cadential interlude" after the third period, presenting two iterations of a IV–V–I cadence, as if reinforcing the previous consequent's close.¹⁰

The preference for fifth-related primary triads creates *harmonic cycles* oscillating between the tonic and a contrasting chord. There is a subtle geometrical logic underlying these cycles. The top system of Figure 6.1.3 is an exact contrary-motion sequence, the bass dividing the octave in half while the upper voices divide it into sixths. Underneath, I show that the major triad exhibits this symmetry in an approximate way. The third staff shows how this approximate symmetry manifests itself in diatonic space: the tritone F♯ major can be diatonicized in either descending or ascending fashion, to F and G major respectively; the pattern achieves stepwise melodic motion by using both quantizations to connect $\hat{5}$ to $\hat{7}$.¹¹ The resulting

---

⁹ In general, the piece exhibits an intriguing and playful mix of scalar inflections. Since it was published in tablature, it is unclouded by questions about *musica ficta*.

¹⁰ Dalza's other Venetian Pavanes—which indeed feel more like variations on a single template than distinct pieces—include similar cadential interludes.

¹¹ For the sake of clarity, my realization includes parallel perfect intervals which would be avoided in practice. The figure's bottom level is very similar to a graph appearing in Rameau's 1737 *Génération harmonique* (Christensen 1993a, p. 194). Unlike Rameau, I consider the sequence a distorted quantization of an exact contrary-motion sequence (Yust 2015a). This recalls the strategy we used to model rock harmony (Figure 2.1.7).

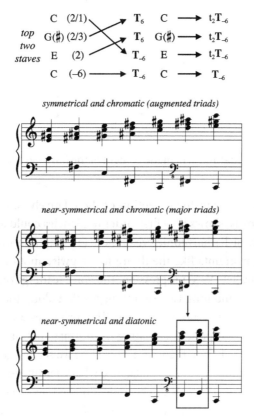

Figure 6.1.3. Upper-voice steps against bass-line fifths.

diatonic structure retains the traces of the chromatic symmetry: melodic steps balanced against a bass that moves by approximately half an octave, cycling from tonic to contrasting sonority and back.

This nearly sequential pattern is remarkable for a number of reasons. First, it exhibits a feature central to Schenkerian theory, the bass acting as a *fifth-divider*, nearly bisecting the octave into consonant intervals, while the melody divides the third into nearly equal steps (a "step divider," we might say). Geometrically, the upper voices articulate a series of *complete circles* in triadic space (i.e., Figure 3.4.1) while the bass divides the octave in half. Second, it gives us an upper-voice analogue to the traditional "rule of the octave"—associating melodic scale degrees with harmonic defaults. These associations are apparent throughout the functional tradition, and particularly important in its earlier stages.[12] Third, the figure's harmonic progressions are closely related to the plagal and authentic cadences, allowing these well-established idioms to appear in other parts of the phrase. Fourth, its progressions are largely non-directional, and can occur either

---

[12] As the tradition develops, $\hat{4}$–$\hat{3}$ is increasingly harmonized by $V^7$–I. Other important possibilities, not appearing on my simple model, include V harmonizing $\hat{5}$, IV harmonizing $\hat{1}$, and vii°6–I harmonizing $\hat{4}$–$\hat{3}$.

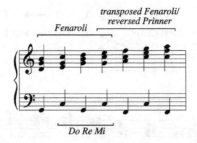

**Figure 6.1.4.** Sequential and schematic content of the fifths-and-steps arrangement.

forward or backward, with the exception of the relatively rare melodic $\hat{7}$–$\hat{6}$. The figure, in other words, shows how first-order tendencies could arise from the conjunction of zeroth-order harmonic preferences (an emphasis on I, IV, and V) and simple melodic constraints like the desire for stepwise motion. Fifth, other than the completely parallel IV–V progression, the voice leadings on Figure 6.1.3 have the form $t_2 T_{-3 \text{ or } -4}$, combining two-step transposition along the chord with three- or four-step transposition along the scale. This produces a sequential structure, the V–I–V–I ($\hat{7}$–$\hat{1}$–$\hat{2}$–$\hat{3}$) pattern repeating in contrary motion at the interval of a fifth as I–IV–I–IV ($\hat{3}$–$\hat{4}$–$\hat{5}$–$\hat{6}$, Figure 6.1.4).[13] Here we see the germ of several later schemas: $\hat{7}$–$\hat{1}$–$\hat{2}$–$\hat{3}$ under V–I–V–I is related to what Gjerdingen calls the "Fenaroli"; while $\hat{3}$–$\hat{4}$–$\hat{5}$–$\hat{6}$ under I–IV–I–IV can be understood either as a transposed Fenaroli or a reversed "Prinner." (Similarly, $\hat{1}$–$\hat{2}$–$\hat{3}$ under I–V–I resembles Gjerdingen's "Do-Re-Mi.") Our figure grounds these schemas in the basic geometry of triadic counterpoint, suggesting that we will find them in any style that makes use of the fifths-and-step defaults.

Michaelis's "Passando per una rezzola" is a brief frottola published in Petrucci's 1504 collection (Figure 6.1.5). Notated in cut-C mensuration, the harmonies articulate a clear triple meter and three four-bar phrases—the first ending on IV, the second with a weak cadence on I, and the third with a stronger close on the tonic.[14] All but two chords are root-position major triads, and the overall harmonic progression is strikingly functional—indeed, the sounding upper voice, considered together with the harmony, traces out a $\hat{5}$–$\hat{6}$–$\hat{5}$–$\hat{4}$–$\hat{3}$–$\hat{2}$–$\hat{1}$ melody harmonized almost entirely with the options in Figure 6.1.3: the exceptions are the I$^6$ chord replacing the root position I in m. 6 (to be discussed shortly), and the two harmonizations of $\hat{4}$–$\hat{3}$—the first a quasi-cadential vii$^{o6}$–I and the second a retrofunctional ♭VII–I. The combination of regular phrasing and familiar progressions anticipates not just the strict functionality of the eighteenth and nineteenth centuries, but also the looser

---

[13] Including the octave repeat, the entire structure can be seen as a near sequence whose interval of repetition changes from a fourth (B–E) to a fifth (E–B).

[14] For a justification of my rebarring, see Boone 2000, pp. 36ff.

**Figure 6.1.5.** The frottola "Passando per una rezzola" by Michaelis.

**Figure 6.1.6.** The opening of Tromboncino's frottola "Se ben hor non scopro el foco."

functionality of our own time: add drums, change the words, and you almost have a pop song.

Figure 6.1.6 shows the opening of Bartolomeo Tromboncino's "Se ben hor non scopro el foco" from the same collection. (Tromboncino, "the little trombonist," would have been better nicknamed "Birichino" or perhaps "Assassino.") Once again we have regular phrases and a clear formal structure. The first phrase ends with a Prinner variant substituting ♭VII for V$^6$. The middle section, shown in Figure 6.1.7, is notable for its four-voice canonic sequence; Figure 6.1.8 analyzes this sequence using a technique from §4.3, applying rhythmic displacement and contrary-motion distortion to antiparallel tenths.[15] In the coda, the middle two voices ascend in canon to form a series of F and B♭$^5_3$ chords, delicately balanced between F and B♭ major, and exploiting the round in Figure 4.5.6.

---

[15] This same sequence appears in many other Renaissance pieces, including Monteverdi's 1610 *Vespro della Beata Vergine* (Rotem and Schubert 2021).

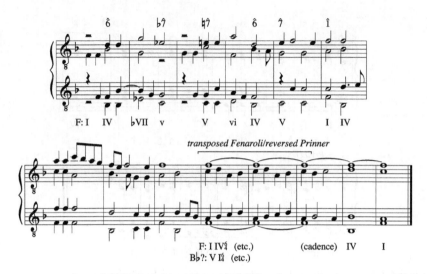

Figure 6.1.7. The end of "Se ben hor non scopro el foco," omitting the repeat of mm. 4–6 on Figure 6.1.6.

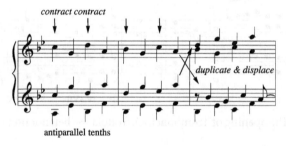

Figure 6.1.8. Deriving the four-voice canon: starting with an ascending-fifth sequence, every other chord is contracted by contrary motion. Rhythmic displacement allows one voice to be duplicated at the unison.

## 2. Similarities and differences

These pieces are so bewilderingly functional that they seem to challenge the thesis of gradual evolution—suggesting perhaps that functional tonality *did* spring forth fully formed in this early vernacular tradition. But on closer inspection, it is clear that we are dealing with a distinctive *protofunctional* dialect that both resembles and differs from later styles.

We can start with the resemblances.

First, these pieces seem to be harmonic in conception: the heavy use of root-position triads, often in close position and related by "default" voice leading, coupled with the deemphasizing of contrapuntal devices such as imitation, all

**Figure 6.2.1.** Parallelism in Dalza's second *Pavana alla Venetiana* (mm. 53–55).

**Figure 6.2.2.** Phrase structure in which a stronger V–I follows a weaker V–I (from the opening of Dalza's *Pavana alla Ferrarese*).

suggest that chords are genuine objects of compositional focus.[16] Unapologetic parallelism reinforces the centrality of harmony (Figure 6.2.1).

Second, these pieces are dominated by primary triads, with root-position I, IV, and V accounting for 70%–80% of all chords. These primary triads tend to behave more or less as in later music: phrases frequently start with the tonic, exploit weak contrasts with IV, ♭VII, or V (Figure 6.2.2), then move to a more decisive contrast that features a robust dominant, which is either resolved at the start of the next phrase (e.g., a half cadence, as in Figure 6.1.2, mm. 7–8), at the end of the phrase (full cadence, as in m. 15 of Figure 6.1.2), or by a surprise move to vi (deceptive progression, Figure 6.3.1). Tonics are stable, dominants provide the most powerful contrast, and subdominants provide a weaker contrast: in this sense, the basic pillars of functional harmony are in place—though in a simple, oscillatory context that typically cycles from tonic to contrasting sonority and back.[17]

There is an interesting question about the role of IV: is it a subdominant that moves to I, a *predominant* that moves to V, or a *post-tonic* to which I tends to move? The conceptual challenge is that the zeroth-order and first-order harmonic properties interact: we would expect music with a lot of I, IV, and V chords to feature a lot of IV–I, IV–V, and I–IV motion. What we need to know is, *given* the prevalence of IV, V, and I, are certain progressions especially likely? We can explore this question by calculating the difference between the overall likelihood of a chord (its zeroth-order probability) and its (first-order) likelihood after a specific harmony: this tells us, for example, whether V is particularly likely to occur after IV.

---

[16] Dahlhaus 1990, p. 288: "Many details [of the frottolas] cannot be explained without recourse to the concept of a chord."

[17] "The I–IV, IV–I, and V–I fifth-relations in [Dalza's] *Pavanna alla ferrarese* are so strikingly marked that Lowinsky was unquestionably right to see in them something new" (Dahlhaus 1990, pp. 109–10).

|       | Dalza | Frottola |
|-------|-------|----------|
| IV–V  | +19.9 | +6.7     |
| IV–I  | –28.5 | –9.4     |
| I–IV  | +6.5  | +14.7    |

**Figure 6.2.3.** The "tendency" of IV–V and IV–I progressions. The number +19.9 indicates that the likelihood of a V chord increases by +19.9 percentage points after a IV, relative to its overall likelihood—or in other words, that IV chords "tend" to go to V chords. Negative values indicate progressions that are suppressed.

|   | Dalza | Frottola |
|---|-------|----------|
| 5 | 99.1  | 97.7     |
| 1 | 95.8  | 97.4     |
| 4 | 94.2  | 97.6     |
| 6 | 87.6  | 58.8     |
| 2 | 70.1  | 53.3     |
| 3 | 14.0  | 40       |
| 7 | 11.1  | 0        |

**Figure 6.2.4.** The likelihood of root-position triads on the various ionian-mode scale degrees. The mediant is, after the leading tone, the *least* likely to support a root-position triad, indicating a preference for $I^6$ over iii, even in genres that typically favor root-position triads.

Figure 6.2.3 shows that the subdominant tends to act more like a predominant in Dalza while being more neutral in the frottola, largely moving in accordance with its zeroth-order probability.[18] We will return to this idea later.

Third, these pieces exhibit a precursor to inversional equivalence in the form of a substantial zeroth-order preference for $I^6$ over iii, despite the otherwise heavy reliance on root-position triads. Figure 6.2.4 shows the proportion of root-position and first-inversion triads appearing above each of the bass degrees: for the primary degrees $\hat{1}$, $\hat{4}$, and $\hat{5}$, root positions occur more than 90% of the time; for the secondary degrees $\hat{2}$ and $\hat{6}$ the percentage is considerably lower; for $\hat{3}$, first inversion occurs more often than root position (60% of the time in the frottola and about 85% of the time in Dalza). One can hypothesize that this asymmetry reflects the aural similarity between I and $I^6$: perhaps, in this harmonically limited music, the $I^6$ chord simply sounds more consistent with the primary triads that dominate the rest of the harmony.[19] This zeroth-order preference for $I^6$ also allows for stepwise bass motion, particularly when combined with the idiomatic Renaissance $vii^{o6}$–I cadence. Figure 6.2.5 combines bass $\hat{4}$–$\hat{3}$–$\hat{2}$–$\hat{1}$ with upper-voice $\hat{6}$–$\hat{5}$–$\hat{4}$–$\hat{3}$ to produce the basic voice leading of Gjerdingen's "Prinner," as characteristic of the Renaissance as of the eighteenth century (cf. Figures 6.1.5 and 6.5.1a, mm. 7–9).

---

[18] This is a relatively small sample so things might change if we looked at more music.

[19] Recall Gjerdingen's remarks about $I^6$, iii, and the rise of functional tonality (§1.5). It is also possible that the preference for $I^6$ reflects the influence of the mixolydian mode, where root-position mediant triads are unavailable.

**Figure 6.2.5.** The Prinner combines two standard ionian features, I⁶ as a default harmonization of $\hat{3}$ and the vii°⁶–I cadence.

**Figure 6.2.6.** A harmonic map for simple functional music.

In all these respects, I think it is appropriate to locate the origins of functional harmony in this repertoire—some of the first music ever printed, and some of the earliest popular music to survive.[20] But we should also recognize the important *differences* from the complex functionality of later centuries.

First, mature functionality is a matter not just of what happens, but of what does *not* happen, with its "harmonic grammar" underwritten by the virtual absence of progressions like V–IV, ii–IV, and so on. This early music exhibits harmonic preferences that evoke those of later functional music, but there is no sense that nonfunctional progressions are forbidden: one can easily find progressions like I–ii–I, or root-position dominants moving to root-position subdominants, and so on. We are dealing with flexible tendencies rather than rigid rules.

Second, there is no strong commitment to a single diatonic collection, with ♭VII common even in ionian contexts. The relevant conception of mode, or tonal area, is one that draws freely on tonic, dominant, subdominant, and subtonic. The ♭VII chord functions much as it does in our own popular music, providing an alternate harmonization for $\hat{4}$ and $\hat{2}$.[21]

Third, the harmonic routines are very simple. There is, for example, no real sense that the ii chord is a predominant: it can of course play this role, but in Dalza it more often moves to I than to V or vii°. Nor is there a sense that the submediant has a characteristic role to play. We are dealing with the fairly rudimentary set of options in Figure 6.2.6 rather than the more complex routines of later music.

Related to this is the importance of IV: the two harmonic cycles I–IV–I and I–V–I are, if not equal, then at least comparable in significance. Furthermore, IV–I progressions sometimes have a subtle "dominant" quality by virtue of an ascending $\hat{6}$–$\hat{7}$–$\hat{8}$ line. In other cases, I–IV progressions have a tonicizing character, with tonic moving to subdominant so as to evoke cadential formulae (e.g., the end of Figure 6.1.7). Figure 6.2.7 compares the relative proportion of IV and V chords in a range

---

[20] Compare McClary 2004, p. 15.
[21] Compare Figure 6.1.5, m. 9; Figure 6.1.6, m. 4; Figure 2.4.1; Pinter 2019; and McClary 2004, p. 218.

268    TONALITY: AN OWNER'S MANUAL

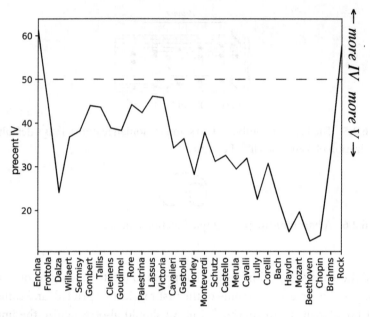

**Figure 6.2.7.** The relative proportion of IV and V: 100% means only IV is used, 0% means only V is used, and 50% represents an even balance between the two.

of ionian and major-mode music from the sixteenth century to the present. In some genres, IV is almost as common as V, falling from about 45% in my sample of Lassus to something more like 15% in Beethoven—a change due to both the declining use of IV and the increasing preference for V.

Fourth, though it is not apparent from the preceding musical examples, the different modes feature different harmonic patterns. In dorian, for example, the subdominant is often deemphasized relative to the subtonic, and pieces often revolve around i, ♭VII, III, and V.[22] Here again we might think of contemporary popular music, where major, minor, and mixolydian all emphasize different chord progressions. Early protofunctionality is a mode-bound option rather than an inviolable law governing all music—analogous perhaps to the blues in 1960s rock, a package of musical moves that can be adopted or avoided according to taste.

Fifth, inversional equivalence does not play a robust compositional role, for the simple reason that the harmonic vocabulary is so restricted: there can be no question about the equivalence of vi and vi⁶ in genres where vi⁶ hardly appears. Instead we have a proliferation of root-position primary triads that deemphasize the melodic function of the bass in favor of its harmonic role in articulating roots. It follows that *simple harmonic functionality does not require inversional equivalence*; the basic prerequisite for harmonic function is harmonic limitation.

Sixth, the melodic tendency of noncadential leading tones is weak. In functional music, outer-voice leading tones almost always move to the tonic. In protofunctional music, noncadential leading tones are less constrained, often progressing

---

[22] For example, Dalza's "Calata ala spagnole 1" and the "Caldibi Castigliano."

**Figure 6.2.8.** A descending leading tone in Dalza's *Tastar de Corde* 1, mm. 85ff.

downward (Figure 6.2.8). This suggests that there are important differences between cadential and ordinary dominants: leading-tone resolution is a function of the cadential suspension rather than the dominant as a harmonic entity or the leading tone as a melodic scale degree.

Seventh, there is no notion of modulation as an orderly progression through secondary keys; the music rarely modulates, and sometimes does so in ways that seem undirected or haphazard. Pieces sometimes begin in one key and end in another.

None of which should dislodge the claim that the origins of functionality can be found in this music. We can find evidence of protofunctional thinking whether we focus on analytical details or zoom out to consider larger statistical features of the genre as a whole. This protofunctional tendency can be found throughout sixteenth-century homophony, in pieces such as Willaert's *Villanesche* (1545) or Goudimel's 1564 setting of the Geneva psalter—all of which place a heavy emphasis on root-position triads supporting stepwise melodic motion. We can also find echoes of this protofunctionality in vernacular styles from Sacred Harp polyphony to the Carter family and three-chord rock-and-roll. Recognizing a distinct protofunctional practice is important not just for understanding the origins of functional harmony but also the nature of functionality itself.

## 3. Origin and meaning

Carl Dahlhaus has cautioned that we should not take these resemblances at face value, since some of these pieces originated with a cantus-tenor duet to which additional voices were later added.

> Provided that the significance of a composition depends on the tradition out of which it arose—*provided therefore that a procedure's origin determines its meaning*—then a frottola like *Oimè et cor* must be characterized as a two-voice composition with a supplemental bass.[23]

---

[23] Dahlhaus 1990, p. 281 (my italics). In a similar vein, Bent writes that "the failure to acknowledge a discant-tenor duet . . . can invalidate an analysis" (1998).

**Figure 6.3.1.** Tromboncino's frottola "Ah partiale e cruda morte!" I have eliminated a repeat of mm. 5–8.

Tromboncino's "Ah partiale e cruda morte!" is one of the pieces Dahlhaus describes as originating with a two-voice framework (Figure 6.3.1). Like "Se ben hor non scopro el foco," it is a quasi-rounded binary form with a sequential coda, largely emphasizing primary-triad harmony; throughout, cantus and tenor form a syntactical two-voice pair complete with cadences (Figure 6.3.2). But the three upper voices *also* tend to articulate close-position triads, supported by a bass that mostly sounds roots. The music thus seems to embody two forms of musical organization simultaneously.

**Figure 6.3.2.** The cantus/tenor duet, and close-position triads, in the first phrase of Tromboncino's "Ah partiale e cruda morte!"

**Figure 6.3.3.** Close position upper voices in mm. 23–27 of Tromboncino's "Ah partiale e cruda morte!" The repeated cadences are attractive in the full arrangement, but oddly pedestrian in the cantus/tenor duet.

A little thought reveals that this is not so mysterious, for as long as upper voices form complete close-position major and minor triads, then cantus and tenor will *necessarily* form an acceptable dyadic sequence of fifths and sixths; conversely, as long as the tenor forms a third, fifth, or sixth with the cantus, the alto can add the note that completes the close-position triad. (In the opening of "Ah partiale e cruda morte!" the tenor is usually a third below the cantus, falling to the fifth/sixth before the cadences.) Looking at Tromboncino's music, it is very difficult to know whether he began with a two-voice framework or some analogue to OUCH theory that produced a two-voice framework as byproduct. The deceptive cadence in the second-to-last line provides some evidence in favor of the second option, for in the cantus/tenor framework there is no deception and the passage repeats to puzzling effect (Figure 6.3.3). This suggests that even if Tromboncino started with a two-voice framework, he was already imagining the four-voice structure. We should not put too much interpretive weight on these questions of compositional method, as their importance tends to recede once we recognize that different paths can lead to similar destination.

Similarly, the *origin* of Renaissance cadential formulae lies in a number of dyadic schemas, particularly the converging-voice idiom known as the *clausula vera*. Dahlhaus and Bent observe that as late as 1532, Petro Aron was describing

272  TONALITY: AN OWNER'S MANUAL

**Figure 6.3.4.** A cadence in which voices converge on E, but which modern listeners will likely hear as emphasizing A.

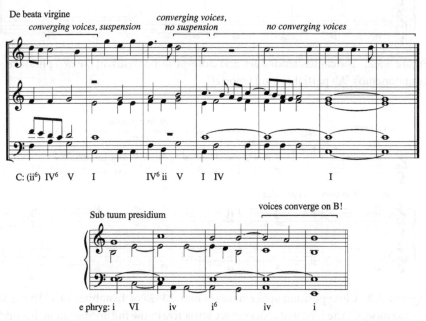

**Figure 6.3.5.** (*top*) The end of Josquin's mass *De beata virgine*. The final V–I and IV–I progressions lack the suspension formula and the final IV–I has no converging pair. (*bottom*) The end of the mass *Sub tuum presidium*, attributed to Josquin. This is an E phrygian piece that ends with a cadence in which upper voices converge on B, not used as a tonal center in the Renaissance.

Figure 6.3.4 as a cadence on E, not A. By that time, however, there was abundant evidence that the meaning of these converging voices was already in flux: (a) pieces ending with or without converging voices (Figure 6.3.5); (b) cadential formulations where the converged-upon note is not used as a tonal center (Figure 6.3.5); (c) a preference for the bass to sound the converged-upon note, as revealed by the *absence* of cadences where voices converge on the sixth above the bass (Figure 6.3.6); (d) the use of deceptive-style cadences in contexts that suggest cadential evasion and phrase elongation (Figure 6.3.1); and (e) theoretical lists of cadences that lack converging voices.[24] Further, the auditory system will lend salience to the bass of a root-position triad through the phenomenon of "tonal fusion"—a psychological effect that was as real in the Renaissance as it is today.[25]

---

[24] Thanks here to David Cohen. Richard Taruskin (2005, vol. 2, pp. 465–72) makes a similar point.
[25] Parncutt 1988.

| Ockeghem: | 86 | 13 | 1 | 0 |
| Josquin: | 79 | 19 | 1 | 1 |
| Palestrina: | 79 | 16 | 3 | 2 |
| Victoria: | 88 | 10 | 1 | 1 |

**Figure 6.3.6.** Possible bass notes under a converged-upon C, along with the percentage of cadences with that bass. The cadences on the sixth above the bass are very rare.

This divergence between theory and practice reminds us that earlier music theorists are not "native informants" who provide authoritative information about their musical culture, but rather *theory builders* who try to describe, systematize, and explain that culture.[26] Rather than taking their assertions at face value, we should check their theories against the data provided by music itself. Doing the history of theory without evaluating theoretical claims is like doing the history of science without considering how experiments turned out. It is also vital to bear in mind that earlier theorists operated in an intellectual environment substantially different from our own: in the early 1500s it was still possible to uphold Aristotle's view that the equatorial regions were uninhabitable, even though European sailors had actually been there, or that heavy objects fall faster than lighter objects, even though anyone could demonstrate the contrary.[27] If Renaissance thinkers upheld tradition over evidence in these matters, how sensitive should we expect them to be to subtle changes in musical practice? The question is not meant to be contemptuous but rather to acknowledge that early sixteenth-century minds had their own ideas about the relative weight of evidence and authority, that the habit of empirical thinking was still in its infancy, that they did not have our tradition of accumulating intellectual progress, that they lacked common terms for "discovery" and "innovation," and that they were largely unacquainted with probabilistic inference.[28] Aron's remarks about the cadence were thus constrained by tradition in ways we may not fully appreciate.[29] All of which presents a fascinating topic for historians of science, and a dangerous pitfall for unwary historicists. Music historians have chided their "presentist" colleagues for unthinkingly projecting contemporary concepts onto the music of the past, but they have been much less sensitive to the equally

[26] See Powers 1992a, pp. 43–4 for a similar view.
[27] See Wootton 2015, pp. 72–73.
[28] Hacking 1975.
[29] Even in 1597 Thomas Morley was describing the consonance of the perfect fourth with a long list of tenor-based precepts like "the fourth above the tenor is consonant only if the bass is a third or fifth below the tenor," paying homage to the dyadic tradition despite his own music's manifestly triadic and functional qualities.

274 TONALITY: AN OWNER'S MANUAL

erroneous assumption that earlier theorists operated with contemporary standards of descriptive accuracy.[30]

One final example of the complex interplay between origin and meaning. We have reason to believe that Renaissance composers had at least *some* notion of inversional equivalence, for the repeating contrapuntal patterns in chapter 4 are defined precisely by the fact that structurally analogous notes move in similar ways: in the Josquin passage in Figure 4.2.2, root moves down by step while third moves up by third, while in Figure 3.4.6 and mm. 20–24 of Figure 3.6.6, root and third move down by step while fifth stays fixed. To construct these sequences a composer has to understand which motions go in which voices, and this is tantamount to an implicit notion of inversional equivalence. (It is difficult to repeatedly lower the root if you cannot identify it!) Imitation thus provides one potential route toward inversional equivalence, for in asking "how can I create a consonant three-voice transposing round?" composers could easily be led to contrapuntal patterns in which roots, thirds, and fifths moved in characteristic ways.

Does it follow that composers thought of inversionally related chords as having the same musical function? Not at all, for it is entirely possible to have an abstract understanding of concepts like "root," "third," and "fifth," while still believing that *register is fundamental to a chord's contextual function and meaning*. But at the same time, it seems likely that this weaker version of inversional equivalence formed the foundation for the later and more robust notion. (Furthermore, it is plausible that the early preference for $I^6$ over iii results from a perceived resemblance between E–G–C and C–E–G.) The interesting question is how the version of inversional equivalence implicit in sixteenth-century practice developed into the stronger form explicit in the eighteenth century. This is a story of gradually shifting musical meaning, written jointly by composers and theorists, and it begins in weak and untheorized tendencies such as the favoring of $I^6$.

Against Dahlhaus's carefully hedged historicism I would therefore propose an alternative in which "origin" and "meaning" can come apart—one in which composers follow their ears as they grope toward the new, sometimes using earlier techniques to create music that exemplifies innovative and untheorized structure. If we believe music can develop in the way that natural language often does, if we believe that composers sometimes develop novel techniques—sometimes without an abstract understanding of their own musical practice, and with written theory trailing behind—then we need something more sophisticated than Dahlhaus's identification of origin and meaning. And if Renaissance music exhibits weaker versions of tendencies that strengthen throughout the sixteenth and seventeenth centuries, then it is futile to make invidious contrasts between approaches that "rely on common-practice tonality as a prism through which to view early music" and

---

[30] Compare Bent 1998 and Dahlhaus's remarks on the relation between $V^7$ and vii°, discussed at the end of the next section. Bent requires that "analytical tools be harmonized with early techniques and vocabulary, to the extent that these can be recovered and extended, just as what is incompatible with how they parsed their music should be avoided" (1998, p. 24).

"methods that respect the integrity and self-sufficiency of the languages of early music."[31] Used cautiously, contemporary theory and data-driven analysis can help us toward a genuinely historical perspective, revealing as-yet-undiscovered regularities in early music, and leading to a more nuanced view of functional harmony itself. To label this project "anti-historicist" or "presentist" is implicitly to reserve the term "history" for the study of verbal discourse. The history of practice is part of the history of theory.

## 4. Harmony and polyphony

A basic question about the development of functionality is the role of genre: was early functionality largely confined to secular and homophonic styles, or does it also appear in the polyphonic tradition? Both answers, I think, have an element of truth. Certainly, the earliest and most obviously functional music is popular, secular, and homophonic, employing techniques that were somewhat inimical to counterpoint. But it is also true that we can find statistical evidence for increasing functionality throughout sixteenth-century polyphony.

To frame our study of this issue, and to set our expectations for the sorts of patterns we might find in analysis, I want to consider the raw triadic progressions in a large sample of music by Ockeghem, Josquin, and Palestrina. Here I have used a computer to record all the instances of a complete vertical triad (major, minor, augmented, or diminished) followed by a second vertical triad, categorized by the inversions of the chords and the interval between their lowest notes. In performing this analysis, I permitted one or two nontriadic sonorities between the triads, to account for passing or other nonharmonic tones. The analysis was completely automatic and devoid of human judgment, neutral with respect to mode and centricity; the only question was whether the vertical intervals, sounding at any one time, formed a triad. For this reason, it gives a relatively raw perspective on the kinds of verticalities we might expect to find in sixteenth-century music, unadulterated by human interpretation.

Figure 6.4.1 considers the zeroth-order chord distributions in the corpora, showing a dramatic increase in root-position major triads from Ockeghem to Palestrina; in fact, root-position major triads and second-inversion triads are the *only* sonorities that increase between the two composers.[32] Figure 6.4.2 records

---

[31] Jesse Anne Owens, in the preface to Wiering 2001, p. ix.

[32] Interestingly enough, this seems to reflect both an increasing preference for "major" modes and an increasing preference for major triads within those modes. Major-mode pieces—interpreted as "pieces ending on a major triad that is in the key signature, and which is the most-frequent chord in the piece"—rise from a total of about 14% in Ockeghem, to 18% in Josquin, to 30% in Palestrina. Meanwhile, the proportion of major triads among the consonances within a broad selection of minor-mode pieces (i.e., pieces whose last root supports a minor triad in the key signature) changes from 22% in Ockeghem to 19% in Josquin to 29% in Palestrina; the corresponding numbers for ionian and mixolydian are 24% for Ockeghem, 34% for Josquin, and 51% for Palestrina.

| | Ockeghem | Josquin | Palestrina |
|---|---|---|---|
| Major $^5_3$ | 28 | 34 | 45 |
| Major $^6_3$ | 16 | 11 | 9 |
| Minor $^5_3$ | 31 | 39 | 31 |
| Minor $^6_3$ | 13 | 9 | 7 |
| Dim $^5_3$ | 2 | 1 | 0 |
| Dim $^6_3$ | 6 | 4 | 4 |
| Any $^6_4$ | 3 | 3 | 4 |

**Figure 6.4.1.** The prevalence of various sonorities in a broad selection of works by Ockeghem, Josquin, and Palestrina. Numbers represent the percentage of complete triadic sonorities.

| | Ockeghem | Josquin | Palestrina |
|---|---|---|---|
| $^5_3 \rightarrow \, ^5_3$ (D5) | 4 | 8 | 13 |
| $^6_3 \rightarrow \, ^5_3$ (0) | 11 | 7 | 5 |
| $^5_3 \rightarrow \, ^5_3$ (A5) | 4 | 7 | 9 |
| $^5_3 \rightarrow \, ^6_3$ (0) | 13 | 11 | 8 |
| $^6_4 \rightarrow \, ^5_3$ (0) | 1 | 1 | 4 |

**Figure 6.4.2.** The progressions whose frequency changes most from Ockeghem to Palestrina. The bass interval is given in parentheses with D5 = descending fifth or ascending fourth, 0 = no motion, and A5 = ascending fifth or descending fourth. Numbers are percentages of all two-chord complete-triad progressions.

the five largest differences in first-order frequencies among the repertoires, sorted by the difference between their likelihood in Ockeghem and their likelihood in Palestrina. We see a substantial increase in descending-fifth root progressions, tripling from 4% in Ockeghem to 13% in Palestrina, while ascending fifths increase to a smaller degree, roughly doubling from 4% to 9%.[33] Meanwhile, there is an impressive decline in motion between $^5_3$ and $^6_3$ sonorities over the same bass—with 6–5 progressions declining faster than 5–6. (In modern terminology: ascending-third root progressions decline more quickly than descending-third root progressions.) The last progression on the list, $^6_4$–$^5_3$ over a fixed bass, was discussed in §5.2: this is almost completely absent in Ockeghem, rising to a respectable 4% of all progressions in Palestrina. To put that number in perspective, $^6_4$–$^5_3$ progressions in Palestrina are about as common as descending-fifth progressions between complete root-position chords in Ockeghem.

Jeppesen writes that in Palestrina "the vertical, harmonic requirements assume merely the exclusively consonant, full harmony of the chords, in which modulatory

---

[33] Some but not all of this is due to Ockeghem and Josquin's greater preference for progressions that move from a complete triad to an open fifth. In Palestrina, 27% of root-position major triads move down by fifth to a root-position triad vs. only about 9% for minor triads, a difference that is too large to be due to cadences alone.

| | Ockeghem |
|---|---|
| $\frac{5}{3} \rightarrow \frac{5}{3}$ (0) | 13 |
| $\frac{6}{3} \rightarrow \frac{5}{3}$ (0) | 11 |
| $\frac{6}{3} \rightarrow \frac{5}{3}$ (D2) | 8 |
| $\frac{6}{3} \rightarrow \frac{5}{3}$ (A2) | 7 |
| $\frac{6}{3} \rightarrow \frac{5}{3}$ (D2) | 6 |
| $\frac{5}{3} \rightarrow \frac{6}{3}$ (A2) | 5 |
| $\frac{6}{3} \rightarrow \frac{6}{3}$ (D2) | 5 |

**Figure 6.4.3.** The most common progressions in Ockeghem are those in which the bass moves by unison or step. Numbers are percentages of all two-chord complete-triad progressions. A2, D2, and 0 identify bass motion.

relations [i.e., progressions] play only a small part."[34] This description of purely contrapuntal harmony-free music seems better suited to Ockeghem, where the bass typically moves by unison or step—exactly as we would expect if it were just another voice, not charged with the dual responsibility of supporting meaningful vertical harmonies (Figure 6.4.3).[35] By contrast Palestrina has a notable preference for major triads over minor, for root-position over first-inversion chords, and for bass leaps by fourth or fifth—leaps that almost invariably support root-position triads.[36] To my mind, this suggests that harmonies are becoming objects of compositional concern, and that the lowest voice is starting to embrace a second role in supporting the overall harmony. This change from pure counterpoint toward counterpoint-with-harmonic-patterning represents a genuine difference within the *prima prattica*, to the point where one might say that Ockeghem, Josquin, and Palestrina speak different musical dialects. And this remains true even if these changes are largely implicit and unselfconscious—a matter of internalized routines rather than explicit thinking.

Figure 6.4.4 catalogues the total duration spent on complete triads in ionian-mode pieces by Josquin and Victoria.[37] As we move backward in time, chord distributions flatten: Josquin spends less time on the tonic and subdominant and more time on first-inversion triads; and Ockeghem's chord-distributions would be flatter still. Victoria's distribution shows both a telltale emphasis on IV and preference for I⁶ over iii. The bass degrees most likely to support root-position triads are $\hat{1}$, $\hat{4}$, and $\hat{5}$, the roots of the three primary triads, while $\hat{7}$ and $\hat{3}$ are most likely to

---

[34] Jeppesen (1931) 1939, p. xi.

[35] The relative balance between major and minor, root position and first inversion, likewise suggests that consonance is the primary harmonic consideration, as if Ockeghem had only weak preferences among the different vertical possibilities.

[36] Carl Dahlhaus claimed that Renaissance harmony is marked by "bass formulas" in which "the difference between $\frac{5}{3}$ and $\frac{6}{3}$ sonorities over the same bass has little or no importance" (1990, p. 145): in Palestrina, however, bass motion by fourth or fifth overwhelmingly tends to support root-position triads. Meier (1988, p. 51) argues that the bass voice, along with the concept of the chord, becomes increasingly important during the sixteenth century.

[37] I used my computer to select one-flat pieces ending on an F triad and with F major as the most common chord, and zero-flat pieces ending on C and with C major as the most common triad; I then averaged the behavior in these two groups. Roig-Francolí 2018 considers some of Victoria's proto-baroque tendencies.

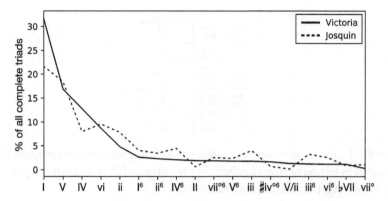

**Figure 6.4.4.** The frequency of complete triads in ionian music by Josquin and Victoria.

support first-inversion triads.[38] This is strongly reminiscent of Dalza and the frottola, once again suggesting a degree of harmonic thinking.

At the level of progressions, functionality can be said to involve both *forward-looking* tendencies for chords to progress in specific ways (e.g., for V to go to I) and *backward-looking* tendencies for chords to *be approached* in certain ways (e.g., for I to be approached by V). Dominants tend to be "constrained toward the future" while tonics are "constrained toward the past"; this is, indeed, key to the dominant's tension and the tonic's release—when we hear a dominant, we have a pretty good idea about what is coming, while a tonic gives us comparatively little sense of what might happen. Figure 6.4.5 looks at some forward- and backward-looking tendencies in Palestrina's C ionian mass movements.[39] Notable here is the $V^6$ chord, which tends to be preceded (57%) and followed (55%) by tonic chords, its neighboring role coming into focus. The $vii^{o6}$ chord is similarly constrained in both temporal directions: 60% of these chords move to C, and about 80% of them are approached by ii (41%), IV (18%), or $I^6$ (21%).

One nice way of visualizing these harmonic tendencies is with a *tendency histogram*, a graph that compares chord's zeroth-order frequencies to their frequencies either *before* or *after* a particular chord. Figure 6.4.6 presents tendency histograms for the $vii^{o6}$ chord in Palestrina's ionian-mode mass movements. When the dotted line lies above the solid line, as at the left of each graph, that means that a particular progression happens more than its zeroth-order probability: thus the graphs show a very strong tendency for both ii→$vii^{o6}$ and $vii^{o6}$→I.[40] When the two lines are nearly the same, as at the center of each graph, that means that a chord's frequency of appearance is unchanged by the presence of the other chord; the second graph

---

[38] The preference for $^6_3$ chords over $^7$ is unsurprising, since the root-position triad is diminished.

[39] That is, pieces with no key signature and which end on a C triad.

[40] For clarity, I eliminate a number of chords whose zeroth-order tendency is very similar to their tendency before or after $vii^{o6}$.

| →chord | | | chord→ | | |
|---|---|---|---|---|---|
| →chord | prog. | % | chord→ | prog. | % |
| V$^6$ | I–V$^6$ | 57 | vii° | vii°–I | 80 |
| vi$^6$ | I–vi$^6$ | 46 | vii$^{o6}$ | vii$^{o6}$–I | 60 |
| vii° | V$^6$–vii° | 43 | V$^6$ | V$^6$–I | 55 |
| vii$^{o6}$ | ii–vii$^{o6}$ | 41 | V | V–I | 40 |
| I | V–I | 36 | | | |
| vii° | IV$^6$–vii° | 36 | | | |
| iii$^6$ | V–iii$^6$ | 36 | | | |

**Figure 6.4.5.** Chords that are most often approached and left in specific ways in Palestrina's masses (C-final movements, no signature).

shows that IV appears before vii$^{o6}$ at about its typical rate, and hence that the relatively large number of IV→vii$^{o6}$ progressions is likely due to the popularity of the IV chord itself. Finally, when the first-order line lies below the second-order line, as at the right of each graph, that means the progression is suppressed: there are many fewer I→vii$^{o6}$ and vii$^{o6}$→V progressions than we would expect on the basis of zeroth-order probability alone.

I find these graphs to be endlessly fascinating, encapsulating a wealth of musical information I know only tacitly; I can easily while away the hours exploring the tendencies in different repertoires.[41] (Particularly interesting is the divergence between raw frequency and tendency: some common progressions, such as IV→I in Palestrina's ionian music, seem to be common largely because of the popularity of their individual chords.) Here we can see a congealing of a substantial portion of the vii$^{o6}$ chord's standard functional behavior—what we might call the "vii$^{o6}$ subsystem." Yet we also see that the chord's functional role is not completely settled: bass scale degrees $\hat{1}$–$\hat{2}$–$\hat{3}$, for example, are typically harmonized by I–ii–I$^6$ rather than with a functional dominant; this is because I→vii$^{o6}$ is suppressed and vii$^{o6}$→I is favored. In this music, vii$^{o6}$ has a downward tendency.

Carl Dahlhaus and Margaret Bent both point to the vii$^{o6}$–I progression as demonstrating the *inapplicability* of functional-harmonic concepts to Renaissance music: for them, functional theory requires assimilating the vii$^{o6}$ to an incomplete V$^7$, but this assimilation is blocked by the Renaissance habit of resolving the fourth scale degree upward.[42] This argument reveals a number of misunderstandings. First, functionally tonal composers often treat vii° as an independent chord separate and distinct from V and V$^7$. This is most obvious in sequences, where we find patterns like I–IV–vii°–iii which would become nonsequential if vii° were

---

[41] This is a good place to reiterate that all my code and data are available online.

[42] Dahlhaus (1990, p. 63) and Bent (1998, p. 44). Dahlhaus views the Renaissance "parallel cadence" as combining 3–5 and 6–8 interval progressions, endowing the third above the bass with an ascending tendency. The classical seventh-above-the-root, by contrast, has a descending tendency and is rarely doubled.

280　TONALITY: AN OWNER'S MANUAL

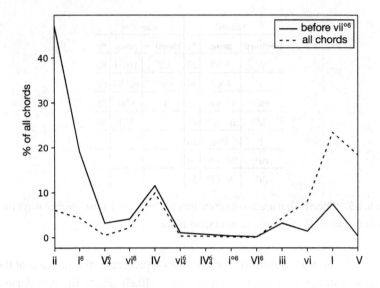

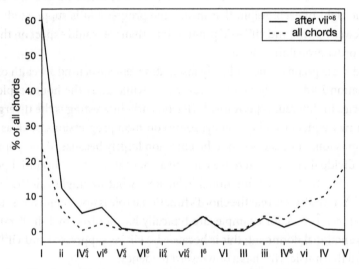

**Figure 6.4.6.** Tendency histograms for chords that precede and follow vii$^{o6}$.

to be replaced with V or V$^7$.[43] But it is also true in nonsequential contexts: in J. S. Bach's chorales, for example, the fifth of vii$^{o6}$ is more likely to ascend than descend, whereas the seventh of V$^7$ almost invariably resolves down (Figure 6.4.7). Second, the shift from vii$^{o6}$ to V$^4_3$ as the preferred dominant over $\hat{2}$, rather than being a *precondition* for functional composition, is actually a change that occurs *during* the functional era, as root-functional thinking increasingly takes hold (Figure 6.4.8).[44]

---

[43] See Tymoczko 2011a, chapter 7.
[44] V$^4_3$ is awkward from an earlier perspective since the fourth above the bass is dissonant, yet its tone of resolution, the third above the bass, is present in the chord; in Renaissance music it is very rare, usually arising

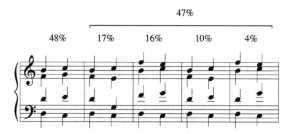

**Figure 6.4.7.** The five most common voice leadings for vii°⁶–I progressions in Bach's chorales. Of these, the majority involve $\hat{4}$ rising to $\hat{5}$, rather than resolving downward.

|        | Corelli | Bach | Haydn | Mozart | Beethoven | Chopin |
|--------|---------|------|-------|--------|-----------|--------|
| vii°⁶  | 97      | 87   | 27    | 33     | 27        | 3      |
| V$^4_3$ | 3      | 13   | 74    | 67     | 73        | 97     |

**Figure 6.4.8.** The frequency of the two most common dominant chords over the supertonic, vii°⁶ and V$^4_3$.

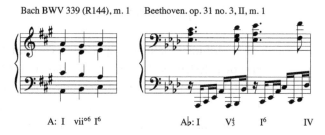

**Figure 6.4.9.** In the nineteenth century, V$^4_3$ gradually comes to replace vii°⁶ as the primary dominant over $\hat{2}$. However, it inherits its voice leading from the earlier chord.

Third, even after nineteenth-century composers came to prefer V$^4_3$ to vii°⁶, the later chord inherited the voice leading of its ancestor—rather than resolving downward, the seventh often ascends (Figure 6.4.9). Here V$^4_3$ acts like vii°⁶, with its root a quasi-pedal tone and the chordal "seventh" less a dissonance-relative-to-the-root than a consonance-relative-to-the-bass. (Indeed, thoroughbass pedagogues explicitly describe the V$^4_3$ as an optional embellishment of vii°⁶.[45]) Thus, rather than establishing a gulf between modal music and functional music, Dahlhaus and Bent isolate a clear point of continuity between the two traditions—indeed, a case where

from a double suspension (i.e., D and F suspended against G, resolving downward to C and E, with B forming the Renaissance seventh and moving up to C). I suspect composers like Corelli and Bach still shared this point of view.

[45] See Buelow 1992, p. 35, and Holtmeier 2007, p. 36. C. P. E. Bach writes: "to the chord of the major sixth and the minor third, the perfect fourth is sometimes added without express indication" ([1762] 1949, p. 239). Thinking of V$^4_3$ as an (optional) *extension* of vii°⁶ is very different from thinking of vii°⁶ as a *subset* of V$^4_3$.

282    TONALITY: AN OWNER'S MANUAL

understanding early music can help clarify the difference between baroque and classical dialects.

To my mind, the moral is a general one: much of the perceived conflict between harmonic theory and early-music analysis arises out of an overly rigid understanding of functionality. Functional harmony is not a logical system but an army of frozen idioms, and the story of its origin is one of gradually congealing conventions, with its strict norms appearing first as subtle preferences, sometimes invisible to the naked eye. Statistics are indispensable here because they are humanity's best tool for observing subtle regularities. Of course, its evidence is provisional, particularly when we crudely search through large amounts of music using computers; it goes without saying that readers should focus on broad trends rather than precise numbers. At the same time, however, crudity can be a kind of strength: for if clearly protofunctional patterns appear in rudimentary statistics, and if these same patterns also show up when we look closely at individual works, then we have converging evidence that there was indeed a gradual turn toward protofunctionality within sixteenth-century music.

### 5. The *Pope Marcellus* Kyrie

Let us therefore search for protofunctionality in a specific piece. It might seem perverse to choose the Kyrie of Palestrina's *Pope Marcellus Mass* (~1562), since the movement shows no sign of the homophonic textures that have been the focus of so much critical commentary. But the choice is strategic in the following sense: if even the polyphonic Kyrie turns out to have protofunctional tendencies, then this will help to loosen the association between functionality and homophony.[46] Furthermore, if extraversion and populism are characteristic of the mass as a whole, and not just its homophonic moments, this would be significant in light of the various legends (still possibly true) about the music's role in defending liturgical polyphony.

I hear each of its three sections as having the same basic form: an introductory idea leads to an accelerating and more intense second idea, followed by an extended cadence. Figure 6.5.1 analyzes the opening "Kyrie." The music sounds its opening note three times before leaping up by fourth and then stepping back downward. This motive appears four times in the lowest voice, always generating similar harmonies: the opening note supports a stable and ringing root-position triad (sometimes briefly touching upon a first-inversion triad), the fourth leap is always accompanied by a pair of root-position triads, and the descending steps are always harmonized in parallel thirds leading to a cadence on the initial note, a version

---

[46] Taruskin (2005, vol. 2, p. 655) articulates a common texture-based view: "the style of Palestrina's Kyrie does not differ especially from the *ars perfecta* idiom [i.e., the Renaissance polyphonic style beginning with Josquin] with which we are familiar, because the Kyrie is a sparsely texted, traditionally melismatic item where textual clarity was not of paramount concern. [ . . . ] It is in the 'talky' movements of the Mass—the Gloria and the Credo—that the special post-Tridentine qualities emerge."

THE ORIGINS OF FUNCTIONAL HARMONY 283

**Figure 6.5.1a.** The opening of Palestrina's *Pope Marcellus Mass*. Each cadence is marked by an asterisk.

of Gjerdingen's "Prinner." The preference for fourth-based harmonic structures, rooted in primary triads, is critical for the overall effect, as we can see by imagining contrapuntally plausible alternatives such as vi⁶–ii⁶–iii–ii–I.

The bass sounds the theme twice in G mixolydian—which is to say, with entries on the G–D fifth and cadences on G—and twice in C ionian, though the pervasive F naturals may tempt modern ears into hearing the entire opening in C.[47] The music then accelerates, introducing the material in Figure 6.5.2 while increasing the cadential energy. Here there are no fewer than five irreducible seventh chords, all supporting cadences that survive into the eighteenth century. (The up-by-step/

---

[47] Jeppesen (1944–1945) 1975 agrees with this reading, arguing that the movement is in mixolydian for the first eight measures and ionian thereafter.

284  TONALITY: AN OWNER'S MANUAL

**Figure 6.5.1b.** The end of the first section of the Kyrie.

**Figure 6.5.2.** In mm. 15–18, overlapping "up by step, down by third" melodies create a one-measure unit supported by a $\hat{4}$–$\hat{5}$–$\hat{1}$ bass.

down-by-third melody will return in the final Kyrie.) The lower voices then pick up the falling thirds, now on G rather than E, leading to the final cadence. Throughout, the melodic and harmonic material is consistent with functional norms.

The "Christe" opens with four statements of a three-voice, eight-beat figure in which a first-inversion chord acts as a neighbor to a root-position primary triad (Figure 6.5.3). These are grouped into fifth-related pairs C–F and G–C, with the second adding chord-roots in the bass; this suggests an at-least-tacit understanding of roots and inversional equivalence. Palestrina then introduces a descending scalar motive that dominates the rest of the section. This creates a series of three- and four-measure phrases each of which ends with a $\hat{6}$–$\hat{3}$–$\hat{4}$–$\hat{1}$ bass, articulating either an ascending-subdominant or an evaded ii⁶–I cadence—an unusual progression that could be a deceptive resolution in phrygian. The rolling, tumbling descent evokes the Shepard-tone passacaglias of chapter 2. Figure 6.5.4 arranges the lines to form a

THE ORIGINS OF FUNCTIONAL HARMONY 285

Figure 6.5.3. The Christe from Palestrina's *Pope Marcellus Mass*.

Figure 6.5.4. The Christe as a Shepard-tone passacaglia.

canon; in Palestrina's music, these melodic fragments are divided among the voices and displaced in register—as if the endless descending sequence were an abstract background that was distorted on its way to the musical surface.

Figure 6.5.5 annotates the final Kyrie. The section opens with paired voices in close canon, each articulating the descending form of the diatonic third's basic voice leading; because that voice leading produces a canon at the fifth, the motive's two transpositions sound almost the same notes (Figure 6.5.6). The bass supports this fifth-based structure to create iconic harmonic cycles, rather like Figure 4.10.2, with the canonic lines either the upper or lower third of the governing triad. This is a wonderful example of the inseparability of sixteenth-century harmony and counterpoint, the music being at once harmonically significant and *also* generated by melodic imitation. The next motive picks up the end of this figure, repeating entries on C and G to create an accelerating (G, B) → (E, C) → (F, A) loop that lasts until the end of the movement (Figure 6.5.7, cf. the lower-right pattern in Figure 3.1.10). Measure 75 is of particular interest, with a IV$^6_4$ chord decorating the piece's final V–I progression; that chord is itself embellished with a irreducible seventh I have labeled vii$^6_5$. Here the F, while dissonant with the bass, serves both as resolution of the suspension G and as preparation of a suspension that resolves to E—a second-inversion triad that cannot be dismissed as merely nonharmonic.

What is striking is the idiomatic character of the piece's protofunctionality: beyond the general fondness for primary triads and fifth progressions, we find a relatively small set of schematic figures in which harmony and melody are inextricably linked. In the opening Kyrie the "up by fourth, down by step" motive gives rise to Prinner figures, IV–I$^6$–ii–vii$^{o6}$–I, followed by an ascending-step/descending-third motive that generates repeated cadential progressions. In the "Christe," we have the two-measure neighboring figure and the endlessly descending triads, while in the last section it is dyadic voice leading and simple harmonic cycles. Throughout, the close imitation creates a sense of near repetition; underneath the ever-changing surface, we can hear something like a harmonic ground, endlessly circulating through familiar harmonies. The overall impression is less of functionality congealing from the top down (for example in the form of greater attention to regular phrase structure or large-scale melodic templates) than of bubbling up from the bottom—of an

THE ORIGINS OF FUNCTIONAL HARMONY 287

**Figure 6.5.5.** The end of the Kyrie in the *Pope Marcellus Mass*. Each cadence is marked by an asterisk.

288   TONALITY: AN OWNER'S MANUAL

**Figure 6.5.6.** The basic voice leading in the final Kyrie. The fifth-related entry pairs sound almost the same notes.

**Figure 6.5.7.** Motivic entries at the end of the Kyrie of Palestrina's *Pope Marcellus Mass*.

increasing focus on a small number of voice-leading patterns. This music is neither purely linear nor purely harmonic, but an inseparable amalgam of the two.

In all, about 85% of the movement's progressions conform to functional norms, with most of the exceptions falling into just two categories: 6–5 motions over a fixed bass, and progressions involving the mediant. These numbers are characteristic of

**Figure 6.5.8.** The end of the first Agnus Dei of Palestrina's "In minoribus duplicibus."

the Mass as a whole and higher than is typical for Palestrina: in his other ionian-mode pieces, the proportion of functional progressions is typically closer to 75% than to 85%. (In fully functional music, the number would be closer to 95%.) By way of contrast, Figure 6.5.8 shows the close of a less-functional movement, the first Agnus Dei from the mass *In minoribus duplicibus*.[48] This music is suffused with nonfunctional passages: prominent mediants; dominants that almost seem to be avoiding the tonic; retrofunctional ascending fifths; a dramatic subtonic–tonic progression; and a meandering lowest voice that seems to be avoiding the low C3 from m. 17 to m. 29. It is almost completely devoid of the subdominant emphasis of so much early functionality. Here we see another side of Palestrina's musicality, not so much "regressive" as learned or introverted. The contrast between these movements reminds us that Renaissance musicians were free to explore a vast

---

[48] This belongs to the same "tonal type" as the earlier Kyrie: it uses high clefs, has no signature, and ends on a C triad (Powers 1981).

290 TONALITY: AN OWNER'S MANUAL

harmonic territory, with parameters like strength of centricity and degree of functionality varying from one piece to another.

## 6. A broader perspective

I am proposing that there is a distinctively sixteenth-century form of protofunctionality, evident as early as 1500 and particularly characteristic of the "paratonal century" from 1550 to 1650. This ionian-mode style features: (a) an emphasis on primary triads moving by fifth, articulating simple I–V–I and I–IV–I cycles; (b) the favoring of I$^6$ over iii as the default harmonization of $\hat{3}$ in the bass; (c) the concomitant *dis*favoring of harmonies like vi$^6$ and iii$^6$; (d) a wealth of simple predominant-dominant-tonic progressions in which the predominant can be either ii, IV, or vi, with relatively little preference among them; (e) the frequent use of vii$^{o6}$–I, often preceded by I$^6$, IV, or ii; (f) precursors to later schemas like the "Fenaroli" and "Prinner" rooted in the primary steps-and-fifths defaults of Figure 6.1.3; and (g) the use of half, full, and deceptive cadences playing familiar roles. Not all these features are equally prominent in every repertoire, let alone every piece, and for many decades they coexist with nonfunctional modes of musical organization. In other words, they are optional idioms rather than rigid rules.

Ionian mode provides the paradigm for two reasons. First, its major triads occupy the positions of tonic, subdominant, and dominant, so that a preference for major chords will reinforce the main functional poles. By contrast, this same preference can have a centrifugal effect in dorian or aeolian, as we will explore in chapter 8. The favoring of fifth-progressions among C, F, and G major triads, *regardless of which white-note mode is being used*, is one of the most challenging features of sixteenth-century music: we are so used to a Copernican universe, in which chord-meaning is relative to the tonic, that it is hard to imagine the absolute space of earlier times, in which particular chords could have their own tonic-independent tendencies. Second, the leading tone lies within the key signature, not requiring explicit accidentals or implicit signaling via cadential suspensions.[49] Accidentals are thus a prerequisite for the transmission of ionian routines to other modes: if alterations are primarily a matter of *musica ficta*, they remain linked to specific cadential formulae, and hence cannot proliferate throughout the phrase. It follows that modal homogenization could scarcely occur before about 1550.

The decision to focus on *local* harmonic structure is motivated by my belief that pieces can sound functional even while eschewing conventional modulatory trajectories—John Coltrane's *Giant Steps*, for example, combines local ii–V–I organization with a key scheme that moves by major third.[50] (This is also consistent

[49] Lowinsky, by contrast, favors a double-mode theory where functional harmony arises simultaneously in both ionian and aeolian (1961, pp. 8–10).

[50] Stein 2002.

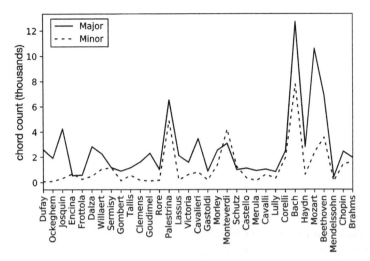

**Figure 6.6.1.** My corpus of hand-analyzed pieces; "major" refers to modes with a major third above the final, "minor" to modes with a minor third above the final.

with psychological research that has called into question listeners' ability to track modulatory relations over even moderate lengths of time.[51]) Furthermore, I believe many of the other parameters that have been proposed as crucial to early functionality—for instance, homophony or regular phrase structure—are somewhat secondary: it is easy to come up with examples of polyphonic or irregularly phrased music that are still strongly functional, from the Kyrie of the *Pope Marcellus Mass* to the more functional fugues of Frescobaldi.[52] The development of functionality was a bottom-up process that began with local details and gradually encompassed larger and larger timespans, ultimately including phrase structure, modulatory patterns, and new formal templates.

To understand these changes, we need something between the raw statistical data of §6.4 and the particular analyses of §6.5. To that end I have created, over many years and with the help of more than a hundred collaborators, a database of Roman numeral analyses matched to musical scores, consisting of about a thousand pieces from Dufay to Brahms. Figure 6.6.1 shows the collection as it currently stands. In building it I have tried to combine breadth and depth, analyzing a large number of pieces by paradigmatic composers (Josquin, Palestrina, Monteverdi, J. S. Bach, Mozart, Beethoven) and a smaller number of pieces by a wider range of composers—with particular attention to the decades between Josquin and Palestrina. For methodological details, consult appendix 4.

---

[51] Cook 1987, Marvin and Brinkman 1999.
[52] Long (2018, 2020) emphasizes the role of rhythm and phrasing in engendering harmonic expectation. But it seems to me that the phenomena she discusses can appear in both modal and functional contexts: regularly phrased eight-bar dance music, like irregularly phrased polyphony, can be more or less functional. For this reason, I think we need an account of functionality that is separable from issues of phrasing and rhythm, even if in actual historical practice these phenomena were often intertwined.

292  TONALITY: AN OWNER'S MANUAL

| | Josquin | | Goudimel | | Monteverdi | |
|---|---|---|---|---|---|---|
| $\hat{6}\ \hat{5}$ | ii→iii | 20.3 | IV→I | 46.2 | IV→I | 38.7 |
| | | | V/V→V | 24.2 | | |
| $\hat{5}\ \hat{4}$ | I→ii | 29.3 | I→IV | 43.3 | I→ii | 43.6 |
| | iii→ii | 23.2 | I→ii | 43.3 | | |
| $\hat{4}\ \hat{3}$ | ii→I | 21.4 | IV→I | 55.6 | vii°→I | 25 |
| $\hat{3}\ \hat{2}$ | I→V | 38.9 | I→V | 84.8 | I→V | 40 |
| | iii→V | 20 | | | | |
| $\hat{2}\ \hat{1}$ | V→I | 28.4 | V→I | 56.2 | V→I | 55.8 |
| | V→vi | 21.6 | V→vi | 34.7 | | |
| $\hat{1}\ \hat{7}$ | I→V | 20.0 | I→V | 39.3 | I→V | 28.6 |
| | vi→V | 20 | IV→V | 26.8 | | |
| | IV→V | 20 | | | | |

**Figure 6.6.2.** The most common harmonizations of descending scale steps in ionian-mode passages of Josquin, Goudimel, and Monteverdi.

Figure 6.6.2 shows the most common harmonizations of descending scale steps in three not-fully-functional corpora: Josquin's ionian-mode pieces, Goudimel's 1564 setting of the *Geneva Psalter*, and a collection of Monteverdi madrigals from Books 3, 4, and 5.[53] The change from Josquin to the later composers is quite striking, the mediant triad and supertonic deemphasized in favor of primary triads. Again, one finds a similar primary-triad emphasis in a wide range of quasi-functional music from Palestrina to rock.

Figure 6.6.3 shows how composers treat different bass degrees—in general, $\hat{1}$ and $\hat{5}$ are most likely to support root-position chords, and $\hat{3}$ and $\hat{7}$ least likely to use root position. Between these poles are the subdominant scale degrees $\hat{2}$, $\hat{4}$, and $\hat{6}$, which can support either root-position or first-inversion chords. Here we can see a slight rise in first-inversion chords as we move toward the classical period, with ii[6] eventually eclipsing IV as principal subdominant. All of this suggests the congealing of the conventions that were eventually to be codified as the seventeenth-century "rule of the octave" (§7.5). These regularities start to appear in musical practice long before they were described by theorists or pedagogues.

Figure 6.6.4 shows the proportion of diatonic triads found in a broad range of music. Here I have anachronistically categorized chords by root, considering I, I[6], and I$\natural$ as forms of the same chord.[54] What emerges is a fairly dramatic increase in the number of V chords across the entire era. There is also a clear emergence of IV as a privileged third sonority: up through about Gombert, the subdominant chord is just another chord, no different from ii, vi, or iii. After this point it starts to

---

[53] For the Goudimel pieces, I have taken the preexisting melody as primary; it mostly appears in the tenor but sometimes in the upper voice; for Monteverdi, I have used the upper voice, with no implication that it is preexisting.

[54] One gets a reasonably similar graph if one considers only root-position triads, or just first-inversion chords.

THE ORIGINS OF FUNCTIONAL HARMONY 293

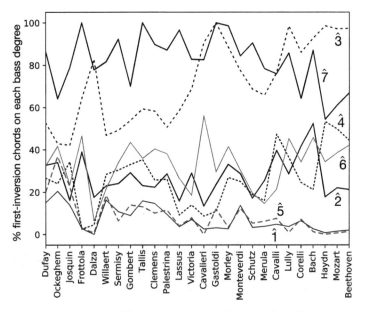

**Figure 6.6.3.** The percentage of first-inversion chords on each scale degree.

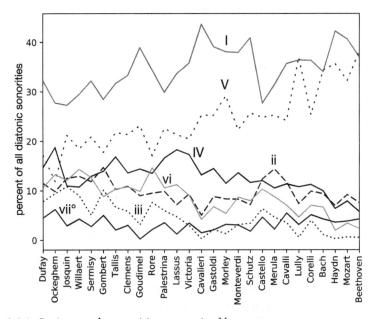

**Figure 6.6.4.** Ionian-mode sonorities categorized by root.

emerge as special, only to be supplanted by the supertonic in the seventeenth century. Again we see the prehistory of functionality moving through distinct phases, with the late sixteenth century being relatively subdominant-focused, and the seventeenth century being comparatively more oriented toward the supertonic. If this is so, then we need to be careful not to generalize about functional harmony *as such*.

294 TONALITY: AN OWNER'S MANUAL

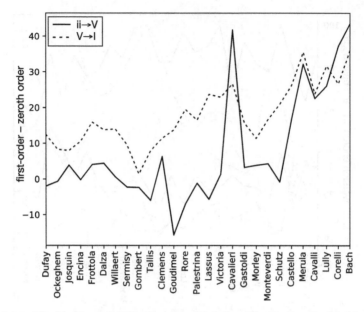

**Figure 6.6.5.** The "tendency" of V→I and ii→V, defined for V→I as the likelihood of I following a V minus the simple likelihood of V. This is the increase in the probability of one chord given that you have just heard the other.

Instead, we will want to recognize the existence of multiple functionalities, some featuring IV and others ii.[55]

Turning now to first-order properties, we see in Figure 6.6.5 that dominants increasingly tend to progress to tonics.[56] In much the same way, ii increasingly tends to V, with its attraction-to-the-dominant eventually matching the dominant's attraction-to-the-tonic. It is interesting that vii$^{o6}$ neither increases in frequency nor in its tendency to I—it has already settled into its role as a dominant-functioned chord. Figure 6.6.6 shows the likelihood that a dominant chord will be approached by IV, vi, and ii: in much sixteenth-century music, there is rough parity among these options, while in the seventeenth century, ii starts to supplant IV and the predominant vi disappears almost entirely (Figure 6.6.7). Indeed, vi gradually adopts a new role as a *pre-predominant* which usually moves to ii or IV prior to moving on to the dominant: thus the harmonic cycles of harmonic functionality gradually lengthen, from the simple oscillations of protofunctionality (e.g., I–IV–I and I–V–I), to the standardization of the four-chord I–ii–V–I, to the eventual inclusion of the vi chord in the five-chord cycles I–vi–(ii or IV)–V–I. This process terminates with the baroque's seven-chord sequence of thirds, I–vi–IV–ii–vii°–V–I, to be discussed in chapter 7.

---

[55] Rock and jazz represent twentieth-century poles of this dichotomy: rock musicians favor IV and jazz musicians ii.

[56] Tendency here is the difference between the chord's probability after a dominant and its overall zeroth-order probability, as in Figure 6.4.6.

THE ORIGINS OF FUNCTIONAL HARMONY 295

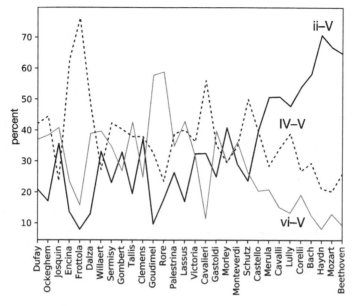

**Figure 6.6.6.** The relative popularity of the ii–V, IV–V, and vi–V progressions.

| Palestrina | Monteverdi | Corelli | Bach | Haydn | Mozart | Beethoven | Brahms |
|---|---|---|---|---|---|---|---|
| 21 | 27 | 21 | 8 | 5 | 5 | 3 | 14 |

**Figure 6.6.7.** Percentage of all root-position vi (or vi$^7$) chords that move directly to root-position V (or V$^7$).

Figure 6.6.8 shows the proportion of progressions that conform to the full-fledged grammar of functional harmony described in §7.1. The picture here is of a very gradual transition from modality to functional harmony: a gentle and consistent rise from the early polyphony of Ockeghem and Josquin to the music of Haydn, Mozart, and Beethoven, punctuated by outliers such as Dalza, the frottolists, and Juan del Encina—and, in the other direction, figures such as Castello. This data suggests it would be foolish to try to draw a sharp line between modality and functionality; instead there is a very slow evolution that takes place over several centuries, and which is particularly dramatic in the century from 1550 to 1650. (As Jeppesen put it: "the entire course of the development of music in the sixteenth and seventeenth centuries was toward harmonic stability and tonal centralization."[57]) We find independent evidence for this process in individual pieces, crude computational surveys, and large collections of human analyses. It is hard to understand how scholars could once have favored a sudden or saltationist perspective, for the data is as close to evolutionary as one could possibly imagine.[58]

---

[57] Jeppesen (1944–1945) 1975, p. 100.
[58] Fétis (1840) 1994 (pp. 30ff) was an early advocate for the saltationist view. More recently, Harold Powers (1981, p. 467) argued against the gradualist picture—in retrospect, placing too much weight on theoretical statements, and not enough on musical practice. Long 2020 makes a similar point.

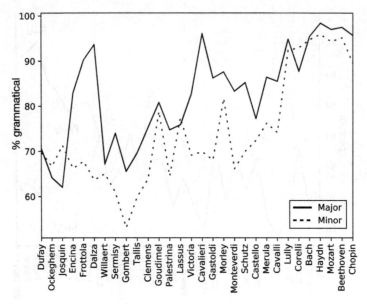

**Figure 6.6.8.** The proportion of progressions conforming to my grammar of functional tonality.

## 7. "I cannot follow"

Marenzio's "Ahi dispietata morte" (1585) sets a text written more than two centuries earlier, one of a large group of sonnets lamenting the death of Laura de Noves, Petrarch's muse and unrequited love.[59] In many madrigals the specter of death is a metaphor for consummated desire or a gambit in the game of sexual persuasion; here, Laura is really dead, and the poet is left to reflect on grief, loneliness, and the consolations of memory. Besides being intrinsically worthy of contemplation, Marenzio's setting provides an opportunity to review many of the topics we have been exploring.

Like many pieces of its time, it is composed of fragments that individually conform to functional conventions, but are juxtaposed in surprising ways. The piece begins and ends with E triads, and was likely conceived as E centered. However, many of the E chords are major triads proceeding directly to A: in this sense, they are "constrained toward the future" (§6.4, §8.6), acting like dominants even though they may have been intended as tonics; for this reason, I have analyzed the opening in an anachronistic A minor. The piece opens with the pair of phrases in Figure 6.7.1, one outlining E–a–E, the second answering with a–E–a. The soprano soars far above the lower voices (an effect Monteverdi used in "Cruda Amarilli"), and

---

[59] Einstein 1948, p. 659, notes that this same text was set by Palestrina.

THE ORIGINS OF FUNCTIONAL HARMONY 297

Figure 6.7.1. The opening of Marenzio's "Ahi dispietata morte."

each voice sings a scale fragment, two ascending and two descending. The cadence uses an irreducible seventh, introducing the suspension E with the metrically weak $\smash{^6_4}$ chord and blurring harmony and counterpoint into an idiomatic whole.[60]

The second phrase again features A minor scale fragments, but more straightforwardly; I have analyzed the opening C–E dyad as A minor even though the A does not arrive for two-and-a-half quarter notes. At the end of the phrase, the upper voices prolong the word "vita," overlapping with the next phrase ("L'una m'à posto in doglia" / "The one plunged me into grief"). Here we leave the A minor/E major orbit, the tenor/bass third A–C slipping down to inaugurate a sequence of basic voice leadings, (G, B) → (E, C) → (F♯, A), forming a harmonic cycle in G. The upper voices then repeat this music up by fourth, a simple sequence grounded in imitation. As Figure 6.7.2 shows, the diatonic third's basic voice leading continues throughout the passage, shifting from (F♯, A) to (F♯, D) and continuing with thirds on G and C; this superimposing of dyads is reminiscent of Figure P4.3. The dyads lead to a deceptive cadence decorating vi with IV⁶, initiating a series of fauxbourdon sixths and ending with a firm cadence on A.

The fifth phrase ("l'altra mi tèn"/"the other holds me here") is another imitative sequence, an ascending-third pattern that brings D minor to C major (Figure 6.7.3). Figure 6.7.4 shows that it is a three-note, two-voice canon at the distance of a quarter note, with the different iterations projected into different voices. Here again imitation produces harmonic patterning, an ascending-third sequence familiar in functional tonality. This sequence is immediately balanced by a gentle

---

[60] Note the similarity to Figure 5.1.5, which is in many ways its mixolydian counterpart.

298    TONALITY: AN OWNER'S MANUAL

**Figure 6.7.2.** The diatonic third's descending-fifth basic voice leading in mm. 8–10.

**Figure 6.7.3.** The second part of Marenzio's "Ahi dispietata morte."

**Figure 6.7.4.** The ascending-third sequence in mm. 14–16, leading to a IV$^6_4$–I alternation.

alternation between I and IV$^6_4$ whose inner voices suggest a canonic A–G–F–E descent. This Prinner variant is a widespread triadic schema rather than a localized eighteenth-century idiom. The pattern will be the focus of the last section of the piece, and its appearance here is a subtle bit of foreshadowing. We end with a

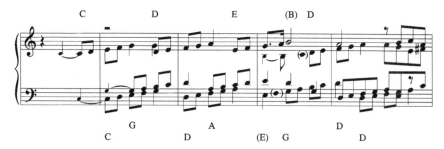

**Figure 6.7.5.** The Chase schema in the seventh phrase of the madrigal.

wonderful right angle, the bass ascending to E for a V–I cadence on an unexpected A major.[61]

The piece's next phrase sets the words "et lei che se nè gita seguir non posso" / "and she who has gone I cannot follow." This virtuosic music is based on the Chase schema, with the underlying melodic pattern appearing canonically eleven times as the music moves from A minor to C major (§4.4). Canon here is a metaphor for following, with the notes portraying what the words claim is impossible—a moment of negative text-painting embodying the fantasy of mortality overcome. Figure 6.7.5 unpacks the mechanics, rebarring the music to group the entries into ascending-step triples (C–C–G, D–D–A, E–E–B). The final entries extend up by seventh rather than fifth, leading to a cadence on C. This piece was my first encounter with the Chase schema, and I remember being dumbfounded by Marenzio's contrapuntal and expressive virtuosity—admiration that was later tempered by the realization that he was reusing a well-known piece of Renaissance vocabulary.

At this point, more than halfway into the piece, we have had almost no signs of E centricity, save an opening phrase that is easily heard in A minor. Instead, the music has offered a trio of strong cadences on A (mm. 7, 13, 20) and two less-marked turns to C (mm. 16 and 24). This is not to suggest that it is impossible to hear the phrygian signals; on the contrary, I imagine that cognoscenti would interpret the score as E centered. My point is that the music does very little to establish E as a genuine, psychologically real center; a casual listener from any culture would be hard pressed to single out the E as the primary tone.

What is fascinating is that the second half of the piece starts to insist on a recognizably phrygian modality (Figure 6.7.6).[62] The contrapuntal virtuosity of "I cannot follow" gives way to a homophonic passage on "ch'ella nol consente" ("she will not let me," a slightly odd blaming of the deceased for a problem not of her making). The details of this little passage are fascinating: it begins with what seems like functional music in G, ii–IV–V–i supporting $\hat{2}$–$\hat{1}$–$\hat{7}$–$\hat{1}$ in the melody, but the cadential

---

[61] The third quarter of m. 18 is harmonically obscure, with my preferred reading being a IV$^{6}_{4}$ whose root F is decorated by a suspension G.

[62] Coluzzi 2015 explores modal flexibility (*commixtio tonorum*) in another Marenzio madrigal.

**Figure 6.7.6.** The third part of "Ahi dispietata morte."

tonic is a minor chord that progresses to A major, evoking a phrygian close.[63] (The continuation, which stays on A rather than moving to D, solidifies this impression.) The effect is of an overlapping cadence, but without the standard suspension—a surprising harmonic turn where the phrase seems to acquire an extra chord.

The next bit of music is transitional and tonally unstable. The lower two voices sing "Ma pur ogni or presente" ("But in every moment") in canon at the fifth, using the basic voice leading to move through thirds and sixths on D, G, C, and F. This is yet another example of the connection between the basic voice leading and canon. The top three voices then vary this material in singing "nel mezzo del meo cor" ("in the middle of my heart"), leading to a cadence on a phrygian E that cannot be interpreted as a dominant. We immediately turn to homophonic declamation with the C major "madonna siede" ("my lady sits"), setting the stage for the final section.

That music, based on the words "et qual è la mia vita, ella sel vede" ("and what my life is now, she sees"), proposes that the dead live on in our remembrance (Figure 6.7.7). The texture is wonderfully suspended, slowing the harmonic rhythm to luxuriate in a series of prolonged third-related harmonies, enlivened by stepwise oscillation (e.g., the four A–G motions in mm. 33–34, the four F–E motions in mm. 34–35, etc.).[64] Here there are almost no hints of (proto-)functional harmony. The basic contrapuntal technique is shown in Figure 6.7.8; it is based on a four-note descending figure that was first presented in mm. 11–12. Harmonically, the figure appears in two forms: in one, the sustained voice creates oscillations between fifth-related triads ("option 1" on the figure, used in the middle of the phrase). The second and more modal version adds a second sustained voice a third below

---

[63] See §7.4 on the ii–IV progression, which is largely eliminated in later music. Here again we see functional practice coming gradually into focus: in this music, the poles of tonic, subdominant, and dominant are fairly clear, but many peripheral conventions are absent.

[64] Newcomb 2007 describes this (perhaps uncharitably) as "chordal noodling."

THE ORIGINS OF FUNCTIONAL HARMONY 301

Figure 6.7.7. The end of "Ahi dispietata morte."

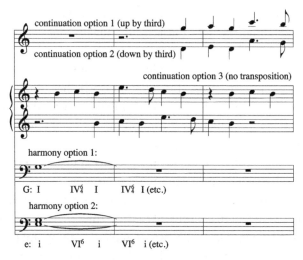

Figure 6.7.8. The contrapuntal logic behind the final passage of Marenzio's "Ahi dispietata morte."

the first, leading to a series of third-related triads, usually arranged to form VI⁶–i progressions in which $\hat{6}$ acts as a descending tendency tone (mm. 33–35, 41–43). To my ear, these VI⁶–i progressions recall the vocabulary of minor-mode rock (e.g., Patti Smith's "Ask the Angels").

I have listed the appearances of the figure above the score, labeled by its highest note, since the beginning is variable. The basic pattern can support a unison canon at the distance of one half-note, but a third unison entry cannot be introduced until three half-notes after the second—as at the end of the piece, where we have four E entries in a row. However, it is possible to accelerate the canon by bringing in an entry at the third (Figure 6.7.8). This leads the music down by third from C to A for a phrygian cadence, the third such cadence in less than ten measures; we then move downward to F and back, but instead of continuing on from A to C, the soprano entry in m. 40 is distorted to reach a high E. This opens onto a deeply spiritual ending and the most extended phrygian passage in the piece—transforming the earlier E-as-possible-dominant to an unmistakable E-as-phrygian-tonic. It is heartfelt and expressive, music that is as alive today as it was more than four hundred years ago: a poem of the mind in the act of making peace with death.

But is it functionally tonal? I confess that the more I think about this question, the more confused I become. It largely depends on whether we think the glass is half empty or half full: clearly, Marenzio's music is not "functionally tonal" if we require that music treat the harmonic norms of the eighteenth and nineteenth centuries as if they were inviolable musical laws. But at the same time, it is clearly music where notions of tonic, dominant, and subdominant, not to mention harmony, sequence, and deceptive cadence, have some use. It is music that seems to move purposefully through key areas, starting on an E-as-quasi-dominant, exploring the white-note A and C areas, before introducing the phrygian flavors of its second half. If "functionally tonal" means "music where the concepts of functional harmony can be useful and enlightening," then the music is functionally tonal—despite the fact that it is in the phrygian mode.

Which should we emphasize: the differences from eighteenth-century practice or the similarities? In some sense, the question is whether functionality comes in degrees. To me, the affirmative answer is natural: this music's departures from later norms do not nullify the equally clear continuities with that tradition. But in saying this I am conscious that I am drawing on a twenty-first-century conception of functional harmony as heterogeneous and largely conventional. (And perhaps more to the point: I am drawing on my enculturation into popular styles that treat functionality as an option rather than a requirement.) To a nineteenth-century musician who had been taught to conceive of musical rules as natural laws, comparable to the as-yet-unchallenged laws of Newtonian physics, things might well seem different. Perhaps from that perspective, little departures would have a much greater significance—as alienating and shocking as minor departures from the laws of nature. Perhaps from that perspective, genuine functionality would require that music rid itself of *all* errors and fully embody the truth. That perspective may be gone at the level of our conscious thinking, and yet still survive in our unconscious habits, preventing us from acknowledging protofunctionality when we hear it.

# Prelude
## Could the Martians Understand Our Music?

Gottfried Weber argued that Western music was pervasively ambiguous, as analysts have a choice about which notes to consider nonharmonic. The fragments in Figure P7.1, for example, can be given either concise or verbose readings depending on how one treats the labeled notes. Take a moment to think about how you would analyze this music. Along the way consider how the desire for consistency influences your judgments: for example, the second and third progressions are loose retrogrades; should they be analyzed so as to reflect this?

My answers are as follows. In the first progression, I choose the concise reading, treating the melodic D as an ornament to a IV–I progression. In the second, I favor the verbose reading because I–ii–vii°6–I6 is an important J. S. Bach idiom, appearing once every three chorales or so.[1] In the third, I choose the concise I–vii°6–I6 interpretation. Meanwhile in the last, I reject *both* concise and verbose options, treating the bass F as harmonic and the tenor A as passing to obtain V–V2–I6. In each case I identify nonharmonic tones to obtain what I consider the most plausible reading, avoiding progressions I believe to be rare. (As Weber said, the ear chooses the "most convenient, simple, easy, and suitable" explanation.[2]) This is justified by my general conviction that functionally tonal music involves a small number of characteristic progressions embellished by a small number of contrapuntal formulae.

Ian Quinn has observed that this process raises a question of *epistemic circularity*.[3] All my readings avoid labeling ii–I progressions present on the musical surface, justifying these decisions by claims about "what typically happens."[4] Yet those justifications are themselves dependent on my readings of specific passages like those in the example. Perhaps if I habitually labeled ii–I progressions I would believe ii–I progressions to be more common, which would in turn encourage me to find ii–I progressions elsewhere. Weber said the ear chooses the simplest analysis: but what if our notion of "simplicity" depends on prejudices not themselves

---

[1] Compare Figure 3.1.7. Appendix 4 discusses Huron's reading of this idiom.

[2] Weber (1817–1821) 1846, p. 658, and Saslaw 1992.

[3] Quinn's skepticism lies behind the approach taken in Quinn 2018, which attempts to do without the notion of nonharmonicity; he and I had a profitable and longstanding debate about these issues over the course of many years, relatively little of which found its way into print. Temperley 2018 (p. 35, fn. 10) notes a similar circularity.

[4] The holistic and skeptical philosopher W. V. O. Quine argued that theoretical terms were severely underdetermined by empirical evidence: his (long-I) "Quinean skepticism" (1953) is in some respects a generalized version of (short-I) Quinnian skepticism—which suggests that our harmonic and contrapuntal beliefs are underdetermined by objective musical facts.

*Tonality.* Dmitri Tymoczko, Oxford University Press. © Oxford University Press 2023. DOI: 10.1093/oso/9780197577103.003.0012

Figure P7.1. Possible analyses of four one-bar passages.

justified by objective data? Would intelligent Martians, if granted access to our music but not our pedagogy, be able to do harmonic analysis?

The issue is that Western classical music combines two different syntaxes: a *contrapuntal* syntax regulating dissonance and a *harmonic* syntax governing the progression of "genuine harmonies." The contrapuntal system does not require any distinction between "genuine consonances" and "consonances produced by nonharmonic embellishment"; it governs the behavior of any and all dissonances. The harmonic system developed after the contrapuntal system had stabilized; it does not govern consonances as such, but only that subset qualifying as genuine. This *does* require that we distinguish law-abiding harmonies from the merely "apparent" chords that are the byproduct of nonharmonic motion. This is made all the more difficult by composers' tendency to ensure that simultaneous nonharmonic tones are mutually consonant (§5.5).[5] The avoidance of clashes inevitably leads to "apparent chords" that do not participate in the harmonic syntax.

Incomplete sonorities are another important source of analytical ambiguity.[6] J. S. Bach's "Jesu, du mein liebstes Leben" makes extensive use of a one-measure contrapuntal fragment that occupies fully a quarter of the piece (see mm. 2, 5, 6, 10, and 14 in Figure P7.2, with variants in mm. 3, 11, and 13).[7] Its third beat contains a bare third, consistent with a triad missing either its root or fifth. What is interesting is that the piece seems to play with these possibilities: in mm. 2, 6, and 14, it sounds like it is missing its fifth, while in mm. 5 and 10, it sounds like it is missing its root.[8] And "sounds" really is accurate: to many listeners, not looking at the score, the B♭–D in m. 3, and the D–F in m. 5, really do *sound*, intuitively and pretheoretically, like B♭ major triads.[9] It is almost as if the piece were trying to prove that the same scale degrees can be given different meanings.[10] One might say that the ambiguity of its

---

[5] Weber (1817–1821) 1846, p. 677.

[6] Weber (1817–1821) 1846, pp. 192–94.

[7] Note the ascending subdominants in mm. 3, 11, and 13, the "slippery figure" (§5.1) in the tenor of m. 8, here a decorated quarter-note anticipation, and the "Renaissance seventh" idiom in m. 15 (VI$^{maj7}$–iv$^6$).

[8] The mediant is a common destination in minor and the F♮ and E♭ on beat 2 of m. 6 combine to suggest V$^6_5$/III; by contrast, the rarity of the major-mode mediant encourages us to hear a rootless tonic in m. 10.

[9] To test this, I asked two generous friends to label the chords in a recording of the chorale. Both heard asymmetrically as described in the text. (As Weber would say, their ears really *did* choose the simplest explanation!) See Goldenberg 2021 for more on incomplete chords.

[10] Consider how mm. 2–3 are echoed in the relative major at mm. 5–6, so that m. 6 is functionally analogous to m. 3, while also containing virtually the same notes as m. 2.

PRELUDE: COULD THE MARTIANS UNDERSTAND OUR MUSIC? 305

**Figure P7.2.** "Jesu, du mein liebstes Leben" (BWV 356, Riemenschneider 243).

*syntax* is intrinsic to its *semantics*, the goal being to create a miniature and multivalent musical kaleidoscope.[11]

Sometimes we can experience these multiple interpretations simultaneously. In Figure P7.3, Bach's descending-fifth sequence arrives on a (B♭, D) that, conceived as IV, continues the harmonic pattern. Yet this measure is also the start of another

---

[11] The same thing happens with larger sonorities as well: in mm. 42–44 of the F♯ minor fugue from book 2 of *The Well-Tempered Clavier*, we hear a long series of descending fifths, E–a♯–D♯–g♯–c♯–f♯–B–E–A, followed in m. 45 by the progression D$^{maj7}$–b–c♯$^7$–A, leading to another long sequence of descending fifths, b–E–A–D–g♯–C♯–f♯. If we read the triads in m. 45 as rootless sevenths (D$^{maj7}$–g♯$^{ø}_5$–c♯$^7$–f♯$^6_5$), the entire passage becomes a descending-fifth progression.

306  TONALITY: AN OWNER'S MANUAL

**Figure P7.3.** Bach's D minor two-part invention, BWV 775, mm. 7–14. I analyze m. 11 as ii and IV simultaneously.

descending-fifth sequence that retrospectively suggests G minor. Here we face an uncomfortable choice between analytical consistency and psychological accuracy: consistency suggests that m. 11 be analyzed like the very similar m. 13, and that it contain just a single chord, like most of the other measures in the piece. And yet I have the overwhelming impression of arriving on a B♭ that is immediately reinterpreted as G minor. The B♭–D is what we might call a *pivot third*, a chord that can be heard in two incompatible ways. My analysis superimposes these hearings like the dual analyses of a pivot chord, even though the passage does not modulate.[12]

Key changes are a third source of ambiguity, as some listeners are relatively quick to adopt a new tonal center while others retain the tonic even through fairly long modulatory digressions. Common modulatory strategies trade on this ambiguity in various ways. Standard *pivot-chord modulations* present overlapping progressions that are each syntactical in different keys: thus we experience the key change only after it has already happened (Figure P7.4). (Even the comparatively unambiguous *direct modulation* can have a similar effect, as listeners cannot know whether a foreign dominant seventh is an applied chord or the start of a new key.) More unusual are what I call *garden-path modulations*, where key areas are juxtaposed to create the impression of an anomalous harmonic hiccup.[13] Figure P7.5 presents a pair of examples: the first produces a V–iii progression that sounds modal even though everything before the D minor is syntactical in B♭ major, while everything after it is syntactical in F major.[14] The passage from Grieg's *Gade* (Op. 57, no. 2) is more dramatic, creating an unmistakably mixolydian cadence that is immediately and retrospectively demystified.[15]

Here Grieg seems to use functional harmony against itself, juxtaposing key areas to create an *effect* of modality even without violating functionally tonal laws.

---

[12] Other pivot thirds can be found in m. 22 (A–C as F major and A diminished) and (arguably) m. 42 (F–A as both F major and D minor).

[13] A "garden-path sentence" is one in which an apparent syntactical violation results from misconstruing an ambiguous phrase: in "the old man the boat," "old man" can be either adjective-noun or noun-verb, with the former reading statistically more likely but producing a nonsyntactical sentence.

[14] A good number of Bach's supposedly "modal" progressions occur across what can be retrospectively understood as key boundaries. They present a challenge of *segmentation*, or the placement of key boundaries; this is a tonal analogue to a familiar problem of atonal analysis (Hasty 1981).

[15] Here the effect is reinforced by the thematic structure and phrase rhythm: the passage is a rewriting of the opening four-measure theme, which uses a G♯ and ends with a standard V–I cadence.

PRELUDE: COULD THE MARTIANS UNDERSTAND OUR MUSIC? 307

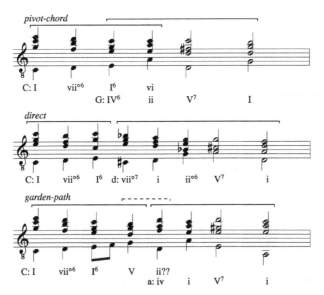

**Figure P7.4.** Three modulatory strategies. In pivot-chord modulation, there is an overlap between syntactical progressions in two different keys. In direct modulation, keys do not overlap, but the new key begins with an unambiguous dominant. Garden-path modulations do not strongly signal the start of the second key, creating a nonsyntactical progression across the key boundary.

**Figure P7.5.** Seemingly modal progressions occurring across key changes: Bach's "In allen meinen Taten" (BWV 13.6, Riemenschneider 103, mm. 3–4) and Grieg's "Gade" (Op. 57, no. 2, mm. 99–103).

This is analogous to the way nineteenth-century composers used nonharmonic tones to extend their harmonic vocabulary, writing music where the supposedly "nonharmonic" notes create musically meaningful sonorities. Such examples remind us that we need to consider syntax in the context of aesthetics: when we discuss functional music, we often take it for granted that composers *wanted* to create clear musical structures and law-abiding harmonic progressions. But sometimes they wanted to write dominant thirteenth chords or mixolydian subtonics. Where twentieth-century composers were free to do exactly that, nineteenth-century composers often maintained a degree of deniability, creating the *impression* of nonfunctionality even while conforming to the prevailing system of musical laws.

These ambiguities greatly complicate the project of harmonic analysis. Earlier I argued for an objective and nonpsychological labeling of scale degrees; now I am talking about "how we hear" and making complex intuitive judgments about nonharmonicity. It would seem that "analytical objectivity" is strongly dependent on context: rather than mechanically treating similar passages in exactly the same way, we have to balance local details with a more general sense of what is to be expected in a genre, or in a particular composer's work. The challenge here is not so much *subjectivity* as it is *holism*, the need to resolve ambiguities by drawing upon stylistic knowledge external to the piece at hand.

What is needed, in other words, is the benign form of circular reasoning that is sometimes called "hermeneutic." For the interdependence of the general and the specific can be unproblematic so long as there are enough unambiguous passages to calibrate our expectations. In the case of the Bach chorales, we can model this circularity with a two-stage process: we begin by treating *every* consonance as a harmony, performing a raw analysis that simulates the background expectations formed by a lifetime of learning. This first-pass analysis is then used in a second pass that adjudicates among allowable readings. Figure P7.6 shows how this works in two passages discussed earlier. I began by programming a computer to identify keys on the basis of scalar content, analyzing A harmonic minor passages in A minor, C diatonic passages either in C major or A minor, and so on. I then counted up all the chords and progressions to be found, treating every consonance as a harmony. These raw counts served as input to a second stage that tried to assign the most probable analysis to every progression (subject to the requirement that all nonharmonic tones obey standard rules).[16] This approach reproduces all the readings I proposed in both Figure P7.1 and P7.2, holistic computation capturing the subtle asymmetries of human judgment.[17]

[16] When comparing progressions of different lengths, I compare the average frequency of their two-chord subprogressions.

[17] Readers can consult the online materials for the other progressions. My approach is inspired by Bayesian analysis, which emphasizes the importance of prior knowledge in interpreting new evidence (Gelman et al. 2013). Ongoing work with the physicist Mark Newman uses hidden Markov models to identify chords from raw notes and keys from chords; this almost completely assumption-free approach manages to produce remarkably accurate analyses (cf. Nápoles López et al. 2019).

| Progression |     | Count |
|-------------|-----|-------|
| IV          | I⁶  | 67    |
| IV          | ii⁶ | 39    |
| ii⁶         | I⁶  | 19    |
| IV ii⁶      | I⁶  | 8     |

| Progression |     | Count |
|-------------|-----|-------|
| ii          | I⁶  | 11    |
| ii          | vii°⁶ | 112 |
| vii°⁶       | I⁶  | 238   |
| ii vii°⁶    | I⁶  | 58    |

**Figure P7.6.** Counts of various progressions in an automatic analysis of J. S. Bach's chorales, treating every consonance as harmonic and using scale membership to identify keys. The top table shows that IV→I⁶ is more common than either of the two-chord subprogressions of IV→ii⁶→I⁶; this is a reason to declare the ii⁶ "merely passing." By contrast, both two-chord subprogressions of ii→vii°⁶→I⁶ are substantially more popular than ii→I⁶, as is the three-chord sequence itself. This is a reason to consider the vii°⁶ harmonic.

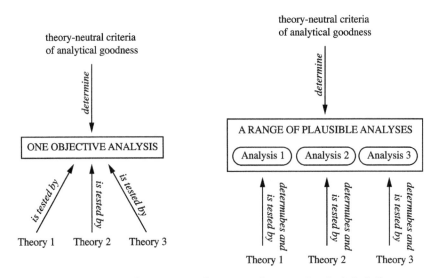

**Figure P7.7.** Two approaches to testing harmonic theories. On the left, different theories are evaluated by a single objective analysis; on the right, different theories determine different optimal analyses, with theory and analysis evaluated as a package.

Thus it may still be reasonable to aspire to a fairly objective labeling of harmonies, subject to the following caveat: that the resolution of ambiguity needs to be carried out on the basis of background knowledge. This caveat greatly complicates the evaluation of harmonic theories: intuitively, one might have thought that theory and analysis could be separated as shown on the left of Figure P7.7, where a single theory-neutral analysis can be used to evaluate many different potential syntaxes.

310 TONALITY: AN OWNER'S MANUAL

Instead, *what counts as the best analysis* may itself be theory-dependent, with the identification of nonharmonic tones itself influenced by the harmonic syntax. This would mean that we have to evaluate theory and analysis together as a single package. What is surprising is that computational methods can capture this holism, modeling the presuppositions essential to expert analytical judgment. Intelligent Martians might not *initially* understand our music, but with enough experience they could probably learn.

Of course, the Martians are a metaphor: in reality, aliens would quite likely lack the biological equipment to make sense of our music—even if they heard air vibrations in the same range that we do, they would likely lack the perception of octave equivalence, consonance and dissonance, our enjoyment of rhythmic entrainment, and so on. Rather than being a universal language, music is fundamentally tied to human biology and culture.[18] Why we put it on spaceships is beyond me.

---

[18] For musical universals see McDermott and Hauser 2005, Savage et al. 2015, and Jacoby et al. 2019. Alexander Rehding and Daniel Chua are insightful and entertaining in imagining potential alien responses to the Voyager spacecraft's "golden record" (2020).

# 7

# Functional Progressions

We now turn to the principles governing chord-to-chord progressions in functional tonality, the tradition beginning roughly with Corelli, dominating European music for almost two centuries, and surviving to this day as an important set of harmonic options. That there are such rules is doubly a point of contention: Schenker denied it, asserting that many apparently harmonic events are in fact the byproducts of linear motion, while contemporary practitioners of "microtheory"—enemies of abstraction and partisans of idiom—have suggested that we can describe functionality using a small collection of schemas. I will instead suggest that we can construct a simple, approximately true, and *heterogeneous* grammar of chord-to-chord possibilities, combining the three independent subsystems of harmonic cycles, fauxbourdon, and sequence. Thus I argue that functional tonality involves broadly grammar-like rules even while acknowledging that it is not governed by a single principle.

These local harmonic constraints underwrite an aesthetic picture of functional harmony as repetitive and nearly sequential, cycling through the same small map of harmonic options and changing just enough so that the ear stays intrigued. This mechanical quality is obvious in baroque music, somewhat sublimated in the classical era, and returns, transformed, in the music of Beethoven and Chopin. By the start of the twentieth century, repetition and sequence are viewed with suspicion—encouraged, in part, by a tendency to link "genius" with the organic. Perhaps as a result, contemporary textbooks tend to deemphasize the repeating harmonic structures at the core of this music—a repression that is aesthetically and politically problematic, pushing high-art functionality away from more manifestly cyclic styles, and drawing too sharp a line between the covert repetition of the classical tradition and the unapologetic repetition of our own time.

## 1. A theory of harmonic cycles

Figure 7.1.1 shows the distribution of major-mode sonorities in J. S. Bach's chorales and Mozart's piano sonatas. It is interesting that the submediant appears almost exclusively in root position: the near disappearance of vi$^6$, combined with the absence of iii and iii$^6$, ensures that bass notes $\hat{1}$ and $\hat{3}$ are harmonized almost exclusively by tonic chords, $\hat{5}$ by either dominant or tonic, and $\hat{7}$ by dominant (Figure 7.1.2). In

*Tonality.* Dmitri Tymoczko, Oxford University Press. © Oxford University Press 2023. DOI: 10.1093/oso/9780197577103.003.0013

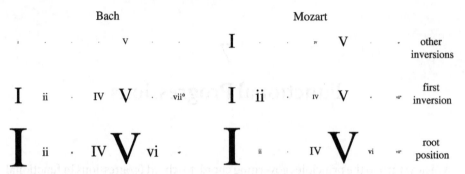

Figure 7.1.1. The frequency of diatonic chords in Bach and Mozart, combining triads and sevenths.

Figure 7.1.2. In functional tonality, bass degrees $\hat{1}$, $\hat{3}$, $\hat{5}$, and $\hat{7}$ typically support tonic and dominant, while the remaining degrees support the other harmonies.

other words, the norm is for the bass to support tonic or dominant whenever it can, with $\hat{2}$, $\hat{4}$, and $\hat{6}$ providing the bulk of the harmonic variation.[1] The submediant can support the broadly similar vi and IV⁶ chords, while the subdominant allows for both IV and ii⁶. The supertonic is unique in permitting the functionally distinct sonorities ii and vii°⁶ (or V$^4_3$ in later styles). Bass strongly correlates with harmonic function.

We have seen that the simplest forms of functionality are built around elementary subdominant and dominant cycles: I–IV–I, I–V–I, and I–IV–V–I, all articulated by root-position chords. As functional harmony develops, the dominant cycle increases in complexity, coming to play a greater and greater role, while the subdominant cycle remains static or even decreases in prominence. Figure 7.1.3 provides a theory of harmonic cycles in baroque and classical music, adapted from *A Geometry of Music*.[2] Here I arrange the diatonic triads in a chain of thirds descending from tonic to dominant: chords are completely free to move rightward and vertically, but leftward motion must proceed along one of the arrows. The size of each symbol corresponds to its frequency. In a typical functional piece, more than 95% of the progressions will conform to this model, particularly if we exclude sequence and fauxbourdon; conversely, all the root progressions allowed by the model are common.[3] This two-way fit poses a challenge for those who would like to

---

[1] This preference for tonic and dominant is embedded in the traditional "rule of the octave," to be discussed shortly; the connection supports Holtmeier's 2007 contention that the rule of the octave is not simply a schema but a theory of functional tonality.

[2] My theory is indebted to a long tradition of "harmonic maps" (Riemann 1896, Piston 1941, McHose 1947, Kostka and Payne 2003).

[3] Some bass lines are rare for linear reasons, such as ii⁶–V⁶ with its leaping tritone or V⁶–I⁶ with its unresolved leading tone.

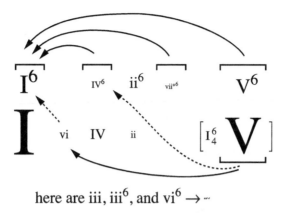

Figure 7.1.3. A model of functional harmony where rightward and vertical motion is unrestricted but leftward motion follows the arrows.

replace Roman numerals with particular schemas, as one would need a fine-tuned collection of idioms—no doubt varying with genre—to reproduce the progressions on the map.

This model incorporates a variety of earlier approaches to functional harmony. Inversionally equivalent chords are placed above one another, meaning that they act similarly. Functional categories are encoded by horizontal position, with neighboring sonorities (e.g., IV and ii, or vii° and V) participating in similar progressions. The model also privileges certain types of root progression: since the "strong" progressions (descending third, descending fifth, and ascending step) move rightward by one, two, or three steps, the model will permit more of these motions than their "weak" counterparts (ascending third, ascending fifth, and descending step). Where the simple protofunctionality of §6.1 was decidedly Riemannian, privileging primary triads as *locations* in harmonic space, our more sophisticated model is more Rameauian, highlighting a specific *way of moving* from tonic to dominant.[4]

With just eleven chords, the map can be learned by example and without explicit instruction. It is also consistent with figured-bass theory, as its guiding principle is that bass lines move along an abstract chain of descending thirds from $\hat{3}$ to $\hat{5}$, with $\frac{5}{3}$ preceding $\frac{6}{3}$ over the same bass, and ascending thirds permissible only when they support $\frac{5}{3} \rightarrow \frac{6}{3}$ progressions (e.g., from root position to first inversion, Figure 7.1.4). Interested readers might try constructing alternative models that produce an approximately root-functional output without making any overtly root-functional assumptions: they will find, I suspect, that a thirds-based arrangement is virtually unavoidable. And while the model includes a few progressions that occur only in specific inversions, it can be approximately reformulated using roots (Figure 7.1.5).

---

[4] See Christensen 1993b, p. 97.

314 TONALITY: AN OWNER'S MANUAL

$$\begin{array}{cccccc} \hat{3}^6 & \hat{1}^6 & \hat{6}^6 & \hat{4}^6 & \hat{2}^6 & \hat{7}^6 \\ \hat{1} & \hat{6} & \hat{4} & \hat{2} & \hat{7} & \hat{5} \end{array}$$

$$\begin{array}{cccccc} \text{C/E} & \text{a/C} & \text{F/A} & \text{d/F} & \text{b°/D} & \text{G/B} \\ \text{C} & \text{a} & \text{F} & \text{d} & \text{b°} & \text{G} \end{array}$$

**Figure 7.1.4.** The descending-thirds arrangement as a figured-bass composer might conceive it, along with a translation into contemporary chord symbols. The main numbers represent bass degrees; the superscripts represent vertical configurations: $\smash{\substack{6\\3}}$ chords on $\hat{1}$ and $\smash{\substack{5\\3}}$ position chords on $\hat{7}$ are rare.

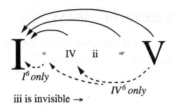

**Figure 7.1.5.** A root-functional version of the model, with some arrows requiring specific inversions.

**Figure 7.1.6.** The functional flexibility of the mediant, which can act as a pre-predominant, a dominant, and a tonic substitute.

I conceive of this map not as a set of universal laws but as first-order defaults surrounded by a penumbra of second-order idioms and practices. Some features of the penumbra remain fixed throughout the functional tradition: for instance, mediants have a rare but conventional role as post-tonic chords moving to vi or IV, as alternative dominants, and as substitutes for the tonic (Figure 7.1.6).[5] Similarly, V–vii°7 can support melodic $\hat{7}$–$\hat{6}$–$\hat{5}$ against bass $\hat{5}$–$\hat{4}$–$\hat{3}$, parallel tenths often decorated by octave displacement.[6] In other cases we can trace the penumbra's historical evolution, as harmonic practice congeals over the course of the eighteenth century (leading to a decrease of vi–V and nonsequential iii) and then expands throughout the nineteenth (leading to an increasing use of ct°7 and ii°7 and the recovery of iii).

---

[5] It is possible that the mediant's harmonic flexibility helps explain its infrequency: by blurring tonic and dominant, it undercuts the dichotomy at the heart of functional syntax. Nonsequential mediants are most common at the beginning and end of the functional tradition, virtually disappearing during the classical style.

[6] See mm. 32–33 of Mozart's Piano Sonata in C major, K.279, II, or m. 13 of his C minor sonata K.457, I (with the leading tone in an inner voice); the tenths often evoke the Prinner schema.

| | baroque | classical | romantic |
|---|---|---|---|
| precadential suspension | ii⁶₅ | I⁶₄ | |
| dominant over $\hat{2}$ | vii°⁶ | V⁴₃ | |
| vi–V | decreasing→ | | |
| root position vii°⁽⁷⁾ | increasing→ | | |
| secondary dominants | increasing→ | | |
| iii | decreasing→ | rare | increasing→ |
| iv, ii°⁷ | rare | increasing→ | |
| ct°⁷ | rare | increasing→ | |
| I–vi–I | very rare | | sometimes |
| nonharmonic tones | mostly melodic and connective | | sometimes quasi-harmonic |

**Figure 7.1.7.** Some salient major-mode differences between earlier and later functional dialects.

Figure 7.1.7 suggests that the functional tradition is like an hourglass, with Haydn, Mozart, and Beethoven the point of maximal harmonic regimentation.[7]

In some styles, harmonic vocabulary depends on mode: in rock, for example, VI–VII–i is common in aeolian but rare in ionian, while I–V–IV–I is common in ionian but rare in aeolian. Functional tonality exhibits an unusual degree of modal symmetry, using virtually the same repertoire of progressions in both major and minor. One distinctive feature of minor-mode harmony is its greater attraction to the mediant—both as a modulatory destination and as a tonicized chord within phrases. As a student, I was puzzled by this asymmetry, wanting some principled justification for this minor-mode behavior. I now think this desire was misplaced: rather than a deviation from an established default, the minor mode never fully abandoned its preexistent modal attraction toward the mediant, with III remaining the primary harmonization of bass $\hat{3}$ until well into the seventeenth century (§8.6). If this is right, then it shows the importance of understanding functional harmony as a historically contingent development, rather than a self-consistent logical system.

I should emphasize that I am not suggesting that local harmonic constraints are the *only* principles animating this music: on the contrary, composers aim to produce compelling music *while also* satisfying the harmonic grammar. The next chapters will consider a host of musical principles not captured by simple chord-to-chord graphs: for instance, that certain progressions will preferentially be found in specific parts of the phrase, that melodies articulate stepwise connections between nonadjacent notes, that phrases will sometimes be governed by the two-voice logic of the imperfect system (§3.1), and so on. And of course, any collection of

[7] Horn and Huron (2015) make a related point about modal homogenization, which occurs on an even larger timescale.

genre-wide principles needs to be supplemented by composer-specific preferences. Past a certain point, it is foolish to talk about functional harmony in general, instead of a specific musician's idiolect.

## 2. A more principled view

Figure 7.2.1 shows a simple but beautiful piece of musical mathematics, a sequence of falling fifths perturbed so that it returns to its starting point after seven notes, its final interval tempered to a diminished "near fifth" almost but not quite the same as the others. Reinterpreted as a sequence of four-step diatonic intervals, these falling fifths can in turn be halved to form a cycle of descending thirds. Because the diatonic scale has seven notes, the bifurcation can be repeated again and again, the thirds splitting into steps which can themselves be factored (more abstractly) into descending fifths and ascending fourths—a circular nesting of interval cycles each contained within its predecessor, a musical *ouroboros*.[8] Figure 7.2.2 shows a passage containing four levels of the pattern, steps inside thirds inside fifths inside steps.

Two aspects of this structure are particularly relevant. First, its layers can be rearranged to produce the basic voice leadings for the primary sonorities of functional harmony (Figure 7.2.3). Indeed, each layer of the ouroboros can be extended to form a "maximally even" diatonic chord, with overlapping collections linked by their basic voice leading.[9] Second, the tertian layer can be used to reformulate the

**Figure 7.2.1.** Nested interval cycles, with each staff dividing the staff above it into two equal intervals.

---

[8] John Clough (1979b and 1994) and Jason Yust (2009) have explored this structure as it relates to prolongation (§9.1–§9.3). I will be more concerned with its role in generating harmonic and melodic patterns, including sequences and near sequences. An unpublished paper by Yust, written when he was a graduate student, anticipates several features of my approach.

[9] Because the size of the diatonic scale is a prime number, every "maximally even" chord is a near interval cycle and every interval cycle can be extended to form a maximally even chord. Since the ouroboros contains fifths, thirds, and steps, it contains basic voice leadings for nearly even chords of every size.

**Figure 7.2.2.** Nested interval cycles in *The Well-Tempered Clavier*'s first A major prelude.

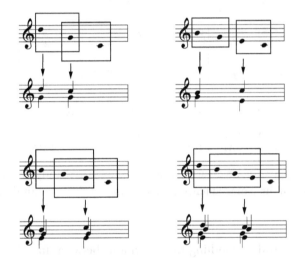

**Figure 7.2.3.** Basic voice leadings for the fifth, third, triad, and seventh chord, derived by rearranging contiguous segments of the interval cycles on Figure 7.2.1.

third-based harmonic grammar: rather than taking triads to be indivisible musical atoms, we can describe music as moving along the descending-third chain of *pitch classes* as shown in Figure 7.2.4. In other words, harmonic cycles often generate complete chains of diatonic pitch classes, descending by third through two abstract octaves.[10] This descending chain of thirds will often continue across harmonic cycles to produce an ongoing pitch-class sequence.

This in turn suggests a path from simpler protofunctionality to the more sophisticated system of the eighteenth century. In chapter 3, we noted that third-related triads and seventh chords are *harmonically* close insofar as they share all but one of their notes, with the last moving by step. Functional tonality exploited this relationship to expand the protofunctional I–IV–V into the richer I–vi–IV–ii–vii°–V,

---

[10] For example, I–IV–V$^7$ forms the cycle (G–E–C)–(C–A–F)–(F–D–B–G), returning to its starting note two octaves below. Very simple cycles such as I–V–I and I–IV–I skip a few notes on this chain of thirds.

318   TONALITY: AN OWNER'S MANUAL

**Figure 7.2.4.** The harmonic grammar expressed with pitch classes. Again, rightward moves are unrestricted while leftward motion follows the arrows.

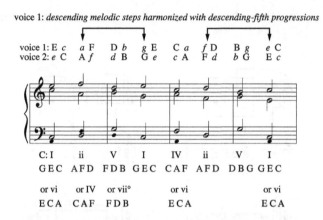

**Figure 7.2.5.** Upper-voice regularity harmonized to form slightly irregular triads. The two staves present the same sequence of descending thirds in slightly different ways.

the additional chords smoothing the transitions between functional poles. (The unsmoothed progressions V–I and IV–I remain primary signifiers of functionality.) The result is a system in which nearly equal divisions of the octave play two separate roles: simple root-position exchanges like I–IV–I and I–V–I divide the *registral* octave nearly evenly, bass moving by approximately half octave while melody moves by approximately one sixth of an octave (§6.1). Meanwhile, paradigmatic four-chord progressions like I–IV–V–I and I–ii–V–I divide the *circle of diatonic triads* into three nearly even segments, creating a functional sequence of tonic, subdominant, and dominant, whose pitch classes articulate a chain of descending thirds (§3.4).

These nested interval cycles allow composers to titrate the degree of sequential repetition in their music. Some functionality is not at all sequential on the surface, its regularity evident only at the abstract level of pitch-class content; in simple I–IV–V–I protofunctionality, even this level of sequential structure is fairly obscure. In other passages, however, we find overtly sequential structure: a single voice articulating falling thirds, two voices chaining the diatonic third's basic voice leading, and a variety of regular and quasi-regular three- and four-voice sequences. Figure 7.2.5 supposes a variety of bass notes underneath the diatonic third's basic voice leading; this is the schema that was discussed in §4.10. In effect, the staves

**Figure 7.2.6.** Roy Orbison's "Oh, Pretty Woman."

parse the chain of descending thirds differently: the two upper-staff voices take turns playing successive notes from the descending-third chain, combining to form a perfectly regular descending-fifth dyadic sequence; the lower staff parses the third-chain as a sequence of triads whose largely descending-fifth root progressions are perturbed by the occasional ascending step or descending third. Here we start to understand how functional music can move seamlessly between monodic, dyadic, and triadic logics.

These ideas can be used to interpret "Oh, Pretty Woman," Roy Orbison's 1964 ode to sexual objectification (Figure 7.2.6). The melody descends through a single octave, moving downward by three thirds and a step; underneath it, the harmony moves by third through *two* abstract octaves, initially in parallel with the melody, but then inserting an $E^7$ between D major and A major. These descending thirds extend from the end of the first statement through the beginning of the second, continuing the sequence across the verse's repetition. The bridge's "down by third, up by step" melody can be derived by omitting notes from the descending-third sequence (e.g., F D b c E C a f, etc.); here it is supported by a pair of nonsequential harmonic cycles—articulated in the electric guitar by a series of ascending triadic voice leadings.[11] Once again the pattern continues through the repeat, the melody skipping only one note on the circle of thirds (or, if we view it as an elided two-voice pattern, switching voices from bottom to top). Orbison's short song thus presents all three levels of the ouroboros: descending steps on the melodic surface, embellishing descending thirds in the abstract progression of pitch classes, mostly grouped into descending-fifth triadic progressions, and supporting a descending-step melodic

---

[11] The A major triad at the end of the bridge sounds like C: V/ii, suggesting another repeat; instead, it becomes the global tonic by compositional fiat.

**Figure 7.2.7.** One of the second themes of the first movement of Beethoven's Op. 22, twice descending by thirds from F to F.

sequence in the bridge.[12] The beauty of this music is its multivalence: it is not based on fifths or thirds or steps but rather on a delicate balance of all three, requiring only the slightest compositional nudge to bring out one or another of these aspects.

Such music is repetitive in two different ways. First, and most obviously, it passes repeatedly through the same abstract set of harmonic possibilities. Second, and more subtly, its phrases can be more or less sequential depending on how a composer chooses to parse the abstract chain of descending thirds. This sequential structure is latent in the grammar, available for composers to exploit if they choose—rather than something *put into* a particular piece, it can be *drawn out* of its generic fabric (cf. §4.3). At some basic level, mature functionality simply *is* the descending sequence of thirds—sometimes manifest on the musical surface and sometimes locked away in the musical subconscious (Figure 7.2.7).[13] The magic of this style lies in the interaction between overt and covert, symmetry and asymmetry, sequential melodic descent filtered through a nonsequential grammar.

All of which might start to suggest that functional tonality is a natural language—deriving from diatonic geometry and resting ultimately on the acoustic pillar of the perfect fifth. This is not exactly wrong: functional tonality is *a* manifestation of *one* set of affordances given by the preexisting geometry of musical possibility. But there are two important caveats. First, the chain of reasoning we have been following is not one of necessity, but rather possibility: having tempered a series of falling fifths, we are not *required* to subdivide the fifths into thirds, nor to construct progressions by grouping this sequence into triads. Nor need we employ fifth-based modulations between nearby scales, nor limit ourselves to just the major and minor modes, nor take any of the thousand other steps that jointly produced functional harmony. Rather than grounding style directly in nature or mathematics, the best we can hope for is to describe musical evolution as a series of small but conventional leaps, some seizing upon possibilities that may be suggested (but not directly required) by cultural, biological, or mathematical phenomena.

---

[12] Temperley 2018 notes the bridge's sequential structure.
[13] There are many well-known examples of descending-third melodies, including the opening of the Hammerklavier's first-movement development (Rosen 1971, pp. 407–13), the opening of Brahms's Fourth Symphony, and Brahms's Op. 121, no. 3.

Second, triadic functionality is not the *only* language that can make a claim to naturalness. We have seen that there is something equally natural about progressions formed from the *ascending* sequence of diatonic thirds—which can be rearranged to form the stepwise descent central to so much melodic behavior. These "retrofunctional" progressions—the very opposite of those found in the functional tradition—are equally natural, and equally suited to human music-making.[14] Here we have two opposed musical regimes, a tonally functional system exploiting descending-third harmony and requiring special melodic treatment, and a modal regime exploiting ascending-third harmony and giving rise to descending melodies. The question is not whether one is "more natural" than the other, but how musicians in different styles make thoughtful use of the possibilities available to them.

## 3. Rameau and Bach

It is in this context that we can start to appreciate the virtues of Rameau's theory of harmony. Rameau proposed that functional music depends on the repeating contrapuntal pattern shown in Figure 7.3.1, where root and third stay fixed while fifth and seventh descend by step. This sequence can be short-circuited by the *double emploi*, in which a single triad like F–A–C stands for F major and d minor simultaneously. This leads to a blurring of harmonies separated by diatonic third.[15] Rameau was not always clear about the circumstances under which this blurring was permitted, and

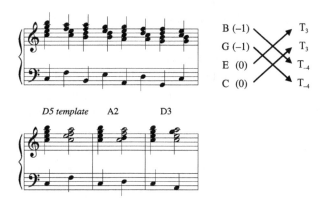

**Figure 7.3.1.** Rameau's descending-fifth paradigm on the top staff with third substitution underneath. Replacing the F major seventh with the D minor seventh produces an ascending-step progression; replacing it with the A minor seventh produces a descending-third progression. Each substitution preserves three common tones, shown here by open noteheads, with the fourth note moving by step.

---

[14] One could of course make an analogous point about many non-Western styles.

[15] This blurring of third-related harmonies is already present in the 1722 *Treatise on Harmony*, which derives the deceptive cadence by noting that C–E–A can replace C–E–G (Rameau [1722] 1971). In that book, C–E–A can have a fundamental bass of either A or C.

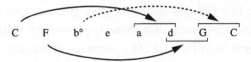

**Figure 7.3.2.** A model of functional progressions inspired by Rameau. Chords can use third substitution to move forward along the arrows to either bracketed chord, inserting either a descending third or ascending step into the sequence of descending fifths (e.g., C–a–d–G or C–d–G). This graph allows for seven progressions, all but one of which is common in functional music; all but one make a single rightward pass through Figure 7.1.3.

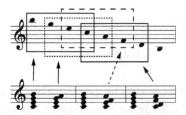

**Figure 7.3.3.** Each of Rameau's three basic progressions articulates a segment of the descending-third chain of pitch classes.

his views evolved over time, but he explicitly favored progressions by descending third and ascending step, both of which can be generated by applying third substitution to a descending-fifth progression.[16] In the spirit of rational reconstruction, let us stipulate that well-behaved Rameauian progressions start with the tonic and move *forward* on the sequence of fifths to vii° or V, either by descending fifth or using the *double emploi*. (See Figure 7.3.2, where the stipulation is that there be no left-pointing arrows, so that the *double emploi* shortens rather than lengthens the descending-fifth journey from tonic to dominant.) What results are seven progressions using descending fifths, descending thirds, and ascending steps: the full circle of fifths, three four-chord progressions consisting of one descending third and three descending fifths, and three progressions consisting of one ascending step and two descending fifths. This reconstructed Rameauianism is both a reasonable approximation to functional practice and extremely close to the theory I have been expounding.

This is because every progression allowed by the neo-Rameauian model articulates a consecutive segment of the descending-third chain pitch classes (Figure 7.3.3). So long as we are willing to follow Rameau in accepting triads as

---

[16] This is particularly clear if one examines the musical examples Rameau offers, which sometimes add content to his explicit theorizing. These examples, like my own reconstruction, highlight the centricity-defining role of I and V$^7$.

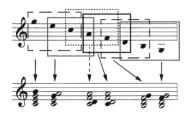

**Figure 7.3.4.** Derivation of the I–vi–IV–ii–vii°–V–I progression from Rameau's descending-fifth paradigm. The boxed progressions can be interpreted as elided versions of the seventh-chord progression on the bottom staff. Black noteheads on the bottom staff are missing from the associated triads.

four-note sonorities lacking either a sixth or a seventh, we can analyze every rightward progression allowed by the descending-third model in terms of Rameau's paradigmatic progression. In other words: a theory based on the descending-fifth sequence of seventh chords, whose roots and sevenths are sometimes omitted, is necessarily going to resemble a theory based on the descending-third sequence of triads, which can sometimes be extended through the addition of sevenths. Figure 7.3.4 goes through the derivation for one specific progression; a similar analysis could be given for virtually every other functional progression, including most of the sequences in §7.6.[17] If there is a weakness of Rameau's theory, it is its inability to deal with simple interchanges like I–V–I and I–IV–I, treating them as elisions of more complex progressions. My approach avoids this problem by tracing Rameau's seventh-chord paradigm to an even more basic object, the chain of descending diatonic thirds.

Rameau's descending-fifth template runs through *The Well-Tempered Clavier*'s first D major prelude like a murmuring *cantus firmus*, a musical "core" that is extended to the three-measure fragment shown in Figure 7.3.5. Bach employs two distortions of the melody's tail, transposing it either upward or downward by third; this introduces a descending third, locally I–vi, into the otherwise-omnipresent fifths.[18] While chords descend by fifth, the keys move in the opposite direction, ascending by fifth from D major to A major and then further up the ladder to E minor, B minor, and F♯ minor. This pattern of distorted fifth-progressions is well-suited to a prelude, and readers may enjoy improvising with it—or perhaps programming it into a computer.[19]

---

[17] Nathan Martin has referred to Rameau's "astonishing ingenuity" in deriving common progressions from his descending-fifth paradigm (Martin 2018). But if functional music tends to move along the descending circle of thirds, then this ingenuity is easily explained; what makes it seem astonishing is the nonobvious relation between Rameau's descending-fifth paradigm and (what I take to be) the more basic circle of descending thirds.

[18] Since the second distortion undoes the first, quarter notes 8–10 are shifted up by third relative to the underlying pattern. The second distortion avoids the tonic chord's seventh, abandoning the leading tone to create a brief moment of triadic arrival; my analysis includes this missing seventh in parentheses.

[19] Readers can visit my https://www.madmusicalscience.com to hear artificially generated music using Bach's template. Those who find Bach's figuration challenging can use another pattern, relaxing whatever stylistic rules they want—the important thing is guiding the perpetually descending sevenths through a range of keys.

324  TONALITY: AN OWNER'S MANUAL

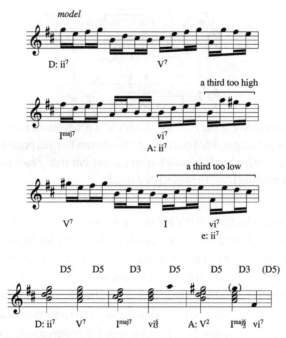

Figure 7.3.5. (*top*) The basic sequential melody of the first D major prelude in *The Well-Tempered Clavier*, with its implied chordal voice leading (*bottom*).

Figure 7.3.6. The fundamental harmonic progression of the prelude, with the descending scalar bass. The bass line here derives from the A major statement.

The result is vaguely sequential and yet never entirely predictable, an unusually clear look at the regularity at the heart of tonal-functional syntax. Indeed, Bach assembles his quasi-sequential phrases into a higher-level near-sequence that would be completely regular were the first statement on E (Figures 7.3.6–7); the perpetually descending stepwise bass flows naturally from the sequence, loosely shadowing one of the upper voices, which themselves articulate a baroque analogue to the "Shepard-tone-passacaglias" of §2.5 (Figure 7.3.8). Here we see three levels of semi-regular harmonic movement: chords descending mostly by fifth,

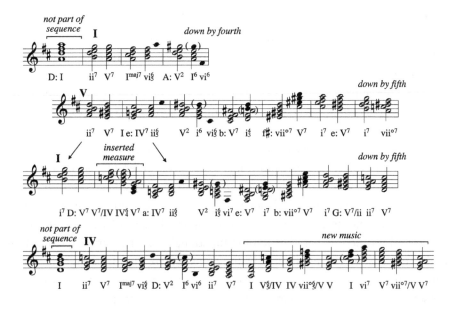

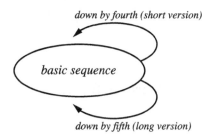

**Figure 7.3.7.** The D major prelude makes four passes through this flowchart.

**Figure 7.3.8.** The prelude's constantly descending bass line, with each beat representing a measure.

keys largely modulating upward by fifth, and larger phrases descending mostly by fifth again.

Though Bach was hardly a loyal Rameauian, the choices available in his open-form prelude closely track the basic concepts of Rameau's theory. There are no ascending thirds or fifths in Figure 7.3.7, but rather a preponderance of descending fifths (65%) and descending thirds (19%), with a smaller number of ascending and descending steps (10% and 5% respectively, the latter mostly moving from tonic to leading-tone seventh).[20] For me, the root motions are salient: it feels as if the dancer is *moving in a particular way* rather than *visiting a collection of familiar places*. In other words, it exhibits a Rameauian functionality based on types of root progression rather than a Riemannian functionality based on locations such as "subdominant." Yet the churning motion-oriented music also conforms to the precepts of the thirds-based grammar, presenting no anomalous moves and touching on a large fraction of the permitted progressions.

The near-equivalence between Rameau's theory and my own is an example of *theoretical underdetermination*, our ability to construct different theories to account for one and the same set of observable facts. In physics we have the Lagrangian, Hamiltonian, and vector formulations of Newtonian mechanics. In music we have Rameau's descending-fifth theory, my own descending-thirds theory, and many others besides: theories based on idioms, functional categories, linear relationships, and so on. The interesting thought is that none of these theories is right or wrong; instead, they offer different perspectives on a musical practice that was largely understood tacitly. In choosing among them we must ask which gives the simplest and most compelling explanation of the broadest range of musical behavior. Different theorists will make different choices, reflecting preferences that are as much aesthetic as scientific.

## 4. Functional melody, functional harmony

Seventh chords are intrinsic to Rameau's theory, not just in providing a tool for analyzing descending-third progressions, but also in coordinating descending-step melody with functionally tonal harmony. In reality, however, seventh chords are not nearly so prevalent as Rameau's theory suggests. How then do real-life functional composers manage the tension between *triadic* functionality and descending melody, given the tendency of "strong" progressions to generate ascending melodic steps? That is, how do functionally triadic composers negotiate the fact that efficient triadic voice leading often leads to ascending melodies?

Here I think we can give five separate answers, each of which helps us understand something different about the style. The first is that functional composers use a wide range of root progressions, including "weak" progressions that give rise to descending triadic voice leading. While it is true that ascending thirds are generally rare, descending steps are reasonably common, and ascending fifths ubiquitous: progressions like IV–I and I–V are important in virtually all functional genres.[21] Functional tonality does not so much avoid ascending-fifth progressions *per se* as ascending fifths *not involving the tonic triad*.

---

[20] Rameau himself might not have considered them true descending-step progressions, as he considered vii° an incomplete $V^7$.

[21] The most common ascending-third progression is vi–I$^6$, and the most common descending-step progressions are vi–V and V–IV$^6$. The functionally anomalous cadential six-four allows for vi–I$^6_4$ and ii–I$^6_4$ (§9.5), while vii° (sometimes thought to be a metonym for $V^7$) allows for I–vii°.

The second answer is that functional harmony involves a norm of larger voice leading, expressed by larger motions on the triadic circle; in particular, simple harmonic cycles like I–V–I and I–IV–I often make a complete circle through the space (Figure 7.4.1). These larger voice leadings permit the addition of passing tones that create brief seventh chords, turning contrapuntal lemons into harmonic lemonade. Thus, insofar as functional composers have to negotiate a conflict between harmonic and melodic forces, this is largely a matter of avoiding obvious contrapuntal possibilities—ascending-third progressions and ascending fifths not involving the tonic. Practically speaking, the remaining options are more than sufficient to produce effective music.

Third, functional composers often write melodies that embed or disguise the circle of descending thirds (e.g., Figures 7.2.2, 7.2.6–7, 9.1.1, 10.2.13). These third-based melodies allow a harmonizing voice either to reorder the thirds (producing the "Ludwig" schema) or move in parallel with them, either a third above or a third

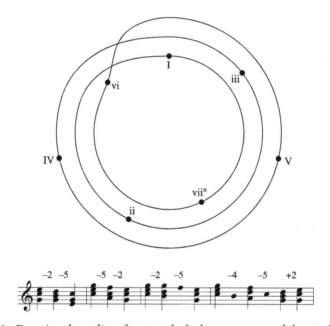

Figure 7.4.1. Functional tonality often travels the long way around the triadic circle.

Figure 7.4.2. Harmonizing a descending-third melody with either contrary or parallel motion.

**Figure 7.4.3.** Measure 5 of the first A♭ major fugue in *The Well-Tempered Clavier*.

**Figure 7.4.4.** Modal possibilities for melodic $\hat{5}$–$\hat{4}$–$\hat{3}$ over harmonic V–?–I.

below (Figure 7.4.2). Figure 7.4.3 shows Bach using both techniques in the opening of *The Well-Tempered Clavier*'s first A♭ major fugue. [22]

A fourth answer is that functional tonality coordinates melody and harmony by *expanding its harmonic vocabulary*. The most common technique is to use seventh chords to fill in the descending thirds that often arise from larger motions on the triadic circle. Imagine, for example, that you are a modal composer who has just used a V chord to harmonize melodic $\hat{5}$; your melody is $\hat{5}$–$\hat{4}$–$\hat{3}$ and you are aiming to place a I chord under $\hat{3}$. What chord goes under $\hat{4}$? The available triadic options are IV$^6$, ♭VII, vii$^{o6}$, and ii (Figure 7.4.4). Functional music fuses the two chords of the V–vii° progression into a dominant-seventh composite (Figures 7.4.5–6). Virtually the same reasoning applies when the melody is $\hat{2}$–$\hat{1}$–$\hat{7}$ and the first note supports a supertonic triad; here standard modal solutions include ii–IV–V and ii–I$^6$–V while common functional solutions are ii–ii$^7$–V and ii–I$^6_4$–V: again, ii–ii$^7$–V fuses ii and IV while I$^6_4$ embellishes the dominant (§9.5).[23] Yet a third instance of this phenomenon has $\hat{8}$–$\hat{7}$–$\hat{6}$ supporting I–?–IV; here the functional tradition retains both the modal solution I–iii–IV (sometimes as I–III–IV) and the fifth progression I–I$^{maj7}$–IV.

---

[22] Compare the second B major fugue, which exploits the double counterpoint latent in the two parallel options.

[23] For modal ii$^{(6)}$–IV–V progressions see Figures 6.5.5 (m. 56) and 6.7.6 (m. 25).

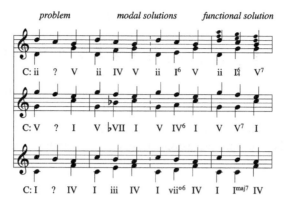

Figure 7.4.5. Modal and functionally tonal approaches to similar musical problems.

| Melody | Progression | Bach | Mozart |
|---|---|---|---|
| $\hat{1} \to \hat{7}$ | $I(\substack{6\\4}) \to V^{(7)}$ | 46.5 | 77.2 |
| | iii→IV | 40.9 | 13.3 |
| $\hat{7} \to \hat{6}$ | vii°→vi | 0 | 46.7 |
| | $V^{(7)} \to$ vii° | 0 | 40.0 |
| | IV→I | 33.6 | 17.7 |
| $\hat{6} \to \hat{5}$ | $IV \to V^{(7)}$ | 30.3 | 4.7 |
| | ii→I$^6_4$ | 0.4 | 31.5 |
| $\hat{5} \to \hat{4}$ | $V^{(7)} \to V^7$ | 30.8 | 14.4 |
| | $I(\substack{6\\4}) \to V^7$ | 5.6 | 44.8 |
| $\hat{4} \to \hat{3}$ | $V^7 \to I$ | 47.1 | 40.8 |
| | vii°→I | 30 | 15.5 |
| $\hat{3} \to \hat{2}$ | $I(\substack{6\\4}) \to V^{(7)}$ | 59.9 | 69.9 |
| | I→ii | 19.2 | 8.5 |
| $\hat{2} \to \hat{1}$ | V→I | 82.2 | 73.9 |

Figure 7.4.6. Harmonizing descending melodic steps in the Bach chorales and Mozart piano sonatas. The notation I($^6_4$) indicates that the tonic chord could be in any inversion including second, whereas I$^6_4$ requires second inversion.

This suggests that functional-harmonic restrictions likely drove the expansion from triads to seventh chords, partly as a way of recovering lost melodic possibilities: scale-degree progressions such as $\hat{2}$–$\hat{1}$–$\hat{7}$, which had indigenous modal harmonizations, gradually acquired functional alternatives involving sevenths and I$^6_4$, alternatives that allowed descending-fifth progressions to harmonize a greater range of melodic possibilities.[24] If this is right, then it seems unlikely that we can *derive* functional rules from voice-leading considerations, as some

---

[24] The ascending use of $\hat{4}$ in I–V$^4_3$–I$^6$ is also relevant here, as it allows I–V–I to harmonize $\hat{3}$–$\hat{4}$–$\hat{5}$.

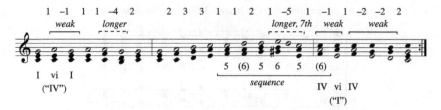

**Figure 7.4.7.** An outline of Leonard Cohen's "Hallelujah." The numbers above the example show the steps each progression takes along the circle of diatonic triads (Figure 7.4.1).

theorists have wanted.[25] Instead something like the opposite is true: at the most general level, melodic goals generate *nonfunctional* triadic progressions; to counteract this tendency, composers need to replace those triadic progressions with more complex alternatives involving seventh chords and the cadential $^6_4$.

A final answer is that surface voices sometimes descend relative to an ascending background. Leonard Cohen's "Hallelujah" uses this strategy alongside the others discussed in this section. The reduction in Figure 7.4.7 is largely determined by the melody, whose primary notes are shown with open noteheads; these ascend by sixth from G4 before falling back to C5.[26] I analyze the final phrase as descending through the triadic background, moving soprano–alto–tenor before cadencing on a C4 that is the same abstract voice as the C5 that ends the second phrase, only now in a lower octave.[27] The strategy here is essentially the inverse of Neil Young's "Helpless": there we found omnipresent descending voice leading giving rise to modal harmony, with the vocal melody ascending by triadic step against a descending triadic background; here we have omnipresent melodic ascent, with the vocal melody *descending* through the voices from one verse to the next. The two songs, with their two different harmonic languages, are in effect mirror images, with "Helpless" descending while "Hallelujah" rises toward the heavens.

## 5. Fauxbourdon and linear idioms

Fauxbourdon begins in the fourteenth century and persists throughout the functional era—parallel triadic motion beholden to no further harmonic laws. As such

---

[25] See Headlam 2012 and Yust 2018, chapter 10, for expressions of this Schenkerian hope.

[26] The only descents come from "weak" progressions in both more and less conventional forms (a IV–I–V found in virtually all functional music, and I–vi–I and IV–vi–IV progressions more idiomatic to rock) and slightly longer voice-leading paths (IV–V and V/vi–vi, the latter using a seventh). I hear I–vi–I and IV–vi–IV as weaker versions of subdominant-tonic oscillation, with vi substituting for IV in the first case and I in the second. These variants start to become popular in the middle of the nineteenth century (§10.7).

[27] This ascending voice leading continues through the repeat even while the vocal melody disguises it, with the middle voice now sounding the melodic G4. This is illustrated, on my example, by the two open noteheads in the final chord, one representing the last note of the first verse, the other the first note of the second verse.

**Figure 7.5.1.** Fanny Mendelssohn Hensel's, *Sechs Lieder*, Op. 1, no. 2, mm. 24–27, contains "decorative" fauxbourdon audibly connecting IV⁶ to V⁶.

it is Exhibit A for the thesis of continuity between modal and functional practice, and a clear example of the multiple syntactical systems comprising functional harmony.[28] In the simplest cases it is decorative, gliding from one syntactic harmony to the next as in Figure 7.5.1. Here we can imagine removing the parallel chords to reveal a functionally permissible residue. (In much the same way, popular musicians sometimes use stepwise motion to embellish familiar progressions, as when IV–I becomes IV–iii–ii–I.) In other cases, fauxbourdon serves a textural function, creating a palette-cleansing wash long enough to interrupt the connection between first chord and last.

One of fauxbourdon's main roles is as the source for an idiom that harmonizes descending bass lines, a schema that is perhaps the most important exception to the general principles governing harmonic cycles. The joyous opening of Bach's Fifth Brandenburg Concerto uses the idiom to move from the high D4 tonic down to the low D3; the bass line uses parallel first-inversion chords with the exception of the root-position chord above $\hat{4}$ (Figure 7.5.2).[29] Early theorists had devised "the rule of the octave" to govern such situations, calling for an applied dominant on $\hat{6}$ and dominants on $\hat{5}$ and $\hat{4}$ (Figure 7.5.3). But many functional composers preferred an alternative that uses fauxbourdon to move *through* a weaker chord on

---

[28] Traditional theorists rarely distinguished fauxbourdon from harmonic cycles: Rameau ([1722] 1971, p. 126), for example, adds a fundamental bass to fauxbourdon, while Weber ([1817–1821] 1846, p. 457) includes fauxbourdon passages in his discussion of chord grammar. Later theorists such as Schenker and Lerdahl also conceive of functional harmony as unified.

[29] The contrary-motion outer voices are a common idiom; see Figures 3.2.5 ("fauxbourdon") and 10.6.9, or Beethoven's Op. 18, no. 5, IV, m. 59ff.

332   TONALITY: AN OWNER'S MANUAL

Figure 7.5.2. The opening of Bach's Fifth Brandenburg Concerto.

Figure 7.5.3. Two approaches to harmonizing a descending scale: the traditional rule of the octave (*top*) creates harmonic accents on metrically weak beats, while the fauxbourdon-based alternative (*bottom*) does not.

Figure 7.5.4. The "fauxbourdon ROTO" and some common variants.

$\hat{5}$ to a metrically strong arrival on $\hat{4}$, which can then continue downward to I via Gjerdingen's "Prinner."[30]

This "fauxbourdon rule of the octave" (or "fauxbourdon ROTO") admits several variants: substituting IV for ii$^6$, V$^2$/IV for V$^6$, and, most importantly, I$^6_4$ for iii$^6$ (Figure 7.5.4). This last yields the I–V–IV–I chord progression of Neil Young's

---

[30] It is sobering to contemplate the divergence between this musical "rule of the octave" and the alternative found in historical treatises—a theoretical construct that is perhaps more accurate as a description of general functional principles than of musical practice (Christensen 1992, Holtmeier 2007; see Sanguinetti 2012, p. 20, who cites a rare discussion of the fauxbourdon ROTO in Valente). Once again we find an embodied and untheorized musical knowledge, idioms learned by ear or by score study, passed on from composer to composer without leaving clear theoretical traces.

**Figure 7.5.5.** In the second theme of the first movement of Brahms's G major violin sonata, Brahms uses the fauxbourdon ROTO to create a strong sense of retrofunctionality.

"Helpless," recreating a ubiquitous modal progression within a functional context—an idiom that is statistically common even while being theoretically puzzling.[31] And while classical composers often skirt past the V–IV, grouping chords in pairs so that V$^6$–IV$^6$ occurs across a phrase boundary, they occasionally milk it for its retrofunctional qualities—as in Brahms's G major violin sonata Op. 78 (Figure 7.5.5), whose melodic-harmonic core would not sound out of place on a classic-rock playlist.[32] The resonance is real, with similar theoretical constraints giving rise to similar solutions.[33]

The IV$^6$–I$^6_4$–ii$^6$ idiom is sometimes reversed in the course of what might be called "standing on the predominant"; usually, predominant chords on $\hat{6}$ and $\hat{4}$ are connected by I$^6_4$, delaying the arrival of the cadential dominant (Figure 7.5.6).[34] In such contexts, theorists often invoke the doubly problematic notion of a "passing $^6_4$ chord." The first issue here is that we do not see a widespread proliferation of "passing $^6_4$ chords" of which IV$^6$–I$^6_4$–ii$^6$ is just one example; instead, the vast majority of "passing $^6_4$s" are instances of the fauxbourdon ROTO schema (Figure 7.5.7). This suggests we are dealing with a specific idiom rather than a more general musical technique. A second problem is that many purportedly "passing $^6_4$" progressions are perfectly well formed from a root-functional perspective: progressions such as I–V$^6_4$–I$^6$, IV$^6$–I$^6_4$–ii$^6$, and V$^2$–vi$^6_4$–V$^4_3$, like the "neighboring" I–IV$^6_4$–I and V–I$^6_4$–V, are largely in accordance with Figure 7.1.3, and merely occur over an unusual bass. (This is particularly clear in the case of I–V$^6_4$–I$^6$, where the dominant simply lacks its

---

[31] Both Temperley (2011) and Rothgeb (1975) describe the fauxbourdon ROTO progression as unusual.

[32] Brahms frequently uses retrofunctional V–IV progressions in his second themes; often these involve some version of the "fauxbourdon ROTO," but sometimes they do not. For other examples, see the second themes of the first movements of the G major string sextet, Op. 36, and the C minor piano quartet, Op. 60.

[33] Compare the fauxbourdon ROTO harmonization of $\hat{8}$–$\hat{7}$–$\hat{6}$–$\hat{5}$ to the template in Figure 6.1.3.

[34] My label is a play on the term "standing on the dominant," coined by Erwin Ratz and popularized by Caplin 1998; Gjerdingen's "Indugio" schema (2007) is closely related. For similar examples from Mozart, see K.279, I, mm. 25ff; K.283, III, mm. 33ff; and K.309, I, mm. 47ff.

**Figure 7.5.6.** Standing on the predominant in the Symphony Op. 11, no. 2, I, mm. 108–115, by Joseph Bologne, Chevalier de Saint-Georges.

|       | Bach | Mozart | Beethoven |
|-------|------|--------|-----------|
| I$^6_4$  | 93   | 82     | 77        |
| V$^6_4$  | -    | 14     | 21        |
| vii$^6_4$ | 7    | 2      | 2         |
| other | -    | 2      | -         |

**Figure 7.5.7.** "Passing $^6_4$" chords in Bach, Mozart, and Haydn. More than 90% involve tonic or dominant.

seventh.) It is not obvious that these progressions have any special "passing" quality, as opposed to simply evincing a greater tolerance for second-inversion triads.[35]

Fauxbourdon also plays a crucial role in the development of sequences. In Corelli's Op. 1, a substantial proportion of the sequential passages use fauxbourdon—usually first-inversion triads descending by step, but occasionally root-position or ascending triads.[36] The descending-step passages are usually decorated with quasi-harmonic 7–6 suspensions that give the impression of a chord change.[37] In figured-bass notation, the suspensions are represented using two figures, and perhaps for this reason, the dissonant sevenths sometimes take on a harmonic character; when accompanied by a perfect fifth, they become very difficult to analyze (Figure 7.5.8). Indeed, this idiom is a direct descendant of the Renaissance seventh (Figure 7.5.9): read literally, roots alternately ascend by step and descend by third, but, as with its Renaissance predecessor, the progression feels suspended between the harmonic and nonharmonic realms. Even more harmonic is the bottom staff of

---

[35] Even in the sixteenth century, Zarlino encouraged composers to be freer in their use of second-inversion harmonies ([1558] 1968, p. 193).

[36] Harrison 2003 explores this connection in detail; Allsop 1992 explores the prehistory of the Corelli style.

[37] William Caplin has noted that the "7" sonorities in these passages have a quasi-harmonic character (1998, p. 31, footnote 29), and I have argued for the importance of the underlying down-a-third-up-by-step root-pattern (2011a, chapter 7).

**Figure 7.5.8.** A fauxbourdon sequence with 7–6 suspensions, along with two variants.

**Figure 7.5.9.** The $^7_5$–$^6_3$ fauxbourdon sequence in mm. 34–37 of Monteverdi's madrigal "Longe da te, cor mio" (Book IV).

Figure 7.5.8, where the stepwise 7–6 descent is embedded in a sequence of seventh chords descending by fifth. One of the analytical challenges posed by baroque harmony is the seeming interchangeability of these options, with sequences spanning the continuum from "merely linear" fauxbourdon to "robustly harmonic" fifths, presenting a full range of intermediate cases.[38] And though these intermediate cases largely vanish in the classical period, they occasionally resurface: in his Op. 17, no. 4 Mazurka (shown in Figure 9.3.6), Chopin updates the effect for the chromatic era, creating a sequence in which all the 7–6 sevenths *sound* harmonic, and half of them ($G^7$ and $E^7$) clearly are.[39]

One final idiom shares fauxbourdon's emphasis on parallel motion, two voices moving in thirds against a fixed pedal point; its tonic and dominant forms are shown in Figure 7.5.10, and an example appears in Figure 7.7.6. The idiom is again delicately balanced between harmonic and nonharmonic, mostly articulating well-behaved harmonies, but with the parallel thirds suggesting "merely linear" motion.

---

[38] The "Crucifixus" from Bach's B minor mass uses the 7–6 and $^7$–$^4_3$ options almost interchangeably (Biamonte 2012).

[39] Examples can also be found in Brahms: Op. 76, no. 4, mm. 28–30 (discussed in Tymoczko 2011a, chapter 8), and Op. 119, no. 2, mm. 15–16.

**Figure 7.5.10.** The "pseudochord" idiom in its tonic and dominant forms.

The D–F–C sonority is particularly interesting since it seems to contravene the general prohibition on I–ii–I$^6$ progressions.[40] It feels uncomfortable to dismiss the chord as "merely nonharmonic," since it occupies the same rhythmic duration as the other harmonies; the phrase does not *sound* like a I–I$^6$–IV progression in which the first chord lasts twice as long as the others. For this reason I call the apparent "ii$^7$" a *pseudochord*, neither harmonic nor nonharmonic but suspended between those worlds.[41]

## 6. Sequences

Chapter 4 contains a general theory of repetition applicable to both modal and tonal composition, and extensible to contemporary music as well. Functional composers did not use all these options with equal frequency. Figure 7.6.1 counts the sequences in Corelli's Op. 1, Bach's *Well-Tempered Clavier*, and the Mozart piano sonatas, classified by the interval of transposition from one grand period to the next.[42] We see that sequences typically move by small intervals and that descent is preferred to ascent; this is the familiar preference for stepwise descending melody, but now governing larger spans of musical time. From Corelli to Mozart there is a substantial increase in descending-third motion, rising to almost a quarter of the latter composer's sequences. Fourth motion and ascending-third motion are rare for all composers, generalizations that continue to hold throughout the tradition. This is likely because of the large registral motions involved; most so-called fifth sequences are actually step sequences—often using permutation in the upper voices, with the bass alternating ascending fourths and descending fifths.

Sequences typically move through a diatonic space that may itself be modulating. For a given diatonic interval of transposition, there are four possible two-chord

---

[40] One might think that this idiom counts as evidence against that prohibition, except that the vast majority of apparent I–ii–I$^6$ progressions occur in precisely this context, with the predominant invariably lacking its fifth.

[41] The second G major prelude in *The Well-Tempered Clavier* contains an extended example of the idiom in which the parallel thirds exceed their usual bounds.

[42] To generate this list, I programmed my computer to identify passages of melodic repetition; I then analyzed each sequence by hand, eliminating the relatively small number that I considered not to be true sequences. I also compared the results to my own analyses of individual pieces to check for completeness (appendix 4).

|        | Corelli | | Bach | | Mozart | |
|--------|---------|-----|------|-----|--------|-----|
|        | *down*  | *up* | *down* | *up* | *down* | *up* |
| step   | 74 | 17 | 61 | 15 | 48 | 19 |
| third  | 6  | 0  | 12 | 5  | 27 | 1  |
| fourth | 2  | 2  | 1  | 6  | 1  | 4  |

**Figure 7.6.1.** Sequences by interval of transposition in Corelli, Bach, and Mozart. Numbers are percentages in the work of each composer.

| First Interval | Second Interval | Name |
|:-:|:-:|:-:|
| D2 | – | **fauxbourdon** |
| D3 | A2 | **"descending third, ascending step"** |
| D4 | A3 | **descending 6–5** |
| D5 | A4 | **descending fifths** |

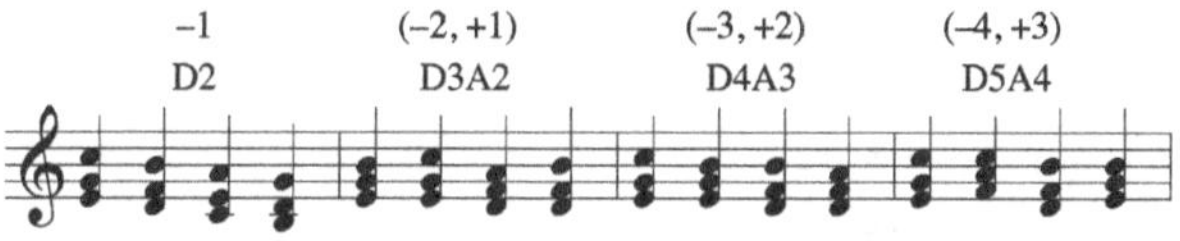

**Figure 7.6.2.** The four diatonic descending-step sequences with two or fewer chords per unit. Here I neglect order and treat octave-related intervals as equivalent (e.g., ascending sixth and descending third). Note that D3A2 and D4A3 both juxtapose $\frac{6}{4}$ and $\frac{6}{3}$ chords over a stepwise descending bass, but with the vertical shapes in different orders.

sequences.[43] The four descending-step options are shown in Figure 7.6.2, while Figure 7.6.3 counts them in our three corpora: in Corelli, fauxbourdon is the most popular, supplanted by descending fifths in the later styles. The down-a-third-up-by-step sequence is present in Bach but largely disappears later; the last possibility, the "descending 6–5," appears throughout the Renaissance but is mostly absent from functional music. Turning to ascending steps, the four possibilities are shown in Figure 7.6.4. Fauxbourdon and the ascending 5–6 are by far the most common; the second possibility, D2A3, contains two weak progressions and is all but unknown. Ascending fifths are particularly characteristic of Bach—indeed, many striking passages in *The Well-Tempered Clavier* are ascending-fifth sequences (Figure 7.6.5). In other styles this sequence is rare but not unheard-of, a second- or perhaps third-level default, usually lacking Bach's omnipresent tonicizations.

---

[43] Hook 2020 uses a similar system of categorization. Longer sequences can usually (but not always) be reduced to just the first and last chord in the repeating unit.

|  | Corelli | Bach | Mozart |
|---|---|---|---|
| D5D5 | 27 | 77 | 80 |
| Fauxbourdon | 56 | 10 | 18 |
| D3A2 | 12 | 5 | 0 |
| D4A3 | 2 | 0 | 0 |
| other | 3 | 7 | 2 |

Figure 7.6.3. Distribution of descending-step sequences in Corelli, Bach, and Mozart.

|  | Corelli | Bach | Mozart |
|---|---|---|---|
| D3A4 | 57 | 60 | 48 |
| fauxbourdon (A2) | 43 | 12 | 52 |
| D4A5 | 0 | 26 | 0 |
| other | 0 | 2 | 0 |

Figure 7.6.4. Distribution of ascending-step sequences in Corelli, Bach, and Mozart. Note the unusually high percentage of D4A5 in Bach.

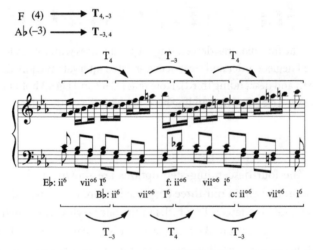

Figure 7.6.5. An ascending-step sequence in *The Well-Tempered Clavier*'s first C minor fugue, mm. 13–14; the two-chord unit is itself a near-contrary sequence moving its voices apart by octave.

Descending-third sequences use all four of the two-chord possibilities shown in Figure 7.6.6: fauxbourdon creates descending-third sequences when the melodic period is two chords long and pure descending-third sequences can be understood as dividing the descending fifth in half (e.g., Figure 4.6.5). The Pachelbel pattern D4A2 comes in two varieties, one in which sequential units act like I–V resolving deceptively, the other containing vii°–I pairs; occasionally, composers combine the two (Figure 7.6.7). Finally, there is the "ascending third, descending

|       | Corelli | Bach | Mozart |
|-------|---------|------|--------|
| D3    | 14      | 21   | 5      |
| D2D2  | 43      | 9    | 49     |
| D5A3  | 29      | 21   | 19     |
| D4A2  | 14      | 24   | 24     |
| D5D5D5D5 | 0    | 21   | 3      |

Figure 7.6.6. Descending-third sequences in Corelli, Bach, and Mozart.

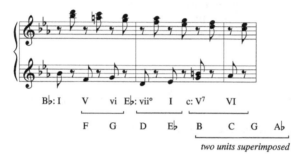

Figure 7.6.7. A mixed descending-third sequence from the first movement of Haydn's Keyboard Sonata, Hob. XVI/49, mm. 50–52. The ascending step is initially a deceptive V–vi progression, then a dominant-tonic vii°–I; the third unit combines these possibilities, the deceptive bass G–A♭ appearing one sequential unit too early, subposed underneath the authentic b°–c progression.

fifth" (A3D5) sequence, C–E–a–C–F . . ., which often uses seventh chords to create stepwise descending voices (Figure 7.6.8).[44] The popularity of all four possibilities reflects the descending third's importance: virtually *any* two-chord pattern sounds functional when it repeats down by third. Ascending-third sequences are considerably rarer, almost always using the D2A4 root progression (Figure 7.6.9).[45] This is the retrograde of the standard Pachelbel progression, and hence supports thirds ascending by step (Figure 7.6.10). True fourth- and fifth-sequences are rare, though we will find that A2D5 ascending-fifth sequences are characteristic of developments (§8.5).

This survey reveals an important higher-level harmonic regularity, with all but a few common functional sequences featuring descending-fifth progressions repeating at some regular interval. The main exceptions are pure descending thirds, whose connection to harmonic cycles is clear, and the Pachelbel sequence,

---

[44] This sequence appears commonly in Beatles songs, for instance "You Never Give Me Your Money."
[45] Interestingly, Bach uses the A5D3 sequence, the inversion of the common D5A3, at least twice in *The Well-Tempered Clavier*: in the first F major fugue (m. 13) and in the second C♯ minor fugue (m. 23).

340  TONALITY: AN OWNER'S MANUAL

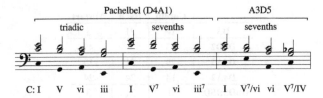

Figure 7.6.8. The use of seventh chords allows for a greater variety of stepwise descending thirds.

|            | Corelli | Bach | Mozart |
|------------|---------|------|--------|
| D2A4       | 0       | 69   | 0      |
| fauxbourdon| 0       | 8    | 100    |
| D5D5D5     | 0       | 15   | 0      |
| D3A5       | 0       | 8    | 0      |

Figure 7.6.9. Ascending-third sequences in theory and practice.

where the engine of repetition is deceptive rather than authentic.[46] This favoring of descending fifths produces notable asymmetries between ascent and decent. For example, the ascending 5–6 (or D3A4) is common, while its retrograde, the descending 6–5 or (A3D4), is all but unknown—even though both are equally useful from a linear point of view, and even though the descending 6–5 was popular in the Renaissance. The rarity of these contrapuntally plausible options means that sequences cannot be *merely* linear, but rather have harmonic content.[47]

Many theorists have argued that sequential progressions have an attenuated functional significance. Less common is the Rameauian suggestion I have been making here, that nonsequential harmony is *itself* quasi-sequential, an oblique and disguised reworking of the circle of descending thirds. It is, to be sure, distinct from the sequential system—a *branching* set of possibilities that allows for a number of different paths through the same basic map, and one that is usually expressed only harmonically. But these differences should not lead us to overlook the system's fundamental regularity: sequence and harmonic cycle are poles in a continuum, rather than separate countries demarcated by a clear border.

---

[46] To these we can add fauxbourdon and the "down a third up a step" sequence, though the latter is rare after the baroque.

[47] See Riemann 1896, pp. 120ff, and Caplin 1998, p. 29, for the view that sequences are almost entirely linear. Schenker went further, denying that sequences existed and speaking of linear progressions instead; see Schenker (1935) 1979, Slottow 2018, and Sprick 2018. Weber (1817–1821) 1846 argues that sequential progressions are similar to those used by harmonic cycles (p. 430), though somewhat looser (p. 432).

**Figure 7.6.10.** A disguised ascending-third sequence at the opening of Pergolesi's *Stabat Mater*, P. 77. The stepwise upper voices are decorated by voice exchanges and octave displacement (E6→E5). The sequence calls for ii° instead of iv on the second beat of m. 3.

This continuity is nicely illustrated by the second half of "Ich grolle nicht," the seventh song from Robert Schumann's *Dichterliebe*, Op. 48 (Figure 7.6.11). We begin with a harmonic cycle that highlights its quasi-sequential structure: the bass descending almost by thirds from tonic to dominant, C–A–F–D–[B]–G, and articulating a I–IV–ii–V–I progression: descending by fifth from tonic to predominant (I–IV), descending by fifth from predominant to tonic (ii–V–I). The descending-third bass continues into the following sequence, an A3D5 pattern whose units combine in pairs to form a contrary-motion fifth-sequence. Figure 7.6.12 connects the figure to Gesualdo's trick, two voices moving in parallel with the other two forming thirds alternately above and below this dyadic core; disregarding the octave displacement, we can think of it as a single repeating transformation operating at two different timescales.

This leads to a two-chord contrary-motion sequence whose outer voices ascend by minor seventh and descend by major second, divided in half to create ascending fourths and descending semitones—a Romantic-harmony pair of subdominant-dominant progressions, with contrary motion producing extended and unusual sonorities.[48] We then hear a *third* contrary-motion pattern that brings us closer to the world of harmonic cycles, a I–V⁷/vi–IV–V near sequence.[49] The music ends with ascending plagal progressions that evoke the Fenaroli/Prinner round (Figure 4.5.6), though here in a three-voice configuration, culminating in a gloriously sarcastic V–I cadence. Listening to the piece I do not sense any grinding of gears as it passes

---

[48] Note that here it is important to consider the melodic E5 as at least quasi-harmonic, as it continues the sequential pattern of mediants-acting-like-dominants, even though it quickly resolves to an orthodox V⁷.

[49] This pattern uses both the ascending-third (I–V⁷/vi) and ascending-step patterns (V⁷/vi–IV–V) in Figure 4.4.1.

342  TONALITY: AN OWNER'S MANUAL

Figure 7.6.11. An outline of the second half of Schumann's "Ich grolle nicht" from *Dichterliebe*.

between harmonic cycles and sequence: the harmonic cycles have sequential qualities, while the sequences articulate harmonic functions.

My purpose is not to deny the audible differences between the disguised repetition of harmonic cycles and the more obvious repetition of the sequential system. Rather, it is to emphasize that both use repetition in complementary ways—and that they are embedded within a language that deploys larger and equally repetitive formal, rhythmic, motivic, and phrasal schemata. As a student, I inherited from my teachers a tendency to devalue repetition in favor of constantly developing variation. Now that I am older, I realize that repetition can be an affirmatively enjoyable musical good.[50] The magic of functional music lies in the way it balances identity and difference, disguising its omnipresent repetition just enough to keep our ears on their toes.

[50] Margulis 2013.

Figure 7.6.12. A derivation of the main sequence in "Ich grolle nicht." At the top, the open-notehead voices descend in parallel, with the other two voices creating seventh chords alternately above and below; on the second line, these voices are placed in register as in §1.1. At the bottom, the actual piece, where the third and voices ascend, and one of the descending voices is displaced by octave. The arrows show that we can think of the entire sequence as a repeating contrapuntal pattern with one pair of voices moving every half note (dotted arrows) while the other pair of voices moves every quarter note (solid arrows).

## 7. Bach the dualist

Schenkerians have warned that a focus on chord-to-chord regularities can lead to impoverished analysis—as if too much attention to grammar would tempt a literary critic to obsess over syntax rather than a novel's inner meaning. Though I am an aficionado of harmonic theory, I think the criticism has merit: earlier composers internalized Roman-numeral norms so deeply that they were virtually second nature, obeyed the way a writer unthinking observes subject-verb-object ordering. As a result, Roman-numeral analysis is often more *correct* than *informative*. The real question is how innovative musical thinking manifests itself *within* the constraints of the syntactic system. I agree with Schenker's suggestion that this is often a matter of voice leading: a single line moving stepwise so as to determine harmonic trajectories (§2.1), a pair of voices articulating basic voice leadings (§3.1), voices articulating long-range melodic connections between nonadjacent notes (§9.1), and so on. The spiral diagrams blend Schenkerian and traditional harmonic

**Figure** 7.7.1. The diatonic third's descending and ascending basic voice leadings and their functional uses.

theory, allowing for both chord-to-chord laws and idiomatic contrapuntal patterns arising from the geometry of musical possibility.

C. P. E. Bach once wrote that the third of a major triad generally has a "tendency to ascend."[51] When I first read this, I dismissed it as a sloppy attempt at theorizing the leading tone—half convincing myself that he had somehow forgotten the subdominant, whose third, I was taught, had a descending tendency.[52] But it is hard to feel entirely comfortable with the hypothesis that a musician as gifted as C. P. E. Bach, dedicated enough to write a figured-bass treatise, would somehow overlook one of the primary diatonic triads. (I am, as readers know, prepared to think that earlier theorists went wrong, but this seems like a step too far.) As I grew to appreciate the role of ascending subdominants in baroque tonality, I began to wonder whether $\hat{6}$ might have an ascending tendency in some styles—with the diatonic third's ascending basic voice leading acting as a counterweight to its more familiar descending form. In other words, I started to wonder whether C. P. E. Bach's puzzling claim might be a reference to dyadic schemas such as those in Figure 7.7.1.

These patterns resonate with the music-theoretical tradition known as "dualism," which conceives of ascending fifths as inversions of descending fifths, their "upside-down" counterparts. Dualist music theorists typically operate in chromatic space, interpreting the major key's dominant as the chromatic inversion of the minor key's subdominant; however, the two forms of the basic voice leading can also be related by *diatonic* inversion around the supertonic. From this point of view, the "ascending subdominant" is the inversional counterpart of the V–I progression (Figure 7.7.2). But this oversimplifies things, since both dominant and subdominant permit a passing note that forms a resolving tritone: paradoxically IV–I is *both* a musical antipode to V–I, and *also* an alternative expression of the same functional logic. Could there be functional dialects where "dominant" is a superordinate genus containing both descending- and ascending-fifth species?[53]

---

[51] Bach (1762) 1949, p. 205.

[52] Alternately, Nathan Martin has suggested to me that it may be an echo of the pre-Renaissance idea that imperfect consonances resolve to perfect consonances.

[53] Delair's 1690 figured-bass treatise recommended the diatonic third's ascending basic voice leading for ascending-fifth bass lines (Nicolas 2019).

**Figure 7.7.2.** The descending G–C voice leading is the diatonic inversion of the ascending F–C voice leading; both permit a passing tone that creates a resolving tritone.

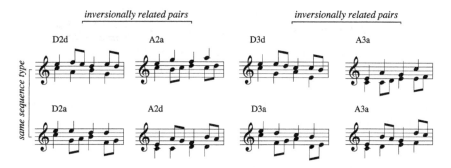

**Figure 7.7.3.** Descending and ascending step- and third-sequences using the two kinds of voice leading. The first two letters indicate the type of sequence, while the last indicates whether the descending or ascending basic voice leading is used. Thus A2a indicates an ascending-step sequence using the ascending form of the diatonic third's basic voice leading.

In J. S. Bach's chorales, approximately a third of the root position IV–I progressions incorporate an ascending leading tone, while in the Beethoven string quartets, the ascending subdominant occurs just a handful of times. (It is similarly rare in other classical-era repertoires.) While composer-to-composer variation is hardly surprising, this suggests a drastically different conception of a basic functional progression. Perhaps the picture of two opposite functions derives from later musical dialects, rather than being intrinsic to functional harmony itself. Perhaps we can recover the earlier perspective by considering patterns such as those in Figure 7.7.3. Here, horizontally related pairs are related by inversion, highlighting the contrast between "right side up" and "upside down." Vertically related pairs use the two forms of the basic voice leading to express the same sequential logic, moving by the same interval and showing that the two voice leadings can function similarly.

To contemporary musicians, reared on the triadic logic of Riemann and Rameau, this way of thinking might seem bizarre. But we will examine four different pieces where J. S. Bach seems to thematize these dyadic relationships, basing sections and even entire pieces on the contrast between ascending and descending fifths. The resulting music is almost always *consistent* with root-oriented triadic grammar;

Figure 7.7.4. Measures 3–4 of the first two-part invention (BWV 772), along with its inversion in measures 19–20.

but it seems to arise from a very different, dyadic thought process. In these pieces, Roman numerals stop short of musical meaning.

(a) *The first two-part invention, BWV 772.* One of the clearest expressions of Bachian dualism can be found in the first two-part invention, whose initial sequence is a lightly disguised Pachelbel progression, moving downward by third from tonic to V/V. Shortly before the end of the piece, the sequence is inverted around B; though the new version sounds unimpeachably functional it is very difficult to analyze, particularly if one imagines the inversion to operate triadically—that is, turning the first version's root-position triads into second-inversion triads (Figure 7.7.4). The harmonic mystery dissipates when we attend to the diatonic third's basic voice leading: in the first sequence, it tonicizes C major in the initial unit while becoming nonharmonic afterward; in the second, it produces a pair of ascending-subdominant progressions with perceptible dominant-tonic energy.[54] (Note that on my analysis several notes that were harmonic in the original become nonharmonic in the inversion.) Here we have an almost-explicit representation of the double relation between the two forms of the basic voice leading, as both inversions and bearers of the same harmonic energy. An analogous dualism can be heard in the piece's two "alternating hands" episodes, the first using the inverted theme to express the ascending-fifth basic voice leading, the second alternating theme and inversion to outline the descending-fifth basic voice leading (Figure 7.7.5). This succession of tension-increasing ascending fifths followed by tension-releasing descent is characteristic of Bach's music.

---

[54] This analysis echoes some of Schoenberg's observations about the piece (Neff 2012).

FUNCTIONAL PROGRESSIONS 347

Figure 7.7.5. Two episodes from the first invention, the first using the inverted theme to ascend by fifth; the second using theme and inversion to descend by fifths.

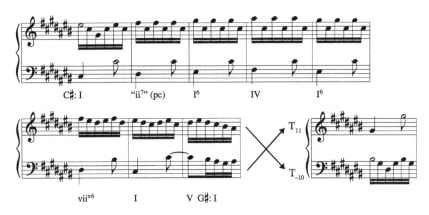

Figure 7.7.6. The opening sequence of the first C♯ major prelude from *The Well-Tempered Clavier*. Open noteheads show the diatonic third's ascending basic voice leading.

*(b) The C♯ major prelude from Book I of* The Well-Tempered Clavier. This prelude begins with a long ascending-fifth sequence based on the "pseudochord" idiom and without any tonicization of new sequential units (Figure 7.7.6); the ascending-fifth basic voice leading can be read from the start of one unit to the next, though this is not obvious to the ear. These ascending-fifth modulations ratchet up the tonal tension, ascending from C♯ to G♯ to d♯ to a♯, arriving at a descending-fifth sequence that releases the accumulated energy. This second sequence is unusual insofar as its four-bar unit modulates up by fifth and then down by step, so that it initially seems to continue the opening sequence up to e♯ (Figure 7.7.7). Here the outer voices clearly delineate the ascending basic voice leading (a fragment of pattern A2a on Figure 7.7.3) while also hinting at the descending form. Where the

348    TONALITY: AN OWNER'S MANUAL

Figure 7.7.7. The second sequence of the C♯ major prelude.

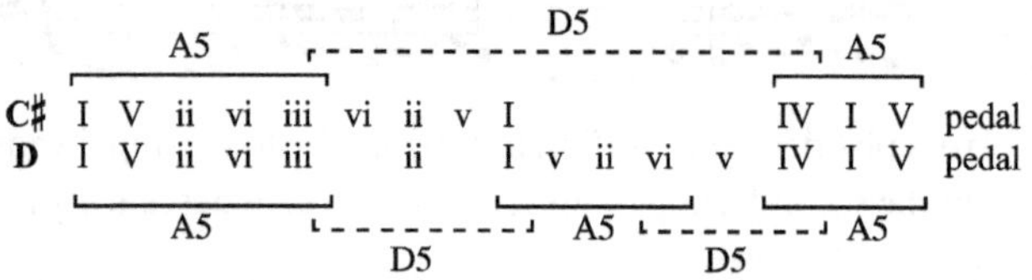

Figure 7.7.8. The tonal plans of the C♯ and D major preludes compared. Solid brackets indicate ascending-fifth modulations; dotted brackets indicate descending-fifth progressions that produce descending-step or descending-fifth modulations.

initial ladder-of-fifths ascent was weightless and independent of tonicization, these last ascending-fifth motions have more energy, as if extra force were required to keep the music moving in that direction. Descending fifths eventually win out, falling past the tonic and down to the subdominant, whereupon the initial music takes us from F♯ to C♯ to G♯ for a long dominant pedal. This pairing of ascending- and descending-fifth sequences anticipates what I will call, in §8.5, the "up-and-down-the-ladder" schema; it is also reminiscent of the D major prelude's tonal plan, though that piece has another trip up and down the ladder of fifths (Figure 7.7.8).[55]

(c) "Ach, lieben Christen, seid getrost" (BWV 256, Riemenschneider 31). The previous pieces contrast the two forms of the diatonic third's basic voice leading, but in different ways: the two-part invention presents the ascending fifth as both the descending fifth's inversional dual and functional equivalent, while the C♯ major prelude uses ascending and descending fifths as contrasting directions in an orderly modulatory path. "Ach, lieben Christen, seid getrost," a freestanding chorale based on an anonymous sixteenth-century melody, gives us a third approach, moving quickly from ascending-fifth progressions to descending-fifth cadences, as

---

[55] The F major two-part invention has a very similar harmonic plan, modulating upward by fifths I–V–ii–vi, descending by fifth-related chords vi–ii–V–V/IV–IV to reach the subdominant, and ending by modulating back up by fifth.

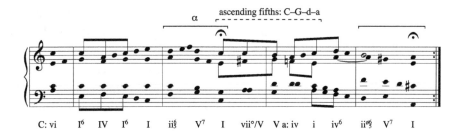

**Figure 7.7.9.** "Ach lieben Christen, seid getrost," highlighting the diatonic third's basic voice leading.

if compressing the prelude's harmonic narrative down to the phrasal level. Its mercurial contrasts feel spontaneous and embodied, the product of internalized keyboard routines rather than a series of chord changes we are intended to follow.

The music begins on A minor but immediately switches to C major for the rest of the phrase (Figure 7.7.9); this is a standard chorale gambit, inserting the global tonic at the start of an opening phrase in a subsidiary key, as if paying lip service to monotonality.[56] The IV–I ascending subdominant features the diatonic third's basic voice leading, supporting a "merely passing" note that "just happens" to create a resolving tritone. The phrase ends with a cadential schema reused by four of the chorale's five phrases, with the inner-voice leading tone falling by third.[57] The second phrase returns from the relative major to the relative minor by a sequence of ascending fifths, C–G–d–a. This is a favorite Bach schema, the diatonic third's basic voice leading allowing for the tonicization of each successive fifth; it is closely

---

[56] Typically these "orphan tonics" also participate in the harmonic narrative of the opening phrase, though sometimes in an unorthodox way (e.g., a vi–I⁶ progression).

[57] To call this "non-normative" is to engage in speculative fiction; in reality, this is a standard cadence that should be included in any realistic description of leading-tone behavior.

related to the four-voice Chase-schema variant in §4.6. Relative to that schema, the seemingly superfluous vii°/V is both standard and expected—sandwiched inside the ascending basic voice leading (C5, E4) → (B4, G4).

The next phrase cancels the Picardy third with Renaissance decisiveness, shifting directly from the cadence on A major to the dominant of C. Once again, we return to the relative minor by the ascending-fifth schema, C–G–d–a, now extended to a half cadence in A minor. The next phrase modulates to G major by descending fifths, arriving at a dominant that moves to G by way of a $IV^6$–$vii^{ø7}$–I progression. Many analysts would consider the $IV^6$ "merely passing," but the chorale contains three $C^6$–$f\sharp^{ø7}$–G progressions, only one of which is preceded by D; it is a particular schema that uses the ascending basic voice leading, not a generic process of prolongation.[58] This last phrase loosely echoes the second, beginning with two more repetitions of the four-voice Chase schema. In the D–a progression, the thirds switch roles so that each staff twice articulates the diatonic third's basic voice leading: (G, B) → (F♯, D) → (A, C) and (D, B) → (F♯, A) → (E, C).[59] At this point the fifths reverse direction, descending to the final cadence as in m. 4.

Here, much more than in the previous pieces, one can start to feel the inadequacy of triadic Roman-numeral theory. For while virtually everything in the chorale can be made *consistent* with that theory, this requires a series of analytical tricks— the delicate placement of key boundaries, the use of secondary dominants to license unusual triadic progressions, and so on. Such tricks will not completely erase the sense of mismatch between triadic grammar and Bach's practice: theory tells us to value descending-fifth progressions and smooth progressions between keys, whereas Bach seems to delight in ascending-fifth progressions that meander from one key to another. There is no path to the music that starts from the precepts in a standard harmony text. But once we focus on the basic voice leading, it starts to clarify: for here we find a systematic contrast between the familiar ascending-fifth schema, appearing in both explicit and disguised form, and the descending-fifth logic of the cadence.

*(d) The second B minor fugue from* The Well-Tempered Clavier. The last piece of *The Well-Tempered Clavier* paints a similar picture on a bigger canvas, using the two forms of the basic voice leading to articulate large formal regions. Its episodes all use the diatonic third's basic voice leading, with episodes 1, 3, and 7 ascending and the rest descending. The subject has two parts, the first an inverted arch combining basic voice leadings in near-contrary motion, the second a $\hat{6}$–$\hat{5}$–$\hat{4}$–$\hat{3}$–$\hat{2}$ descent. The piece presents two harmonizations of this descent, each exploiting a different dyadic pattern (Figure 7.7.10).[60] The first uses sequence D3a on Figure 7.7.3

---

[58] Burstein (2018, p. 6) writes that the $IV^6$–I progression is "atypical," but by my count I is the second most common successor to $IV^6$ in Bach's chorales.

[59] This could be described as a variable sequence with changing permutation.

[60] *The Well-Tempered Clavier*'s second F♯ minor fugue also juxtaposes these harmonic strategies, initially harmonizing $\hat{6}$–$\hat{5}$–$\hat{4}$–$\hat{3}$–$\hat{2}$ with the descending-third sequence before shifting to descending fifths for the rest of the piece. In that fugue, however, the descending-third harmonization is fleeting and momentary, with the bulk of the piece tracing out long sequences of descending fifths.

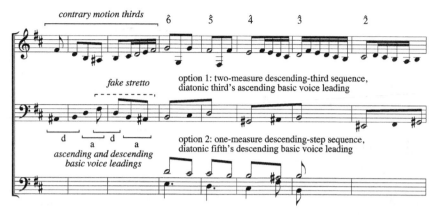

**Figure 7.7.10.** The subject of the second B minor fugue from *The Well-Tempered Clavier*, along with two harmonizations of the linear descent.

and leads to a series of energetically charged ascending-fifth episodes while the second uses seventh chords and the diatonic fifth's basic voice leading; this produces a variety of harmonizations spanning the gamut from fauxbourdon to descending fifths.[61] The music thus charts a path from unusual to conventional, gradually relaxing in intensity over the course of its ninety-nine measures—much as our earlier examples balanced ascending-fifth tension with descending-fifth release.

Formally, the piece is in three large sections: the first twenty-six measures contain a single episode and state the subject on B, F♯, and B; this music is dominated by an energetic, trilling countersubject and the diatonic third's ascending basic voice leading. The central second section lasts from m. 27 to m. 80 and introduces the oscillatory, descending-fifth countersubject. Here we have very little B minor, with two entries on F♯ and one each in D major, A major, and E minor; this music is dominated by descending-fifth progressions. The third section is a transposed and condensed repeat of the second, supplemented by a cursory final cadence.

Figure 7.7.11 uses open noteheads to highlight two fundamental voice-leading patterns: the contrary-motion near sequence harmonizing the subject's opening and the countersubject's basic voice leading. The abundance of white shows how completely the two schemas saturate the music. The first episode warps the subject's final measure into an episode that exploits pattern A2a on Figure 7.7.3, moving along the chain of ascending fifths from A major to its relative minor. The m. 26 arrival on C♯[7] signals the end of the first section and the disappearance of the trilling countersubject. Bach's willingness to drop this motive contradicts compositional nostrums about unity and motivic consistency: instead, the piece simply moves on to something new.

The first half of the second section is outlined in Figure 7.7.12. In some ways this can be considered a second beginning, the counterpoint finally having achieved its

---

[61] Compare the two harmonizations of the descending tenths in Figure 3.4.11.

352   TONALITY: AN OWNER'S MANUAL

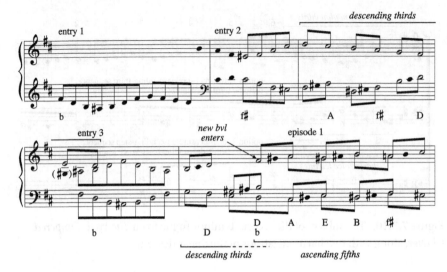

Figure 7.7.11. An outline of the fugue's first section.

Figure 7.7.12. An outline of the first half of the fugue's middle section.

final form. It is interesting that this new countersubject appears only after the piece has left the tonic, as if reserving its home-key debut for the recapitulatory third section. Bach's countersubject has a characteristic baroque flexibility, appearing once as fauxbourdon, three times as descending fifths, and twice as the intermediate $\frac{7}{5}$–$\frac{6}{3}$ sequence (Figure 7.7.13).[62] One weakness of triadic theory is its inability to capture this flexibility: fauxbourdon is purely linear, the descending-fifth sequence paradigmatically harmonic, and the $\frac{7}{5}$–$\frac{6}{3}$ D3A2 sequence is an uncomfortable hybrid

---

[62] These intermediate forms typically thwart the turn to the relative major that otherwise characterizes the minor-mode entries, the III$^{+\text{maj}7}$ a second-level Baroque dominant (e.g., A$^{+\text{maj}7}$–f♯ in m. 29 and G$^{+\text{maj}7}$–e in m. 73). Compare Rings (2011, p. 152) on the evanescent nature of fugal key areas.

**Figure 7.7.13.** The six appearances of the 7–6 pattern, transposed to B.

that cannot easily be assimilated to either category. Like the Renaissance seventh, this eighteenth-century idiom challenges the distinction between harmonic and nonharmonic, opening a gap between Bach's thinking and our own.

The fourth entry gives way to a descending-step episode whose bass has the same oscillating character as the second countersubject, as if echoing the new musical mood (see Figure 7.7.12, and pattern D2d on Figure 7.7.3). It is a canonic sequence whose upper voices outline the descending form of the diatonic third's basic voice leading, highlighted here for the first time. The following A major entry gives us a descending-fifth harmonization of the second countersubject, a diatonic $\smash{^6_5}$–$\smash{^4_2}$ sequence in sevenths. This is followed by a return of the diatonic third's ascending basic voice leading, embedded in a highly chromatic sequence, with the voices outlining exactly the same notes that featured in the earlier ascending-fifth episode. (Compare the reduction of episode 3 in Figure 7.7.12 to that of episode 1 in Figure 7.7.11.) Like that earlier passage, the music ascends by fifths from A to F♯, once again moving from major to relative minor. Discounting the recapitulatory third section, this is the last ascending-fifth sequence in the piece: having dominated the first half of the fugue, its nonstandard logic gives way to descending-fifth convention.

The rest of the piece has some wonderful moments: a joyous cascade with outer voices in a lightly disguised canon (episode 4 on Figure 7.7.14); a brief ascending-fourth sequence based on the first two measures of the theme, creating the false impression of stretto (entry 8 on the same figure); and a final descending-fifth episode in which the bass loops the end of the subject under a florid upper-voice countermelody, with the outer voices decorating the diatonic third's descending basic voice leading (episode 5). With the return to the tonic, the fugue settles into a recapitulation. The expressive effect is somewhat unclear, the recapitulation functioning neither as a triumphant return nor a counterweight to any lengthy tonal excursion;

354   TONALITY: AN OWNER'S MANUAL

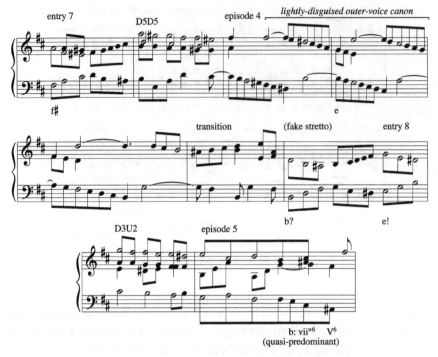

Figure 7.7.14. An outline of the second half of the middle section of the fugue.

instead, it is a slight tweaking of the degree-of-sameness in a relatively homogeneous piece. The final close is perfunctory, the subject shrinking to its first four notes and appearing in the lower voices before the entire *Well-Tempered Clavier* careens to a halt on an unexpected Picardy third.

*　*　*

If it is true that J. S. Bach's music is often governed by a dualistic contrast between ascending and descending fifths, then what consequences follow? A blunt answer is that for all its accuracy, Roman-numeral thinking is often *boring*, insensitive to the contrapuntal structures that give direction to its atomic and independent harmonic cycles. Rather than mere conventions, these contrapuntal structures reflect a preexisting musical geometry; thus, though they may sometimes appear in historical sources or partimento manuscripts, they can also be rediscovered independently by musicians as they learn their way around the keyboard. This independent rediscovery is part of the process of developing a distinctive compositional voice.

A sense for this contrapuntal logic is a prerequisite for enlightening analytical reduction. Consider the opening of Petzold's Minuet in G, not composed by Bach but evidently valued by him. Every Schenkerian analysis I know treats the opening melody as embellishing a neighboring $\hat{5}$–$\hat{6}$–$\hat{5}$ progression, the E–F♯–G ascent a superficial prolongation of the primary E (Figure 7.7.15).[63] The assumption seems

---

[63] See for example Proctor 2004 or Schachter 2016.

Figure 7.7.15. Carl Schachter's reading of the opening of Petzold's Minuet in G.

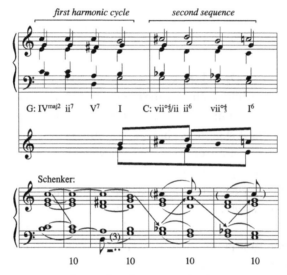

Figure 7.7.16. A sequence of ascending basic voice leadings in mm. 8–15 of *The Well-Tempered Clavier*'s first prelude, along with Schenker's reading.

to be that the subdominant's third has a tendency to *descend*, acting as a neighbor to $\hat{5}$. The preceding analyses suggest that the progression is instead an expressively marked illustration of C. P. E. Bach's *ascending* tendency. On this hearing, the tonic and stable G–A–B–C–D is answered by a more active ascending-subdominant C–D–E–F♯–G, the C–B bass and E–F♯–G melody creating a subdominant-dominant hybrid. Habits formed by Haydn and Mozart will not help us hear this music, nor adjudicate among our interpretive options. Nor will it do to retreat to subjectivity, declaring analysis the record of our own responses to decontextualized notes: for interpretation should be cognizant of a composer's vocabulary—or at a minimum, not conducted in ignorance thereof.

A similar point could be made about Figure 7.7.16, which at first glance seems to juxtapose two unrelated syntactical units, IV$^{maj2}$–ii$^7$–V$^7$–I in the dominant and a descending-step sequence that returns to the tonic. To a traditional theorist, the progression from V to vii°$^4_3$/ii is an inessential juncture, a pair of words belonging to different sentences. To a Schenkerian, the local progressions and modulations are superficial, generated by a deeper linear process in which the tenth (C4, E5) descends by step through the octave to (C3, E4). Those who have been sensitized to the diatonic third's basic voice leading, however, may notice the descending-step dyadic

356    TONALITY: AN OWNER'S MANUAL

Figure 7.7.17. Measures 9–14 of the prelude to the G major cello suite, BWV 1007.

sequence (G, B) → (F, D) and (F, A) → (E, C): this gives higher-order direction to the harmonic cycles while continuing the modulatory journey up the ladder of fifths (C major→G major→D minor→ . . .). Bach embeds the dyadic sequence in a series of nonsequential triads, superimposing the first-unit (F, D) with the second-unit (F, A), so that (G, B) is root-third of a G major triad while (F, A) is third-fifth of D minor (c.f. Figure P4.3). This dyadic logic joins two Roman-numeral cycles and cuts across the parallel tenths of Schenker's analysis. The compositional thinking here is recognizably similar to that which produced the four-voice Chase schema in "Ach, lieben Christen, seid getrost," or the ascending-fifth sequences of the B minor fugue; indeed, virtually the same progression occurs in the G major cello suite, extending the ascending fifths past the supertonic to the relative minor (Figure 7.1.17).[64]

Should the ubiquity of these schemas lead us to postulate corresponding structures in the minds of listeners, as Meyer, Gjerdingen, and Byros have suggested? Here I think we should be cautious. It is plausible that an experienced listener might judge the bottom staff of Figure 7.7.1 to "sound like Bach"—just as enculturated audiences might say that a I–♭III–♭VII–IV–I progression "sounds like rock." But there is a huge leap from this kind of tacit recognition to an *explicit* awareness of schemas as specific items of musical vocabulary: "oh, that is an ascending subdominant pattern, oh, now we are hearing an ascending-fifth sequence, oh, here's a Prinner." Anyone who has taught ear training will know just how rare such awareness is, even among talented musicians with substantial education. For this reason, I suspect that the transmission of schemas occurs predominantly from composer to composer, through explicit instruction, implicit learning, and score study—augmented by a substantial helping of independent rediscovery. Readers who are familiar with Bach might ask themselves how much they thought about the diatonic third's ascending basic voice leading prior to this book. If the answer is "not at all," then music is not a straightforward transmission of information from composer to listener; rather, it is a more complex mixture of implicit and explicit.

---

[64] Note that Figure 7.7.11 contains the same pattern we have been considering, (E, G♯)→ (D, B) and (D, F♯)→ (C♯, A), with (D, B) and (D, F♯) superimposed.

# Prelude
## Chromatic or Diatonic?

A famous passage from the second movement of Beethoven's Ninth Symphony arranges eighteen descending-third progressions into four-chord groups (Figure P8.1). The result is an intriguing mixture of diatonic and chromatic, never establishing a clear tonic and wandering through tonal space—yet spelling out a long series of fifth-related diatonic scales. My analysis postulates a nested pair of repeating contrapuntal patterns, triads moving inside diatonic scales that are themselves moving. This hierarchical analysis helps simplify the description of the melody: if we conceive the passage chromatically, we have to say that major and minor triads move differently, the fifth of every minor triad ascending by semitone, and the fifth of every major triad ascending by two semitones; if we postulate diatonic scales we can instead say that the fifth of every triad ascends by *scale step* to become the root of the next.[1] Sometimes this scale step is a minor second, sometimes it is a major second, but from a diatonic perspective it is always one step. It goes without saying that a very large amount of music is structured in exactly this way; my analysis simply assumes that Beethoven's passage exhibits the same sort of hierarchy found throughout his work.

In this case, the diatonic scale's notes are *themselves* descending sequentially so as to create a series of descending-fifth modulations. When the A4 in m. 2 moves to B♭ rather than B♮, it reveals that an abstract object, a scale step or melodic slot, has moved down by semitone from B to B♭. Because of these shifts, the chordal pattern never reaches the diminished triad and the music does not arrive at a clear dominant, though to my ear it still has a distinctly diatonic cast. These scalar progressions are somewhat more goal directed than the triadic progressions: the chords move down by third from C major to A major (spelled B♭♭), making a right-angle turn to $V^7$ of E minor, while the keys move by fifth from C down to E where the music remains.

We can use our spiral diagrams to represent the motion of scales within the twelve-tone chromatic collection (Figure P8.2). The recipe in §2.1 allows us to calculate the descending basic voice leading: sliding downward from C to F gives us $T_{-7}$, revisiting our initial angular position four times for $t_4$. The resulting voice

---

[1] This is exactly the same reasoning that allows us to analyze "doe, a deer" as a single diatonic pattern moving up by scale step (Figure P2.1).

*Tonality.* Dmitri Tymoczko, Oxford University Press. © Oxford University Press 2023. DOI: 10.1093/oso/9780197577103.003.0014

358  TONALITY: AN OWNER'S MANUAL

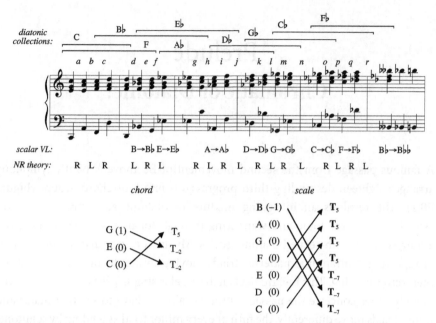

**Figure P8.1.** Measures 143–176 of the scherzo of Beethoven's Ninth Symphony, along with the composite diatonic collections. Below the music I show the repeating contrapuntal patterns at the level of both chord and scale. "T" represents diatonic transposition while T represents chromatic transposition. I also include a neo-Riemannian analysis.

leading, $T_{-7}t_4$ or $T_5 t_{-3}$, lowers the leading tone semitonally while keeping every other note fixed. It follows that Beethoven's passage uses two hierarchically nested basic voice leadings: the *chordal* voice leading takes a clockwise step in its spiral diagram, connecting third-related triads by an ascending diatonic step; the *scalar* voice leading moves counterclockwise in its diagram, connecting fifth-related scales by a descending chromatic step (Figure P8.3). These are hierarchically self-similar transformations occurring on two different structural levels.[2]

My account contrasts with one of the foundational analyses of neo-Riemannian theory, which models the passage with two chromatic voice leadings: the "R transform," which either raises the fifth of a major triad by two chromatic semitones, or lowers the root of a minor triad by the same amount; and the "L transform," which either raises the fifth of a minor triad by semitone or lowers the root of a major triad by semitone.[3] Thus where I identify two hierarchically nested transformations, the neo-Riemannian analysis has two nonhierarchical transformations in alternation, operating directly on chromatic triads and unmediated by the diatonic collection. Neither of these is correct as a matter of simple fact. The advantages of my

---

[2] These nested diagrams recall Figure 3.7.4 but represent different musical levels: where the earlier figure depicted *dyads* moving inside scale-like *triads*, our new diagram represents chord-like *triads* inside seven-note *scales*.

[3] See Cohn 1997 for the analysis and appendix 3 for the neo-Riemannian transformations.

PRELUDE: CHROMATIC OR DIATONIC? 359

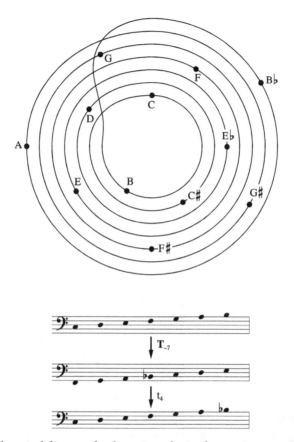

**Figure P8.2.** The spiral diagram for diatonic scales in chromatic space. Sliding clockwise along the spiral from C to F passes seven points for $T_{-7}$ while passing twelve o'clock four times for $t_4$. The combination $T_{-7}t_4$ shifts B to B♭ while keeping all other melodic slots fixed; this is the basic voice leading.

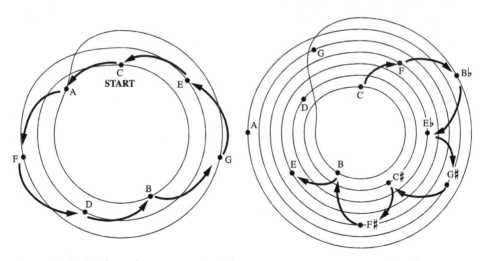

**Figure P8.3.** Beethoven's passage takes eighteen counterclockwise steps along the triadic spiral and eight clockwise steps along the spiral of diatonic scales.

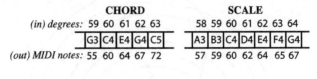
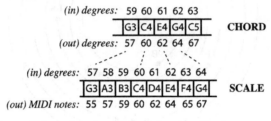

Figure P8.4. Flat and hierarchical models of chord and scale.

interpretation are, first, that it describes Beethoven's sequence using standard harmonic procedures, second, that it offers a unified explanation of the triadic voice leadings, with each triad's fifth moving up by scale step, and third that it generalizes easily to any chord in any scale. The advantage of the neo-Riemannian analysis is that it connects Beethoven's procedures to nineteenth-century chromaticism. The two analyses thus highlight Beethoven's position at the fulcrum between classical and Romantic eras.

From this perspective, scale degrees and pitch classes are fundamentally analogous. Before writing this book, I thought of them as ontologically different, scale degrees labeling movable positions in a collection while pitch classes labeled notes. This conception went along with a relatively flat view of musical hierarchy, in which scales of various sizes sat side-by-side, each mapping their own scale degrees directly to pitch classes (Figure P8.4). Surface voices, on this picture, move within scales, coming together to form chords as byproducts. Having written this book, I have come to believe that musical objects can participate in more complex hierarchies, with *any* collection's output available to serve as the input of the next. This gives us a unified perspective on phenomena from modulation to subchordal voice leading (e.g., the diatonic third's basic voice leading, or the contrary-motion patterns in Figures 4.7.1–3). This idea sounds simple when written on the page but is extremely difficult to implement at the speed of music, whether in improvisation or at the slower pace of notation—and all the more so when one is exploring unfamiliar collections. Music theory can help musicians internalize this abstract perspective, explaining how to replace specific idioms with more general techniques applying to all levels of the collectional hierarchy.

# 8

# Modulation

This chapter uses the spiral diagrams to model scales and modulation. We begin with some conceptual issues surrounding key changes, including the notion of "modulatory distance" and the meaning of enharmonic spelling in a fixed chromatic universe. We then construct a circular model of key relations, using it to describe several common modulatory schemas. This leads to a reconsideration of the seventeenth-century process of modal homogenization, by which other modes take on the characteristics of ionian. Finally, we survey some features of scalar thinking in the twentieth and twenty-first centuries. In many ways, the conceptual work has already been done; the task is simply to apply familiar techniques to new musical problems.

## 1. Two models of key distance

What does it mean for two modes to be "close"? One answer focuses on modulations that minimize the motion of *scale degrees*, reducing the overall sum of distances as measured from tonic to tonic, supertonic to supertonic, and so on. From this point of view C major and G major are not close, since their scale degrees are almost half an octave apart; instead, the most proximate keys are the parallel major and minor—as well as semitonally related keys such as C and D♭ major (Figure 8.1.1). This notion of key distance is most relevant when instruments do the same thing before and after the modulation: one singer, for example, singing the same melody in both old key and new. (If you can sing a tune in C major, you can probably sing it in D♭ major whereas G major may be out of your range.) It underlies modulatory practices such as "sidestepping" or "pumping-up," familiar in jazz and popular music but sometimes found in classical music as well.[1]

A second answer focuses on modulations that minimize the motion of *pitch classes* irrespective of their scale-degree roles. Here the nearest major keys are related by fifth, while the nearest major/minor pairs are in the "relative" relationship (Figure 8.1.2). This notion of key distance is implicit in classical modulatory norms,

---

[1] Lewin 1984 and McCreless 1996; two familiar examples are the end of the scherzo of Beethoven's *Hammerklavier* Op. 106 and Miles Davis's "So What."

*Tonality.* Dmitri Tymoczko, Oxford University Press. © Oxford University Press 2023. DOI: 10.1093/oso/9780197577103.003.0015

**Figure 8.1.1.** Scale-degree preserving mappings from C major to C minor and D♭ major. The open notehead is the tonic.

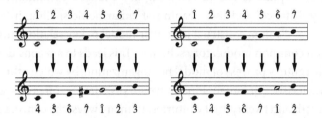

**Figure 8.1.2.** Scale-degree changing voice leadings from C major to G major and A minor.

and most useful when different material is presented in the two keys—for example in the first and second themes of a textbook sonata—or when composers have a wide variety of instruments at their disposal. For in this case no problems arise from the nearly half-octave scale-degree shift. This second approach links "key distance" and pitch-class content, with nearby keys sharing a large number of common tones; the earlier conception leads to a definition of "key distance" in which nearby keys need not share many notes at all.

Underlying both is the idea that scales can be modeled as collections of musical voices, circularly ordered by pitch class and able to change both pitch class and scale-degree role (§1.2, Figure 8.1.3).[2] The two approaches emphasize different kinds of motion on the spiral diagrams. For modally matched keys, the scale-degree-preserving voice leadings are *slides* along the spiral; for mode-changing modulations, we combine these slides with the parallel modulation connecting keys sharing a tonic. What results is a model in which abstract voices never change scale-degree roles (Figure 8.1.4).

The second notion of key distance permits voice leadings that do change roles—represented by *loops* on the spiral diagram. For major keys, distance is given by iterations of the diatonic scale's basic voice leading, which either lowers the leading tone (clockwise) or raises the fourth scale degree (counterclockwise). The nearest

---

[2] These pairings are the primary theoretical objects studied in Brinkman 1986, Agmon 1989, and Rings 2011. These earlier theorists do not associate them with abstract musical voices as I do here; for Agmon they are formal mathematical objects, and for Rings they are subjective perceptions.

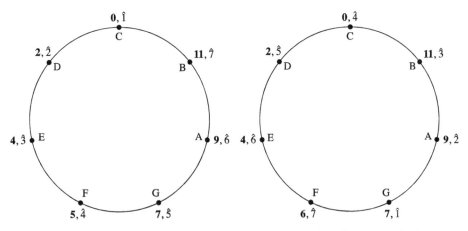

**Figure 8.1.3.** Each abstract voice is associated with a pitch class (bold), a scale degree, and a letter name. The two circles represent C major (left) and G major (right).

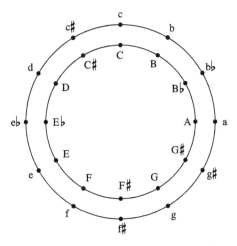

**Figure 8.1.4.** A model of key distance based on the motion of scale degrees.

major/minor pairs are now linked by the *relative* relationship. The diagram in Figure 8.1.5 dates back to the eighteenth-century work of Heinichen and Kellner; indeed, Heinichen's "Musicalische Circul" is one of the earliest geometrical representations of musical structure, antedating the Tonnetz by almost a decade (Figure 8.1.6).

To get a feel for this second approach, it is useful to play the scales at the piano with a fixed fingering; different scalar voice leadings will correspond to different ways of shifting your fingers as you modulate from one key to another, with each finger tracking an abstract voice.[3] Suppose for example you play a C major scale with the fingering shown at the top of Figure 8.1.7. The simplest flatward modulation lowers the leading tone by semitone, lowering the note played by the fourth finger of the right hand, and moving the tonic from third left-hand finger to the

---

[3] Each *finger* plays a *note* that has a *scale-degree role*, corresponding to the three basic elements of the model.

364  TONALITY: AN OWNER'S MANUAL

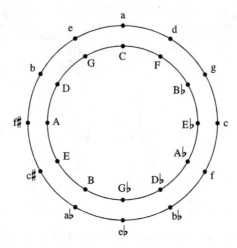

Figure 8.1.5. A model of key distance based on the motion of pitch classes.

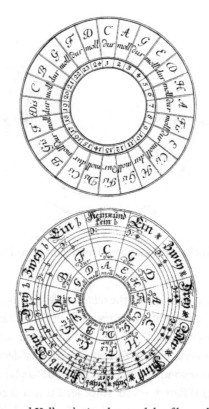

Figure 8.1.6. Heinichen and Kellner's circular models of key relations.

right-hand thumb. A series of five such modulations sends the tonic of the first key to the leading tone of the last, but a series of seven *sharpward* modulations maps the tonic of C major to the tonic of C♯ major. In both cases, the fingers embody the melodic slots, taking on new scale-degree roles as you modulate. The size of the modulation corresponds to the total distance moved by all fingers.

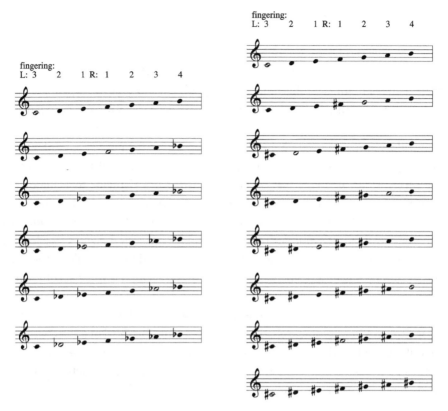

**Figure 8.1.7.** Two paths between the same points on the scale circle. (a) The 150° (five pie-slice) clockwise path from C major to D♭ major. (b) The 210° (seven pie-slice) counterclockwise path from C major to C♯ major. The first maps the tonic to the leading tone; the second tonic to tonic.

Two warnings. First, there is an inherent ambiguity in identifying scalar voice leadings, as any change of scale can be nullified by an equal-and-opposite change in the surface motion of the voices (appendix 1); the best we can say is "*if* scales move like *this*, then surface voices move like *that*"—or perhaps, "this choice of scalar voice leadings rationalizes the logic of the surface voices better than the alternatives." Second, while abstract voices often trace specific paths through pitch-class space, scale degrees typically do not. Consider a modulation from tonic to dominant: at the level of pitch classes, it is easy to see why we might want to say "the fourth scale degree has been raised by semitone to become the leading tone of the new scale" (cf. Figure 1.2.5). By contrast, it is unclear whether the "tonic role" has moved down by fourth or up by fifth—indeed, that can seem to be a fundamentally misguided question. Changes in scale degree do not imply determinate trajectories through musical space: instead, pitch classes simply take on new scale-degree roles without occupying any intermediate points, tonicity passing directly from one note to another.

## 2. Enharmonicism and loops in scale space

Consider a series of modulations, modeling scale degrees on the piano as just described. Start with C diatonic and lower the second, third, sixth, and seventh scale degrees to form A♭ diatonic; then repeat that modulation again, lowering the new second, third, sixth, and seventh scale degrees to form E (F♭) diatonic; then repeat the procedure one more time to return to the white notes (D♭♭). You will find that your left-hand third finger, which formerly played the tonic, is now playing the leading tone (Figure 8.2.1). Contrast that modulation with the series of key changes that ascends by fifth from C major to E major and then returns to the white notes as above, by lowering the second, third, sixth, and seventh scale degrees. Here each finger ends up back on its initial note. We can say that the first sequence of modulations forms a *nontrivial* voice leading from the C diatonic scale to itself, moving each voice downward along the scale; the second produces a trivial voice leading that leaves each voice exactly where it began.

All of which is very clear on the spiral diagram in Figure 8.2.2. The first sequence moves in a complete clockwise circle, taking one third of a turn with each modulation, while the second takes four counterclockwise steps before moving four steps clockwise; the different outcomes thus reflect the geometrical fact that loops represent transpositions along the chord. Here, however, the "chord" is

Figure 8.2.1. Two modulatory sequences; solid arrows are descending major-third modulations that lower the second, third, sixth, and seventh scale degrees; dashed arrows raise the fourth scale degree.

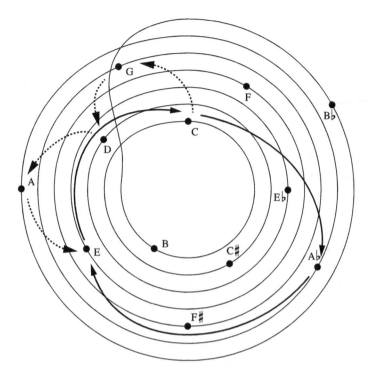

**Figure 8.2.2.** The two modulatory sequences from Figure 8.2.1 graphed in 7-in-12 space.

what we would usually call a "scale," a seven-note diatonic collection embedded within the twelve-note chromatic aggregate. Other than that, there is nothing unusual going on: if a series of modulations makes a complete loop surrounding the center of scale space, then it will change the scale-degree function of the abstract voices (here represented by our seven fingers); if the modulations do not make such a circle, then the abstract voices will return to their original scale-degree functions. The spiral diagram allows us to see this as a specific manifestation of a more general phenomenon that applies to both chords and scales. Enharmonic equivalence is produced by loops in scale space, just as chordal inversion is produced by loops in chord space. Indeed, enharmonicism just *is* chordal inversion at the scalar level.[4]

What is confusing is that notation normally *but not always* tracks the underlying scalar voice leading, with the seven letter names A–G corresponding to the seven abstract voices or melodic slots. Thus when we lower the white-note scale's leading tone we add a flat to B, indicating that melodic slot B has moved down by semitone. Each one-step clockwise motion on the circle adds a flat or subtracts a sharp;

---

[4] Yust 2018 pursues similar considerations using different mathematics; Tymoczko and Yust 2019 detail the close connections between voice-leading spaces and Yust's Fourier models.

counterclockwise moves add a sharp or subtract a flat. If we rigorously follow this rule, then nontrivial modulatory sequences will connect different spellings of the same scale: the modulations on the left of Figure 8.2.1 produce C major, A♭ major, F♭ major, and D♭♭ major. The spelling does not indicate the presence of two distinct harmonic objects, for in a fixed chromatic universe, C major and D♭♭ major are one and the same—acoustically, conceptually, and in every other sense. Rather, the spelling indicates the presence of a *nontrivial path*, a loop in voice-leading space that changes the voices' scale-degree roles: in C major, the C slot (or "voice" or finger) has tonic function, while in D♭♭ major, the D slot is tonic.[5] The modulatory sequence on the right of Figure 8.2.1 adds four sharps and then subtracts them, sending C major to C major, with the identity of the spelling reflecting the triviality of the associated voice leading. This is conceptually the same phenomenon we encountered in Figure 1.2.2, where a series of background voice leadings made a complete loop in chord space, so that a single pitch acquired a new scale-degree label; in both cases, surface voices need to move in order to remain in the same place.

However, there are also *merely notational* enharmonic changes that do not correspond to any scalar voice leading. In Gottschalk's *Le Mancenillier* (Op. 11, Figure 8.2.3), the music shifts from G♯ minor to the parallel major (spelled as A♭) and then down by fifth to C♯ minor; this entire passage then repeats down by fourth, passing through D♯ major (spelled as E♭) before returning to the initial G♯ minor. The underlying scale-degree logic is not at all puzzling, and would be unremarkable if transposed into C minor or D minor. In C♯ minor, however, Gottschalk's sequence takes him through G♯ and D♯ major, both requiring double sharps. His flat-side respelling of these keys is merely notational in the sense that it does not record any genuine pitch-class voice leading: if we were listening to the piece, or watching a pianist depress keys in slow motion, we would have no way of knowing that the respelling had occurred. Similarly, if we were to model its scalar voice leadings with our fingers there would be no difference between playing G♯ major and A♭ major; the switch from sharps to flats has no observable consequence. By contrast, genuine enharmonicism involves an observable change in the melodic slots' scale-degree roles.

The contrapuntal significance of enharmonicism has been obscured by its historical connection to issues of tuning and temperament. Absent a fixed chromatic background, a sequence of twelve fifths will take us close, but not exactly back, to our starting point—in a Pythagorean framework, for instance, C major and D♭♭ major differ by about a quarter of a semitone. (Geometrically we could represent this as in Figure 8.2.4, with B♯ major slightly to the left of C major, and A♯♯♯ major to the left of that: fifth-related diatonic collections are found approximately 34.4° around the circle rather than 30°, so that a sequence of fifth modulations never returns to

---

[5] In isolation we cannot distinguish between C major and D♭♭ major. But we can distinguish a modulation taking C major to C major from one taking C major to D♭♭ major. We could of course rewrite these as modulating from D♭♭ major to D♭♭ major and from D♭♭ major to E♭♭♭♭ major, respectively.

MODULATION 369

**Figure 8.2.3.** Scalar voice leadings in Gottschalk's *Le Mancenillier*, Op. 11. The flat-side respellings are merely notational and do not represent scalar voice leading.

C major.) These are genuinely different scales. When we work in a universe with twelve fixed chromatic pitch classes enharmonic spelling acquires a new meaning: instead of signifying a difference in musical identity it signifies the presence of a *nontrivial route* from a chord to itself. And this is true whether we are using equal or unequal temperament.

The habit of thinking of enharmonic spelling as representing different locations, rather than different paths between the same musical location, persisted long after it was obviated by the advent of a fixed chromatic universe. For example, both David Lewin and Richard Cohn have noted that it is impossible to notate the progression in Figure 8.2.5 such that (a) each voice leading is written in analogously (for instance as a major-third progression rather than diminished fourth); and (b) the final chord is spelled the same way as the first. From this Cohn draws the conclusion that "classical methods of analysis" and "diatonically based models" are inadequate.[6] Cohn

---

[6] The words here come from Cohn 1996 and echo the sentiment in Lewin 1984, a very challenging and obscure paper; Cohn 2012, pp. 2–3, reiterates the view. Waltham-Smith 2018 also seems to endorse a similar perspective. Klumpenhouwer 2011 argues that we can avoid any sense of paradox if we simply label keys chromatically.

370 TONALITY: AN OWNER'S MANUAL

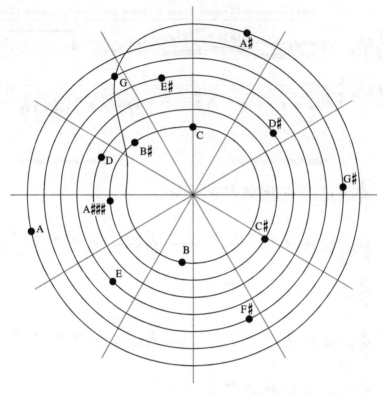

**Figure 8.2.4.** A Pythagorean space places B♯ and C major at distinct spatial locations.

**Figure 8.2.5.** (*left*) A progression dividing the octave equally, which is awkward to spell; (*right*) a two-leveled repeating contrapuntal pattern involving a three-note chord (stemmed) inside a seven-note scale.

MODULATION    371

is correct that these sorts of modulations exploit chromatic voice leading—and specifically the proximity of C major and E major in 3-in-12 space (Figure 2.1.3). But it does not follow that we need to abandon the very idea that chords can be embedded inside diatonic collections, nor the hierarchical organization characteristic of so much Western music. That might be true if one believed that diatonicism and classical analysis *necessarily presuppose* something like a Pythagorean picture of scales floating freely in a continuous and unquantized chromatic universe. But in a fixed chromatic universe it is entirely possible to repeat the two-tiered voice-leading schema on the right of Figure 8.2.5, operating with chord and scale simultaneously: all we have to do is apply one voice-leading schema at the level of the chord and another at the level of the scale. What is new in these progressions is that chords take the lead, moving by efficient chromatic voice leading and pulling scales alongside them.[7]

Indeed, the spiral diagrams show us exactly when a repeating contrapuntal pattern can return each voice to its starting pitch: this will be possible only when it moves purely radially, and hence can occur only when the relevant circular space has *multiple chords at the same angular position*. For if the repeating contrapuntal pattern takes a nonzero number of angular steps, then further repetitions will always increase the total quantity of angular motion. (It cannot change direction, since §4.2 showed that a repeating contrapuntal pattern corresponds to a pattern of geometrical motion in a spiral diagram.) The space of chromatic triads contains three chords at each filled radial position, allowing us to find repeating voice-leading schemas that return each voice to its starting point (§2.1). The existence of this pattern is a simple consequence of the fact that 3, the size of the triad, divides 12, the size of the chromatic scale. By contrast, any repeated modulatory move, when embodied by the pianist's hands, will necessarily return to its starting scale in a new registral position. For exactly the same reason, there can be no diatonic voice-leading schema connecting distinct triads that, when iterated, returns each voice to its starting pitch.

### 3. Minor keys

So far we have constructed two models of key distance, one emphasizing the proximity of parallel major and minor, the other emphasizing the proximity of relative major and minor. Since both relationships are important, it would be nice to be able to model them simultaneously. This led the eighteenth-century theorist F. G. Vial to propose the structure in Figure 8.3.1; one of its diagonal axes corresponds to motion along the circle of fifths while the other alternates between parallel and relative

---

[7] As a keyboardist, J. S. Bach daily confronted an instrument in which the diatonic scale is a subset of the twelve chromatic notes, and indeed celebrated this embedding in his most famous composition. Were E♭ minor and D♯ minor different places then there would be little sense in the E♭ minor/D♯ minor prelude-and-fugue pair in Book I of *The Well-Tempered Clavier*.

372  TONALITY: AN OWNER'S MANUAL

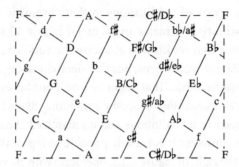

**Figure 8.3.1.** F. G. Vial's model of major and minor keys. The NE/SW diagonal represents motion between fifth-related keys; the NW/SE diagonal alternates between relative and parallel modulations.

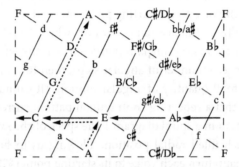

**Figure 8.3.2.** The two progressions in Figure 8.2.1 look abstractly similar in Vial's space but produce very different effects: the solid path moves every abstract voice down one scale degree while the dashed path returns each voice to its starting position. This difference is not apparent in Vial's geometry.

modulations. Vial's graph is an accurate model of functional practice—which is to say, it represents the most common modulations as short-distance geometrical paths. But it obscures the circular geometry of enharmonic equivalence: after all, the two paths in Figure 8.3.2 look similar, but only one returns its scale degrees to their initial position. The model gives us no insight into the unified logic governing both chord and scale.

For this reason, I favor an alternative that more closely resembles the spiral diagrams. Figure 8.3.3 derives this model in three stages. The first superimposes the circular spaces for the diatonic, acoustic (i.e., melodic-minor ascending), and harmonic minor scales, using dotted lines to connect the collections belonging to G and D minor; as in Figure 3.3.9, I represent each spiral with a single circle whose arcs apply the basic voice leading. The top-right circle improves on the model by duplicating the diatonic collection and rearranging the scales' radial positions: now the circular arcs represent shifts between a single key's scale-forms rather than applications of a basic voice leading. The lowest graph reflects this same

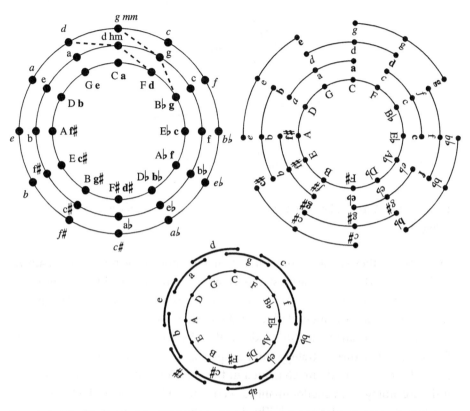

**Figure 8.3.3.** Three models of key space. Top left: the superimposed diagrams for the diatonic, harmonic minor, and melodic minor collections, moving outward. Top right: a version that rearranges each scale's radial positions while separating major and natural minor. In both of these graphs, boldface type indicates natural minor, regular type is harmonic minor, and italic is melodic minor. Bottom: a more compact diagram that does not distinguish the three specific minor-scale forms.

information more compactly, no longer distinguishing the minor scale-forms. In all three models, *spatial extension* allows minor keys to provide shortcuts between otherwise-distant keys. This nonlocality arises not from deep features of musical geometry but rather the convention of treating distinct scales as *syntactically* equivalent, with changes between minor scale-forms not counting as modulations even though they move through scale space.

These models reconcile circular voice-leading logic with the insight that parallel and relative keys are both closely related. Because A minor is spatially extended, it can be close to C major, G major, D major, and A major. The first and last are the relative and parallel relationships. The proximity to G major reflects the single-semitone voice leading that turns a G major tonic into an A melodic-minor leading tone.[8] And though modulations from D major to A minor are uncommon in D

---

[8] Nowadays we tend to think that Kellner's model puts the minor keys in the correct position, but Heinichen's model, which highlights the proximity of G major and A minor, has some benefits.

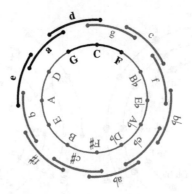

**Figure 8.3.4.** Circular key space, with key areas darkened to reflect proximity to C major.

major pieces, they are quite common in G major: indeed, the modulatory pathway I–V–ii (G–D–a) is one of the most important in functional tonality. Thus the model is reasonably accurate analytically, even though it is a two-dimensional simplification of a vastly more complicated seven-dimensional space.[9]

It is useful to augment this model with information about the global tonic. Figure 8.3.4 borrows a strategy from chapter 2, using darker colors to represent keys whose tonic triads are contained in the C major scale; these form a stack of fifths ascending from subdominant to mediant, F–C–G–d–a–e, all clustered in a single region of circular space.[10] This in turn shows that enharmonicism requires chromaticism: because modulation typically uses efficient scalar voice leadings, there is no obvious sharpward path from iii (the sharpest of the diatonic keys) to IV (the flattest). Hence a sequence of diatonic modulations will tend to cancel out, adding and subtracting the same small collection of sharps and flats, and not requiring enharmonic respelling. This means that composers who understand key areas diatonically—limiting themselves to the triads contained in a single diatonic scale—will not travel in complete circles through key space. It is only once key areas are conceived chromatically, allowing for sharpward motion from mediant to subdominant, that enharmonicism becomes commonplace. This is what I take to be the truth behind Lewin and Cohn's claim that such modulatory sequences force us to abandon "diatonically based models": not that we need to abandon the basic picture of chords inside scales, but rather that we need to consider modulatory destinations in chromatic space, rather than limiting ourselves to keys whose tonics inhabit a single diatonic collection.

With this model in hand, we see that the coordinated motion of Beethoven's Ninth, rather than being unusual, is in fact necessary for modulatory sequences to generate repeating patterns of Roman numerals. Consider Chopin's D major

---

[9] These models are consistent with, but more intuitive than, the three-dimensional lattice used in §7.4 of Tymoczko 2011a. Some readers may prefer even simpler concentric models like Figure 8.1.5, which is fine so long as one remembers that minor keys are "smeared."

[10] Compare Agmon 2013, building on observations made by the eighteenth-century musician Joseph Riepel.

**Figure 8.3.5.** Chopin's D major prelude.

prelude: here, the sequential units articulate I–IV–V–[vi or I]–V/V–V progressions that ascend by fifth along the D major scale, from D major to A major, E minor, B minor, and the dominant of B minor (Figure 8.3.5).[11] As in Beethoven's Ninth, we have coordination between levels. Beethoven's passage is exceptional because each level uses its basic voice leading, taking a single angular step in the relevant spiral diagram. Chopin's looser and more general coordination-between-levels is commonplace—indeed, essential to modulatory sequences as we know them. For if chords and keys move differently, then sequential units will move relative to the underlying scale, leading to different tonal functions and different Roman numerals.

Chopin's prelude ascends the ladder of fifths to F♯ major, the point of maximal distance from the tonic, before sliding chromatically to A[7] and returning to the opening; the repeat is largely faithful, except that the penultimate chord, vii°[7]/iii, is reinterpreted as a common-tone diminished seventh of D. These last progressions illustrate the difference between *chordal* and *scalar* approaches to modulation: the initial key changes exploit scalar proximity, moving by fifth between closely related key areas for a very smooth modulatory effect; by contrast, the phrases end with modulations that exploit the voice-leading properties of *chords themselves*—at the end of the first phrase the root of the F♯ minor chord moves semitonally to form the G–A–C♯ subset of A[7], while at the end of the second phrase the vii°[7]/iii resolves chromatically to I. Here it is the chordal subsets that are close: F♯–A–C♯ to G–A–C♯, and E♯–G♯–B–D to F♯–A–A–D. In *A Geometry of Music*, I distinguished "scale-first" from "chord-first" modulations in twentieth-century music; Chopin's prelude exploits the same mechanisms in a more traditional style.

---

[11] Note the IV–V[7]–I harmonization of the ascending basic voice leading for diatonic thirds (§3.1).

# 4. Modulatory schemas

As functional tonality develops, its syntax starts to encompass larger and larger stretches of musical time. In the Renaissance, chords and tonal centers progress relatively unsystematically, with the nonharmonic system providing a good portion of the harmonic energy: the oscillation between stability and tension, "home" and "away," is largely produced by the motion of non-chord tones to chord tones. By the late sixteenth century, chord progressions provide a higher level of motion away from home and back again. But it is only toward the middle of the seventeenth century that we start to find a grammar of modulatory destinations that is broadly analogous to its grammar of chord-to-chord successions (Figure 8.4.1). A related development, to be discussed in chapter 9, is the increasing use of regular phrase templates such as "sentence" and "period."

In their details, the grammars of chord and key are mirror images: chords tend to progress from tonic to secondary destinations to dominant, while keys move from tonic to dominant to secondary destinations. Chordal norms are more stable than the modulatory norms: from 1600 to the present we can find pieces deploying TSDT harmony in recognizably similar ways, even while patterns of modulation change: for example, classical phrases often end by tonicizing the dominant, but this modulation is rare in jazz or rock-and-roll. Modulatory norms are also form-dependent in a way that chord grammar is not: sonatas are structured as journeys from tonic to foreign keys and back, while fugues and rondos permit more frequent returns to the tonic.

Beyond these very general conventions are some more specific modulatory schemas. These typically occur in sonata-form developments, where the majority of classical-style modulations are found. One of the simplest is what I call the *helicopter drop*, a sudden and dramatic turn to a distant key, followed by a gradual return to the tonic. The first-movement development of Beethoven's *Pathétique* starts by jolting the listener from G minor to E minor, whereupon it descends by fifths back to the tonic (Figure 8.4.2).[12] The first-movement development of the

|  | first key | second key | subsequent keys | final key |
|---|---|---|---|---|
| *major:* | I | V | v, ii, vi, iii | I (often visiting IV) |
| *minor:* | i | III or v | v, III, iv, VI | i (often visiting I and iv) |

**Figure 8.4.1.** A schematic outline of standard modulations in baroque and classical music.

[12] Other examples include the first-movement developments of Beethoven's Op. 7, no. 1 (deceptive cadence to ♭VI followed by a descending-third sequence to ♭II, skipping ahead one sequential step to V), Op. 31, no. 2 (§10.3), and Op. 31, no. 3 (shift to VI followed by a descending fifth movement to IV, which immediately ascends to the ii⁶ that starts the recapitulation.

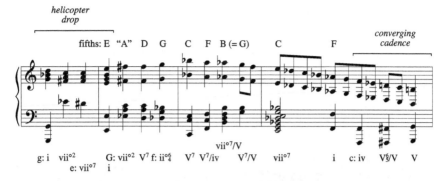

**Figure 8.4.2.** The development of Beethoven's *Pathétique* sonata, Op. 13, I. Enharmonic reinterpretation of the diminished seventh takes us to a distant E minor, from which the music descends by fifths back to a converging cadence and the tonic.

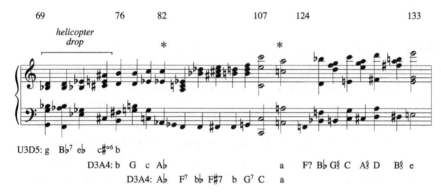

**Figure 8.4.3.** The development section of Beethoven's Op. 59, no. 2, I.

second Razumovsky quartet is similar, moving through a circle of major-third related minor triads (g–e♭–b) to arrive at a B minor that feels more distant than it actually is. The remaining seventy measures pursue a single ascending-step near sequence (Figure 8.4.3). Particularly interesting are the reinterpretations of the A and A♭ chords, marked by asterisks on the example: in both cases, sequential logic dictates that the chords should be dominants moving up by fourth; instead, they act as tonics moving down by third (§4.9). These transformations extend the long sequential climb so that it twice ascends from A to C before finally breaking free to rise to the tonic. (Note also the two enharmonic respellings, signifying two loops in scale space and a recapitulation in G𝄫 minor.) The embedding of diverse thematic material within a single modulatory sequence is characteristic of Beethoven's practice.

Another important schema is what I call a *paired-sequence design*, a balanced pair of sequences with the second largely undoing the work of the first.

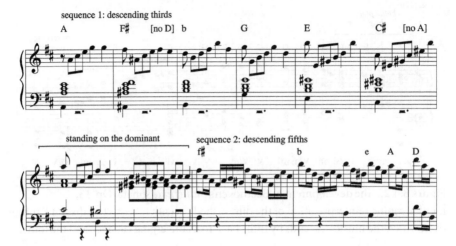

Figure 8.4.4. A paired-sequence design in the development of Haydn's Symphony no. 62, I.

The pivot is often rhetorically marked, a "point of farthest remove," where the music delays for a while—standing on the dominant, introducing a new theme, or reaching a strong cadence. The first-movement development of Haydn's Symphony no. 62 is typical, beginning with an ascending arpeggio that moves through the harmonies $A^7$–$F\sharp^7$–[D]–b–G–$E^7$–C♯ (Figure 8.4.4). This is a near sequence by descending third, the fifth-progression $F\sharp^7$–b omitting a sequential step. The point of farthest remove features an augmented sixth, a standing-on-the-dominant and a brief caesura; a descending arpeggio then takes us down the ladder of fifths, $C\sharp^7$–$F\sharp^7$–$B^7$–$E^7$–$A^7$, discharging harmonic tension as the recapitulation arrives. (Note the nice correspondence between key and motive, an ascending arpeggio for the first sequence and a descending arpeggio for the second.) Compared to the helicopter drop, the departure and return are more equal and balanced: where the former takes a large leap on circular scale space, followed by a series of short steps back, the latter involves a pair of broadly comparable motions.

The development of the first movement of Beethoven's Op. 2, no. 1, uses the same basic pattern (Figure 8.4.5). Here the initial sequence ascends by step from the relative major A♭ to B♭ minor to C minor, both modulations using the i–Ger$^6_5$/ii–V/ii progression even while deploying different themes. Instead of pausing on the antipodal point, Beethoven immediately retraces his modulatory steps: we begin in C minor, still referencing the second theme, and descend by fifths to A♭ whereupon the modulation stops while the chords continue, the music's thematic content liquidated into generic tonal material. If we imagine a pair of spiral diagrams, as in Figure P8.3, the chords continue to move along their circle while the keys stop. The introduction of E♮ brings a standing-on-the-dominant that features a characteristic contrary-motion pattern (§10.1).

MODULATION 379

**Figure 8.4.5.** A paired-sequence design in the development of Beethoven's Op. 2, no. 1, I.

## 5. Up and down the ladder

The most elaborate modulatory schema is a version of the paired-sequence design that I call the *up-and-down-the-ladder*. Originating in the baroque, this schema pairs ascending- and descending-fifth sequences: the ascending fifths increase the tension and often employ the diatonic third's ascending basic voice leading; the descending fifths release the tension and return us to equilibrium. This pattern becomes a central classical-era developmental schema, surviving into the nineteenth century as a common modulatory template.[13] The "up-then-down"

---

[13] Examples include *The Well-Tempered Clavier*'s first C♯ and D major preludes, its second C major fugue, Bach's F major two-part invention, and the opening of the G major cello suite. Romantic examples include Chopin's D major prelude, discussed earlier, and the second song of Schumann's *Dichterliebe*.

380 TONALITY: AN OWNER'S MANUAL

organization can be understood as a byproduct of the linear ordering of diatonic keys, arranged in fifths from flat to sharp (IV–I–V–ii–vi–iii). The keys at either end are not close by any definition, and composers rarely modulate directly from one to the other. Thus diatonic tonal journeys are typically bounded, requiring a there-and-back-again structure, with up-then-down (or tension-then-relaxation) being energetically preferable to down-then-up (or relaxation-then-tension).

In the classical period the schema most often appears in sonata-form developments, where it acquires a few additional characteristics:

1. An early turn to the dominant's parallel minor.
2. A two-step ascending-fifth sequence moving from v to ii to vi.
3. Continuation of the ascending fifths to a tonicization of V/vi, often utilizing the augmented sixth and sometimes preceded by an $\hat{8}$–$\hat{7}$–$\sharp\hat{6}$–$\flat\hat{6}$–$\hat{5}$ bass descent.
4. An arrival on vi, the point of farthest remove for the development as a whole; this can be either a thematic passage, a cadence, or standing on the dominant.
5. Return to the tonic key in one of several ways:
   a. a descending-fifth sequence (i.e., moving down the ladder);
   b. a quick, surprising turn to the global dominant (e.g., V/vi–vi–V⁷);
   c. direct motion from V/vi to the tonic.[14]

The ascending fifths ratchet up the tension, their sonic signature a sequence of *Sturm-und-Drang* i–V⁷/V progressions; this leads to an energetic peak that is discharged by more conventional harmonic movement. In larger pieces the schema sometimes occupies only one part of the development.

The appearance of V/vi as a point of farthest remove has sometimes been identified as a characteristic of the early eighteenth century; however, the up-and-down-the-ladder schema appears throughout classical music, particularly in the relatively simple developments of Mozart's piano sonatas.[15] Figures 8.5.1–3 provide some shorter examples from the sonatas of Haydn, Mozart, and Beethoven. The development of the first movement of K.332 is notable in that Mozart alters an expositional sequence to conform to the ascending-fifth schema—an unusual rewriting that testifies to the idiom's gravitational pull (Figure 8.5.4). Figure 8.5.5 lists a few other notable examples; we will encounter several more in chapter 10.

Though largely indigenous to development sections, the up-and-down-the-ladder can occasionally appear in transitions as well. The exposition of the first

---

[14] The nineteenth-century theorist Ernst Friedrich Richter cites Mozart's K.533, I, an "up-and-down-the-ladder," as a paradigmatic development; his analysis closely tracks my description of the schema (Richter 1852, pp. 32–34). Richter's discussion is cited in Beach 1983, which provides a Schenkerian discussion of developments that emphasize or close on V/vi. This option creates something like the opposite of the helicopter drop: a gradual journey away from the tonic followed by a quick and surprising return.

[15] See Rosen 1988. In the online supplement to this book, I summarize the developments of all of Mozart's piano sonatas.

MODULATION 381

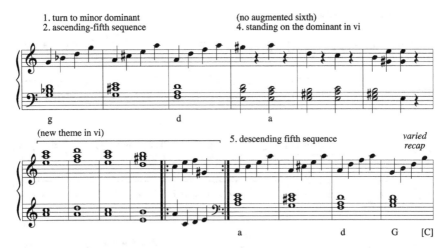

**Figure 8.5.1.** The development of the first movement of Haydn's Divertimento in C major, Hob.XVI:1.

**Figure 8.5.2.** The development of the first movement of Mozart's K.332, I.

**Figure 8.5.3.** The development of the first movement of Beethoven's Op. 49, no. 2.

**Figure 8.5.4.** In the development of K.332, I, Mozart changes a descending-fifth sequence into an ascending-fifth sequence.

movement of Beethoven's C major piano sonata Op. 2, no. 3, is in three parts (Hepokoski and Darcy's "trimodular block"): the first medial caesura leads to G minor and the music in Figure 8.5.6, modulating up the circle of fifths to D minor and A minor, before returning down the ladder (a–D–g), ending with an augmented sixth and standing on the dominant of G. It is interesting to imagine this as displaced developmental rhetoric, a familiar template that usually though not always occurs elsewhere in the form. Similar moments occur in the recapitulation of Beethoven's Op. 18, no. 2, I, and the transition of Op. 59, no. 2, I.

MODULATION 383

| Haydn | Sonata 18, I, Hob. missing (E♭ maj) |
| --- | --- |
| | Sonata 57, III, Hob. XVI/47 |
| Mozart | K.283, III |
| | K.284, I |
| | K.310, II |
| | K.311, I |
| | K.333, I |
| | K458, I ("Hunt" quartet) |
| | K.533, I |
| | K.545, I |
| | K.547a, I |
| | K.550, I, IV |
| Beethoven | Op. 10 no. 2, I, mm. 99ff (?) |
| | Op. 10 no. 2, III, mm. 47ff |
| | Op. 21, I, mm. 152ff |
| | Op. 24, I ("Spring" sonata) |
| | Op. 28, I |

Figure 8.5.5. Some other developments that use the up-and-down-the-ladder schema.

Figure 8.5.6. The middle section of the exposition of Beethoven's Op. 2, no. 3, I. Each unit of the initial sequence expands the fauxbourdon ROTO, i–v⁶–iv⁶–i⁶₄–ii°⁶ becoming i–V²/V–V⁶–V⁶₅/iv–iv⁶–i⁶₄–V⁶/V.

## 6. Modal homogenization and scalar voice leading

This theory of modulation can also help elucidate the phenomenon of modal homogenization, by which the various Renaissance modes came to take on the characteristics of ionian. This process maps ionian-mode procedures into a new domain, implying something like a voice leading between scalar collections—a "modulation," as it were, taking place over the span of decades rather than seconds. Our two notions of key distance correspond to the two ways in which this can happen: in a scale-degree-preserving transformation, the modal tonic stays fixed while other degrees change position—as when the seventh degree is raised from a modal subtonic to a functional leading tone (Figure 8.6.1). In a scale-degree-changing transformation, we have a fixed vocabulary of pitches that change meanings, centricity shifting from one note to another. This necessarily involves ambiguity during the transition, the multiplicity of interpretive possibilities reflecting a gradual change of scale-degree roles.[16]

Ambiguity about tonal centers is common in music that admits a wide variety of modes, and particularly when musical styles are changing. Satie's third "Gnossienne" is a good example, its main motto potentially either iv–i in E minor or i–v in a chromaticized A minor (Figure 8.6.2). Context suggests it is meant to be heard in A minor, though the pull of the harmonic-minor scale is strong enough to allow the more old-fashioned hearing. By contrast, when Stravinsky uses the same mode at the start of *The Firebird*'s "Infernal Dance," the tonal center is unmistakable. In much the same way, Laurie Anderson's "O Superman" can be heard in A♭ major with contrasting C minor; or in C minor with contrasting A♭. Here the ambiguity is not a product of stylistic innovation, but of the role of rhythm, phrasing, and expectation in producing popular-music centricity (§2.5).[17]

Figure 8.6.1. Scale-degree-preserving and scale-degree-changing models of modal homogenization for mixolydian. In the first, G mixolydian becomes G ionian; in the second it becomes C ionian.

---

[16] This ambiguity is facilitated by the fact that centricity in Renaissance polyphony is often fairly subtle (Powers 1958).

[17] On *Shady Grove*, Jerry Garcia and David Grisman perform the song "Wind and Rain" in a way that I hear as strongly mixolydian; Crooked Still, on *Crooked Still Live*, plays a very similar version—almost a transposition of Garcia and Grisman's—that I nevertheless hear in ionian. Brittany Haas, who played on Crooked Still's recording, told me she initially heard the piece in mixolydian even while the other musicians heard it in ionian.

**Figure 8.6.2.** Satie's third *Gnossienne* can be heard in either A minor or E minor.

| ionian | | mixolydian | | dorian | | aeolian | |
|---|---|---|---|---|---|---|---|
| I | 26 | I or i | 24 | I or i | 21 | I or i | 24 |
| V | 18 | IV | 17 | V or v | 19 | IV or iv | 15 |
| IV | 9 | V or v | 14 | IV or iv | 9 | V or v | 9 |
| vi | 8 | ii | 7 | VII | 7 | III | 8 |
| ii | 5 | VII | 6 | III | 6 | VI | 7 |
| | | | | | | VII | 6 |
| | | | | | | iv⁶ | 5 |

**Figure 8.6.3.** Common complete triads in Palestrina's masses. In ionian and dorian, V is substantially more common than IV; in mixolydian/aeolian, IV is somewhat more common than V. Modal identity was determined by computer.

Seventeenth-century modal homogenization is also bound up with a deeper shift from what I have termed absolute musical space, in which particular chords have their own tonic-independent tendencies, to the tonic-relative (or "Copernican") perspective of our own time. In Palestrina's style, for example, there are five tonal centers available in the white-note scale, C–G–d–a–(e), with the last allowing only the weaker phrygian cadence. Secondary emphasis groups these into modally matched pairs, affiliating C with G (each solmized as "ut" in their respective hexachords) and D with A (each solmized as "re"), with the E (or "mi") tonality in its own category (emphasizing A as a secondary center).[18] Signs of this affiliation can be seen in a wide variety of statistical features, including chord distributions and cadential destinations (Figures 8.6.3–4).[19] Thus we have a pair of authentic modes emphasizing the fifth as a secondary scale degree, with the remainder emphasizing the fourth.[20] In other words, the major triads on C and G tend to affiliate regardless

---

[18] These affiliations may reflect the presence of structurally similar pentachords, with the C diatonic scale containing an 02457 pentachord on C and G, and an 02357 pentachord on D and A (Judd 1992). These pairs are broadly consistent with those noted by Meier 1988 and Ceulemans 2017.

[19] In determining the mode of a mass movement, I looked at key signature, final chord, and most frequent chord. Thus my "mixolydian" pieces had no key signature with G major as the final and most frequent chord. The frequency constraint was meant to eliminate ionian pieces that happened to end on G. I also checked mode assignments by hand for plausibility.

[20] The subdominant emphasis in mixolydian is noted by Kerman (1981, pp. 69–70) and Jeppesen ([1931] 1939, pp. 81–82); the subdominant emphasis in phrygian is noted by Zarlino ([1558] 1983, chapters 20 and 30). Jeppesen (1931) 1939, pp. 59–82, is largely consistent with my own account. Meier (1988, p. 135) notes Palestrina's tendency to cadence on C even in mode 7 (mixolydian rather than hypomixolydian).

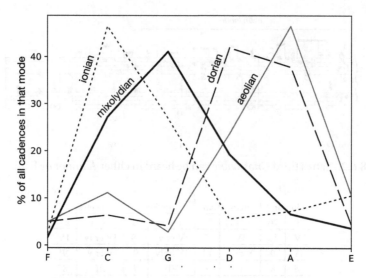

**Figure 8.6.4.** Cadential destinations in Palestrina's zero-flat modes as determined by computer. Ionian and dorian have many dominant cadences and relatively few subdominant cadences; mixolydian and aeolian have fewer dominant cadences and more subdominant cadences. Note the general scarcity of cadences on E and F.

of which is tonic: mixolydian G emphasizes C as subdominant where ionian C emphasizes G as its dominant.

By contrast, the major-minor system involves a double relativity: first, all major keys, and all minor keys, emphasize the same secondary degrees; second, the two modes are very similar to one another (e.g., both major and minor emphasize the dominant). Gioseffo Zarlino foreshadowed this more homogeneous conception when he argued that every Renaissance mode *should* emphasize the fifth and third above its tonic, a view that was less an accurate description of his contemporaries' practice than a programmatic statement about how music could be.[21] This led him to suggest that purportedly phrygian pieces had hypoaeolian elements: since a pure phrygian would emphasize the fifth above the tonic, an E mode that emphasized A necessarily had an aeolian quality.[22] Zarlino's analysis suggests that late Renaissance modality may have been ambiguous even for enculturated listeners: a listener who accepted plagal patterns of emphasis might hear E-music-that-emphasized-A as being in E, whereas a listener who demanded authentic emphasis might hear the same piece in A, even if it happened to end on E.

With these issues in mind, let us consider the modes individually.

(a) *Mixolydian*. Since it is just a single accidental away from ionian, the mixolydian mode can readily incorporate ionian routines by raising its seventh degree; but since it tends to emphasize I and IV, it can *also* adopt ionian qualities

---

[21] See Christensen 1993b, who also emphasizes Zarlino's classification in terms of the quality of the third above the root.
[22] Zarlino (1558) 1983, chapters 20 and 30.

**Figure 8.6.5.** The last phrases of the first two verses of Scheidt's 1624 "Gelobet siest du, Jesu Christ." The first-verse phrase is easily heard in C, the second is more strongly in G.

by exchanging primary and secondary tonal centers, gradually evolving from "G music that also emphasizes C" to "C music that emphasizes G."[23] These two possibilities can both be heard in the opening of Scheidt's 1624 setting of the mixolydian "Gelobet seist du, Jesu Christe" (SSWV 135, Figure 8.6.5). The end of the first verse has a strong C major quality, beginning an eighteen-measure passage with no F♯; the second verse presents series of harmonic cycles in G major. It is likely that Scheidt conceptualized the entire piece in G mixolydian; yet it contains substantial passages that are reasonably heard in C major.[24]

As a general rule, mixolydian tends to move toward ionian by way of scale-degree-preserving mappings. Marenzio's 1586 three-voice villanelle "Vorria parlare e dire" is representative: F♯ outnumbers F♮ almost 5-to-1, with the mixolydian seventh appearing only in mm. 4–5 (Figure 8.6.6). The harmonic progressions can mostly be parsed into functionally plausible cycles, though there are a few nonfunctional moments (e.g., IV–vi–V in mm. 2–3 and I–ii–I⁶ in mm. 13–14, the shift from D to A in m. 11). The most striking is the V–♭VII–V in mm. 4–6, with its staggered parallelism (reminiscent, perhaps, of pop-music power chords).[25] Here we have a mixolydian that could be described as substantially ionian, but with a strong subtonic emphasis.

---

[23] Dorian is two accidentals away (F→F♯, C→C♯), while aeolian is three. Phrygian is four semitones from ionian if we fix the tonic (i.e., raise $\hat{2}$, $\hat{3}$, $\hat{6}$, and $\hat{7}$), but only three if we allow the tonic to move (i.e., lower $\hat{1}$, $\hat{4}$, and $\hat{5}$).

[24] Bach's settings of the melody are similarly ambivalent: in BWV 91.6 (Riemenschneider 51) the opening melodic note is a tonic; whereas in BWV248.28, it is a dominant (though I hear it gradually acquiring tonicity as the chorale progresses). See Burns 1993 and 1995 for more.

[25] Einstein 1948, chapter 8, contains numerous examples of early *canzone villanesca* with extensive passages in parallel root-position triads; Einstein notes that these fifths "almost completely" disappear in Marenzio (p. 586), though one remains in Figure 8.6.6.

388 TONALITY: AN OWNER'S MANUAL

Figure 8.6.6. Marenzio's "Vorria parlare e dire" (1586).

*(b) Phrygian.* At the other end of the spectrum is phrygian, maximally distant from ionian and the only mode not permitting an authentic cadence. If we go back far enough, we can find phrygian music with a strong secondary emphasis on the fifth scale degree, just as Zarlino described. The phrygian of Hildegard of Bingen's twelfth-century "Laus Trinitati" is not entirely dissimilar from that of Stravinsky's *Symphony of Psalms*, with both emphasizing the tonic/fifth pair (Figure 8.6.7).[26] Here there is little danger of mistaking E for any sort of dominant; it is a genuine phrygian that emphasizes its first and fifth scale degrees in a way that is analogous to ionian.

By contrast, the secondary A emphasis of much phrygian-mode music, from the mid-sixteenth century on, creates an ambiguity between phrygian and hypoaeolian. Consider Johann Schein's 1627 setting of "Aus tiefer Noth," shown as Figure 8.6.8.[27] Our sense that the E has a dominant quality is partly a matter of exposure to later music, but it is also a feature of the music itself. Recall that dominants are typically constrained toward the future while tonics are constrained toward the past (§6.4). Now ask how Schein's E chords behave: of the four E major

---

[26] The need for a term (like "phrygian mode") to describe the similarities between Hildegard and Stravinsky stands as a point against Powers's suggestion that we abandon the term "mode" as a musical descriptor, replacing it instead with "tonal type." Hildegard and Stravinsky do not use the same "tonal type," but both their pieces can reasonably be said to be in phrygian.

[27] Schein's setting is likely the model for Bach's.

**Figure 8.6.7.** Hildegard of Bingen's "Laus Trinitati."

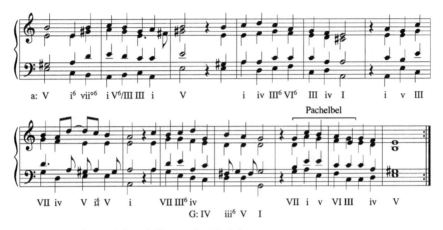

**Figure 8.6.8.** Johann Schein's "Aus tiefer Noth."

chords in the piece, all but the last proceed directly to A minor (first inversion in m. 1, root position in mm. 4 and 8). Furthermore, the E chord that starts the piece is audibly similar to the G♯°⁶ chord that occurs at the end of that measure, a seeming dominant of A. The only E minor chords are found in sequential passages, pairing with A minor as ascending-fifth units: a–e–C–G in m. 6 (perhaps suggesting tonic-dominant pairs ascending by third) and the (G)–a–e–F–C–d Pachelbel sequence in the final phrase (perhaps suggesting tonic-dominant pairs with deceptive resolutions). Meanwhile the piece's E chords are approached variously (from A minor and D minor), but never by a phrygian cadence. The A minor chord is in many ways its mirror image: typically approached by E (or g♯°⁶) but progressing in a number of different ways.

All of which suggests that even if E is being *conceived* as a tonic, it may not be *behaving* as one: like a classical dominant, these "phrygian tonics" are constrained in how they move, while the purportedly nontonic A minor chord is constrained in how it is approached. *In its statistical behavior, the phrygian tonic is evolving into a minor-key dominant* (Figure 8.6.9). In this respect, phrygian is the opposite of mixolydian, evolving toward ionian by a change of scale-degree roles.

*(c) Aeolian and dorian.* Between these two poles lie the aeolian and dorian modes, which are somewhat slow to adopt the full suite of ionian-mode conventions. As with mixolydian, the transition typically occurs in a scale-degree-preserving way, with the aeolian and dorian tonics evolving into minor-key tonics. But this process requires more extensive adjustments, and the emphasis on the secondary major triads often pulls the music away from its ostensible center.

390 TONALITY: AN OWNER'S MANUAL

**Figure 8.6.9.** Scale-degree-preserving and scale-degree-changing models of modal homogenization for phrygian.

**Figure 8.6.10.** The Introit from Schütz's *St. Matthew Passion*.

Figure 8.6.10 shows a late modal piece, the Introit from Schütz's *St. Matthew Passion* (ca. 1665). This ostensibly G-based music emphasizes major triads on C, F and B♭, all but effacing the sense of G as a genuine center. After the initial i–iv–I progression, the music tonicizes C; this initially leads me to hear C–F–B♭–F as I–IV–♭VII–IV in C mixolydian, with the C centricity eventually overwritten by the cadence on B♭. The quasi-palindromic piece then reverses direction with an ascending-fifth Chase schema rising past G to D. (As in much Renaissance music, melodic direction correlates with harmonic progression, ascending melodic steps harmonized with descending fifths, while descending melodic steps are harmonized with ascending fifths—here forming a phrasal up-and-down-the-ladder analogous to those of classical developments.) The sequence's final fifth-progression, g–d, dovetails with a descending 6–5 that is not part of the palindrome (Figure 8.6.11).[28] All in all it is a wonderfully compressed exemplar of baroque modality, elusive and

---

[28] The bass/alto canon begins in mm. 11–12 and continues across the sequential boundary. Overlapping ascending fifths and the "descending 6–5" also occur in the Kyrie of Byrd's Mass in Three Voices (§3.5).

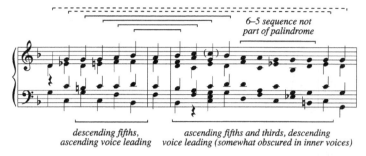

Figure 8.6.11. The palindrome hidden in Schütz's piece.

familiar, modal and harmonic, major and minor. Central to its mystery is the sense that the forces of minor-mode centricity are weak, liable to being dislodged by the scale's major triads.

This issue is subtle enough to deserve clarification. I am not arguing that aeolian or dorian music is "really" in major, or that minor-mode centricity is somehow illusory: Renaissance dorian and aeolian often place a perceptible emphasis on minor-mode primary triads—i, iv, and v and their major parallels—which are typically more prevalent than secondary triads such as III, VII, and VI. Nevertheless, secondary major triads play a more significant role than in later functional music, exerting a tonic-independent gravitational pull (Figure 8.6.12). Indeed, for many composers, the mediant triad remains the primary minor-mode harmonization of bass $\hat{3}$ until well into the seventeenth century, being displaced by i$^6$ long after I$^6$ has become a major-mode default (Figure 8.6.13); and of course, a fondness for the mediant is one of the main modal asymmetries remaining in mature functionality (§7.1). Ears accustomed to functional tonality will naturally tend to hear modal music as "emphasizing" these secondary major triads, whereas it would be more accurate to use a double negative: it *deemphasizes them less than J. S. Bach*. Our sense of the music "digressing into major" is a reflection of our having acclimated to the scarcity of secondary major triads in later music.

At the same time, there are some remarkably early examples of minor-mode functionality. Morley's "Leave, alas, this tormenting" is composed out of short harmonic cycles which are unusual mainly in that they modulate somewhat faster than we might expect (Figure 8.6.14). We begin with very clear G minor, but immediately move to a stereotypical cadence in C minor, only to be wrenched immediately into D minor before settling back into G minor for eighteen measures. The III chord on the second system is a slight but noteworthy inclination toward major. There are a few other moments where Morley uses major triads in not-completely-functional ways (VI$^6$–III$^6$ on the third system, perhaps VII instead of v$^6$ shortly thereafter, VII$^6$ on the bottom system), but these are exceptional; overall the music is strongly functional, particularly when compared to pieces like Schütz's *St. Matthew Passion*.

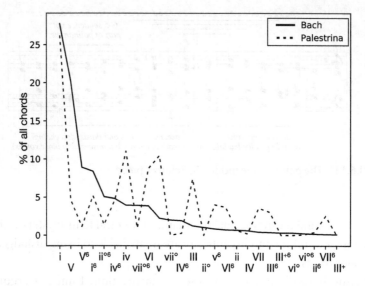

**Figure 8.6.12.** Diatonic triads in the minor-mode passages of Bach's chorales and in Palestrina's mass *Spem in alium*. Sonorities such as VI, III, VII are significantly more common in Palestrina than in Bach.

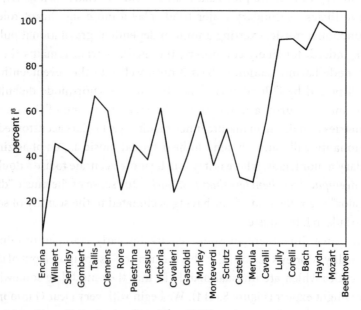

**Figure 8.6.13.** The relative frequency of $i^6$ and III in minor mode.

Future theorists will digitize and analyze a much larger quantity of sixteenth- and seventeenth-century music, allowing them to tell the story of modal homogenization in fine-grained detail. But I think the outlines are already clear: the process of homogenization is comparatively straightforward in the case of mixolydian, but more crooked and halting in the case of the remaining modes. For a time, it

**Figure 8.6.14.** The harmonies in Morley's 1600 "Leave, Alas, This Tormenting."

is almost as if the composers choose between major and modal rather than major and minor. During the transition, we find functional and modal techniques existing side-by-side, producing fascinating music whose basic principles are liquid and negotiable—with highly functional pieces like Morley's antedating highly modal pieces like Schütz's by the better part of a century. Historians may once have looked upon the paratonal century from 1550 to 1650 as a time of confusion, a rudimentary groping toward the absolute truths of classical harmony; now it seems like a flexible, nondogmatic, and open period in which multiple syntaxes overlap. Pieces differ primarily in the balance between the two forces, and not in the fact of pluralism as such.

## 7. Generalized set theory

Grieg's *Elegie* begins with an eight-bar parallel period showcasing the composer's fondness for chromatically descending bass lines (Figure 8.7.1). The ear hears virtually the same music presented over B minor and what sounds like G minor—harmonically distant yet surprisingly logical. The G minor is a musical pun, for while B harmonic minor does not contain G minor as a stack of thirds, it *does*

394 TONALITY: AN OWNER'S MANUAL

Figure 8.7.1. The opening of Grieg's *Elegie*, Op. 47, no. 7.

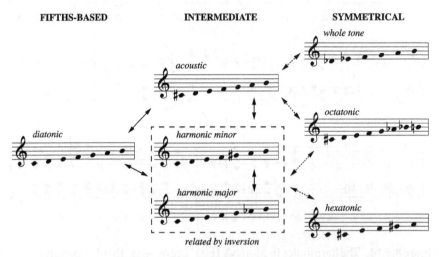

Figure 8.7.2. Seven scales common in twentieth-century music. Solid arrows mean scales of that type can be linked by single-semitone voice leading. Dashed arrows mean scales of that type share all but one of the notes in the smaller collection.

contain its enharmonic equivalent as a stack of scalar fourths, A♯–D–G. Grieg's music thus manages to evoke two incompatible hearings, a chromatic hearing according to which G minor and B minor are related by transposition (reflecting the fact that they sound alike), and a harmonic-minor hearing according to which they are not (reflecting the fact that the collection of notes A♯–D–G sounds like it belongs to B harmonic minor). It is not simply that we are forced to choose between these two different interpretations but rather that *both are equally important for our understanding*. Like a linguistic pun, it requires us to process two incompatible meanings at one and the same time.[29]

Grieg's piece, like Satie's third *Gnossienne*, represents an early example of scalar exploration, treating nondiatonic scales as objects in their own right rather than mere variants of the diatonic. I have argued that twentieth-century music generalizes the traditional three-scale system to include the scales in Figure 8.7.2. Four of these

---

[29] In other words, the piece exploits the fact that the harmonic minor scale contains collections related by chromatic but not scalar transposition, a property often referred to as "ambiguity" (Rothenberg 1978 and Balzano 1980).

are the most-even seven-note collections in twelve-tone equal-temperament: the diatonic, acoustic (or melodic-minor ascending), harmonic minor, and harmonic major. Three are symmetrical: the eight-note octatonic and the six-note whole-tone and hexatonic. These scales are interesting for a number of reasons. They contain all and only the "nonchromatic" sets (i.e., those that do not contain a chromatic cluster), providing a way station between traditional diatonicism and complete atonality. The scales are also linked by interesting voice-leading relationships (Figure 8.7.3). Its seven-note collections have a systematic structure when expressed on the circle of fifths, reflecting both their intervallic makeup and the "heights" of

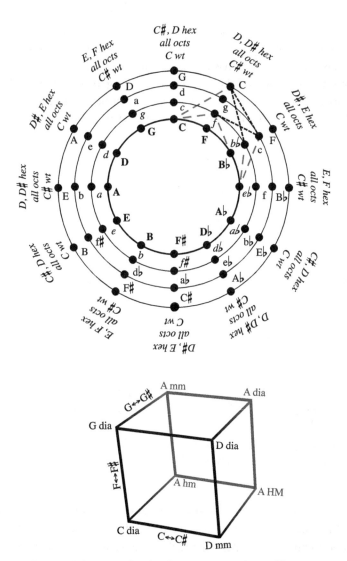

**Figure 8.7.3.** The spiral diagrams for the diatonic, acoustic, and harmonic scales (bold, italic, and plain text from center outward), with the symmetrical scales on the outside. Lines show single-semitone voice leadings among the seven-note collections. Below, the single-semitone voice leadings represented on a cube.

| height | C dia. | C ac. | D hm | G HM |
|---|---|---|---|---|
| 41 | | | | E♭ |
| 40 | | B♭ | B♭ | |
| 39 | F | | F | |
| 38 | C | C | | C |
| 37 | G | G | G | G |
| 36 | D | D | D | D |
| 35 | A | A | A | A |
| 34 | E | E | E | |
| 33 | B | | | B |
| 32 | | F♯ | | F♯ |
| 31 | | | C♯ | |

Figure 8.7.4. This table can be read in two ways. First, each column shows the notes of the column-label scale as they appear on the circle of fifths: the diatonic scale is a compact stack of seven fifths, the acoustic scale has a compact core of five fifths (a pentatonic scale) with two outliers, and so on. Second, the table records the "brightness" of those scales' modes, expressed as the sum of its intervals above the tonic pitch; here each cell labels the tonic of a *mode* of the column-label scale, whose "height" is given by the row label. See Figure 8.7.5.

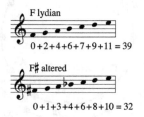

Figure 8.7.5. Mode height as the sum of the intervals above the tonic.

Figure 8.7.6. The principles of chord-scale compatibility associate chords with scales containing them; here, four common scales that accompany G–B–F, functioning as $G^7$.

their modes (Figures 8.7.4–5). And the scales can be integrated with functional harmony via the principles of "chord-scale compatibility" (Figure 8.7.6). We should not be surprised to find these scales reappearing in a wide range of styles from impressionism and jazz to minimalism and postminimalism.

The spiral diagrams allow us to expand our horizons beyond this particular collection, showing us the voice-leading possibilities of *any* chord in any scale, and *any* scale in chromatic space. The diagrams also allow us to consider more complex

**Figure 8.7.7.** A triply nested sequence from *Wheels within Wheels* in which a seven-note scale (*bottom*) iterates its ascending basic voice leading inside the eleven-note scale lacking F♯ ($T_8 t_{-5}$). Inside this scale, a six-note scale (*middle*) moves according to its ascending basic voice leading ($T_6 t_{-5}$); inside this, a four-note scale (*top*) moves according to the voice leading $T_3 t_{-2}$. Chords with open noteheads are generalizations of the melodic minor scale as discussed in the text.

collectional hierarchies: thus, rather than using a ten- or eleven-note scale directly (which often leads to chromatic saturation), we can consider five-, six-, or seven-note collections moving *inside* these larger collections, their chromatic intervals subtly distorting as they move around the space. Figure 8.7.7 contains a triply nested chord progression I used in a piece called *Wheels within Wheels*: the largest wheel (lowest layer) contains seven-note scales moving inside an eleven-note scale (all the notes except F♯); the middle wheel contains six-note chords moving inside those seven-note scales; while the smallest wheel has four-note chords moving inside those six-note scales. The music presents an ever-changing sequence whose structure is aurally discernable even while remaining unpredictable. This arrangement generalizes the nested hierarchy of Beethoven's Ninth to an additional layer, using three basic voice leadings simultaneously.

Beyond that, the spiral diagrams reveal analogies between different chord-and-scale domains. While the full picture is too complex to explain here, it is worth surveying briefly. Suppose we have a spiral diagram with just one chord at each angular position—that is to say, an $n$-note chord in an $o$-note scale, with $n$ not dividing $o$ and the two numbers not sharing any common factor: 3 in 7, 7 in 10, 5 in 12, and so on. In that case, the most-even $n$-note chord will be a near interval-cycle, a circular ordering of notes all but one of which are the same size, with the unusual interval one scale step larger or smaller than the others. For example, the diatonic

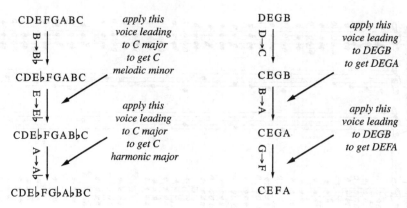

Figure 8.7.8. Scrambling the generalized circle of fifths to obtain analogous chords in different musical domains.

seventh chord E–G–B–D is a near interval cycle, a stack of three two-step intervals (E–G, G–B, B–D) with the fourth interval being just one step smaller (D–E, a step rather than a third). Similarly, the diatonic scale is a stack of seven-semitone perfect fifths (F–C, C–G, G–D, etc.) with the final interval (B–F) again just a chromatic step too small. In this sense the seventh chord E–G–B–D is the structural analogue of the C diatonic collection. Because both are near interval cycles, we can form a generalized "circle of fifths" by shifting the position of the unusual interval: with the diatonic seventh chord, we move D down by step to C, connecting E–G–B–D to E–G–B–C, with the C major collection we move B down by semitone to B♭, connecting C diatonic and F diatonic; this is the descending basic voice leading for each collection. Thus we have both harmonic and contrapuntal analogies between E–G–B–D and C diatonic: harmonically, both are near interval cycles, contrapuntally both are linked by a generalized circle of fifths.

To extend this analogy to other collections, we exploit the fact that we can generate nearly even chords by scrambling the voice leadings on the generalized circle of fifths.[30] For example, the melodic minor scale is the second-most even seven-note chord in twelve-tone equal temperament; it can be generated by applying the voice leading E→E♭, which links the F major scale to the B♭ major scale, one step too early on the circle of fifths: that is, to C major rather than F major (Figure 8.7.8). The stack of fourths D–E–G–A is the second-most even diatonic tetrachord; it can be generated by applying the voice leading B→A one step too early on the circle of diatonic thirds, to the E diatonic seventh chord rather than to the C major seventh chord. In exactly the same way, we can obtain the third-most-even seven-note scale, the harmonic major scale, by applying the voice leading A→A♭ *two* steps too early (i.e., once again to C major, rather than to B♭ major).[31] This procedure gives

---

[30] Tymoczko 2004 and 2011a. Junod et al. (2009) note some of these relationships in the 7-in-12 context.
[31] To obtain the inversion of the harmonic minor scale, we do the same in the sharpward direction, applying the displacement G→G♯ not to D major but to C major.

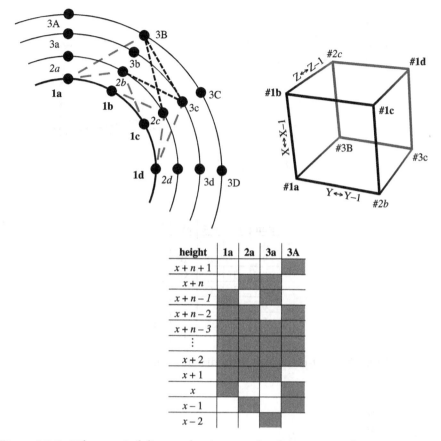

**Figure 8.7.9.** When a spiral diagram has just one chord at every angular position, the four most-even chords will be linked by the same single-step voice-leading relationships and will have the same structure. Chord 1 is the most-even chord with a, b, c, connected by the basic voice leading ("the generalized circle of fifths"). Chord 2 is the second most even chord, with its basic voice leading linking 2a to 2b, and so on. Chord 3 comes in two inversionally related variants, 3a and 3A. This is the abstract pattern shared by Figures 8.7.3–4 and 8.7.10–12.

us a generalized recipe for producing chordal analogues in different chord-and-scale domains. Once again, these "analogues" will be similar both in their internal structure and their contrapuntal relationships. The second-most even chord, for example, will be "gapped" when expressed in terms of the interval that characterizes the maximally even chord (Figure 8.7.9). The third-most even sonority will be an inversionally related pair forming a doubly gapped stack of the characteristic interval. And all of these objects will be linked by an analogous system of single-step voice leadings. Thus one and the same description can be applied to familiar seven-note scales, three- and four-note diatonic collections, and countless other collections as well—a remarkable system of analogies linking different chord-in-scale domains (Figures 8.7.10–12).

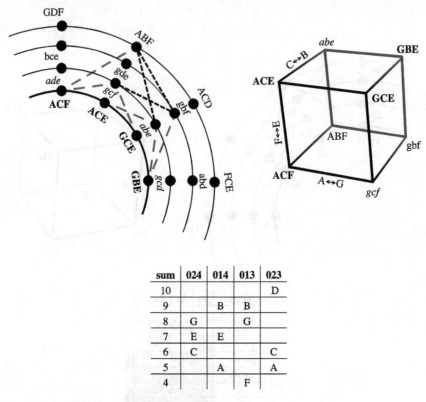

| sum | 024 | 014 | 013 | 023 |
|---|---|---|---|---|
| 10 |  |  |  | D |
| 9 |  | B | B |  |
| 8 | G |  | G |  |
| 7 | E | E |  |  |
| 6 | C |  |  | C |
| 5 |  | A |  | A |
| 4 |  |  | F |  |

**Figure 8.7.10.** The most-even triads in the diatonic scale.

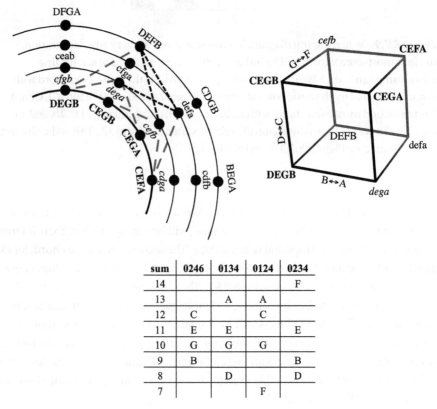

| sum | 0246 | 0134 | 0124 | 0234 |
|---|---|---|---|---|
| 14 |  |  |  | F |
| 13 |  | A | A |  |
| 12 | C |  | C |  |
| 11 | E | E |  | E |
| 10 | G | G | G |  |
| 9 | B |  |  | B |
| 8 |  | D |  | D |
| 7 |  |  | F |  |

**Figure 8.7.11.** The most-even four-note chords in the diatonic scale.

MODULATION 401

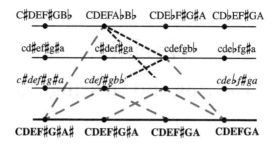

Figure 8.7.12. The most-even six-note chords in the eleven-note scale containing all the standard chromatic pitch classes except B. For legibility, the circles have been straightened into lines.

These relationships hint at a music theory that has yet to be written, a generalized set theory going beyond taxonomy to illuminate abstract structures reappearing across different chord-and-scale domains. We have not yet taught ourselves how to think in this way, much less to explore the aesthetic significance of these ideas. But one way in which we can take ownership of the functional tradition is to ask how its techniques might be adapted to new harmonic realms. Earlier composers made knowing and intelligent use of the quadruple hierarchy, moving voice in chord, chord in scale, and scale in chromatic aggregate. Inspired by the Prime Directive, we can adapt their techniques to arbitrary collections, using the spiral diagrams to chart interesting paths through a new world of musical possibility.

# Prelude
## Hearing and Hearing-As

Music bumps against the limits of human possibility. It is easy to write rhythms that performers cannot play, and possible to play rhythms that listeners cannot understand. Composers regularly devise pitch systems that elude even the most sensitive ear. The history of music is a tug-of-war between the aspirational force of the musical imagination and the gravitational pull of practical limitation, energized by the fact that audiences generally do not like hard work. The result is genuine confusion about what we hear: we may *think* we hear the organization in a complex piece of total serialism, or the relationships described by set theory, or a sense of long-term resolution in a sonata recapitulation, even while psychological experiments suggest we are wrong. Music is unique among the arts, and rare among human perceptual situations generally, in demanding skepticism about first-person testimony.

Or perhaps it is not so unique. The history of science shows that observations can be contaminated by expectations, and it is now standard practice to ensure that experimentalists do not know what they are expected to see. Judges and lawyers have come to understand that eyewitness testimony can be surprisingly unreliable. For centuries, belief in the supernatural led intelligent people to think they were witnessing miracles and acts of witchcraft. An extensive literature on "implicit bias" suggests we can be prejudiced even when we think we are not. Many oenophiles believe they can distinguish cheap from expensive wine while failing to do so in controlled circumstances. Perhaps the challenges of music perception are just a specific manifestation of the more general problem of self-knowledge.[1]

Here it is important to distinguish two issues. The first is that we can sometimes *think* we are sensitive to musical features even when we demonstrably are not—we might, for example, think we can hear sonatas returning to the tonic key even while being vulnerable to clever tricks (for instance, rewriting a piece so that it ends in a foreign key). This problem is relatively tractable: to find out what I can hear, you can just run an experiment. The second and more difficult issue is that we are sometimes capable of passing empirical tests *even without being able to hear the relationship as such*. In this case, experiments will not tell us what we need to know.

Imagine a student with very good absolute pitch who is insensitive to intervallic quality: asked to identify the interval D–F♯, they count on their fingers—"let's see,

---

[1] Compare Brewer 2015 ("N-rays"), National Research Council 2014 (eyewitnesses), Thomas 1971 (the supernatural), Jost et al. 2009 (implicit bias), Goldstein et al. 2008 (wine).

*Tonality*. Dmitri Tymoczko, Oxford University Press. © Oxford University Press 2023. DOI: 10.1093/oso/9780197577103.003.0016

D to E♭, E♭ to E, E to F, F to F♯, that's four semitones so . . . um . . . *a major third!*" This student might pass simple or even advanced ear-training tests, identifying intervals, chords, and progressions with a high degree of accuracy. But we may legitimately feel they are missing something. (They might encourage our suspicion by saying things like "I don't really experience a melody in one key as being similar to its transposition into another.") Rather than being directly sensitive to the inherent sound of intervals, the way they directly perceive colors or smells, the imaginary student *calculates* interval on the basis of absolute-pitch information.[2]

Contrast this sort of calculational experience with direct sensitivity to interval and chord quality as such. When I hear a dominant seventh chord, I experience it as a perceptual whole: its character seems immediate, forceful, and present. Often the sense of dominantness precedes any specific awareness of the component pitches; I might know that I am hearing a dominant before I realize what scale degree is in the melody; and I might not be able to identify its inner voices at all. Furthermore, the perception of dominantness is connected with a range of style-dependent expectations and responses: in a classical context the chord will feel tense and full of implication; in a blues it might sound like an energetic yet stable tonic. These phenomena seem to be *embedded in the perceptual experience* rather than generated by conscious calculation: I feel the tension as it were *in the chord itself*.

Philosophers distinguish *hearing as* from *hearing plus thinking*: the question is whether we hear a major third *as* a major third, or whether we hear a pair of notes that allow us to *think the thought* "that is a major third."[3] Though not a common music-theoretical topic, it is arguably foundational to the entire enterprise: for if we are committed to the idea that art is experiential, then we have reason to be less concerned with *what we can calculate* and more concerned with *what we hear directly*. This is why we spend so much time teaching ear training rather than allowing students to use scores or other technology.

The issue is relevant to questions about long-term key structure. For here there is a fundamental and perhaps biological difference between two different groups: the small number of absolute-pitch listeners who are directly sensitive to keys, able to hear that a piece has returned to the tonic, and the much larger group of relative-pitch listeners who have access to this information only by way of explicit calculation. This inability to directly hear keys should make us wary of statements like: "the most radical transformation of a theme is from dissonance to resolution [ . . . ] this is basically what happens in a sonata when the second group is recapitulated at the end in the tonic."[4] And we should remain suspicious *even if* some relative-pitch listeners are able to reliably identify the return of the tonic key on the basis of

---

[2] Of course, most absolute-pitch listeners are directly sensitive to interval quality. I have, however, met some who reported the sort of insensitivity discussed here.

[3] The distinction originates with Wittgenstein's (1953) distinction between "seeing as" and "seeing plus thinking" which in turn was inspired by the earlier movement of Gestalt psychology. See DeBellis 1999 for related discussion.

[4] Rosen 1988, p. 197.

404 TONALITY: AN OWNER'S MANUAL

rhetoric, instrumentation, score study, or conscious tracking of modulations.[5] For the experience of dissonance is felt and immediate in a way that the calculation of keys is not. Indeed, it is reasonable to wonder whether absolute-pitch listeners genuinely experience a recapitulation as a release of tension, psychologically comparable to the resolution of a dominant.[6]

All of which presents a profound challenge to music theory. We should take seriously those experiments suggesting that our powers of long-range musical perception are less impressive than theorists have traditionally believed. We should be sensitive to the social and institutional forces that encourage us to hide our limitations, exaggerating the power of our musical ears. And we should be genuinely worried that so many music-theoretical claims seem to be rooted in unverifiable introspection: that experts confidently claim to hear vast stretches of music "representing" or "prolonging" a single note; that they claim to hear a note in one measure directly connecting to another fifty measures away; or that they claim to hear a sense of return to the tonic after ten or more minutes. The danger is that some substantial proportion of these claims might not be grounded in anything real.

Yet at the same time we should recognize that theory can sometimes change our experience.[7] One of my favorite examples involves the track "In" by the electronic musician Brothomstates (Lassi Nikko). At first listen, the music sounds like a synthesized flute echoing in a gently lilting triple meter. But as you tap along you invariably find yourself making small adjustments, responding to subtle irregularities that bely the music's placid and ambient surface. Transcription is useless, yielding a jagged irregularity completely foreign to one's lived experience (Figure P9.1). Here we have two perceptions both true and contradictory: a palpable sense of echo and the unsteadiness of one's tapping fingers. It is a perceptual impossibility, comparable to those psychology experiments that convince people they are seeing something completely red and completely green at one and the same time.[8]

The paradox evaporates once we attend to the distance between pitch-repetitions, revealing a regular 3 + 2 pattern not at all obvious in standard notation (Figure P9.2). What we are hearing, in other words, is an *irregular echo*, a phenomenon unusual in both art and nature. The entire passage likely results from just five notes

---

[5] Repeated listening is not the answer, as it gives the listener cognitive access to information they may not be able to perceive directly. Suppose a non-absolute-pitch listener learns a piece well enough that they know what key they are in at any one time. This is compatible with their not having an immediate and palpable sense of long-term tonal closure: they may know *that* a piece is returning to the tonic, while having absolutely no sense of "dissonance being resolved." In the same way, they could memorize a twelve-tone piece accurately enough to identify, by ear, any divergences from the score. But this tells us nothing about whether listeners are sensitive to twelve-tone structure in the aesthetically relevant sense. Repeated experience allows us to *think the thought* "now I am back in the home key" (or "now I am hearing the retrograde inversion of the row, starting on B♭"), but this is different from being sensitive to the relevant musical properties.

[6] Cook 1987, Marvin and Brinkman 1999. It is entirely possible to notice that the music has returned to the tonic key without any associated sense of release.

[7] Davies 1983. Hansberry 2017 argues, correctly in my view, that scale-degree identity is to some extent under our conscious control; indeed, I recall hearing about a new-music soprano who assigned scale degrees to twelve-tone pieces, hearing them in relation to imaginary tonics.

[8] Crane and Piantanida 1983.

**Figure P9.1.** The opening of "In" from Brothomstates' *Claro*.

played on a synthesizer, with the quintuple-meter echoes forming a melodic composite both energetic and relaxed: intuition filtered through algorithm to produce a psychologically compelling result. This realization allows us to harmonize our seemingly incompatible percepts: that the music sounds like it is produced by an echo, but that the composite is rhythmically irregular. And this in turn can genuinely change our experience, for instance by teaching our fingers when to tap, or changing our sense of which notes belong together—helping us understand, for example, that the C in mm. 5 and 6 is not just a neighbor but also an echo of the C in the previous measures.

I cannot offer any general theory of musical perception, nor any reliable way to separate "hearing as" from "hearing plus thinking." But a lifetime of experience has convinced me of two facts. First, that it can be genuinely difficult to know whether

**Figure P9.2.** The music as the product of a 3 + 2 echo. Accented notes are played on the synthesizer; the rest are produced by the echo.

we are thinking something or experiencing it directly—and hence that we can be drastically mistaken about what we hear. (Indeed, I suspect that this confusion explains why so many ambitious composers wasted so much energy manipulating inaudible pitch-relationships.) And second, that theory can sometimes enrich our experience, leading us to understand music in a way that genuinely increases our enjoyment. The challenge for theory is to stretch our ears while remaining realistic about human limitation. Done badly, it is like playing tennis without a net, elevating blatantly implausible claims to the status of institutional common sense. Done well, it is a delicate and intimate form of science that increases the world's supply of aesthetic value. No hard-and-fast rules determine the boundary between these two activities, only taste and good judgment.

# 9

# Heterogeneous Hierarchy

Music theory offers diverse tools for conceptualizing longer spans of musical time: principles of motivic development, models of key relations, theories of long-range melodic connection, and *Formenlehre* both old and new. This chapter will explore these approaches in light of the theoretical framework we have been developing. I begin by suggesting that the concept of *melodic strategy* allows us to incorporate insights from Schenkerian theory within the generally sequential framework of my harmonic grammar. I then consider some connections between phrase structure and voice leading.

The general picture I offer is one of *heterogeneous hierarchy*. Rather than Schenker's vision of many fundamentally similar musical levels, guided by a unified logic and nested like the layers of an onion, I see diverse forms of organization superimposed: a harmonic system directing the flow of chords, a contrapuntal system overseeing the motion of surface voices (and largely inherited from the Renaissance), a melodic system creating longer-range linear coherence, a modulatory system governing the progression of keys, a sequential system generating varied repetition, formal systems concerned with phrasing and long-term development, and so on. To focus on one is in no way to discount the others: after all, when we walk, our legs obey a local alternation of left and right, and yet our journeys are nevertheless directed. Nor is it disrespectful to say that these systems are relatively simple when considered in isolation, for they come together to form a wonderfully complex set of musical resources.[1]

## 1. Strategy and reduction

Rameau once wrote that it is almost impossible to give definite rules for melody, as good taste plays a central role in its development.[2] Schenker took perhaps the single largest step toward unraveling this mystery when he proposed that music typically involves a slower melody taking place beneath the musical surface, with phrases often embellishing stepwise descents from one tonic-triad note to another, and with bass lines moving from tonic to dominant before leaping back to the tonic. This template is so ubiquitous that examples are almost superfluous, but Figure 9.1.1

---

[1] For similar views see Meyer 1996, p. 259, and Webster 2010 ("multivalence"). The approach also resembles the "post-human organicism" of Watkins (2017) and Arndt (2019).
[2] Rameau (1722) 1971, p. 155.

*Tonality.* Dmitri Tymoczko, Oxford University Press. © Oxford University Press 2023. DOI: 10.1093/oso/9780197577103.003.0017

**Figure 9.1.1.** The opening of Mozart's Symphony no. 40, K.550 features a linear descent from $\hat{5}$ to $\hat{7}$.

provides one anyway—the opening phrase of Mozart's G minor symphony K.550, embedding a linear descent from D down to F♯, while reserving the strong root-position dominant for the end of the phrase.

I am firmly convinced that this idea can help us understand a wide range of music, and I regularly encourage young composers to listen for this "slower melody" in styles both old and new. What is more challenging is understanding its significance. Attention to melodic structure has sometimes been set in opposition to the recognition of local harmonic patterns, as if the two were somehow incompatible. To my mind, however, there is no conflict at all: the art of functional composition consists in writing satisfying phrases *while also satisfying the constraints of the local harmonic grammar*. This sort of double organization is familiar from the world of sports and games. In basketball, players execute higher-order aims (driving to the basket, advancing the ball to the other end of the court, blocking an opponent's lanes) within the constraints given by the rules (no more than two steps per dribble, no contact with opposing players, etc.). Similarly, chess players pursue strategic goals (developing pieces, controlling the center) within local constraints governing pieces' motions. If the harmonic grammar provides the rules of the game, then phrase-level melodic templates are the higher-level goals.

What makes a melody directed? Schenker's answer, which I endorse, is that directed melodies often articulate coherent voice-leading structures. Simple melodies, such as "Helpless," have just one structural voice, descending stepwise

Figure 9.1.2. Dual transpositions in the opening of Mozart's Symphony no. 40.

from one tonic-triad note to another. More complex melodies, such as "Eight Days a Week," dance between multiple voices of an abstract background that itself moves in a coherent way—somewhat like an Alberti bass, but less predictably. Still more complex is the technique of moving contrary to a background voice leading, as when Beethoven ascends along the predominantly descending *Waldstein* progression (§3.7). This produces a dual melodic logic superimposing multiple directed narratives: in the *Waldstein*, the two hands take separate paths from tonic to dominant, bass descending by step while the melody ascends by thirds.

These facts imply that directed melodies will often articulate the doubly parallel motion represented by our spiral diagrams—that is, the combination of big-T transposition along the scale, and little-t transposition along the chord. The nonharmonic system ensures that out-of-chord notes resolve by step to in-chord notes; and registral limitations ensure that these within-chord notes tend to outline close-position triads and seventh chords. The resulting "background" provides melodic destinations, points of rest between which the surface moves. (Again, I think of this as a kind of dancing, surface voices leaping among background voices in an aesthetically pleasing way.) Figure 9.1.2 analyzes the opening of Mozart's Fortieth Symphony, where hierarchical transposition is intrinsic to melodic directedness, the glue binding harmony and melody together.

Mozart's melody also exhibits another important technique, the application of double transposition to specifically *thematic* objects with distinctive rhythmic and registral profiles: the melody of mm. 2–5 is transformed by double transposition into that of mm. 6–9. Figure 9.1.3 identifies the most common possibilities available to functional composers. Though this technique is as old as functionality itself, it becomes increasingly important as musical culture shifts from a polyphonic to a homophonic default: double transposition of prominent thematic material is relatively rare in *The Well-Tempered Clavier*, more common in C. P. E. Bach, and ubiquitous in Mozart and Haydn. One sign of its importance is its appearance in three of the eleven schemas in the appendix of Robert Gjerdingen's *Music in the Galant Style* (Figure 9.1.4).[3]

The quadruple hierarchy thus underwrites a *collectional analysis* that is more precise than its Schenkerian antecedents. Figure 9.1.5 shows that the opening of Mozart's piano sonata K.284 presents a pair of ascending arpeggiations along the tonic triad, D–F♯–A. The introductory fanfare is a two-octave near sequence of

---

[3] The technique seems to be genuinely schematic insofar as it is usually applied to phrase-initial motives using tonic and dominant harmonies rather than motives more generally.

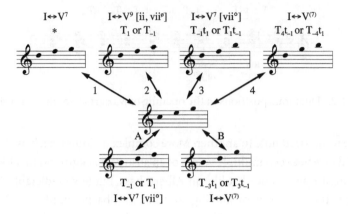

**Figure 9.1.3.** Thematic transformation by dual transposition. The starred transformation maps the tonic-triad notes into a nontriadic subset of the dominant seventh.

**Figure 9.1.4.** (*top*) Three schemas that employ double transposition between tonic and dominant; the labels above the solfege names refer to Figure 9.1.3. (*bottom*) The Do-Re-Mi in a melodic context.

falling thirds that manages to sound iconic and functional without implying any specific harmonies (§7.2). The first arpeggiation is a near sequence moving the third D–F♯ along the scale D–F♯–A; as in Figure 4.5.7, Mozart skips the perfect consonance to produce an ascending sequence of thirds and sixths.[4] The music then descends by thirds to a tonic pedal, completing a four-measure sentence. The second arpeggiation begins by harmonizing its melody with a contrary-motion version of

---

[4] The upper-voice dyad moves by a loop ($t_1$) and a slide ($T_1$) on the 2-in-3 spiral diagram; the three-note scale itself oscillates between D–F♯–A and C♯–E–G.

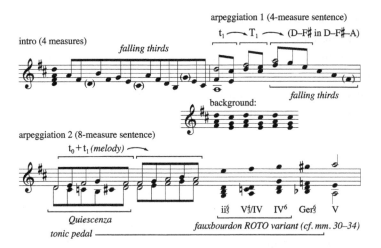

**Figure 9.1.5.** An analysis of the opening of Mozart's K.284, I.

Gjerdingen's "Quiescenza" (see Figures 3.1.10 and 4.7.4).[5] This sentence ends with a fauxbourdon ROTO variant replacing I$^6_4$ with V$^4_3$/IV, leading to an outer-voice arrival on A. Here the large-scale strategic goal, ascent to the fifth, is achieved using familiar dyadic and seventh-chord voice-leading schemas—while also remaining consistent with functional-harmonic norms. This is not so much a generic process of "arpeggiation," existing independent of and prior to the conventions of functional harmony, but rather something more specific, a careful arrangement of schematic building blocks that themselves exploit the fundamental geometry of musical possibility.

Proceeding in this way I think we can have many of the benefits of Schenkerian theory while jettisoning its problematic metaphysics. The key is, first, to use the quadruple hierarchy to reconceive the notion of the "background" in scale-theoretic terms, as a matter of surface voices moving along abstract alphabets: subchord, chordal, scalar, and chromatic, each nested within the next. Second, to reconceive reduction as a kind of paraphrase, a speculative hypothesis about the longer strategic goals that might animate a passage. We need not say less-important material "represents" more-important material, any more than we say that omitted material "represents" the events in a paraphrase. Instead, what is important is simply that our reductions serve as plausible blueprints, their notes connecting the way one scene in a movie might continue an earlier narrative. A good blueprint is an analytical way station: simple enough that we can imagine ourselves inventing it, and yet rich enough that we can imagine expanding it into the finished piece.

If I am right, then a certain amount of musical hierarchy has an irreducibly *melodic* character. It is easy to find evidence for long-range melodic relationships, notes that seem to connect despite not being adjacent on the musical surface. While

---

[5] My analysis highlights the ascending basic voice leading (B, G) → (D, F♯) to emphasize the continuity with the following gesture.

I do not say that harmonies lack such hierarchy, I do believe it is less common, in large part because functional music obeys a strict set of local harmonic rules. Melody is locally free but hierarchically structured, which is precisely why it is so hard to describe. Harmony is its mirror image, largely nonhierarchical but locally constrained, and hence more amenable to syntactic theorizing. Broadly speaking, Schenker was right about melody but wrong about harmony.

## 2. Two models of the phrase

It follows that composers do not wander aimlessly through harmonic space, moving from chord to chord without memory or thought of the future.[6] Instead, they arrange outer voices to build satisfying melodies while repeatedly passing through the same basic map of harmonic possibilities. Different kinds of harmonic cycles will therefore tend to appear in different parts of the phrase: early-phrase cycles will typically avoid melodic $\hat{2}$–$\hat{1}$ in favor of other scale degrees, just as the bass $\hat{5}$–$\hat{1}$ will likely be reserved for the final cadence (Figure 9.2.1). Some contemporary theorists describe the early-phrase progressions as "prolongational," as distinct from late-phrase "cadential" progressions, but to the traditional harmonic theorist they are essentially similar, alternative paths through a single harmonic map. The difference between them is the result of large-scale strategy rather than syntax.

One way of putting this is that individual harmonic cycles have different degrees of *cadential weight*, with phrases moving from less-conclusive to more-conclusive over the course of a phrase. Figure 9.2.2 quantifies this notion in a rough-and-ready way, considering whether a harmonic cycle contains a predominant, ends with a root-position tonic-dominant progression, and so on.[7] Cadential weight, thus defined, generally increases throughout a phrase, with the final cycle longer and stronger than its predecessors. We can use this approach to construct a

**Figure 9.2.1.** Some common early-phrase and cadential progressions.

---

[6] Of course, no sensible person would imagine this to be so: traditional harmonic theory was never meant as a recipe for producing beautiful music, any more than English grammar provides a paint-by-numbers kit for producing beautiful poetry; the grammar plays a *necessary* but not *sufficient* role in the production of compelling functional music. Critics of traditional harmonic theory sometimes treat its limitations as fundamental flaws (Schenker [1930] 1997, pp. 1–9, Gjerdingen 1996 and 2015).

[7] To be clear, this is only a very rough approximation of a complex issue; cadential weight is affected by such factors as rhythm and temporal duration.

| feature | strength |
|---|---|
| tonic scale degree in melody of final tonic | 1 |
| final tonic in root position | 1 |
| final tonic preceded by vii° | .25 |
| final tonic preceded by V | .5 |
| final tonic in root position | .5 |
| final dominant accompanied by seventh | .5 |
| final dominant with $\hat{2}$ in melody | .5 |
| final dominant preceded by IV or ii | .5 |

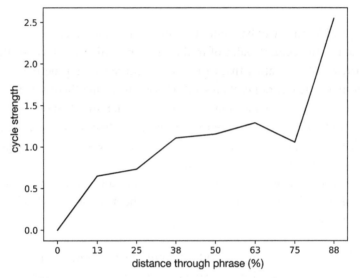

**Figure 9.2.2.** (*top*) A simple model of cycle strength, assigning "strength points" to various features of the cycle. (*bottom*) Modeled in this way, cycles increase in strength throughout the phrase in Bach's chorales.

simple-but-effective algorithm for harmonizing chorale-style melodies. Suppose we have a series of melody notes $n_1, n_2$, and so on, to be harmonized by a series of chords $C_1, C_2, \ldots$ Given a chord $C_i$ harmonizing melodic note $n_i$, we can choose a new chord $C_{i+1}$ by multiplying two probabilities, the (first order, phrase-independent) probability that a particular chord follows chord $C_i$ according to a harmonic grammar and the (zeroth order) likelihood that that chord is found at that point in the phrase. Figure 9.2.3 shows that this fairly simple algorithm can produce a reasonably idiomatic output, comparable to the efforts of a good second-semester undergraduate.[8]

Chapter 6 argued that the earliest functional styles are so harmonically limited that the question of inversional equivalence does not arise. We now see why it is more important in more complex styles. Fundamentally, inversional equivalence is a conceptual technology that synthesizes harmonic and polyphonic ideals,

---

[8] Here the algorithm chooses a voice leading $C_i \to C_{i+1}$ from the actual voice leadings in Bach's chorales.

**Figure 9.2.3.** A computer-generated harmonization of the opening two phrases of the melody of "Christus, der ist mein Leben" (BWV 281, Riemenschneider 6).

allowing a wide variety of bass lines to express the same small collection of chord progressions. The central claim of traditional harmonic theory is not that inversion is irrelevant, but rather that early-phrase and cadential progressions are similar, differing in degree rather than kind. This is why earlier theorists often used the term "cadence" to refer to harmonic cycles more generally.[9] And this is why the full power of traditional harmonic theory only appears when we interpret early-phrase and cadential progressions as more and less conclusive journeys through a single map of harmonic possibilities (Figure 9.2.4).

All of which starts to narrow the gap between traditional harmonic theory and the Schenkerian alternative, at least as concerns the structure of individual phrases. For both parties can agree on the following:

P1. Phrases tend to begin and end with root-position tonic chords;
P2. Melodies tend to decorate stepwise descents from one note of the tonic chord to another, perhaps after an initial ascent;
P3. Melodies often jump between the degrees of a series of abstract scalelike chords that articulate close-position harmonies connected by familiar voice leadings (§9.1);
P4. Bass lines tend to reserve the root-position dominant for the final cadence.

These principles imply that traditional harmonic theorists will often find the phrase-level structures emphasized by Schenkerian analysis. Similarly, they will often be able to reinterpret orthodox Schenkerian graphs as highlighting these features of functional phrases. From a practical point of view, the two approaches are speaking a very similar language.[10]

However, they differ over subtle questions about the *meaning and scope* of these features. Where traditional theory asserts that harmonic cycles are concatenated sequentially, placed one after another like beads on a string, Schenkerians argue

---

[9] Caplin 2004 rejects this term, but I think it captures the point that functional tonality extends the harmonic logic of the cadence to the rest of the phrase. Caplin also tends to draw a sharp distinction between "cadence" and "noncadence," whereas I think the distinction is inherently fuzzy.

[10] Sewell 2021 notes that Schoenberg provided simple melodic reductions along the lines I have been describing.

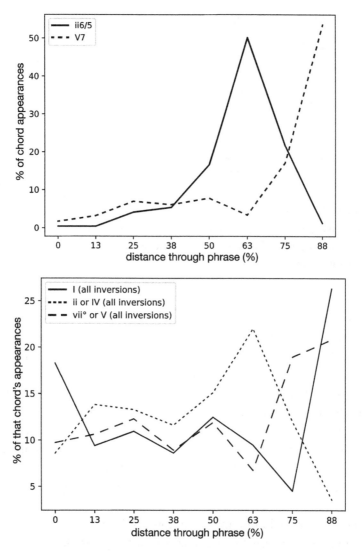

**Figure 9.2.4.** (*top*) Specific inversions are highly likely to be found at specific phrasal positions in J. S. Bach's chorales. (*bottom*) When we ignore inversions and group chords by functional category, we find a much more even distribution.

that early-phrase progressions are *nested inside* a single "structural" progression that lasts for the duration of the phrase (Figure 9.2.5). This view is described with admirable clarity in a pair of recent textbooks, Steven Laitz's *The Complete Musician* and Jane Clendinning and Elizabeth West Marvin's *The Musician's Guide to Theory and Analysis*.[11] Both use the term "the phrase model" to describe the recursive conception: what makes the final dominant cadential, on this view, is not its rhythmic role within the conventions of the eight-bar phrase, or its use of root-position dominant chords and $\hat{2}$–$\hat{1}$ melody, but rather the fact that it "connects" syntactically to

---

[11] Laitz 2008, Clendinning and Marvin 2016. Caplin 1998 has a similar view.

416   TONALITY: AN OWNER'S MANUAL

**Figure 9.2.5.** Steven Laitz's interpretation of the opening of Haydn's G minor sonata, Hob. XVI:44, II (from *The Complete Musician*). Where a traditional theorist would see four successive harmonic cycles, Laitz postulates that three of the cycles are embedded within the fourth. Above the staff, I note the use of a schema from Figure 9.1.3 to relate tonic and dominant.

the initial tonic, with the earlier T–S–D–T cycles *hierarchically embedded* within a higher-level "structural" progression.[12] Harmonic analysis thus requires us to determine which chords belong to the structural progression and which do not.

As a general rule, I do not find it useful to imagine chords lasting longer than they do. At best this strikes me as a confusing metaphor for centricity, a phenomenon that has much more to do with emphasis and expectation than with hierarchy and persistence.[13] (It may also reflect phrase-level expectations that arise in certain functional subgenres, as we will discuss shortly.) In other aspects of life, there is little temptation to connect stability and representation: after all, when we travel we may feel unsettled, but we do not say that our trips "represent" the state of being-at-home.

I suspect the desire to fuse these concepts results from two factors. The first is a failure to consider alternative explanations for the phrase-level linear structures so rightly emphasized in Schenkerian theory. The second is a desire for a *unified* approach to musical structure in which phenomena such as melodic directedness, centricity, harmonic function, phrase-level expectations, and nonharmonicity can *all* be explained as manifestations of the same basic principles. In Figure 9.2.6, for example, Schenkerian analysis is presented as a later stage in a sequence of progressive reductions: the top level removes nonharmonic tones to obtain a harmonic skeleton, while the third level removes consonant chordal skips to obtain a melodic outline. Up to this point, Schenkerian and non-Schenkerian theorists can agree. The next levels, however, continue to remove harmonies in accordance with the phrase model: the fourth reveals a single TD(T) harmonic cycle governing the

---

[12] Though it derives from Schenker, the Laitz-Clendenning-Marvin phrase model is often presented in starkly harmonic terms, shorn of the linear features fundamental to traditional Schenkerianism.
[13] Tymoczko 2011a, chapter 5.

HETEROGENEOUS HIERARCHY 417

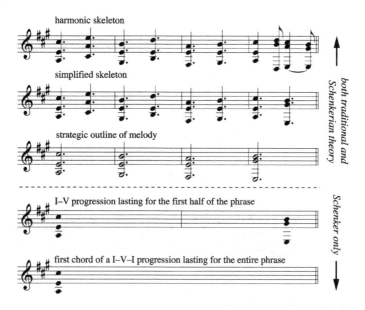

**Figure 9.2.6.** Lerdahl and Jackendoff's five-stage reductional analysis of the opening of Mozart's K.331, I. Above the staves I add my own description of the reductional level. The first three are compatible with traditional theory.

antecedent (resolving to the tonic in m. 5), while the fifth eliminates the dominant to obtain a single TDT governing the whole phrase.[14] The approach thus extends nonharmonic reduction to larger time scales.

Deciding between these two conceptions of the phrase is perhaps the single most pressing problem of contemporary music theory, as it directly affects elementary pedagogy. Empirically, the question is what evidence supports the claim that initial tonics "attach" to final dominants: in Figure 9.2.5, tonic chords are almost all unaccented, appearing only on the last quarter note of every measure, yet the bulk of the phrase is taken to embellish the opening tonic. Nor is it obvious, in the case of more flexibly phrased music such as that in Figure 9.2.7, how to identify the initial tonic that supposedly attaches to a given cadence; here Schenkerian analysis seems to require fundamentally different mechanisms for the perception of regularly and irregularly phrased music. There are also deeper methodological questions about the foundations of the entire approach: in chapter 5, I argued that nonharmonic tones do not necessarily "stand for" or "prolong" harmonic tones; if even the simplest forms of reduction are problematic, then there is all the more reason to be concerned about its Schenkerian generalizations. Finally, there is the fundamental philosophical question about hearing and hearing-as, for while it is possible to

[14] These later reductional stages tend to eliminate all the nontonic chords between the initial tonic and the final cadence, regardless of the musical surface.

418  TONALITY: AN OWNER'S MANUAL

Figure 9.2.7. Measures 39–48 of the first A minor fugue in *The Well-Tempered Clavier*. Here we have a flexible musical texture without clearly articulated phrase breaks, making it difficult to determine what initial C major chord should attach to the strong final cadence.

think "this initial tonic connects to the final dominant," it is much less clear that we genuinely *hear* such connections. How could we even test whether the recursive picture is true? Does "I feel the tonic as persisting" mean anything more than "tonic chords are generally stable"?

The upshot is that although Schenkerian theory has dominated American music-theoretical discourse for more than half a century, there is little or no solid evidence supporting it—and no historical evidence that earlier composers in fact thought in this way.[15] Thus as far as anyone knows, it may be possible to hear functional harmony in two fundamentally different ways: sequentially, as a sequence of harmonic cycles placed one after another, or recursively, as a collection of "prolongational"

---

[15] As recently as 2011, it was possible to publish an article in a prominent music-theory journal broaching the question of how Schenkerian theory *might*, in principle, be tested (Temperley 2011a). Morgan 1978 considers antecedents to Schenkerian analysis, all of which are compatible with the version of traditional theory I articulate here; the distinctively Schenkerian focus on very long-range pitch connections has little or no theoretical precedent.

cycles nested within one another. It may be that these different ways of hearing are uncorrelated with the quality of one's musicianship—that one can be an excellent performer, composer, or theorist and hear in either way. That would argue for a pluralism in music theory, with different listeners perceiving a single piece in fundamentally different ways. Another possibility, closer to Schenker's own view, is that both modes of hearing are available, but that sequential hearing is a sign of inferior musicianship; if that is right, then there are multiple ways to interact with music but some of them are objectively worse than others. Still another possibility is that people generally hear in only one of these ways, in which case many of us are wrong about what we hear. After all I am convinced that I hear harmonic cycles sequentially, while many of my friends and colleagues seem equally confident about the hierarchical perspective.

That there can be pervasive disagreement over such a fundamental issue is nothing short of alarming—as if linguists regularly disagreed about which nouns attached to which verbs. And that these competing views have been embedded in competing educational institutions is doubly concerning, for depending on what conservatory one attends, or which textbook one reads, one may encounter just one perspective, often presented as incontrovertible and obvious.[16] This is not so much an individual failing as a cultural issue, evidence of an intellectual community insufficiently devoted to discovering the truth. The problem, I suspect, is that Schenkerian theory appeals to a powerful sense of how music *should* be: in this respect, it recalls the Platonic faith that nonharmonic tones *must* be "merely decorative," or that recapitulations *must* create a sense of long-term resolution—convictions that survive not because they are supported by evidence, but because they satisfy intellectual and emotional needs.

## 3. Chopin and the Prime Directive

My view is that melody and harmony are heterogeneous, independent forces that can be combined in a wide variety of ways. While it might be true that *certain kinds of melodies* naturally suggest functional harmonization—for example, those that embellish the chain of descending thirds—the same cannot be said for melodies in general; indeed, a major theme of this book is that stepwise descending melodies often generate *retrofunctional* harmonies that contravene functional expectations. If that is right, then we should expect to find composers employing one and the same melodic strategy to produce a range of harmonic effects—for instance, using descending melodic steps to move between diatonic modality, functional harmony, and chromaticism.

---

[16] The fact that Schenkerian theory is associated with racist aesthetic opinions adds moral urgency to these already pressing problems (Ewell 2020).

420  TONALITY: AN OWNER'S MANUAL

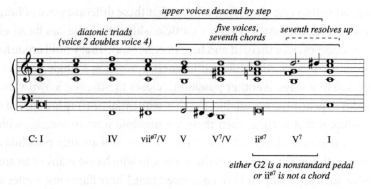

Figure 9.3.1. The opening of Chopin's first etude uses stepwise descending voice leading, first with diatonic triads and then with chromatic seventh chords.

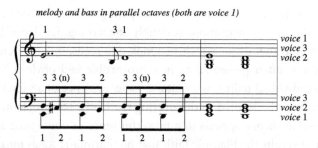

Figure 9.3.2. Chopin's structured arpeggiation embellishes three underlying voices, each of which appears in two octaves. This is represented by the networks, which start in the center, move left, and then move right.

This is exactly what happens in Chopin. At one end of the spectrum are passages like the opening of the first etude, where stepwise descending voice leading is fully compatible with the constraints of functional harmony (Figure 9.3.1).[17] At the other end are pieces like the A minor prelude, a famously baffling miniature that avoids any intimations of A minor until its final bars. Yet on closer inspection it is based on a very similar logic, its voice leading disguised by the elaborate "nonharmonic tone machine" in Figure 9.3.2. The background is a sequence of third-related triads e–G–b–D–(F)–a, with each triad's root descending by step to become the fifth of the next (Figure 9.3.3). The G and D triads give rise to $I^6_4$–V–(I) progressions that continue the sinking counterpoint, with the latter inaugurating a series of seventh chords linked by semitonal voice leading.[18] These slithering sevenths are utterly typical of

---

[17] Note that the bass reaches $\hat{5}$ for the cadence while the melody hints at a $\hat{3}$–$\hat{2}$–($\hat{1}$) descent, returning to the third scale degree for the repeat. Carl Czerny ([1830] 1848, I, p. 92) has an alternative voice-leading reduction that departs more radically from the musical surface.

[18] These chords, A–d♯$^{ø4}_3$–d♯$^{ø4}_3$–d♯$^{o6}_5$–d♯$^{o6[♭3]}_5$, transform A-as-dominant into A-as-tonic by way of a French sixth that continues the ascending-third triadic sequence. Rings 2011 considers these sorts of changes of scale-degree function.

Figure 9.3.3. Three increasingly detailed outlines of Chopin's A minor prelude.

Chopin and mid-nineteenth-century chromaticism more generally; what is new here is the implied connection to an earlier *diatonic* voice leading more characteristic of modality—another contrapuntal tradition, adjacent to functionality, but utilizing a different scalar and chordal repertoire.[19] Ultimately, the entire prelude is built on descending melodic steps: in the opening, diatonic steps connect mysterious triads that just barely conform to functional norms; in the middle, chromatic steps connect functionally anomalous sevenths (Figure 9.3.4). It is as if Chopin were telling us that these two worlds were not so far apart as we might have thought.

---

[19] For more on the "second practice," see Kinderman and Krebs 1996 and Cohn 2012. The particular idiom used here is the descending major-third version of the game described in §8.5 of Tymoczko 2011a. My analysis has many points of overlap with that in Meyer 1996 (pp. 93–97); it contrasts with those of Kramer (1990) and Subotnik (1991), who both read this piece as challenging the very idea of analytical reconstruction. Hatten 2014 offers a sensitive discussion of the work's poetics.

422　TONALITY: AN OWNER'S MANUAL

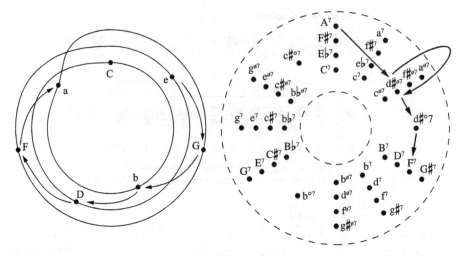

**Figure 9.3.4.** The A minor prelude takes short clockwise moves in two different geometrical spaces.

The first A minor mazurka (Op. 7, no. 2) is similar, interpolating VI$^6$ into iv$^6_4$–i to create a strikingly modal opening, but proceeding onward to a functional phrase with a clear $\hat{5}$–$\hat{4}$–$\hat{3}$–$\hat{2}$–$\hat{1}$ linear descent.[20] Once again these descending diatonic triads lead to nonfunctional sevenths, descending voice leading now chromatic and futuristic rather than modal and nostalgic (Figure 9.3.5). The second A minor mazurka is similar but with the diatonic triads giving way to chromatic trichords; the tetrachords are reserved until the piece's coda (Figures 9.3.6–7). An interesting wrinkle here is the scrambling of the stepwise descents: rather than repeating the diatonic triad's basic voice leading, (A, C, F) → (A, C, E) → (G, C, E) → (G, B, E), Chopin gives us (A, C, F) → (G, C, F) → (G, B, F) → (G, B, E), moving along the dotted lines in Figure 8.7.10. This is the technique of Chopin's E minor prelude, now expressed with diatonic triads rather than chromatic sevenths.[21] Here we see something like an explicit awareness of the Prime Directive.

One final example allows for a more direct comparison with Schenker. The first contrasting phrase of the Revolutionary Etude again features descending stepwise voice leading embodied by triads and sevenths. Schenker and I both identify the same initial voice leading, a chromatic 6–5 sequence using minor triads (Figure 9.3.8). But my analysis continues the stepwise descent through the following dominant sevenths, while Schenker instead follows the surface, inventing a 5–6 sequence to rationalize its voice leading. His graph includes a provocative footnote:

> all conventional concepts, such as functional harmony, modulation, etc., fail in regard to measures 21–41. It would be wrong, for instance, to speak of a modulation

---

[20] The Op. 24, no. 4 mazurka similarly decomposes its final V–I cadence into a pair of descending thirds in accordance with the logic of the 3-in-7 spiral diagram. Like the opening of Op. 7, no. 2, the V–iii–I can likewise be understood either as a nod toward modality or as a drawn-out suspension.

[21] See §4.10, Tymoczko 2011a.

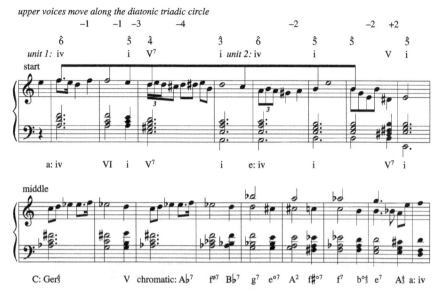

**Figure 9.3.5.** The A minor Mazurka, Op. 7, no. 2, opens with a series of short descending moves on the triadic spiral, creating a iv–VI–i progression; the eight bars feature two loosely parallel iv–i–V–i progressions in A and E minor. The contrasting middle section uses descending semitonal voice leading between seventh chords.

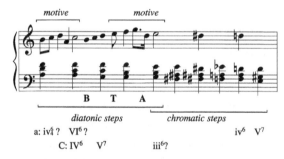

**Figure 9.3.6.** The opening of the A minor Mazurka, Op. 17, no. 4. The move from A–C–F to G–B–E, instead of taking place in the order Alto–Bass–Tenor, occurs in the order Bass–Tenor–Alto, producing a series of nontriadic harmonies.

**Figure 9.3.7.** Chromatic seventh-chord descent in the coda of Op. 17, no. 4.

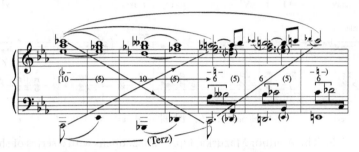

Figure 9.3.8. (*top*) My analysis of mm. 28–35 of Chopin's "Revolutionary" etude Op. 10, no. 12. The bottom staff shows an idealized background voice leading, while the top staff shows the actual upper voices, rising in thirds against the descending background. (*bottom*) Schenker's analysis of the same passage emphasizes a persisting C(♭).

to B-flat major, a-flat minor, etc. The voice leading of the middleground alone offers the correct solution to the problem.[22]

I agree that it would be perverse to describe this music as resulting from standard tonal-functional strategies, as if Chopin began with the intention to modulate to B♭ major, A♭ minor, D♭ minor, or to embody those keys with unusual modal progressions. Instead, it manifests a fundamentally *contrapuntal* logic that exploits stepwise descending voice leading, taking short clockwise motions in a pair of spiral diagrams (Figure 9.3.9). This descending background is further embellished by an ascending melodic voice as in the opening of the *Waldstein* (§3.7).

Yet Schenker and I disagree in our characterization of that logic. When Schenker speaks of "middleground voice leading," he is not referring to the continuous process of chromatic descent; instead, he is claiming that the music *derives from* or *prolongs* a persistent C (or C♭) shown by the arrows and open noteheads on his reduction. For Schenker, the unusual surface is essentially nonharmonic and decorative, with the real structure lying elsewhere. For me the *process* is instead basic and irreducible: the relevant middleground is a sequence rather than a static harmony;

---

[22] Schenker (1933) 1969, p. 58.

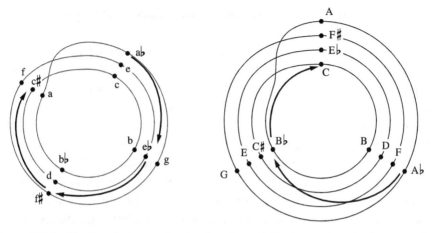

Figure 9.3.9. The Revolutionary Etude takes short clockwise motions in the space of chromatic triads (*left*) and chromatic seventh chords (*right*).

furthermore, I conceive of this sequence as creating a series of abstract, scale-like objects within which the surface voice ascends, rather than as a chorale made up of specific pitches. Finally, I believe that the background *does* in fact intimate a variety of functional phenomena: it is not "wrong" to hear modulations, tonics, or dominants; it is just that these functional effects are guided by a deeper logic.

When Schenker says that traditional concepts "fail," he is, I think, expressing a holistic conviction that his linear and prolongational approach could *replace* the ideas of traditional theory. It was this belief that led him to cast aspersions on such commonplace concepts as scale, sequence, motive, modulation, and functional-harmonic convention.[23] Recent Schenkerianism tacitly softens his radicalism, presenting Schenkerian theory as an extension of traditional music theory rather than a replacement for it. But this leads to the methodological challenge of synthesizing two very different views of musical structure: for how could one and the same chord be merely linear and *also* a dominant obeying a local chord-to-chord grammar? How could Chopin's Revolutionary Etude simultaneously be the mere byproduct of middleground voice leading and *also* modulate to A♭ major? My approach tries to ease this conflict by placing the two forms of explanation on different conceptual levels, treating local harmonic constraints as rule-like and syntactical, and larger linear relationships as strategic. For many Schenkerians, tonality just *is* prolongation, and the passages we have just considered are all functionally tonal. For me, Chopin's varied harmonic palette shows that style depends not just on musical goals, but also on the chordal and scalar environment in which the goals are pursued. We see this in the fact that Chopin can use a single melodic strategy to produce a wide range of harmonic effects.

---

[23] See Schmalfeldt 1991 and Cohn 1992.

## 4. An expanded vocabulary of reductional targets

Schenkerian templates were originally presented as something like laws of nature, rooted in the overtone series and applicable to all great music. By reconceiving them as melodic strategies, we can open the door to other forms of musical organization, including some that do not emphasize stepwise descent.[24]

Consider the variations theme of Beethoven's E major piano sonata, Op. 109 (Figure 9.4.1). Figure 9.4.2 reads each four-measure unit as a *near sequence by contrary motion*, presenting thirds on E, B, E, and A(♯), with each third accompanied by a voice exchange.[25] The two four-bar units combine to produce an eight-bar phrase featuring three distinct presentations of its opening two-measure idea. On my reading, the first four-bar pattern involves two octave displacements, one shifting G♯3 to G♯4 in m. 3, the other displacing the repeated cadence to arrive on (B2, B4) instead of (B3, B3). The second four-bar phrase has no displacements, the surface voices switching hands to arrive at the expected cadence on (B2, B3).[26] My drawing

Figure 9.4.1. The theme of the variations movement of Beethoven's Op. 109.

---

[24] See Neumeyer 1987, Temperley 2006 and 2011, and Froebe 2015 for related views. It may be that Schenkerian schemas have their origins in something more than arbitrary convention—for example, the preference for descending stepwise melodies may be rooted in the physiology of respiration (chapter 2).

[25] Beethoven's theme also recalls his earlier Op. 18, no. 5 minuet. Its I–V–I–IV progression would be a falling fifth sequence were the initial chord F♯ instead of E. This same near sequence appears as a chord progression in Figure 6.1.3 and as a succession of keys in Bach's D major prelude (§7.3).

[26] The location of the final cadence is interesting, and one could make the case that it belongs on the downbeat, with both melody and bass delaying the arrival until beat 3.

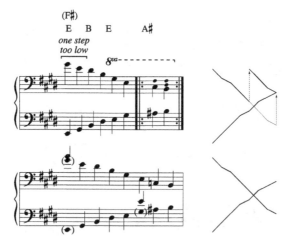

**Figure 9.4.2.** (*left*) My analysis of the opening of Beethoven's theme. (*right*) A graphical representation, with the vertical axis in scale steps and the horizontal axis in quarter notes.

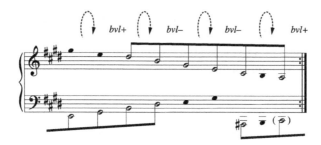

**Figure 9.4.3.** The theme as a superimposition of two thirds cycles. Vertical dyads are connected by either a basic voice leading (bvl+ or bvl−) or the two-step voice exchange (curved arrow).

perhaps expresses this more clearly than conventional notation. Figure 9.4.3 shows that the theme is composed of two overlapping chains of thirds: ascending thirds in the left hand, overlapping with descending thirds in the right.

Three pieces of evidence support this analysis. First, Beethoven makes the contrary-motion design explicit in the piece's third variation, where the music articulates exactly the reduction I have proposed—the composer helpfully analyzing his own music (Figure 9.4.4). This unveiling of covert sequential structure is reminiscent of the Op. 1, no. 3 variations, which also use the diatonic third's basic voice leading (§4.10). Second, this kind of thematic design, based on contrary motion and diatonic thirds, is characteristic of Beethoven: we have already encountered examples in §3.2, and will encounter many more in the next chapter. And third, the exploration of dyadic logic continues throughout the theme: in mm. 9–10, we have a curious descending-step sequence combining the two forms of the diatonic third's basic voice leading (Figure 9.4.5, compare pattern D2a on Figure 7.7.3). So the basic

428  TONALITY: AN OWNER'S MANUAL

**Figure 9.4.4.** The third variation of Op. 109 (bottom staves of each line) exposes the contrary-motion structure of the theme (top two staves).

**Figure 9.4.5.** My analysis of the second half of Beethoven's theme. Inward-pointing stems show the descending form of the diatonic third's basic voice leading; outward-pointing stems represent the ascending form.

voice leading, which initially alternates with voice exchanges, now appears more explicitly and without the voice exchanges.

I chose this passage because I think it demonstrates the core Schenkerian technique of analyzing complicated passages as decorations of simpler templates. Standard Schenkerianism, however, with its single-minded focus on stepwise melody—and its concomitant disdain for sequential structure—is not well-equipped to analyze it, in large part because the music's vocabulary lies outside the Schenkerian catalogue of acceptable reductive targets.[27] Hence Forte and Gilbert

---

[27] As Robert Morgan put it, in Schenker's theory, "stepwise motion forms the basis for all melodic content" (Morgan 2014, p. 19).

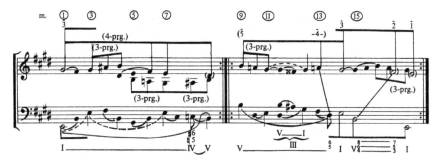

**Figure 9.4.6.** Forte and Gilbert's analysis of Beethoven's theme.

**Figure 9.4.7.** The Op. 22 minuet opens by decorating the ascending form of the diatonic third's basic voice leading.

promote the first measure's weak F♯ to primary melodic status and ignore the theme's notable close on $\hat{3}$ (Figure 9.4.6). This is a first example of what I take to be a broader incompatibility between Beethoven's lexicon and the generic expectations of Schenkerian theory—and a reminder that we need to consider a composer's individual vocabulary when producing musical reductions.

The minuet from the Op. 22 piano sonata is broadly analogous to the Op. 109 theme, again emphasizing contrary motion and the diatonic third's basic voice leading (Figure 9.4.7). Here, however, it opens with an ascending-fifth contrary motion pattern E♭–B♭–F, again decorated with voice exchanges but now with each dyad preceded by its diatonic lower neighbor. Note that on my analysis the initial melodic D belongs to the lower voice and continues in the left hand. The underlying schema appears in many of Beethoven's compositions, including the preceding opus number (Figure 9.4.8); it is easily missed if one is not expecting it.[28]

---

[28] It is also the diatonic inversion of the two-voice fauxbourdon framework at the start of the fifth Brandenburg concerto (Figure 7.5.2). Yust 2015b refines Schenker's reading of the piece.

430  TONALITY: AN OWNER'S MANUAL

**Figure 9.4.8.** The opening of the minuet of Beethoven's First Symphony, Op. 21.

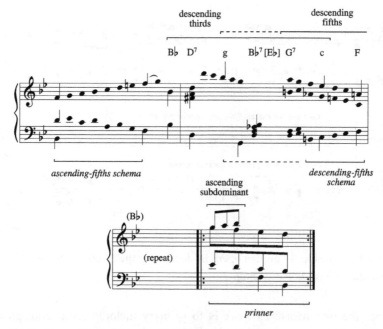

**Figure 9.4.9.** An analysis of the Op. 22 minuet.

The sequential antecedent dissolves into a curiously static consequent that sits on a V$^9$ chord resolving to I without any linear descent. We then move to a middle section that is a doubly distorted A3D5 near sequence: instead of the purely sequential B♭–D$^7$–g–B♭$^7$–E♭–G$^7$–c–E♭–a°– ... , Beethoven gives us B♭–D$^7$–g–B♭$^7$–[E♭]–G$^7$–c–F$^7$–B♭, omitting the E♭ and adjusting the final unit upward by step so that it returns to the tonic after four iterations (Figure 9.4.9).[29] There are also hints of an antiparallel contrary-motion sequence, with the upper-voice thirds moving from B♭5 to E♭5 to A4 while the bass roots ascend G2–C3–F3.[30] The repeat brings us to a coda

---

[29] The direct shift from B♭$^7$ to G$^7$ is an example of what I have called "the minor-third system" (Tymoczko 2011a). The switch from descending thirds to descending steps occurs in many Beethoven pieces, including Op. 31, no. 3, I, mm. 68–70.

[30] The middle section answers $\hat{5}$–$\hat{4}$–$\hat{3}$–$\hat{2}$–$\hat{1}$ in G minor with $\hat{6}$–$\hat{5}$–$\hat{4}$–$\hat{3}$–$\hat{2}$ in C minor, shifting the rhythmic emphasis from tonic to dominant in preparation for the I$^6_4$–V arrival.

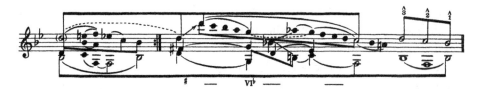

Figure 9.4.10. Schenker's reading of Beethoven's Op. 22 minuet.

in which the hanging G5 is doubly resolved: upward to B♭ by way of the "ascending subdominant," and downward to D (harmonized by the tenor $\hat{4}$–$\hat{3}$–$\hat{2}$–$\hat{1}$ to generate a Prinner). Once again, the upper-voice melody never reaches the tonic; insofar as there is a descent, it is in an inner voice, and postponed to the coda rather than presented in the main body of the piece.

Schenker's analysis is largely insensitive to its sequential structure (Figure 9.4.10). The most obvious issue is his choice of primary note D5, the sixth note of the upper voice's eight-note melodic sequence: if one knows the idiom, F is a more obvious choice. (Schematically, the initial D4 belongs to the lower voice, even though Beethoven initially presents it in the right hand.) Equally problematic is the interpretation of the middle section as a generic descending-fifth progression D–g–c–F rather than a distorted near sequence by descending third: not only does the latter reading engage more musical details but it is more responsive to Beethoven's sequential vocabulary.[31] The resulting analysis ends up flattening this highly personal music into something generic.[32]

All of which raises three methodological questions. The most important is whether sequences are essential or merely superficial. Schenkerian analysis is often presented as a process of *removing notes*, reducing music to a nonsequential chorale-like background whose melodies invariably move according to principles of good voice leading.[33] I have argued that sequences can also be legitimate targets for musical reduction, comparable to the stepwise melodic connections that feature in Schenkerian analysis: for me, the inner life of these pieces, their deepest semantics, consists in the juxtaposition of schematic and sequential material. I take these sequences to be atomic units, pieces of vocabulary comparable to English phrases like "it is what it is."[34] Idioms are analytical end-states requiring no further reduction.

---

[31] Schenker's reading ignores the B♭$^6_3$ in the middle section, reducing it to a G minor triad.

[32] Schenker's invention of C[7] in the opening is reminiscent of Dahlhaus's denial of the autonomy of vii°[6] (§6.4).

[33] "It should be evident now that the analytic procedure is one of *reduction*; details which are subordinate with respect to larger patterns are gradually eliminated" (Forte 1959). Arndt (2018, p. 39) argues that the focus on surface-to-depth reduction is a later accretion; Schenker proposed an idealist theory of the Genius's creative process, which proceeds from the background to foreground. In this book, I am concerned with Schenker as he has been received rather than the historical figure.

[34] Gjerdingen and Bourne 2015.

432  TONALITY: AN OWNER'S MANUAL

Here, the two philosophies lead to very different perspectives on voice exchanges. If the target of reduction is a chorale-like structure, then voice exchanges must ultimately be reduced away. By contrast I think the familiar picture of "surface" voice exchanges decorating stepwise melody, while often useful, is misleading here: the point of Figure 9.4.2 is that the basic voice leading and voice exchanges combine to produce a *near contrary-motion fifth sequence*, with the voice exchange and the basic voice leading producing very similar melodic intervals (§10.1). I claim this sequence is a recurring schema important throughout functional music and crucial to Beethoven's language in particular— a unified idiom not *representing* anything deeper. Indeed, the next chapter will argue that the schema is one of a small number of contrary-motion patterns basic to functionally tonal counterpoint. If I am right, then this is a case where the analytical habit of eliminating voice exchanges can lead us astray.

A second question concerns the ontology of our reductional targets. Schenkerian reduction produces a chorale-like output where specific pitches are arranged in the manner of species counterpoint. I have instead proposed a method that yields a scalar background, whose abstract "voices" are melodic slots available in every octave (e.g., Figure P5.3 or P5.7). Thus my analysis of the middle section of Chopin's Revolutionary Etude featured an ascending surface pattern within a descending harmonic field; Schenker's alternative features specific *pitches* which are projected into other octaves by a process of register transfer. One could complain here that standard Schenkerian analysis is *insufficiently hierarchical*, ignoring the ontological difference between chord and scale—and flattening multileveled musical structures in the process.

The last question concerns the degree of similarity to be expected among functionally tonal pieces. I believe there are considerable differences from composer to composer and genre to genre. Acknowledging these differences might lead us to reconsider, for example, whether every functional piece needs to articulate a linear descent to the tonic. Absent a preexisting conviction about this matter, it is difficult to understand why any analyst would identify a $\hat{3}-\hat{2}-\hat{1}$ descent in the two pieces we have just considered. Here, Schenkerian analysis seems to suffer from the desire to make every piece tell the very same story, an aspiration virtually explicit in the motto "semper idem sed non eodem modo."[35] A better view, I think, describes composers as deploying a range of strategies and schemas that vary with time and place: rather than a single "language of tonality," it paints a picture of overlapping networks of context-dependent practice—an hourglass shape with baroque tonality comparatively closer to the Renaissance, classical practice more regimented and conventional, and more expansive in the nineteenth century. Where Schenkerian metaphysics requires unity, the melodic strategies allow for variability.

---

[35] "Always the same but not in the same way," Schenker's motto, appearing at the front of *Der Tonwille* and later works.

## 5. Simple harmonic hierarchy

Though I believe functional harmony obeys chord-to-chord laws, I do not claim that its grammar is completely and utterly nonhierarchical. I have already mentioned that fauxbourdon often embellishes functional progressions, as when IV–iii–ii–I decorates IV–I (§7.5). Furthermore, I agree with the standard view that the cadential six-four should be understood hierarchically, with progressions like ii⁶–I$^6_4$–V moving from a supertonic to a dominant that is itself embellished by a second-inversion triad; in symbols ii⁶–(I$^6_4$⇒V), with (I$^6_4$⇒V) indicating that the six-four is hierarchically dependent on the following dominant. This perspective brings a host of otherwise anomalous progressions under the umbrella of standard functional principles; sequences such as V$^6_5$/V–I$^6_4$–V or vi–I$^6_4$–V can be understood to move from the initial chord to the final dominant *by way of* a subsidiary or decorative $^6_4$.[36] The view gains further support from the fact that second-inversion triads can decorate the final tonic in cadential idioms like V–IV$^6_4$–I (Figure 9.5.1). It is more enlightening to view this as V–(IV$^6_4$⇒I) rather than a retrofunctional V–IV progression. Indeed, in earlier music we find first-inversion triads functioning in this way (e.g., m. 12 of Figure 6.5.1).

Figure 9.5.1. While the standard cadential $^6_4$ chord decorates the dominant, an alternative decorates the tonic: m. 30 of the first Agnus of Palestrina's mass *Quando lieta sperai*; Chopin's Mazurka, Op. 17, no. 3, mm. 39–40; the opening of the slow movement of Mozart's A minor piano sonata, K.310, where the G–B♭ suspensions embellish a deceptive resolution.

---

[36] This is precisely why some theorists like the notation V$^{6-5}_{4-3}$; my own preference is to notate the scale degrees and trust that readers understand the idiom.

**Figure 9.5.2.** Two analyses of the opening of Bach's "Herr Jesu Christ, dich zu uns wend" (BWV 332, Riemenschneider 136).

Secondary dominants often require a similar approach. Consider the two analyses in Figure 9.5.2. The first is not so much wrong as incomplete, for while it correctly notes the presence of harmonic cycles in G major, D major, and E minor, it implausibly postulates four separate key changes, as if the mere presence of a dominant were sufficient to immediately cancel the prevailing key. The better analysis depicts a multileveled structure—identifying E minor both as the tonic of its own IV$^6_5$–V$^6_5$–i cycle *and also* as vi in a higher-level G major cycle. This description recognizes the psychological reality that very brief excursions to foreign keys do not fully dislodge our memory of the home tonality: when we return to the tonic after a short digression to E minor, we are capable of experiencing the entire progression in a persisting G major. (It is not known whether listeners experience the E minor as having any tonic quality, or whether we simply accept V$^7$/vi–vi as an idiom, perhaps a substitute for iii–vi.) We might say that centricity is "sticky," changing more slowly than harmonies themselves. Musicians exploit this stickiness by briefly digressing from the home key, a technique that is as old as secondary dominants and as recent as "playing outside" (§5.6).[37]

Rhythm, phrasing, and sequence can reinforce this hierarchical structure in interesting ways. In Figure 9.5.3, for example, a two-unit sequence moves from tonic to supertonic, embellishing each chord with its own dominant.[38] The phrase structure reinforces the harmonic hierarchy: since mm. 9–16 mirror mm. 1–8, it is much easier to hear the entire unit moving upward from I to ii, creating a large-scale I–ii–V progression decorated by lower-level tonic-dominant oscillations. The third eight-bar unit is particularly interesting, as it does not involve secondary dominants; instead it is an example of "standing on the dominant," in which hypermetrically weak tonics may be felt to embellish rhythmically stable dominants. Here we have harmonic hierarchy *without* secondary dominants or exact sequential parallelism.[39]

---

[37] It is also clear that musical experience is often multileveled and hierarchical: we can hear a tonic scale degree as decorating the third of a V chord that is itself unstable relative to the tonic. My explanation of this phenomenon is that the tonic scale degree is unstable relative to the local harmony while the local harmony is itself unstable relative to our functionally tonal harmonic expectations (§7.1).

[38] This example comes from Muns 2008.

[39] Other examples include the opening of the B♭ major prelude from the first book of *The Well-Tempered Clavier* (featuring diatonic chords with a very weak dominant function), Chopin's Mazurka Op. 50, no. 3, mm.

HETEROGENEOUS HIERARCHY 435

**Figure 9.5.3.** The opening of the last movement of Haydn's final piano sonata, Hob.XVI:52.

Such examples clearly show that Western music can exhibit a limited degree of hierarchical embedding, with subsidiary progressions decorating larger patterns that can be felt to follow familiar harmonic trajectories. This sort of recursive organization has generated significant interest among both musicians and cognitive scientists, as it evokes the structure of natural language: the hierarchy in Figure 9.5.2 seems analogous to that in a phrase like "the kitten *we got at the shelter* has grown into an affectionate cat," where the sentence "we got the kitten at the shelter" is embedded inside "the kitten has grown into an affectionate cat." This suggests that music may exploit the same cognitive capacities as natural language, with musical "sentences" like I–V–I capable of being embedded inside one another to form progressions like (I–V–I)–(vi–V/vi–vi)–... [40]

---

53–61 (featuring secondary *sub*dominants), and Figure 9.6.6 (secondary dominants embellishing descending thirds). Salzer (1952) 1962 uses these brief moments of harmonic recursion to argue against traditional harmonic theory.

[40] Among those who have made this connection are Bernstein 1976, Lerdahl and Jackendoff 1983, Katz and Pesetsky 2011, and Rohrmeier 2011 and 2020.

436 TONALITY: AN OWNER'S MANUAL

This analogy has led some theorists to propose that secondary dominants *generally* decorate the chords to which they apply.[41] If so, it is wrong to hear a direct relationship between a secondary dominant and the preceding chord: instead, we should hear X–V⁷/Y–Y as a version of X–Y, with the second harmony embellished by a V⁷/Y chord at a lower level, symbolically X–(V⁷/Y⇒Y). (This is analogous to the way we connect "the kitten" but not "the shelter" to the verb phrase "has grown"; it is the kitten rather than the shelter that has grown.) Thus in the penultimate measure of Figure 9.5.2, the meaningful progression is from G major to E minor, and not from G major to A♮. The G–A♮ is like the misleading adjacency "the shelter has grown" in the English sentence.

Once again, however, the complexity of musical practice thwarts simple generalizations. For if secondary dominants invariably worked as just described, then we would not find progressions of the form X–(V⁷/Y⇒Y) unless we *also* found X–Y. Yet virtually any nonsyntactical progression X–Y can be normalized by the insertion of the appropriate secondary dominant, including V–IV, V–ii, I♮–vi, and so on. Figure 9.5.4 provides a pair of examples from the Bach chorales in which secondary dominants cancel the implications of the preceding chord, allowing the music to rescind its outstanding harmonic obligations.[42] The paradox is that secondary dominants are simultaneously a clear example of harmonic recursion *and also* evidence for its limited scope: it is not much of an exaggeration to say that any secondary dominant could signal *either* a momentary digression to a foreign key, hierarchically embedded within a persisting tonic, *or* a shift to a new key that simply abandons any existing implications. This suggests harmonies have only weak implications for chords beyond their immediate successors.

To my mind, this difference underscores a fundamental feature of functional harmony: where human language cannot be characterized in a word-to-word fashion, a good deal of music does seem to exhibit chord-to-chord structure. One can imagine linguistic utterances that thwart expectations in a manner similar to the previous examples: "The beautiful and ... yesterday we went to the ... and the kitten we got at the shelter has grown into an affectionate ..." The incomprehensibility we feel here, the palpable frustration generated by unrealized implications, is unlike anything one experiences in any of the musical examples.

The failure of hierarchical analysis, in even simple cases, speaks volumes. In many ways, secondary dominants are comparable to nonharmonic tones: both phenomena initially seem clearly hierarchical, yet turn out to involve unexpected complexities. Nonharmonic tones do not always represent harmonic partners, and secondary

[41] Brown 2005 (pp. 76ff) and Rohrmeier 2011 both make this argument, though they stop short of explicitly demonstrating that their recursive principles actually account for the regularities in functional pieces—or, what is more difficult, demonstrating that their recursive grammars *rule out* the patterns we do not find in functional tonality. Rohrmeier 2020 seems to acknowledge that the hierarchical approach does not expand our ability to describe what happens in actual pieces, merely functioning as a theory of analytical intuitions *about* music.

[42] For more examples, see Figures 10.4.7 (I–ii–IV–V upon removing the applied dominant) and 10.6.5 (V–ii⁶) and the end of the trio of Beethoven's Op. 28, III, where D♮, functioning locally as a cadential ♮, moves via secondary dominant to B minor and the end of the movement.

HETEROGENEOUS HIERARCHY 437

**Figure 9.5.4.** Secondary dominants licensing unusual harmonic progressions: "Wie schön leuchtet der Morgenstern" (BWV 36.4, Riemenschneider 86) has a V–ii if the applied dominant is removed; "Fröhlich soll mein Herze springen" (BWV 248.33, Riemenschneider 139) has a I$^6_4$–vi without the applied dominant.

dominants do not always embellish their successors. The issue, in both cases, is the limits of musical perception: where we perceive language with almost crystalline accuracy, transforming sound into meaning without error, we perceive music through a low-fidelity haze. We are simply not *accurate* enough to be bothered by the fact that the "Renaissance seventh" cannot be reduced to a consonant background, or that the progression ii–V/IV–IV contravenes the principles of functional harmony when the secondary dominant is eliminated. What is remarkable is that music can move us so deeply despite our perceptual limitations.

## 6. The four-part phrase

Classical phrases often exhibit a quadruple grouping structure inherited from Western European dance music.[43] Figure 9.6.1 shows how four durational units can be arranged to satisfy two constraints: that one unit repeats or varies another, and that the final unit forms a cadence. When the third unit recalls the first, we have an ABA′C or "period" structure—often further organized into two loosely parallel halves, with a weak close after AB and a stronger close after A′C. When

---

[43] Rothstein 1989 emphasizes the classical style's eight-bar norm.

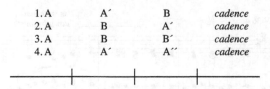

**Figure 9.6.1.** Four ways to divide eight measures into four two-bar groups, with a cadence at the end, and at least one group echoing another.

the recall is immediate, we have an AA′BC "sentence," again often articulated as (AA′) and (BC). The third possibility occurs when the third unit echoes the second for an ABB′C arrangement. This structure has no standard name and is considerably less common than the others, but it does occasionally appear (Figure 9.6.2); we might call it "tail-development form," because the phrase proceeds by developing the "tail" of the initial four-measure idea. The fourth possibility, AA′A′′C, is reasonably common, appearing for example in Beethoven's Op. 109 variations (Figure 9.4.1).[44] This is a nice example of how abstract reasoning can serve concrete analysis: rather than postulating sentence and period as unexplained schemas, we can understand them as filling out an abstract space of possibility—sensitizing our ears to new possibilities along the way.

Though not unknown in earlier music, quadruply divided phrases become popular in the late eighteenth century and remain so in our own time (Figure 9.6.3).[45] Longer themes often nest these templates inside one another so that similar structures appear on multiple temporal levels. The most common approach is to embed an eight-bar sentence inside a sixteen-bar period (Figure 9.6.4). In the rondo of his D major piano sonata K.311, Mozart takes things one step further: the opening four bars are organized as a small period that is continued by a four-bar sentence; together, they form an eight-bar sentence that is embedded in a sixteen-bar period, triply nesting the standard four-part templates (Figure 9.6.5).[46]

More complex construction can arise from elision, with one or more bars shared by overlapping formal units. I hear the opening of the *Hammerklavier*'s scherzo as a four-bar AA'A'A" that ends with a weak cadence: heard on its own, these measures outline a weakly closed I–vi–IV–V–I harmonic cycle, with the first three chords hierarchically decorated by their own dominants (Figure 9.6.6). The final bar starts a second schema, a four-bar "Ludwig" featuring outer-voice contrary motion and organized as four-bar sentence; heard on *its* own, it would make a reasonably convincing opening.[47] To understand this music, we therefore need to recognize the weak close in m. 4: whether we refer to it as a "cadence" or a form of "noncadential

---

[44] Richards 2011 calls these "trifold sentences."
[45] Rothstein 1989, pp. 125–30, considers the origin of these phrase templates.
[46] Lerdahl 2020, p. 89, makes the same point.
[47] Note that this is the same ascending-fifth schema I identified in the Op. 22 minuet, on the same pitches: IV–I–V in B♭ major (§10.1).

**Figure 9.6.2.** Four classical-style ABB′C phrases: A, Haydn's Hob. XVI:8, IV; B, the opening of Mozart's violin sonata K.304; C, the opening of Beethoven's Op. 31, no. 3; and D, the opening of Beethoven's Op. 79.

closure" is immaterial; the important point is its role in dividing the phrase into two overlapping halves, 4 + 4 somehow adding up to 7.

Here I have been using the terms "sentence" and "period" to refer to very general grouping strategies that can exist on a variety of temporal levels. William Caplin, our most influential theorist of phrase structure, instead defines "sentence" and "period" as thematic patterns of what he calls "formal functions," largely determined by bass motion and always having a length of eight "real" bars.[48] This has, in my opinion, three problematic consequences. First, it deemphasizes one of the most interesting features of the classical style, the reuse of similar grouping strategies on different

---

[48] Caplin 2013 observes that we can analyze phrase structure in terms of motivic material, melodic strategy, or harmony and bass. Temperley 2018, p. 90, favors a grouping-based strategy for reasons similar to mine. Brody 2016 pursues the issue in a more general way, proposing "thematic design" and "tonal structure," as axes along which different theoretical approaches might disagree. In this section I focus mostly on thematic design and motive; in the next I consider tonal structure.

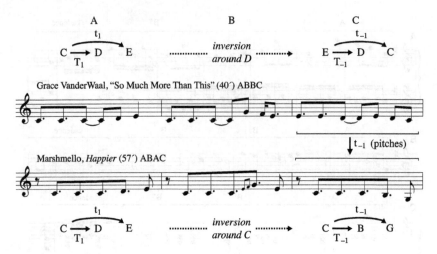

**Figure 9.6.3.** Grace VanderWaal's 2017 "So Much More Than This" arranges the three units A, B, and C to form an ABBC phrase, while Marshmello's 2018 "Happier" arranges similar units to form an ABAC period.

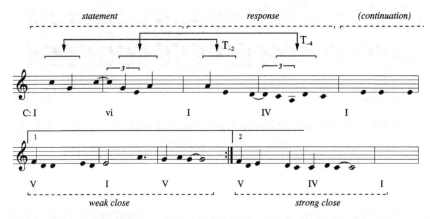

**Figure 9.6.4.** Sam Cooke's 1961 "Cupid" nests two eight-bar sentences inside a sixteen-bar period. The initial motive is transposed relative to the prevailing chord, changing harmonic notes to nonharmonic notes and vice versa.

temporal levels.[49] Second, it deprives us of vocabulary for expressing similarities between classical-style phrases and those in nonclassical styles such as rock. Third, it directs our attention away from relatively intersubjective features of musical structure, such as the contrast between ABA′C and AA′BC grouping, and toward much more subjective judgments about rhetorical role.

The second theme of the first movement of Beethoven's Op. 31, no. 3, illustrates the difficulties that can arise. From the perspective of melody, motive, and

---

[49] Caplin 2009b allows for nested formal functions, but conceives them as generalized "beginning/middle/end" patterns rather than the specific grouping strategies characteristic of sentence and period.

HETEROGENEOUS HIERARCHY 441

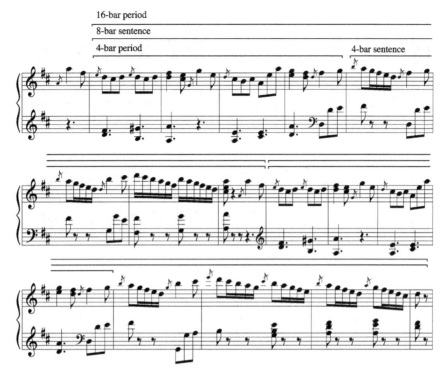

Figure 9.6.5. Triply nested groupings in Mozart's K.311, III.

Figure 9.6.6. The opening of the scherzo of Beethoven's *Hammerklavier*, Op. 106. The first four measures and the last four measures each sound like coherent four-bar phrases.

grouping, Figure 9.6.7 is a period, an (AB)(A′C) phrase with an unmistakable pause on an unstable ii⁶. Caplin, however, does not recognize it as such, taking its lightly embellished $\hat{3}$–$\hat{4}$–$\hat{5}$–$\hat{1}$ bass to indicate that the entire structure is "cadential," lacking "initiating function" altogether.[50] But his writing also justifies another

---

[50] See Caplin 1998, p. 111. Although Caplin in principle allows that cadential function is determined by myriad factors, in practice he is almost exclusively focused on the bass: this leads him to describe Beethoven's entire theme as having cadential function although it is the start of the second group. In this context, Richards argues that tonic chords are only "weak indicators of cadential function" (2010, p. 26).

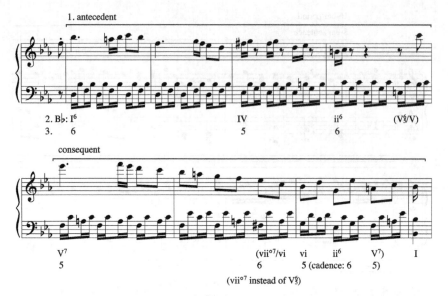

Figure 9.6.7. Three features of the second theme of Beethoven's Op. 31, no. 3, I, suggesting three different formal interpretations. First, its rhythmic and motivic antecedent/consequent design; second, its cadential bass line; third, its disguised sequential structure. This last feature may explain the decision to begin with a first-inversion triad.

interpretation that highlights the left hand's ascending-step sequence. This would make the phrase functionally *medial*, a continuation without proper beginning.[51] Thus we could interpret one and the same phrase as a standard period, a cadential structure lacking initiating function, or a sequence expressing medial function.

While I incline toward the first of these interpretations, I am much more strongly committed to the view that they are all reasonable: motivically, Beethoven has given us a period built from a largely sequential progression over a bass line that usually signals a cadence. All these descriptions are true, all are potentially available to listeners, and none need take priority over the others. The advantage of thinner, more objective definitions of "sentence" and "period"—based on grouping rather than a nebulous and subjective concept of "function"—is that they give us relatively neutral categories with which to express our differing perceptions: whatever we may think about its formal function, we can agree that this theme is a period in the sense of having a loosely parallel (AB)(A′C) grouping structure, with a weak close on ii⁶ answered by a stronger close on the tonic. To my mind, that is reason to favor the simpler and more objective terminology.

---

[51] Caplin analyzes the sequential second theme of Beethoven's Op. 2, no. 2, I as a "continuation" (1998, pp. 112–13).

## 7. Grouping, melody, harmony

Here, finally, we start to glimpse the full complexity of the classical style, which obeys a local harmonic grammar while articulating longer-range melodic connections and *also* grouping music into conventional four-unit patterns, sometimes instantiated on multiple temporal levels, all occurring inside scales that follow higher-level modulatory pathways and alongside complex networks of motivic and thematic relationships which may themselves make topical and generic references, while invoking the large-scale conventions of forms such as the sonata. And that is completely ignoring rhythm, orchestration, timbre, and any number of vitally important phenomena. Music is difficult not so much because of the complexity of its syntactical systems, but because it juggles so many simultaneously.

And though we can consider these systems separately, they sometimes interact in complex and interesting ways. One example is when the local harmonic grammar is overridden across phrase boundaries. In the first eight bars of Figure 8.5.2, a V–ii progression occurs across mm. 4–5 of a sentence form. Here the rhetorical structure ameliorates the harmonic hiccup: rather than a baldly retrofunctional V–ii, I hear a first musical thought that ends on the dominant followed by a new thought beginning on the supertonic. Such examples show what is at stake in questions about the nature and location of cadences; for whatever we call these $I_4^6$–V progressions, we want to recognize them as punctuations, important junctures that weaken the grip of the local harmonic constraints.[52]

More common are those cases in which harmony supports grouping structure. Chapter 6 noted that dominants and tonics are oriented oppositely in time: dominants are approached freely, but constrained in how they move; tonics move freely, but are approached in only a small number of ways (§6.4). This differential orientation is fundamental to the logic of the period, which begins with maximum harmonic stability, and hence maximal uncertainty about the future, progresses to a high degree of harmonic instability (and hence predictability), and then retraces its steps to achieve repose.[53] From this point of view, one might be tempted to consider Figure 9.7.1 an eight-measure period in which IV plays the role of the dominant, appearing as the final chord of the first four-bar unit and leading to I at the end of the second. This intuition motivates Drew Nobile to *define* "dominant" and "tonic" in terms of the phrasal and entropic tendencies in Figure 9.7.2. In effect, Nobile uses "dominant" to refer to a particular position *within the phrase*, rather than within the more abstract *harmonic cycles* that make up the phrase. I prefer the more traditional terminology, in part because I prefer its linking of functional names to particular scale-degree collections. Nevertheless, I feel the force of Nobile's insight: there are genres in which phrasal convention can lead us to hear

---

[52] This provides another reason to reject Caplin's strict division between "cadence" and "noncadence."

[53] The association of tension with certainty about the future, and repose with uncertainty, may seem counterintuitive; but recall that the tension is associated with the sense that the chord *has to move* in a particular way. The uncertainty of repose is associated with the fact that the tonic has no analogous obligations.

**Figure 9.7.1.** Drew Nobile analyzes this passage from the Eagles' "Take It Easy" as a period structure with the subdominant chord playing the role of the dominant.

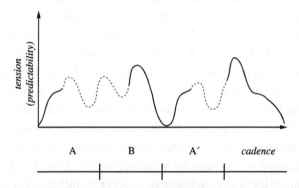

**Figure 9.7.2.** The energetic trajectory of an abstract period; it begins with low tension, moves to high tension at the half cadence; and retraces its steps to end with low tension.

a wider range of harmonies as functioning like "dominants" in the broadest sense of the term—unstable sonorities creating strong expectations of a coming tonic.[54] Both phrase structure and harmonic cycles can create tension and release.

It is sentences, however, that present the most complex interaction between the musical systems. We saw in §9.1 that classical composers use dual transpositions $T_x t_y$ to transfer material from one harmony to another. This gives rise to a fundamental sentence-form default whereby a melodic fragment, harmonized by I–V, is answered by V–I.[55] Here the demands of thematic parallelism often lead to an interesting phenomenon: if the I–V statement uses, say, descending voice leading (options A–B on Figure 9.1.3), then the response will typically use descending voice leading from V to I (options 1–4); and taken together the sentence will traverse a loop in chord space, answering "V just below I" with "I just below V" (or

---

[54] Nobile's perspective derives from Lerdahl 2001, and recalls Long's (2018, 2020) proposal that we consider rhythm and phrasing as essential to functional tonality. These perspectives are closely related to the ideas discussed in §9.2; indeed, one way of interpreting the Schenkerian notion of a "structural dominant" is as "the dominant that occurs when we are expecting the end of the phrase." Here, phrasal role supersedes note-content as a determiner of function. This approach works best with very regularly phrased music.

[55] Caplin and Schoenberg present the opening of Beethoven's Op. 2, no. 1, as a model sentence; to my mind, however, it is unusual insofar as its basic idea has just one chord, giving it a more urgent and developmental character than the typical Mozartian sentence (I–V, V–I). See BaileyShea 2004.

HETEROGENEOUS HIERARCHY 445

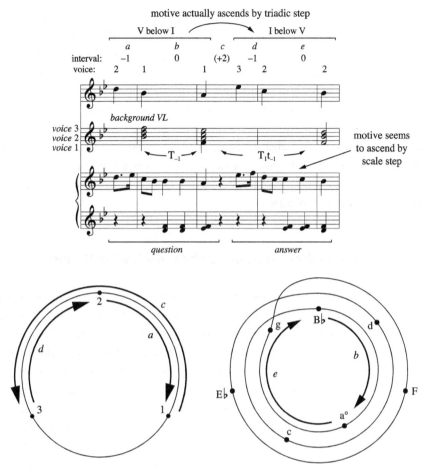

Figure 9.7.3. The opening of Mozart's K.282, II.

alternatively, answering "V just above I" with "I just above V"). The requirement of motivic similarity thus ensures that motives will ascend by step along a descending chordal background, producing scale steps at the surface.[56]

Chapters 6 and 7 argued that functional tonality makes particular use of I–V–I voice leadings that travel a full circle in triadic space, rather than more efficient voice leadings that often feature in modal counterpoint. We now see that the conventions of sentence form endow these circular journeys with rhetorical significance, the first half of the circle posing a musical question that is answered by the second. Figure 9.7.3 analyzes the melody of the second movement of Mozart's K.282 as moving inside harmonies that act like very small scales; its core claim is that the surface voices move *contrary* to the underlying voice leading, ascending by chordal

---

[56] This is the origin of the "changing-note archetype" discussed in Gjerdingen 1988, later rechristened the "Meyer" schema.

446    TONALITY: AN OWNER'S MANUAL

step as the chords descend. Here we also have a clear example of a nonadjacent melodic connection, the m. 1 D5 and the m. 3 C5 belonging to the same abstract voice.

This sort of analysis makes no reference to organicism, prolongation, representation, verticalization, register transfer, obligatory register, or any other controversial concepts of Schenkerian theory; instead, its assumptions are those of standard scalar discourse, albeit at an unusual hierarchical level. And though we are far from Schenker's complete theory, we can see glimmerings of a characteristic insight: that even when chords act like abstract fields-of-play for concrete voices, they can still articulate interesting contrapuntal structures. Schenker the musician was right to point to this phenomenon, even if Schenker the metaphysician described it in ways that may now seem problematic.


## 8. Beyond the phrase: hierarchy at the level of the piece

My belief is that large-scale form is produced by collage-like arrangements of smaller sections whose differences in mood, mode, rhythm, and texture, conjoined with thematic returns and contrasts, collectively form a coherent and pleasingly dramatic experience.[57] This play of energetic trajectories, of similarity and contrast, is at the core of musical storytelling, equally present in classical symphonies, free improvisation, and well-sequenced rock albums. Its resistance to enlightening general description is one of the main embarrassments of music theory—for the very features that most powerfully stoke our musical interest, leading us to sit quietly for long stretches of time, are also the most resistant to rational elucidation. Which is not to say that they are beyond description, but rather that our words tend to add little to what is obvious from simply listening.

This, I think, creates pressure to fill the void, to find something useful to say about the nature of musical form. Earlier theorists often turned to motive, proposing that nonobvious thematic connections contributed to a sense of musical unity, explaining why some pieces are formally convincing while others are not.[58] This has always seemed bizarre to me, as it feels obvious that a great piece can contain multiple unrelated themes or motives, much as a great novel can contain many different episodes. Another option is to follow Schenker in asserting that entire movements embellish the same harmonic-contrapuntal templates that govern individual phrases. What makes for large-scale continuity, on this account, is ultra-long-range connection between pitches.

This approach is not obviously wrong in principle. Imagine for example that classical sonata-forms tended to follow a first theme emphasizing $\hat{3}$ with a second theme, in the dominant, that emphasizes $\hat{2}$ (locally $\hat{5}$). And imagine, furthermore, that these emphases were strong enough that listeners, performers, and

---

[57] See Levinson 1997. Explaining what makes a piece "coherent and pleasingly dramatic" is no easier than explaining what makes a good movie.

[58] Reti 1951.

analysts tended to agree about them, even without any special training. Such a situation would suggest that composers were indeed concerned with constructing movement-long trajectories of melodic emphasis. (Whether listeners could hear these relationships, and whether they were aesthetically significant, are of course further questions.) In actual fact, however, the process of Schenkerian reduction is a good deal less straightforward than this: constructing a long-term Schenkerian narrative requires a host of nonobvious decisions about which notes are structural, and these are often influenced by the desire to construct a satisfactory analysis.[59] One reasonable conclusion is that functional music simply does not exhibit intersubjectively identifiable trajectories of the sort Schenker postulated. Any appearance to the contrary is made possible only because analysts put their finger on the scale, gathering data with one eye toward making the results vindicate the theory.

Putting that aside, there is a more important question about the *aesthetic relevance* of large-scale pitch structure—about why anyone should care whether a given piece contains the nonobvious relationships that Schenkerian analysis purports to uncover. Imagine a long piece that exhibits these kinds of long-range connections while presenting a satisfying sequence of themes, moods, local pitch structures, and characters. Now suppose we introduce small modulations that distort the pitch structure while preserving the sequence of themes, moods, and characters. If the long-term pitch relationships are aesthetically important, then these shifts should have a significant impact on our appreciation for the overall work, yet it seems implausible that they would: indeed, a non-absolute-pitch listener, not intimately familiar with the piece, might not even notice them. How could aesthetic value rest so squarely upon relationships with such little perceptual import? Schenkerian theory seems caught between the empirically implausible claim that we *are* sensitive to long-term prolongational structure (without realizing it) and the equally implausible philosophical claim that unheard relationships can be primary bearers of musical value.[60] In this respect, it is comparable to twelve-tone composition, two modernist ideologies placing a heavy emphasis on relationships that are difficult if not impossible to hear.

Many theorists therefore prefer to model long-term harmonic relationships using *keys* and *scales* rather than Schenkerian linear connections.[61] This is a significant improvement, for it is indisputable that a large number of functionally tonal pieces nest local chord progressions within formally similar motion on the level of the scale. We have seen that the two processes can be represented using the very same spiral diagrams, a hierarchical self-similarity linking local musical details to progressions

---

[59] Marvin 2012–2013 points out that this challenge is particularly acute in the case of sonata-form recapitulations. There is also the additional challenge of devising a Schenkerian analysis that is compatible with traditional formal divisions (P. Smith 1994, C. Smith 1996, and Brody 2021).

[60] This thought experiment is inspired by the experiment of Cook 1987, later repeated by Marvin and Brinkman 1999. Gjerdingen 1999 expresses skepticism about some details of Cook's experiment even while endorsing his general conclusions.

[61] Yust 2018 emphasizes keys within a largely Schenkerian framework, though this does not lead to major changes in analytical practice.

448    TONALITY: AN OWNER'S MANUAL

spanning entire movements. Furthermore, scales and keys are empirically unproblematic to the point where computers can identify them; by contrast, we have achieved essentially no success at automating Schenkerian analysis.[62] Thus at a purely conceptual level, key relationships deliver uncontroversial long-term hierarchical structure at least broadly analogous to that hypothesized by Schenkerians.

Yet once again there are significant issues of perceptibility and aesthetic relevance. Hepokoski and Darcy write that sonata-form recapitulations deliver "the *telos* of the entire sonata—the point of *essential structural closure* (ESC), the goal toward which the entire sonata-trajectory has been aimed . . . the exposition's structure of promise (presented there in the dominant) finds here its goal and resting-point (in the tonic)."[63] For Caplin, recapitulation "functions to resolve the principal tonal and melodic processes left incomplete in earlier sections" and "resolves [the] fundamental conflict of tonalities when the subordinate theme is transposed back into the home key."[64] When I read these sorts of claims, I try to imagine myself as a young student who does not find long-term key relations to be particularly salient. Would I worry that my perception was inadequate? Would that lead me to contemplate leaving music? Or would I be tempted to misdescribe my own perception, pretending to hear the relations that the experts told me to hear? The language of "ultimate goal" and "resolution" suggests that listeners who do not experience recapitulatory closure are in some sense *defective*.

There is also the worry that sonata-form recapitulations involve a degree of repetition that is out of character with the dynamic qualities of the rest of the form, particularly in those pieces with fairly literal recapitulations.[65] In shorter pieces, repetition can create a pleasurable rhythm of departure and return; but as we consider larger timescales, the expressive purpose of repetition becomes increasingly obscure—comparable, perhaps, to ending a movie by repeating its first twenty minutes.[66] Here we can start to sense a conflict between the classical style's twin inheritances of dance music and opera, the one emphasizing sectionalized repetition, the other musical storytelling.[67] This conflict was aptly diagnosed by John

---

[62] Kirlin 2014.

[63] Hepokoski and Darcy 2006, p. 232. On the same page they write: "The attaining of the ESC is the most significant event within the sonata . . . It is here that the presence of the tonic becomes finally secured as real rather than provisional." In private conversation, Hepokoski stressed that he is speaking of a *compositional* norm and making no claims about perception; nevertheless, he continues to use the term "resolution" in this context (Hepokoski 2021, p. 12).

[64] The first quote is from Caplin 1998, p. 161, continuing "and to provide symmetry and balance to the overall form by restating the melodic-motivic material of the exposition." The second is from Caplin 1998, p. 163.

[65] Scott Burnham speaks of "the embarrassment of trying to fit a large-scale repetition into a dramatic narrative" (1995, p. 18). This embarrassing combination of drama and formulaic repetition is echoed by Debussy's alleged wisecrack about smoking a cigarette during classical-form developments (cf. Rosen 2001, p. 117, suggesting the piece was by Beethoven, or Taruskin 2005, vol. 3, p. 22, suggesting it was by Brahms). William Marvin (2012–2013) notes that an analogous problem arises within the confines of Schenkerian theory.

[66] Margulis 2013.

[67] Rothstein observes that the classical style's origins in dance music and opera were emphasized by Leonard Ratner and Charles Rosen respectively (1989, p. 130); to these, he adds popular music as a third source.

Philip Sousa, one of the first composers to regularly begin and end pieces in different keys:

> As a child I was brought up on band music. As I grew I noticed something about the marches of that day—they did not climax. Speaking gastronomically, when they got through with the ice cream they went back to the roast beef. And the beef had no new sauce on it, no new flavor.[68]

Sousa bequeathed this attitude to ragtime composers like Joplin, yielding a short-lived and uniquely American rebellion against recapitulation and long-term tonal closure—a musical flexibility not heard since the sixteenth and seventeenth centuries.[69] This rebellion reflected the theoretical conviction that long-term tonal closure is *not* necessary for the creation of satisfying musical statements.

To be clear, *Formenlehre* theorists have made vitally important contributions to recent theory, providing a wealth of new analytical concepts that help sensitize us to classical-style conventions—including "medial caesura," "continuous exposition," "trimodular block," "standing on the dominant," "'tight' vs. 'loose' organization," and the "one more time technique." This work is broadly schema-theoretical in character, supplementing Gjerdingen's more local additions to our analytic vocabulary.[70] Like Gjerdingen's work, it has reoriented theory away from long-term pitch-narratives, whether scalar or Schenkerian, and toward more concrete and palpable gestures. One benefit of this shift is that it deemphasizes *justification*, the project of explaining why "masterworks" are great, in favor of a more constructive and concrete goal of informed listening. If there is a difficulty here, it is the philosophical question of whether it is important for the listener to *consciously* track these formal markers and conventions.[71]

For a music theorist, learning to live without aesthetic reassurance is like tightrope-walking without a net. It leaves us in a place where nothing *guarantees* the aesthetic quality of the music we love: not motivic consistency, not the Urlinie, and not the long-term resolution of modulatory dissonance. But this is where we stand with respect to most of the arts. Nothing guarantees the coherence of *Guernica*, or *To the Lighthouse*, or *The Blues Brothers* other than our love for the work itself. The amazing thing is that musical discourse has managed for so long to nurture the hope that there might be something more—that we might be able to *prove* through

---

[68] The quotation comes from a 1918 interview with the *Boston Post*, quoted in Warfield 2011, p. 299.

[69] In a fascinating 2017 article, Yoel Greenberg suggests that recapitulations arose from a concatenation of two different practices: "the double return of the opening theme in the tonic in the middle of the second half of a two-part form, and the thematic matching between the ends of the two halves of two-part form."

[70] Byros 2015 also makes the connection between formal conventions and scale-degree schemas.

[71] Hepokoski writes: "To feel this music musically—to identify with this music as music—is to monitor the moment-to-moment tensions of the drives toward the succession of boundary cadences" (2021, p. 8). I find it difficult to believe that typical eighteenth-century classical-music audiences engaged in this sort of "monitoring."

reasoning and analysis that a piece was satisfactory or coherent or organic or a masterwork. These efforts have gone hand-in-hand with an unquestioned conviction that the classical sonata is the paradigm of musical coherence, with recapitulation providing a powerful sense of resolution or completion. I do not expect to convince readers to share my doubts about any of this, but I would hope to convince them that those doubts are reasonable, and that students who share them are not defective but merely different. Otherwise, we risk making agreement with orthodoxy a prerequisite for admission into the discipline.

# Prelude
## Why Beethoven?

Leonard Bernstein's *The Joy of Music* opens with a question about Beethoven's pre-eminence. Acknowledging that the composer's materials are often simple—even simplistic—Bernstein wonders how it could be that Beethoven is still the paradigmatic classical composer. (The assumption seems to be that complexity is inherently valuable, foreclosing the possibility that Beethoven's music could be attractive *because of* its simplicity, but we will put that aside.) Bernstein's answer is *form*, understood as the ability to write music that seems like the perfect or inevitable continuation of what had come before; this leads to the inevitable reflections on genius, artistic perfection, and the existence of God.[1]

The preschool motto "don't yuck my yum" warns against criticizing musical theodicies. But I think we can find a more practical approach to Beethoven's form. Figure P10.1 compares the density of attacks in the exposition of the first movement of Beethoven's *Waldstein* and the entire first movement of Mozart's first piano sonata. There are two notable differences. First, the variation in Beethoven's rhythm is more *extreme* than Mozart's, passing through a wider range of musical states; second, the cycles of change are *slower* in Beethoven, with rhythm helping to demarcate formal regions. Indeed, the *Waldstein* could hardly be more obvious about this, with the first theme moving from eighths to sixteenths and the second theme accelerating from half notes to triplet eighths to sixteenths to a trill. Rhythm not only differentiates the exposition's main formal zones, but also marks the progression within them. It is hard to think of a previous composer who habitually manipulated such large spans of musical time.

Much the same point could be made about the use of register in the first movement of the *Tempest* (Figure P10.2). Once again we see Beethoven's music oscillating dramatically, where a typical classical piece would stay in a narrower range. And once again we see Beethoven using a basic musical parameter in a form-defining way, most notably by constructing a long registral arch linking transition and second theme—eliding the medial caesura that typically separates those two formal regions. Registral *separation* also seems to be a significant parameter, with the hands expanding to the edges of Beethoven's piano in the middle of the second theme; this then initiates a grand contrary-motion sequence that returns to a more normal configuration.[2]

---

[1] Bernstein 1956.

[2] We would find a similar contrast were we to consider dynamics, with Beethoven's ranging from pianissimo to fortissimo rather than the forte-and-piano opposition of many classical sonatas.

*Tonality.* Dmitri Tymoczko, Oxford University Press. © Oxford University Press 2023. DOI: 10.1093/oso/9780197577103.003.0018

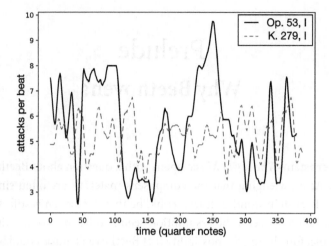

**Figure P10.1.** Attack density in the *Waldstein*'s first-movement exposition and the first movement of Mozart's first piano sonata.

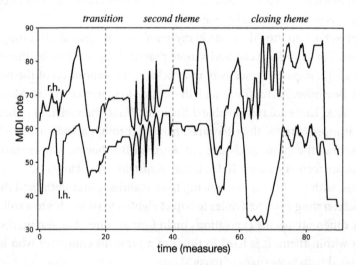

**Figure P10.2.** Registral position of the two hands, averaged over a four-beat window, in the first movement of the *Tempest* sonata.

This interest in extremes evokes the opposition between *beauty* and *sublimity*. Eighteenth-century philosophers associated beauty with the pleasant and well-formed: flowers, landscapes, small birds. The sublime was a form of aesthetic pleasure associated with the overwhelming, awesome, or incomprehensible: storms and mountain ranges, the ruins of a great city, the idea of distant galaxies, Shelley's Ozymandias. In music, beauty was associated with the decorous: elegant major-key melodies stated at a moderate tempo and dynamic.[3] Even during his lifetime

---

[3] Edmund Burke (1757) 1999, Part 3, chapter 25: "the beautiful in music will not bear that loudness and strength of sounds, which may be used to raise other passions; nor notes which are shrill, or harsh, or deep; it agrees best with such as are clear, even, smooth, and weak. [In addition,] great variety, and quick transitions

**Figure P10.3.** The second theme of the *Waldstein*'s first movement.

Beethoven was recognized as the great composer of the sublime—wild and almost out-of-control, exploiting unprecedented contrasts to create extremes of emotional response.[4] In this respect, his formal innovations are precisely *not* a matter of "inevitability," at least insofar as "inevitable" is kin to "appropriate" or "tasteful": instead they are closer to *provocations*, a willingness to tolerate excesses other composers avoided—and in some cases, to embrace an obviousness that might seem naïve.

This gives us a vantage from which to think about Beethoven's oft-noted antimelodic impulse. Where Mozart and Haydn frequently oriented their music around clear and singable tunes, Beethoven had a fondness for material that was almost deliberately generic. Consider Figures P4.2, 3.2.4, or 7.2.7. Here we have something like sub- or proto-music, unrefined nuggets of musical ore. Similarly, the second theme of the *Waldstein* is deliberately featureless, singable but not worth singing, and harmonized by a stock Pachelbel progression (Figure P10.3). For me, the frequent banality of Beethoven's themes is inseparable from his focus on long-term formal processes, as if he deliberately subordinated local interest to long-term narrative.[5] (In much the same way Beethoven's harmony often consists of simple tonic and dominant alternations, with many fewer secondary diatonic triads than in J. S. Bach or Brahms.) Twenty-first-century listeners are familiar with the gestural music of Xenakis and Penderecki, who rejected serial pitch manipulations in favor of striking trajectories of force and line. Strange though it may seem, I hear Beethoven as a kindred spirit, a composer emphasizing larger shapes over local ornament and detail. Indeed, there exists an atonal recomposition of the *Waldstein*'s exposition that preserves a remarkable amount of its formal clarity and expressive intensity, being surprisingly enjoyable in its own right.[6] Atonal Mozart would just sound awful.

All of which gives us reason to suspect that Beethoven's aesthetic concerns may differ from those of his predecessors—and in particular, that he was interested in loosening the formal schemas governing the classical style.[7] Hepokoski and

---

from one measure or tone to another, are contrary to the genius of the beautiful in music. Such transitions often excite mirth, or other sudden and tumultuous passions; but not that sinking, that melting, that languor, which is the characteristic effect of the beautiful as it regards every sense."

[4] Hoffmann 1989.
[5] Dahlhaus makes a similar point (1991, p. 83).
[6] Lalite et al. 2009.
[7] Dahlhaus 1991, Schmalfeldt 1995 and 2011.

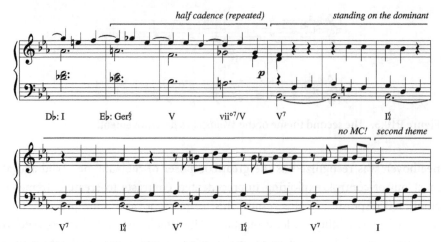

**Figure P10.4.** Measures 44–66 of Beethoven's Op. 10, no. 1, I, which move from transition to second theme with no medial caesura. Hepokoski and Darcy describe this moment as a "caesura fill" even though it could also be a "standing on the dominant" (albeit at a quiet dynamic); had the music proceeded to a pause before its second theme, this passage almost certainly would have been identified as such.

Darcy orient their sonata theory around the perception of a "medial caesura," the articulating pause that conventionally precedes second themes. Yet Beethoven's tendency to avoid this gesture can be seen as early as his first C minor sonata, where a passage of "standing on the dominant" leads without pause to the second theme (Figure P10.4).[8] And while the *Waldstein* contains a pause between transition and second theme, its "filled caesura" articulates a rhythmic deceleration linking the sixteenth-note transition to the quarter- and half-note second theme. Here the *fact* of the caesura takes a back seat to its *function* in carrying out the form-defining deceleration (Figure P10.5).[9] The danger is that we will interpret Beethoven as more beholden to formal convention than he actually was: paradoxically he is simultaneously eccentric and archetypal, an extreme outlier and the classical composer *par excellence*.

*Formenlehre* theorists would no doubt respond that I am hearing ahistorically, failing to grapple with sonata form as an a priori norm governing the expectations of historically situated listeners. My response is that we have very little evidence that sonata form in fact functioned this way, particularly for listeners who were

---

[8] Similar points can be made about the second theme of the first movements of the *Eroica* (where there is no pause at all between the beat 1 dominant arrival and the beat 2 start of the main theme) and the *Tempest*, to be considered subsequently. See Richards 2013a.

[9] Compare the medial caesura in the first movement of the Fifth Symphony, which expands and transforms the "knock of fate" motive into the start of the second theme (§10.4): here the caesura is again doing formal work over and above its conventional function.

Figure P10.5. The *Waldstein*'s "filled medial caesura" features rhythmic deceleration.

not professional musicians.[10] No doubt there were some who enjoyed tracking a piece's progress through its preordained stations, just as some contemporary audio engineers consciously attend to the mixing and production of songs on the radio. But it seems unlikely that this mode of listening was either a default or an ideal, or that early nineteenth-century musical culture prioritized the technical signposts of sonata form over and above its affective sequence of moods and gestures. And even if that could be shown for the more conventional music of the late eighteenth century, it is not at all clear that the conclusion would generalize to Beethoven, a self-conscious revolutionary whose music evinces a lifelong interest in new modes of musical continuity.

Thus I would argue that there is a conflict between Beethoven's nascent Romanticism, his compositional self-reliance, and recent approaches to musical form. Caplin, Hepokoski, and Darcy all seem to want theories that apply equally to Haydn, Mozart, and Beethoven, but Beethoven may have been more ironic, more historically conscious, and more iconoclastic than his predecessors.[11] And so

---

[10] In fact, we have some evidence that this is not the case, as contemporaneous "programmatic" readings do not emphasize the medial caesura (e.g., the "Eroica" program in Marx [1859] 1997; see Burnham 1995).

[11] The subtitle of Caplin 1998 is "A Theory of Formal Functions for the Instrumental Music of Haydn, Mozart, and Beethoven," while Hepokoski and Darcy introduce their book by writing "from one perspective the *Elements* is a research report, the product of our analyses of hundreds of individual movements by Haydn, Mozart, Beethoven, and many surrounding composers of the time" (2006, p. v).

we find him starting pieces *in medias res*, writing the *Heilige Dankgesang*, putting second themes in unusual keys, writing periods without root-position cadences, omitting the medial caesura, expanding the nonharmonic domain, and generally exploring alternatives to inherited convention. To read him as a *classical* composer, a courtier elegantly retracing a preordained sequence of sonata-form dance steps, is to neglect those aesthetic qualities that can still inspire us, two hundred years later. For his attitude seems to have been that music is fundamentally under our control, that we can change the rules when we want to—that we can, for want of a better phrase, *take ownership* of style itself. The result is music with genuine philosophical content, implicitly humanist where so much theory inclines toward scholasticism.

# 10

# Beethoven Theorist

As an undergraduate, I took an ill-fated independent study with David Lewin, a dazzling speculative theorist and a fine practical musician. My goal was to write Bach-style fugues, but Lewin thought it would be more fun to try to imitate Beethoven, a composer I had never really understood. Predictably, my efforts were hopeless: while I had some minimal sense of how to impersonate Bach, I was completely stymied when it came to Beethoven. Over and over, I wrote overcomplicated, histrionic, and entirely unmusical exercises; each week, Lewin would look at my work and say something like "it's really not about harmony, you know"—invariably pointing to some marvelous passage consisting almost entirely of tonic and dominant. Afterward, I would go home and once again fail to put simple chords together in a way that sounded even remotely interesting. My problem was that I had been made to understand what Beethoven's music wasn't, but not what it *was*. What makes it work if not harmony?[1]

Almost three decades later I have the beginnings of an answer: sequences, schemas, and patterns in general, and a specific set of contrary-motion idioms in particular. As the first classical composer to grow up playing J. S. Bach, Beethoven seems to have inherited the baroque love for mechanism—to which he added his own distinctive emphasis on contrary-motion counterpoint and primary-triad harmony, all filtered through a uniquely forceful musical personality. Like Corelli, Beethoven was exquisitely sensitive to the nearly sequential character of basic functional procedures, which need only the slightest nudge to become manifestly repetitive. The resulting play of near and exact repetition poses a challenge for theories that deemphasize sequence or reject its harmonic significance, as patterns are at the core rather than the periphery of Beethoven's language.[2]

It is just here that we are liable to be distracted by the stereotype of Beethoven as a composer of overwhelming force, whether divinely inspired or oppressively patriarchal.[3] For Beethoven was an intellectual who took pleasure in the artful juxtaposition of schematic content—a composer who poured his admittedly torrential energy through a sieve of utterly standard devices. What is surprising, perhaps, is that this sort of intellectual play can coexist with unprecedented rhetorical power. Humans like to put each another into boxes, imagining that excellence in one

---

[1] Eventually, Lewin gave up and I spent the rest of the semester happily writing fugues.
[2] For example, Caplin 2004, p. 69.
[3] McClary 1991 and Fink 2004.

*Tonality.* Dmitri Tymoczko, Oxford University Press. © Oxford University Press 2023. DOI: 10.1093/oso/9780197577103.003.0019

458    TONALITY: AN OWNER'S MANUAL

domain implies limitation in another, and it can be difficult to accept that one and the same figure is *both* highly cerebral and highly expressive—as when the supposedly dumb jock turns out to have a talent for mathematics, or when Scott Burnham's "Beethoven *Hero*" turns out to be Dmitri Tymoczko's Beethoven *theorist*.

This chapter will try to recover Beethoven the pattern-maker, highlighting his ability to spin compelling music out of commonplace material. My fundamental concern will be to explore how Beethoven built a personal vocabulary from ready-to-hand material—drawing a life's worth of music out of theoretical relationships that other composers might dismiss as trivial. After two introductory sections, I consider three famous opening movements: the *Tempest*, the Fifth Symphony, and the Op. 28 "Pastorale." I then turn to Schubert's *Quartettsatz* and the prelude to Wagner's *Lohengrin*, two pieces that pursue Beethovenian arguments amid the dissolution of the classical consensus. In Schubert this is largely a matter of continuing Beethoven's quest for greater formal flexibility, but in Wagner it comes to affect the musical details as well. The five analyses can be read in any order, and readers will benefit if they study the pieces ahead of time.

One thing I will not emphasize is Beethoven's tendency to reuse motivic material, recycling the same ideas, sometimes in nonobvious ways, throughout a piece. This is partly because I find motivic unity to be aesthetically uninteresting: to me, it does not matter whether some wonderful new theme bears a cryptic and nonobvious relationship to some other music occurring elsewhere in a piece; what matters instead is whether that new theme *fits* with what has come before, contributing to a satisfying energetic and expressive trajectory.[4] And partly it is because I am less interested in motives than in the structures they decorate: when I imitate or improvise classical-style music, motive feels superficial, a way of stamping an almost illusory distinctiveness onto a preexisting vocabulary. Reusing a motive feels neither challenging nor virtuous, whereas constructing a satisfying melodic-harmonic core feels much more difficult. I worry that Beethoven's obsession with motivic unity distracts from his deeper and more elusive virtues—primarily his ability to construct large-scale statements out of familiar building blocks. What fascinates me are the features that recur from piece to piece, rather than the motives distinguishing one piece from another.

## 1. Meet the Ludwig

If a chord divides the octave very evenly, then it can be linked by efficient voice leading to its transpositions. If its notes are clustered close together, then its voice exchanges will be small. The minor third is interesting insofar as it is balanced between these two extremes, being halfway between the unison and the tritone—or in other words exactly *one fourth* of an octave. This means that the most efficient

---

[4] Burnham 1995.

**Figure 10.1.1.** Measure 17 of Fanny Mendelssohn Hensel's "April," from *Das Jahr*, H. 385, presents a contrary-motion sequence in which outer voices move by minor third to form similar harmonies (minor thirds or major sixths, 3 or 9 = 12 − 3 semitones). On the right, the schema's diatonic quantization.

voice leading connecting it to its tritone transposition is exactly the same size as its smaller voice exchange. Two contrary-motion voices, when restricted to this interval class, will alternate between these two possibilities: (E♭4, C5) → (C4, E♭5) → (A3, F♯5) → (F♯3, A5) → (E♭3, C6) and so on.[5] In Figure 10.1.1, Fanny Mendelssohn Hensel uses this pattern in an exact contrary-motion sequence in which the outer voices always move by minor third.[6]

The diatonic third, being *approximately* one quarter of an octave, inherits this symmetry in an approximate way, allowing for sequences in which one voice sounds thirds while the other alternates thirds and steps. Figure 10.1.2 embellishes this dyadic template using contrary motion, lower neighbors, and a mixture of the two. In the descending-fifth sequence, one of the lower neighbors creates note-repetition and is rarely used; in the ascending-fifth version, both lower neighbors are common. The resulting patterns are ubiquitous throughout Beethoven's music, appearing in almost every movement and producing a characteristically Beethovenian sound. To honor schema theory's penchant for cutesy names, I will refer to them collectively as *the Ludwig*. A significant portion of Beethoven's intellectuality involves these patterns; when combined with parallel motion, the Ludwig is not so much an

---

[5] One can add transpositions to this template but that does not change the basic Tinctorian situation.
[6] Small intervals like the minor second have a small voice exchange but a large voice leading to their tritone transposition; large intervals have large voice exchanges, but a small voice leading to their tritone transposition. The minor third is perfectly balanced between these two poles.

460 TONALITY: AN OWNER'S MANUAL

Figure 10.1.2. The Ludwig embellishes the basic contrary-motion pattern by adding stepwise contrary motion and lower neighbors.

idiom as a conceptual scheme, a very general way of approaching tonal-functional counterpoint.

In development sections, this pattern is often used to produce overtly sequential passages.[7] More interesting are the many thematic statements that embed it covertly. The simplest Ludwigs create V–I–IV or IV–I–V progressions as in Figure 10.1.3. Here contrary motion endows primary-triad harmony with new contrapuntal depth, replacing its fifths-and-steps defaults with novel outer-voice possibilities (Figure 10.1.4). This fusion of contrapuntal fifth-progressions, deriving from dyadic voice-leading geometry, and harmonic fifth-progressions, deriving from functional convention, is the Ludwig's essential feature. More complex Ludwigs can act as V–I–vii°/V or as V/IV–IV–vii°, replacing Gjerdingen's oscillatory "Quiescenza" with a more energetic expansion (Figure 10.1.5).[8] The second theme of the first movement of Beethoven's first piano sonata uses a hybrid descending-fifth Ludwig to expand the registral range by three octaves; this culminates in a second contrary-motion passage returning the hands to close position (Figure 10.1.6). The *Pathétique* sonata uses the schema at the start of its first two movements, giving the second movement the character of a major-mode variation on the opening allegro (Figure 10.1.7).[9]

---

[7] Examples include the first-movement developments of the Kreutzer (or perhaps "Bridgetower") sonata, the Second Symphony, the *Waldstein*, the *Eroica*, and the Fifth Symphony (discussed later).

[8] Thanks here to Nathan Mitchell, who also pointed out the relevance of Rink's "Morte" schema (Figure 4.7.4).

[9] Steve Taylor points out that the second half of the opening adagio melody is similar to the third-movement antiparallel episode discussed in the prelude to chapter 4—thus linking all three movements thematically. The first-movement introduction can also be interpreted as a disguised Ludwig variant over a perpetually descending bass; mm. 7–8 are a potential source for Figure 4.6.1 and *Tristan* more generally.

BEETHOVEN THEORIST   461

**Figure 10.1.3.** Primary-triad Ludwigs: the opening of the string quartet Op. 18, no. 3, and the second theme of the *Appassionata* sonata's first movement, Op. 57, mm. 36–40.

**Figure 10.1.4.** The Ludwig as an alternative to the fifths-and-steps pattern of Figure 6.1.3. Here "D" refers to a generic dominant (V or vii°).

It is also common to find nonsequential Ludwigs that combine an ascending fourth with an ascending fifth (Figure 10.1.8). Here it can be useful to distinguish *octave-focused* Ludwig units where the octave or unison is the primary harmony from *third-focused* units that emphasize imperfect consonances (Figure 10.1.9). Figure 10.1.10 shows a contrary-motion theme from the end of the exposition of the D major sonata, Op. 10, no. 3, I; it is a hybrid, ascending-fifth Ludwig, moving

**Figure 10.1.5.** The Ludwig as a variant of Gjerdingen's "Quiescenza."

**Figure 10.1.6.** The Ludwig schema in the second theme of Op. 2, no. 1, I, mm. 25–32. On the middle line, the basic thirds-and-sixths structure; beneath that, the embellishing chords. The schema appears twice so that the hands expand by two octaves.

from V/IV to IV to I, whose first unit is octave-focused. Analysts who approach this passage chordally will miss the significance of the "merely passing" B–G dyad, which is essential to the schema but not the Roman-numeral harmony.[10] The Rondo of Op. 31, no. 1, opens with the lower-neighbor version of the same pattern,

---

[10] Beethoven exploits the schema's contrary-motion potential by continuing it through multiple octaves: in this case, the descending line appears on A4 to A3 and A2, while the ascending line moves from A1 to A3 and A4.

**Figure 10.1.7.** The Ludwig in the first two movements of the *Pathétique* Sonata, Op. 13.

**Figure 10.1.8.** Octave-repeating Ludwigs often found in thematic contexts.

again treating some schematic dyads as nonharmonic; it progresses to a version of the schema that recalls the "Morte" (Figures 10.1.11–12).

If there is a historical precedent here, it is likely Clementi, in many ways the progenitor of Beethoven's style. Like Beethoven, Clementi deemphasized tunes in

464 TONALITY: AN OWNER'S MANUAL

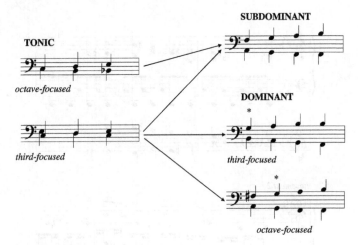

Figure 10.1.9. Third- and octave-focused Ludwig units on the primary triads. Asterisks mark emphasized harmonies.

Figure 10.1.10. The ascending-fifth Ludwig near the end of the exposition of the first movement of Beethoven's Op. 10, no. 3, mm. 93–96.

Figure 10.1.11. The ascending-fifth Ludwig in the opening of Op. 31, no. 1, III. Here the voice leading ascends while the chords descend.

**Figure 10.1.12.** Another contrary-motion pattern in Op. 31, no. 1, IV, mm. 28–31. The D–F♯ dyad appears one step higher than in the standard schema.

favor of registrally expansive gestures, and like Beethoven he favored simple tonic-dominant alternation enriched with secondary dominants. Thematic and sequential Ludwigs can be found throughout Clementi's early sonatas, which can sometimes sound uncannily like the work of his more famous successor. Indeed, Beethoven is said to have remarked that those who study Clementi make themselves acquainted with the techniques of Mozart, but not the converse—as if the Ludwig were a secret that could be acquired only in that composer's work.[11] If Clementi's themes are less strongly etched than Beethoven's, his larger forms less clearly defined, then this may reflect the difference between someone who blazes a trail and someone who walks along afterward.

## 2. From schema to flow

It is also possible to understand the Ludwig as a more flexible network of compositional options. Figure 10.2.1 augments the basic third-to-sixth unit by providing a choice about whether to move by descending fourth or fifth. This new flowchart represents the Ludwig not as a fixed idiom, a precomposed chunk of music waiting to be plugged into a composition, but as something malleable: not so much "*the* Ludwig schema" as "Ludwig-*ing*," a particular kind of musical flow. This figure contains all those consonances that are invertible at the octave—or, equivalently, those which can be expanded by third to produce another consonance.[12] This

---

[11] Schindler 1840, p. 197; 1841, II, pp. 83–84. For a generally Beethovenian piece, see Clementi's minuet from Op. 10, no. 1; for some Clementi Ludwigs, see Op. 7, no. 2, I, mm. 4–5, Op. 10, no. 1, III, mm. 1–2, Op. 13, no. 4, mm. 45–49 (initially published as Op. 14, no. 1). For a Beethovenian use of the diatonic third's basic voice leading, see Op. 7, no. 2, I, mm. 78–79 (compare Figure 3.2.4).

[12] That is, the one consonance that is not invertible at the octave, the fifth, is also the only consonance that cannot be expanded by a third: C–G is consonant, but C–B is dissonant.

466  TONALITY: AN OWNER'S MANUAL

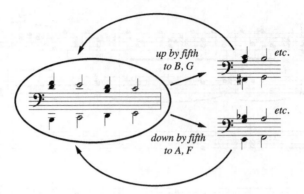

**Figure 10.2.1.** A flowchart for invertible counterpoint at the octave. If two notes share a stem, choose one.

**Figure 10.2.2.** Replacing tritones with perfect fifths in the Ludwig's basic unit.

means not just that the hands can be swapped but also that any passage of two-voice Ludwiging can have either of its voices doubled at the third. Figure 10.2.2 expands the chart to include the fifth: when the sequence is contracting, the fifth comes before the third at the beginning of each unit; when it is expanding, it comes after the third at the end of each unit. In some sense Ludwiging is just contrary motion itself, exploiting the fifth-based geometry of diatonic dyads (cf. Figure 3.3.8).

Earlier, I described the second theme of Beethoven's Op. 2, no. 1, as a V–I–vii°/V descending-fifth Ludwig repeating at the octave. We can now say that the underlying dyadic progression in Figure 10.1.6, E♭–A♭–D–A♭, makes four passes through the Ludwig network, comprising a *single* near sequence rather than two exact sequences stuck together. The same basic strategy can be found in a huge range of passages, from the opening of the second piano sonata to the Op. 109 variations theme (Figures 10.2.3–4). What makes these passages so characteristically Beethovenian is their unidirectionality, harmonic and thematic repetition *continuing* an ongoing process of registral expansion.[13] Other composers are more likely

---

[13] Due to registral limitations, continuous contrary-motion Ludwiging is often disguised by octave displacements.

**Figure 10.2.3.** Measures 25–31 of Op. 2, no. 2, I, present five successive Ludwig units, with the left hand octave-displaced.

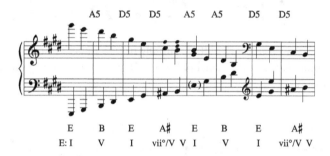

**Figure 10.2.4.** The Op. 109 variations theme contains eight consecutive units (§9.4).

to change direction: for example, in mm. 11–18 of the Courante from Élisabeth Jacquet de La Guerre's Suite in D minor (1687), we have five Ludwig units whose top voice alternates between descending and ascending, interleaved with descending-fifth sequences built on the third's basic voice leading (Figure 10.2.5).[14]

Contrary-motion Ludwiging can be augmented by the parallel-motion options shown in Figure 10.2.6; together, these provide a simple but comprehensive set of outer-voice defaults for functionally tonal music-making. Here we have essentially adopted the Tinctorian perspective from the prelude to chapter 3, analyzing functional counterpoint not in terms of independent voices, but rather parallel and contrary patterns, isolating those contrapuntal possibilities consistent with the harmonic grammar. And while the resulting idioms have a schematic character, they are more general than the independent atoms that usually go by that name, being closer a complete list than an arbitrary set of building blocks.[15]

---

[14] Beethoven sometimes uses this change-of-direction strategy in developmental passages, including the first-movement developments of his second (mm. 146ff) and third (mm. 186ff) symphonies.

[15] Note that the two kinds of motion exploit two different geometries: the logic of contrary motion is essentially a dyadic note-against-note logic, while the logic of parallel motion is more robustly triadic.

Figure 10.2.5. Measures 11–18 of the Courante from Élisabeth Jacquet de La Guerre's Suite in D minor (*Pièces de clavecin*, book 1, 1687) present five Ludwig units that alternate directions.

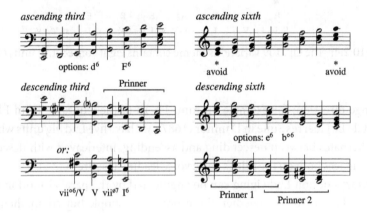

Figure 10.2.6. Functionally tonal parallel-motion schemas.

The interesting question is how the Ludwig can be both fundamental to functional counterpoint *while also* characteristic of Beethoven's music. If the Ludwig reflects the basic geometry of contrapuntal possibility, then why is it not equally ubiquitous in Mozart or Haydn or Monteverdi?

I have three answers that can be arranged in order of increasing interest. The first is that the Ludwig was part of Beethoven's improvisational practice, a favorite lick or riff that he drew upon when needed. The Ludwig can thus be understood as one specific manifestation of his more general fondness for contrary-motion

**Figure 10.2.7.** A contrary-motion wedge in Beethoven's E minor piano sonata Op. 90, I, mm. 105–107.

**Figure 10.2.8.** A passage from Op. 2, no 3, IV, mm. 127–133, that begins with contrary motion along the F major triad and progresses to an ascending-fifth Ludwig, itself moving by near-contrary motion along the diatonic scale.

patterns (Figures 10.2.7–9). Though these patterns are often simple, they occasionally achieve extraordinary complexity, as in Figure 10.2.10, which combines free 5–6 ascent in the left hand with a melody that descends through thirds and sixths. By contrast, a composer like Mozart was more partial to outer-voice parallelism.

Slightly more interesting is the idea that the Ludwig functions as a tool for producing the dramatic gestural waves characteristic of Beethoven's style. The repeating passage from mm. 57–60 in the first movement of the *Eroica* is exemplary, part of a massive sonic accretion using register (expanding by two octaves), dynamics (full-orchestra crescendo), rhythm (quarter notes to repeating eighth notes and ultimately sixteenths), and orchestration (trumpets and timpani, Figure 10.2.11).[16] From this perspective the Ludwig is a pitch-domain analogue of the crescendo.

---

[16] This is the second theme in Hepokoski and Darcy's reading.

470  TONALITY: AN OWNER'S MANUAL

Figure 10.2.9. (*top*) The contrary-motion pattern from Figure 1.5.6 can be doubled at the third and extended through a complete octave to produce a series of mostly functional harmonies. (*bottom*) Beethoven uses this strategy in the opening of Op. 130, I, mm. 18–19.

Figure 10.2.10. The second theme of Op. 2, no. 1, IV, mm. 34–42, combines free 5–6 ascent in the left hand with a right-hand contrary-motion melody that descends through thirds and sixths.

Figure 10.2.11. Measures 57–60 of the *Eroica* first movement, containing three consecutive Ludwig units with the last two linked across voices.

**Figure 10.2.12.** Tonic-dominant-tonic progressions as contrary-motion, near-fifth sequences in mm. 73–76 of Op. 10, no. 2, I.

**Figure 10.2.13.** One of the second themes in the *Hammerklavier*'s first movement (mm. 66–68) is a four-unit Ludwig that connects smoothly back to itself.

The third answer is that Beethoven was theoretically fascinated by the quasi-sequential qualities of basic functional idioms. I have at various points mentioned his tendency to make music out of "unrefined tonal ore."[17] It seems likely that this tendency in turn reflects an intellectual fascination with phenomena other composers took for granted—leading him to fashion music that highlighted the beauty of basic musical mathematics. Figure 10.2.12, for example, seems to announce that the I–V–I progression can be a contrary-motion near sequence, dividing the octave almost in half. Similarly, the *Hammerklavier*'s second theme is a four-unit contrary-motion Ludwig whose fifth-progressions (a) exploit the melodic third-cycle sounded by one of the Ludwig's voices; (b) dramatize the underlying mechanisms of functional harmony, raising its descending thirds to melodic salience, and (c) insert a descending-third progression to create Rameau's *double emploi*, all without disrupting the melodic thirds (Figure 10.2.13).[18] Such passages

---

[17] This is broadly speaking a devotion to musical poverty, a kind of asceticism or humility; some theorists have connected this to Beethoven's interest in popular or revolutionary music (Biamonte 2006, Ferraguto 2019).

[18] This theme resembles one of the second themes of Op. 7, I, mm. 60–68.

are both elementary and extraordinary, utter trivialities that happen to clarify the fundamental logic of functional harmony. Beethoven's incessant Ludwiging may therefore represent a kind of *musical understanding*, an implicit knowledge that teeters on the edge of the explicit. If so, it is another manifestation of a fundamentally intellectual musicianship, an obsessive circling around theoretical ideas expressed with an unusual compositional clarity.

## 3. The *Tempest*

The first movement of the *Tempest* is one of Beethoven's most characteristic productions—all violence and gesture, largely amelodic, and almost entirely sequential in its harmony. The reference to Shakespeare is icing on the cake, connecting two giants of Western culture through a pair of their most iconic productions. But if the piece manifests the violent and aggressive Beethoven, then it also hints at a subtler figure—the humorist who repeats musical fragments beyond what is reasonable, or deliberately lingers on seemingly wrong notes, or builds extended movements out of quirkily simplistic material. This is the composer who responded to his brother's "Johann Beethoven, land owner" with a sarcastic "Ludwig Beethoven, brain owner."[19]

There is a moment in the recapitulation that epitomizes this more complex figure: at m. 189, the ascending-fourth transposition would bring the music past the edge of Beethoven's piano (F6). Rather than transposing down by octave, Beethoven fixes D6 as an upper-voice pedal, creating unusual dissonances as the notes crunch against the piano's edge (Figure 10.3.1).[20] Here the music seems to put itself into question, as if asking about the source of its power. Sublimity is about exceeding limits, the storm destroying the harbor's sea walls or the musician pounding the keys so hard that "the piano must break."[21] Here, however, the edge

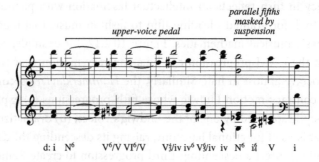

Figure 10.3.1. The upper-voice pedal in mm. 190–192 of the *Tempest*.

---

[19] Kinderman 2009a, p. 357.

[20] Cavett-Dunsby 1988 considers register in the transposed second-theme recapitulations of Mozart's "Haydn" quartets. Bergé and D'hoe 2009 note the registral issue here.

[21] Beethoven's description of how a pianist should play the piece (Burnham 2009).

of Beethoven's keyboard seems impervious to his raging, a real-life barrier easily capable of withstanding the force that human fingers can bring to bear. How is this failure in any way sublime?

The answer requires a detour into eighteenth-century aesthetics. While most philosophers identified the sublime with overpowering *external* forces, Immanuel Kant instead associated it with the human drive to transcend our own finitude—the *internal* capability that allows us, for any actual cataclysm, to imagine one even greater. This is the impulse that lets the toddler ask for a number larger than any you can mention, revealing a concept of infinity greater than anything instantiated in nature. Kant's suggestion was that external forces can sometimes lead us to recognize our inner resources: contemplation of an external object such as "the starry skies above" sometimes reveals our physical limits ("annihilates as it were my importance as an animal creature"), which in turn provokes us to recognize our "infinite" rational nature ("infinitely elevates my worth as an intelligence").[22] For Kant it was the *human spirit* that was truly sublime and awe-inspiring, rather than external objects or events: monumentality and excess are the false and illusory sublime.[23] True sublimity instead looks elsewhere, *negating* the finite and external in favor of a transcendent interiority. This suggests that art may be able to achieve sublimity by undermining itself.

I like to imagine that Beethoven fashioned his upper-voice pedal as a reflection of this more spiritual view. For in this moment the edge of the piano, symbolized by the pedal, annihilates the music's physical aspect and with it the notion that sound could reach beyond itself—its audible warpings a subtle and humorous jab at Beethoven's heroic aspirations. But at the same time, it slyly hints at an esoteric message, a negative theology in which musical failure points beyond music itself. Indeed, Beethoven alluded to Kant's discussion of sublimity in his conversation books, and had on his writing desk a famously self-defeating inscription from an Egyptian temple—"I am all that is, that was, and that will be. No mortal man has raised my veil"—that Kant singled out as "most sublime."[24] Whether Beethoven got this attitude directly from Kant or whether the two figures independently shared a similar outlook is relatively unimportant: what matters is that Beethoven's sublimity lies not just in extremity and extravagance, volume and length, but also in a kind of self-conscious reflection. Beyond the tempestuous Beethoven lies a more thoughtful figure.

*(a) Exposition.* The exposition is a locus of intense disagreement and a test for recent ideas about form: some analysts put the main theme at m. 1, others at m. 21; some hear a second theme at m. 41, while others argue that the piece has a continuous exposition with no second theme; some identify a closing theme at m. 75,

---

[22] Kant (1788) 1997, p. 133.

[23] On Beethoven and monumentality, see Rehding 2009 and Dahlhaus 1991.

[24] An 1820 conversation book contains the phrase "the starry skies above and the moral law within—KANT!" (Thayer 1967, p. 747). For the inscription, which Kant considered among the most sublime ever uttered, see Schindler (1860) 1996, p. 365, and Kant (1790) 1970, p. 160.

474   TONALITY: AN OWNER'S MANUAL

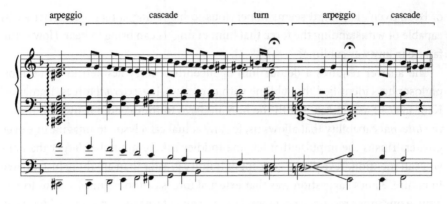

**Figure 10.3.2.** The opening of the *Tempest* uses a Ludwig to articulate three basic motives.

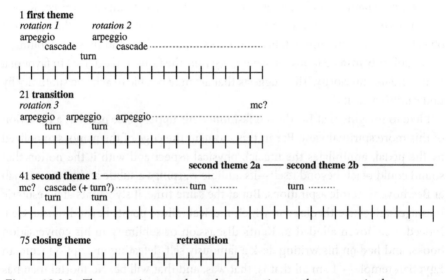

**Figure 10.3.3.** The arpeggio, cascade, and turn motives as they appear in the exposition. Each tick represents one measure.

while others consider that to be a second theme. Part of the issue is that the piece lacks familiar cadential markers—a well-defined medial caesura or a definitive cadence before the closing section. Instead, motive starts to supplant cadence as a determiner of form: the opening phrase, shown in Figure 10.3.2, presents three figures I call "arpeggio," "cascade" (sometimes called "sigh"), and "turn."[25] As many analysts have noticed, these three figures return throughout the exposition in something like the way a development rotates through the exposition's themes (Figure 10.3.3). Particularly interesting are the transition and second theme, which combine to form a single registral arc (Figure P10.2), moving from arpeggio (mm. 21–40) to

---

[25] Bergé and D'hoe 2009 survey approaches to the motivic content.

cascade (mm. 42–54) to turn (mm. 55–63), as if expanding the narrative of the opening.[26]

Yet for all the novelty, it is possible to hear a four-part exposition containing five large paragraphs: a loosely periodic main theme at m. 1, a sequential transition at m. 21, a second group at m. 42 (with another theme starting at m. 55), and a closing section at m. 75.[27] To be sure, there is a sense in which the formal identity of these sections clarifies only gradually: the opening music initially sounds like it could be an improvised introduction, but quickly turns into a thematic allegro, while the transition initially sounds like it could be a thematic statement, but quickly starts modulating.[28] This "becoming clear only in retrospect" continues in various ways throughout the exposition. If we are alive to Beethoven's playful humor, then we will not be shocked by these misalignments between rhetoric and formal function.[29]

I understand the opening twenty-one measures as a large period, two quasi-parallel phrases each beginning with a slow arpeggio, moving to the cascade, and ending with a cadence.[30] The antecedent articulates a Ludwig that continues across the phrase boundary, perhaps motivating the shift from d: V to F: V (Figure 10.3.2). The music continues with an ascending-step sequence whose last unit is repeated and embellished (Figure 10.3.4). That is, the V$^6_5$/V–V appears in two

Figure 10.3.4. The consequent (mm. 7–20) as a disguised ascending-step sequence.

---

[26] Dahlhaus 1991 suggests that the piece represents a decisive break with earlier conceptions of form. See Schmalfeldt 1995 and Horton 2014 for discussion.

[27] This is the parsing given in Tovey 1931. Caplin 2009a also stresses the continuity between the *Tempest* and Beethoven's style. Vande Moortele 2009 surveys readings of the piece's form.

[28] See Dahlhaus 1991 and especially Schmalfeldt 1995 and 2011. Hamilton 2009 connects the opening to the practice of improvised preluding.

[29] Webster 2010 surveys the equally unusual form of Op. 10, no. 3, I.

[30] Schmalfeldt (1995, p. 62) questions the analysis as a period because the consequent is sequential; however, I believe sequential themes are common in Beethoven. Rothstein 2009, following Riemann and Uhde,

**Figure 10.3.5.** The transition (mm. 21–40) as a disguised ascending-fifth sequence using fauxbourdon triads.

slightly disguised forms: first as N$^6$–vii°, then as vii°$^7$/V–(i$^6_4$⇒V$^7$), joined by a semitonally ascending diminished seventh.[31] Melodramatic figuration leads to a powerful cadence and the start of the transition. This begins the third motivic rotation, the ascending arpeggio figure impassioned and in-tempo, and answered by a metricized turn.

The transitional sequence deploys the technique I have called the *disguised model*, altering its initial unit so that the sequential structure clarifies as the music progresses (another instance of "becoming clear only in retrospect"). The sequence uses fauxbourdon triads to ascend by fifth, the phrasing accelerating from four bars to two to one (Figure 10.3.5).[32] It ends with an elongated vii°$^7$/V, discharged on the dominant and ushering in the second theme. This elongation replaces the medial caesura, acting as a temporary suspension before the music snaps back into action: instead of pausing on V before starting a theme on I, Beethoven pauses on vii°$^7$/V before starting a theme on V. Energetically, it lacks the quality of exhalation, feeling more like a climax than a rest—and indeed it is near the high point of the registral arc encompassing both transition and second theme (Figure P10.2).

That second theme features the exposition's only nonsequential harmony, a V–i–V–N$^6$–vii°–i$^6$ progression that leads to a harmonized version of the turn (Figure 10.3.6).[33] Formally, it is a sixteen-bar sentence that arrives at a weak cadence in m. 56; this cadence is immediately repeated as if we were hearing a phrase extension or "postcadential echo." However, its third repetition completes a sentence with a more decisive cadence, leading me to experience a pair of overlapping phrases, with the two-bar cadence of the first theme simultaneously the initial presentation of the second theme—the same technique used in the *Hammerklavier*

---

notes that the entire period forms a 2 + 4 structure if one takes the Largo half as fast as the Allegro. Both the phrase and its constituent halves are examples of Goldenberg's "question/answer pairs" (2020).

[31] James Hepokoski (2009), John Nathan Martin (2010), and David Damschroder (2016) all read C♯–E–G–B♭ in m. 11 as a common-tone diminished seventh of G minor. This reading not only breaks the harmonic sequence but postulates a very rare chord, the minor-key ct°$^7$. Hatten 2009 agrees with my reading: a dominant C♯–E–G–B♭ moving retrofunctionally to a dominant-of-the-dominant. This is a common Beethoven progression (§3.8).

[32] Op. 18, no. 6, II, m. 18, contains the same ascending-fifth pattern. Damschroder's Schenkerian analysis (2016) turns the sequence's parallel motion into a non-parallel chorale. Burnham 2009 notes the near omnipresence of first-inversion triads.

[33] Hepokoski (2009) suggests that the movement has no second theme since it lacks a medial caesura; instead, he hears this music as a "dominant lock" (or "standing on the dominant"). For me it has too much individuality for that, its simple tonic-dominant harmony characteristically Beethovenian.

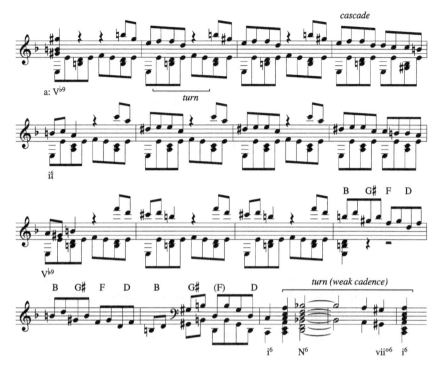

**Figure 10.3.6.** The second theme (mm. 41–57) can be read as a sixteen-bar sentence with a weak cadence.

scherzo (cf. Figure 9.6.6). This sense of overlap is reinforced by a repetition that forms a loosely parallel 8 + 12 period. Thus, the first theme never quite ends while the second never quite begins, and what initially sounds like a cadence turns out, in retrospect, to be the start of something new.[34]

The theme's consequent is tonally subtle. Caplin describes it as an example of "invertible counterpoint," the melodic turn A–B♭–A–G♯–A moving from melody to bass. But since the reregistration would create parallel fifths, the counterpoint is not truly invertible; Beethoven thus changes rhythm and register, introducing a C♯ that allows us to hear (C♯, E) → (D, F) as a tonicization of D minor (Figure 10.3.7).[35] Here the turn, just heard as $\hat{1}$–♭$\hat{2}$–$\hat{1}$–$\hat{7}$–$\hat{1}$, potentially reacquires its original scale degrees ($\hat{5}$–$\hat{6}$–$\hat{5}$–♯$\hat{4}$–$\hat{5}$). For me, this music is highly unstable between A and

---

[34] My reading of the second-theme phrasing is broadly compatible with that of Schmalfeldt and Caplin. Both of them, however, read the m. 63 cadence as the conclusion of a large thematic group stretching back to m. 42, asserting a strong formal juncture *between* the nearly parallel presentations of the second theme: thus they parse the music as (AB)(B′), with the B′ representing, in Caplin's words, "an entirely different thematic region" (Caplin 2009a, p. 111). I find it more natural to imagine something more like (A)(BB′) with A and B briefly overlapping, the A material forgotten as the music takes up a new subject. Thus I would consider m. 55 simultaneously weakly cadential with respect to the preceding music and initiating with respect to what follows.

[35] Caplin's invocation of "invertible counterpoint" is really a metonym for a more general issue, namely the way registral shifts can extinguish (what he considers) cadences by removing the required root-position dominant (as in Example 4.7 of Caplin 2009a).

478    TONALITY: AN OWNER'S MANUAL

**Figure 10.3.7.** Since registral inversion produces parallel fifths (*middle*), Beethoven alters the motive (*bottom*).

D: where the thematic repetition suggests an A tonic, harmonic syntax suggests D minor (a hearing reinforced by the convention of recalling the opening key somewhere near the end of the second group).[36] The magic lies in the availability of both interpretations. It is the rare classical-style passage that can be said to be in two keys at once.

The repeat expands the register by transposing along the dyad, first by $t_1$, then by $t_2$, the right hand constantly ascending but always in a slightly different way (Figure 10.3.8). The continuation reinterprets vii°7 of A minor as vii°7 in the relative major, contracting the register with a descending-third contrary-motion sequence that restarts the left hand's eighth-note motion; Beethoven liked this effect so much he reused it in the first-movement development of his Second Symphony.[37] We arrive, finally, on a two-measure Ludwig fragment repeated no fewer than five times. (Here I take the outer voices to be primary, A–B–C–E against C–B–A–G♯, with the latter voice doubled at the third.) Its fragmentary nature gives this music the character of a closing theme; however, both the quiet dynamic and the dominant-pedal bass undercut the cadential arrival at m. 74.[38]

Figure 10.3.9 summarizes the exposition as a series of six schematic processes, each featuring an ascending bass line—a remorseless ratchet that continues throughout the movement.[39] That line is harmonized with contrary motion at the beginning and end of the exposition, and with parallel motion in the middle. Each

---

[36] I hear the bass articulating Byros's le–sol–fi–sol schema, but on the wrong scale degrees, somewhat like the transition in the first movement of Beethoven's Second Symphony (Byros 2012, 2015). This raises the delicate question, endemic to schematic analysis, of whether to read the passage as a deliberate deforming of a preexisting norm, or as a new Beethovenian norm of its own. Schmalfeldt 1995 hears an A major tonic but notes its potential for dominant function.

[37] The diminished seventh is in m. 165 and the third-sequence starts in m. 166.

[38] Schmalfeldt (1995), Hepokoski (2009), and Rothstein (2009) do not hear closure arriving until m. 87; Caplin (2009a) instead hears those measures as a "post-cadential codetta." Both hearings strike me as reasonable.

[39] Tovey 1931.

**Figure 10.3.8.** (*top*) Registral expansion by transposition along the dyad (mm. 63–69); (*bottom*) the contrary-motion descending-third sequence returning the hands to their original alignment (mm. 69–73).

**Figure 10.3.9.** The exposition as a series of parallel and contrary sequences.

process is in my view a unity, an internalized musical pattern or sequence or schema of the sort that could guide improvisation—and which the *Tempest* knits into a convincing musical argument. These schematic processes lie *underneath* the motivic relationships that are readily available to the ear, endowing the music with a deeper

**Figure 10.3.10.** Janet Schmalfeldt's analysis of the movement.

continuity.[40] Ubiquitous motives, stock musical patterns, avoidance of straightforward melody, and extremes of dynamics and register: that is Beethoven's style in a nutshell.

We can reasonably wonder whether we need any further reduction beyond this. It would be quixotic to suggest that the piece would be aesthetically defective if it possessed no further unity, or that six familiar processes—easily summarized on just a few staves—were inherently *too much* for ninety measures of music. Yet a good deal of analytical effort seems to be driven by just this belief. Schmalfeldt, for example, provides the Schenkerian reduction in Figure 10.3.10. The picture is that the white noteheads stay in force throughout the intervening music, being singled out by the ear despite their inclusion inside sequential processes. This "singling out" has been taken to explain something aesthetically important about the piece, its "organic coherence" or status as a "masterwork." To me this all seems implausible. My schematic reduction is simple enough that I can imagine thinking it up on my own, and yet complex enough that I can almost imagine recomposing the movement on that basis. By contrast it is inconceivable that I would get anywhere starting from Figure 10.3.10. Sequence-based reduction provides a sense of ownership that I do not get from Schenkerian analysis, allowing me to understand how actual human beings might find their way to music as complex and impressive as the *Tempest*.

*(b) Development and recapitulation.* The development is a helicopter drop, the rolled chords taking us far from the tonic ($D^6-f\sharp^{o7}-F\sharp^6_4$), with the six-four bypassing the dominant and progressing directly to a root-position tonic. The compensating sequence follows the transition so faithfully that it sounds more like repetition than a development proper: few other classical-style developments are so completely based on what is arguably a "transitional" sequence. Its ending is perturbed so as to move by fourth rather than fifth, turning the entire pattern into a lightly embellished ascending 5–6: $(([f\sharp\Leftarrow C\sharp^4_3 \Rightarrow f\sharp^6]-b)-(G^6-C)-(A^6-D))$. This leads to a half cadence on A by way of an augmented sixth, followed by twelve measures of standing on the dominant, during which the melody echoes the second theme's E–F–D–E turn (Figure 10.3.11).[41] Finally, almost-parallel triads return us to the opening; as in mm. 55–56, the tonic is surrounded by semitonal neighbors.

---

[40] Cohn 2005 reads many of my "stock patterns" as "introverted motives" rather than schemas.
[41] The $\natural\hat{6}-\flat\hat{6}-\hat{5}$ approach is a common developmental arrival.

Figure 10.3.11. The development, mm. 93–143.

Figure 10.3.12. The recapitulation's two arioso laments, with the second transposed to D minor for comparison.

The recapitulation is one of the more inventive in Beethoven's middle period. The slow arpeggio gives rise to an expressive lament, pedal down, its final F poignantly suggesting D minor; this leads to the cascade, turn, and cadence exactly as before.[42] The next arpeggio is followed by a loosely parallel lament in F minor; to facilitate comparison, Figure 10.3.12 transposes both melodies into the same key. The implied $C^7$–f progression expands to a new chromatic 5–6 sequence that evokes the development: $C^7$–f is followed by C♯–f♯ and D–g.[43] At this point the harmonic sequence could connect smoothly with the $E♭^6$–$c♯^{o4}_3$–$g♯^{o7}$ of the exposition but this would upset the two-chord grouping; Beethoven instead omits the E♭ and proceeds directly to c♯° (Figure 10.3.13). Thus we can trace the ascending-step sequence throughout the movement: E–a, F♯–b, G–C, A–d, [B–e], C–f, C♯–f♯, D–g, E–A, lacking only the tonicization of E.[44] We could say that the recapitulatory *repeat* simultaneously *continues* the ongoing (if difficult-to-perceive) sequential process.

---

[42] Kinderman 2009b observes that the D minor lament anticipates the opening of the baritone recitative in Beethoven's Ninth Symphony.

[43] Since each ascending-step modulation adds five flats, reinterpreting VI of the preceding minor key as V of the next, the three sequential steps add fifteen total flats and complete a full circle in scale space.

[44] Skipping this tonicization is fairly standard, since the supertonic is diminished in minor.

Figure 10.3.13. The ascending-step sequence running throughout the movement.

From there the recapitulation largely repeats the exposition, with the exception of the upper-voice pedal discussed earlier. The parallelism lasts until the retransition, where repeated octaves lead to a spooky coda, compressing the closing theme to a single measure, a fitting depiction of the storm's aftermath.[45] For all its originality, the movement is almost entirely schematic, composed of a handful of sequences stitched together with a few moments of i–V–i functionality. Beethoven arrays these materials in the service of a compelling formal trajectory, the large-scale registral, motivic, and harmonic shapes portraying a musical storm that is sublime in every sense of the term—overwhelming and rigorous music that escapes the gravitational pull of the ordinary to achieve something unprecedented.

## 4. The Fifth Symphony

The first movement of the Fifth Symphony is in many ways cousin to the *Tempest*: largely sequential, with a middle-register minor tonic, interrupting its recapitulation for a doloroso aria, and opening with the juxtaposition of heterogeneous material.[46] The *Tempest*'s arpeggio is replaced by a fortissimo "Knock of Fate," appearing at the start of the form's major sections: exposition, transition, second theme, development, recapitulation, second theme recapitulation, and, in the coda, the final thematic statement. (It is missing from the recapitulation's transition, replaced by the oboe lament.) Both pieces are unusually taut in their overall form, suffused with motivic relationships and exemplifying the analyst's dream of unity. But where the *Tempest*'s sequences are obvious, the Fifth's are covert and disguised.

(*a*) *Exposition.* Schenker and Tovey both warn against taking the main motive to be the first measure's G–G–G–E♭; for them the central theme is this figure

---

[45] Jander 1996 contextualizes the piece's storm tropes.
[46] Hepokoski 2009 notes this connection.

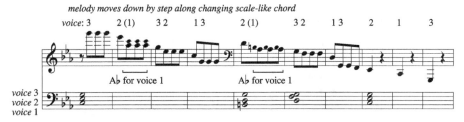

**Figure 10.4.1.** Measures 7–18 as a distorted arpeggio, cycling through three scale degrees that are themselves moving.

*combined* with its repetition down by one diatonic step, the "down by third, up by step" melody so central to functional logic (§7.2).[47] I am not so certain. The opening measure articulates a systematic pattern of chordal intervals that can be traced throughout the first phrase—a disguised patterning, no doubt produced by the compositional subconscious, that lends the music an audible if hard-to-describe consistency (Figure 10.4.1). This pattern of chordal intervals becomes increasingly explicit over the course of the movement, as if Beethoven were gradually revealing the underlying structure (Figure 10.4.2).[48]

Harmonically, the piece opens with an obsessive focus on tonic and dominant: the only other harmony in the first thirty-eight measures is the Italian sixth at the end of the first phrase. This harmonic limitation is offset by rhythmic variety, the piece exploring many different four-measure arrangements of tonic and dominant (Figure 10.4.3).[49] The second phrase is an "accelerating double sentence" whose continuation is itself a smaller sentence: we start with a four-bar presentation that is repeated exactly; the continuation is then constructed as a sentence with a two-bar unit, whose continuation uses a *one*-bar unit (Figure 10.4.4).[50] The continuation's Ludwig recalls the *Pathétique*'s allegro opening, departing from the four-bar hypermeter, and presenting the first sustained series of quickly changing harmonies. Schematic content balances the harmonic acceleration, the complexity of the onrushing chords ameliorated by their idiomatic nature.

We then hear three cascading phrases linked by a twisty maze of contrasts and resemblances: phrases 1 and 3 use the same intervals along the chord, phrases 2 and 3 use seventh chords, while phrases 1 and 2 add an extra descending step to

---

[47] Schenker (1921–1923) 2004. Tovey (1935) 1981 snarkily observes that no piece was ever derived from just four notes.

[48] This same sort of gradual clarification characterizes the second theme of Op. 23, I (Figure 3.1.8), the variations movement of Op. 1, no. 3 (§4.10), the variations movement of Op. 109 (§9.4), and the idea of the "disguised model."

[49] If we disregard rotations, then there are four ways of arranging two harmonies in four bars: AAAA, AAAB, AABB, and ABAB. All four appear on Figure 10.4.3. While I doubt that Beethoven was consciously working through these possibilities, I do believe he was deliberately searching for variety in the context of a limited harmonic vocabulary.

[50] Lerdahl (2020, p. 89) makes a similar observation about the less-symmetrical opening music. William Caplin would likely call this a compound sentence with two stages of fragmentation.

Figure 10.4.2. Several appearances of the (0, 0, –1, –1) interval sequence.

| | | | | |
|---|---|---|---|---|
| mm. 7–10 | i | i | i | i |
| mm. 11–14 | V | V | V | V |
| mm. 15–18 | i | V | i | V |
| mm. 26–29 | V | V | V | i |
| mm. 30–33 | | | | |
| mm. 34–37 | V | V | i | i |

Figure 10.4.3. The symphony's four-bar phrases distribute two harmonies in many different ways.

the third sequential iteration, perturbing their patterns in analogous ways (Figure 10.4.5).[51] These relationships are too fast to process in real time, though the constant changes help keep the music fresh. The modulation, such as it is, consists in the unexpected resolution of c: vii°7/V to E♭: V, the F♯ reconceived as G♭.[52] The following horn call expands the Fate motive so that thirds become fifths, changing minor to relative major without transposition: it does not feel like a medial caesura, in large part because of the impression of being cut off in mid-utterance—the pause more unexplained than preparatory, innovative rhetoric replacing familiar gesture. As in the *Waldstein*, the caesura's novel function seems more important than its conventional ancestry.

---

[51] Schenker (1923–1924) 2005 notes that the dominant form of this arpeggiation gave Beethoven particular difficulties.
[52] Lewin 1986 colorfully describes this moment's enharmonic play.

**Figure 10.4.4.** The second large phrase (mm. 26–44) as an accelerating double sentence.

**Figure 10.4.5.** Intervallic patterns in the three descending arpeggios.

At this point there is an interesting question of hypermeter. Both Tovey and Schenker continue to read four-bar groupings through the transition, so that the second theme starts on the last beat of the hypermeasure (Figure 10.4.6). This puts the tonic arrival on hyperbeat 3 rather than hyperbeat 1. Riemann and Imbrie

**Figure 10.4.6.** Hypermeter at the start of the second theme (mm. 56–66).

instead start the second theme on the second measure of a four-bar group; on this hearing the second theme's sequential units all have a weak-weak-weak-strong design that mirrors the rhythm of the opening motive. This correspondence is underscored by the basses, whose statement of that motive arrives on the accented bar. For performers, the question is whether to emphasize the theme's second bar (encouraging the Tovey/Schenker hearing), or the fourth-bar tonic arrival (encouraging the Riemann/Imbrie alternative).[53]

The second theme is a long ascending-step near sequence (Figure 10.4.7). As in the *Tempest* transition, Beethoven uses a disguised model, creating a chainlike continuity wherein each unit of the sequence has a direct link to its predecessor: the sequence's first statement reworks the pitch classes of the horn call; the second statement uses the same harmonic progression as the first; and the third unit uses the same melody as the second.[54] This third unit appears a step too high, skipping the mediant and moving directly to IV, whereupon it gets stuck on various secondary dominants before arriving at V$^6_5$.[55] The ascending bass continues through the next phrase, a rushing release of pent-up energy, its descending melodic waterfall counterbalancing the sinuous ascent of the preceding sequence. This music uses a hybrid descending-fifth Ludwig, (D, B♭) → (E♭, G) → (G, E♭) → (A♭, C), here acting as V–I–IV and embellished with appoggiaturas; these are linked across the repeat to form

---

[53] Riemann 1903, p. 38; Imbrie 1973. My own preference is for the Riemann/Imbrie reading, though I think both are reasonable. Justin London (2004, p. 92) proposes yet another analysis in which the second theme begins on a hypermetrical strong beat (m. 63). This disagreement suggests that hypermeter can be fairly subjective. Temperley 2008 considers hypermetrical transitions in general.

[54] In the transformation from horn call to violin melody, some harmonic notes become nonharmonic; this leads Auerbach to dismiss the motivic connection as "invalid" (2021, p. 91). Like Reti, I consider it to be significant (Reti 1951).

[55] This near sequence often seems to appear in E♭, as in the second paragraph of the *Eroica*, the second theme of the first movement of the C minor violin sonata, and the end of Op. 31, no. 3—though it is also found in the first movement of the D major violin concerto. The shift from the German augmented sixth to the fully diminished seventh chord, with the slightly odd ♭$\hat{6}$–♮$\hat{6}$–$\hat{5}$ bass, appears in a number of other pieces as well (e.g., Op. 10, no. 3, I, m. 199). Here ♭$\hat{6}$ is "sublimated" (Samarotto 2004).

Figure 10.4.7. The second theme (mm. 71–94) as an ascending-step near sequence.

Figure 10.4.8. The Ludwig at the end of the second theme (mm. 96–102). The repeat creates four units of continuous Ludwiging.

a continuous passage of Ludwiging (Figure 10.4.8). We arrive at an exultant closing passage restoring the major third G–E♭ to its default role as $\hat{3}$–$\hat{1}$ in E♭ major. The exposition's entire second half is thus a single musical gesture, a steadily rising scalar bass beginning in stillness and moving toward climactic affirmation (Figure 10.4.9).

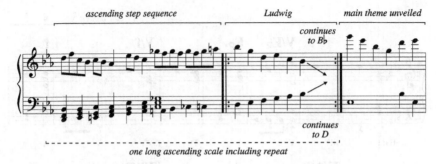

**Figure 10.4.9.** The ascending scalar bass in the second theme.

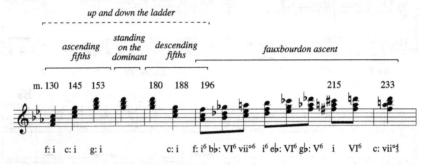

**Figure 10.4.10.** A harmonic outline of the development.

As Bernstein said, there is something inevitable here, a palpably new focus on long spans of musical time. This is not so much a matter of divine inspiration or compositional genius, but rather musical *thought*: unusually long paragraphs formed from entirely schematic material.

(b) *Development*. The exposition transformed G–E♭ from $\hat{5}$–$\hat{3}$ in C minor to $\hat{3}$–$\hat{1}$ in E♭. The development responds with something like the opposite gesture: what initially sounds like $\hat{5}$–$\hat{3}$ in E♭ is undercut by a low D♭–C that turns it into $\hat{4}$–$\hat{2}$ in F minor. This begins a sixty-five-measure "up-and-down-the-ladder," ascending by fifth from F to C to G, standing on the dominant, and descending by fifth to C and F. This leads to a mysterious fauxbourdon passage, a transfigured second theme ascending from F minor to B♭ minor before losing energy, crawling upward through the tritone G♭ minor (respelled as F♯), crabbed and chromatic, only barely reaching E♭ major (notated as D) before grinding to a halt just when the dominant comes into view (Figure 10.4.10).

The ascent up the ladder of the fifths takes place by way of a grand contrary-motion gesture. Figure 10.4.11 provides a reduction, the top staff cascading downward by six octaves from C7 to C1 while the lower ascends from A♭2 to E♭4; at each stage the top staff descends by an octave and a fourth, or ten diatonic steps, while the lower voice ascends by fifth. The voice leading uses a descending-fifth Ludwig that moves from (A♭, C) to (D, F) to (G, B), but the initial dyad is the upper third of F minor rather than the lower third of A♭ major; this converts the A♭–D progression of

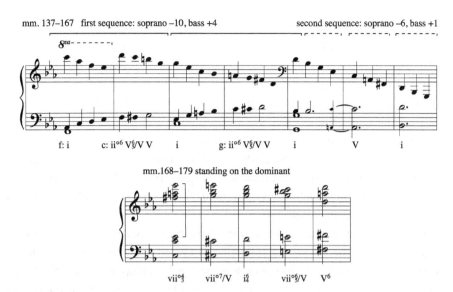

Figure 10.4.11. The two contrary-motion sequences in the first half of the development.

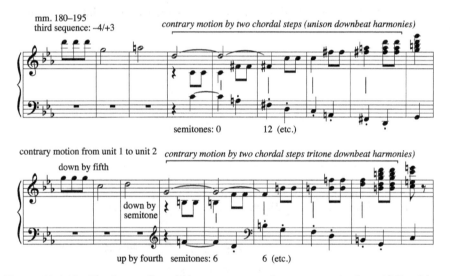

Figure 10.4.12. The descending-fifth, contrary-motion sequence in the middle of the development.

descending-fifth dyads into an f–d° progression of descending-third triads.[56] Once again dyadic logic augments the triadic logic of Roman numerals.

The standing on the dominant begins with a familiar retrofunctional move from vii° to vii°7/V and then to i$^6_4$. The descent down the ladder of fifths, shown in Figure 10.4.12, is less complicated, as befits its role in reducing the musical

---

[56] Beethoven uses almost the same voice leading in the *Eroica* scherzo's ascending-step sequence (m. 143). Schenker (1923–1924) 2005 recognizes a connection between this moment and the closing theme, but not its schematic identity.

tension; it also contains the piece's first syncopation (!), tying the lower strings' incipit across the barline. This music brings back the second theme's version of the Fate gesture, juxtaposing it with another contrary-motion passage, descending lower-register arpeggios against rising upper-register tritones; since each part moves by two steps along the seventh chord, the downbeat interval class is always the same. There is a bit of contrapuntal trickery across the repeat, with the arpeggiated tritone moving down by semitone while the rest of the music moves by fourth and fifth. This leads to a reimagining of the second theme and the movement's first use of fauxbourdon (Figure 10.4.10, last measure).[57] The sequence recalls the *Tempest*'s development, fauxbourdon ascending by fourth before becoming a chromatic 5–6.

Once again, my analytical reductions have sequences and schemas as their targets, reducing the music to a collection of nested patterns—contrary-motion ascending- and descending-fifth sequences arranged as an up-and-down-the-ladder pair. Figure 10.4.13 provides Schenker's more note-based analysis: at the highest level, he connects the A♭ that starts the development to the G that is the first downbeat of the descending-fifth "down-the-ladder" sequence; at the intermediate level

**Figure 10.4.13.** Three of Schenker's development sketches: (*top*) his long-range sketch; (*middle*) a more detailed sketch; (*bottom*) his interpretation of the contrary-motion Ludwig.

---

[57] B♭ minor continues the "down the ladder" portion of the schema one step too far.

he constructs the descending scale shown in the example's middle system; and at the most detailed level, he connects the first Ludwig's initial upper-voice A♭ to the lower-voice G that starts the second unit. I have a number of technical reservations about these reductions: in particular, many of Schenker's choices seem arbitrary, motivated less by internal musical logic than by an external mandate to force the music to confirm to his preconceived reductional templates; this is most obvious in his insensitivity to the Ludwig's schematic unity, repeatedly forcing it into a stepwise mold. Most important, however, is the question of analytical goals. Schenker's aim, it seems to me, is to show that Beethoven is a superhuman genius, and hence better than you. Mine is to demystify Beethoven by showing how you might have written this music yourself. I try to do this by providing reductions that are simple enough so that one could imagine inventing them, while being complex enough to serve as blueprints that could be used to reconstruct the final piece. Schenker's note-based reductions are too far from the surface to serve this purpose—both because they are insufficiently reflective of the piece's details and because there are countless pieces to be written embedding their notes.

*(c) Recapitulation and coda.* Oboe solo aside, the first half of the recapitulation is fairly literal. In part this is because the transition requires only a single change of harmony, vii°$^7$/V moving to V rather than V/III. The major difference is timbral: pizzicato lower strings and an increased role for the winds, leading to the lament that replaces Fate's second knock.[58] The second theme is transformed by the "pattern continues, chord repeats" technique of §4.9; this takes I to IV and an expanded "standing on the dominant" using ♭$\hat{6}$ and ♮$\hat{6}$ (Figure 10.4.14). Amusingly, the second theme's second sequential unit, melodic B♭–C–D♭–C with harmonic C$^7$–F, is the same in both exposition and recapitulation. These changes have the effect of keeping the entire second theme area more squarely in the orbit of C major, delaying the arrival of C minor until the coda.

The coda is most notable for what it does *not* do: in place of schematic cleverness and voice-leading trickery, we have raw compositional force, often featuring a stripped-down texture of octaves or dyads that evoke the Knock of Fate. The overall impression is of accumulating energy: six overlapping phrases grouped into three paragraphs, outlining large scalar trajectories and building to a climax surpassing anything heard so far. Like the *Waldstein*, it presents a long process of rhythmic change, beginning with roughly fifty measures of mostly eighth-note motion, slowing to quarter notes for the next fifty measures, arriving on a singular half-note at the start of the fifth phrase, and reinstating eighth notes for the final thirty bars. Motivically, it separates the opening motive's pitch and rhythm, highlighting its pitch content in the second phrase and focusing on rhythm in the remainder.[59]

---

[58] The introduction to the second theme, which shifts from horns to bassoons, confronts conductors with a delicate decision, as it is distinctly less powerful than the exposition; I might consider adding a single horn to the bassoons, strengthening the texture while still preserving some timbral difference.

[59] The last movement of Brahms's C minor piano quartet Op. 60 also seems to separate the pitch and rhythm of the Fifth Symphony's opening notes.

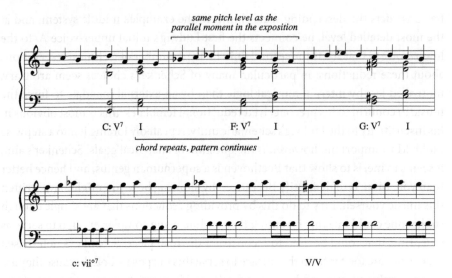

Figure 10.4.14. The recapitulation's version of the second theme (mm. 319ff).

The coda begins with pulsing eighth-note harmony, strings and winds alternately intoning the weak-weak-weak-strong rhythmic motto; the two Ludwig units loosely recall the transition (Figure 10.4.15, compare mm. 34ff of Figure 10.4.4).[60] These arrive on a second-inversion triad that overlaps with the start of the second phrase, simultaneously a cadential $^6_4$ and a tonic-functioning beginning. The lower voice combines the Knock of Fate pitches with the rhythm of the second-theme horn call, abandoning its cadence in favor of a natural-minor descent in tenths, the counterpoint contracting to bare dyads. Once again, we bypass the cadence, scale-fragments instead changing direction and taking up the WWWS rhythmic motto; offbeat eighths add a third voice that converts the tenths into tonic-dominant harmony, as if the language were gradually rebuilding itself. One has the feeling of massive forces reversing direction, an ocean liner slowly coming about, with phrase 2 descending from A5 to D4 and phrases 3 and 4 ascending back to C5.

Phrase 4 returns to the coda's opening, extending the Ludwig and reinforcing its relation to the transition (Figure 10.4.16). The cadential arrival is the coda's sole half-note measure, the gigantic musical mechanism simultaneously slowing and gathering force. Phrase 5 is an unusual example of what might be called "development by reorganization," using virtually the same material as phrase 4, but organized downbeat-to-upbeat rather than upbeat-to-downbeat. Eighth notes return for the final section, reuniting the motive's pitch and

---

[60] Schenker reduces the coda's upper voice to C–D–E♭, rather than the E♭–F–G of the schema; the issues here are largely analogous to those surrounding the Op. 22 minuet (§9.4).

**Figure 10.4.15.** The coda's first three phrases, mm. 374–422.

rhythm (Figure 10.4.17). The music of mm. 6–9 appears twice, repeated in such a way as to clarify the theme's arpeggiated nature; the oboe's A♭5–G5 helps us hear the repeat as a continuation. The repeat also has the effect of withholding the dominant for the final cadence.

All in all, the coda feels somewhat beyond analysis, devoid of the non-obvious relationships that make verbal commentary worth reading. Here Beethoven seems to be well on his way to a music of gesture, made from contrasts of direction, grouping, and density rather than complexities of harmony and melody. Though it uses familiar scales and harmonies, its aesthetics feel genuinely novel, somewhere between the worlds of Haydn and Penderecki. It is interesting that this music completes such a taut and intricate movement, as if Beethoven's

Figure 10.4.16. The coda's fourth and fifth phrases, mm. 423–468.

Figure 10.4.17. The end of the coda, mm. 469–502.

expressive energy could no longer be contained within the idioms of the classical style. The coda breaks its generic bonds, bursting forth in a frenzy of unstructured energy.

## 5. The "Pastorale" sonata, Op. 28

The first movement of the "Pastorale" sonata shows Beethoven exploring similar ideas in a more placid frame of mind. Its most distinctive feature is its rhythm of repetition: almost every phrase is played twice, with the repeat sometimes extended. The piece thus suggests its own formal analysis, articulating structural divisions through repetitive regularity.[61] A second point of interest is the emphasis on parallel motion, with fauxbourdon playing a starring role—augmented occasionally by other sorts of parallelism, and sometimes in dialogue with contrary motion. While many of Beethoven's movements are dominated by sequences or harmonic cycles, the "Pastorale" is the rare piece that is largely devoted to the third system of functional tonality. The combination of repetition and fauxbourdon contributes to its relaxed lack of urgency.

*(a) Exposition.* I parse the exposition as being in six large phrases, with the first two forming the first group, the third the transition, the fourth and fifth the second theme, and the sixth a closing theme. The first phrase begins with descending-third fauxbourdon, IV–ii–vii°–V over a tonic pedal, replacing the suspensions of the standard 7–6 sequence with accented passing tones (Figures 10.5.1–2). Having articulated almost the entire chain of thirds from tonic to dominant, the inverted arch ascends by horn fifths to recapture lost registral space. The lowest voice is displaced downward by octave for the horn call, the unusual spacing setting up the

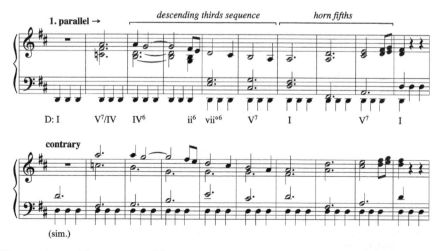

Figure 10.5.1. The opening of the Op. 28 piano sonata.

---

[61] Sommer 1986 reads the form against the rhythm of repetition. Tovey 1931 is much closer to my reading.

**Figure 10.5.2.** The descending 7–6 compared to Beethoven's descending-third fauxbourdon sequence.

repeat's "thinking within the chord." Here the tenor moves upward as the upper voices descend, transforming parallel into contrary motion—a process that will recur throughout the movement (Figure 10.5.3).

The second phrase is also fauxbourdon-based, a variant of the "standing on the predominant" idiom with three voices moving back and forth between ii$^6$ and IV$^6$ while the pedal shifts to the tenor (Figure 10.5.4). I hear this music as responding to the horn fifths of the opening—a kind of "tail development" whereby the second phrase picks up on the ending of the first: Figure 10.5.5 tries to capture the relationship, but the analysis feels pedantic, like pinning a butterfly to a board. The transitional third phrase is also fauxbourdon-based, with three voices descending against a tenor pedal. We hear a four-chord pattern first in A and then in E, moving twice up the ladder of fifths to tonicize V/V. The vii$^6_5$–V$^6$–V$^4_3$/V–V progression crosses fauxbourdon with the Prinner, its two transpositions connecting to form a descending scale—repetition that is again continuation (Figures 10.5.6–7). This whole pattern is then repeated with an oscillating neighbor-tone decoration—leading to a gradual weakening of the tonic, so that the first presentation of b$^6_5$–A$^6$–E$^4_3$–A is clearly in D while its repeat can be heard in A. The final cadence is repeated while the right-hand scale descends to an abrupt halt on E4, once again lending the medial caesura a novel expressive valence: first, because the harmonically unsupported pause has the character of an interruption, as if a performer had somehow gotten lost; and second because the subsequent E♯ seems to resume the melodic thread, the purported medial caesura occurring in the middle of a continuous melodic statement.

Compounding this effect is a serious case of tonal indecision, the music vacillating between A major and F♯ minor for almost thirty measures before finally settling down in A (Figure 10.5.8).[62] The second theme begins with right-hand ascending steps against left-hand descending fifths, stating the defaults in Figures 6.1.3–4.[63]

---

[62] There is a cadence on the dominant of A in m. 59, an F♯ minor theme in m. 63, a weak A major cadence in m. 70, a return to F♯ minor in m. 71, and a half cadence on *its* dominant in m. 77. Longyear and Covington (1988) compare this to "backing slowly into a parking space." See also Hepokoski and Darcy (2006, p. 120) on "tonally migratory" phrases.

[63] The upper three voices move in doubly parallel motion, perhaps developing the fauxbourdon opening; the chordal sevenths resolve up by step in the first and third measures.

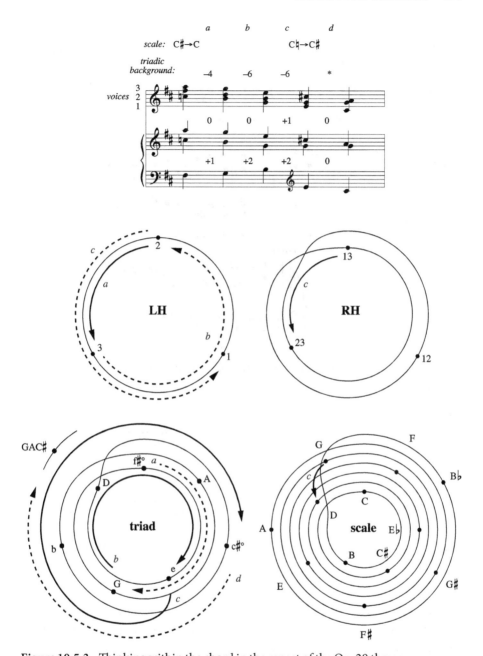

**Figure 10.5.3.** Thinking within the chord in the repeat of the Op. 28 theme.

It is the bass that makes the music interesting, its insistently descending fifths easy to miss if you are not paying attention. But if you are, you can almost hear Beethoven making the music-theoretical point that functional harmony encodes a contrary-motion sequence as one of its basic idioms.[64] This contrary-motion

---

[64] Indeed, it was this passage that inspired Figure 6.1.3, which is as much Beethoven's discovery as it is mine. An analogous passage can be found in the closing theme of the first movement of the A major sonata Op. 2, no. 2, there with $V^7$ supporting $\hat{4}$.

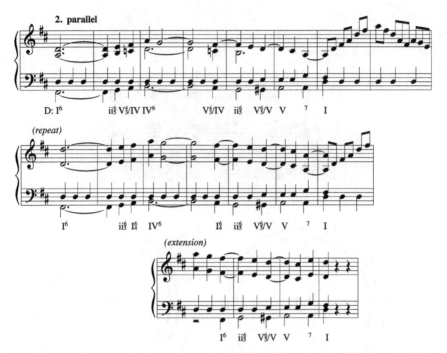

**Figure 10.5.4.** The second phrase (mm. 21–39) is based on the fauxbourdon ROTO schema.

**Figure 10.5.5.** The second phrase loosely echoes the first-phrase horn call.

antecedent leads to a parallel motion consequent, reversing the process heard at the movement's opening: there, the parallel-motion fauxbourdon theme was answered by a contrary-motion variant; here a contrary-motion antecedent is answered by parallel-motion consequent. The half-cadence C♯$^7$ slides to E$^7$, with both sonorities being decorated by lower neighbors to produce common-tone decorations; unusually, they are half-diminished and minor sevenths rather than fully diminished sevenths. This static phrase extension is one of the largest nonrepeated passages in the movement, a treading water before the A major arrival in m. 91.

That arrival occurs in the middle of a continuous forty-eight-measure sweep extending from m. 61 to m. 108—or even longer, for listeners who share my sense that the m. 61 E♯ continues the preceding music. Once again, we have a sequence playing a thematic role: in this case, a standard A3D5 with parallel tenths in the

**Figure 10.5.6.** The fauxbourdon-based transition, mm. 40–62.

**Figure 10.5.7.** The transition as a continuous process, the parallel first-inversion chords continuing through the repeat.

outer voices, fauxbourdon parallelism having been reduced from three voices to two (Figure 10.5.9). The sequence descends by two thirds, moving from A to f♯ to D before reversing direction with two statements of the ascending-fifth Ludwig (Figure 10.5.10).[65] Once again parallel is answered by contrary, here within a single phrase. The second statement shadows the original a third higher, descending by third and then using the descending-fifth Ludwig to arrive at the same chord that completed the first statement. It is fascinating to see Beethoven deliberately juxtaposing two

---

[65] It is also possible to hear a non-octave-repeating Ludwig taking D to D, though that reading cuts against the rhythmic organization.

**Figure 10.5.8.** The off-tonic beginning of the second theme, mm. 63–91.

versions of the Ludwig, as if he considered them variants of the same basic pattern. This restatement also tells us something about Beethoven's conception of musical identity, for this theme is not a specific melody but something more general—a texture, a shape, a sequence of schemas. Here Beethoven seems to declare that he is a composer of patterns rather than melodies.

The brief cadential passage then takes us to a cadence on A and a closing theme that displaces the rhythm of the fourth phrase (Figure 10.5.8) by a quarter note.[66] Figure 10.5.11 shows that the left-hand figuration embeds the horn fifths of the opening theme, a relationship that relatively few pianists choose to emphasize; the right hand almost duplicates this melody at the octave, leading to Gjerdingen's Quiescenza and a brief tonicization of D major; the closing theme thus contains both thematic and tonal references to the opening. This music—repeated an octave below, with the melody doubled at the original pitch level—takes us to the end of the exposition and a descending quarter-note line. The horn fifths will be central to the development, in both its opening-theme and closing-theme variants.

---

[66] Thanks here to Yuqi Liang.

Figure 10.5.9. The second theme's loosely parallel A major phrases, superimposed.

The six large expositional phrases are numbered on Figures 10.5.1–11. Each is in some way sequential or schematic: the first a descending-third fauxbourdon sequence moving to the horn-fifth ascent, embellished contrapuntally in the repeat; the second, a version of the "fauxbourdon ROTO"; the third, another fauxbourdon variant; the fourth, a contrary-motion sequence basic to functional tonality; the fifth, a descending-third sequence (like the opening theme) followed by a Ludwig; and the sixth, horn-fifths followed by the Quiescenza. Half of these phrases move from parallel to contrary or *vice versa*. There is no extended passage of nonsequential, nonschematic, and melodic music to be found in the movement. The ubiquity of patterning, in such a relaxed piece, reminds us that schema and sequence are central features of Beethoven's vocabulary, compatible with a wide range of expressive moods.

*(b) Development and recapitulation.* The development is perhaps the largest "up and down the ladder" in the literature, featuring contrary motion throughout (Figure 10.5.12). It begins two fifths below its usual starting point: the schematic shift from dominant major to dominant minor, which usually takes place across

502    TONALITY: AN OWNER'S MANUAL

Figure 10.5.10. The two continuations of the second theme's A major phrases.

Figure 10.5.11. The closing theme is a loose eight-bar period with syncopated melody.

**Figure 10.5.12.** An outline of the development.

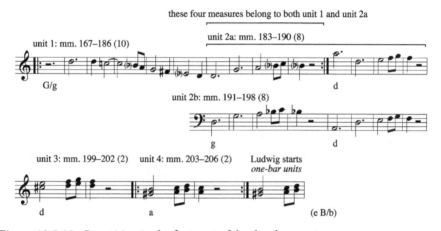

**Figure 10.5.13.** Repetition in the first part of the development.

the exposition/development boundary, here occurs *within* the development and on the *sub*dominant. From there the music ascends through five fifth-related minor keys, arriving at a V/vi that lasts for thirty-eight measures (!), enlivened by a variety of rounds and contrary-motion patterns.[67] This leads to a very brief fragment of the closing theme—once in B major and once in a B minor that moves directly to V[7]. Like the exposition, the development presents a series of immediately repeating statements. Here they shrink as the main theme is liquidated: we begin by reducing the ten-measure main theme to its four-measure "horn fifths" conclusion, arranged in eight-measure pairs, contracting to its last two measures in m. 199, a single measure in m. 207, and ultimately a single note in m. 240. Figure 10.5.13 shows the start of this process. The final reappearance of the closing theme cements its connection to the opening, the left-hand horn fifths more salient after a development largely devoted to that motive.

---

[67] The outer voice round at m. 230 is reminiscent of m. 170 of the first movement of the Second Symphony, which extends the pattern from triad to seventh chord.

504    TONALITY: AN OWNER'S MANUAL

Unlike the previous pieces, the recapitulation involves only minor changes to the exposition: inserting eighth notes into the first statement of the main theme (mm. 279–280), adding an extra flourish in mm. 304–307, and transposing mm. 316–319 so as to remain in the tonic. The coda returns to the main theme and adds a brief cadence. It is difficult for me to perceive this as anything other than perfunctory, for it neither contributes to what I consider a genuine musical narrative, nor resolves anything I hear as long-term tonal dissonance. In this respect it contrasts with the more varied recapitulations of the *Tempest* and the Fifth Symphony. How is it that Beethoven could be simultaneously so radical along some dimensions and so conventional along others? What marked the difference, for him, between unassailable features of sonata form, and those that were available for experimentation? How did he understand the relation between large-scale repetition and musical storytelling?

## 6. Schubert's *Quartettsatz*

These three analyses should convey a sense of the intelligent play I hear in Beethoven's music. While his pieces are not always so pattern-based, nor so heavily Ludwig-focused, these movements reflect an important strand of his thinking—one that I think has been obscured by a fixation on genius, heroism, divine inspiration, the *Idee*, musical unity, and the (Burkean) sublime. I now want to consider how Beethoven's techniques are transformed in two pieces composed in his shadow, Schubert's *Quartettsatz* and the prelude to Wagner's *Lohengrin*. I hear both composers as attempting to match Beethoven's expressive clarity while expanding his musical vocabulary—Schubert in the direction of greater lyricism and formal flexibility, and Wagner through a more thoroughgoing rejection of schematic composition. If Beethoven's language is one of limitation, a redeploying of musical resources toward broader stretches of musical time, then both Schubert and Wagner can be understood as trying to enrich their local vocabulary while preserving Beethoven's command of large-scale architecture.

The *Quartettsatz*'s exposition is divided into three parts: we begin with three phrases in C minor, the last of which moves to A♭; we then hear a lyrical second theme that leads to a two-part transition occurring *after* the second theme. The transition begins with an ascending-step sequence whose dominant sevenths never resolve, arriving at a G dominant that is $V^7$ of the global tonic—as if we were treading water tonally. We then hear a short, repeated phrase that transforms this dominant into a tonic, leading to an authentic cadence and a trio of themes in G major. This three-part structure is in uneasy dialogue with the gestural targets of the classical-era sonata, blurring, rearranging, and otherwise problematizing events such as transition, medial caesura, and the "essential expository cadence."[68]

---

[68] See Grant 2018 for a helpful survey of Schubert's three-part expositions, which generally articulate similar trajectories. Barry 2014 considers whether the piece may be "Schubert's most extreme treatment of

**Figure 10.6.1.** The opening of Schubert's *Quartettsatz*.

Schubert's combination of schematic detail and large-scale freedom has prompted a great deal of criticism, but to a twenty-first-century musician it suggests a genuine theoretical insight, that formal conventions and large-scale key-relations are less significant than one might think.[69] In this respect, Schubert continues a process that begins with Beethoven's more limited problematizing of sonata-form conventions.

*(a) Exposition.* The opening measures present three basic elements: the tremolo texture, the eighth-note neighboring figure, and the four-bar lament bass (Figure 10.6.1). Both the motive and its development have a static character, intrinsically accompanimental and always appearing on the same pitch classes. We open with a four-voice canonic round expanding from middle C to the quartet's full

---

sonata form" (32); Webster 1978 suggests it is not in sonata form. Longyear and Covington (1988) suggest that Beethoven's Op. 28 is a precursor. Other insightful discussions include Bruce 1969, Fieldman 2002, Smith 2006, Mak 2008, and Hunt 2014.

[69] See Fieldman 2002 for a survey of these criticisms.

506    TONALITY: AN OWNER'S MANUAL

**Figure 10.6.2.** The opening fuses Ludwig and fauxbourdon ROTO.

**Figure 10.6.3.** The transition from C minor to A♭ major, mm. 13–26.

four-and-a-half-octave range, low C2 to high G6. Harmonically it articulates a third-focused tonic-subdominant Ludwig, with the substitution of i$^6_4$ for V$^4_3$/iv evoking the fauxbourdon ROTO (Figure 10.6.2). To the attentive analyst, the weak-beat i$^6_4$ signals an interruption, the unaccented second-inversion triad syntactically passing, yet appearing at the end of each two-bar unit. Thus we could in principle infer that the canon, when it breaks, must proceed to something other than V. Eventually, the music satisfies this expectation with a dramatic Neapolitan, the Ludwig continuing to the dominant through a voice exchange. In the next six-bar

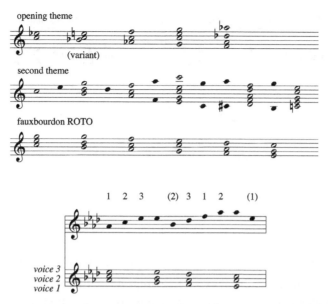

**Figure 10.6.4.** (*top*) Comparison of the C minor and A♭ major themes, and the fauxbourdon ROTO. (*bottom*) The A♭ major theme ascends along a descending background.

phrase, the motive, such as it is, appears for the first time in an upper voice, repeating just once before reaching a cadence with an unaltered predominant. This is a softer and less angry sound, a notable contrast with the previous Neapolitan.

The third phrase is shown in Figure 10.6.3. The ♭$\hat{2}$ appears as part of the cello ostinato, hinting at F minor and foreshadowing the coming A♭ major; the cadence, when it arrives, reinterprets the Neapolitan to swerve to the submediant.[70] At this point a familiar Schubert emerges, a soaring melody against a simple accompaniment in the lower strings—the movement's emotional center, and more sustained lyricism than in any of pieces we have considered so far. If this is a second theme, it is preceded by no real transition: instead, the accompaniment sublimates the neighboring motive, the second violin E♭–F–E♭ inverting the initial C–B♭–C. The effect is of a cinematic dissolve, our attention drawn by an upper-register melody so that the motive gradually fades from consciousness, foreground receding into background and ultimately beyond the horizon of our attention. It is as if the motive has finally accepted its intrinsically accompanimental character.

Figure 10.6.4 details the resemblances among the opening theme, the A♭ major theme, and the fauxbourdon ROTO schema: the opening substitutes V$^2$/IV for V$^6$, bypassing the schema's distinctive V$^6$–IV$^6$ progression, while the second theme supposes new bass notes to avoid the equally characteristic IV$^6$–I$^6_4$–ii$^6$.

---

[70] Webster 1978 notes that these quick transitions are characteristic of Schubert; Bruce 1969, Navia 2016, and Duane 2017 hear an earlier transition starting in m. 13. Smith 2006 considers the various roles of D♭ major and the Neapolitan in the movement.

**Figure 10.6.5.** An analysis of the A♭ major theme (mm. 27–60).

The second-theme melody ascends upward against this descending background, an arpeggiation that continues when it repeats at the octave. This pattern of octave restatement will continue throughout the exposition, which repeats almost as much as the first movement of Beethoven's Op. 28. The cadential phrase-extension provides a classical-music take on the Renaissance ascending-fifth sequence, secondary dominant concealing the V–ii retrofunctionality and minor tonic reinforcing the descending voice leading (Figure 10.6.5).[71] Its repetition is thus a continuation, a single sequence of ascending fifths perturbed by third substitutions.[72]

The long-delayed cadence arrives as the tremolos return and the mode changes to minor, a shocking reversion to the *bravura* opening—with the neighbor-note motive again in the foreground (Figure 10.6.6). This music has the character of a sonata-form transition, and indeed it is possible to imagine moving directly from the E♭⁷ in m. 26 to the A♭ minor in m. 61—an alternative that would be rhetorically if not tonally more straightforward than Schubert's actual composition. As in Beethoven, texture, mode, and gesture serve a thematic function, recalling the opening even in the context of considerable variation.[73] Figure 10.6.7 proposes a stepwise descending background voice leading against which the surface moves; this effect of continuous descent disguised by registral displacement is similar to the Shepard-tone passacaglias considered earlier.[74] We arrive on the dominant in

---

[71] Here is a place where it is helpful to view a I⁶₄ chord as tonic, a functionally tonal analogue to the harmonic ⁶₄ in Figure 5.2.1.

[72] In Roman numerals, IV–I–V–ii–[I replacing vi]–V–ii–[I replacing vi]–V–I. The I–ii–V–I and I–V–ii–I are four-chord *double emploi* progressions: in the more familiar five-chord *double emploi* (e.g., I–IV–ii–V–I or the pop-music I–V–ii–IV–I), we hear third-related chords in succession; in the four-chord version, one such chord replaces another.

[73] Duane 2017 uses computational analysis to argue that texture can signify thematicity in Schubert's expositions.

[74] For example, §2.5 or §7.3. The last movement of Mozart's E♭ major piano sonata, K.282, mm. 48–56, has a similar sequence, lowering the notes of a dominant seventh so that V⁷ becomes iv of the key a step higher.

**Figure 10.6.6.** The beginning of the transition, mm. 61–80.

C minor, as if all the preceding music had gotten us exactly nowhere; I hear this as Schubert's take on the medial caesura, a reference that is clearer in the recapitulation, where the texture contracts to a single voice (Figure 10.6.16).[75]

Stasis is averted at the last minute by two measures in which chords change on every eighth, the movement's quickest harmonies (Figure 10.6.8). Here we have

---

[75] Richard Cohn (1999) has proposed that major-third-related key areas can serve similar functional roles, implying that the second theme's A♭ major could be a tonic substitute. I personally hear A♭ major as a distinct key rather than a flavor of tonic, a hearing that comports with the broader three-key practice surveyed in Grant 2018.

510  TONALITY: AN OWNER'S MANUAL

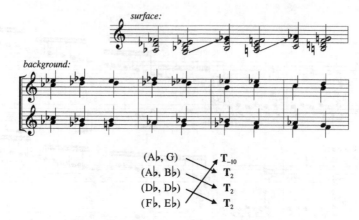

Figure 10.6.7. Descending chromatic voice leading in the transition.

Figure 10.6.8. The end of the transition, mm. 81–92.

the same effect found in the transition of the first movement of Beethoven's Op. 28, a modulating phrase that is immediately repeated. This makes the repeat sound very different from the original: what was III of C minor gradually becomes VI of G minor, a transformation that does not so much occur in musical space as in *interpretive* space, our perceptions revolving around the fixed point of an exact repeat.

The form then becomes a bit mysterious. To my ear, the preceding phrase is transitional rather than thematic, motivically linked to the (faux) medial caesura by the melodic F♯–G–A♭–G, and beginning on III of C minor. But the phrase ends with a perfect authentic cadence and the next phrase, as Aaron Grant notes, could be heard as closing: a six-measure sentence containing a full statement of the fauxbourdon ROTO, bringing to completion a motif present throughout the

**Figure 10.6.9.** The first G major theme, mm. 99–104. The melody alternates sixths and tenths above the descending bass.

exposition (Figure 10.6.9).[76] The reference here is not simply one of motivic content, but of schematic identity: both the C minor opening and the A♭ major melody hint at the fauxbourdon ROTO without stating it clearly, the former descending $\hat{8}$–$\hat{7}$–$\hat{6}$–$\hat{5}$–$\hat{4}$, and latter $\hat{8}$–$\hat{7}$–$\hat{6}$, and continuing the schema's harmony even further.[77] In the G major theme, the schema emerges complete and undisguised, Schubert finally coming clean about his material.[78] The melody, meanwhile, ascends in contrary-motion tenths and sixths against the bass, as in the opening of the Fifth Brandenburg Concerto (c.f. Figure 7.5.2 and the fauxbourdon passage in Figure 3.2.5).

The first G major theme starts on G4 and repeats up an octave; the next theme begins on the higher-octave G5, repeating at a stratospheric G6 (with the cello instead switching to pizzicato). The descending octave moves from bass to melody, sliding chromatically down from tonic to dominant, and then diatonically down to tonic (Figure 10.6.10). Figure 10.6.11 shows that this melody transports the preceding bass line's intervals into the chromatic scale, a subtle continuity that might initially escape the ear. The eight-measure sentence is based on the *Waldstein*/ *Natural Woman* progression, descending (I–V)–(♭VII–IV)–(♭VI–♭III). Normally, this ♭III would proceed to V, as in Morley's "April Is in My Mistress' Face"; here, Schubert drops down to a striking root-position Neapolitan, as if extending the sequence further—a dramatic continuation that transforms the *Waldstein* schema into something novel.[79] There follows a straightforward closing melody, a six-measure

---

[76] Grant 2018 describes a number of Schubertian three-key movements in which the thematic material initially has a closing character that is retrospectively reinterpreted as thematic.

[77] Many commentators have noted the motivic connection, including Beach 1994 and Barry 2014; the schematic relationship is less frequently discussed.

[78] Again, this bears comparison to the gradual revelation of structure we found in Beethoven.

[79] The Neapolitan appears in the next sequential unit, which would continue ♭V–♭II. For a rock analogue see Led Zeppelin's "Kashmir," which similarly extends the 6–5 pattern beyond its standard length. Peter Smith 2006 associates this moment with the prominent Neapolitan of the opening.

**Figure 10.6.10.** The second G major theme, mm. 113–124, along with its underlying voice leading. Numbers show 90° arcs on the circle of chromatic triads (Figure 2.1.3).

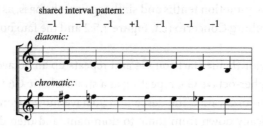

**Figure 10.6.11.** The two G major themes present the same intervals in different scales.

sentence ascending by octave and repeating in the higher register, the cello's double pedal both instantiating the omnipresent three-note motive and introducing an idea that will become important in the development (Figure 10.6.12). This is the exposition's third six-measure sentence.[80]

*(b) Development and recapitulation.* I hear the development in three large sections, a static D♭ major center flanked by two sequential passages (Figure 10.6.13). We start with an ascending-step near sequence that omits the mediant; formally, it fuses the opening tremolo, the coda to the lyrical theme, and the cello's closing ostinato.[81] The phrasing, shown in Figure 10.6.14, is subtle: initially the V–I progressions decorate the sequential units, repeating twice within the A♭ major

---

[80] The others are the second phrase of the opening section and the G major theme.
[81] Compare Figure 10.4.7.

Figure 10.6.12. The closing theme (mm. 125–130) as a six-measure sentence.

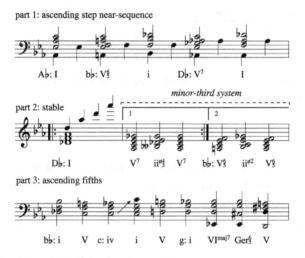

Figure 10.6.13. An outline of the development.

section; in the second unit, we hear the expected V–i progression in B♭ minor—but instead of repeating, the upper voices ascend by third while the bass slides down by step. This means that the second V–I progression, which repeats the previous measure from a rhythmic/motivic perspective, has a different musical function: rather than embellishing the tonic of an already established sequential unit, it is the third unit of the harmonic sequence. This sort of variation is emblematic of functional tonality, subtle irregularity enlivening a fundamentally repetitive substrate.

The following melody picks up the cello pedal, reversing the process at the beginning of the piece: where the transition from C minor to A♭ major steered the neighbor figure from foreground to the background, the cello's accompanimental pattern here moves from background to foreground. The octave displacement also continues the exposition's registral play: where the exposition repeated themes in a higher octave, this theme contains its own higher-octave repeat. The harmony

514　TONALITY: AN OWNER'S MANUAL

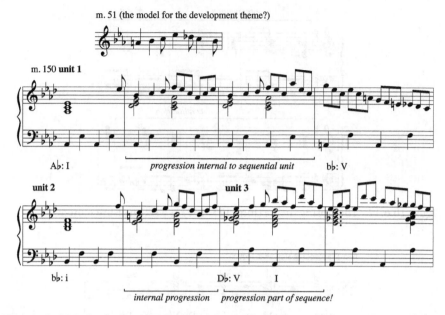

**Figure 10.6.14.** In the first development theme the sequential unit contracts so that its V–I progression changes function.

exploits the minor-third system to arrive at B♭ minor, linking A♭⁷ to F♯⁵₃ by semitonal voice leading across the repeat; its repeated ii°⁴₃–V⁷ progressions evoke the transition's iv⁶–V⁶₅ units (Figure 10.6.7).

The third section contains what would be a textbook "up-and-down-the-ladder" were the piece in B♭ major: melodies descending chromatically as the harmony rises i–v–ii–vi to a V/vi that is approached by augmented sixth. Like the opening of the exposition, the development goes nowhere tonally, starting with the closing theme's G major and ending on the dominant of G minor. This V/vi slides deceptively to the false tonic B♭ major and the recapitulation of the lyrical theme.

Of course, the piece is *not* in B♭ major and the recapitulation begins in the wrong key. One could take this as a sign of Schubert's flexible attitude toward modulation, or perhaps even compositional frivolity: perhaps, having found himself in the midst of a B♭ major up-and-down-the-ladder, he simply followed its local promptings, trusting that he could make his way back to the tonic.[82] A more colorful possibility is that the key represents a confession of musical theft, for the lyrical melody may derive from one of Mozart's more languid and proto-Schubertian concoctions, the adagio of the piano sonata K.332.[83] Figure 10.6.15 shows that the two phrases outline almost the same contrapuntal substrate, both subposing a novel

---

[82] Beach 1994 suggests that the B♭ key area is part of a movement-long C–B♭–A♭–G progression. I do not place much aesthetic weight on these sorts of long-term pitch relations.

[83] There is an extensive literature on Schubert's borrowings, including Cone 1970, Edwards 1997, and Humphreys 1997. Thanks here to René Rusch.

Figure 10.6.15. Comparison of Mozart and Schubert's themes.

bass under the fauxbourdon ROTO's I$^6_4$. Mozart then returns to the schema, giving us ii$^6$ and I$^6$ right where we expect. These last two chords are preceded with pseudo-dominant root-position mediants, which I have labeled III$^+$/ii and iii; Schubert's theme replaces these with standard-issue dominants. Perhaps, having borrowed Mozart's B♭ opening for an A♭ second theme, Schubert felt compelled to restore it to its proper place—presenting it as a *B♭ major beginning* to make clear what he had done. As in a good mystery novel, the confession is hidden, the B♭ major beginning the recapitulation rather than the piece as a whole.

In any case, the theme immediately shifts to E♭ major for its repeat. While close to C minor, this E♭ major will not take us smoothly back to the tonic: the A♭ major theme was a semitone above the exposition's G major destination, while the recapitulation's E♭ is a *minor third* above the desired C major arrival. The transition is therefore altered so that it ascends by just one major second rather than two (B♭ to C$^6_5$ rather than E♭ to F$^6_5$ to G$^6_5$, see Figure 10.6.16); this takes us to C-as-dominant which is then transformed into C-as-tonic for a repeat of the exposition's final section, ending with the opening round.[84]

Looking back at this analysis, I am struck by three things. The first is its schematic familiarity. The main harmonic and contrapuntal devices all appear in earlier chapters: the Ludwig, the fauxbourdon ROTO, descending chromatic sequences, the ascending-step near sequence that skips the mediant, and the "up and down the ladder." If I were ever to teach a course on "composing like Beethoven," or to advise a student struggling with that task, I could imagine using this piece as a model; for like much of Beethoven's music, it illustrates the power of *avoiding* certain kinds

---

[84] This kind of repositioning of the opening music appears famously appears in the first movement of Mozart's D major piano sonata K.311, I. Schubert makes a few other very small changes to the recapitulation, including using minor chords in the second-theme *Waldstein* sequence.

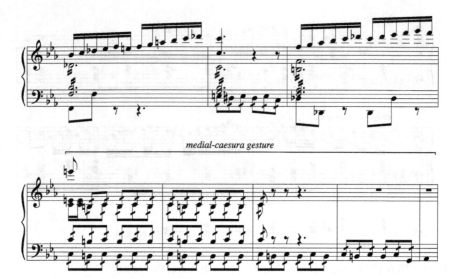

**Figure 10.6.16.** The medial-caesura gesture in the recapitulation's transition, mm. 241–244.

of invention. It is interesting not because of its material, but because of the expressive *use* to which it puts that material. Schubert's comfort with Beethoven's vocabulary is all the more impressive for the fact that it was largely untheorized: he did not learn the Ludwig or the fauxbourdon ROTO from a textbook; instead, he likely discovered them directly in music.

The second feature is the omnipresence of stepwise descending voice leading. Figure 10.6.17 graphs several of the piece's schemas in the relevant spiral diagrams.[85] The similarity of procedure is clear, with all these patterns moving by small clockwise steps. Particularly interesting is the relation between the diatonic fauxbourdon ROTO and the chromatic *Waldstein* sequence, a *geometrical* analogy that Schubert highlights with a clear *thematic* parallelism (Figure 10.6.11). Here we see something like the Prime Directive, an awareness that musical patterns can be transported from one chord-and-scale environment to another. We are not yet in the world of Chopin or Wagner: rather than setting sail onto on the open seas of chromatic counterpoint, Schubert prefers to stick closer to the shores. But we can start to see the glimmerings of a new and more general understanding of musical possibility.

Finally, there is the piece's deconstruction of classical form, with its three separate tonal areas, its two secondary themes, its oddly placed medial caesura, and its rearranged recapitulation. In this respect it continues Beethoven's efforts to loosen the formal conventions of earlier classical music. Schubert's music conveys the sense of sonata form as abstracted and transformed: tonally stable thematic zones interspersed with transitions, any of which might end with a medial caesura. Directed modulatory architecture is giving way to contrasts of character and mood, the piece

---

[85] Yust 2015a also notes the omnipresence of stepwise descending voice leading in Schubert, though he analyzes it differently.

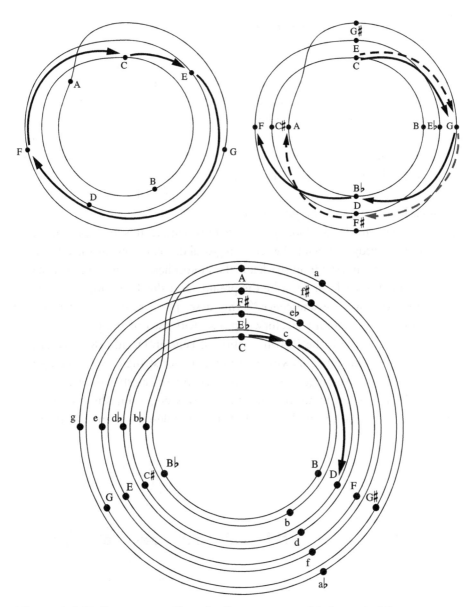

**Figure 10.6.17.** Four passages from the *Quartettsatz* modeled on spiral diagrams. On the top left, the basic "fauxbourdon ROTO" pattern C–e°–F⁶–C⁶₄, used at multiple points in the movement; top right, the two chromatic triadic sequences, the *Waldstein* C–G⁶–B♭–F⁶ (second theme) and the ascending-fifth C–G–D–A (development, dotted line). On the bottom, the seventh chord sequence C⁷–c⁷–D², used in the transition.

presenting not an orderly march from tonic to dominant and back, but a meandering tour through tonal and expressive space. For me this is liberating, suggesting that Schubert was a kindred spirit: someone who did *not* feel that large-scale key relations were central to musical coherence, someone who understood sonata form as optional and conventional, rather than a musical law of nature. The piece, in other words, makes implicit but genuinely theoretical claims about the nature of musical form.

## 7. The prelude to *Lohengrin*

I hear the *Lohengrin* prelude as a slow-motion, otherworldly fugue—the theme stated in A major, E major, and A major in successively lower registers, with the earlier instruments adding countermelodies above each new entry; in this respect it is like an imitative piece opening top-middle-bottom, descending through pitch space—though more dramatic in its registral plummet and with a polyphonic "theme" instead of a monophonic line. Orchestration is the music's lifeblood, with timbre as important as pitch and rhythm: altissimo divisi strings, briefly joined by high winds, dissolving to solo string harmonics. As the music progresses, timbre develops in concert with pitch, each thematic entry assigned to a new instrumental family (strings, winds, and horns), arriving finally at a loosely thematic brass fanfare; this then leads to a giant Beethovenian wedge retracing the earlier registral descent, now mirrored by an ascending bass line, and subliming back into the stratosphere for a nine-measure coda.

Liszt and Wagner both describe the prelude as a slowly waxing vision of the Grail, followed by its evanescence.[86] This description resonates not just with the registral and timbral trajectory, but also with two of the piece's potential inspirations: the first is the "Dawn" section of Félicien David's 1844 symphonic ode *The Desert*, which begins with altissimo A major string chords and a prominent E–F♯–E motive (Figure 10.7.1); the second is Palestrina's *Stabat Mater*, which Wagner arranged around the time he was beginning the orchestration of *Lohengrin*.[87] Like the prelude, Palestrina's double-chorus motet juxtaposes

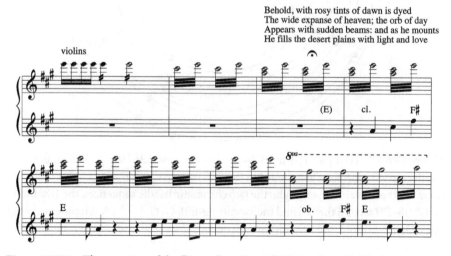

Figure 10.7.1. The opening of the "Dawn" section of Félicien David's *The Desert*.

---

[86] See Liszt 2016, pp. 117–18 (also found in Trippet 2010, p. 19), and Wagner 1907, pp. 232–33. Kramer 2002 discusses the antisemitism of Wagner's program and various efforts to resist this reading.

[87] Deathridge 2008. The connection to the desert suggests that the antisemitism may have been intrinsic to the music's conception, rather than a late-breaking addition: for Wagner, the contemporary world is an antispiritual Jewish-dominated desert.

BEETHOVEN THEORIST 519

**Figure 10.7.2.** Measures 1–12 of the *Lohengrin* prelude. The first three stanzas all begin with this material.

homophonic passages almost as if they were individual voices, generating a similar sense of sacred calm.

It is just here that the music touches on familiar concerns. For if Schubert's *Quartettsatz* is a cubist rearranging of sonata form, its individual phrases recognizable though sometimes out-of-order, then Wagner's piece represents a far greater fracturing of classical language—reaching inside the phrase to its schematic details. The prelude begins with three parallel stanzas of approximately sixteen measures: each opens with a root-position I–vi–I, a progression that is hardly used from 1650 to 1850, but familiar in a good deal of other music (e.g., "Oh, Pretty Woman" or "Hallelujah"). From there each stanza progresses to a short descending passage that hints at the fauxbourdon ROTO, I–V⁶–IV⁶, but moving to V⁷ rather than the expected I$^6_4$; at tempo, the V–IV has the unmistakable character of a harmonic retrogression.[88] The music then restates this descent, continuing to a V⁶/vi that inaugurates a descending-fifth sequence, its dominant thwarted by vii°⁷/ii and a chromaticized converging cadence (Figure 10.7.2). Idiom here has been subjected

---

[88] The anticipations in m. 8 recall the third-based anticipations in the opening of Monteverdi's "Ohimé," while softening the parallel fifths across the phrase break.

520 TONALITY: AN OWNER'S MANUAL

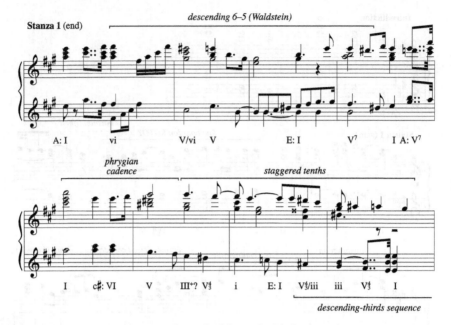

Figure 10.7.3. Measures 13–20, the end of the prelude's first stanza.

to radical reinterpretation: where earlier composers might have imagined classical harmony as a universal musical language, Wagner understands it as historically situated.

After this shared introduction, the stanzas proceed freely, in something like the way the successive voices in Renaissance polyphony diverge after stating a motive. The first is in some ways the most hermetic: what sounds like a repeat of the I–vi–I is interrupted by a descending chromatic 6–5 sequence, F♯–C♯–E–B (Figure 10.7.3). The A major context makes this sound more like free-floating chromaticism than the typical descent from tonic to dominant—a perception reinforced by the tonicization of E major. Having arrived on B, we descend by fifth to A major, leading to an unexpected phrygian cadence on G♯. Outer voices then descend in staggered tenths, moving unsystematically through third-related harmonies to arrive at E major halfway through the bar.

It is easy to overlook how novel this harmony is, particularly when we are thinking about Wagner's later chromaticism. For though functional and diatonic, the prelude is worlds apart from the schematic language of the classical style: the proliferation of secondary triads decenters tonic and dominant, and the music "wanders" even when it remains diatonic. Wagner tends to disguise his schemas, as when he occludes the converging cadence with semitonal motion or presents the *Waldstein* progression on unusual scale degrees. One can draw a contrast with those Romantic composers who present their wandering moments as *departures* from a tonic-dominant background. Already in *Lohengrin*, wandering is becoming the norm.

BEETHOVEN THEORIST 521

Figure 10.7.4. Measures 21–27, the start of the second stanza.

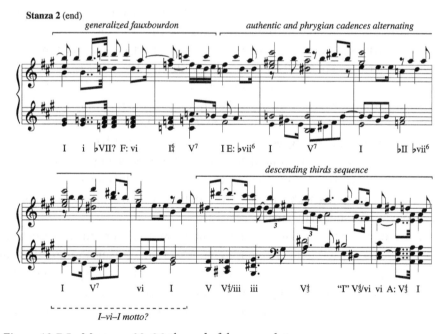

Figure 10.7.5. Measures 28–36, the end of the second stanza.

The second stanza begins as the first, with the winds sounding the theme in the lower register while the strings add a countermelody that, for me, is largely textural (Figure 10.7.4). The second half of the phrase, shown in Figure 10.7.5, uses generalized fauxbourdon to reach a cadence on F. The countermelodies ascend by

**Figure 10.7.6.** Descending-step harmonies and ascending-third melodies in *Lohengrin* and Beethoven's *Waldstein*.

third as the harmony descends, as in the *Waldstein* (Figure 10.7.6). The next four measures juxtapose phrygian and authentic cadences on E, modality and functionality alternating as if they were equally plausible options.[89] The last dominant returns to E by way of vi, hinting at the I–vi–I motto before descending by thirds B–G♯–[E]–c♯–A–f♯. The relation between this music and the end of the first stanza exemplifies Wagner's innovative conception of musical identity: the two passages seem to traverse similar terrain without quite being variations, passing through the same stations in their own individual way. This formal flexibility again recalls the Renaissance.

The third stanza largely repeats the second, though in a new register and with more powerful orchestration: the A major theme enters in the horns, bassoons, and lower strings, centered around middle C and supported by the full force of the winds and strings (Figure 10.7.7). An extra ♭II in m. 49 resolves as an ascending subdominant to an F that moves via the major-third system to A$^7$, the brass entering fortissimo for the arrival on D (Figure 10.7.8). The following music can be heard as a decorated I–vi–I, D–(b⇐F♯⇒b)–(A⇒D), leading to two iterations of the converging cadence suggesting different keys—the first beginning in D and the second ending in A, with no definitive point of modulation in between. (As in the *Quartettsatz* or Beethoven's Op. 28, a repeated modulation can be heard in two different ways.) This takes us to a strong dominant whose deceptive resolution overlaps with the start of the final large phrase.[90]

That music features a giant contrary-motion wedge, more than five octaves from low-bass F♯1 to violin A6, converging over nine measures to less than an octave (Figure 10.7.9). Programmatically, this represents the evaporation of the Grail, ecstatic insight gradually contracting in a poignant release of musical energy.[91] Music-theoretically, it represents the evolution of contrary motion from

---

[89] One could potentially hear this music as juxtaposing full cadences in E with half-cadences in A; I, however, hear an E center throughout.

[90] Kramer 2002 reads this final wedge as the second half of the fourth stanza; to me it sounds new.

[91] Wagner's symbolic use of register bears comparison with the end of Monteverdi's "Cosi sol d'un chiara fonte" (Madrigals, Book 8), where a Ludwig schema generates wide registral separation that mirrors the words "I am so far from my salvation."

**Figure 10.7.7.** Measures 37–50, the third stanza. This music largely repeats the second stanza.

a specific schematic gesture, carefully arranged to be consistent with functional laws, to a more general tool for generating novel harmonic states—the ancestor of early-modern moments such as Figure 10.7.10. On close inspection we can find traces of a familiar descending-third schema: at the beginning, ascending steps in an inner voice against descending thirds and fourths in the upper voice (compare Figures 10.3.8 and 10.2.10), overlapping with descending melodic steps and fifths against ascending steps in the bass, and finally dissolving into a purely harmonic sequence that alternates root-position and first-inversion chords. These are linked by a nonfunctional C♯–E hinge connecting the F♯ minor beginning to an A major continuation that features deceptive rather than authentic resolutions. The arrival at m. 67 is the prelude's first conclusive cadence, prompting a return to the altissimo register and one last version of the I–vi motto, now normalized into a I–vi–IV–I progression (Figure 10.7.11).

Figure 10.7.8. The fourth stanza, mm. 51–57.

Christopher Reynolds rightly associates this music with Beethoven, and there is indeed a clear resonance with many of the passages we have considered.[92] But where Reynolds traces the music to the Ninth Symphony in particular, I would instead point to Beethoven's lifelong fascination with contrary motion—the Ludwig as a manifestation of a broader compositional habit rather than any one particular piece.[93] The main difference is that Wagner's language is much less schematic than Beethoven's: like many nineteenth-century composers, he combines Beethoven's formal clarity with a more varied harmonic vocabulary drawing on a much wider range of historical influences. The atoms of the *Lohengrin* prelude are not the ubiquitous I–V–I progressions of the Fifth Symphony, nor even the more complex sequential formulations we have been examining, but something looser and less definite. Sequences and contrary motion become tools for achieving harmonic novelty.[94]

A good deal of critical commentary has centered on the question of *Lohengrin*'s relation to Wagner's later music. At first hearing they are quite different: *Lohengrin* more triadic and more familiarly functional, its modulations less frequent and its key areas more stable. If we think of "progress" as a vector pointing from *Tristan* to *The Book of the Hanging Gardens*, then *Lohengrin* is clearly "not yet" progressive. But it is possible to hear the piece as progressive in another sense, exploring a flexible fusion of modality and functionality found in our own time. *Lohengrin*, in

---

[92] Reynolds 2015; Gauldin 2004 explores chromatic wedges in Wagner's later music.

[93] In comparison to other Beethoven pieces, the Ninth Symphony does not strike me as being heavily saturated with Ludwigs or other classical schemas; in fact, I suspect that its *nonschematic* character represents its greatest influence on Wagner.

[94] See Figure 4.1.4. Segall 2010 contains an interesting example from Schoenberg's *Verklärte Nacht*.

BEETHOVEN THEORIST 525

Figure 10.7.9. The contrary-motion wedge of mm. 58–72, along with an analysis.

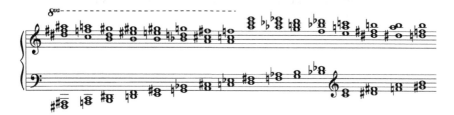

Figure 10.7.10. The death of Kastchei from Stravinsky's *Firebird* (R195). The lower voices feature the repeating contrapuntal pattern shown in Figure 4.2.2, while the upper voices descend chromatically and unsystematically, producing a wide range of sonorities.

Figure 10.7.11. The end of the prelude, mm. 73–75.

other words, intimates a diatonic progressivism whose explorations occur *within* familiar scales rather than outside of them. Here we come full circle, returning to something like the freedom of the modal era—a largely diatonic language in which function contends with other modes of musical organization.

Yet despite these changes, the basic materials of Wagner's prelude are not unfamiliar. Consider some of the idioms it shares with the *Quartettsatz*: the fauxbourdon ROTO, contrary-motion sequences, the *Waldstein* schema, the major-third system, and so on. These patterns can be found wherever intelligent composers use triadic materials, from Renaissance modality to contemporary popular music. This is not so much a matter of historical influence but of constraints inherent in musical space: as we rise to higher levels of abstraction, styles start to converge, with different genres making slightly different use of the same basic musical options.

In the four centuries from Ockeghem to Brahms, these possibilities are constrained and then loosened. Initially the narrowing is harmonic, as the modal freedom of the early sixteenth century is gradually restricted to a smaller set of functionally tonal progressions. In the eighteenth century, we have a gestural narrowing that increasingly focuses on specific schemata: sentence and period, converging cadence, standing on the dominant, sonata form, and all the rest. Beethoven is at the very center of this process, simultaneously the apotheosis of classical condensation and the initiator of the Romantic countermovement—the point of rest at the top of the arc. The *Quartettsatz* was written at the beginning of the expansion, the music's local moves familiar even while its sonata-form architecture is novel. The *Lohengrin* prelude is expansive even at the level of local detail, its schemas distorted and its progressions announcing a new harmonic freedom. A Hegelian would describe it as combining the thesis of local freedom with the antithesis of large-scale formal clarity—a clarity that was initially made possible by a severe restriction of gesture, but which eventually transcended that limitation.

# Conclusion

## Past and Future

For centuries theorists have dreamed of a Platonic and extra-human music, with listening the unwitting contemplation of ratio and number.[1] There is a lot wrong with this picture: to take it literally is to imagine that music could be independent of physics, biology, culture, and history; yet the association of ratio and consonance depends on the physics of vibrating objects, and our pleasure in these relationships depends on our bodies and upbringing. Platonism feeds the temptation to ignore complexity and detail, encouraging us to think that nonharmonic tones *must* "stand for" their harmonic partners, or that the return to the tonic key *must* create a sense of resolution, or that beloved pieces *must* have an *Urlinie*. The very framework of rigid norms not actually embodied in practice, of "geniuses" taking liberties with *a priori* musical laws, reflects an urge to deny the human elements of music-making. It is understandable if twenty-first-century musicians want to put Platonism behind us.

Yet for all that it is not completely misguided. Around the world we can hear musicians deploying an organizational strategy whose origins date to the early Renaissance: surface voices moving inside chords that move inside scales that are themselves moving inside the aggregate. The spiral diagrams provide an elegant tool for visualizing this structure, a unified set of geometrical models revealing the interdependence of harmony and counterpoint: wheels within wheels, each turning independently of the others. Styles can be characterized, in part, by the settings of this complex machine: in a consonant, diatonic, and imitative environment, with little constraint on harmonic progression, it can produce the transcendent stasis of high-Renaissance polyphony; in a more homophonic and slightly less diatonic context, the hedonic yawp of AC/DC. Augmented by a complex harmonic grammar, we can approach the Newtonian clockwork of a Bach prelude, or the Romantic subjectivity of a Beethoven sonata. With extended-tertian sonorities and an expanded modal vocabulary, we move toward impressionism, jazz, and minimalism. No doubt new settings remain to be discovered, new ways of recombining the same basic ingredients.

---

[1] Both Leibniz and Thelonious Monk described music as a kind of unconscious mathematics (Rohrmeier 2020).

*Tonality.* Dmitri Tymoczko, Oxford University Press. © Oxford University Press 2023. DOI: 10.1093/oso/9780197577103.003.0020

## 528 TONALITY: AN OWNER'S MANUAL

The collectional hierarchy can be the explicit object of attention, as when musicians move motives along both chord and scale, or when surface voices ascend against a descending background—as in the *Waldstein* or the Revolutionary Etude. More subtle are pieces like "Eight Days a Week," *Heu me Domine*, or "Helpless," where voices might ascend along a continually descending scale in order to remain stationary—or those moments where composers exploit dyadic rather than triadic logic. For here the quadruple hierarchy can arise not because composers are paying attention to it, but because musical culture has settled upon idioms that exploit its unique characteristics. This is most obviously true of those countless embodied routines that produce efficient voice leading by combining similar operations at multiple hierarchical levels: big-T little-t transposition, or in the case of Gesualdo's trick, big-I little-i inversion (appendix 3). Here the quadruple hierarchy is like a collective unconscious, supplying hidden and non-obvious structure to a vast range of practices and techniques. Some parts of this structure are easily visible, like the tip of an iceberg; others lurk far below the musical surface.

In its full generality, the collectional hierarchy lies beyond the horizon of our intuition: there are few if any musicians today who can sit down at their instrument, choose some arbitrary three-note subset of some arbitrary seven-note scale, and fluently manipulate the resulting possibilities. Instead, we tend to internalize the more limited set of musical routines relevant to a particular style. Over the course of this book, we have identified theoretical origins for nine of the eleven schemas listed in the appendix of Gjerdingen's *Music of the Galant Style*: dyadic space for the Quiescenza, Fonte, and Monte (§3.1), triadic space for the Prinner and Romanesca (§3.4), a canonic fourth-progression for the Fenaroli (Figure 4.5.6), and basic sentential logic for the Meyer, Do-Re-Mi, and Sol-Fa-Me (§9.1).[2] Such patterns are not isolated idioms specific to the galant period but reflections of very general voice-leading possibilities known to composers in many genres. This tracing of schemas to abstract geometrical structure underwrites my claim that musical knowledge is often *implicit*, known in ways that may not be directly accessible to conscious self-reflection. For it is often the case that there are only a small number of ways to achieve basic musical goals, such as harmonizing stepwise descending melodies using closely related triads. Given enough time, musicians will eventually discover these possibilities, thereby internalizing a kind of geometrical knowledge without realizing it. Culture will preserve these discoveries, transmitting them as important idioms or musical figures of speech. Perhaps a particular style will favor some possibilities to the point where they become markers of its sound-world. Listeners, having internalized these routines, may develop a sense for that core vocabulary even without being able to express their knowledge in words.

Many chapters of this story remain untold. In Bebop and later jazz styles, the descending voice leading of the diatonic fifth-sequence is chromaticized, allowing roots to descend by semitone, tritone, or fifth. Here the 2-in-12 diagram of chromatic

---

[2] See appendix 3 for another perspective on both the Fenaroli and the "horn fifths" schemas.

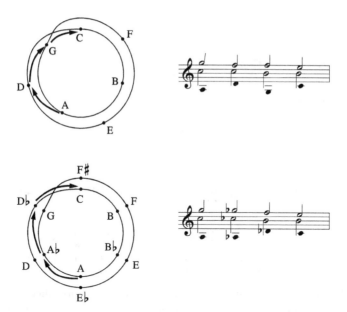

**Figure C1.** Bebop harmony extends the circle of dyadic fifths by allowing tritone substitution. This replaces the 2-in-7 diatonic spiral with the 2-in-12 chromatic spiral. The lower diagram can be read either as referring to root progressions or to upper-voice pairs connected by efficient voice leading.

dyads can model both root progressions and upper-voice pairs (Figure C1). Charlie Parker's "Blues for Alice" uses this chromaticized space to reimagine the blues as a sleek machine, the chord-roots making three complete turns through the 2-in-12 diagram, moving radially or by clockwise step, with upper-voice fifths always sliding downward (Figure C2).[3] This is an ancient musical logic, part of a dialogue beginning before Ockeghem's "generalized fauxbourdon" and still audible in Neil Young's "Helpless" (§2.3, §3.4, §7.3). From this point of view, Bebop is more Romantic than modernist; for rather than rejecting functional convention, Bebop musicians complexified it, adding new stories to the building rather than razing it to the ground.

This book has tried to reconceive musical schemas so as to highlight their deeper structure, taking their most basic forms to be those most closely connected to abstract musical geometry: a mathematical substrate that is then embellished, varied, and refined to produce the more specific idioms characterizing individual styles. Thus we can distinguish the general Pachelbel progression, the ubiquitous progression that harmonizes parallel thirds as root-third and third-fifth in alternation, from the particular "Romanesca" that operates in the galant, a I–V$^6$–vi–I$^6$ opening gambit that is comparatively infrequent elsewhere. In much the same way, we have

---

[3] My diagram factors the upper voices into fifth-related pairs such as third-seventh, fifth-ninth, and so on. When these pairs are related by chromatic transposition (e.g., two tritones or two fifths) they can be modeled by the diagram in Figure C1. In other cases, we have to postulate that upper voices move within a diatonic field whose modulations are directed by the roots.

530   TONALITY: AN OWNER'S MANUAL

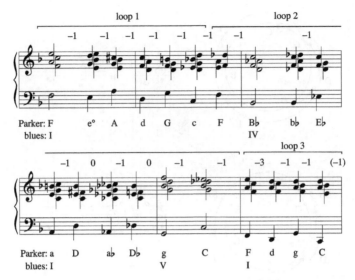

**Figure C2.** The harmonic structure of Charlie Parker's "Blues for Alice." The numbers above the staff refer to motion on the previous example's 2-in-12 circle. Upper voices include the important tones in Parker's melody.

analyzed the "converging cadence" as just one manifestation of the diatonic third's basic voice leading, particularly important in the classical period but belonging to a larger genus. By taking the geometrical substrate to be primary, we can highlight the ways in which different musical dialects exploit the same fundamental core. And we can understand why the same schemas reappear in so many different styles, as composers in different eras exploit the same set of musical relationships.

The collectional hierarchy represents a point of contact between different strands of music theory, including schema theory, scale theory, voice-leading geometry, neo-Riemannian theory, and Schenkerian analysis. The deemphasizing of voice exchanges is fundamental to Schenkerianism, emblematic of its ambition to reduce complex surfaces to simpler templates. Voice exchanges can often be interpreted as the product of motion "on the surface," decorating a crossing-free background that is recognizably scalar. These background patterns can in turn be represented as combining transposition or inversion at multiple levels, a strategy that encompasses the basic moves of "neo-Riemannian theory."[4] Conversely, reconceiving chords as scale-like entities allows us to transcend analytical literalism, permitting "chords" whose notes may not be literally present, or which may appear in multiple octaves while belonging to none. The resulting analyses are at once Schenkerian and scale-theoretical, expressing recognizably Schenkerian insights in less metaphysically freighted language (e.g., Figures 1.2.2, P5.3, P5.7, and 9.7.3).

Compositionally, this approach lets us extend the core techniques of earlier music, including registral inversion, efficient voice leading, contrary-motion

---

[4] See §1.1, appendix 3, and Tymoczko 2023.

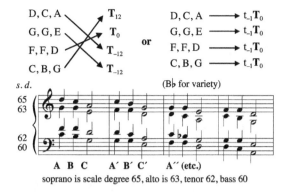

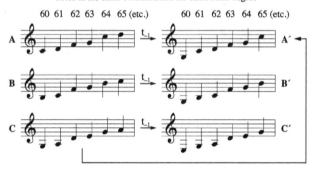

Figure C3. A four-voice round generating a series of scale degrees. In the top-staff chorale, the soprano always sings scale degree 65, alto 63, tenor 62, and bass 60. After each three-chord cycle, the chords are transposed down by step: thus the scale-degree label assigned to a pitch increases by one with each iteration (cf. Figure 1.2.2).

counterpoint, independent voices pursuing their own big-T little-t trajectories, hierarchically nested collections, musical networks containing multiple types of transformations, and sequences. This synthesis could perhaps lead to a new creative practice that detaches compositional technique from its schematic moorings. If I ever write another book, it will be about how we might use these ideas to make new music—including new forms of dissonant and atonal music.

As a preview of that effort, and a conclusion to this one, let us adapt the contrary-motion technique of the *Waldstein* opening in accordance with the Prime Directive. Figure C3 starts with an arbitrary chord progression, the first measure connecting diatonic fourth chords by efficient descending voice leading. Every subsequent measure permutes the voices as shown by the arrows, producing a perpetually descending four-voice canon. This progression in turn defines a series of abstract scales whose degrees appear in every octave, along which a melody might move. Figure C4 composes melodies that move along these scales: here, the top voice sounds offbeat eighths that ascend by scale degree, while the next line plays the repeating pattern + 3, −3, +3, +3 at a delay of six quarter notes. The result is simple

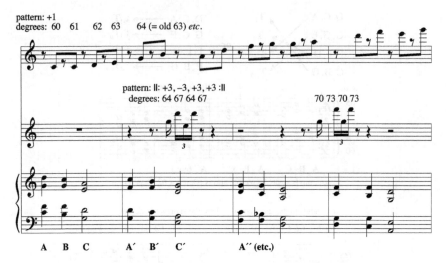

**Figure C4.** Melodies moving relative to the previous example's scale degrees.

and algorithmic but also charming, process music inspired by a classical sonata. By reconceiving the past, we can help revitalize it.

This, I think, is just one of many reasons to be optimistic about the musical future. Computers and abundant musical data are transforming our sense of what we can know, replacing speculative generalization with solid empirical claims.[5] New electronic instruments are allowing us to combine algorithm and intuition in unprecedented ways (e.g., Figure P9.1). Pluralism and multiculturalism are giving rise to a music theory less fixated on European masterworks and a pedagogy better suited to contemporary music-making. Theorists have a chance to nudge culture here, reinterpreting basic musical concepts so that they are more directly relevant to our current needs. We can begin by painting a picture of earlier music not as a cherished museum of unapproachable masterpieces, but as a springboard to music that has yet to be made. In this way we might truly take ownership of the tradition we have ostensibly inherited.

---

[5] Particularly important here is the development of musicxml, a cross-platform format for representing musical scores, and music21, a software package for analyzing and creating scores (Cuthbert and Ariza 2010).

APPENDIX 1

# Fundamentals

Geometry begins in the commitment to take distance seriously. In this book the relevant notion of distance is usually *voice-leading distance*, corresponding to the physical distance a finger moves on an instrument such as the piano. Our analytical atoms are "paths in pitch class space," combining an initial pitch class (such as "D" or "E quarter tone sharp") with a directed magnitude (such as "fourteen semitones up" or "two and a half semitones down"). These objects are conceptually unproblematic and easy to hear; we can notate them using a number to indicate how a pitch class moves: $G \xrightarrow{-4} E\flat$ for the descending four-semitone path, $G \xrightarrow{8} E\flat$ for the ascending eight-semitone path, and so on.[1] Alternatively we can use pitch labels, writing $G4 \rightarrow E\flat4$ and $G4 \rightarrow E\flat5$ to identify the corresponding pitch-class paths. For legibility I will eliminate the numbers when a path connects its pitch classes by the shortest possible route, using $G \rightarrow E\flat$ for the descending four-semitone path.

Distance is always measured in *scale steps*. This means that the size of an interval is measured along some contextually relevant scale: E–G has chromatic size 3, diatonic size 2, pentatonic size 1, and triadic size 1 (e.g., along the C major triad). Notions such as "transposition," "inversion," "path in pitch-class space," and "chord type" are also scale-dependent: in the diatonic scale (C, E, G) is transpositionally related to (D, F, A), and hence the same type of chord, but this is not true in the chromatic scale. I generally use $T_x$, $T_x$, and $t_x$ for chromatic, scalar, and chordal transposition by $x$ steps; sometimes I use $\tau_x$ for transposition along a chordal subset. Pitches are labeled using a generalized "midi note numbering" in which scale steps are size 1 and the number 60 is as close to middle C as possible. For the chromatic scale, this means B3 = 59, C4 = 60, C♯4 = 61, D4 = 62, and so on; for the white-note scale, B3 = 59, C4 = 60, D4 = 61, etc.; and for the C major triad, G3 = 59, C4 = 60, E4 = 61.

This relativity of musical distances underwrites a *hierarchical set theory* in which transposition and inversion can apply not just chromatically or diatonically, but at the chordal level as well. This is represented pictorially in Figure 1.2.6, embedding the C major triad inside a C diatonic scale that is itself embedded in the twelve-tone equal tempered chromatic scale. Transposition is represented by addition on input scale degrees: to transpose (C4, E4, G4) by ascending triadic step, we add

---

[1] These objects differ from the pitch-class intervals of earlier music theory in distinguishing multiple routes between the same points: thus "start at G and move down by four semitones" is different from "start at G and move up by eight semitones," even though both connect G to E♭. See Tymoczko 2011a and 2023.

534    APPENDIX 1: FUNDAMENTALS

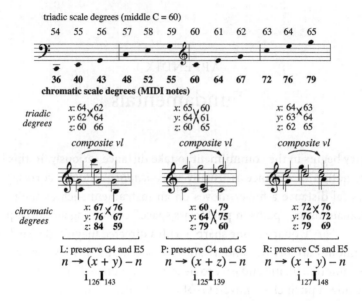

**Figure A1.1.** Inversion occurring at both the triadic and chromatic levels. The two inversions preserve the same pair of notes and combine to produce an efficient voice leading.

1 to its triadic representation (60, 61, 62), producing (61, 62, 63) or (E4, G4, C5) (i.e., $t_1$); to transpose it along the diatonic scale, we add 1 to its diatonic representation (60, 62, 64), obtaining (61, 63, 65) or (D4, F4, A4) ($T_1$); to transpose chromatically, add 1 to get (61, 65, 68) or (D♭4, F4, A♭4) ($T_1$). Inversion is represented by subtraction from a constant value, sending $x$ to $c - x$ for some constant $c$. The pitch $c/2$ is a "fixed point" held constant by this inversion; when C is odd, this fixed point lies halfway between scale degrees (e.g., a quarter tone in twelve-tone equal temperament). To invert (C4, E4, G4) around C4 within the intrinsic scale C–E–G, we subtract each number in its triadic representation (60, 61, 62) from 120, which is twice the fixed point; this produces (60, 59, 58) or (C4, G3, E2). To invert diatonically around C4, we subtract each number in its diatonic representation (60, 62, 64) from 120, producing (60, 58, 56) or (C4, A3, F3). To invert chromatically we do the same with (60, 64, 67), obtaining (60, 56, 53) or (C4, A♭3, F3).

Transformations at one level often counteract their analogues at another. Figure 2.1.4 shows how chromatic transposition by four ascending semitones can nearly counteract transposition downward by one major-triad step, producing efficient voice leading as its residue. Figures 3.1.2 and 3.3.1 show how this works for diatonic dyads, Figure 3.4.1 for diatonic triads, and Figure P8.2 for the diatonic scale considered as a seven-note chord in twelve-note chromatic space. Figure A1.1 shows that inversion can produce the same sort of hierarchical cancellation: we begin by labeling the notes of the C major triad in two different ways, once using triadic scale degrees and once using chromatic scale degrees; choosing two notes $x$ and $y$ to remain fixed, we invert twice, sending each note $n$ to $(x + y) - n$; the figure shows this calculation for each of the three pairs of notes within the triad. Once again the combination of triadic and chromatic transformations nearly cancel out, here keeping two notes fixed and moving the third "parsimoniously," by one or two semitones. The result is a voice leading between two similarly voiced, inversionally related pitch-class sets, known to theorists as "neo-Riemannian transformations." These transformations are generalized as "Gesualdo's trick" in §1.1.[2] There, two voices move in parallel, combining a generalized neo-Riemannian transformation with a transposition. Such voice leadings always preserve the distance between at least two voices, and are discussed further in appendix 3. Interested readers can also download computer code allowing for the arbitrary embedding of arbitrary collections, and providing a variety of set-theoretical transformations at every hierarchical level.[3]

Formally, a *voice leading* can be defined as a collection of paths in pitch-class space, measured along some scale. Voice leadings are an important component of implicit musical knowledge, representing possible routes from one chord to another. We can write $(C, E, G) \xrightarrow{0,1,2} (C, F, A)$, meaning "C, whatever octave it is in, stays fixed, while E, whatever octave it is in, moves up by semitone, and G, whatever octave it is in, moves up by two semitones." This voice leading is measured in chromatic space; measured diatonically it would be $(C, E, G) \xrightarrow{0,1,1} (C, F, A)$, since the distance from G to A is one diatonic step. The written ordering of the paths is immaterial, with $(C, E, G) \xrightarrow{0,1,2} (C, F, A)$ and $(E, G, C) \xrightarrow{1,2,0} (F, A, C)$ equally good representations of one and the same voice leading. As with paths in pitch-class space, the absolute register of the voices is unspecified, but the distance moved by each voice is; given a voice leading and the pitches in the first chord, we can calculate the pitches in the second. We can eliminate the numbers when notes move by the shortest possible distance, writing $(C, E, G) \to (C, F, A)$ for the voice leading described above. Alternatively, we can use pitch-space voice leadings to represent pitch-class voice leadings, writing $(C4, E4, G4) \to (C4, F4, A4)$ to identify general pitch-class paths whose voices could be in any octave.

There are two different reasons why we might use voice leadings as just defined. The first is to group together related but distinct pitch-space transformations, as when we consider the voice leadings $(C4, E4, G4) \to (C4, F4, A4)$ and $(E3, C4, G4) \to (F3, C4, A4)$ to instantiate the same basic pattern. In this case, the notion of voice leading involves a certain amount of abstraction from the musical surface. The second is to model scalar objects whose "notes" are melodic slots available in any octave. Here, the musical object is inherently abstract, and the pitch-class perspective a faithful reflection of its underlying ontology. What is interesting is that the same formalism covers both cases: we can think of the voice leading $(C, E, G) \to (C, F A)$

---

[2] The opening of Schoenberg's Op. 36 violin concerto is a nice example, moving from F♯2, B2, D♯3, E3, A3, B♭3 to the inversionally related A♭2, D3, F3, G3, C4, D♭4, with both hexachords spaced (3, 1, 1, 2, 1) in chordal steps. The registral distance between the three-note chromatic cluster is preserved.

[3] See http://www.madmusicalscience.com/quadruple.html.

**Figure A1.2.** The voices in the leftmost voice leading cross each other; those in the center do not, even though they contain the same paths. The paths on the right will never cross no matter what octave they are in.

*either* as a general description for a class of pitch-space voice leadings, or as a voice leading between two *scales* whose notes exist in every octave.

There are several important categories of voice leading. *Bijective* (or note-to-note) voice leadings send each note in the first chord to exactly one note in the second: thus (C, E, G) → (C, F, A) is a bijective voice leading from C major to F major, while (C, C, E, G) → (A, C, F, A) is a *nonbijective* voice leading between these same chords.[4] I usually focus on bijective voice leadings. A *voice exchange* is a bijective voice leading from a chord to itself whose paths sum to zero, like (C, E, G) → (E, C, G). Voice exchanges can be decomposed into a series of *pairwise voice exchanges* that move two voices in contrary motion by opposite amounts, exchanging their notes.[5] Voice exchanges, thus defined, involve contrary motion (i.e., paths that sum to zero): the voice leading (C4, E4) → (E4, C5) is *not* a voice exchange even though the two voices exchange pitch classes; instead it is a transposition along the chord.

Any voice leading, between any chords whatsoever, can be factored into a voice exchange and a remainder that is *spacing-preserving* or *strongly crossing free*. Spacing-preserving voice leadings preserve chordal-step distance and therefore cannot be arranged in register so that their voices cross: if plotted on the pitch-class circle, each voice can glide smoothly from its starting point to its destination without ever sounding the same pitch class as any other voice, except perhaps at its endpoints. If a voice leading is not spacing-preserving, then its voices will cross when plotted on the pitch-class circle; this means they can be arranged in register to produce literal crossings (Figure A1.2). A spacing-preserving voice leading between transpositionally related chords can always be represented as a combination of transposition along the scale (T) and transposition along the chord (t). Similarly, a spacing-preserving voice leading between inversionally related chords combines inversion along a scale (I) with inversion along the chord (i). For unrelated chords, a spacing-preserving voice leading is called an *interscalar transposition*; all the interscalar transpositions between any two chords can be derived by combining any

---

[4] A subtlety: if we think of chords as *multisets* with specific doublings, then (C, C, E, G) → (A, C, F, A) could be understood as a bijective voice leading from C-with-doubled-root to F-with-doubled-third (Callender, Quinn, and Tymoczko 2008, Tymoczko 2011a).

[5] This conception of "voice exchange" is minimal and technical, referring to a specific type of voice leading. Schenkerian theory uses a more robust notion (Cutler 2009).

one interscalar transposition with transpositions along the chord.[6] Voice crossings never make a voice leading smaller: hence between any two chords, there is always a minimal voice leading that is crossing-free. This means that hierarchical self-similarity can arise as the byproduct of the search for efficient voice leading, in both the melodic and harmonic domains.

The spiral diagrams represent the spacing-preserving voice leadings between the transpositions of one or more chords—in other words, the possibilities that remain when we ignore voice exchanges. Appendix 2 derives the diagrams in two different ways. These representations are abstract and topological rather than concrete and geometrical, more like subway maps than topographical maps. As a general matter, they show us how hierarchically nested transpositions combine: we can see from the 2-in-7 diagram that two applications of $t_1 T_{-4}$ produces $T_{-1}$ and that seven applications produces $t_{-1}$, for any two-note chord in any seven-note scale; similarly, it is clear from the structure of 3-in-12 space that there is always a voice leading that, when repeatedly applied, cycles through the chord's major-third transpositions before returning every voice to its starting note; by contrast, it is clear from the 7-in-12 diagram that there can be no such cycle, which is why enharmonic respelling will always be necessary whenever any modulatory schema is repeated until it returns to its starting key. Perhaps most importantly, the diagrams show us which combinations of transposition-along-the-chord and transposition-along-the-scale come closest to counteracting one another, producing purely radial or nearly radial motion. Of course, the degree to which they actually do so depends on a chord's intervallic structure.

When a chord divides the octave nearly evenly, the two kinds of transposition are similar and the radial voice leadings are efficient or small (Figures A1.3–4). As I emphasized in §2.3, this sort of contrapuntal proximity does not imply any perceptible harmonic relationship. Sometimes, however, the spiral diagrams *do* represent harmonic similarity, or shared note content. This occurs when we have a maximally even chord whose size is relatively prime to the size of our scale: such a chord will be a "near interval cycle" or stack of intervals $k$ scale-steps large, with one additional interval of size $k \pm 1$; the basic voice leading moves one of these notes by just one step, changing the unusual interval to size $k$ and producing another interval cycle that is the $k$-step transposition of the first. (This is the starting point for the "generalized set theory" of §8.7.) It follows that chords adjacent on the spiral diagram share all but one of their notes, with the mismatched note differing by only one step; hence they are similar both contrapuntally (in the sense of being connected by efficient voice leading) and harmonically (in the sense of sharing all but one of their notes). Such chords can often play similar musical roles: the most familiar examples are the diatonic triad, where adjacent (third-related) chords have similar functional roles (§3.4, §7.1),

---

[6] See Tymoczko 2008 and 2011a. In my earlier work I used *scalar* and *interscalar interval matrices* to represent these voice leadings; the spiral diagrams provide a geometrical representation of these algebraic objects.

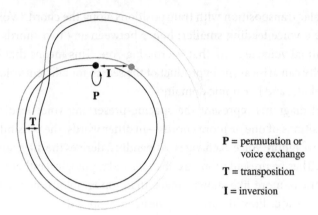

P = permutation or voice exchange
T = transposition
I = inversion

**Figure A1.3.** A symbolic diagram showing how three near symmetries affect the shape of the graph. For a nearly T-symmetrical chord, the distance between the rings of the spiral is small; for a nearly I-symmetrical chord, the distance between a chord and its inversion is small when we superimpose their spiral diagrams; for a nearly P-symmetrical chord, the curved arrow representing one or more pairwise voice exchanges is small. In this book I do not try to represent these distances faithfully.

**Figure A1.4.** Chords sharing the same angular position need not be contrapuntally close in an absolute sense.

and the seven-note diatonic scale, where adjacent collections give rise to similar modes (e.g., mixolydian and ionian, §8.6) and constitute nearby tonal regions (§8.3).[7]

It is in this context that we can best understand the problem of doublings and incomplete chords. For while it is mathematically possible to construct circular spaces for chords with a fixed number of doublings, these inevitably spread sonically similar objects throughout the spiral (e.g., CCEG, CEGG,

---

[7] If we take 7-in-12 space to represent diatonic modes, then angular neighbors are modally similar: for instance, a one-step clockwise move changes C ionian to C mixolydian.

APPENDIX 1: FUNDAMENTALS 539

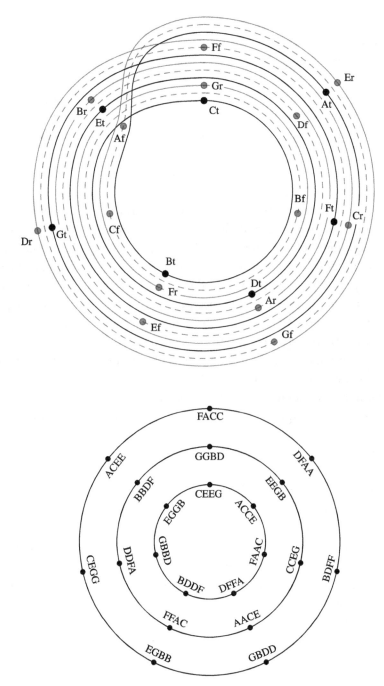

**Figure A1.5.** Circular diagrams for diatonic triads with one doubling. (*top*) Superimposing three copies of 4-in-7 spiral diagram; here r, t, and f indicate whether the root, third, or fifth is doubled. (*bottom*) A more abstract version of the graph.

540 APPENDIX 1: FUNDAMENTALS

and EGCE on Figure A1.5). In other words, *contrapuntal proximity* diverges from *harmonic similarity* in a particularly egregious fashion. There is no easy fix to this problem, since harmonically similar states such as (C, C, E, G) and (C, E, E, G) are genuinely different contrapuntally: the former is two diatonic steps away from an F major triad whereas the latter is not. This means we have to choose whether to model voice-leading distance, harmonic similarity, or some other music-theoretical notion. We cannot do everything at once.

What we can do is model music hierarchically, treating chords as abstract scale-like objects whose notes may not all be present, or may appear in multiple octaves simultaneously. Recall the *Waldstein* analysis in §3.7, where the four voices pass through a range of different harmonic configurations, all represented by a background voice leading with three logical voices. Here, doubling and voice exchanges are a byproduct of the surface-level motion of voices rather than of the deeper counterpoint. The two-tiered picture thus suggests a strategy for implementing what is sometimes called *cardinality equivalence*—the perspective on which CGG and CCG are "the same," and hence represented by a single location in geometrical space.[8] We can model chords like CGG and CCG as different configurations of surface voices within a single underlying two-note "scale" CG, just as we represented the second and third chords in Figure 3.7.2 (GGBD and GGBB) as configurations of surface voices inside a scale-like triad. Similarly, we can postulate background voice leadings containing notes not found on the surface, so that two surface voices (e.g., the third CE) could represent a complete triad at the background level.[9] In this way, the hierarchical perspective can bridge the gap between mathematics and musical intuition. It also suggests the interesting analytical project of providing hierarchical analyses for passages like Figures P5.3 and P5.7.

One possibility, not discussed in this book, is to allow surface voices to move from chord to chord by a process of *quantization*, a useful musical transformation that snaps "out-of-grid" notes into a scale. Consider the Palestrina passage in the upper-left corner of Figure 4.9.6: there the bass was interpreted as alternating between two different moves along the triad ($t_2$ and $t_1$). An alternative conceives the bass as always moving to the next chordal tone by the *smallest possible nondescending interval*: when the fifth is in the bass, it stays fixed to become

---

[8] I sometimes treat doubling as part of chordal identity (so that, for example, CGG and CCG lie on different rings of Figure 3.5.3), representing changes of spacing by curved arrows.

[9] Headlam 2012 criticized voice-leading geometry on the grounds that it could not accommodate cardinality equivalence or incomplete chords. I think that the hierarchical picture allows us to model many of these phenomena.

the root of the next chord (0 steps); when the root is in the bass, it ascends by step to become the fifth of the next chord (+1 step). Instead of a frog hopping along a gently shifting circular arrangement of lily pads (§1.2), we can imagine one set of lily pads sinking under the water while a new set rises, so that the frog has no option to "move with the lily pads"; it must choose to hop clockwise or counterclockwise (or hop vertically when that is possible). The advantage of this approach is that it allows us to deal with situations where different groups of voices move in different ways. Indeed, it allows us to avoid postulating *any* specific voice leading at the background: lily pads rise and fall, while surface voices move in various ways.

Sometimes, however, we do want to postulate specific voice leadings at the scalar level, and sometimes the number of background voices actually changes. This can happen in two ways, depending on whether the change occurs at the arrival of a new chord or while a chord is sounding. In the first and simpler case, a voice simply enters or exits the texture at the start of a new harmony, with the existing voices articulating a bijective voice leading between the smaller chord and a subset of the larger (Figure A1.6).[10] More complex are those situations where the number of voices changes during a chord's lifetime: in the first four right-hand chords of Figure 9.3.1, for example, the alto doubles the bass at the octave, the four right-hand voices implying a three-voice triad at the background level; from the fifth to the sixth chords, however, the two surface B voices move by contrary motion to $D^7$, $(G, B_1, B_2, D) \rightarrow (F\sharp, A, C, D)$. Here we might want to say that

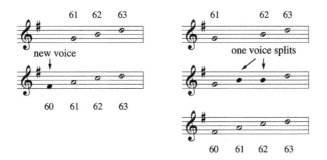

**Figure A1.6.** Two ways in which the number of background voices can change. In the first, a new voice enters at the moment of a chord change; in the second, the number of voices changes while the chord is sounding. On the right, the top line features a three-note scale, whose degrees are numbered above the example; the lower lines feature a four-note scale, whose degrees are numbered below.

---

[10] For example, Figure P5.7 when the bass sounds D. The upper voices continue to move along the three-note subset.

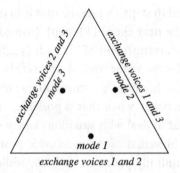

**Figure A1.7.** The cross section of three-note chord space. Each chord appears in all three of its modes; "mode 1" is an ordering with the smallest interval between the first two notes. Each boundary acts geometrically like a mirror, exchanging voices' pitches *and labels*: if voice 1 has C and voice 2 has E, then exchanging them sends voice 1 to E and relabels it voice 2, while sending voice 2 to C and relabeling it voice 1.

a single voice "splits" into multiple voices.[11] In other words, the two right-hand Bs begin as surface-level doublings of a single abstract voice, and end as two different abstract voices—the "splitting" promoting them from surface to the background; the converse process of "merging" moves them from background to surface.

That chords can function in an abstract and scale-like way is an important Schenkerian insight, one that significantly increases the power of our geometrical models. This perspective tends to deemphasize voice crossings by assigning them to the surface. A complementary approach, more Tinctorian or set-theoretical, deemphasizes transposition in order to represent voice crossings more perspicuously. Figure A1.7 shows an abstract graph representing the cross section of three-note voice-leading space, an intrinsically two-dimensional space that is compressed into a line-segment on the circular diagrams. Here each chord appears three times, corresponding to its three modes, while the mirror boundaries represent the three pairwise voice exchanges swapping the chord's adjacent pitch classes. As in Figure 3.5.4, transposition comes out of the page. We can use this figure to represent classes of voice leadings equivalent under the Tinctoris Transform, including those with voice crossings. Figure A1.8 simplifies and analyzes the opening of Beethoven's Op. 109 variations theme. Where a traditional set-theoretic perspective would simply observe the repeated presence of the same set class (here, the diatonic triad 024), our more contrapuntal set theory labels the specific mappings between the notes, assigning different voice leadings to different geometrical paths. These transformations generalize the concept of voice leading from *specific chords* to *generalized chord types*, endowing set theory with rich contrapuntal content.

---

[11] Callender 1998.

APPENDIX 1: FUNDAMENTALS 543

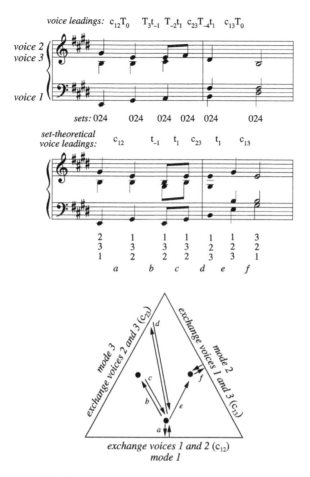

**Figure A1.8.** A simplified version of Beethoven's Op. 109 variations theme, with its voice leadings analyzed into three components: voice crossings ($c_{xy}$, with $x$ and $y$ identifying the crossed voices), transposition along the diatonic scale ($T_x$), and transposition along the triad ($t_x$). Underneath the example, I give a (diatonic) set-theoretical analysis, consisting solely in the observation that every chord is a diatonic triad (024). Beneath that, I identify the passage's set-class voice leadings, obtained by omitting the T component. The second staff of music shows an alternate realization of these same set-class voice leadings, keeping the E major harmony fixed. This music is related by the Tinctoris Transform to Beethoven's original. For clarity, I separate out the two components of the "$c_{23}t_1$" voice leading. When voices cross, they exchange numbers, so that $c_{21}$ exchanges the notes in the first and second voices while also renumbering them accordingly. Below, I graph the music in set class space.

We can construct analogous graphs for chords of any size, using two-dimensional polygons to represent complicated higher-dimensional geometries—and providing subway-style maps for otherwise-incomprehensible spaces.[12]

[12] Tymoczko 2020b.

APPENDIX 2

# Deriving the Spiral Diagrams

The spiral diagrams represent all possible combinations of big-T transposition along the scale and little-t transposition along the chord, for any choice of chord and scale. As we have seen, these transformations are fundamental to a wide range of music, capturing some substantial component of intuitive knowledge. The diagrams can be derived either as the union of helices, or as subspaces of the higher-dimensional space of $n$-note chords.

*(a) The union of helices.* The easiest way to arrive at the spiral diagrams is to build them out of helices.[1] Start with the two-note spiral shown on the upper right in Figure P2.9; we will work in chromatic space for simplicity. Choose some point to represent the chord (C4, G4). Now imagine a third dimension, extending outward from the paper and representing chords' "center of gravity" or pitch sum. In this three-dimensional space, position in the $xy$ plane will represent pitch-class content, so that chords with the same pitch-class content will always be vertically aligned.[2] As we transpose the (C4, G4) dyad upward, we spiral outward from the paper to form a helix or corkscrew, returning to our original position when each voice has moved up by octave. (One can imagine a glissando in continuous space, ascending smoothly between equal-tempered perfect fifths; this gives meaning to every point on the helix.) The helix contains all and only those ordered chromatic dyads whose first note is a perfect fifth below its second; it contains no dyads whose first note is a perfect fourth below its second. Starting at (C4, G4), or (60, 67) in chromatic pitch numbers, we do not return to (C, G) until we reach (C5, G5) or (72, 79). The sum of this second dyad is 151, which is 24 more than the sum of the first, 127.

Now consider the effect of transposition along the chord $(t_1)$. This turns every perfect fifth into a perfect fourth, increasing its sum by 12: (C4, G4) or (60, 67) becomes (G4, C5) or (67, 72), which sums to 139; (D4, A4) or (62, 69) becomes (A4, D4) or (69, 74). Geometrically, this creates a second helix, interleaved with the first, whose points represent fourths rather than fifths (Figures A2.1–2). Every point on this second helix shares the same pitch-class content with the dyad immediately below it vertically, but sums to 12 more than its lower neighbor. Thus as we ascend vertically from any point, we alternate between helices, moving from fourth to fifth and back, repeatedly applying $t_1$ to increase the pitch-sum by 12.[3] Looking down on the double helix from above gives us the two-note spiral diagram

---

[1] Thanks to Nori Jacoby, who helped me work out the multiple-helix derivation.

[2] If we want distance in the $xy$ plane to represent voice-leading distance, we need the $n$-fold spiral arrangement used in the book. This is because $T_{o/n}t_{-1}$ is small for nearly even $n$-note chords.

[3] This double helix is the two-note analogue to Roger Shepard's helical representation of pitches (Shepard 1964).

546   APPENDIX 2: DERIVING THE SPIRAL DIAGRAMS

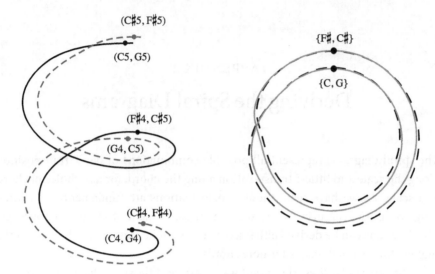

**Figure A2.1.** (*a*) Three-dimensional helices each containing the transpositions of an individual mode. (*b*) When viewed from above these produce the spiral diagrams.

| fifth | | | fourth | | |
|---|---|---|---|---|---|
| notes | numbers | sum | notes | numbers | sum |
| (C4, G4) | (60, 67) | 127 | | | |
| | | | (G4, C5) | (67, 72) | 139 |
| (C5, G5) | (72, 79) | 151 | | | |
| | | | (G5, C6) | (79, 84) | 163 |

**Figure A2.2.** The modes of (C, G). Perfect fifths sum to $7 + 24i$ where $i$ is an integer, while perfect fourths sum to $19 + 24i$. As the sum increases by 12, we move from one mode to the other, hopping between the helices in the previous example.

shown in Figure A2.1. Each helix is *continuous*, with each of its points representing a specific dyad; points not on either helix have no musical meaning.

In this three-dimensional space, every path between helical points represents the voice leading taking the starting pitches to the destination pitches, first note to first note and second to second; the two helices do not intersect themselves or one another. To use the 2D version of the diagram, we need to ensure that different voice leadings can be distinguished when seen from above; this means disallowing purely vertical paths that would disappear from that vantage. We can accomplish this by requiring that paths either move parallel to a helix or horizontally between them. This guarantees that a transposition along the chord will make a "loop" when seen from above; it also creates the misleading impression of a self-intersecting curve.

The same reasoning applies for chords with three or more notes; for an *n*-note chord in an **o**-note scale, transposition by octave adds o*n* to the sum of the chord's scale degrees and creates a helix; transposition along the chord adds **o** to its sum and creates a new helix interleaved with the first. We can do this *n* times before we return to the original helix, creating *n* interleaved helices, one for each mode, and generating the spiral diagram when viewed from above.

*(b) As subspaces of the higher-dimensional space of all chords.* Alternatively, we can derive the spirals as lines passing through the higher-dimensional geometrical space containing all possible *n*-note chords. These are twisted, mirrored donuts, technically known as *orbifolds*, whose structure can be quite hard to intuit. Recipe 1 in Figure A2.3 gives general instructions for forming voice-leading spaces whose points represent objects such as chords or set classes and whose paths represent voice leadings between their endpoints. This recipe allows us to associate any voice-leading-in-a-score with a path-in-the-space; to go from path to voice leading, we need Recipe 2 in Figure A2.4.

1. For *n*-note objects, start with the *n* perpendicular axes of ordinary Euclidean geometry, each representing the pitch played by a different musical voice. This is *n*-note ordered pitch space.

2. Choose some set of symmetries to relate these objects: for chords, reordering and octave shifts; for transpositional set classes, reordering, octave shifts, and transposition; for traditional set classes, those same symmetries plus inversion.

3. Find a region of the space whose interior contains no two points related by the chosen symmetries; isolating any duplicates, or pairs related by the symmetries, on the boundary.

4. Model an *n*-voice chorale by choosing the single point on the interior of the region (or those multiple points on the boundary) corresponding to the notes one is currently hearing; model each voice leading with the path formed by a smooth glissando from start notes to end notes.

**Figure A2.3.** Recipe 1, for constructing a range of musical geometries.

1. Within a region, the voice leading corresponding to a path is simply the one that takes the coordinates of the initial point to those of the destination point: a path that links (5, 7) to (7, 17) raises the first pitch by 2 steps and the second by 10 steps.

2. The boundary points will come in two varieties: mirror singularities *symmetrical* under some voice-leading transformation and duplicate points *related* by some voice-leading transformation. When we touch a boundary point, we apply a voice-leading transformation *to every point* in our region, obtaining new coordinates for the region. This is because we have moved into a new area of ordered pitch space, equivalent to the original but containing different arrangements of pitches.
    a. When we "bounce off" a singularity, we apply that chord's symmetry to every point in our region.
    b. When we teleport from one duplicate point to another, we apply the transformation that turns the *arrival* point into the *departure* point.
    c. We repeat this process every time a path interacts with a boundary point.

3. Having assigned new coordinates to the region, we can calculate the voice leading using rule 1 and the destination point's new coordinates.

**Figure A2.4.** Recipe 2, for interpreting paths in a geometry.

Both recipes exploit the fact that musical space is structured like wallpaper, composed of many equivalent regions containing different versions of the same basic objects (e.g., chords or set classes, illustrated metaphorically by Figure A2.5). We can represent music using any one of these regions, each of which contains just one point for each object (except at their boundaries, which contain multiple points representing the same object). As we move off a region's boundary, we either "bounce off" a mirrorlike point, or "teleport" between boundary points representing the same musical object. In either case, we have to apply some musical transformation to all the coordinates in our region. This is because we have entered a new region of pitch-space that is equivalent to the first but contains different pitches (e.g., reordered and transposed by octave, relative to the previous region). *It follows that geometrical boundaries can be identified with specific musical transformations*, and hence that geometrical modeling can illuminate musically significant operations such as transposition along the chord.

The spiral diagrams are lines or circles in the higher-dimensional spaces containing all the transpositions of some chord. The simplest is pitch-class space, which can be derived from the line representing every conceivable pitch (Figure A2.6). Recipe 1 tells us to choose a region containing one point for every pitch class, with duplications only on the boundary; here, I choose the octave from C4 to C5, 60 to 72 in numbers. This is chromatic pitch-class space. Applying $T_{12}$ turns the left boundary into the right, and applying $T_{-12}$ turns the right boundary into the left. Within the region, a path's length and direction give us the relevant voice leading: one-unit leftward motion lowers a note by semitone, two-unit rightward motion raises it by two semitones, and so on. (For pitches in the region, we can calculate these paths by simply subtracting the starting coordinate from the destination coordinate.) By imagining smooth glissandos, we find that an ascending octave moves off the rightward boundary, reappearing on the left to return to its starting point, while descending-octave motion does the same in the opposite direction.

Figure A2.5. Musical space is like a piece of wallpaper, constructed out of many similar regions. Any path in this larger space can be represented in a single region, though paths may appear to "bounce off" certain boundary points (β), or "teleport" between others (α). These boundaries can be associated with specific musical transformations.

APPENDIX 2: DERIVING THE SPIRAL DIAGRAMS   549

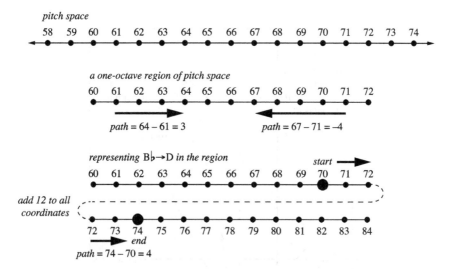

**Figure A2.6.** Representing music using a one-octave region of chromatic pitch space. Within the region, paths can be determined by subtracting start-coordinate from end-coordinate; when moving off the boundary, one first has to apply a transformation to all coordinates.

We can check this using Recipe 2, which tells us that when we move off the right boundary, we need to apply $T_{12}$ to every point's coordinate, since that is the transformation that turns the destination point (left boundary) into the departure point (right boundary); conversely, we subtract 12 from every point when moving off the left boundary. The figure shows the path representing ascending-third motion from B♭ to D.

For two-note chords, we begin with the Cartesian plane representing all ordered pairs of chromatic pitches. The square at the center of Figure A2.7 is defined by the equations $12 \leq x + y \leq 24$, and $0 \leq y - x \leq 12$. Every ordered pair of pitches is equivalent to either a single point in the square's interior or a pair of points on its boundary.[4] Figure A2.8 rotates the square and labels the points representing unisons, major thirds, and their inversions. Points on the left edge (summing to 12) are related by $t_1$ to points on the right (summing to 24): for example, the left-edge sixth (2, 10) is duplicated as the right-edge third (10, 14), and the left-edge third (4, 8) is duplicated as the right-edge sixth (8, 16).[5] According to Recipe 2, moving off the right boundary requires us to apply $t_1$ to every point in the space, while moving off the left boundary requires us to apply $t_{-1}$. (The top and bottom

---

[4] Imagine a pair of pitch classes $x$ and $y$: you can always arrange them in pitch so that one is less than an octave above the other, satisfying $0 \leq y - x \leq 12$. Since transposition along the chord increases or decreases their sum by 12, repeated transpositions will eventually satisfy $12 \leq x + y \leq 24$, producing either a unique point in the interior or a pair of points on the boundaries. The two quantities $x + y$ and $y - x$ are the two Tinctorian coordinates from the prelude to chapter 3.

[5] In each case, the right-edge duplicate has the left edge's second pitch as its first pitch, and the octave-transposition of the left edge's first pitch as its second pitch.

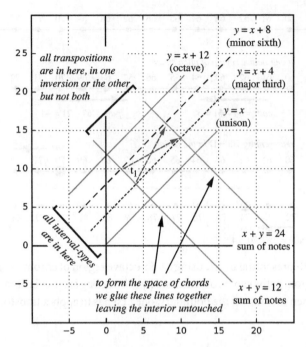

**Figure A2.7.** A derivation of two-dimensional chord space. The square is bounded by the lines $y = x$ (unisons), $y = x + 12$ (octaves), $x + y = 12$, and $x + y = 24$. The two lines $y = x + 4$ and $y = x + 8$ contain major thirds and minor sixths respectively; these are the two strands of the spiral. The dashed arrows represent transposition up by one step along the chord, sending root up to third and third up to root; these link chords on the $x + y = 12$ face with their equivalents on the $x + y = 24$ face.

boundaries meanwhile reorder each dyad while perhaps transposing notes by octave.[6]) Figure A2.8 uses curved lines to represent the process of "teleportation," but this is merely a graphical contrivance that does not substantively alter the figure. The result is recognizable, modulo a little stretching and twisting, as the spiral diagram for chromatic major thirds and minor sixths.

Exactly the same reasoning applies in higher dimensions. Figure A2.9 gives the general equations identifying the region of higher-dimensional Euclidean space containing one point for every chord (except at the boundaries, which have multiple points representing the same chord). Figures A1.10–11 show the line segments containing major triads in three-note (three-dimensional) chord space and four-note seventh chords in four-note (four-dimensional) chord space. Since the extra dimensions are not relevant here, these diagrams simply draw those segments in two dimensions. Once again, we see that points on the left boundaries relate by

---

[6] The bottom boundary swaps a dyad's notes; the top boundary swaps them but also transposes the first note up by octave and the second note down by octave. These octave shifts change as we move from region to region.

APPENDIX 2: DERIVING THE SPIRAL DIAGRAMS 551

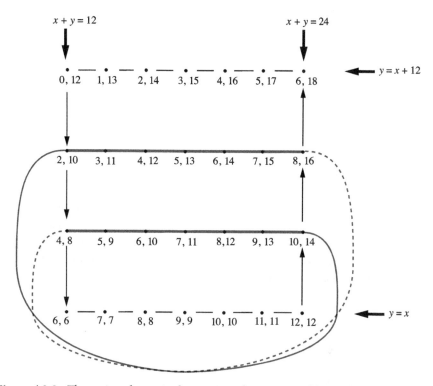

**Figure A2.8.** The region shown in the previous figure, rotated by 45 degrees. For ease of reading, I have shown only the unisons, octaves, major thirds, and minor sixths. Transposition moves horizontally, while chords lying on a vertical line sum to the same value. Chords on the left boundary relate by $t_1$ to chords on the right boundary; when we move off the right to reappear on the left, we need to apply $t_1$ to all the points in the region.

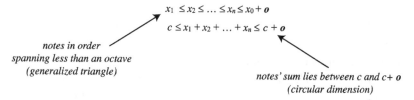

**Figure A2.9.** Two equations that determine the region representing chord space for chords of any size: the first determines a "generalized triangle" containing all set classes whose notes are in order while spanning no more than an octave; the second determines the circular dimension whose coordinate is given by the sum of chords' pitch classes. Here $c$ is an arbitrary constant. In three voices with an octave of size 12, and choosing $c$ as 0, the equations are $x_1 \leq x_2 \leq x_3 \leq x_1 + 12$ and $0 \leq x_1 + x_2 + x_3 \leq 12$.

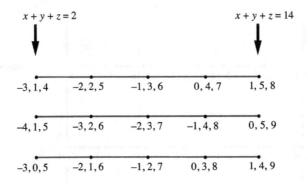

**Figure A2.10.** Chromatic major triads lie on three line segments in the region determined by the equations in Figure A2.9. This region is three-dimensional, though here I draw it in two dimensions. Chords on the same vertical line sum to the same value. Chords on the left boundary are related by $t_1$ to chords on the right. Recipe 2 tells us that as we move off the right boundary we need to apply $t_1$ to every chord in the region.

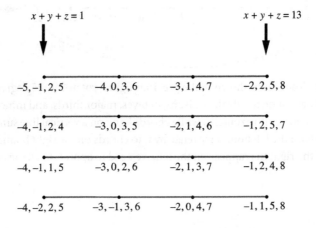

**Figure A2.11.** Dominant seventh chords lie on four line segments in the region determined by the equations in Figure A2.9. This region is intrinsically four-dimensional. Each line contains a different mode of the dominant seventh. Chords on the same vertical line sum to the same value. Chords on the left boundary are related by $t_1$ to chords on the right. Recipe 2 tells us that as we move off the right boundary, reappearing on the left, we need to apply $t_1$ to every chord in the region.

$t_1$ to those on the right.[7] As we move off the right boundary, we reappear on the left, applying $t_1$ to all our coordinates; when moving off the left, we reappear on the right and apply $t_{-1}$. Thus horizontal "loops" have the effect of transposition-along-the-chord. The spiral diagrams connect these horizontal line segments to form a continuous curve, replacing "teleportation" with motion along a spiral. This continuous curve appears to self-intersect, but that is an artifact of representing

---

[7] For details see Tymoczko 2020b.

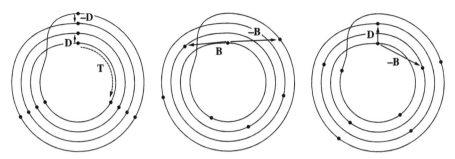

**Figure A2.12.** The three kinds of spiral diagram. (*left*) When the size of the chord (*n*) evenly divides the size of the scale (*o*) we have *n* copies of each chord sharing the same angular position; the *diagonal action* **D** moves inward or outward by one radial unit and generates all the voice leadings connecting chords at the same angular position; these combine with chromatic transpositions (**T**) to generate the remaining voice leadings. (*middle*) When the size of the chord is relatively prime to the size of the scale, no two transpositions share the same angular position; here the *basic voice leading* **B** moves chords by one angular unit; repeated applications of this basic voice leading generate all the voice leadings on the figure. (*right*) When the size of the chord shares a common factor with the size of the scale, there is both a diagonal action and a basic voice leading.

higher-dimensional structures on a 2D sheet of paper. As we have seen, these graphs can be extended by adding multiple chord types, or introducing curved arrows to represent pairwise voice exchanges, incorporating additional features of the higher-dimensional geometry.

The spiral diagrams come in three flavors (Figure A2.12). When the size of the chord *n* divides the size of the scale *o*, then there are *n* distinct chord-forms sharing the same angular position, linked by the transposition *o*/*n*. In this case there is a *diagonal voice leading* ($T_{o/n} t_{-1}$) that moves chords radially.[8] By repeating it, we can generate all the spacing-preserving leadings between chords at the same angular position, passing through each of the chord's inversions or modes and eventually returning each note to its starting pitch. When the size of the chord is instead relatively prime to the size of the scale, there is exactly one chord at each and every radial position; here a *basic voice leading* moves chords by one angular position, generating by repeated application all the voice leadings on the spiral.[9] The third type of graph occurs when the size of the chord shares a common factor with the size of the scale; in this case, there are between 1 and *n* chords sharing the same angular position. We can think of these spaces as having both a diagonal voice leading (which moves radially, passing through some subset of the modes before returning each voice to its starting position) and a basic voice leading (which connects angular neighbors).

---

[8] The adjective "diagonal" comes from mathematics, reflecting the fact that a single group acts simultaneously as a transposition along both chord and scale.

[9] Hook 2008 and 2011 was the first to explore the basic voice leading, beginning with the case of the diatonic scale and eventually extending this idea to other seven-note collections. He also introduced the big-T, little-t notation used in this book. Tymoczko 2008 and 2011a explored the general combination of transposition along both chord and scale, but had no way to represent these relationships geometrically.

APPENDIX 3

# Sequence and Transformation

The topic of sequences belongs to a larger *transformational theory* that extends the apparatus of chapter 4 in two ways: allowing transformations other than transposition and giving arrows an explicit parameter controlling temporal delay.[1] Explicitly notated temporal delays can be used to model nonrepeating canons. In Figure A3.1, for example, the middle voice imitates the top voice down a fourth at a distance of one measure while the lower voice imitates the middle voice down a fifth at a distance of two measures.[2] They are also useful when a sequence contains imitation at a temporal interval smaller than its simple period. For example, the sequential unit in Figure A3.2 is three beats long, but the top voice imitates the middle at the distance of a single beat. The model in chapter 4 is unable to capture the one-beat imitative relationship; an accurate analysis would have the top part imitating the middle part up a sixth and at a one-beat delay, and the bottom parts imitating themselves up a third and at a four-beat delay. These more-complicated arrows move music through pitch and time like the transposing delay lines of modern audio production.

When the temporal delay is zero, we have a *vertical process* in which input and output occur simultaneously. In Figure A3.3 this produces parallel motion along the diatonic scale, the chromatic scale, and both chord and scale together.[3] (As discussed in §3.6, the lower-left passage is characteristic of chorale textures in which the upper voices move in doubly parallel motion along a rapidly changing triad.) Sometimes, however, parallel motion cannot be modeled with vertical arrows: in Figure A3.4, Kabalevsky moves two voices along collections of different sizes, creating constantly changing vertical intervals; here it is easier to use *coupled melodic motion*, horizontal arrows whose subscripts indicate that their melodic intervals are always the same.[4] Figure A3.5 shows a vertical process called *quantization*, a transformation that sends notes downward until they lie within a chosen collection.[5]

[1] Taneyev (1909) 1962 discusses displacements in time as well as pitch.

[2] This canon repeats after nine measures, but we can choose not to observe the repeat. The example comes from Noam Elkies, who notes that the use of multiple temporal delays is unusual; most canons involve just a single temporal delay. See also Gauldin 1996.

[3] The figure's *Petrushka* analysis originates in a collaboration with Rachel Hall and Jason Yust, never published because I felt dissatisfied with its formalism; in retrospect, I was looking for something like the generalized transformational theory described here (Hall, Tymoczko, and Yust 2010).

[4] Horizontal arrows are generally more flexible than vertical arrows. In Figure A3.4, we cannot analyze the Stravinsky passage using arrows as the upper intervals are three times as large as the lower intervals; in the Bartók passage, we can use a vertical inversional arrow, as the two parts move in exact contrary motion. Vertical inversion arrows are characteristic of "K-nets" (Klumpenhouwer 1991 and Lewin 1990).

[5] This "quantization" operation is essentially the mathematical floor function: it leaves notes in the B minor triad untouched, sending any other note downward until it reaches a note in the B minor triad. Avoiding octaves thus requires diatonic transposition by *eight* rather than seven steps: F♯5 quantizes to F♯5, but Pärt harmonizes melodic F♯6 with D5 rather than F♯5.

556 APPENDIX 3: SEQUENCE AND TRANSFORMATION

**Figure A3.1.** The opening of "Non nobis, Domine," an anonymous sixteenth-century canon featuring multiple transpositions and temporal delays. "$D_x$" represents delay by $x$ beats.

**Figure A3.2.** The sequence in mm. 37ff of the second F major fugue in *The Well-Tempered Clavier*.

APPENDIX 3: SEQUENCE AND TRANSFORMATION 557

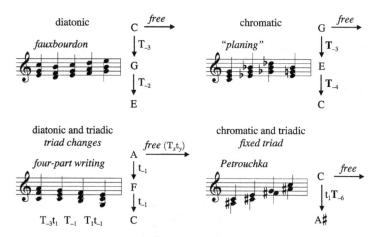

**Figure A3.3.** Vertical sequences involving transposition.

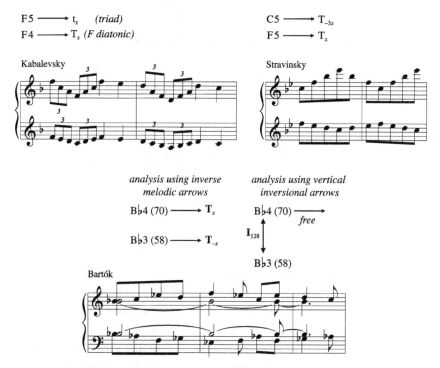

**Figure A3.4.** Vertical sequences represented with coupled melodic intervals. (*top left*) Kabalevsky's "Etude" (Op. 27, no. 24) features parallel motion along two different collections, changing the vertical interval between the parts. (*top right*) Stravinsky's *Rite of Spring* (R46 + 2) features contrary motion in which the upper part takes three steps for every step in the lower part, the two always moving in opposite directions. (*bottom*) Bartók's "Subject and Reflection" (*Mikrokosmos* 141) moves its parts in exact chromatic contrary motion. This last sequence can also be analyzed with vertical *inversional* arrows.

558    APPENDIX 3: SEQUENCE AND TRANSFORMATION

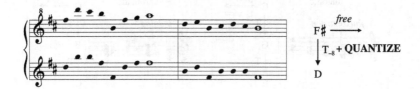

**Figure A3.5.** Pärt's *Für Alina* transposes the top voice down by eight diatonic steps and then quantizes to the B minor triad.

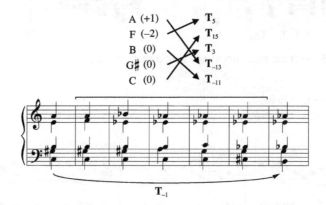

**Figure A3.6.** The harmonies at the start of Schoenberg's *Five Pieces for Orchestra*, Op. 16, III ("Farben"). The middle five chords are a repeating contrapuntal pattern; since it is not harmonically stable it generates a variety of set classes.

We can think of these transformational arrows as algorithms, little chunks of computer code that generate one part of a score from another. Traditional sequences are a special class of algorithm that has the property of being *self-replicating*: since all parts have the same temporal delay, equal to the length of the sequential unit, the resulting structure continues indefinitely, generating an infinite amount of music from a finite source. Twentieth-century composers often use sequences as a tool for accessing unusual harmonic states: in Schoenberg's "Farben," a short melody moves canonically throughout the ensemble, producing a variety of different set classes (Figure A3.6).[6] In this context, harmonically unstable sequences are preferable to harmonically stable sequences as they generate a wider range of harmonies.

Also noteworthy are those harmonically stable repeating contrapuntal patterns that exploit contrary motion. One common idiom uses subsets of the whole-tone scale, conceived as a harmony (typically an extended dominant, $V^{9\sharp 5\sharp 11}$). Two superimposed whole-tone subsets can be transposed by either an even or an odd

---

[6] Ligeti borrowed this technique fifty years later in "Monument."

number of semitones to produce a whole-tone resultant, as in Figure A3.7.[7] In *The Rite of Spring*, Stravinsky applies an analogous technique to diminished seventh chords, descending major seconds in the first violins against rising major thirds in the lower voices (Figure A3.8). He then uses the Principle of Musical Approximation, replacing the completely symmetrical diminished seventh with the *nearly* symmetrical dominant seventh, producing slightly irregular melodies.[8] This

**Figure A3.7.** *The Firebird* (1919 Suite), R7. (*a*) The upper two staves move in exact contrary motion, producing whole-tone subsets; the bottom staff completes the whole-tone scale. (*b*) The strings move within the contrary-motion augmented triads.

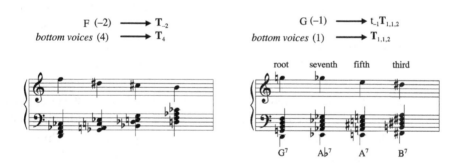

**Figure A3.8.** Contrary motion in the string parts at R70 of *The Rite of Spring*. (*a*) Descending seconds against ascending major thirds, forming a series of diminished seventh chords. (*b*) The same technique applied to nearly symmetrical dominant seventh chords.

---

[7] Russell 2018. Early Stravinsky often moves instrumental lines relative to surface voice leading, as in the opening bassoon parts of *The Firebird* or R43 of *The Rite of Spring*. This orchestrational habit may have led him to consider how the technique could be used in more obviously contrapuntal ways. In Figure A3.7, Stravinsky moves the string parts *within* the augmented triads, forming diatonic melodies. This is not how the passage appears in the original ballet or 1911 suite; it may have been recomposed after *The Rite of Spring*.

[8] Alternatively one could apply this sort of thinking *within* the chord, for instance by playing a two-step interval as measured within a four-note chord (i.e. notes 1–3 or 2–4). The two voices can then be moved by either an even or odd number of tetrachordal steps to produce subsets of just two harmonies (notes 1–3 or 2–4). Versions of this technique are used in the Fenaroli and "horn fifths" schemas, as well as a Prinner variant (cf. Figures 4.5.6, 4.6.1–2, and 4.8.6).

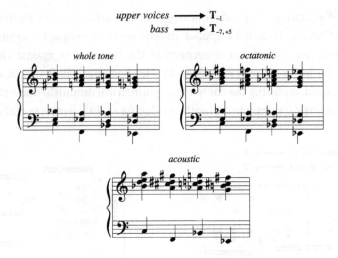

**Figure A3.9.** Jazz sequences in which the upper voices descend semitonally while the bass descends by fifth. As long as the initial scale contains the tritone transposition of the initial bass note, then the resulting harmonies will always belong to one of its transpositions.

suggests a robust though perhaps intuitive understanding of the Prime Directive, applying one and the same technique to the whole-tone scale, the diminished seventh chord, and the nonsymmetrical dominant seventh.[9]

Postwar jazz synthesizes these contrary-motion sequences with tonally functional harmony (Figure A3.9).[10] In Figure A3.10 the left hand plays "Viennese fourth chords," a tritone plus a perfect fourth; if the right hand plays any octatonic subset, then the two hands can move in contrary motion to produce another octatonic subset, ascending whole tones and descending semitones combining to express descending-fifth harmony. A related strategy superimposes stacks of fifths moving independently: because the diatonic scale is a large stack of fifths, the result tends to be diatonic (Figure A3.11).[11] Pioneered by McCoy Tyner, this technique is so distinctive that one can evoke modern jazz simply by combining random fourth chords with equally random melodies composed of quartal trichords.[12]

---

[9] *The Rite of Spring* is full of interesting contrary-motion patterns, for instance at R44 + 4 (seventh chords in contrary motion forming large octatonic subsets), R60 (triads moving in contrary motion in winds and trumpets), throughout the "Sacrificial Dance" (e.g., R192–R194, upper voices against bassoons, or R196, trombones moving down octatonically while winds ascend along the B♭ minor and C major triads forming a nearly octatonic composite). See Russell 2018.

[10] Stuckenschmidt 1965. Here again contrary motion functions to produce harmonic expansion.

[11] Nine of the twelve superimpositions of three-note fourth chords produce a diatonic subset. Different patterns of left-and-right hand motion are more or less likely to preserve diatonicism. Suppose, for example, left and right hand are each playing three-note fourth chords. If they are close together on the circle of fifths, they will belong to the same diatonic or pentatonic collection. If one hand moves up by three semitones while the other moves down by two, their relative position on the circle of fifths will change by only one; by contrast, if one hand stays fixed and the other moves by semitone, their configuration changes by 5. The latter change is more likely to turn a diatonic subset nondiatonic.

[12] See https://www.madmusicalscience.com/robots.html.

APPENDIX 3: SEQUENCE AND TRANSFORMATION 561

**Figure A3.10.** Here the left-hand voicings ascend by two semitones while the right-hand voicings descend by one semitone; because the voicing forms an octatonic subset, the resultant harmonies are octatonic as well. The entire passage expresses a sequence of descending-fifth harmonies.

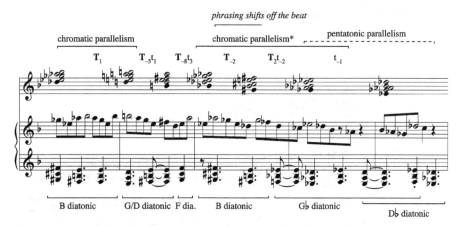

**Figure A3.11.** At 2'57" in "Passion Dance," McCoy Tyner plays four-note pentatonic subsets in his right hand, moving in doubly parallel motion along both chromatic and pentatonic scales; the left hand plays chromatic fourth chords. Though his two hands move independently and in contrary motion, the music articulates diatonic subsets. This need not require deliberate planning as it tends to happen naturally. Compare Figure 1.1.8.

It is also possible to use inversional arrows to form sequences that turn each successive unit upside down. In Figure A3.12 the lines echo one another in both a one-bar canon-by-inversion and a two-bar canon-by-transposition.[13] A closer look shows why these sequences are not very common: since $I_x I_x = T_0$ for any inversion $I_x$, every other unit contains exactly the same pitch classes. It follows that harmonically stable inversional sequences tend to oscillate between unchanging sonorities. For this reason, inversion is usually used to create *near* rather than exact sequences: Figure A3.13, for example, obtains harmonic

---

[13] Since the index numbers are related by octave, this collection of arrows is harmonically stable, preserving the pitch-class intervals between lines.

**Figure A3.12.** A sequence using inversion rather than transposition. Notes are numbered diatonically with C4 = 60, D4 = 61, and so on; $I_x(y)$ sends $x$ to $y - x$. The grand period is six bars long.

**Figure A3.13.** We can obtain greater harmonic variety by transposing each successive unit.

**Figure A3.14.** Measures 15–18 of Bach's first two-part invention present a near sequence combining transposition and inversion (the music is in the lower system of Figure 7.7.5). The transposition moves the upper voice downward by 10 and 11 diatonic steps in alternation; the inversion moves the top note of the original sixteenth-note figure up by octave to become the bottom note of the inverted figure.

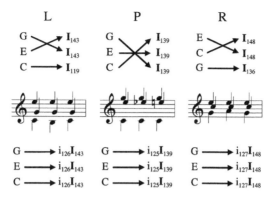

**Figure A3.15.** The neo-Riemannian L, P, and R voice leadings as repeating contrapuntal patterns. See Figure A1.1 for the calculation of index numbers.

variety by transposing each successive unit; this comes at the cost of destroying the one-bar canon-by-inversion, but that was not very salient to begin with. Figure A3.14 shows an interesting canon that combines transpositional and inversional arrows.[14]

When we turn to repeating contrapuntal patterns, we find ourselves unexpectedly close to the concerns of neo-Riemannian theory. The passages in Figure A3.15 analyze the basic neo-Riemannian voice leadings as one-note sequences-by-inversion, repeatedly applying the same operation so that harmonies oscillate between major and minor. As in the transpositional case, we can eliminate the crossed arrows by reconceiving the sequences hierarchically: here, we combine "little i" inversion-within-the-chord and "big I" inversion-within-the-chromatic-scale (compare Figure 4.2.4). The two inversions nearly cancel out, producing an efficient voice leading as residue (cf. Figure A1.1).[15]

As before, we can obtain greater harmonic variety by transposing successive units. Figure A3.16 generates the "Moro Lasso" progression from the "relative" transformation, adding –1 to each chromatic inversion; this causes the sequence to slide down by chromatic step. One and the same set of arrows can be used to produce a number of the three-voice sequences found in §1.1, formalizing the observation they are all "the same" (Figure A3.17).[16] Figure A3.18, meanwhile, analyzes

---

[14] Compare m. 61 of the first A minor fugue in *The Well-Tempered Clavier*.

[15] Crossed $T_x$ and $I_x$ arrows describe sequences using symmetry operations that can apply to extended passages of music; dual transformations like $T_x t_y$ and $I_x i_y$ describe sequences using *voice leadings* that apply to just a single chord. The latter description has the advantage of being insensitive to a chord's registral position and internal intervallic structure. Thus it is often useful to go back and forth between the two. We could, for example, convert a neo-Riemannian voice leading into a large-unit sequence by writing down an instance of that voice leading, describing it with crossed $I_x$ arrows, and using these arrows to form a larger sequence. See Tymoczko 2020b on the difference between the *symmetry group* and the *homotopy group*.

[16] These patterns are *nondualist* since both major and minor chords descend; a dualist sequence would move them in opposite directions (Tymoczko 2020b).

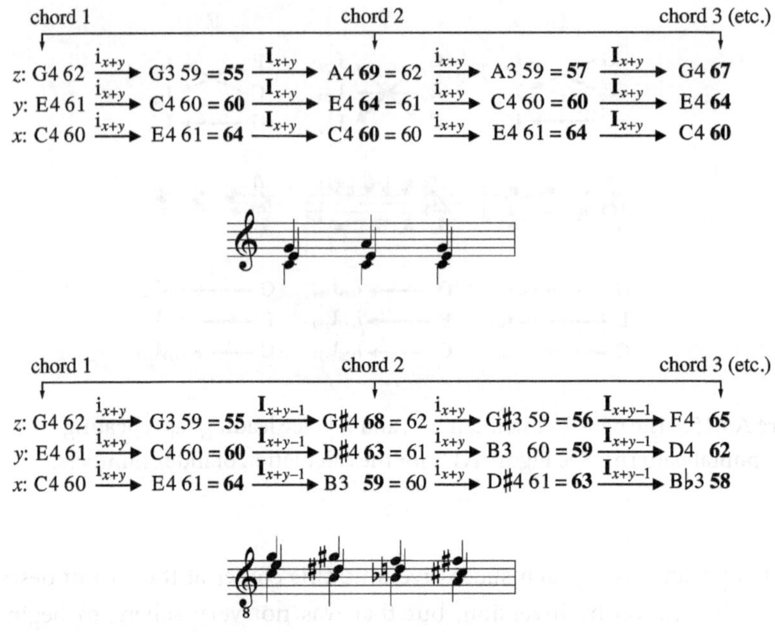

## 564 APPENDIX 3: SEQUENCE AND TRANSFORMATION

**Figure A3.16.** (*top*) The relative transform as pair of hierarchical inversions. (*bottom*) The "Moro Lasso" sequence applies the Tinctoris Transform by subtracting 1 from its chromatic subscripts.

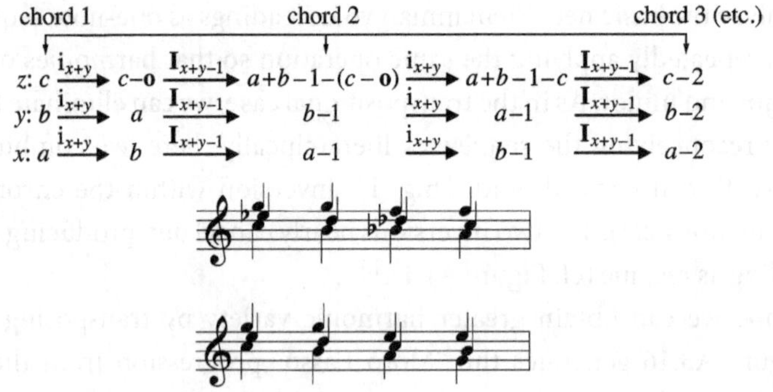

**Figure A3.17.** Two sequences from §1.1, described with the same contextual inversions used in the previous example. In the top sequence, the letters $a$, $b$, $c$ refer to chromatic scale degrees; in the bottom, they are diatonic.

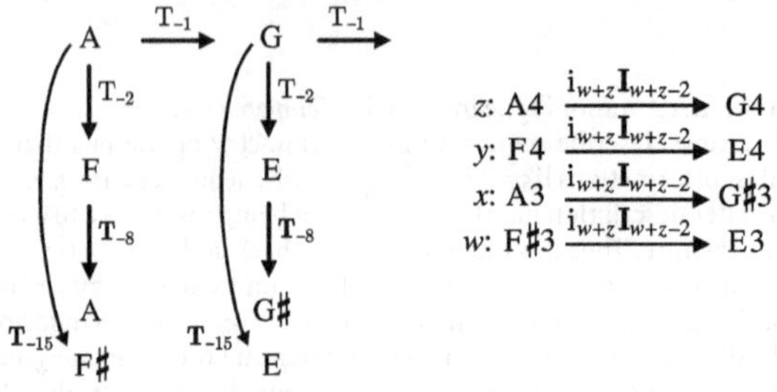

**Figure A3.18.** Two analyses of the sequence in Figure 1.1.7, the first using transposition and the second using inversion.

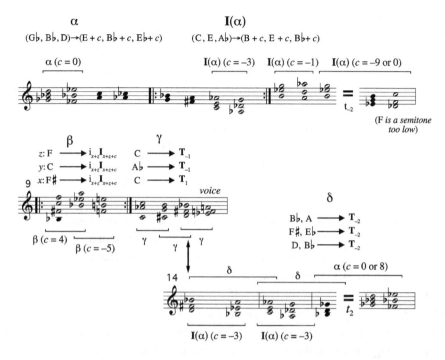

**Figure A3.19.** Some salient progressions in Schoenberg's "Angst und Hoffen." I focus on the piano part and omit mm. 5–6 and 11–12.

the transpositional and inversional relationships at play in Figure 1.1.7. The two analyses capture two different features of the music—first, that the lines move in doubly parallel motion along three separate diatonic scales, and second, that the harmonies are inversionally related. It is unusual to find a single passage possessing both properties.

At this point, what began as a theory of sequences has evolved into a general framework for analyzing a very wide range of transformations. Figure A3.19 illustrates its scope by analyzing "Angst und Hoffen," the seventh song in Schoenberg's *Book of the Hanging Gardens*, Op. 15.[17] The music begins with a voice leading from an augmented triad (perhaps "Angst") to a Viennese fourth chord (perhaps "Hoffen"); I describe this as schema α, modeling it with a diagram that includes a parameter $c$ determining the second chord's transposition.[18] This schema appears right-side-up with $c = 0$, and then upside-down

---

[17] This piece is the subject of two extended analyses by David Lewin (1981, 1987, pp. 128ff) and a third by Jack Boss (2019). Lewin's second analysis prefigures his later interest in K-nets by analyzing contrary motion using vertical inversional arrows. I prefer horizontal transpositional arrows instead.

[18] I do not provide any notation for the pattern's absolute transpositional level. Voice leadings conforming to the schema are related by the Tinctoris Transform.

with $c = -3, -1$ (recreating the ascending-step melody of the opening), and $-9$. The final chord is distorted, its middle voice a semitone too low—a flexible treatment of intervals characteristic of Schoenberg's early atonal music.[19] My analysis imagines the large melodic leap as resulting from an elided transposition-along-the-chord that turns B4–E♭5–G5 into E♭4–G4–B4 ($t_{-2}$), thus relating this voice leading to its predecessor.[20] The rest of the example identifies a series of sequences, the first using Gesualdo's trick, the second a contrary-motion wedge, and the third a two-chord transpositional sequence extending I(α) into a chromatic melody. It ends two chordal steps higher than we expect ($t_2$), overlapping with the final appearance of α. Though this analysis is technical and specific, I feel it captures something of Schoenberg's intuitive play-with-shapes: the basic musical objects here are not sets, abstract collections of disembodied pitch classes, but more specific "hand shapes" or Tinctorian vertical configurations, linked by familiar sequences and voice-leading patterns. These sequences link the music to the past even while generating futuristic harmonies.

Approached in this way, the theory of sequences can be generalized into a transformational theory that is more responsive to information about voice, register, and time.[21] A final generalization permits the transposition and inversion of *any* collection along any other. Figure A3.20 does this with fractional scale degrees.[22] An

**Figure A3.20.** Using fractional scale degrees to transpose an arbitrary collection along the C diatonic scale.

---

[19] Ethan Haimo suggests that the basic objects of this music are more elastic than set classes, neighborhoods containing set classes related by small "perturbations" (i.e., efficient voice leadings); see Haimo 1996 and Tymoczko 2020b.

[20] In other words, the augmented triad (B, E♭, G) allows for an ascending-step melody with both Viennese chords that follow it, the (A, D, A♭) in m. 7 and its near-transposition down by minor sixth, the distorted (D♭, F = G♭, C) in m. 8. In both cases, the ascending registral semitone is audible in the music (G5–A♭5 and B4–C5). The idea of elided inversion is useful at the end of the piece, connecting the final chord of sequence δ to the return of α.

[21] Traditional transformational theory often focuses on disembodied pitch classes, assigned to octave and instrument according to unformalized compositional whim (Lewin 1987).

[22] Tymoczko 2011a, chapter 4.

APPENDIX 3: SEQUENCE AND TRANSFORMATION 567

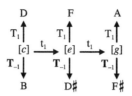

**Figure A3.21.** Using unstated chord tones to transpose an arbitrary collection along the C major triad. Here B and D are interpreted relative to tacit chordal degrees.

alternative and somewhat more intuitive approach allows for intervallic networks containing unstated notes (§4.8). Figure A3.21 moves a two-note motive along an unstated C major triad, the tones of resolution being merely conceptual and implied—observable by their transformational effects, much as a planet might be discovered through its influence on another planet's orbit.

APPENDIX 4

# Corpus Analysis, Statistics, and Grammar

Though it has one foot in the creative arts and the other in the sciences, music theory has been somewhat slow to embrace empirical methods. Figures such as David Huron and Fred Lerdahl have tried to push the field in that direction, the former influenced by empirical psychology, the latter by the introspective methods of Chomskian linguistics. But I think it is fair to say that many theorists do not consider their profession to be even broadly continuous with science. Those who do tend to follow Huron in adopting the language and style of psychological discourse: formalized theories, papers written as experiments, and null-hypothesis significance testing, often in a context of skepticism toward traditional music-theoretical verities. In this book I have instead chosen to adopt a more traditional style, for three reasons.

The first, I admit, is constitutional: I believe I will have more fun and reach more readers if I speak somewhat informally and leave out the significance tests. After all, corpus analysis can be a powerful tool for traditional scholarship—as it was for both Knud Jeppesen and Allen Irvine McHose.[1] Having programmed a computer to identify non-harmonic tones, I discovered the Renaissance sevenths when they caused my algorithm to fail, at which point I was able to theorize about them in a relatively traditional way. Similarly, having programmed a computer to identify cadences in Renaissance music (operationalized as two voices converging stepwise on an octave or unison with one decorated by a suspension), I was able to search hundreds of pieces for patterns like that at the bottom of Figure 6.3.5. Here the computer pointed me toward examples whose analytical significance was intuitively clear. In such cases, machines act as virtual assistants, increasing our access to musical examples. Humans can take advantage of these tools without adopting the language of statistical science.

A second reason is that large effects can often be seen without sophisticated statistics. My Bach-chorale analyses contain 45 instances of $I-X-I^6$, where $X$ is a single chord over bass scale-degree $\hat{2}$; 34 of these are $I-vii^{o6}-I^6$ progressions, 10 are $I-V^4_3-I^6$, and only 1 is $I-ii-I^6$. Meanwhile the Mozart piano sonatas contain about 115 progressions of this form without a single indisputable $I-ii-I^6$. Such regularities speak for themselves. Statistics are necessary when we are dealing with subtle effects not obvious to the naked eye—a new drug that slightly decreases the length of an

---

[1] Working before computers, both scholars had to gather data separately for each music-theoretical question—an earlier study of parallel fifths would not facilitate a later study of root motions, for example. One of the main virtues of computers is that they allow us to ask multiple questions of the same data.

**Figure A4.1.** Three analyses of the sixth measure of Bach's "Liebster Jesu, wir sind hier" (BWV 373, Riemenschneider 328). The first two are considered by David Huron; the third is my preferred analysis.

illness, an early-childhood intervention that slightly improves test scores a decade later, and so on.[2] The musical behaviors I care about tend to be considerably more obvious than this. And even when we are dealing with subtle topics, such as the gradual increase in root-position fifth-progressions over the course of the sixteenth century, we can often observe the relevant phenomena analytically, once we have been alerted to them by corpus study (§6.5).

The final issue is that there are significant methodological questions that need to be resolved before we can profit from rigorous statistical methodology. Consider David Huron's treatment of the ii–vii$^{o6}$ idiom, discussed in connection with Figure P7.1. Huron considers two possible analyses of the passage in Figure A4.1, neither of which I endorse; the best analysis, in my view, recognizes *two* eighth-note chords rather than one quarter-note harmony.[3] Huron's analysis of this idiom underwrites his claim that more than 20% of Bach's supertonic chords progress to tonics—a number that exceeds my own by a factor of at least 10.[4] Or consider the *Tempest*'s m. 11 G–B♭–C♯–E chord, which Hepokoski and Martin call a "ct$^{o7}$/iv" and which Hatten and I consider a vii$^{o7}$/V (m. 11, shown in Figure 10.3.4). These cases show us that simple Roman-numeral labeling, sometimes disparaged as "trivial transliteration of note content," requires a nontrivial sense of a composer's vocabulary. The paradox of analysis is that we have to know what we're looking for in order to find it.

For these reasons, I have decided to follow the philosophy of open data—writing in a relatively informal mode but releasing all my code and data so that readers can reproduce and criticize my results.[5] Those who worry about my

---

[2] There is a "replication crisis" currently unfolding across the social and biomedical sciences, sometimes described as an epidemic of untrustworthy and implausible results. See Simmons, Nelson, and Simonsohn 2011. These difficulties provide another reason to focus on larger effects.

[3] Huron 2007b.

[4] Huron 2007a, p. 266. The other issue is Huron's decision to consider I$^6_4$ a standard tonic rather than an anomalous cadential sonority, hierarchically dependent on the following dominant (§9.5). He and I once had a chance to examine his data, determining that a large proportion of his ii–I progressions belonged to these two categories.

[5] Readers can go to https://www.madmusicalscience.com/taom to download my code, data, and a python program allowing them to reproduce my quantitative examples, as well as the other programs described in the text.

APPENDIX 4: CORPUS ANALYSIS, STATISTICS, AND GRAMMAR    571

subjective choices can reanalyze my data, for instance automatically labeling all the "nonharmonic consonances" in the Bach chorales, or removing any modulations I have introduced into Renaissance pieces. Readers will no doubt discover errors in both my analyses and my code. But a policy of openness allows others not only to correct those mistakes but also to use my data for work I have not anticipated. My hope is that this combination of humanistic writing and data transparency will satisfy both nonspecialists who are primarily interested in high-level conclusions and quantitative researchers who are more interested in the fine details.

This data serves as the input to musical "grammars," or theories of what does or does not typically happen in a particular musical genre. In this book, I have simultaneously tried to bolster traditional theories while identifying their limits. The first effort involves, for example, the suggestion that traditional theories of nonharmonicity work reasonably well in Renaissance, baroque, and classical music, allowing us to identify consonant harmonies decorated by familiar nonharmonic formulae (§5.1–§5.4); the proposal that the descending-third arrangement of triads, from I down to V, captures the most common progressions in functional music (§7.1–§7.3); and the claim that sequential progressions are harmonically significant (§7.6). Such proposals are meant to counter skeptics who want to replace traditional theory with something radically different. The second part of the project acknowledges the schema-theoretical point that music is fundamentally idiomatic, reconceiving traditional precepts not as exceptionless laws but as largely true generalizations. We cannot expect that every passage in every piece will conform to those generalizations, nor even that there will be any explanation for anomalous occurrences. Sometimes exceptions happen.

It is a truism of linguistics that *grammaticality* is not the same as *frequency*: that there can be perfectly grammatical sentences that have never been uttered, and are unlikely ever to be: Noam Chomsky famously gave the example of the rare-but-grammatical "colorless green ideas sleep furiously." Is it wrong to link "grammaticality" with frequency in the musical case?

My first answer is that Chomsky's example was meant to highlight the rarity of particular *sequences of words* rather than sequences of *abstract grammatical categories*. The extremely rare sentence "colorless green ideas sleep furiously" corresponds to the very *common* sequence <ADJECTIVE> <ADJECTIVE> <NOUN> <VERB> <ADVERB>. If we translate this point to the musical domain, then the analogues to word-sequences are something like actual segments of musical notation, with Roman numeral sequences like V–IV being analogous to abstract sequences like <NOUN> <ADJECTIVE>. And at the level of grammatical categories, the question about frequency and grammaticality is by no means resolved. There are some sequences, like <NOUN> <NOUN> <NOUN> <VERB> <VERB> <VERB>, that are almost unknown in English (e.g., "people cats dogs like hate sigh," a description of the sadness expressed by people who are hated by those cats that are liked by dogs). Some linguists *do* take the rarity of this abstract sequence to indicate that it

# 572 APPENDIX 4: CORPUS ANALYSIS, STATISTICS, AND GRAMMAR

is indeed ungrammatical, while others consider the form to be grammatical in an idealized sense.

Second, the linguistic divergence between frequency and grammaticality is underwritten by *semantics*: though we might initially be baffled by "people cats dogs like hate sigh," we can upon reflection extract its meaning. (Even with "colorless green ideas sleep furiously" we can answer questions like: "were the ideas awake?" or "how did they sleep?"[6]) By contrast, it is much harder to extract any meaning from "like hate sigh people cats dogs." Lacking semantics, it is unclear whether music supports any analogous distinction. If asked "is root-position I–V–IV–I a grammatical chord progression?" I can say only that it is common in rock and rare in classical music; in that sense, it is "grammatical in," or "characteristic of," the one style but not the other. At the same time, were I to hear a I–V–IV–I progression in classical music, I would register it as unusual without experiencing any further difficulties.[7] In particular, I have no experience of being able to "comprehend" I–V–IV–I in rock but not classical music; instead, I have the *expectation* that the progression occurs in some styles but not others. Violating these expectations leads to mild surprise rather than genuine perplexity.

It might be possible to separate frequency and acceptability were classical music a living tradition. For suppose two Viennese classical-era composers disagreed about whether the I–ii–I[6] progression was grammatical in their shared language: if one were to compose successful pieces making use of the progression, and if these pieces were accepted by the community as exemplars of the classical style (rather than archaic evocations of earlier music), then this would provide evidence that the progressions were grammatical despite their infrequency. It is not clear that composition can still function in this way, as contemporary ears are no longer capable of delivering eighteenth-century judgments. For suppose that a charismatic music theorist constructed a theory implying that I–ii–I[6] was acceptable (say, because the supertonic was "merely passing"); and suppose that theorist's followers began composing mock-classical music featuring extensive I–ii–I[6] progressions.[8] It seems to me that this would tell us less about the classical style than about the contemporary theoretical community. The question is not what *we* think about classical harmony but what its native speakers thought.[9]

---

[6] See Camp 2004. The issue is complicated, as there are semantically defective sentences that are judged grammatical (e.g., "more people have been to Russia than I have," Wellwood et al. 2018).

[7] For example, there are retrofunctional moments in Brahms (chapter 7, footnote 29) and Bach: "Nun freut euch, lieben Christen g'mein" (BWV 388, Riemenschneider 183), mm. 3–4; "Komm, Gott Schöpfer, Heiliger Geist" (BWV 370, Riemenschneider 187), m. 1; and "So gibst du nun, mein Jesu, gute Nacht" (BWV 412, Riemenschneider 206), mm. 26–27.

[8] Indeed, one periodically finds this progression in theory texts, despite its extreme rarity in actual music.

[9] My suggestion here is vaguely reminiscent of Wittgenstein's "Private Language Argument" (Wittgenstein 1953), which argues that linguistic meaning crucially requires the presence of a community. My argument is that judgments of grammaticality may require the presence of an appropriate community, at least insofar as they depart from judgments about frequency.

For all these reasons, I think it is best to understand musical grammars as *interpretive summaries* of statistical tendencies. That is, they aspire to provide a useful description of musical behavior as being "standard" or "unusual" to varying degrees. (While the simplest grammars might use just two categories, we have seen that it is often useful to adopt a more fine-grained picture in which standardness comes in degrees.[10]) This sorting serves a variety of practical functions. For the analyst, it directs attention toward those features of a piece that are genuinely exceptional, preventing us from wasting time "explaining" common occurrences. For the student, trying to compose in the style, it can provide suggestions about what might come next. For the theorist, it can point toward hypotheses about why musical practice might have developed as it did (e.g., that mature functionality fleshes out the simpler I–IV–V template with a series of descending-third progressions [§7.2]). For the cognitive scientist, it can hint at the mental representations that constitute competence in a musical style.

My word "interpretive" is meant to serve a double function. First, it registers the reality that we can construct multiple theories accounting for the same set of observable facts. For instance, I have proposed that the progression I–ii–I$^6$ is ungrammatical or unusual in mature functional music; I explain most of the exceptions as instances of the pseudochord idiom (§7.5).[11] Others may assert that I–ii–I$^6$ is grammatical, proposing auxiliary explanations that restrict its appearance to the "pseudochord" idiom. This kind of pluralism, or "underdetermination," is endemic to science, where equivalent theories often account for the same observations.

The word "interpretive" also points to the holistic nature of the grammatical enterprise. Consider once again the interdependence of harmonic labeling, nonharmonic-tone identification, and harmonic theorizing discussed in the prelude to chapter 7. This holism gives us yet another reason to be cautious about the prospects for a simple approach to corpus study—and in particular about the possibility of *theory-neutral* datasets of analyzed music. For suppose it is true that the identification of nonharmonic tones needs to be carried out on the basis of expectations about what is common in a particular repertoire; if so, then one of the basic canons of scientific method, the separation of data collection and hypothesis formation, may be inappropriate. If analysis is theory-dependent, then it is circular—though not necessarily *viciously* so.

Music theory is a difficult discipline, requiring equal comfort with the two cultures of art and science, and on occasion the third culture of philosophical reasoning as well. It is also an activity of diminishing cultural prestige, once fit to inhabit the Quadrivium, now demoted to the study of a relatively marginal aspect of

---

[10] Thus the V$^2$–I progression in Figure 1.5.1 can be simultaneously unusual relative to a coarse-grained norm, while still occurring frequently enough to be characteristic of Bach's style. For a very different understanding of "musical grammar" see Zbikowski 2017.

[11] For me, the almost-invariable absence of the ii chord's fifth is an important datum, suggesting a linear configuration rather than a true harmony.

human behavior—extremely marginal if we concern ourselves with notated composition. If the new era of computational corpus study exacerbates the first problem, requiring theorists to master yet another complex skill, it ameliorates the second, putting music theory in dialogue with computer science, information theory, linguistics, 3D visualization, and cognitive science. To me this is yet another reason to be encouraged about its future.

# Terms, Symbols, and Abbreviations

(C, E, G) → (C, F, A). A voice leading from (C, E, G) to (C, F, A) in which the first note in the first chord moves to the first note in the second chord, the second note in the first chord moves to the second note in the second chord, and so on. Here, C stays fixed, E moves up to F, and G moves up to A. These intervals are *paths in pitch-class space* that can occur in any octave (appendix 1).

C4, C♯5, and so on. A method of referring to pitches, combining a pitch class (C) with an octave number. Octave numbers run from written C to the B above, with octave 4 starting at middle C. Thus B3 is the note below middle C, while B4 is a major seventh above.

60, 61, 62 . . . scale degrees are typically numbered so that 60 is as close to middle C as possible. The exact numbering is unimportant; what matters is the difference between scale degrees.

A3D2 (etc.). A sequence in which roots alternately ascend by diatonic third (A3) and descend by diatonic second (D2). Octaves typically do not matter, with ascending fourth (A4) equal to descending fifth (D5).

Abstract voice. A scale degree or "melodic slot" available in every octave and moving in specific ways (§1.2, appendix 1).

Alphabet (musical). A chordal, scalar, or other collection along which surface voices can move.

Basic voice leading. A voice-leading schema that, when repeated, generates all the voice leadings on a spiral diagram; it is found only when the size of the chord is relatively prime to the size of the scale (§3.1, §3.4, appendices 1–2).

Bijective voice leading. A voice leading in which each note of one chord is connected to exactly one note of the other (appendix 1).

Chase schema. A three-voice canonic schema dating back to the Renaissance (§4.4).

Chord. A collection of either pitches or pitch classes, depending on context.

576  TERMS, SYMBOLS, AND ABBREVIATIONS

Chord-loop family. A collection of repeating progressions that can be derived from a single repeating four-chord progression by eliminating chords; the underlying four-chord progression typically moves clockwise through the space of chromatic major triads, selecting one chord at each angular position (§2.3).

Chord type. A collection of chords related by transposition.

Collectional hierarchy. A more general name for the quadruple hierarchy, useful for situations in which there are different numbers of layers.

Concrete voice. See *surface voice*.

Disguised model. A sequence whose initial unit is altered so as to conceal the sequential structure.

Extrinsic scale. A scale in the standard sense, containing smaller chords; contrasts with *intrinsic scale*.

Fauxbourdon ROTO (or Fauxbourdon Rule of the Octave). A schema for harmonizing descending scalar bass lines (§7.5).

Functional analysis. A style of Roman-numeral analysis that tries to record the meaning, origin, or function of chords, as opposed to the more neutral *scale-degree analysis* (prelude to chapter 6).

Functional tonality. A generic term for what is sometimes called "tonal" as opposed to "modal" harmony, or the harmony of the "common-practice period," making frequent use of progressions such as I–IV–I, I–IV–V–I, I–V–I. The term is a very general label that does not favor the views of any particular theorist (§7.1–§7.3, chapters 6–7).

Garden-path modulation. A modulation that juxtaposes two passages, each syntactic in its own key, so as to create the impression of a nonfunctional progression across the key boundary (prelude to chapter 7).

Gesualdo's trick. A sequence of chords sharing the same intrinsic spacing in which two voices move in parallel, while the remainder move so that each chord is the pitch-class inversion of its predecessor (§1.1, prelude to chapter 2, appendix 3).

Harmonic skeleton. What remains when nonharmonic notes are removed.

Helicopter drop. A modulatory schema in which a sudden modulation to a distant key is followed by a long sequence returning to the tonic (§8.4).

$I_x$, $I_x$, $i_x$, $\iota_x$. These symbols refer to $x$-step inversion (pitch-space reflection) along various collections: the chromatic scale ($I_x$), a scale such as the diatonic ($I_x$), a chord ($i_x$), and a chordal subset ($\iota_x$) (appendix 1).

Index number. A tool used in calculating the effects of inversion (pitch-space reflection). If we number the notes in a collection, inversion along that collection sends every note $x$ to note $c - x$ for some fixed $c$ known as the *index number* (appendix 1).

Intrinsic scale. The octave-repeating scale formed by a chord's own notes (prelude to chapter 2, appendix 1).

Intrinsic spacing. See *spacing in chordal steps*.

Inversion. An ambiguous term referring to two unrelated phenomena: *registral inversion*, the rearranging of notes into different octaves (prelude to chapter 2); and *pitch-space reflection*, which turns a collection of intervals upside down (appendix 1).

Inversional equivalence. The view that chordal identity is determined by pitch-class content. Here, C3–G3–E4 is the same chord as E3–G3–C4 as they both contain the pitch classes C, E, and G. This view is often associated with Rameau, though it was anticipated by earlier theorists such as Lippius.

Irreducible seventh. See *Renaissance seventh*.

Loop family. See *chord-loop family*.

The Ludwig. An outer-voice contrary-motion schema that exploits the intrinsic geometry of diatonic space (§10.1–§10.2, §4.7, and §3.2).

Melodic slot. A scale degree or abstract voice.

Modality. Largely diatonic music in which each diatonic collection can have a wide range of tonal centers; typically chords progress freely.

Morte. A contrary-motion schema moving from tonic to dominant (Figure 4.7.4).

Neo-Riemannian progression. A spacing-preserving voice leading between inversionally related chords; it can be decomposed into a pair of inversions along intrinsic and extrinsic scales (prelude to chapter 2, appendix 3). Any such progression will preserve the distance between at least two voices, and can be used in Gesualdo's trick.

578    TERMS, SYMBOLS, AND ABBREVIATIONS

Nonharmonic. A tone that is not part of the underlying harmony, according to standard contrapuntal theory. It is a misleading term insofar as nonharmonic tones (in the technical sense) can produce harmonic effects (in the nontechnical sense). Yet it is accurate insofar as it captures the thinking of many theorists and composers.

OUCH theory. A configuration-based strategy for writing four-voice counterpoint (§3.6).

Pachelbel progression. A descending-fourth, ascending-step sequence of root progressions (D4A2) allowing two voices to descend in parallel. It can be analyzed as an instance of Gesualdo's trick (§1.1).

Paired-sequence design. A pair of sequences of comparable size, one of which undoes the other (§8.4).

Pairwise voice exchange. A voice exchange in which two voices move along equal and opposite paths to exchange pitch classes, as in (C4, E5) → (E4, C5); here, the first voice moves up by major third from C4 to E4 and the second moves down by major third from E5 to C5. More complicated voice exchanges can be expressed as the product of pairwise voice exchanges.

Paratonal century. The period from 1550–1650 when modal and functionally tonal techniques mix freely. Similar to our own time in some respects.

Path in pitch-class space. A combination of an octave-free pitch class with a distance and direction in pitch space, for example, "C, in any octave, moves down by eight semitones" (appendix 1).

Pitch class. An octave-free note type such as C, C♯, or D. Spelling does not matter and the note can occur in any octave.

Prime Directive. "Whenever you find an interesting musical technique, try to generalize it to every possible chordal and scalar environment" (§1.1).

Principle of Musical Approximation. The technique of viewing nonsymmetrical chords as perturbations of, or approximations to, symmetrical chords (§2.1, Figure A3.8).

Prinner. A common schema in which $\hat{6}$–$\hat{5}$–$\hat{4}$–$\hat{3}$ and $\hat{4}$–$\hat{3}$–$\hat{2}$–$\hat{1}$, in two different voices, are harmonized by IV–I–vii°–I. This schema plays different roles in different styles, serving as a cadential progression in the Renaissance and a "riposte" in the Galant. I use the term to refer to the general progression rather than its style-specific manifestation.

# TERMS, SYMBOLS, AND ABBREVIATIONS 579

Protofunctionality. A set of ionian-mode harmonic routines first appearing around 1500 and emphasizing root-position I, IV, and V chords (§6.1).

Quadruple hierarchy. A hierarchical arrangement of nested collections, or alphabets, in which *surface voices* can move along collections of various types (§1.2).

Renaissance seventh. A sounding seventh chord in which the seventh acts like a suspension but which cannot be reduced to a triad according to standard contrapuntal theory (§5.1).

Retrofunctional. Harmonic techniques that reverse the descending-fifth norm of functional tonality, often motivated by voice leading (chapter 2, §3.8).

Rogue note. A nonharmonic tone that is leapt-to and leapt-away-from; rare from 1500 to 1900.

Roman-numeral analysis. A very general style of musical analysis that labels tertian harmonies relative to a tonal center (prelude to chapter 6).

Scale. An abstract musical object whose notes can appear in any octave; it can be modeled as a circular ordering of pitch classes.

Scale degree. A way of identifying the abstract voices in a scale. A scale's pitch classes are typically labeled relative to the tonic, which is scale degree 1 (e.g., Figure 8.1.3). Its specific pitches are typically numbered so that note 60 is as close to middle C as possible.

Scale-degree analysis. A style of Roman-numeral analysis that aspires to a relatively theory-neutral labeling of chords' scale-degree content, as opposed to *functional analysis* (prelude to chapter 6).

Sequential reduction. A style of analysis that traces a quasi-regular surface back to a regular sequential background (§4.10).

Set class. A collection of chords related by transposition or inversion. On its own, *set class* usually refers to collections of pitch classes while *pitch-set set class* refers to collections of pitches. The term *transpositional set class* refers to collections related by transposition but not inversion.

Shepard-tone passacaglia. A repeating passage articulating a nontrivial voice leading across the repeat, producing the effect of continual descent or ascent (§2.5). I believe the phenomenon was first described by David Feurzeig.

# 580 TERMS, SYMBOLS, AND ABBREVIATIONS

SNAP system. A system of nonharmonic tones comprising Suspensions, Neighbor tones, Anticipations, and Passing tones (§5.1).

Spacing in chordal steps. The intervals between a collection of pitches as measured along the intrinsic scale; a transpositional pitch-set set-class measured intrinsically (prelude to chapter 3).

Spiral diagram. The main theoretical models used in this book, representing the geometry of a pair of hierarchically nested transpositions (prelude to chapter 2, prelude to chapter 3, §2.1, appendices 1–2).

Structured arpeggiation. A melodic sequence in which a voice moves regularly along a shifting chordal background (§4.8, prelude to chapter 5).

Surface voice. A surface melodic stream containing notes that are felt to connect.

$T_x, T_x, t_x, \tau_x$. These symbols refer to $x$-step transposition along various collections: the chromatic scale ($T_x$), another scale such as the diatonic ($T_x$), a chord ($t_x$), and a chordal subset ($\tau_x$) (prelude to chapter 2).

Thinking within the chord. Treating chords as scale-like collections along which surface voices move (§1.2, prelude to chapter 2, §3.7).

Tinctoris Transform. The independent transposition of each chord in a voice leading (prelude to chapter 3). Two progressions are related by the Tinctoris Transform if they exhibit the same sequence of vertical configurations.

Tonal. An ambiguous term that can refer to music that is functionally tonal (see above), or non-atonal. In addition the adjective sometimes refers to keys and modes ("tonal center," "tonal region," "tonal plan"). I typically use the term as a synonym for "non-atonal," encompassing techniques common to a range of modal and functionally tonal styles.

Up-and-down-the-ladder. A paired-sequence design in which a tension-increasing series of modulations up the circle of fifths is undone by a tension-releasing series of modulations down the circle of fifths (§8.5).

Voice. An ambiguous term that can either refer to *abstract* or *concrete* voices.

Voice exchange. A voice leading from a chord to itself in which the sum of all the intervals moved by all voices equals zero.

Voicing. A way of arranging a chord in register, which can be formalized as a pattern of *spacing in chordal steps.*

Voice leading. A collection of paths in pitch class space that indicate how the notes of one chord move to those of another; see (C, E, G) → (C, F, A) (appendix 1).

Voice-leading schema. A collection of voice leadings related by transposition, such as (C, E, G) → (C, F, A) and (G, B, D) → (G, C, E). It can be modeled as a set of instructions for moving chordal elements: "hold the root fixed, move the third up by step, and move the fifth up by step."

# Bibliography

Aarden, Bret, and Paul T. von Hippel. 2004. "Rules for Chord Doubling (and Spacing): Which Ones Do We Need?" *Music Theory Online* 10(2).

Agmon, Eytan. 1989. "A Mathematical Model of the Diatonic System." *Journal of Music Theory* 33(1): 1–25.

Agmon, Eytan. 1995. "Functional Harmony Revisited: A Prototype-Theoretic Approach." *Music Theory Spectrum* 17(2): 196–214.

Agmon, Eytan. 2013. *The Languages of Western Tonality*. New York: Springer.

Agmon, Eytan. 2020. "The Webern in Mozart: Systems of Chromatic Harmony and Their Twelve-Tone Content." *Music Theory Spectrum* 42(2): 173–92.

Aldwell, Edward, and Carl Schachter. (1969) 2002. *Harmony and Voice Leading*. 3rd ed. Belmont: Wadsworth.

Allsop, Peter. 1992. *The Italian "Trio" Sonata: From Its Origins until Corelli*. New York: Oxford University Press.

Arndt, Matthew. 2011. "Schenker and Schoenberg on the Will of the Tone." *Journal of Music Theory* 55(1): 89–146.

Arndt, Matthew. 2013. "Schenker and Schoenberg on the Eye of the Genius." *Theoria* 20: 39–120.

Arndt, Matthew. 2018. *The Musical Thought and Spiritual Lives of Heinrich Schenker and Arnold Schoenberg*. New York: Routledge.

Arndt, Matthew. 2019. "Schoenberg—Schenker—Bach: A Harmonic, Contrapuntal, Formal Braid." *Zeitschrift der Gesellschaft für Musiktheorie* 16(1): 67–97.

Arthur, Claire. 2021. "Vicentino versus Palestrina: A Computational Investigation of Voice Leading across Changing Vocal Densities." *Journal of New Music Research* 50(1): 74–101.

Auerbach, Brent. 2021. *Musical Motives: A Theory and Method for Analyzing Shape in Music*. New York: Oxford University Press.

Babbitt, Milton. 1987. *Words about Music*. Edited by Stephen Dembski and Joseph N. Straus. Madison: University of Wisconsin Press.

Bach, Carl Philipp Emanuel. (1762) 1949. *Essay on the True Art of Playing Keyboard Instruments*. Edited and translated by William Mitchell. New York: W. W. Norton.

BaileyShea, Matthew. 2004. "Beyond the Beethoven Model: Sentence Types and Limits." *Current Musicology* 77: 5–33.

Balzano, Gerald. 1980. "The Group-Theoretic Description of 12-Fold and Microtonal Systems." *Computer Music Journal* 4(4): 66–84.

Barry, Barbara. 2014. "Schubert's 'Quartettsatz': A Case Study in Confrontation." *Musical Times* 155(1928): 31–49.

Bass, Richard. 1996. "From Gretchen to Tristan: The Changing Role of Harmonic Sequences in the Nineteenth Century." *19th-Century Music* 19: 263–68.

Beach, David. 1967. "The Functions of the Six-Four Chord in Tonal Music." *Journal of Music Theory* 11(1): 2–31.

Beach, David. 1974. "The Origins of Harmonic Analysis." *Journal of Music Theory* 18(2): 274–306.

Beach, David. 1983. "A Recurring Pattern in Mozart's Music." *Journal of Music Theory* 27: 1–29.

Beach, David. 1994. "Harmony and Linear Progression in Schubert's Music." *Journal of Music Theory* 38(1): 13–17.

Bent, Margaret. 1998. "The Grammar of Early Music: Preconditions for Analysis." In *Tonal Structures in Early Music*, edited by Cristle Collins Judd, 15–59. New York: Garland.

## 584 BIBLIOGRAPHY

Bergé, Pieter, and Jeroen D'hoe. 2009. "To Play or Not to Play: Motivic Connections in the First Movement of Beethoven's *Tempest* Sonata." In *Beethoven's* Tempest *Sonata: Perspectives of Analysis and Performance*, edited by Peter Berge, Jeroen D'hoe, and William Caplin, 9–38. Walpole: Peters.

Bernhard, Christopher. (~1640) 1973. "The Treatises of Christoph Bernhard." Translated by Walter Hilse. *The Music Forum* 3: 1–197.

Bernstein, Leonard. 1956. *The Joy of Music*. New York: Simon and Schuster.

Bernstein, Leonard. 1976. *The Unanswered Question*. Cambridge, MA: Harvard University Press.

Besseler, Heinrich. 1950. *Bourdon und Fauxbourdon*. Leipzig: Breitkopf und Härtel.

Biamonte, Nicole. 2006. "Modality in Beethoven's Folk-Song Settings." *Beethoven Forum* 13(1): 28–63.

Biamonte, Nicole. 2010. "Triadic Modal and Pentatonic Patterns in Rock Music." *Music Theory Spectrum* 32(2): 95–110.

Biamonte, Nicole. 2012. "Variations on a Scheme: Bach's 'Crucifixus' and Chopin's and Scriabin's E-minor Preludes." *Intégral* 26: 47–89.

Bobbitt, Richard. 1955. "Harmonic Tendencies in the *Missa Papae Marcelli*." *The Music Review* 14: 273–88.

Boone, Graeme. 2000. "Marking Mensural Time." *Music Theory Spectrum* 22(1): 1–43.

Boretz, Benjamin. 1970. "Sketch of a Musical System (Meta-Variations, Part II)." *Perspectives of New Music* 8(2): 49–111.

Boretz, Benjamin. 1972. "Meta-Variations, Part IV: Analytic Fallout (1)." *Perspectives of New Music* 11(1): 146–223.

Boss, Jack. 2019. *Schoenberg's Atonal Music: Musical Idea, Basic Image, and Specters of Tonal Function*. Cambridge: Cambridge University Press.

Brewer, William F. 2015. "Perception Is Theory Laden: The Naturalized and Philosophical Implications." *Journal for General Philosophy of Science* 46: 121–38.

Brinkman, Alexander R. 1986. "A Binomial Representation of Pitch for Computer Processing of Musical Data." *Music Theory Spectrum* 8: 44–57.

Brody, Christopher. 2016. "Parametric Interaction in Tonal Repertoires." *Journal of Music Theory* 60(2): 97–148.

Brody, Christopher. 2021. "Second-Reprise Opening Schemas in Bach's Binary Movements." *Music Theory Spectrum* 43(2): 257–79.

Brown, Matthew. 2005. *Explaining Tonality*. Rochester, NY: University of Rochester Press.

Bruce, Robert. 1969. "The Lyrical Element in Schubert's Instrumental Forms." *Music Review* 30(2): 131–37.

Buelow, George. 1992. *Thorough-Bass Accompaniment According to Johann David Heinichen*. Lincoln: University of Nebraska Press.

Bukofzer, Manfred. 1947. *Music in the Baroque Era: From Monteverdi to Bach*. New York: W. W. Norton.

Burke, Edmund. (1757) 1999. *A Philosophical Enquiry into the Origins of the Sublime and Beautiful and Other Pre-Revolutionary Writings*. London: Penguin.

Burnham, Scott. 1995. *Beethoven Hero*. Princeton: Princeton University Press.

Burnham, Scott. 2009. "Singularities and Extremes: Dramatic Impulse in the First Movement of Beethoven's *Tempest* Sonata." In *Beethoven's* Tempest *Sonata: Perspectives of Analysis and Performance*, edited by Peter Berge, Jeroen D'hoe, and William Caplin, 39–60. Walpole: Peters.

Burns, Lori. 1993. "J. S. Bach's Mixolydian Chorale Harmonizations." *Music Theory Spectrum* 15(2): 144–72.

Burns, Lori. 1995. *Bach's Modal Chorales*. Hillsdale: Pendragon Press.

Burstein, L. Poundie. 2015. "The Half Cadence and Related Analytic Fictions." In *What Is a Cadence? Theoretical and Analytical Perspectives on Cadences in the Classical Repertoire*, edited by Markus Neuwirth and Pieter Bergé, 85–116. Leuven: Leuven University Press.

Burstein, L. Poundie. 2018. "The Practice of Music Theory, and Music Theory versus Practice." In *Teaching Music Theory*, edited by Rachel Lumsden and Jeffrey Swinkin, 1–12. New York: W. W. Norton.

BIBLIOGRAPHY 585

Burstein, L. Poundie. 2020. "Those Boring, Arcane Part-Writing Exercises." *Gamut: Online Journal of the Music Theory Society of the Mid-Atlantic* 9(1).

Burstein, L. Poundie. forthcoming. "Analysis nach Schenker." In *Handbuch Musikanalyse. Methode und Pluralität*, edited by Ariane Jeßulat, Oliver Schwab-Felisch, Jan Philipp Sprick, and Christian Thorau, translated by Oliver Schwab-Felisch. Kassel: Bärenreiter.

Byros, Vasili. 2012. "Meyer's Anvil: Revisiting the Schema Concept." *Music Analysis* 31(3): 273–346.

Byros, Vasili. 2015. "Hauptruhepuncte des geistes: Punctuation Schemas and the Late-Eighteenth-Century Sonata." In *What Is a Cadence? Theoretical and Analytical Perspectives on Cadences in the Classical Repertoire*, edited by Markus Neuwirth and Pieter Bergé, 215–51. Leuven: Leuven University Press.

Byros, Vasili. 2017. "Mozart's Vintage Corelli: The Microstory of a Fonte-Romanesca." *Intégral* 31: 63–89.

Callender, Clifton. 1998. "Voice-Leading Parsimony in the Music of Alexander Scriabin." *Journal of Music Theory* 42(2): 219–33.

Callender, Clifton, Ian Quinn, and Dmitri Tymoczko. 2008. "Generalized Voice Leading Spaces." *Science* 320: 346–48.

Camp, Elisabeth. 2004. "The Generality Constraint, Nonsense, and Categorial Restrictions." *Philosophical Quarterly* 54(215): 209–31.

Camp, Elisabeth. 2017. "Perspectives in Imaginative Engagement with Fiction." *Philosophical Perspectives* 31: 74–102.

Camp, Elisabeth. 2018. "Why Maps Are Not Propositional." In *Non-Propositional Intentionality*, edited by A. Grzankowski and M. Montague, 19–45. New York: Oxford University Press.

Caplin, William E. 1998. *Classical Form: A Theory of Formal Functions for the Instrumental Music of Haydn, Mozart, and Beethoven*. New York: Oxford University Press.

Caplin, William E. 2004. "The Classical Cadence: Conceptions and Misconceptions." *Journal of the American Musicological Society* 57(1): 51–118.

Caplin, William E. 2009a. "Beethoven's Tempest Exposition: A Springboard for Form-Functional Considerations." In *Beethoven's Tempest Sonata: Perspectives of Analysis and Performance*, edited by Peter Berge, Jeroen D'hoe, and William Caplin, 87–125. Walpole: Peters.

Caplin, William E. 2009b. "What Are Formal Functions?" In *Musical Form, Forms & Formenlehre: Three Methodological Reflections*, edited by Pieter Bergé, 71–89. Leuven: Leuven University Press.

Caplin, William E. 2013. "Teaching Classical Form: Strict Categories versus Flexible Analyses." *Tijdschrift voor Muziektheorie* 18(3): 119–35.

Caplin, William E. 2015. "Harmony and Cadence in Gjerdingen's 'Prinner.'" In *What Is a Cadence? Theoretical and Analytical Perspectives on Cadences in the Classical Repertoire*, edited by Markus Neuwirth and Pieter Bergé, 17–58. Leuven: Leuven University Press.

Cavett-Dunsby, Esther. 1988. "Mozart's 'Haydn' Quartets: Composing Up and Down without Rules." *Journal of the Royal Music Association* 113(1): 57–80.

Ceulemans, Anne-Emmanuelle. 2017. "Lasso, Meier, Powers. The Reality of the Modes under Scrutiny." Paper presented to the 9th European Music Analysis Conference, Strasbourg.

Chafe, Eric. 1992. *Monteverdi's Tonal Language*. New York: Schirmer.

Christensen, Thomas. 1992. "The 'Règle de l'Octave' in Thorough-Bass Theory and Practice." *Acta Musicologica* 64(2): 91–117.

Christensen, Thomas. 1993a. *Rameau and Musical Thought in the Enlightenment*. Cambridge: Cambridge University Press.

Christensen, Thomas. 1993b. Review of Carl Dahlhaus's *Studies on the Origins of Harmonic Tonality* and Joel Lester's *Between Mode and Keys*. *Music Theory Spectrum* 15(1): 94–111.

Christensen, Thomas. 2019. *Stories of Tonality in the Age of François-Joseph Fétis*. Chicago: University of Chicago Press.

Chua, Daniel K. L., and Alexander Rehding. 2021. *Alien Listening: Voyager's Golden Record and Music from Earth*. New York: Zone Books.

586 BIBLIOGRAPHY

Clendinning, Jane Piper, and Elizabeth West Marvin. 2016. *The Musician's Guide to Theory and Analysis*. 3rd ed. New York: W. W. Norton.

Clough, John. 1979a. "Aspects of Diatonic Sets." *Journal of Music Theory* 23: 45–61.

Clough, John. 1979b. "Diatonic Interval Sets and Transformational Structures." *Perspectives of New Music* 18(1–2): 461–82.

Clough, John. 1994. "Diatonic Interval Cycles and Hierarchical Structure." *Perspectives of New Music* 32(1): 228–53.

Clough, John. 2000. "Flip-Flop Circles and Their Groups." Paper presented to the national meeting of the Society for Music Theory, Toronto.

Cohn, Richard. 1992. "The Autonomy of Motives in Schenkerian Accounts of Tonal Music." *Music Theory Spectrum* 14(2): 150–70.

Cohn, Richard. 1996. "Maximally Smooth Cycles, Hexatonic Systems, and the Analysis of Late-Romantic Triadic Progressions." *Music Analysis* 15(1): 9–40.

Cohn, Richard. 1997. "Neo-Riemannian Operations, Parsimonious Trichords, and Their 'Tonnetz' Representations." *Journal of Music Theory* 41(1): 1–66.

Cohn, Richard. 1999. "As Wonderful as Star Clusters: Instruments for Gazing at Tonality in Schubert." *19th-Century Music* 22(3): 213–32.

Cohn, Richard. 2005. "'This Music Crept by Me upon the Waters': Introverted Motives in Beethoven's 'Tempest' Sonata." In *Engaging Music: Essays in Analysis*, edited by Deborah Stein, 226–35. New York: Oxford University Press.

Cohn, Richard. 2012. *Audacious Euphony*. New York: Oxford University Press.

Collins, Denis. 2015. "Taneyev's Theories of Moveable Counterpoint in the Music of J. S. Bach." *Bach* 46(2): 22–45.

Collins, Denis. 2018. "Approaching Renaissance Music Using Taneyev's Theories of Movable Counterpoint." *Acta Musicologica* 90(2): 178–201.

Collins Judd, Cristle. 1992. "Modal Types and 'Ut, Re, Mi' Tonalities: Tonal Coherence in Sacred Vocal Polyphony from about 1500." *Journal of the American Musicological Society* 45(3): 428–67.

Coluzzi, Seth J. 2015. "Speaking in (and out of) Mode: Structure and Rhetoric in Marenzio's *O Mirtillo, Mirtillo anima mia* (1595)." *Music Theory Spectrum* 37(2): 253–74.

Cone, Edward T. 1970. "Schubert's Beethoven." *The Musical Quarterly* 56(4): 779–93.

Cook, Nicholas. 1987. "The Perception of Large-Scale Tonal Closure." *Music Perception* 5(2): 197–205.

Cook, Nicholas. 1989. "Music Theory and 'Good Comparison': A Viennese Perspective." *Journal of Music Theory* 33(1): 117–41.

Crane, Hewitt D., and Thomas P. Piantanida. 1983. "On Seeing Reddish Green and Yellowish Blue." *Science* 221: 1078–80.

Cuthbert, Michael Scott, and Christopher Ariza. 2010. "Music21: A Toolkit for Computer-Aided Musicology and Symbolic Music Data." In *Proceedings of the 11th International Society for Music Information Retrieval (ISMIR 2010), August 9–13, 2010, Utrecht, Netherlands*, edited by J. Stephen Downie and Remco C. Veltkamp, 637–42.

Cutler, Timothy. 2009. "On Voice Exchanges." *Journal of Music Theory* 53(2): 191–226.

Czerny, Carl. (1830) 1848. *School of Practical Composition*. Translated by John Bishop. London: Robert Cocks & Co.

Dahlhaus, Carl. 1967. "Zur chromatischen Technik Carlo Gesualdos." *Analecta Musicologica* 4: 77–96.

Dahlhaus, Carl. 1990. *Studies in the Origins of Harmonic Tonality*. Translated by Robert Gjerdingen. Princeton: Princeton University Press.

Dahlhaus, Carl. 1991. *Ludwig van Beethoven: Approaches to His Music*. Translated by Mary Whittall. New York: Oxford University Press.

Damschroder, David. 2016. *Harmony in Beethoven*. Cambridge: Cambridge University Press.

Damschroder, David. 2018. *Tonal Analysis: A Schenkerian Perspective*. New York: W. W. Norton.

Danto, Arthur. 1981. *The Transfiguration of the Commonplace: A Philosophy of Art*. Cambridge, MA: Harvard University Press.

Davies, Stephen. 1983. "Attributing Significance to Unobvious Musical Relationships." *Journal of Music Theory* 27(2): 203–13.

de Clerq, Trevor, David Temperley, David Lustig, and Ethan Tan. 2011. "A Corpus Study of Rock Music." http://rockcorpus.midside.com. Accessed September 26, 2020.

Deathridge, John. 2008. *Wagner Beyond Good and Evil*. Berkeley: University of California Press.

DeBellis, Mark. 1999. "The Paradox of Musical Analysis." *Journal of Music Theory* 43(1): 83–99.

Deutsch, Diana, and John Feroe. 1981. "The Internal Representation of Pitch Sequences in Tonal Music." *Psychological Review* 88(6): 503–22.

Doll, Christopher. 2017. *Hearing Harmony: Toward a Tonal Theory for the Rock Era*. Ann Arbor: University of Michigan Press.

Douthett, Jack, and Peter Steinbach. 1998. "Parsimonious Graphs: A Study in Parsimony, Contextual Transformations, and Modes of Limited Transposition." *Journal of Music Theory* 42(2): 241–63.

Duane, Ben. 2017. "Thematic and Non-Thematic Textures in Schubert's Three-Key Expositions." *Music Theory Spectrum* 39(1): 36–65.

Edwards, George. 1997. "A Palimpsest of Mozart in Schubert's Symphony No. 5." *Current Musicology* 62: 18–39.

Einstein, Alfred. 1948. *The Italian Madrigal*. Princeton: Princeton University Press.

Everett, Walter. 2004. "Making Sense of Rock's Tonal Systems." *Music Theory Online* 10(4).

Everett, Walter, and Tim Riley. 2019. *What Goes On: The Beatles, Their Music, and Their Time*. New York: Oxford University Press.

Ewell, Philip A. 2020. "Music Theory and the White Racial Frame." *Music Theory Online* 26(2).

Ferraguto, Mark. 2019. *Beethoven 1806*. New York: Oxford University Press.

Fétis, François-Joseph. (1840) 1994. *Esquisse de l'histoire de l'harmony*. Translated by Mary Arlin. Hillsdale: Pendragon Press.

Feurzeig, David. 2010. "On Shifting Grounds: Meandering, Modulating, and Möbius Passacaglias." Paper presented to the national meeting of the Society for Music Theory, Indianapolis.

Fieldman, Hali. 2002. "Schubert's Quartettsatz and Sonata Form's New Way." *Journal of Musicological Research* 21: 99–146.

Fink, Robert. 2004. "Beethoven Antihero: Sex, Violence, and the Aesthetics of Failure, or Listening to the Ninth Symphony as Postmodern Sublime." In *Postmodern Modes of Hearing*, edited by Andrew Dell'Antonio, 109–53. Berkeley: University of California Press.

Flew, Antony. 1975. *Thinking about Thinking: Do I Sincerely Want to Be Right?* London: Collins Fontana.

Forte, Allen. 1959. "Schenker's Conception of Musical Structure." *Journal of Music Theory* 3(1): 1–30.

Forte, Alan, and Stephen Gilbert. 1982. *Introduction to Schenkerian Analysis*. New York: W. W. Norton.

Froebe, Folker. 2015. "On Synergies of Schema Theory and Theory of Levels: A Perspective from Riepel's Fonte and Monte." *Zeitschrift der Gesellschaft für Musiktheorie* 12(1): 9–25.

Fux, Johann. (1725) 1971. *The Study of Counterpoint*. Edited and translated by Alfred Mann. New York: W. W. Norton.

Gauldin, Robert. 1995a. *A Practical Approach to Sixteenth-Century Counterpoint*. Long Grove: Waveland.

Gauldin, Robert. 1995b. *A Practical Approach to Eighteenth-Century Counterpoint*. Long Grove: Waveland.

Gauldin, Robert. 1996. "The Composition of Late Renaissance Stretto Canons." *Theory and Practice* 21: 29–54.

Gauldin, Robert. 1997. *Harmonic Practice in Tonal Music*. New York: W. W. Norton.

Gauldin, Robert. 2004. "The Theory and Practice of Chromatic Wedge Progressions in Romantic Music." *Music Theory Spectrum* 26(1): 1–22.

Gelman, Andrew, John Carlin, Hal Stern, David Dunson, Aki Vehtari, and Donald Rubin. 2013. *Bayesian Data Analysis*. New York: Chapman and Hall.

588 BIBLIOGRAPHY

Georgiades, Thrasybulos. 1937. *Englische Diskantetheorie aus der ersten hälfte 15. Jahrhunderts*. Munich: Musikwissenschaftliches Seminar der Universität München.

Gjerdingen, Robert. 1988. *A Classic Turn of Phrase: Music and the Psychology of Perception*. Philadelphia: University of Pennsylvania Press.

Gjerdingen, Robert. 1996. "Courtly Behaviors." *Music Perception* 13(3): 365–82.

Gjerdingen, Robert. 1999. "An Experimental Music Theory?" In *Rethinking Music*, edited by Nicholas Cook and Mark Everist, 161–70. New York: Oxford University Press.

Gjerdingen, Robert. 2007. *Music in the Galant Style*. New York: Oxford University Press.

Gjerdingen, Robert. 2015. "Musical Grammar." In *The Oxford Handbook of Critical Concepts in Music Theory*, edited by Alexander Rehding and Steven Rings, 651–72. New York: Oxford University Press.

Gjerdingen, Robert. 2020. *Child Composers in the Old Conservatories: How Orphans Became Elite Musicians*. New York: Oxford University Press.

Gjerdingen, Robert, and Janet Bourne. 2015. "Schema Theory as a Construction Grammar." *Music Theory Online* 21(2).

Goldenberg, Yosef. 2020. "Continuous Question-Answer Pairs." *Music Theory Online* 26(3).

Goldenberg, Yosef. 2021. "Intriguing Interpretation of Dyads in Common-Practice Tonal Music." *Gamut: Online Journal of the Music Theory Society of the Mid-Atlantic* 10(1).

Goldstein, Robin, Johan Almenberg, Anna Dreber, John Emerson, Alexis Herschkowitsch, and Jacob Katz. 2008. "Do More Expensive Wines Taste Better? Evidence from a Large Sample of Blind Tastings." *Journal of Wine Economics* 3(1): 1–9.

Gosman, Alan. 2009. "Canonic Patterns: Reframing the Puzzle." *Theory and Practice* 34: 1–29.

Gosman, Alan. 2012. "Canonic Threads and Large-Scale Structure in Canons." *Gamut: Online Journal of the Music Theory Society of the Mid-Atlantic* 5(1).

Grant, Aaron. 2018. "Schubert's Three-Key Expositions." PhD diss., Eastman School of Music.

Greenberg, Yoel. 2017. "Of Beginnings and Ends: A Corpus-Based Inquiry into the Rise of the Recapitulation." *Journal of Music Theory* 61(2): 171–200.

Guillotel-Nothmann, Christophe. 2018. "Conditional Asymmetry and Spontaneous Asymmetry of Harmonic Progressions: The Changing Status of the Directional Tendency of Root Progressions in Madrigal Cycles from Verdelot to Monteverdi (c. 1530–1638)." *Music Theory Online* 24(4).

Hacking, Ian. 1975. *The Emergence of Probability: A Philosophical Study of Early Ideas about Probability, Induction and Statistical Inference*. Cambridge: Cambridge University Press.

Hadjeres, Gaëtan, François Pachet, and Frank Nielsen. 2017. "DeepBach: A Steerable Model for Bach Chorales Generation." *Proceedings of Machine Learning Research* 70: 1362–71.

Haimo, Ethan. 1996. "Atonality, Analysis, and the Intentional Fallacy." *Music Theory Spectrum* 18(2): 167–99.

Hall, Rachel, Dmitri Tymoczko, and Jason Yust. 2010. "Upright Petrouchka, Sideways Neapolitans, and Proper Scales." Paper delivered to the national meeting of the Society for Music Theory, Indianapolis.

Hamilton, Kenneth. 2009. "Beethoven's *Tempest* Sonata in Performance." In *Beethoven's Tempest Sonata: Perspectives of Analysis and Performance*, edited by Peter Berge, Jeroen D'hoe, and William Caplin, 127–62. Walpole: Peters.

Hansberry, Benjamin. 2017. "What Are Scale-Degree Qualia?" *Music Theory Spectrum* 39(2): 182–99.

Harrison, Daniel. 1988. "Some Group Properties of Triple Counterpoint and Their Influence on Compositions by J. S. Bach." *Journal of Music Theory* 32(1): 23–49.

Harrison, Daniel. 1994. *Harmonic Function in Tonal Music: A Renewed Dualist Theory and an Account of Its Precedents*. Chicago: University of Chicago Press.

Harrison, Daniel. 2003. "Rosalia, Aloysius, and Arcangelo: A Genealogy of the Sequence." *Journal of Music Theory* 47: 225–72.

Harrison, Daniel. 2016. *Pieces of Tradition: An Analysis of Contemporary Tonality*. New York: Oxford University Press.

## BIBLIOGRAPHY 589

Hasty, Christopher. 1981. "Segmentation and Process in Post-Tonal Music." *Music Theory Spectrum* 3: 54–73.

Hatten, Robert S. 2009. "Interpreting Beethoven's *Tempest* Sonata through Topics, Gestures, and Agency." In *Beethoven's Tempest Sonata: Perspectives of Analysis and Performance*, edited by Peter Berge, Jeroen D'hoe, and William Caplin, 163–80. Walpole: Peters.

Hatten, Robert S. 2014. "Performing Expressive Closure in Structurally Open Contexts: Chopin's Prelude in A minor and the Last Two Dances of Schumann's Davidsbündlertänze." *Music Theory Online* 20(4).

Headlam, David. 2012. Review of *A Geometry of Music. Music Theory Spectrum* 34(1): 123–43.

Hepokoski, James. 2009. "Approaching the First Movement of Beethoven's *Tempest* Sonata through Sonata Theory." In *Beethoven's Tempest Sonata: Perspectives of Analysis and Performance*, edited by Peter Berge, Jeroen D'hoe, and William Caplin, 181–212. Walpole: Peters.

Hepokoski, James. 2010. "Sonata Theory and Dialogic Form." In *Musical Form, Forms & Formenlehre: Three Methodological Reflections*, edited by Pieter Bergé, 71–89. Leuven: Leuven University Press.

Hepokoski, James. 2021. *A Sonata Theory Handbook.* New York: Oxford University Press.

Hepokoski, James, and Warren Darcy. 2006. *Elements of Sonata Theory: Norms, Types, and Deformations in the Late-Eighteenth-Century Sonata.* New York: Oxford University Press.

Hinton, Stephen. 2010. "The Emancipation of Dissonance: Schoenberg's Two Practices of Composition." *Music & Letters* 91(4): 568–79.

Hodes, Jeffrey. 2012. "A New Roman-Numeral Analyzer for Classical Music." Undergraduate thesis, Princeton University.

Hoffmann, E. T. A. 1989. *E. T. A. Hoffmann's Musical Writings.* Edited by David Charlton. Translated by Martyn Clarke. Cambridge: Cambridge University Press.

Holtmeier, Ludwig. 2007. "Heinichen, Rameau, and the Italian Thoroughbass Tradition: Concepts of Tonality and Chord in the Rule of the Octave." *Journal of Music Theory* 51(1): 5–49.

Holtmeier, Ludwig. 2011. Review of Robert Gjerdingen's *Music in the Galant Style. Eighteenth-Century Music* 8(2): 307–48.

Hook, Julian. 2002. "Uniform Triadic Transformations." *Journal of Music Theory* 46(1/2): 57–126.

Hook, Julian. 2003. "Signature Transformations." Paper presented to the national meeting of the Society for Music Theory, Madison.

Hook, Julian. 2008. "Signature Transformations." In *Music Theory and Mathematics: Chords, Collections, and Transformations*, edited by Jack Douthett, Martha M. Hyde, and Charles J. Smith, 137–60. Rochester, NY: University of Rochester Press.

Hook, Julian. 2011. "Spelled Heptachords." In *Mathematics and Computation in Music, Proceedings of the Third International Conference of the Society for Mathematics and Computation in Music*, edited by Carlos Agon, Emmanuel Amiot, Moreno Andreatta, Gérard Assayag, Jean Bresson, and John Mandereau, 84–97. New York: Springer.

Hook, Julian. 2020. "Generic Sequences and the Generic Tonnetz." *Journal of Music Theory* 64(1): 63–103.

Horn, Katelyn, and David Huron. 2015. "On the Changing Use of the Major and Minor Modes 1750–1900." *Music Theory Online* 21(1).

Horton, Julian. 2014. "Dialectics and Musical Analysis." In *Aesthetics of Music: Musicological Perspectives*, edited by Stephen Downes. New York: Routledge.

Huddleston, Rodney, and Geoffrey Pullum. 2002. *The Cambridge Grammar of the English Language.* Cambridge: Cambridge University Press.

Humphreys, David. 1997. "Something Borrowed." *Musical Times* 138(1853): 19–24.

Hunt, Graham G. 2014. "When Structure and Design Collide: The Three-Key Exposition Revisited." *Music Theory Spectrum* 36(2): 247–69.

Huovinen, Erkki. 2002. *Pitch-Class Constellations: Studies in the Perception of Tonal Centricity.* Turku: Acta musicologica Fennica.

Huron, David. 1991. "The Avoidance of Part-Crossing in Polyphonic Music: Perceptual Evidence and Musical Practice." *Music Perception* 9(1): 93–104.

590 BIBLIOGRAPHY

Huron, David. 2007a. *Sweet Anticipation: Music and the Psychology of Expectation*. Cambridge, MA: MIT Press.

Huron, David. 2007b. "On the Role of Embellishment Tones in the Perceptual Segregation of Concurrent Musical Parts." *Empirical Musicology Review* 2(4): 123–39.

Huron, David. 2016. *Voice Leading: The Science behind a Musical Art*. Cambridge, MA: MIT Press.

Imbrie, Andrew. 1973. "'Extra' Measures and Metrical Ambiguity in Beethoven." In *Beethoven Studies*, edited by Alan Tyson, 45–66. New York: W. W. Norton.

Jacoby, Nori, Eduardo A. Undurraga, Malinda J. McPherson, Joaquín Valdés, Tomás Ossandón, and Josh H. McDermott. 2019. "Universal and Non-Universal Features of Musical Pitch Perception Revealed by Singing." *Current Biology* 29: 3229–43.

Jander, Owen. 1996. "Genius in the Arena of Charlatanry: The First Movement of Beethoven's Tempest Sonata in Cultural Context." In *Musica Franca: Essays in Honor of Frank A. D'Accone*, edited by Irene Aim, Alyson McLamore, and Colleen Reardon, 585–630. Hillsdale: Pendragon Press.

Jeppesen, Knud. (1931) 1939. *Counterpoint: The Polyphonic Vocal Style of the Sixteenth Century*. Translated by Glen Haydon. Englewood Cliffs, NJ: Prentice Hall.

Jeppesen, Knud. (1944–1945) 1975. "Problems of the Pope Marcellus Mass." In *Palestrina: Pope Marcellus Mass*, edited and translated by Lewis Lockwood, 99–130. New York: W. W. Norton.

Jeppesen, Knud. (1946) 1970. *The Style of Palestrina and the Dissonance*. New York: Dover.

Jost, John, Laurie A. Rudman, Irene V. Blair, Dana R. Carney, Nilanjana Dasgupta, Jack Glaser, and Curtis D. Harding. 2009. "The Existence of Implicit Bias Is beyond Reasonable Doubt: A Refutation of Ideological and Methodological Objections and Executive Summary of Ten Studies That No Manager Should Ignore." *Research in Organizational Behavior* 29: 39–69.

Junod, Julien, Pierre Audétat, Carlos Agon, and Moreno Andreatta. 2009. "A Generalization of Diatonicism and the Discrete Fourier Transform as a Mean [*sic.*] for Classifying and Characterising Musical Scales." In *Mathematics and Computation in Music*, edited by Elaine Chew, Adrian Childs, and Ching-Hua Chuan, 166–79. New York: Springer.

Kant, Immanuel. (1788) 1997. *Critique of Practical Reason*. Edited and translated by Mary Gregor. Cambridge: Cambridge University Press.

Kant, Immanuel. (1790) 1970. *Critique of Judgment*. Translated by John Henry Bernard. New York: Free Press.

Katz, J., and David Pesetsky. 2011. "The Identity Thesis for Language and Music." Unpublished manuscript available at https://ling.auf.net/lingbuzz/000959.

Kerman, Joseph. 1981. *The Masses and Motets of William Byrd*. Berkeley: University of California Press.

Kinderman, William. 2009a. *Beethoven*. 2nd ed. New York: Oxford.

Kinderman, William. 2009b. "The First Movement of Beethoven's *Tempest* Sonata: Genesis, Form, and Dramatic Meaning." In *Beethoven's Tempest Sonata: Perspectives of Analysis and Performance*, edited by Peter Berge, Jeroen D'hoe, and William Caplin, 213–34. Walpole: Peters.

Kinderman, William, and Harold Krebs, eds. 1996. *The Second Practice of Nineteenth-Century Tonality*. Lincoln: University of Nebraska Press.

Kirlin, Phillip B. 2014. "A Probabilistic Model of Hierarchical Music Analysis." PhD diss., University of Massachusetts.

Kloss, Jürgen. 2012. "'. . . Tell Her to Make Me a Cambric Shirt': From the 'Elfin Knight' to 'Scarborough Fair.'" https://www.justanothertune.com/html/cambricshirt.html.

Klumpenhouwer, Henry. 1991. "A Generalized Model of Voice-Leading for Atonal Music." PhD diss., Harvard University.

Klumpenhouwer, Henry. 2011. "History and Structure in Cohn's *Audacious Euphony*." *Intégral* 25: 159–75.

Korte, Werner Fritz. 1929. *Die Harmonik des frühen XV. Jahrhunderts in ihrem Zusammenhang mit der Formtechnik*. Münster: Suhrbier & Bröcker.

Kostka, Stefan, and Dorothy Payne. 2003. *Tonal Harmony*. 4th ed. New York: Alfred A. Knopf.

Kramer, Lawrence. 1990. *Music as Cultural Practice: 1800–1900*. Berkeley: University of California Press.

Kramer, Lawrence. 2002. "Contesting Wagner: The *Lohengrin* Prelude and Anti-Anti-Semitism." *19th-Century Music* 25(2–3): 190–211.

Labov, William. 1975. "Empirical Foundations of Linguistic Theory." In *The Scope of American Linguistics*, edited by Robert Austerlitz, 77–134. Lisse: Peter de Ridder Press.

Laitz, Steven. 2008. *The Complete Musician*. New York: Oxford University Press.

Lalite, Philippe, Emmanuel Bigand, Joanna Kantor-Martynuska, and Charles Delbé. 2009. "On Listening to Atonal Variants of Two Piano Sonatas by Beethoven." *Music Perception* 26(3): 223–34.

Laukens, Dirk. 2019. *Jazz Guitar Chord Dictionary*. Antwerp: Jazz Guitar Online. Free ebook available from http://www.jazzguitar.be.

Lawrence, John Y. 2020. "Toward a Predictive Theory of Theme Types." *Journal of Music Theory* 64(1): 1–36.

Lendvai, Erno. 1971. *Bela Bartók: An Analysis of His Music*. London: Kahn and Averill.

Lerdahl, Fred. 1988. "Cognitive Constraints on Compositional Systems." In *Generative Processes in Music: The Psychology of Performance, Improvisation, and Composition*, edited by John Sloboda, 231–59. New York: Oxford University Press.

Lerdahl, Fred. 2001. *Tonal Pitch Space*. New York: Oxford University Press.

Lerdahl, Fred. 2020. *Composition and Cognition*. Berkeley: University of California Press.

Lerdahl, Fred, and Ray Jackendoff. 1983. *A Generative Theory of Tonal Music*. Cambridge, MA: MIT Press.

Lester, Joel. 1998. "J. S. Bach Teaches Us How to Compose: Four Pattern Preludes of the *Well-Tempered Clavier*." *College Music Symposium* 38: 33–46.

Levine, Mark. 1989. *The Jazz Piano Book*. Petaluma: Sher Music.

Levinson, Jerrold. 1997. *Music in the Moment*. Ithaca, NY: Cornell University Press.

Lewin, David. 1981. "A Way into Schoenberg's Opus 15, Number 7." *In Theory Only* 6(1): 3–24.

Lewin, David. 1984. "Amfortas's Prayer to Titurel and the Role of D in 'Parsifal': The Tonal Spaces of the Drama and the Enharmonic C♭/B." *19th-Century Music* 7(3): 336–49.

Lewin, David. 1986. "Music Theory, Phenomenology, and Modes of Perception." *Music Perception* 3(4): 327–92.

Lewin, David. 1987. *Generalized Musical Intervals and Transformations*. New Haven, CT: Yale University Press.

Lewin, David. 1990. "Klumpenhouwer Networks and Some Isographies That Involve Them." *Music Theory Spectrum* 12: 83–120.

Lewis, Christopher Orlo. 1983. "Tonality and Structure in the Ninth Symphony of Gustav Mahler." PhD diss., University of Rochester.

Lewis, Clive Staples. 1964. *The Discarded Image*. Cambridge: Cambridge University Press.

Liszt, Franz. 2016. *The Collected Writings of Franz Liszt*, vol. 3, part 2. Edited and translated by Janita R. Hall-Swadley. Lanham, MD: Rowman & Littlefield.

London, Justin. 2004. *Hearing in Time*. New York: Oxford University Press.

Long, Megan Kaes. 2018. "Cadential Syntax and Tonal Expectation in Late Sixteenth-Century Homophony." *Music Theory Spectrum* 40(1): 52–83.

Long, Megan Kaes. 2020. *Hearing Homophony*. New York: Oxford University Press.

Longyear, Rey M., and Kate R. Covington. 1988. "Sources of the Three-Key Exposition." *Journal of Musicology* 6(4): 448–70.

Lowinsky, Edward. 1961. *Tonality and Atonality in Sixteenth-Century Music*. Berkeley: University of California Press.

Lund, Jeb. 2014. "Is a Hot Dog a Sandwich? An Extended Meditation on the Nature of America." *Guardian*, July 3. Available at https://www.theguardian.com/commentisfree/2014/jul/03/is-a-hot-dog-a-sandwich-nature-america.

Mak, Su Yin. 2008. "Et in Arcadia Ego: The Elegiac Structure of Schubert's Quartettsatz in C Minor (D. 703)." In *The Unknown Schubert*, edited by Barbara M. Reul and Lorraine Byrne Bodley, 145–53. New York: Routledge.

Margolis, Eric, and Stephen Laurence. 2003. "Concepts." In *The Blackwell Guide to the Philosophy of Mind*, edited by Stephen P. Stich and Ted A. Warfield, 190–213. Oxford: Blackwell.

592  BIBLIOGRAPHY

Margulis, Elizabeth. 2013. *On Repeat*. New York: Oxford University Press.

Martin, Nathan John. 2010. Review of *Beethoven's 'Tempest' Sonata: Perspectives of Analysis and Performance. Theory and Practice* 35: 169–89.

Martin, Nathan John. 2018. "Schenker and/or Rameau." Paper presented to the national meeting of the Society for Music Theory, San Antonio.

Marvin, Elizabeth West, and Alexander Brinkman. 1999. "The Effect of Modulation and Formal Manipulation on Perception of Tonic Closure by Expert Listeners." *Music Perception* 16(4): 389–408.

Marvin, William. 2012–2013. " 'Und so weiter': Schenker, Sonata Theory, and the Problem of the Recapitulation." *Theory and Practice* 37–38: 221–40.

Marx, Adolf Bernhard. (1859) 1997. *Musical Form in the Age of Beethoven: Selected Writings on Theory and Method*. Translated by Scott Burnham. Cambridge: Cambridge University Press.

McClary, Susan. 1991. *Feminine Endings: Music, Gender, and Sexuality*. Minneapolis: University of Minnesota Press.

McClary, Susan. 2004. *Modal Subjectivities*. Berkeley: University of California Press.

McCreless, Patrick. 1996. "An Evolutionary Perspective on Nineteenth-Century Semitonal Relations." In *The Second Practice of Nineteenth-Century Tonality*, edited by William Kinderman and Harald Krebs, 87–113. Lincoln: University of Nebraska Press.

McCreless, Patrick. 2011. "Ownership, in Music and Music Theory." *Music Theory Online* 17(1).

McDermott, Josh, and Marc Hauser. 2005. "The Origins of Music: Innateness, Uniqueness, and Evolution." *Music Perception* 23(1): 29–59.

McEnery, Tony, and Andrew Wilson. 1996. *Corpus Linguistics*. Edinburgh: Edinburgh University Press.

McHose, Allen. 1947. *The Contrapuntal Harmonic Technique of the 18th Century*. New York: Crofts.

Meeùs, Nicolas. 2000. "Toward a Post-Schoenbergian Grammar of Tonal and Pre-Tonal Harmonic Progressions." *Music Theory Online* 6(1).

Meeùs, Nicolas. 2018. "Harmonic Vectors and the Constraints of Tonality." *Music Theory Online* 24(4).

Meier, Bernhard. 1988. *The Modes of Classical Vocal Polyphony: Described According to the Sources, with Revisions by the Author*. Translated by Ellen S. Beebe. London: Broude Brothers.

Meyer, Leonard. 1956. *Emotion and Meaning in Music*. Chicago: University of Chicago Press.

Meyer, Leonard. 1982. "Process and Morphology in the Music of Mozart." *Journal of Musicology* 1(1): 67–94.

Meyer, Leonard. 1996. *Style and Music*. Chicago: University of Chicago Press.

Milsom, John. 2005. "Imitatio, Intertextuality and Early Music." In *Citation and Authority in Medieval and Renaissance Musical Culture: Learning from the Learned*, edited by Suzannah Clark and Elizabeth Eva Leach, 141–51. Woodbridge: Boydell.

Mirka, Danuta. 2015. "The Mystery of the Cadential Six-Four." In *What Is a Cadence? Theoretical and Analytical Perspectives on Cadences in the Classical Repertoire*, edited by Markus Neuwirth and Pieter Bergé, 157–84. Leuven: Leuven University Press.

Moore, Alan. 2012. *Song Means: Analyzing and Interpreting Popular Song*. Burlington: Ashgate.

Moreno, Jairo. 1996. "Theoretical Reception of the Sequence and Its Conceptual Implications." PhD diss., Yale University.

Morgan, Robert. 1978. "Schenker and the Theoretical Tradition: The Concept of Musical Reduction." *College Music Symposium* 18(1): 72–96.

Morgan, Robert. 2014. *Becoming Heinrich Schenker*. Cambridge: Cambridge University Press.

Morris, Robert D. 1995. "Equivalence and Similarity in Pitch and Their Interaction with PCSet." *Journal of Music Theory* 39(2): 207–43.

Muns, Lodewijk. 2008. "Why I Am Not a Schenkerian." Unpublished manuscript available at https://lodewijkmuns.nl/WhyIamNotaSchenkerian.pdf.

Nápoles López, Néstor, Claire Arthur, and Ichiro Fujinaga. 2019. "Key-Finding Based on a Hidden Markov Model and Key Profiles." In *6th International Conference on Digital Libraries for Musicology*, 33–37. New York: Association for Computing Machinery.

Narmour, Eugene. 1988. "Melodic Structuring of Harmonic Dissonance: A Method for Analysing Chopin's Contribution to the Development of Harmony." In *Chopin Studies*, edited by Jim Samson, 77–114. Cambridge: Cambridge University Press.

National Research Council. 2014. *Identifying the Culprit: Assessing Eyewitness Identification*. Washington, DC: National Academies Press.

Navia, Gabriel Henrique Bianco. 2016. "The Medial Caesura in Schubert's Sonata Forms: Formal and Rhetorical Complications." PhD diss., University of Arizona.

Neff, Severine. 2012. "Schoenberg as Theorist." In *Schoenberg and His World*, edited by Walter Frisch, 55–84. Princeton: Princeton University Press.

Neumeyer, David. 1987. "The Ascending *Urlinie*." *Journal of Music Theory* 31(2): 275–303.

Newcomb, Anthony. 2007. "Marenzio's Riffs." In *Luca Marenzio e il madrigale romano*, edited by Franco Piperno, 115–43. Rome: Accademia Nazionale di Santa Cecilia.

Nicolas, Patrice. 2019. "Challenging Some Misconceptions about the *Règle de l'octave*." *Music Theory Online* 25(4).

Ninov, Dimitar. 2016. "Functional Nature of the Cadential Six-Four." *Musicological Annual* 52(1): 73–96.

Nobile, Drew. 2015. "Counterpoint in Rock Music: Unpacking the 'Melodic-Harmonic Divorce.'" *Music Theory Spectrum* 37(2): 189–203.

Nobile, Drew. 2016. "Harmonic Function in Rock Music: A Syntactic Approach." *Journal of Music Theory* 60(2): 149–80.

Nobile, Drew. 2020. "Double-Tonic Complexes in Rock Music." *Music Theory Spectrum* 42(2): 207–26.

Nolan, Catherine. 2003. "Combinatorial Space in Nineteenth- and Early Twentieth-Century Music Theory." *Music Theory Spectrum* 25(2): 205–41.

Okazaki, Miles. 2015. *Fundamentals of Guitar*. Fenton, MO: Mel Bay.

Osborn, Brad. 2017. "Rock Harmony Reconsidered: Tonal, Modal and Contrapuntal Voice-Leading Systems in Radiohead." *Music Analysis* 36(1): 59–93.

Palisca, Claude. 1956. "Vincenzo Galilei's Counterpoint Treatise: A Code for the *Seconda Pratica*." *Journal of the American Musicological Society* 9(2): 81–96.

Palisca, Claude. 1994. *Studies in the History of Italian Music and Music Theory*. New York: Oxford University Press.

Parncutt, Richard. 1988. "Revision of Terhardt's Psychoacoustical Model of the Root(s) of a Musical Chord." *Music Perception* 6: 65–94.

Perry, Jeffrey, and Paul Lansky. 1996. "The Inner Voices of Simple Things: A Conversation with Paul Lansky." *Perspectives of New Music* 34(2): 40–60.

Pinter, D. 2019. "The Magnificent Flat-Seventh." *Soundscapes* 22. Available at https://www.icce.rug.nl/~soundscapes/VOLUME22/Magnificent_flat-seventh.shtml.

Piston, Walter. 1941. *Harmony*. New York: W. W. Norton.

Powers, Harold. 1958. "Mode and Raga." *The Musical Quarterly* 44(4): 448–60.

Powers, Harold. 1981. "Tonal Types and Modal Categories in Renaissance Polyphony." *Journal of the American Musicological Society* 34(3): 428–70.

Powers, Harold. 1992a. "Is Mode Real? Pietro Aron, the Octenary System, and Polyphony." *Basler Jahrbuch für Historische Musikpraxis* 16: 9–52.

Powers, Harold. 1992b. "Modality as a European Cultural Construct." In *Secondo convegno europeo di analisi musicale: Atti*, edited by Rosanna Dalmonte and Mario Baroni, 207–20. Trento: Università degli studi di Trento, Dipartimento di storia della civiltà europea.

Proctor, Gregory. 2004. "A Schenkerian Look at Lully." *Journal of Seventeenth-Century Music* 10(1).

Putnam, Hilary. 1988. *Realism and Reason*. Cambridge: Cambridge University Press.

Quine, Willard van Orman. 1953. *From a Logical Point of View*. Cambridge, MA: Harvard University Press.

Quinn, Ian. 2005. "Harmonic Function without Primary Triads." Paper presented to the national meeting of the Society for Music Theory, Boston.

Quinn, Ian. 2018. "Tonal Harmony." In *The Oxford Handbook of Critical Concepts in Music Theory*, edited by Alexander Rehding and Steven Rings, 467–97. New York: Oxford University Press.

## BIBLIOGRAPHY

Rabinovitch, Gilad. 2018. "Gjerdingen's Schemata Reexamined." *Journal of Music Theory* 62(1): 41–84.

Rabinovitch, Gilad. 2019. "Implicit Counterpoint in Gjerdingen's Schemata." *Music Theory & Analysis* 6(1): 1–49.

Rabinovitch, Gilad. 2020. "Hidden Polyphony, Linear Hierarchy, and Scale-Degree Associations in Galant Schemata." *Indiana Theory Review* 36(1–2): 114–66.

Rameau, Jean Paul. (1722) 1971. *Treatise on Harmony*. Translated by Philip Gossett. New York: Dover.

Reef, John. 2020. "A 'Proto-Theme' in Some of J. S. Bach's Fugal Works." *Music Theory Online* 26(4).

Rehding, Alexander. 2009. *Music and Monumentality: Commemoration and Wonderment in Nineteenth-Century Germany*. New York: Oxford University Press.

Reti, Rudolf. 1951. *The Thematic Process in Music*. New York: Macmillan.

Reynolds, Christopher Alan. 2015. *Wagner, Schumann, and the Lessons of Beethoven's Ninth*. Berkeley: University of California Press.

Ricci, Adam. 2004. "A Theory of the Harmonic Sequence." PhD diss., University of Rochester.

Rice, John. 2015. "The Morte: A Galant Voice-Leading Schema as Emblem of Lament and Compositional Building-Block." *Eighteenth-Century Music* 12(2): 157–81.

Richards, Mark. 2010. "Closure in Classical Themes: The Role of Melody and Texture in Cadences, Closural Function, and the Separated Cadence." *Intersections: Canadian Journal of Music* 31(1): 25–45.

Richards, Mark. 2011. "Viennese Classicism and the Sentential Idea: Broadening the Sentence Paradigm." *Theory and Practice* 36: 179–224.

Richards, Mark. 2013a. "Beethoven and the Obscured Medial Caesura: A Study in the Transformation of Style." *Music Theory Spectrum* 35(2): 166–93.

Richards, Mark. 2013b. "Sonata Form and the Problem of Second-Theme Beginnings." *Music Analysis* 32(1): 3–45.

Richards, Mark. 2017. "Tonal Ambiguity in Popular Music's Axis Progressions." *Music Theory Online* 23(3).

Richter, Ernst Friedrich. 1852. *Die Grundzige der musikalischen Formen und ihre Analyse*. Leipzig: Georg Wigand.

Riemann, Hugo. 1896. *Harmony Simplified*. London: Augener.

Riemann, Hugo. 1903. *System der musikalischen Rhythmik und Metrik*. Leipzig: Breitkopf and Härtel.

Rings, Steven. 2011. *Tonality and Transformation*. New York: Oxford University Press.

Rings, Steven. 2013. "A Foreign Sound to Your Ear: Bob Dylan Performs 'It's Alright, Ma (I'm Only Bleeding),' 1964–2009." *Music Theory Online* 19(4).

Rohrmeier, Martin. 2011. "Towards a Generative Syntax of Tonal Harmony." *Journal of Mathematics and Music* 5(1): 35–53.

Rohrmeier, Martin. 2020. "The Syntax of Jazz Harmony: Diatonic Tonality, Phrase Structure, and Form." *Music Theory & Analysis* 7(1): 1–62.

Roig-Francolí, Miguel A. 2003. *Harmony in Context*. New York: McGraw-Hill.

Roig-Francolí, Miguel A. 2018. "From Renaissance to Baroque: Tonal Structures in Tomás Luis de Victoria's Masses." *Music Theory Spectrum* 40(1): 27–51.

Rosch, Eleanor. 1978. "Principles of Categorization." In *Cognition and Categorization*, edited by Eleanor Rosch and Barbara Bloom Lloyd, 28–49. Hillsdale, NJ: Erlbaum.

Rosen, Charles. 1971. *The Classical Style*. New York: W. W. Norton.

Rosen, Charles. 1988. *Sonata Forms*. New York: W. W. Norton.

Rosen, Charles. 1998. *The Romantic Generation*. Cambridge, MA: Harvard University Press.

Rosen, Charles. 2001. *Critical Entertainments*. Cambridge, MA: Harvard University Press.

Rotem, Elam, and Peter Schubert. 2021. "Stretto fuga—How to Make a Masterpiece out of Two Intervals." Video, 17:50. https://youtu.be/zGZjzBvXCzg.

Rothenberg, David. 1978. "A Model for Pattern Perception with Musical Applications. Part I: Pitch Structures as Order-Preserving Maps." *Mathematical Systems Theory* 11: 199–234.

Rothgeb, John. 1975. "Strict Counterpoint and Tonal Theory." *Journal of Music Theory* 19(2): 260–84.

Rothgeb, John. 1996. "Re: Eytan Agmon on Functional Theory." *Music Theory Online* 2(1).

Rothstein, William. 1989. *Phrase Rhythm in Tonal Music*. New York: Schirmer.

Rothstein, William. 2009. "Riding the Storm Clouds: Tempo, Rhythm, and Meter in Beethoven's *Tempest* Sonata." In *Beethoven's* Tempest *Sonata: Perspectives of Analysis and Performance*, edited by Peter Berge, Jeroen D'hoe, and William Caplin, 235–72. Walpole: Peters.

Rowe, Dorothy. 1983. *Depression: The Way Out of Your Prison*. New York: Routledge and Kegan Paul.

Russell, Jonathan. 2018. "Harmony and Voice-Leading in *The Rite of Spring*." PhD diss., Princeton University.

Sailor, Malcolm, and Andie Sigler. 2017. "The Insufficiently Stimulated Ear: A Corpus Study of Dissonance Treatment from DuFay to Victoria." Paper presented to the national meeting of the Society for Music Theory, Arlington.

Salzer, Felix. (1952) 1962. *Structural Hearing*. New York: Dover.

Salzer, Felix. 1983. "Heinrich Schenker and Historical Research: Monteverdi's Madrigal Oimè, se tanto amate." In *Aspects of Schenkerian Theory*, edited by David Beach, 135–52. New Haven, CT: Yale University Press.

Samarotto, Frank. 2004. "Sublimating Sharp 4: An Exercise in Schenkerian Energetics." *Music Theory Online* 10(3).

Sanguinetti, Giorgio. 2012. *The Art of Partimento*. New York: Oxford University Press.

Saslaw, Janna. 1992. "Gottfried Weber and the Concept of *Mehrduetigkeit*." PhD diss., Columbia University.

Savage, Patrick E., Steven Brown, Emi Sakai, and Thomas E. Currie. 2015. "Statistical Universals Reveal the Structures and Functions of Human Music." *Proceedings of the National Academy of Sciences* 112(29): 8987–92.

Savage, Patrick, Adam Tierney, and Annirudh Patel. 2017. "Global Music Recordings Support the Motor Constraint Hypothesis for Human and Avian Song Contour." *Music Perception* 34(3): 327–34.

Schachter, Carl. 1990. "Either/Or." In *Schenker Studies*, edited by Heidi Siegel, 165–80. Cambridge: Cambridge University Press.

Schachter, Carl. 2016. *The Art of Tonal Analysis*. Edited by Joseph Straus. New York: Oxford University Press.

Schenker, Heinrich. (1910) 1987. *Counterpoint*, vol. 1. Edited by John Rothgeb. Translated by John Rothgeb and Jürgen Thym. New York: Schirmer.

Schenker, Heinrich. (1921–1923) 2004. *Der Tonwille: Pamphlets in Witness of the Immutable Laws of Music*, vol. 1. Edited by William Drabkin. Translated by Ian Bent, William Drabkin, Joseph Dubiel, Timothy Jackson, Joseph Lubben, and Robert Snarrenberg. New York: Oxford University Press.

Schenker, Heinrich. (1923–1924) 2005. *Der Tonwille: Pamphlets in Witness of the Immutable Laws of Music*, vol. 2. Edited by William Drabkin. Translated by Ian Bent, William Drabkin, Joseph Dubiel, Joseph Lubben, William Renwick, and Robert Snarrenberg. New York: Oxford University Press.

Schenker, Heinrich. (1926) 1996. *The Masterwork in Music*, vol. 2. Edited by William Drabkin. Translated by Ian Bent, William Drabkin, John Rothgeb, and Heidi Siegel. Cambridge: Cambridge University Press.

Schenker, Heinrich. (1930) 1997. *The Masterwork in Music*, vol. 3. Edited by William Drabkin. Translated by Alfred Clayton and Derrick Puffett. Cambridge: Cambridge University Press.

Schenker, Heinrich. (1933) 1969. *Five Graphical Music Analyses*. Translated by Felix Salzer. New York: Dover.

Schenker, Heinrich. (1935) 1979. *Free Composition*. Edited and translated by Ernst Oster. New York: Longman.

Scherer, Josh. 2015. "A Bro and a Philosopher Debate the True Meaning of a Sandwich." https://firstwefeast.com/eat/2015/04/philosophy-of-meat-bread.

## 596 BIBLIOGRAPHY

Schindler, Anton. 1840. *Biographie von Ludwig van Beethoven*. Münster: Achendorff.

Schindler, Anton. 1841. *The Life of Beethoven*. Translated by Ignaz Moscheles. London: Henry Colburn.

Schindler, Anton. (1860) 1996. *Beethoven as I Knew Him*. Edited by Donald W. MacArdle. Translated by Constance S. Jolly. Mineola: Dover.

Schmalfeldt, Janet. 1991. "Towards a Reconciliation of Schenkerian Concepts with Traditional and Recent Theories of Form." *Music Analysis* 10(3): 233–87.

Schmalfeldt, Janet. 1995. "Form as the Process of Becoming: The Beethoven-Hegelian Tradition and the *Tempest* Sonata." *Beethoven Forum* 4: 37–71.

Schmalfeldt, Janet. 2011. *In the Process of Becoming*. New York: Oxford University Press.

Schoenberg, Arnold. (1911) 1983. *Theory of Harmony*. Berkeley: University of California Press.

Schoenberg, Arnold. 1984. *Style and Idea*. Edited by Leonard Stein. Translated by Leo Black. Berkeley: University of California Press.

Schubert, Peter. 2008. *Modal Counterpoint, Renaissance Style*. New York: Oxford University Press.

Schubert, Peter. 2018. "Thomas Campion's 'Chordal Counterpoint' and Tallis's Famous Forty-Part Motet." *Music Theory Online* 24(1).

Schuijer, Michiel. 2008. *Analyzing Atonal Music: Pitch-Class Set Theory and Its Contents*. Rochester, NY: University of Rochester Press.

Segall, Christopher. 2010. "K-Nets, Inversion, and Gravitational Balance." *Theory and Practice* 35: 119–45.

Segall, Christopher. 2014. "Sergei Taneev's Vertical-Shifting Counterpoint: An Introduction." *Music Theory Online* 20(3).

Sewell, Ian. 2021. "When All You Have Is a Hammer: Surface/Depth as Good Comparison." *Music Theory Spectrum* 43(2): 197–220.

Shepard, Roger. 1964. "Circularity in Judgements of Relative Pitch." *Journal of the Acoustical Society of America* 36(12): 2346–53.

Simmons, Joseph P., Leif D. Nelson, and Uri Simonsohn. 2011. "False-Positive Psychology: Undisclosed Flexibility in Data Collection and Analysis Allows Presenting Anything as Significant." *Psychological Science* 22(11): 1359–66.

Simon, Herbert, and Kenneth Kotovsky. 1963. "Human Acquisition of Concepts for Sequential Patterns." *Psychological Review* 70(6): 534–46.

Simon, Herbert, and Richard Sumner. 1968. "Pattern in Music." In *Formal Representation of Human Judgment*, edited by Benjamin Kleinmuntz, 219–50. New York: Wiley.

Slottow, Steven. 2018. "To Be or Not to Be: Schenker's Versus Schenkerian Attitudes towards Sequences." *Gamut: Online Journal of the Music Theory Society of the Mid-Atlantic* 8(1).

Smith, Charles. 1986. "The Functional Extravagance of Chromatic Chords." *Music Theory Spectrum* 8: 94–139.

Smith, Charles. 1996. "Musical Form and Fundamental Structure: An Investigation of Schenker's *Formenlehre*." *Music Analysis* 15: 191–92.

Smith, Peter. 1994. "Brahms and Schenker: A Mutual Response to Sonata Form." *Music Theory Spectrum* 16: 77–71.

Smith, Peter. 2006. "Harmonic Cross-Reference and the Dialectic of Articulation and Continuity in Sonata Expositions of Schubert and Brahms." *Journal of Music Theory* 50(2): 143–79.

Sommer, Heinz-Dieter. 1986. "Beethovens kleine Pastorale Zum 1. Satz der Klaviersonate op. 28." *Archiv für Musikwissenschaft* 43(2): 109–27.

Sprick, Jan Philipp. 2018. "Sequences: Between Affirmation and Destruction of Tonality." *Music Theory Online* 24(4).

Stein, Beverly. 2002. "Carissimi's Tonal System and the Function of Transposition in the Expansion of Tonality." *Journal of Musicology* 19(2): 264–305.

Stephenson, Kenneth. 2002. *What to Listen for in Rock: A Stylistic Analysis*. New Haven, CT: Yale University Press.

Strunk, Oliver. 1950. *Source Readings in Music History*. New York: W. W. Norton.

Stuckenschmidt, Hans Heinz. 1965. "Debussy or Berg? The Mystery of a Chord Progression." *The Musical Quarterly* 51(3): 453–59.

Subotnik, Rose Rosengard. 1991. *Developing Variations: Style and Ideology in Western Music*. Minneapolis: University of Minnesota Press.

Sutcliffe, W. Dean. 2003. *The Keyboard Sonatas of Domenico Scarlatti and Eighteenth-Century Musical Style*. Cambridge: Cambridge University Press.

Swinden, Kevin. 2005. "When Functions Collide: Aspects of Plural Function in Chromatic Music." *Music Theory Spectrum* 27(2): 249–82.

Taneyev, Sergei. (1909) 1962. *Convertible Counterpoint in the Strict Style*. Translated by G. Ackley Brower. Boston: Bruce Humphries.

Taruskin, Richard. 2005. *The Oxford History of Western Music*. New York: Oxford University Press.

Taylor, Benedict. 2019. *Towards a Harmonic Grammar of Grieg's Late Piano Music*. New York: Routledge.

Telesco, Paula J. 1998. "Enharmonicism and the Omnibus Progression in Classical-Era Music." *Music Theory Spectrum* 20(2): 242–79.

Temperley, David. 2006. Review of *Music in the Galant Style*. *Journal of Music Theory* 50(2): 277–90.

Temperley, David. 2007. "The Melodic-Harmonic 'Divorce' in Rock." *Popular Music* 26(2): 323–42.

Temperley, David. 2008. "Hypermetrical Transitions." *Music Theory Spectrum* 30(2): 305–25.

Temperley, David. 2011a. "Composition, Perception, and Schenkerian Theory." *Music Theory Spectrum* 33(2):146–68.

Temperley, David. 2011b. "The Cadential IV in Rock." *Music Theory Online* 17(1).

Temperley, David. 2018. *The Musical Language of Rock*. New York: Oxford University Press.

Thayer, Alexander Wheelock. 1967. *Thayer's Life of Beethoven*. Edited by Elliot Forbes. Princeton: Princeton University Press.

Theune, Michael. 2007. *Structure & Surprise: Engaging Poetic Turns*. New York: Teachers & Writers Collaborative.

Thomas, Keith. 1971. *Religion and the Decline of Magic*. New York: Scribner.

Tierney, Adam, Frank Russo, and Annirudh Patel. 2008. "Empirical Comparisons of Pitch Patterns in Music, Speech, and Birdsong." *The Journal of the Acoustical Society of America* 123: 3721.

Tierney, Adam, Frank Russo, and Annirudh Patel. 2011. "The Motor Origins of Human and Avian Song Structure." *Proceedings of the National Academy of Sciences of the United States of America* 108(37): 15510–15.

Tomlinson, Gary. 1990. *Monteverdi and the End of the Renaissance*. Berkeley: University of California Press.

Tovey, Donald. (1935) 1981. *Symphonies and Other Orchestral Works: Essays in Musical Analysis*. New York: Oxford University Press.

Tovey, Donald. 1931. *A Companion to Beethoven's Pianoforte Sonatas*. London: Associated Board of the Royal Schools of Music.

Trippet, David. 2010. "Liszt on Lohengrin (or: Wagner in absentia)." *The Wagner Journal* 4(1): 4–21.

Tymoczko, Dmitri. 2003. "Progressions Fondamentales, Functions, Degrés, une Grammaire de l'Harmonie Tonale Élémentaire." *Musurgia* 10(3–4): 35–64.

Tymoczko, Dmitri. 2004. "Scale Networks in Debussy." *Journal of Music Theory* 48(2): 215–92.

Tymoczko, Dmitri. 2008. "Scale Theory, Serial Theory, and Voice Leading." *Music Analysis* 27(1): 1–49.

Tymoczko, Dmitri. 2011a. *A Geometry of Music*. New York: Oxford University Press.

Tymoczko, Dmitri. 2011b. "Dualism and the Beholder's Eye." In *The Oxford Handbook of Riemannian and Neo-Riemannian Music Theories*, edited by Ed Gollin and Alex Rehding, 246–67. New York: Oxford University Press.

Tymoczko, Dmitri. 2020a. "Review-Essay on Fred Lerdahl's *Composition and Cognition*." *Music Theory Online* 26(1).

Tymoczko, Dmitri. 2020b. "Why Topology?" *Journal of Mathematics and Music* 14(2): 1–56.

Tymoczko, Dmitri. 2023. "Hierarchical Set Theory." *Journal of Mathematics and Music* 17(2): 282–90.

598 BIBLIOGRAPHY

Tymoczko, Dmitri, and Jason Yust. 2019. "Fourier Phase and Pitch-Class Sum." In *Proceedings of the 7th International Conference of Mathematics and Computation in Music*, edited by Mariana Montiel, Francisco Gómez-Martín, and Octavio A. Agustín-Aquino, 46–58. New York: Springer.

Vande Moortele, Steven. 2009. "The First Movement of Beethoven's *Tempest* Sonata and the Tradition of Twentieth-Century *Formenlehre*." In *Beethoven's* Tempest *Sonata: Perspectives of Analysis and Performance*, edited by Peter Berge, Jeroen D'hoe, and William Caplin, 293–314. Walpole: Peters.

Varricchio, David J., and Frankie D. Jackson. 2016. "Reproduction in Mesozoic Birds and Evolution of the Modern Avian Reproductive Mode." *The Auk* 133(4): 654–84.

Vicentino, Nicola. (1555) 1996. *Ancient Music Adapted to Modern Practice*. Edited by Claude V. Palisca. Translated by Maria Rika Maniates. New Haven, CT: Yale University Press.

Von Hippel, P., and David Huron. 2000. "Why Do Skips Precede Reversals? The Effect of Tessitura on Melodic Structure." *Music Perception* 18: 59–85.

Wagner, Napthali. 2003. "'Domestication' of Blue Notes in the Beatles' Songs." *Music Theory Spectrum* 25(2): 353–65.

Wagner, Richard. 1907. *Richard Wagner's Prose Works*, vol. 3. Translated by William Ashton Ellis. London: Kegan, Paul.

Waltham-Smith, Naomi. 2018. "Sequence." In *The Oxford Handbook of Critical Concepts in Music Theory*, edited by Alexander Rehding and Steven Rings, 577–601. New York: Oxford University Press.

Warfield, Patrick. 2011. "The March as Musical Drama and the Spectacle of John Philip Sousa." *Journal of the American Musicological Society* 64(2): 289–318.

Watkins, Holly. 2017. "Toward a Post-Humanist Organicism." *Nineteenth-Century Music Review* 14: 93–114.

Weber, Gottfried. (1817–1821) 1846. *Theory of Musical Composition*. Translated by James F. Warner. Boston: Wilkins, Carter, and Company, and O. C. B. Carter.

Webster, James. 1978. "Schubert's Sonata Form and Brahms's First Maturity." *19th-Century Music* 2(1): 18–35.

Webster, James. 2010. "Formenlehre in Theory and Practice." In *Musical Form, Forms & Formenlehre: Three Methodological Reflections*, edited by Pieter Bergé, 123–39. Leuven: Leuven University Press.

Wellwood, Alexis, Roumyana Pancheva, Valentine Hacquard, and Colin Phillips. 2018. "The Anatomy of a Comparative Illusion." *Journal of Semantics* 35(3): 543–83.

Westergaard, Peter. 1975. *An Introduction to Tonal Theory*. New York: W. W. Norton.

Wiering, Franz. 2001. *The Language of the Modes: Studies in the History of Polyphonic Modality*. New York: Routledge.

Wittgenstein, Ludwig. 1953. *Philosophical Investigations*. Edited by G. E. M. Anscombe and R. Rhees. Translated by G. E. M. Anscombe. Oxford: Blackwell.

Wolff, Christoph. 2001. *Johann Sebastian Bach: The Learned Musician*. New York: W. W. Norton.

Wootton, David. 2015. *The Invention of Science*. New York: HarperCollins.

Yellin, Victor. 1998. *The Omnibus Idea*. Warren, MI: Harmonie Park Press.

Yust, Jason. 2009. "The Step-Class Automorphism Group in Tonal Analysis." In *Mathematics and Computation in Music: MCM 2007*, edited by T. Klouche and T. Noll, 512–520. New York: Springer.

Yust, Jason. 2015a. "Distorted Continuity: Chromatic Harmony, Uniform Sequences, and Quantized Voice Leadings." *Music Theory Spectrum* 37(1): 120–43.

Yust, Jason. 2015b. "Voice-Leading Transformation and Generative Theories of Tonal Structure." *Music Theory Online* 21(4).

Yust, Jason. 2018. *Organized Time: Rhythm, Tonality, and Form*. New York: Oxford University Press.

Zarlino, Gioseffo. (1558) 1968. *The Art of Counterpoint*. Translated by Guy A. Marco and Claude V. Palisca. New Haven, CT: Yale University Press.

Zarlino, Gioseffo. (1558) 1983. *On the Modes*. Edited by Claude V. Palisca. Translated by Vered Cohen. New Haven, CT: Yale University Press.

Zbikowski, Lawrence M. 2017. *Foundations of Musical Grammar*. New York: Oxford University Press.

# Index

*For the benefit of digital users, indexed terms that span two pages (e.g., 52-53) may, on occasion, appear on only one of those pages.*

Notes are indicated by "n" following the page number. Figures are indicated by *f* following the page number.

Aarden, Bret  130–31, 131n.41
AC/DC
  "Back in Black"  61, 527
Acuff, Roy and his Smokey Mountain
    Boys  83–84
aggregate (chromatic)  15, 42, 45–46, 366–67,
    401, 527
Agmon, Eytan  75n.34, 117n.19, 362n.2, 374n.10
Alberti bass  205, 206n.5, 408–9
Aldwell, Edward  237n.49
Allsop, Peter  334n.36
alphabet, musical  15n.15, 25*f*, 206–7, 250–51,
    411
Anderson, Laurie
  "O Superman"  384
Andriessen, Louis
  *De Staat*  179–81, 180*f*
Armstrong, Louis  37, 189, 250–51
  "West End Blues"  38*f*, 189*f*
Arndt, Matthew  21n.36, 170n.20, 248n.67,
    407n.1, 431n.33
Arthur, Claire  211n.6
Artusi, Giovanni  226–27, 234, 235, 249
Ashley, Clarence "Tom"
  "Rising Sun Blues"  83–84, 83*f*, 248–49
Auerbach, Brent  486n.54
"Autumn Leaves" (Kosma)  138–40

Babbitt, Milton  3, 136n.46, 222–23
Bach, C. P. E.  113n.14, 120n.21, 154n.4,
    281n.45, 344, 354–55, 409
Bach, J. S.  3, 16n.20, 27–28, 34, 141, 154n.4,
    161–62, 168*f*, 173–75, 173n.22, 175*f*,
    181–83, 182*f*, 188, 190, 203, 209n.9,
    210–11, 215n.15, 218–20, 223–24,
    224*f*, 237–39, 257, 258–59, 259*f*, 291,
    Ch. 7 (prelude), §7.3, 334*f*, 335n.38,
    336–40 §7.7, 371n.7, 388n.27, 391,
    392*f*, 412–13, 451, 453, 527, 573n.10
  Brandenburg Concerto No. 5  331–32, 332*f*,
    429n.28, 510–11

Cello Suite No. 1 in G major  188–89, 189*f*,
    355–56, 356*f*, 379n.13
chorales  28*f*, 118n.20 §3.6, 144n.53, 208*f*, 217*f*,
    218*f*, 225*f*, 238*f*, 254*f*, 279–82, 281*f*, 307*f*,
    311–12, 312*f*, 314*f*, 329*f*, 387n.24, 413*f*,
    415*f*, 434*f*, 436, 437*f*, 569–71, 570*f*, 572n.7
  "Ach, lieben Christen, seid getrost" §7.7*c*
  "Es woll uns Gott genädig sein"  77*f*
  "Ich dank' dich, lieber Herr"  128, 129*f*
  "Jesu, du mein liebstes Leben"  304–5, 305*f*
  "Was mein Gott will, das g'scheh
    allzeit"  181–83, 183*f*
  computational imitation of  412–13, 414*f*
  dualism of § 7.7
  Partita in B♭  204*f*
two-part inventions
  C major §7.7*a*,  562*f*
  D minor  204*f*, 305–6, 306*f*
  F major  348n.55, 379n.13
*The Well-Tempered Clavier*  23–24, 24*f*,
    144n.53, 173n.22, 176n.23, 177–78,
    190n.31, 371n.7, 379n.13, 409
Book I:
  Fugue in C minor  166*f*, 338*f*
  Fugue in E minor  162–63, 163*f*
  Fugue in F major  186–87, 187*f*
  Fugue in A♭ major  327–28, 328*f*
  Fugue in G♯ minor  157*f*
  Fugue in A minor  418*f*, 563n.14
  Fugue in B♭ major  237*f*
  Fugue in B♭ minor  27*f*, 191*f*
  Prelude in C major  13, 355–56, 355*f*
  Prelude in C♯ major §7.7*b*, 379n.13
  Prelude in D major §7.3, 379n.13, 426n.25
  Prelude in G major C5.0F3 *f*, 336n.41
  Prelude in A major  317*f*
  Prelude in B♭ major  434–35n.39
Book 2:
  Fugue in C major  169*f*, 379n.13
  Fugue in C♯ minor  171–72, 173*f*
  Fugue in E major  141n.49

## 600 INDEX

Bach, J. S. (*cont.*)
    Fugue in F major  141n.49, 177*f*, 556*f*
    Fugue in F♯ minor  169*f*, 305n.11, 350n.60
    Fugue in B♭ major  237*f*
    Fugue in B minor  §7.7d
    Prelude in C minor  144n.52
    Prelude in E minor  158*f*, 167*f*
BaileyShea, Matthew  444n.55
"The Ballad of the Green Berets" (Sadler and
    Moore)  82–83
Balzano, Gerald  394n.29
Barry, Barbara  504–5n.68, 511n.77
Bass, Richard  158n.4, 178n.25
Beach, Amy
    "Fire-Flies" (Op. 15, no. 4)  189–90, 190*f*
Beach, David  221n.20, 253n.3, 380n.14,
    511n.77, 514n.82
The Beatles  76, 147–48, 148*f*, 339n.44
    "A Day in the Life"  71–72
    "Eight Days a Week"  10–11, 11n.11, 58–59,
        147–48
    "Here Comes the Sun"  71–72
    "I'm a Loser"  63–64
    "She Loves You"  148n.58
    "With a Little Help from My Friends"  78–79,
        78*f*, 147–48
    "You Never Give Me Your
        Money"  339n.44
    "You Won't See Me"  66, 66*f*
Beethoven, Ludwig van  3, 17, 20n.31, 23–24,
    33, 34, Ch. 4 (prelude), 159–60, 172–73,
    188, 197*f*, 200–1, 206n.5, 241, 258–59,
    267–68, 291, 295, 311, 314–15, 345,
    380 §9.4, 448n.65, Ch. 10 (prelude),
    Ch. 10, 527
    Piano Sonata, Op. 2, no. 1  107–9, 108*f*,
        110–11, 144–46, 145*f*, 378, 379*f*,
        444n.55, 460, 462*f*, 466–67, 470*f*
    Piano Sonata Op. 2, no. 2  442n.51, 466–67,
        467*f*, 497n.64
    Piano Sonata Op. 2, no. 3  208*f*, 383*f*, 469*f*
    Piano Sonata Op.7, no. 1  376n.12
    Piano Sonata Op.10, no. 1  144n.53,
        166n.13, 454*f*
    Piano Sonata Op. 10, no. 2  471*f*
    Piano Sonata Op. 10, no. 3  177–79, 178*f*,
        179*f*, 461–63, 464*f*, 486n.55
    Piano Sonata Op. 13 (*Pathétique*) Ch. 4
        (prelude), 160*f*, 167–68, 167n.14,
        198–200, 201–2, 376–77, 377*f*, 460,
        463*f*, 483
    Piano Sonata Op. 22  320*f* §9.4
    Piano Sonata Op. 26  105–6, 106*f*
    Piano Sonata Op. 27, no. 1  100*f*

    Piano Sonata Op. 28 (*Pastorale*)  436n.42,
        458 §10.5, 504–5n.68, 507–8, 509–10,
        522
    Piano Sonata Op. 31, no. 1  63–64, 461–63,
        464*f*, 465*f*
    Piano Sonata Op. 31, no. 2 (*Tempest*)  169–70,
        376n.12, 451, 452*f*, 454n.8, 458 §10.3,
        482, 486–88, 489–90, 504
    Piano Sonata Op. 31, no. 3  C8P23
        n.12,  439*f*, 440–42, 442*f*, 486n.55
    Piano Sonata Op. 49, no. 2  382*f*
    Piano Sonata Op. 53 (*Waldstein*)  63–64,
        132–36, 408–9, 451, 452*f*, 453, 453*f*,
        460n.7, 483–84, 491, 516, 520, 521–22,
        522*f*, 526
    Piano Sonata Op. 54  10*f*, 204*f*
    Piano Sonata Op. 57 (*Appassionata*)  461*f*
    Piano Sonata Op. 79  439*f*
    Piano Sonata Op. 81a (*Lebewohl*)  224–26,
        240
    Piano Sonata Op. 90  469*f*
    Piano Sonata, Op. 106
        (*Hammerklavier*)  186–87, 187*f*,
        320n.13, 361n.1, 438–39, 441*f*, 471–72,
        471*f*, 476–77
    Piano Sonata Op. 109  §9.4,  437–38, 466–67,
        467*f*, 542–43, 543*f*
    String Quartet Op. 18, no. 3  461*f*
    String Quartet Op. 59, no. 1  144*f*, 170n.19
    String Quartet Op. 59, no. 2  194, 376–77,
        377*f*
    String Quartet Op. 59, no. 3  142*f*
    String Quartet Op. 127  20n.30
    String Quartet Op. 130  470*f*
    String Quartets Op. 18  331n.29, 380–82
    Symphony No. 1  194–95n.35, 429, 430*f*
    Symphony No. 2  142n.51, 173n.22, 460n.7,
        467n.14, 478, 478n.36, 503n.67
    Symphony No. 3 (*Eroica*)  175*f*, 240, 460n.7,
        467n.14, 469, 470*f*, 489n.56
    Symphony No. 5  194, 454n.9, 458, 460n.7
        §10.4, 504, 524
    "Knock of Fate"  454n.9, 482, 491, 492
    Symphony No. 7  5*f*, 207*f*
    Symphony No. 9  240, 241*f*, Ch. 8 (prelude),
        374–75, 396–97, 481n.42, 524,
        524n.93
    Trio, Op. 1, no. 3  §4.10
    Violin Concerto, Op. 61  486n.55
    Violin Sonata, Op. 23  101–2, 101*f*
    Violin Sonata, Op. 30, no. 2  486n.55
    Violin Sonata, Op. 47 (*Kreutzer*)  460n.8
Bent, Margaret  258n.5, 269n.23, 271–72,
    274n.30, 279–82

INDEX   601

Bernhard, Christoph 204n.2, 221n.20, 227n.31, 235n.46, 236n.47
Bernstein, Leonard 435n.40, 486–88
   *The Joy of Music* 451
Besseler, Heinrich 257n.1
Biamonte, Nicole 66n.23, 335n.38, 471n.17
von Bingen, Hildegard
   "Laus Trinitati" 388, 389*f*
*The Blues Brothers* 449–50
Bobbitt, Richard 259n.7
Bologne, Joseph, Chevalier de
      Saint-Georges 334*f*
Boone, Graeme 262n.14
Boretz, Benjamin 223n.23
Boyce, Tommy and Hart, Bobby
   "Steppin' Stone" 72–74, 73*f*
Brahms, Johannes 23, 227, 291, 448n.65, 453, 526, 572n.7
   *Fantasien* Op. 116, no. 2 176n.23
   *Klavierstücke* Op. 76, no. 4 335n.39
   Piano Quartet, Op. 60 491n.59
   Symphony No. 4 320n.13
   *Vier ernste Gesänge* Op. 121, no. 3 320n.13
   Violin Sonata in G major, Op. 78 332–33, 333*f*
Brewer, William 402n.1
Brinkman, Alexander 16n.17, 291n.51, 362n.2, 404n.6, 447n.60
Brody, Christopher 439n.48, 447n.59
Brothomstates (Lassi Nikko) 404
   *Claro,* 405*f*
Brown, Matthew 20n.32, 35n.57, 436n.41
Bruce, Robert 504–5n.68, 507n.70
Buelow, George 113n.14, 120n.21, 281n.45
Bukofzer, Manfred 257n.1
Bunting, Edward 83n.47
Burke, Edmund 452–53n.3, 504
Burnham, Scott 448n.65, 455n.10, 457–58, 472n.21, 476n.32
Burns, Lori 387n.24
Burstein, L. Poundie 20n.30, 21n.34, 35n.56, 205n.4, 350n.58
Byrd, William
   Mass in Three Voices 121*f*, 124, 211–12, 390n.28
Byros, Vasili 16, 29n.52, 74, 77n.37, 356, 449n.70, 478n.36

cadence 19–21, 28, 30, 61–63, 99–101, 211n.6, 218, 219*f*, 233, 254*f*, 258n.4, 261–62, 265, 266, 267*f*, 270–74, 276n.33, 283*f*, 287*f*, 290, 296–97, 302, 348–49, 349n.57, 377–78, 380, 386*f*, 422n.20, 437–39, 438*f*, 442, 443,
   449n.71, 455–56, 473–75, 476–77, 477n.35, 477*f*
   as harmonic cycle 413–14
   authentic 388–89, 521–22
   converging 102–3, 151–52, 201–2, 377*f*, 519–20, 529–30
   deceptive 253, 265, 270–74, 290, 321n.15
   final 412, 414
   half 78, 265, 290, 444*f*
   mixolydian 306–8
   perfect authentic 510–11
   Phrygian 301–2, 385–86, 388–89, 520, 521–22
   Renaissance 256n.9, 279n.42, 569
   Schenkerian interpretation 416–18, 418*f*
caesura 377–78
   filled 453–54, 454*f*, 455*f*
   medial 17, 20, 380–82, 449, 451, 453–54, 454*f*, 455*f*, 455–56, 473–75, 476, 483–84, 496, 504–5, 508–9, 516*f*, 516–17
Callahan, Homer
   "Rounder's Luck" 83–84
Callender, Clifton 155n.2, 536n.4, 542n.11
Camp, Elizabeth 52n.6, 234n.43
Campion, Thomas 91, 91*f*
Caplin, William 20, 21–22, 116n.17, 151n.1, 333n.34, 334n.37, 340n.47, 414n.9, 415n.11, 439–42, 443n.52, 444n.55, 448, 455–56, 457n.2, 475n.27, 477–78, 477n.34, 478n.38, 483n.50
The Carter Family 269
Carthy, Martin 85
Cavett-Dunsby, Esther 472n.20
centricity 68, 148–49, 247–48, 275, 288–90, 299, 322n.16, 384, 390–91, 416–17, 434
Ceulmans, Anne-Emmanuelle 385n.18
Chafe, Eric 229–11nn.35–6, 235n.45
Chopin, Frederic 3, 9–10, 17, 34, 116n.18, 200–1, 224–26, 247–48, 249, 311, 334–35, 379n.13 §9.3, 516
   Etude, Op. 10, no. 1 420–21, 420*f*
   Etude, Op. 10, no. 12 (*Revolutionary*) 136 §9.3, 432, 528
   Prelude, Op. 28, no. 2 (A minor) 188–89 §9.3
   Prelude, Op. 28, no. 4 (E minor) 198, 198*f*, 201–2
   Prelude, Op. 28, no. 5 (D major) 374–75, 375*f*
   Mazurka, Op. 6, no. 2 227n.31
   Mazurka, Op. 6, no. 3 213*f*, 225*f*
   Mazurka, Op. 7, no. 2 422, 423*f*
   Mazurka, Op. 17, no. 3 433*f*

602   INDEX

Chopin, Frederic (*cont.*)
  Mazurka, Op. 17, no. 4  334–35 §9.3
  Mazurka, Op. 24, no. 4  422n.20
  Mazurka, Op. 30, no. 2  207*f*
  Mazurka, Op. 33, no. 1  236*f*
  Mazurka, Op. 41, no. 1  225*f*
  Mazurka, Op. 41, no. 2  225*f*
  Mazurka, Op. 50, no. 2  144*f*
  Mazurka, Op. 50, no. 3  434–35n.39
  Nocturne, Op. 27, no. 2  250*f*
chorale(s)  13, 35, 82, 96, 134–36, 149–50, 149*f*,
      188–89, 203, 204–5, 205*f*, 206–7, 412–13,
      424–25, 431, 432, 476n.32, 531*f*
chord
  added-sixth  236*f*, 241–42
  as objects of compositional focus  264–65
  as scale §1.2, Ch. 2 (prelude),  53 §3.10,
      Ch. 5 (prelude), 540
  augmented  52–53, 53*f*, 69, 70–71, 71*f*, 275,
      559*f*, 565–66
  augmented sixth  141, 186*f*, 377–78, 380,
      480, 486n.55, 514
  common-tone diminished seventh  96–97
      §3.11, 375, 476n.31, 496–98
  common-tone dominant seventh
      §3.11,  242–44
  common-tone (other chords)  496–98
  diatonic distance between§2.2
  dyads, geometry of §§3.2–4
  Farben  95*f*, 558*f*
  fourth  9–10, 227n.31, 228*f*, 560, 561*f*
  grammar  29–30, 119, 239 §6.6, Ch. 7,
      Appendix 4
  pivot  305–6, 307*f*
  power  387
  seventh  12, 19–20, 27, 28 §3.11, 257–58
      §7.3, 329–30
  seventh chords, geometry of §3.11
  seven-note  137, 149–50, 149*f*, 240, 241*f*,
      366–67, 396–97, 534–35
  six-four  214–16, 222, 226, 257–58, 286,
      333–34, 508n.71
  So What  95*f*
  symmetrical  52–53, 394–96, 538*f*, 558–60
  thinking within  31–33 §3.10, 179–81, 231,
      495–96, 497*f*, 559n.8
  triads, geometry of §§3.6–10
  Tristan  224–26, 225*f*
  unprepared seventh  173–75, 218n.18,
      228–29, 228*f*
  voicing Ch. 3 (prelude)
Christensen, Thomas  202n.38, 218n.18,
      221n.20, 257n.2, 259n.7, 260n.11,
      313n.4, 332n.30, 386n.21

chromatic  4–5, Ch. 2 (prelude), 59–60,
      63–64n.20, 87, 89*f* §3.12, 190n.32,
      198, 242–44, 246–48, 249, 250*f*, 251*f*,
      254*f*, Ch. 8 (prelude), §§8.1–3, 384
      §8.7, §9.3, 511–12, 512*f*, 514, 519–20,
      524n.92, 525*f*, 565–66
  cluster  68–69
  figures, transposing diatonically  11–12,
      566–67
  neighbor  40*f*, 204–5, 204*f*
  sequence §1.1,  53*f*, 63–64, 64*f*, 69–71,
      147–48, 163–65, 164*f*, 260–61, 334–35,
      353, 481, 488, 489–90, 510*f*, 515–16,
      517*f*, 520, 528–29, 563–65
  set theory  14–15, 94–95, 95*f*
  sevenths  140, 140*f*, 420*f*
  space  10, 68–69, 134, 137, 344
  substitution  114, 114*f*, 118–19
  transposition Ch. 2 (prelude),
      §2.1,  107, 135*f*
  triad  33, 45–46, 49*f* §2.1, 69–70, 92
  *see also* modulation
chromaticism  75, 78–79, 96, 132–34, 148–49,
      227, 242–44, 358–60, 374, 419, 422, 520
  heavily diatonic  75, 146
Chua, Daniel  310n.18
circle of fifth(s)  54–55, 99–100, 198, 199*f*,
      321–22, 371–72, 380–82, 394–96, 396*f*,
      398*f*, 399*f*, 560n.11
  generalized  397–99
*clausula vera*  99–100, 271–72, 555
Clementi, Muzio  463–65
Clendinning, Jane
  *The Musician's Guide to Theory and
      Analysis*  142n.50, 414–16
Clough, John  6n.6, 15n.15, 316n.8
Cobain, Kurt  59
Cohen, Leonard
  "Hallelujah"  330, 330*f*
Cohn, Richard  3, 4n.5, 21–22, 60n.17, 75n.34,
      78–79, 147n.57, 148–49, 149n.63,
      358n.3, 369–71, 374, 421n.19, 425n.23,
      480n.40, 509n.75
Collins, Denis  156n.3
Collins, Shirley  85
Collins Judd, Cristle  385n.18
Coltrane, John
  *Giant Steps*  290–91
Coluzzi, Seth  299n.62
computational analysis  212, 214, 238–39,
      240*f*, 255 §6.4, 295, 308, 309–10,
      336n.42, 385*f*, 386*f*, 447–48, 508n.73,
      532, 534–35, 569, 573–74
computational harmonization  412–13, 414*f*

INDEX   603

Cone, Edward  514n.83
contrary motion  3, 31, 31*f*, 32*f*, 53, 69, 87,
  90–91, 93–94, 104, 105–6, 105*f*, 110–11,
  125–26, 134, 137, 151–52, 153–54,
  153*f*, 155, 158–60, 158*f*, 165, 167–68,
  171, 175–76, 178–81, 178*f*, 180*f*, 181*f*,
  182*f* §4.7, 260–62, 263, 264*f*, 331n.29,
  341–42, 350–51, 360, 409–11, 427–28,
  428*f*, 429, 430–31, 432, 438–39, 451,
  457, §§10.1–3, 478–80, 489–91, 489*f*,
  495–98, 501–3, 510–11, 518, 522–24,
  525*f*, 526, 530–31, 536, Appendix 3
Cook, Nicholas  16n.17, 209n.8, 291n.51,
  404n.6, 447n.60
Cooke, Sam
  "Cupid"  440*f*
Corelli, Archangelo  75–76, 257, 280–81n.44,
  311, 334–35 §7.6, 457
  Op. 1  336
counterpoint  2–3, 33, 60, 74, 87, 89*f*, 90–91,
  96–98, 104, 113, 119–20, 122*f*, 125–26,
  128–29 §3.10, §3.12, Ch. 4 (prelude),
  161–62, 186, 203, 227, 231, 234–35,
  238–39, 249, 275, 276–77, 286, 296–97,
  351–53, 420–21, 432, 459–60 §10.2,
  492, 527, 530–31, 540
  Baroque  11–12
  chromatic  516
  geometry of elementary functional  261–62
  instruction  2, 23, 24, 205–6, 212n.8
  invertible Ch. 4 (prelude),  158–59, 158*f*,
    167n.17, 169*f*, 328n.22, 466*f*, 477–78,
    477n.35
  of J.S. Bach  3 §7.7
  language of  8–9
  of Mahler  246
  modal  203–4, 222–23, 445–46
  Morte schema  186, 186*f*
  negative and positive  90–91, 93–94, 154
  parallel  6–8, 265*f*, 387, 468–69, 495,
    498–500
  parallel and contrary  110–11, 126*f*, 467–68
  Renaissance  222–23
  species  47, 209, 214n.14, 218, 432
  of Stravinsky  6–8
  *see also* chord (thinking within), contrary
    motion, doubly parallel motion,
    OUCH theory
Crane, Hewitt  404n.8
Cuthbert, Michael Scott  3, 532n.5
Cutler, Timothy  536.5
Czerny, Carl  420n.17

Dahlhaus, Carl  26n.46, 149n.63, 223n.23,
  256n.9, 257, 257n.1, 259n.7, 265n.16,

265n.17, 269, 269n.23, 270, 271–72,
  274–75, 274n.30, 277n.36, 279–82,
  431n.32, 453n.5, 453n.7, 473n.23,
  475n.26, 475n.28
Dalza, Joan Ambrosio  259–60, 260*f*, 265–66,
  265n.17, 265*f*, 266*f*, 267, 268n.22,
  277–78, 295
  *Pavana alla Venetiana*  259–60, 260*f*, 265*f*
  *Tastar de Corde*  269*f*
Damschroder, David  202n.39, 254n.4,
  476n.31, 476n.32
Danto, Arthur  234n.43
Darcy, Warren  20, 21–22, 380–82, 448, 453–54,
  454*f*, 455–56, 455n.11, 469n.16
Davies, Stephen  404n.7
Davis, Miles  66n.22
  "So What"  361, 361n.1
De Clerq, Trevor  56n.11
Deathridge, John  518n.87
DeBellis, Mark  403n.3
Debussy, Claude  4, 79–81, 84–85, 88–89, 192,
  203, 226–27, 247–48, 448n.65
  *Prelude to the Afternoon of a Faun*  5*f*
Deutsch, Diana  15n.15
disguised model  198, 476, 483n.48, 486–88
Doll, Christopher  68n.26, 72n.32, 247n.66
doubly parallel motion  41–42, 53, 54*f*, 60,
  125–26, 132, 195–96, 496n.63, 555,
  561*f*, 563–65
Douthett, Jack  70n.28
Duane, Ben  507n.70, 508n.73
Dufay, Guillaume  23, 214–16, 215–16n.16, 291
Duran Duran
  "Rio"  63–64, 67*f*
Dylan, Bob
  "The House of the Rising Sun"  84–85,
    84*f*, 84n.48
  "Knockin' on Heaven's Door"  59–60, 60*f*
  "Tangled Up in Blue"  61

Edwards, George  514n.83
Einstein, Alfred  296n.59, 387n.25
Ellington, Duke
  "Satin Doll"  194, 196*f*
del Encina, Juan  295
enharmonicism  34 §8.2
epistemic circularity  303–4
Evans, Bill
  "So What"  95*f*
Everett, Walter  78n.39, 148n.58
Ewell, Philip  82n.46, 419n.16

Faithfull, Marianne  85
Farrenc, Louise
  *Souvenir des Huguenots*, Op. 19  193, 194*f*

## 604 INDEX

fauxbourdon 34, 107–9, 108*f*, 165–66, 177n.24, 178*f*, 191–92, 233–34, 241–42, 297, 311, 312–13 §7.5, 336–39, 340n.46, 350–53, 429n.28, 433, 476, 476*f*, 488, 489–90, 495–500, 496*f*, 496n.63, 498*f*, 499*f*, 501
  generalized 114–16, 521–22, 528–29
  rule of the octave (ROTO) 76, 77n.36, 116, 148n.60, 331–32, 383*f*, 409–11, 498*f*, 501, 506*f*, 507*f*, 507–8, 510–11, 514–16, 517*f*, 519–20, 526
Fekaris, Dino
  "I Will Survive" 138–40, 140*f*
Fenaroli, Fedele 221n.20
Feroe, John 15n.15
Ferraguto, Mark 471n.17
Fétis, François-Joseph 21–22, 218–20, 227n.32, 257, 295n.58
Feurzeig, David 65–66, 158n.4
Fieldman, Hail 504–460nn.68–9
Fink, Robert 457n.3
Flew, Antony 20n.33
flow 17, 407 §10.2
folk music 21n.35, 23, 82–84, 85–86, 227n.31
*Formenlehre* 21, 407, 449, 454–55
Forte, Allen 35n.58, 428–29, 429*f*, 431n.33
Foster, Gwen
  "Rising Sun Blues" 83–84, 83*f*
Franklin, Aretha 63–64, 74–75
Froebe, Folker 426n.24
frottola 262–66, 265n.16, 269–71, 270*f*
Fux, Johann 221n.20

Gauldin, Robert 120n.21, 215–16n.16, 237n.49, 257n.1, 524n.92, 555n.2
Gaynor, Gloria
  "I Will Survive" 138–40, 140*f*
Gelman, Andrew 308n.17
Geneva Psalter 269, 292
Georgiades, Thrasybulos 257n.1
genius 2, 21n.36, 35–36, 173–75, 311, 431n.33, 451, 452–53n.3, 486–88, 490–91, 504, 527
Gesualdo, Carlo §1.1, 41, 69–70, 96
  "Moro Lasso" 4–5, 147–48
  trick of §1.1, 15, 63–64n.20, 202, 341, 528, 534–35, 537
Gibbons, Orlando 172–73
  *In Nomine a* 4 174*f*
Gilbert, Stephen 428–29, 429*f*
Gjerdingen, Robert 3, 6, 16–17, 21–22, 25n.45, 67n.24 §1.5, 74, 151–52, 209n.9, 210n.3, 255n.6, 261–62, 266, 331–32, 333n.34, 356, 409–11, 412n.6, 431n.34, 445n.56, 447n.60, 449, 460, 462*f*, 500

*Music in the Galant Style* 102–3, 409, 528
  *see also* schema
Glass, Philip
  *Einstein on the Beach* 66n.22
Goffin, Gerry
  "Natural Woman" 63–64, 63*f*, 67–68
Goldenberg, Yosef 304n.9, 475–76n.30
Goldstein, Robin 402n.1
Gottschalk, Louis
  *Le Mancenillier*, Op. 11 368, 369*f*
Goudimel, Claude 269, 292, 292*f*
grammar 1–2, 3, 17n.21, 22, 29–30, 47, 64–65, 76, 81*f*, 205–6, 220–21, 226–27, 235, 239, 250–51, 253, 258, 267, 295, 296*f*, 311, Ch. 7, 376, 407, 408, 412–13, 412n.6, 425, 433, 436n.41, 443, 467, 527, Appendix 4
  construction 26–27
Green, Al
  "Take Me to the River" 71–72
Grieg, Edvard 76, 79–81
  Op. 12, no. 3 ("Watchman's Song") 75–76, 76*f*
  Op. 43, no. 3 ("In My Homeland") 75*f*–76, 79–81, 81*f*
  Op. 47, no. 7 ("Elegie") 84n.48, 393–96, 394*f*
  Op. 57, no. 2 ("Gade") 306–8, 307*f*
  Op. 65, no. 4 ("Salon") 146n.55
  Op. 68, no. 3 143*f*
  Op. 68, no. 4 143*f*
Guarini, Giovanni Battista 227
Guns-N-Roses
  "Sweet Child O' Mine" 63–64

Hamilton, Kenneth 475n.28
Hansberry, Benjamin 404n.7
harmonic cycle 34, 191–92, 198, 199*f*, 260–61, 265, 267–68, 286, 290, 294, 297, 311, §§7.1–3, 327, 331–32, 331n.28, 339–42, 354, 355–56, 386–87, 391, 412–16, 413*f*, 416*f*, 418–19, 434, 438–39, 443–44, 451, 495
harmonic skeleton 128, 203, 210, 212, 217–18, 217*f*, 220–21, 228–29, 241, 246, 249, 416–17
Harrison, Daniel 68n.26, 156n.3, 158n.4, 186n.28, 223n.25, 334n.36
Hasty, Christopher 306n.14
Hatten, Robert 421n.19, 476n.31, 570
Haydn, Franz Joseph 75–76, 141–44, 211, 295, 314–15, 334*f*, 354–55, 380, 409, 453, 455–56, 468, 472n.20, 493–95
  Divertimento in C major, Hob.XVI: 1 381*f*

Divertimento in G major, Hob.XVI:8  439*f*
Quartet in C major, Op. 50, no. 2 Hob.
    III:45  178n.25
Sonata in E minor, Hob. XVI:34  181, 182*f*
Sonata in G minor, Hob. XVI: 44  416*f*
Sonata in E♭ major, Hob. XVI: 49  339*f*
Sonata in E♭ major, Hob. XVI: 52  435*f*
Symphony No. 62, Hob. XVI:62  377–78,
    378*f*
Symphony No. 100, Hob.I:100  142n.51,
    207*f*
Headlam, David  148n.61, 330n.25, 540n.9
hearing as Ch. 9 (prelude),  417–18
Heath, Gordon  85, 85*f*
"Heavenly Spark"  109–10, 109*f*
    *see also* Sacred Harp
Heinichen, Johann David  362–63, 364*f*,
    373n.8
Hendrix, Jimi  71–72, 74–75
Hensel, Fanny Mendelssohn  4, 31–33, 458–59
    "April" (*Das Jahr*, H. 385)  459*f*
    "January" (*Das Jahr*, H. 385)  32*f*
    "October" (*Das Jahr*, H. 385)  192*f*
    *Sechs Lieder*, Op. 1, no. 2  331*f*
Hepokoski, James  17n.22, 20, 21–22, 380–82,
    448, 449n.71, 453–54, 454*f*, 455–56,
    469n.16, 476n.31, 476n.33, 478n.38,
    482n.46, 496n.62, 570
hierarchy
    collectional  10, 14–15, 360, 396–97, 409–11,
        528, 530
    quadruple §1.2,  401, 409–11, 528
Hinton, Stephen  248n.67
Hodes, Jeffrey  239n.54
Hoffmann, E.T.A.  453n.4
holism  308, 309–10
Holtmeier, Ludwig  27n.48, 29n.52, 30n.54,
    103n.7, 124n.30, 210n.3, 255n.6,
    281n.45, 312n.1
Hook, Julian  6n.6, 42n.5, 156n.3, 337n.43,
    553n.9
Horn, Katelyn  315n.7
Horton, Julian  475n.26
"The House of the Rising Sun"  72–74, 83–85,
    83*f*, 84*f*
Huddleston, Rodney  18n.23
Humphreys, David  514n.83
Hunt, Graham  504–5n.68
Huron, David  3, 23–24, 24n.44, 56n.9,
    124–97nn.31–2, 131n.40, 303n.1,
    315n.7, 569, 570, 570*f*

Imbrie, Andrew  485–86
impressionism  12, 527

inversional equivalence  19, 21, 124, 161–62,
    223n.24, 256, 257–58, 266, 268, 274,
    284–86, 313, 413–14

Jackendoff, Ray  135n.45, 417*f*, 435n.40
Jacoby, Nori  310n.18, 545n.1
Jacquet de La Guerre, Élisabeth
    Sonata no. 1  213*f*
    Suite in D minor  466–67, 468*f*
Jagger, Mick  61
Jander, Owen  482n.45
jazz  2–3, 4, 12, 21n.35, 31–33, 94–95, 107–10,
    226–27, 244n.61, 246–47, 294n.55,
    361, 376, 394–96, 527, 528–29
Jeppesen, Knud  214n.14, 221n.20, 222n.22,
    276–77, 283n.47, 295, 385n.20, 569
Joplin, Scott  1, 449
    *Pine Apple Rag*  145*f*
Jost, John  402n.1
Josquin  23–24, 93*f*, 122, 159–60, 172–73,
    211–12, 212n.8, 214n.12, 218–20,
    259, 274, 275, 275n.32, 276–78, 276*f*,
    276n.33, 278*f*, 282n.46, 291–92, 292*f*,
    295
    *Benedicite, omnia opera* (motet)  174*f*
    *Liber generationis* (motet)  212*f*
    Mass *De beata virgine*  272*f*
    Mass *L'ami baudichon*  160*f*
    Mass *Sub tuum presidium*  272*f*
Junod, Julien  398n.30

Kamakawiwoʻole, Israel
    "Over the Rainbow"  111*f*, 114–16
Kant, Immanuel  473, 473n.24
Katz, Jacob  435n.40
Kellner  362–63, 364*f*, 373n.8
Kerman, Joseph  385n.20
Kern, Jerome
    "All the Things You Are"  138–40, 139*f*
Kinderman, William  421n.19, 472n.19,
    481n.42
King, Carole  4, 63–64
    "Natural Woman"  63–64, 63*f*, 67–68
Kirlin, Phillip  209n.11, 448n.62
Kloss, Jürgen  85n.52
Klumpenhouwer, Henry  156n.3, 369n.6,
    555n.4
knowledge  96, 237, 528
    background  309–10
    conscious  41
    geometrical  528
    implicit  47, 257, 471–72
    intuitive  90–91
    musical  1–4, 45–46, 332n.30, 528

606 INDEX

knowledge (*cont.*)
  public 188
  self 402
  stylistic 308
Korte, Werner Fritz 257n.1
Kostka, Stephen 128n.36, 237n.49, 312n.2
Kramer, Lawrence 421n.19, 518n.86, 522n.90

Labov, William 22n.38, 211n.6
Laitz, Steven
  *The Complete Musician* 414–16, 416*f*
Lalite, Philippe 453n.6
Lansky, Paul 65n.21
Laukens, Dirk 94n.10
Lawrence, John 20n.29
Led Zeppelin
  "Kashmir" 511n.79
  "Stairway to Heaven" 61, 85n.50
Lendvai, Erno 60n.17, 140n.48
Lerdahl, Fred 15n.15, 15n.16, 16, 135n.45,
      149n.63, 209n.11, 220n.19, 249n.71,
      256n.7, 331n.28, 417*f*, 435n.40,
      438n.46, 444n.54, 483n.50, 569
Levine, Mark 94n.10, 244n.61
Levinson, Jerrold 446n.57
Lewin, David 11n.11, 361n.1, 369–71, 374,
      457, 484n.52, 555n.4, 565n.17, 566n.21
Lewis, Christopher 244n.61, 245n.65
Lewis, C.S. (Clive Staples) 87–88
Ligeti, György 12, 17, 66n.22
  *Passacaglia Ungherese* 162–63, 163*f*
Liszt, Franz 518–19
"Locomotive Breath" (Jethro Tull) 61
London, Justin 486n.53
loops
  chord-loop families §§2.3–5, §2.7
  and enharmonicism §8.2
  and functional harmony 444–45
  in spiral diagrams Ch. 2 (prelude), 92,
      98–99
Lowinsky, Edward 257, 265n.17, 290n.49
Lund, Jeb 21n.34
Lusitano, Vicente
  *Heu me Domine* 12–13, 13*f*, 528

MacColl, Ewan 85
Maggio, Antonio
  "I Got the Blues" 145*f*
Mahanthappa, Rudresh 4, 6
  "The Decider" 7*f*
Mahler, Gustav 96, 210–11 §5.5, 247–48
  Symphony no. 2 240n.57
  Symphony no. 9 34, 142*f* §5.5
Marenzio, Luca 34, 227 §6.7

"Ahi dispietata morte" §6.7
"Vorria parlare e dire" 387, 388*f*
Margulis, Elizabeth 342n.50, 448n.66
Marshmello
  "Happier" 440*f*
Martin, Nathan 323n.17, 344n.52, 476n.31,
      570
Martines, Marianna
  Sonata in A major 208*f*
  "Vo solcando un mar crudele" 157*f*
Marvin, Elizabeth West 16n.17, 142n.50,
      291n.51, 404n.6
  *The Musician's Guide to Theory and
      Analysis* 414–16
Marvin, William 447n.59, 448n.65
Marx, Adolf Bernhard 455n.10
mathematics 2, 45–46, 96, 320, 367n.4, 457–58,
      540, 553n.8
  musical 154, 183–84, 316, 471–72, 527n.1
McClary, Susan 227–10nn.32–3, 234n.43,
      267n.20, 267n.21, 457n.3
McCreless, Patrick 4n.3, 361n.1
McDermott, Josh 310n.18
McEnery, Tony 23n.40
McHose, Allen 128n.36, 312n.2, 569
Meeùs, Nicolas 48n.2, 259n.7
Meier, Bernhard 79n.42, 277n.36, 385n.18
melodic slot 12, 13–14, 14*f*, 134–36, 357, 359*f*,
      363–64, 367–68, 432, 535–36
Meyer, Leonard 3, 16, 24n.44, 26n.47,
      74, 202n.38, 240n.59, 356, 407n.1,
      421n.19
Michaelis
  "Passando per una rezzola" 262–63, 263*f*
Milsom, John 162n.9
minimalism 201–2, 394–96, 527
Mirka, Danuta 211n.7
modernism 1–2, 85–86, 184, 249n.70
modes 2, 56*f*, 98, 257–58, 268, 275n.32, 290,
      291*f*, 320, 361, §§8.6–7, 537–38
modulation 2–3, 15, 34–35, 45–46, 68, 151–52,
      269, 320, 347–48, 348*f*, 355–56, Ch. 8
      (prelude), Ch. 8, 403–4, 422–25, 447,
      481n.43, 483–84, 522, 524–26, 529n.3,
      570–71
  choral and scalar 375
  chord-first 375
  direct 306, 307*f*
  garden-path 306, 307*f*
  pivot-chord 306, 307*f*
Monk, Meredith 4, 31–33, 104
  *Anthem* 32*f*
Monk, Thelonious
  "Pannonica" 109–10, 109*f*, 527n.1

Monteverdi, Claudio  19–20, 23–24, 104,
        210–11, 218n.18 §5.3, 237–38, 248–49,
        257, 291, 292, 292*f*, 468
    controversy with Artusi  226–27, 234
    "Cosi sol d'un chiara fonte" (Madrigal
        8.4)  194–95n.35, 522n.91
    "Cruda Amarilli" (Madrigal 5.1)  296–97
    "Longe da te, cor mio"
        (Madrigal 4.19)  335*f*
    "Ohimè, se tanto amate" (Madrigal 4.11)  34
        §5.3, 241–42, 519n.88
    "Tu se' morta" (*Orfeo*)  224–26
    *Vespro della Beata Vergine*  263n.15
Monteverdi, Giulio Cesare  212n.8, 234
Moore, Alan  63n.19
Morgan, Robert  169n.18, 418n.15, 428n.27
Morley, Thomas  79–81
    "April Is in My Mistress' Face"  79, 80*f*, 81*f*,
        173n.22, 227, 273n.29, 511–12
    "Leave, alas, this tormenting"  391–93
Morris, Robert  94n.11
Mozart, W.A.  6, 69–70, 76–77, 141–44,
        161–62, 166n.13, 188, 191–92, 206n.5,
        206*f*, 226–27, 237, 291, 295, 311–12,
        312*f*, 314–15, 314n.6, 329*f*, 333n.34,
        334*f*, 336, 337*f*, 338*f*, 339*f*, 354–55, 380,
        380n.15, 409–11, 444n.55, 453, 455–56,
        463–65, 468–69, 472n.20, 515n.84,
        569–70
    Clarinet Concerto, K.622  144n.53
    Piano Fantasy, K.475  178n.25
    Piano Concerto, K.488  207*f*
    Piano Sonata, K.279  193, 195*f*, 239, 240*f*,
        451, 452*f*
    Piano Sonata, K. 282  445*f*, 445–46,
        508n.74
    Piano Sonata, K. 283  14*f*
    Piano Sonata, K. 284  409–11, 411*f*
    Piano Sonata, K. 309  6*f*, 143*f*
    Piano Sonata, K. 310  20n.30, 191*f*, 433*f*
    Piano Sonata, K. 311  438, 441*f*
    Piano Sonata, K. 331  417*f*
    Piano Sonata, K. 332  381*f*, 382*f*, 514–15,
        515*f*
    Piano Sonata, K. 333  77*f*, 208*f*
    Piano Sonata, K. 533  193*f*, 380n.14
    Piano Sonata, K. 545  166*f*
    String Quintet, K. 516  116n.18
    Symphony no. 36, K.425  250*f*
    Symphony no. 40, K.550  176n.23, 408–09,
        414
    Violin Sonata, K. 304  439*f*
Muns, Lodewijk  434n.38
*musica ficta*  218, 260n.9, 290

Nápoles López, Néstor  308n.17
Narmour, Eugene  24n.44, 210n.2, 224n.27
Navia, Gabriel  507n.70
Neff, Severine  346n.54
neo-Riemannian theory  41, 42n.6, 50–51,
        358–60, 358*f*, 530, 534–35, 563, 563*f*
Neumeyer, David  426n.24
Newcomb, Anthony  300n.64
Newman, Mark  308n.17
Newman, Randy
    "When She Loved Me"  147–48, 147*f*
Newton, Isaac  26–27
Nicolas, Patrice  100n.4, 344n.53
Ninov, Dimitar  253n.3
Nobile, Drew  68n.26, 247n.66, 256n.7, 443–44,
        444*f*
Nolan, Catherine  91n.7
nonharmonic consonance  212, 254–55, Ch. 7
        (prelude), 570–71

Ockeghem, Johannes  93*f*, 114–16, 212n.8,
        275–78, 276*f*, 277*f*, 295, 526, 528–29
    Mass *De plus en plus*  116*f*
oenophile(s)  402
orbifold  547
ornament  303
Osborn, Brad  78n.39
OUCH theory  96–97 §3.6, 132, 136–37, 271
O-Zone
    "Dragostea Din Tei"  68

Pachelbel, Johann  6
    *see also* sequence
Palestrina, Giovanni Pierluigi da  1, 4, 22,
        130–31, 161–62, 197*f*, 203, 210–11
        §5.1, 222–23, 226, 227, 237–38, 259,
        275–77, 276*f*, 278–79, 279*f*, 291–92,
        296n.59, 385–86, 385*f*, 386*f*, 540–41
    masses of  23–24, 24*f*, 90–91, 93*f*, 122, 126,
        127*f*, 128, 130–31, 131*f*, 223*f*, 385*f*
    Mass *Aeterna Christi munera*  220*f*
    Mass *Assumpta est Maria*  217*f*, 220*f*
    Mass *Ave regina coelorum*  99–100, 100*f*, 162*f*
    Mass *De beata Marie virginis*  213*f*, 214*f*, 255*f*
    Mass *Descendit angelus Domini*  116*f*, 222*f*,
        222
    Mass *Dilexi quoniam*  215*f*
    Mass *Fratres ego enim accepi*  173n.22
    Mass *In duplicibus minoribus*  214*f*
    Mass *In minoribus duplicibus*  255*f*, 289*f*
    Mass *In semiduplicibus majoribus*  220*f*
    Mass *Io mi son giovinetta*  215*f*
    Mass *Papae Marcelli*  34, 216*f*
    Mass *Quando lieta sperai*  433*f*

608  INDEX

Palestrina, Giovanni Pierluigi da (*cont.*)
  Mass *Spem in alium*  114, 115*f*, 128–29,
    130*f*, 392*f*
  Mass *Veni Sancta Spiritus*  213*f*
  *Stabat Mater*  114n.15, 518–19
Palisca, Claude  71n.31, 73n.33, 221n.20,
  235n.45
parallelism (thematic)  434, 444–45, 482, 516
Parncutt, Richard  272n.25
"Paranoid" (Black Sabbath)  61
Paul Revere and the Raiders
  "Steppin' Stone"  72–74
Payant, Lee
  "Scarborough Fair"  85, 85*f*
Perren, Freddie
  "I Will Survive"  138–40, 140*f*
Perry, Jeffrey  65n.21
Petrucci, Ottaviano  259–60, 262–63
Petzold, Christian
  Minuet in G  354–55, 355*f*
philosophy §1.3,  33, 61, 126, 203, 218–20,
    253–55, 303n.4, 403, 417–18, 432, 447,
    449, 452–53, 455–56, 473, 570–71,
    573–74
  analytic  3
Picardy third  350, 353–54
Picasso
  *Guernica*  449–50
Pinter, D.  56n.11, 267n.21
Piston, Walter  312n.2
Plato  2, 210–11, 220–21, 419, 527
polyphony  74–75, 96, 205–6, 291n.52
  liturgical  282
  in the Renaissance  2–3, 25–26 §6.4, 295,
    384n.16, 520, 527
  in Sacred Harp  23–24, 86n.53, 269
postminimalism  394–96
Powers, Harold  21n.35, 273n.26, 289n.48,
    295n.58, 384n.16, 388n.26
pre-predominant  294
Principle of Musical Approximation  52–53,
    176, 558–60
Prime Directive  5, 6, 9–10, 15, 96–97, 149–50,
    172–73, 251–52, 401 §9.3, 516, 531–32,
    558–60
protofunctionality  34, 257, §§6.1–3, 282,
    286–88, 290, 294, 302, 313, 317–19
Prout, Ebeneezer  17–19, 18*f*, 221n.20
pseudochord  335–36, 336*f*, 347–48, 573
Pullum, Geoffrey  18n.23
Putnam, Hilary  19n.27

quadruple grouping structure  437–38
Quine, Willard van Orman  303n.4

Quinn, Ian  25n.45, 117n.19, 155n.2, 204n.1,
    210n.2, 223n.24, 303–4, 536n.4

Rabinovitch, Gilad  29n.52, 103n.7
Rameau, Jean-Philippe  26–27, 33, 34, 201–2,
    221n.20, 253, 259n.7, 260n.11, 313
    §7.3, 326, 331n.28, 340, 345–46,
    407–8
  *double emploi*  68, 471–72
  reduction  13, 35, Ch. 5 (prelude), §9.1, 416–18,
    420n.17 §9.4, 480
  nonharmonic  214, 215–16n.16, 218–20, 227,
    228–29, 237, 238–39, 241, 245–46,
    248–49, 250
  scalar  330
  schematic  175*f*, 480, 490–91
  Schenkerian  446–47
  sequential §4.10,  202n.38, 490–91
Reef, John  209n.9
Rehding, Alexander  310n.18, 473n.23
Reich, Steve  12
Renaissance  2–3, 26, 33–34, 79, 83, 85, 86,
    88–89, 114–16, 114n.15, 124–25, 124*f*,
    125n.34, 128–29, 146–47, 154, 155,
    162n.9, 172–73, 178–79, 181, 218,
    222–24, 227, 231–32, 255, 263n.15,
    271–75, 288–90, 299, 344n.52, 350,
    376, 407, 432, 520, 521–22, 526, 527,
    570–71
  cadence  30, 256n.9, 266, 271–72, 272*f*,
    279–82
  counterpoint  222–23, 230n.36
  harmony  230n.37, 233, 277n.36, 279–82
  inversional equivalence in  124, 161–62,
    256, 266, 268, 274, 284–86
  modes §8.6
  sequences  79–81, 336–37, 339–40, 507–8
  *see also* polyphony, schema
Renaissance (band)  82–83
repeating contrapuntal pattern  31–35, 155,
    §§4.2–3, 172*f*, 181–83, 184, 197*f*, 274,
    321–22, 342, 357, 358*f*, 370*f*, 371, 525*f*
Reti, Rudolf  446n.58, 486n.54
retrofunctional  56–57, 61, 68, 74–75, 76–77,
    77*f* §2.9, 84–85, 116, 128–29, 138–40,
    144–48, 148n.62, 244, 262–63, 288–90,
    321, 332–33, 333*f*, 419, 433, 443,
    476n.31, 489–90, 507–8
Reynolds, Christopher  524
Ricci, Adam  158n.4
Rice, John  188n.29
Richards, Mark  20–3nn.30–1, 72n.32,
    438n.44, 441n.50, 454n.8
Richter, Ernst  380n.14

Riemann, Hugo 34, 210n.3, 221n.20, 259n.7, 312n.2, 313, 325–26, 340n.47, 345–46, 475–76n.30, 485–86
*see also* neo-Riemannian theory
Rings, Steven 84n.48, 352n.62, 362n.2, 420n.18
*The Rocky Horror Picture Show*
"Time Warp" 71–72
rogue note 204–5, 228–29, 239n.54
Rohrmeier, Martin 135n.45, 435n.40, 436n.41, 527n.1
Roig-Francolí, Miguel 277n.37
Roman-numeral analysis 19–20, 21, 23, 25–26, 33, 34–35, 56–57, 57f, 101–2, 114n.15, 119, 223–24, 241, Ch. 6 (prelude), 291, Ch. 7 (prelude), 312–13, 343–44, 345–46, 350, 354, 355–56, 374–75, 461–63, 488–89, 508n.72, Appendix 4
Rosch, Eleanor 20n.29
Rosen, Charles 16n.17, 154, 320n.13, 380n.15, 403n.4, 448n.65, 448n.67
Rotem, Elam 263n.15
Rothenberg, David 394n.29
Rothgeb, John 249n.71, 250n.72, 253n.1, 254f, 254n.4, 255n.5, 256n.10, 333n.31
Rothstein, William 437n.43, 438n.45, 448n.67, 475–76n.30, 478n.38
Rowe, Dorothy 59
Russell, Jonathan 193n.34, 559n.7, 560n.9
Rydell, Bobby
"Forget Him" 147–48

Sacred Harp 23–24, 25f, 269
"Heavenly Spark" 109–10, 109f
Sailor, Malcolm 212n.9
Salzer, Felix 229n.35, 230n.37, 233n.41, 434–35n.39
Samarotto, Frank 59n.14, 486n.55
Sanguinetti, Giorgio 221n.20, 332n.30
Saslaw, Janna 303n.2
Satie, Erik
*Gnossienne* no. 3 384, 385f, 394–96
Savage, Patrick 47n.1, 310n.18
"Scarborough Fair" 82–83, 85, 85f
Scarlatti, Domenico 37, 188, 210–11, 224–26
Sonata in A minor, K. 3 39f
Schachter, Carl 208f, 237n.49, 254n.4, 354n.63, 355f
Scheidt, Samuel
"Gelobet siest du, Jesu Christ" 386–87, 387f
Schein, Johann
"Aus tiefer Noth" 388–89, 389f

schema 3, 5f, 8–9, 15, 16, 17 §1.5, 34–35, 74, 77n.37, 96, 102–3, 103f, 104–6, 107–9, 116, 151–52, 154, 157f, 159, 163–66, 171, 205–6, 207–9, 286–88, 290, 297–99, 311, 312–13, 331–32, 356, 371, 409–11, 416f, 432, 437–38, 449, 457, 467, 478–80, 478n.36, 482, 483, 486–88, 492n.60, 498–500, 501, 504–5, 510–11, 514–15, 516, 519–20, 522–24, 526, 528, 529–31, 565–66, 571
ascending-fifth 56–57, 67–68, 74, 76–77, 96–97, 114–16, 161–62, 222, 229–30, 336–39 §7.7, §8.5, 429, 438n.47, §§10.1–2, 476f, 507–8, 517f
ascending subdominant 117–18, 223–24, 241–42, 284–86 §7.7, 430–31, 522
basic voice leading, dyadic §§3.1–3, 118–19, 124, 152–53 §4.2, 154n.4, 165–66, 174f, 187f, 198–201, 228–29, 233–34, 286, 297, 300, 316–17, 318–19, §7.7, 379, 411n.5 §9.4, §§10.1–2, 529–30
cadential 349–50
Chase 172–75, 174f, 175f, 181–83, 201–2, 299f, 299, 349–50, 355–56, 390–91
contrary-motion 32f, 106 §4.7, §6.1, 331–32, 457, §§10.1–2, 478, 496–98, 501, 526, 530–31, 560
deep 67–68
descending-third 522–23
development 379–80
Do-Re-Mi 261–62, 410f, 528
Fenaroli 178–79, 221n.20, 261–62, 290, 341–42, 528, 559n.8
Fonte 102–3, 528
formal 342, 449, 453–54, 516–17
helicopter drop 376–78, 480
hidden 183f, 209
horn fifths 192n.33, 192f, 495–96, 500, 501–3, 528n.2, 559n.8
Indugio 207–9, 333n.34
Ludwig 33, 110–11, 186, 327–28, 428n.27, 429, 431, 432, 438–39 §10.1, 465–66, 489n.56, 490–91, 522n.91
Ludwiging §10.2
Meyer 410f, 445n.56, 528
modulatory 361, 362, §§8.4–5, 537
Monte 102–3, 528
Morte 186, 186f, 207–9, 460n.8, 461–63
nonharmonic 220–21
omnibus 10, 10f, 132–34, 181, 181f
one more time 449
paired-sequence design 377–78
parallel motion 113, 327f, 335–36, 467, 468f, 555

610  INDEX

schema (*cont.*)
  pedal tone  237, 242–44, 279–82, 335–36
  Prinner  30, 116, 118–19, 178–79, 207–9,
      261–62, 263, 266, 267*f*, 282–83, 286–88,
      290, 297–99, 314n.6, 331–32, 341–42,
      356, 430–31, 496, 528, 559n.8
  protofunctional  260–62, 262*f*
  Quiescenza  96–97, 102–3, 409–11, 460,
      462*f*, 500–1, 528
  Renaissance seventh  19–20, 214–17,
      216*f*, 217*f*, 218–20, 222, 226, 261–62,
      280–81n.44, 296–97, 304n.7, 334–35,
      351–53, 436–37
  Romanesca  6, 29–30, 29*f*, 528, 529–30
  Schenkerian  426n.24
  Sol-fa-mi,  410*f*, 528
  Standing on the dominant  178–79, 377–78,
      380–82, 434, 449, 454–55, 476n.33,
      480, 488, 489–90, 491, 526
  Standing on the predominant  333–34, 496
  two-tiered  371
  up and down the ladder  101–2, 152n.2,
      323, 347–48, 355–56, 375, 377–78 §8.5,
      390–91, 488–91, 501–3, 514–16
  voice-leading  30, 369–71
  *Waldstein*  63–64, 76, 511–12, 515n.84, 516,
      520, 526, 531–32
  *see also* cadence (converging), *clausula*
      *vera*, fauxbourdon ROTO, Gjerdingen
      (Robert), pseudochord, repeating
      contrapuntal pattern
Schenker, Heinrich  19, 21–22, 25n.45, 33,
    34–35, 135n.45, 171, 221n.20, 249–50,
    311, 331n.28, 340n.47, 343–44, 355–56,
    355*f*, 407–9, 411–12, 416n.12, 418–19,
    422, 424–25, 424*f*, 429n.28, 431, 431*f*,
    431n.33, 432, 432n.35, 446–47, 482–83,
    484n.51, 485–86, 489n.56, 490–91,
    490*f*, 492n.60
Schenkerian  13, 20n.32, 21, 22n.37, 33, 34–35,
    48–49, 103–4, 106, 119, 134–36,
    148–49, 171, 202, 202*f*, 205n.3, 209,
    249n.70, 261–62, 330n.25, 331n.28,
    343–44, 354–56, 380n.14, 407, 409–11,
    414–19, 425–26, 428–29, 431, 432,
    444n.54, 446–48, 448n.65, 449,
    476n.32, 480, 530, 536n.5, 542–43
Scherer, Josh  21n.34
Schindler, Anton  465n.11, 473n.24
Schmalfeldt, Jane  425n.23, 453n.7, 475n.26,
    475n.28, 475–76n.30, 477n.34,
    478n.36, 478n.38, 480, 480*f*
Schoenberg, Arnold  19, 21–22, 25n.45,
    95*f*, 131n.41, 210n.2, 213n.11 §5.2,

    227, 246, 248n.67, 346n.54, 414n.10,
    444n.55, 565–66
  "Angst und Hoffen" (Op. 15, no. 7)  158*f*,
    565–66, 565*f*
  *The Book of the Hanging Gardens*, Op.
    15  524–26
  "Farben" (Op. 16, no. 3)  95*f*, 558, 558*f*
  *Harmonielehre*  221
  *Verklarte Nacht*, Op. 4  524n.94
  Violin concerto, Op. 36  535n.2
Schubert, Franz  23, 34, 63–64, 75, 88–89
  C major string quintet, D. 956  227n.31
  "Morgengruss," D. 795.8  5*f*, 11n.11
  *Quartettsatz*, D. 703  136, 458 §10.6,
    519–20
Schubert, Peter  91n.8, 123n.28, 137n.47,
    155n.1, 263n.15
Schuijer, Michiel  91n.7
Schumann, Clara Wieck
  "Liebesfrühling" (Op. 12, no. 4)  118–19,
    119*f*
  *Soirées Musicales*, Op. 6  101–2, 102*f*
Schumann, Robert
  "Am Kamin" (Op. 15, no. 8)  254*f*
  *Dichterliebe*, Op. 48  341, 379n.13
  "Estrella" (Op. 9, no. 14)  144n.52
  "Ich grolle nicht" (Op. 48, no. 7)  341, 342*f*
  "Liebesfrühling" (Op. 37, no. 4)  118–19,
    119*f*
Schütz, Heinrich  4, 75–76
  *St. Matthew Passion*, SWV 479  390*f*, 390–91,
    391*f*, 392–93
  "Wie lieblich sind deine Wohnungen,"
    SWV29  74–75, 75*f*
Seals and Crofts
  "Summer Breeze"  61
Seeger, Peggy  85
Segall, Christopher  156n.3, 524n.94
set theory  14–15, 37–38, 41, 91, 94–95, 96,
    121–22 §8.7, 402, 533–34, 537–38,
    542–43
sequence
  Baroque  109–10, 334–35, 351–53
  canonic  92, 92*f*, Ch. 4 (prelude), Ch. 4, 222,
    227, 229–30, 230*f*, 263, 290, 422
  chromatic  4–5, 53*f*, 69–70, 481, 515–16,
    517*f*, 520
  contrary-motion  3, 31, 31*f*, 32*f*, 105–6,
    105*f* §4.7, 260–61, 426–27, 432, 451,
    §§10.1–2, 478, 489*f*, 496–98, 526
  endless  12, 57–58, 64–66, 70–72, 284–86
  melodic  134–36 §4.8, 205*f*, 208*f*
  modulatory  366, 367–68, 367*f*, 374–75,
    376–77

near 61, §§4.8–9, 262n.13, 324–25, 351,
377–78, 409–11, 426–27, 430–31, 432,
486–88, 512–13
Pachelbel 6, 7*f*, 29–30, 116, 118–19, 194,
231–32, 338–40, 346, 388–89, 453,
529–30
Renaissance 29–30, 30*f*, 79–81, 222, 274
*see also* schema
Sewell, Ian 205n.3, 209n.8, 414n.10
Shelley, Percy Bysshe
Ozymandias 452–53
Shepard, Roger 545n.3
Shepard-tone passacaglias 12 §2.5, 72–74,
171–72, 284–86, 286*f*, 324–25, 508–9
Shostakovich, Dmitri 4, 66n.22, 70–71, 71*f*,
76, 190n.32, 247–48
Ninth String Quartet 246–47, 247*f*
Simmons, Joseph 570n.2
Simon and Garfunkel 85
Simon, Herbert 15n.15
sliding (on a spiral diagram) 44, 50–51,
50n.3, 68–69, 90, 92, 97–98, 137,
357–58, 359*f*
Slottow, Steven 171n.21, 340n.47
Smith, Charles 149n.63, 447n.59
Smith, Elliot
"Rose Parade" 59
Smith, Patti 300–1
Smith, Peter 447n.59, 504–5n.68, 507n.70,
511n.79
SNAP system §5.1, 239n.54
Sommer, Heinz-Dieter 495n.61
Sousa, John Philip 448–49
sonata (form) 2, 15–16, 17, 20, 35–36, 82,
361–62, 376–77, 380, 402, 403–4, 443,
446–47, 448–50, 453–56, 495, 504–5,
508–9, 516–17, 519–20, 526
*see also* caesura
spacing (in chordal steps) Ch. 2 (prelude), 60,
70n.29, 94, 95*f*, 103–4, 106, 107*f*, 113,
124–25, 128, 149–50, 162–63, 165n.11,
195–96, 197*f*, 495–96, 536–37, 540n.8,
553
Sprick, Jan Philipp 158n.4, 340n.47
"Stand by Your Man" (Sherrill and
Wynette) 82–83
Starr, Ringo 78
Status Quo
"Pictures of Matchstick Men" 61
Stein, Beverly 290n.50
Steinbach, Peter 70n.28
Stephenson, Kenneth 17n.21, 48n.2, 57n.13
Stravinsky, Igor 4, 6–8, 88–89, 159–60, 247–48,
555n.4

*The Firebird* 160*f*, 384, 525*f*
*The Rite of Spring* 8*f*, 240, 241*f*, 250–51,
557*f*, 558–60
*Symphony of Psalms* 388
Strozzi, Barbara
"L'amante modesto" (Op. 1, no. 13) 171–72,
173*f*
"Il Contrasto dei Cinque Sensi" (Op. 1,
no. 14) 170*f*
"Gli amanti falliti" (Op. 1, no. 16) 172*f*
structured arpeggiation 15, 188–89, 189*f*,
192, 204–5, 420*f*
Strunk, Oliver 212n.8
Stuckenschmidt, Hans 560n.10
subjectivity 23, 74, 245–46, 256, 308, 354–55,
362n.2, Ch. 9 (prelude), 439–40, 442,
446–47, 570–71
Subotnik, Rose 421n.19
Sutcliffe, W. Dean 210n.1
Swinden, Kevin 256n.8
"Sympathy for the Devil" (Rolling
Stones) 61–63, 62*f*, 78
synthesizer 68, 404–5, 405*f*
Szymanowska, Maria
Polonaise no. 1, from *18 Dances of Different
Genres* 169–70

Tallis, Thomas
*Spem in alium* 91n.8, 136–37, 138*f*
Taneyev, Sergei 155–57, 159n.5, 555n.1
Taruskin, Richard 212n.8, 256n.9, 257n.2,
258n.4, 272n.24, 282n.46, 448n.65
Taylor, Benedict 75n.35
Taylor, Steve 151n.1, 240n.57, 460n.9
Telesco, Paula 10n.9
Temperley, David 29n.52, 56n.11, 61n.18,
63–64n.20, 67n.24, 78n.39, 209n.8,
247n.66, 303n.3, 320n.12, 333n.31,
418n.15, 426n.24, 439n.48, 486n.53
Thayer, Alexander 473n.24
Theune, Michael 233n.40
thinking within the chord 31–33 §3.7, 179–81,
231, 495–96, 497*f*, 559n.8
Thomas, Keith 402n.1
"Three Blinde Mice" (traditional) 157–58,
157*f*
Tierney, Adam 47n.1
Tinctoris, Johannes Ch. 3 (prelude), 220–21
*Liber de arte contrapuncti* 87–88
Tinctoris Transform Ch. 3 (prelude), 110–11,
119–20, 141, 172*f*, 178*f*, 184–86, 187–88,
459n.5, 467, 534–35, 542–43, 543*f*,
549n.4, 564*f*, 565–66
Tomlinson, Gary 235n.44

612  INDEX

tonicization  132–34, 151–53, 193, 336–37,
    347–48, 349–50, 380, 477–78, 481,
    500, 520
Tovey, Donald Francis  475n.27, 478n.39,
    482–83, 485–86, 495n.61
transcription  83n.47, 85, 404
Trevathan, Charles
    "Bully Song"  145f
triad
    *see* chord
Trippet, David  518n.86
Tromboncino, Bartolomeo  271
    "Ah partiale e cruda morte!"  270, 270f,
        271f
    "Se ben hor non scopro el foco"  263, 263f
Turner, Georgia  83–84
Tymoczko, Dmitri  16n.18, 41n.4, 42n.6,
    44n.8, 50n.4, 70n.29, 155n.2, 367n.4,
    398n.30, 457–58, 530n.4, 533n.1,
    536n.4, 537n.6, 543n.12, 552n.7,
    553n.9, 555n.3, 563n.15, 563n.16,
    566n.19
    *A Geometry of Music*  13–14, 44n.8, 48–49,
        50n.4, 55n.8, 75n.34, 91, 97n.2, 110n.12,
        148n.59, 148n.61, 155n.2, 198, 213n.11,
        280n.43, 312–13, 334n.37, 335n.39,
        374n.9, 375, 398n.30, 416n.13, 421n.19,
        422n.21, 430n.29, 533n.1, 536n.4,
        537n.6, 553n.9, 566n.22
    *The Thousand Faces of Form*  149–50
    *Wheels within Wheels*  396–97, 397f
Tyner, McCoy  4, 9–10, 9f, 114–16, 560
    "Pursuance" (*A Love Supreme*)  248f
    "Passion Dance" (*The Real McCoy*)  9f, 561f

Vande Moortele, Steven  475n.27
VanderWaal, Grace
    "So Much More Than This"  440f
Van Ronk, Dave  72–74, 84–85
Varricchio, David  257n.2
Vial, F.G.  371–72, 372f
Vicentino, Nicola  211n.6
Victoria, Tomas Luis da  122, 277–78, 278f
Victorian  227
voice
    abstract  13–14, 25f, 132–34, 204n.2, 330,
        362, 363–64, 363f, 365, 366–68, 372f,
        445–46, 541–42
    surface  10, 13–14, 132–36, 137, 188–89,
        204–5, 207n.6, 330, 360, 365, 367–68,
        407, 409, 411, 424–25, 426–27, 445–46,
        527, 528, 540–41, 559n.7
    *see also* melodic slot

voice exchange  34–35, 45–46, 79, 81f §3.3,
    §3.7, 134–36, 151–52, 152f, 164f §4.3,
    341f, 426–27, 427f, 429, 432, 458–59,
    505–7, 530, 536–37, 538f, 540, 542–43,
    550–53
    pairwise  125f, 164f, 536, 538f, 542–43, 550–53
voicing Ch. 2 (prelude), Ch. 3 (prelude),  120,
    128, 561f
von Hippel, Paul  23–24, 24n.44, 130–31,
    131n.41

Wagner, Napthali  84n.49
Wagner, Richard  34, 35–36, 88–89, 516
    *Lohengrin*  136, 458, 504 §10.7
    *Parsifal*  147n.57
    *Tristan und Isolde*  79n.43, 136f, 137f, 180f,
        460n.9, 524–26
Waltham-Smith, Naomi  158n.4, 369n.6
Warfield, Patrick  449n.68
Watkins, Holly  407n.1
Watson, Doc  83–84
Weber, Gottfried  18n.23, 22n.39, 131, 207n.7,
    211n.4, 253n.3, 303–4, 304n.5, 304n.6,
    331n.28, 340n.47
Webster, James  407n.1, 475n.29, 504–5n.68,
    507n.70
Wellwood, Alexis  572n.6
Westergaard, Peter  13n.14, 223n.23
White Stripes
    "The Air Near My Fingers"  61, 62f, 67–68
The Who
    "I Can See for Miles"  61
    "I Can't Explain"  61–63, 78
Wiering, Franz  275n.31
Wittgenstein, Ludwig  19–20, 403n.3, 572n.9
Wolff, Christoph  154n.4
Woolf, Virginia
    *To the Lighthouse*  449–50
Wootton, David  22n.37, 235n.44, 273n.27

Yellin, Victor  10n.9, 188n.29
Young, Neil  76
    "Helpless"  47f, 57–58, 64, 70–71, 330,
        332–33, 528–29
    "Keep on Rockin' in the Free World"  72–74,
        73f
Yust, Jason  53n.7, 148n.61, 202n.38, 209n.10,
    260n.11, 316n.8, 330n.25, 367n.4,
    429n.28, 447n.61, 516n.85, 555n.3

Zarlino, Gioseffo  123, 334n.35, 385n.20, 386,
    388
Zbikowski, Lawrence  573n.10